S0-BGH-955

LAW ENFORCEMENT
IN-SERVICE TRAINING PROGRAMS

LAW ENFORCEMENT IN-SERVICE TRAINING PROGRAMS

Practical and Realistic Solutions to Law Enforcement's In-Service Training Dilemma

By

NEAL E. TRAUTMAN, B.S., M.S.

Doctorate Student, Police Science Instructor, Training Officer, Winter Park Police Department, Winter Park, Florida. Formerly, President of the Florida Police Training Officer's Association and Editor of the Florida Law Enforcement In-Service Training Newsletter

CHARLES C THOMAS • PUBLISHER
Springfield • Illinois • U.S.A.

Published and Distributed Throughout the World by

CHARLES C THOMAS • PUBLISHER
2600 South First Street
Springfield, Illinois 62794-9265

ISBN 0-398-05287-5

Library of Congress Catalog Card Number: 86-14558

With THOMAS BOOKS *careful attention is given to all details of manufacturing and design. It is the Publisher's desire to present books that are satisfactory as to their physical qualities and artistic possibilities and appropriate for their particular use.* THOMAS BOOKS *will be true to those laws of quality that assure a good name and good will.*

Printed in the United States of America
SC-R-3

Library of Congress Cataloging-in-Publication Data

Trautman, Neil E.
Law enforcement in-service training programs.

Bibliography: p.
Includes index.
1. Police training—Study and teaching—United States.
2. Police—In-service training—United States. I. Title.
HV8142.T73 1987 363.2'2'0683 86-14558
ISBN 0-398-05287-5

To
Laurie
Martha
Heather
and
Jim

The author wishes to acknowledge
his sincere gratitude to Laurie Trautman,
his wife, for her untiring effort and endless
inspiration during the writing of this book.

He also conveys appreciation for the
virtually endless assistance from fellow trainers
during the completion of this book.

PREFACE

Law enforcement in-service training has become desperately needed and incredibly difficult for most police departments. The public demands professionalism. The possibility of devastating civil suits is ever present. Crippling budget limitations never cease. Man power restrictions are a constant source of difficulty. The time when you could give an officer a badge and gun, then tell him to just go out and put someone in jail is long gone.

All officers realize and understand the necessity for effective and regular in-service training. Few, however, can appreciate the responsibility of those who are assigned to conduct training. Standards of training expertise have never been at such a demanding level. Contemporary civil litigation accepts no excuses and allows no second chances. The complexities of today's law enforcement is often overwhelming.

The majority of American law enforcement agencies have less than twenty-five officers. Most can't afford a full-time training officer, let alone a training staff. Realistically, whomever is assigned training may also be a shift supervisor or the community relations officer. Being under paid, overworked and having multiple responsibilities is undoubtedly frustrating. In addition, not knowing how to train can make the job virtually impossible.

To provide trainers with a solid foundation, **LAW ENFORCEMENT IN-SERVICE TRAINING PROGRAMS** begins with a thorough explanation of how to develop and administer training programs. Topics such as training strategies, goals and objectives, reasons for failure, training equipment, budgeting and obtaining support from management are included. The lack of understanding fundamental principles of training can cripple every in-service program an agency developes.

Practicality and realism are stressed throughout every chapter. The most prevalent and useful in-service programs are presented: street survival, stress management, driving, firearms, field training officers programs, supervision training, computer training, first aid, physical fitness and video tape training.

Trainers will learn how to transform sound theoretical principles into productive and effective in-service training. Their officers will soon take pride in the innovation and progressiveness of the training division. An application of the knowledge contained within, will provide any training officer with the satisfaction of knowing his efforts really do make a difference. Without such knowledge, an agency is destined to become stagnant and frustrated; a victim of its own ignorance.

CONTENTS

LAW ENFORCEMENT
IN-SERVICE TRAINING PROGRAMS

1.

DEVELOPING AND ADMINISTERING TRAINING PROGRAMS

Every law enforcement agency has a training program of some sort. There are a variety of differences, however, in the degree to which these programs are formalized. In some agencies they are very unproductive and disorganized, consisting of demonstrating to the new officer a few things about his job, then "turning him loose." The remainder of the training takes place as he runs into difficulties where he is forced to ask questions or be given instructions.

Other agencies have organized an extensive training program for new officers. Thorough orientation and field training officer programs await them. A complete training staff is able to ensure that a variety of quality in-service training programs meet the needs of not only new officers, but the entire department as well.

No matter what form a training program takes, its purpose is always the same: To teach the trainee something he would not learn by his own unaided efforts, or to teach him quick, for less money, and more efficiently. Developing the ability to do job related skills and promote further understanding is the general objective of training. The efficient development of a training program will condense the long, expensive and sometimes painful process of learning through one's own experience into a shorter and more efficient program of learning.[1]

DEVELOPMENT OF TRAINING PROGRAMS

The training function in law enforcement agencies should be established to meet legitimate training needs. Needs which contribute to the organization's overall goals should be organized to execute the training process in the most effective cost efficient manner. Should each departmental division and section be responsible for the training of its personnel, or can the job be done more efficiently and economically through one highly specialized training section? Should small or medium sized agencies have a departmental training officer? Should a training program be developed and organized on a division wide or department wide basis?

While there are sound guidelines essential to the development of a training program, a mixture of plans usually provide the best results. A mixture is certainly adaptable to more agencies than any one guideline alone.

No one at a particular agency is more likely to know its particular needs, resources, internal funds, and operating conditions as well as the department head and his staff. On the other hand, developing a quality training program is, in itself, a highly specialized skill requiring extensive expertise which can not be substituted by an excellent knowledge of the department's internal circumstances.[2]

The developmental process is important to ensure that predetermined learning needs are accomplished. Other program development can be flexible to meet the particular circumstances of individual agencies. Development remains a very complex task and should be conducted by following these major steps for all programs:

- establish goals
- define objectives
- select training strategies
- select instructional technics
- select training aids
- develop lesson plans
- budgeting
- evaluating and improvement

THE DISTINCTION BETWEEN GOALS AND OBJECTIVES

It is important that the trainer fully understand the difference between goals and objectives. To summarize, goals are broader statements or purpose than are objectives. Objectives are more precise aims to achieve goals. If you were developing an in-service training course on management, your goal might be to improve management within the department.

The objectives can fall in one of three categories: learning objectives, planning objectives and process objectives. Examples are:

Figure 1. Effective development of training will condense the long and expensive learning process of experience into a shorter and more efficient program of learning.

Learning Objectives:	That the officer be able to:
	Define the difference between process and content;
	Describe ten common management problems and how to solve them.
Planning Objectives:	That the course be ready by a certain date;
	That the course not take longer than one week;
	That video equipment be used.
Process Objectives:	That the learners:
	Develop confidence in management skills;
	Assume greater responsibility for learning.[3]

ESTABLISHING GOALS

Establishing goals and defining objectives create a framework for the trainer to design and implement a training program. Instructional goals or a goal statement should be general in nature. Two or more specific performance objectives should be derived from an instructional goal. An example of this would be "administer emergency first aid," as opposed to "apply a tourniquet."

Goal statements should include a general behavior the trainee will be able to perform upon the completion of the training. Thus, they should be expressed as a trainee outcome. An example might be "prepare presentence reports," as opposed to "appreciate the need for presentence reports." Another example is "enforce jail rules and regulations."

Training goals should not include any conditions or standards. They should state only behavior. Nor should goals refer to conditions which must be formed for successful completion. "Administer first aid," would be appropriate, while "administer first aid according to the red cross first aid manual," would be inappropriate.[4]

Any training goal should be based upon the overall goals of the police department. Consequently, the most pertinent question is whether the goals of the agency are realistic. They must also support organizational activities. These two basic needs suggest that three steps are necessary to ensure that both an agency's overall goals and the more specific training goals are accomplished.

First, make certain that a needed change calls for training. What many police organizations need is not training, but detailed, operational planning and implementation of plans.

The second step in this process is to determine what part police training can play in the change. In other words, what changes can be acquired through systematic training? Training strategy will ascertain which goals can be reached through a training program and which are unattainable. Training goals, on the other hand, determine which training strategy would be most appropriate.

The third, and most difficult step is to determine which police personnel should be trained to achieve the concerned change. Training of a single officer will seldom be enough to achieve the sought after change. While one officer may attend a special training program, funding or manpower restrictions may prevent many others who are equally in need, from attending. If the training program as a whole does not reach the minimum number of officers required to achieve the change, your efforts will do nothing more than amount to futile frustration.[5]

DEFINING OBJECTIVES

Now that the trainer has established goals, he is ready to develop more specific performance objectives. A performance objective is the specific behavior expected of a student after instruction.

In defining your objectives, decide what you expect your students to be able to know, do, think and feel by the end of the course. Avoid such vague statements, "A student will appreciate the procedures of conducting a felony stop." Instead, ask yourself, "What are the procedures needed to conduct a felony stop?" Should an officer be able to conduct a felony stop, follow certain rules, apply certain methods, and manipulate required equipment? What are they and what degree of expertise could be expected to manage all the necessary skills? What background knowledge would an officer need to know in order to handle a felony stop?

The aforementioned manner of determining the right objectives can be easily applied to any type of training process. If you start with the final product and then work backwards, it will be much easier to plan the objective steps.[6]

It is important to be specific when writing your objectives. Learn to use "action verbs" when describing the student's behavior. Action verbs tend to be less "vague." Rather than understanding or appreciating, use words such as describe, change, invite, decide, state or spell.

Learn to use your objectives while both planning your course and actually presenting it. Sharing the objectives with your students will enable you to realize greater benefits such as these:

A. The basis for evaluation of your students' performance is formed from your objectives.
B. Once enrolled, students know what to expect and what is expected of them.
C. Knowing the objectives will allow potential students to be more informed as to whether or not they wish to participate in your training course.
D. Departmental staff personnel can easily assess the course by reviewing the list of objectives. This will become important when you need to justify your training program for needed funding.[7]

Doctor Robert Mager, educator, and author of **Preparing Instructional Objectives**, states that three important questions should be answered when developing course objectives: What should we teach? How will we know when we have taught it? What materials and procedures will work best to teach it? Doctor Mager believes that very few police training programs answer these questions.

After performance objectives have been determined, they must be communicated to the officer. Objectives are fully realized only after the officer can demonstrate the aim of the objective. A totally stated objective will succeed in advising the officer a visual conception of the learned skills. A statement of course objectives is not explicit enough to be useful until it explains how the trainer intends to achieve understanding. The objective that communicates most effectively will be the one which describes the expected behavior of the officer. Such statements will identify and define the desired behavior as well as specify the criteria of accepted performance.

The criteria of successful performance may be found in a variety of ways. It can be a principle applied to a given situation, correct responses, a time limitation, or principles that must be identified.

It is crucial that there be a reliable, accurate method to measure officer trainee performance according to the stated performance objectives. An example may be that the evaluation of rapid fire during a firearms training course is directly contingent upon completion within a specified period of time.[8]

SELECTING TRAINING STRATEGIES

A number of factors should be taken into account when selecting a training strategy. The first is your departmental training goals. Once an agency is clear about its goals, it can choose a strategy that will lead to it.

A second consideration is the various resources available for your agency's training. A study of the business world determines that management training technics commonly used by corporations and companies use a variety of training technics in developing their management sections.[9]

The studies indicated that "on the job training" was used more frequently than any other technic. Other technics or strategies used for training, in descending order of frequency, were job rotation, special projects, case studies, management gains, role playing, and sensitivity training. The following table will relate general characteristics of training strategy.

The International City Manager's Association conducted an extensive

Figure 2. Proper training program development requires thorough research and planning.

survey of teaching technics used nation wide during recruit training.[11] It should be noted that 18 percent of the 1,475 municipal police departments surveyed indicated that no recruit training at all was provided in 1968.

A strategy is a method for obtaining a specific result or goal. The specific goal of a training program is training. An instructional strategy is a method or combination of methods used to facilitate training and learning.

Strategy may be viewed as the vehicle which transfers instructional input into an improved behavioral change. Instructional strategy comes in many shapes and sizes. Some strategies may be labeled more traditionally, such as lectures, role playing, case study, etc. Other strategies are called techniques, such as questioning, practice, or a conference. Still other strategies are thought of in terms of aids, or equipment, such as overhead projectors, chalkboards, movie projectors, video cassette recorders, etc. Their differences are found in the uses they provide to enhance the achievement of instructional goals.[12]

Instructional strategies not only exist in a variety of forms, but can also be mixed with other strategies to form a totally new strategy. An

TABLE I
CHARACTERISTICS OF TRAINING STRATEGY

1. Academic.	Transmitting content and increasing conceptual understanding.	Lecture Seminar Individual reading.	1. Content and understanding can be passed on from those who know to those who are ignorant. 2. Such knowledge and understanding can be translated in practice.	Examination of test retained knowledge and understanding.
2. Laboratory.	Process of function and change. Process of learning.	Isolation. Free exploration and discussion. Experimentation.	1. It is useful and possible to pay attention to psychological factors for separate attention. 2. Understanding of own and other's behavior help in the performance of the jobs.	Unfreezing participants from their usual expectations and norms. Helping participants see and help others see own behavior and develop new habits.
3. Activity.	Practice of specific skill.	Work on the job under supervision. Detailed job analysis and practice with aids.	1. Improvement in particular skill leads to better performance on the job. Production and training can be combined rather simply.	Analyzing skill and dividing it into parts. Preparing practice tasks, standards, and aids.
4. Action.	Sufficient skills to get organizational action.	Field work, setting and achieving targets.	1. Working in the field develops people. 2. Individual skills and organizational needs will fit together.	Preparation of field programs. Participation according to schedule.

TABLE I Continued

5. Person development.	Improved individual competence in wide variety of tasks and situations.	Field training, simulation methods, incident and case sessions, and syndicate discussion.	1. Training in job requirements with emphasis on process will help a participant develop general skills and understanding. 2. Organization will support the individual in using understanding and skills acquired.	Identifying training needs, Preparing simulated data.
6. Organization development.	Organizational improvement.	Study of organizational needs. Work with small groups from the organization.	1. Attention to organizational needs as process develops understanding. 2. Organizational change will result in individual's change.	Survey of organizational needs. Determining strategic grouping for training. Working on organizational requirements.

Rolf P. Lynton and Udai Pareek, Training for Development (Homewood, Illinois: Richard D. Irwin, Inc., 1967), pg. 50–51.

example would be a demonstration or role playing session combined with a round table discussion and group critique to form an inner active type of strategy.

Without an instructional strategy, the trainer has no way of bringing the officer and the training program within reach of each other. Accurate strategy selection, based upon preconceived criteria we have discussed, can increase the probability of effectiveness. The selection of strategy is frequently based upon tradition or the saving of time. However, if you are planning for your officers to acquire new skills and information, or you wish them to alter their attitudes or feelings, the training strategies should be totally different.

Every training topic has its own appropriate teaching technique. A demonstration-practice session is more effective if officers are to acquire new specific skills. Developing or changing attitudes about something is best accomplished through role playing followed by a group discussion.

TABLE II
TEACHING TECHNIQUES FOR RECRUIT TRAINING (990 CITIES REPORTING)

Teaching Technique	*Rank for All Cities over 10,000*	*Number of Cities Using Technique*	*Rank by Population Groups* 10,000 to 25,000	25,000 to 50,000	50,000 to 100,000	100,000 to 250,000	250,000 to 500,000	Over 500,000
Lecture and discussion	1	973	1	1	1	1	1*	1
TV, films, recordings, and other audio visual aids	2	874	2	2	2	2	1*	1*
Actual practice (field experience under supervision of selected police officers)	3	796	3	3	5*	4	6	3*
Practice in use of work devices	4	782	4	4	4	6	5	5*
Simulation of practice (such as acting out the apprehension and arrest of a shoplifter)	5	764	5	5	3	5	1*	5*
Field observations of police facilities (such as communication facilities, lab facilities, etc.)	6	704	7	7	5*	3	1*	3*
Discussion of assigned readings	7	699	6	6	7	8	8	5*
Field observations of street problems (such as traffic control, crowd engineering, etc.)	8	673	8	8	8	7	7	8

*Ranked equally

Source: J. Robert Hovlick, "Recruit Training: Police Chiefs' Dilemma," *Public Management*, 50 (December 1968)

Certain strategies are more suitable for certain learning objectives. The following are suggestions for the use of particular teaching strategy techniques to accomplish specific objectives:

A. To help the officer develop knowledge regarding facts, figures, concepts, and various other information, the strategies of paneled debates, field trips, field projects, simulation exercises, and group discussions would be useful.

B. To assist officers in developing thorough understanding, applying information and making connections between classroom training and real life experiences, the techniques of role playing, group discussions, field projects, and surveys would be useful.

C. To help an officer develop skills in performing certain tasks, operating equipment, handling tools, and practicing new skills, training techniques such as role playing, knowledge surveys, field projects, and group discussions should be used.

D. For officers to develop or change attitudes towards various issues and situations, the strategies of role playing, group discussions, field projects, and learning contracts should be used.

E. In assisting officers to develop new values and adapt priorities to certain important beliefs, assisted research, role playing, discussion groups, and learning contracts may be used.

F. To encourage officers to participate in the learning process, knowledge surveys, learning contracts, research papers, brain storming, role playing, group discussions, paneled debates, field trips, simulation exercises, field projects, and an assortment of evaluation techniques may be helpful.

G. To obtain feed-back on officer's thoughts and feelings regarding a training program, surveys, questionnaires, examinations, memorandums, discussion groups, and private interviews can be used.[13]

EVALUATING AND IMPROVEMENT

Results are what matters in any training program. Results can be measured in terms of officer learning and ultimately officer performance. Evaluation processes can usually be extended beyond the concerned training program to produce worthwhile information on officer performance for other than training purposes. An efficient evaluation program can be a valuable quality control instrument for management. It can determine information on how to improve training and supervision, and be of great assistance in counseling officers on how to improve their work. It can also provide useful information for officer promotions or terminations.

There are two basic types of evaluations: testing and performance. Examination type evaluations are useful in determining how much knowledge an officer has regarding a subject. Performance evaluations indicate the degree of skill the officer has acquired in applying his knowledge to his work. Examinations are accomplished by subjective or objective tests, while evaluations are generally accomplished by observation using a rating scale.[14]

Subjective, or essay, examinations are easy to construct but very difficult to grade accurately. While they offer an excellent opportunity for an officer to demonstrate his ability to organize and express his ideas in writing, grading them may just as likely reflect the weaknesses of the trainer at grading as much as it may show the knowledge of the officer taking the examination.

Observation is sometimes used as the means of evaluation. A rating scale which lists the factors on which highly accurate observations can be documented, is used. It is the most popular form of rating evaluation.

A rating is usually depicted by numbers which provide descriptions of various levels of quality. Yet, even the best scale can give no more valid and reliable results than the validity and reliability of the person applying it. Maximum accuracy in using observation rating scales can be achieved by following three principles:

1. Rate each factor independently; avoid the halo effect.
2. Compare ratings of different raters. Be suspicious of one rater who consistantly rates higher or lower than others.
3. Be certain that raters do not give ratings based upon their own personal standards rather than standards established by the department.

Objective tests are not affected by the weaknesses of a grader as much as many other types of tests. They do, however, require considerable skill in construction. Multiple choice examinations are widely used even though they are time consuming to construct, because of their superiority to most other types of examinations.

The following are intended as guidelines to assist you in writing a quality multiple choice examination:

1. Determine the major points you wish to convey to the students before composing your examinations. Base your questions on these training points. Test on the knowledge that really makes a difference to the officer's effectiveness.
2. Limit the multiple choices that an officer has to choose from to one or two words. Minimizing the number of words they have to think through for each question allows an officer to concentrate on the real essence of the question.
3. There is a tendency for instructors to state the correct answer in a more lengthy manner, while the wrong answers are very brief. Take care not to do this, as the correct answer would then be conspicuous due to its length.
4. If you choose to use words such as "not," "all except," or other

negative expressions in a question, emphasize them by underlining these words so that they will not be overlooked.

5. When appropriate, use a picture or diagram in place of or along with certain words, to simulate reality more closely.[15]

True/false examinations allow coverage of many training points and are considerably easier to construct than multiple choice examinations. If composed with care, true/false tests will provide a good understanding of an officer's achievement and knowledge. The following are guidelines for the construction of such exams:

1. Cover only one fact or subject matter at a time.
2. Avoid making true/false questions very complicated. The purpose of such examinations are not to measure intelligence or reading ability. The purpose is to measure knowledge of specific facts.
3. Be as exact and precise with your wording as possible. Avoid expressions which could be interpreted differently by officers.

Training programs should be concluded with examinations in order to estimate the success of the subject presentation, the ability of the instructor, and the acquired knowledge and potential of officers during training. Such evaluation results should become a part of every officer's personnel record.

For best results, a training officer should develop provisions for on-going program evaluation. In effect, this means that all new training programs and methods should be regarded as experimental.

The most widely used evaluative techniques involve before and after comparisons of work performed, attitudes, and other criteria that indicate effects of the training program upon personnel, along with the benefits to participating police agencies. An evaluation should attempt first to determine whether ideas, skills, and operating procedures presented in training programs are not being applied. Second, it should determine the overall worth of training to the department. It should also establish future training needs, both in general and in respect to individual police officers.

DEPARTMENTAL TRAINING POLICY

If your agency should require that a training policy be written, it should be sufficiently broad to include individual officers, all administrators and supervisors, the department itself, the city or county personnel department, and the city or county commission. Such a policy could be as follows:

There is an obligation by the police department to its employees and the citizens of its community to develop and utilize to its fullest extent, the ability and talent of all agency employees. Supervisory and managerial officers are accountable for the utilization and development of all human resources, just as they are accountable for the other administrative rules, instructions, and state statutes. Responsibility for the agency's training and development shall be the employees, the police training staff, the police administrators, the police chief, the city personnel department, and the city manager and commission.

DEVELOPING A TRAINING COURSE

A great deal of law enforcement training has been dictated by the reaction to crisis. Often when a police crisis or a public incident takes place, the attention given the situation will result in a training program being developed regarding that particular subject. The lack of forethought concerning the need for a particular training program usually occurs as the result of training officers being removed from daily police operations. To be sensitive to current operational needs, training officers should be required to occasionally conduct field operations with all divisions of an agency and keep as close a relationship as possible. Attending regular departmental staff meetings, performing tours of field duty, attending roll call and devoting time to furthering relationships with fellow officers, will assist in eliminating the "living in an ivory tower" syndrome.

If the subject matter for a particular in-service training course involves technical, complex, specialized skills or knowledge, there is seldom a substitute for a full-fledged, thorough training program. Such a program offers the department the opportunity to select its own qualified instructors, teach a standardized course curriculum, use a variety of instructional methods, and require officer trainees to perform and participate in an assortment of practical exercises. Developing your own in-service course is more adaptable to complex or higher level skills than many other instruction methods.

Unfortunately, if specific training programs are not fully supported by top management, training officers may be forced to consider not organizing or conducting them at all. Training efforts should be devoted to other types of training programs in the absence of top level support.

Morale, a desire to learn, and interest will be absent when officers are excused from attendance due to other priorities. If officers being trained recognize that training courses are of a second-rate importance, the probability of obtaining high motivation, holding close attention for inspiring work that leads to comprehension is almost impossible. If this takes place, no one besides the training officer is likely to realize the reason courses failed was the initial lack of commitment, which resulted in these negative factors. Instead, the training officer will be held accountable for its failure. Unfortunately, this "training trap" takes place more often than is necessary. Additional emphasis will be placed on obtaining support from management in the latter section of this chapter.

The previously discussed steps of conducting a needs assessment, setting course goals and objectives, and selecting appropriate instructors are the next steps to developing a quality training program. Following the selection of course instructors, it is recommended that the training officer discuss the course material with each instructor. This will allow the training officer to have a direct hand in determining the actual content of the course. There are four basic considerations which should be taken into account when determining the content:

1. Consider what the supervisors of the officers to be trained believe are the main deficiencies in the training area. A supervisor's expectation of improved performance should be matched by his willingness to reward the positive change. Future reinforcement is an important consideration. Real change will not take place without on-the-job reinforcement by the concerned supervisor.
2. Consider the views of officers to be trained. Determine their attitudes and values regarding the subject. Ascertain specifically what additional knowledge they need to know in order to improve their job performance.
3. Develop into the course outline a section, which will explain to the officers being trained, that certain areas are of vital concern because they and their supervisors are in agreement as to their importance. The officers should also understand that part of mastering the concerned skill is learning how to demonstrate them on the job.
4. Establish a set of informal and uncomplicated documentation. An officer should keep simple records and notes during the course.

> Supervisors should be informed to keep records of noticeable changes in an officer's performance following the course. They should also be advised to document reinforcements they make in these particular training areas. Reinforcement makes it more likely that the training will become a permanent part of an officer's job performance.[16]

Standardization is another concern associated with in-service training. The lack of uniform instruction of standard operating procedures within law enforcement agencies are common. Quality, standardized police training usually requires that a single resource be used and presented by the instructor.

Providing the in-service instructor with a well researched lesson plan, based on good, up to date material, is crucial. Without current resource material, the instructor will find it almost impossible to prepare necessary lesson plans which ensure standardization from course to course.

Providing officers being instructed with duplicate copies of written materials is also useful in ensuring standardization.

Copies of both lesson plans and written materials provide officers with permanent records for legal purposes, should civil litigation pertaining to the concerned training area occur in the future. Officers should be required to keep a constantly growing professional notebook. This will allow them to have a quick reference whenever there is a need to refresh their memory on a training area.[17]

There are many considerations to consider when determining the best method of scheduling in-service training. Monthly sessions, weekly sessions, and daily sessions are all possible.

Holding uninterrupted two to four hour training sessions each month is a distinct possibility. The sessions could be routinely scheduled for what is normally a slow day, during a time just prior to the officer's reporting for a scheduled shift. Conducting training prior to the officer's scheduled tour of duty will ensure that each officer is fresh and alert.

If you choose to have training sessions on a weekly basis, they should be shorter in length, lasting thirty to sixty minutes each. This type of training session is usually conducted by a shift supervisor or agency training officer. Again, immediately prior or immediately following a schedule tour of duty is the recommended manner. Since weekly training sessions are of short duration, physical fatigue should not be a problem.

Due to many considerations, some agencies depend on daily roll call training. A brief ten minute training period amounts to approximately forty hours of in-service training for a year. Learning retention research has proven that a well structured and delivered training program of ten minutes in length with one or two specific objectives will be absorbed and be remembered longer than an annual in-service program of a one week duration.

The roll call instructor should consider the use of slides, films, video tape, or material handouts in his ten minute delivery. Topics should be timely and be carefully matched with the current "street scene."

Each session's purpose should be stated at the onset of the presentation and should be briefly summarized at its conclusion. The shift supervisors in some agencies routinely assign officers on their shift various roll call presentations. The instructing officer should prepare a working bibliography of all materials associated with the topic. An evaluation of these materials will allow him to choose those items dealing more directly on the subject.

The instructor should now write the entire speech and review it to familiarize himself with the context. The next step will be to prepare an outline used for the actual presentation. Thirty to sixty percent of the words used in the presentation should appear on the outline. Investment in time required for conducting an organized roll call training program is minimal compared with the positive results to be obtained.[18]

TRAINING DEVELOPMENT MISCONCEPTIONS

All police trainers will occasionally need to re-adjust their own performance as classroom situations change. The following are misconceptions which may be easily misunderstood, followed by the associated facts:

- **Training is a program.** Fact—Even though we all usually refer to the term "training program," the overall scope of training itself is not a program. It is actually a process that continues long after an officer returns back to his usual job.
- **Training is a fixed overhead expense.** Fact—Training should be an accountable task of verifiable performance improvements and cost savings data. It should not be viewed by management as a fixed overhead.
- **Everybody needs training.** Fact—Everyone can benefit by training,

yet not everyone needs training at any given time. Training officers should consider the use of their limited resources as too valuable to use indiscriminately without considering the individual needs of officers. Trainers should concentrate on training efforts with respect to high-need areas first.

- **Trainers are the best people to do the training.** Fact—Trainers can often be perceived as having a relatively low credibility due to the fact that they are not considered experts in many particular areas. The best instructors within a department are usually those who are the best performers in particular specialty areas.
- **The best departments offer the most in-service courses.** Fact—Quantity, at the expense of quality, is a serious mistake. Often the most productive training divisions are those which spend considerable time in evaluating and assessing their needs prior to the delivery of training courses.
- **Participation in training should be voluntary.** Fact—Voluntary participation by officers usually provide those officers who wish to be there, to begin with. It does not provide the officers who usually need the concerned training the most. Real results usually come from training those who need it the most, not by training those who simply want it the most.
- **Training is the same as education.** Fact—Education tends to have long term and often vague overall goals. Training, must be immediately applicable on the job. Education tends to benefit the individual, whereas, training tends to benefit the organization. Training must be verifiable in terms of short range, on the job performance improvement.[19]

CONTEMPORARY TRENDS IN POLICE TRAINING DEVELOPMENT

With the influx of excessive funding made possible by the Law Enforcement Assistance Administration during the 1970's, training prospered. Now that those funding resources are non-existent, a continued effort for the development of the police training function during the 1980's is more necessary than ever.

Another beneficial result of LEAA funding was the enormous growth in the law enforcement courses offered by local colleges and universities. Unfortunately, these proved to be "short lived" following the elimination of federal funding. Most local law enforcement agencies came to expect the luxury of universities providing needed training courses. These same agencies were caught off guard when such programs were terminated. There now exists a danger of the return to mediocre in-service training programs which were common during and prior to the 1960's.

Future emphasis in law enforcement training must be focused upon its relevance to the needs of officers "on the street." There is currently a wide spread use of training fads sweeping the nation.

This wide variety of gimmicks may sometimes offer new and innovative programs, yet also has directed law enforcement training emphasis away from the basics. Gimmicks in training tend to gain considerable attention, but they soon lose their appeal if field officers remain without the basics necessary to do a good job.

We sometimes concentrate on new and innovative techniques but do not tackle the less appealing or controversial issues that training sometimes seem to overlook.

Some of the issues we can not continue to ignore include:

- Educating officers who have never learned basic english.
- Increasing the supervisory ability of staff members.
- Tackling the issue of mental health and suicide among officers.
- Providing more quality police driving training.
- Law enforcement alcoholism and drug addiction.

THE ROLE OF THE TRAINING OFFICER

Nationally, the role of a training officer varies from agency to agency. American law enforcement currently views the role of a training officer in a variety of ways, usually depending upon the size of the agency. While some departments have a training staff larger than another department's entire force, the responsibilities tend to be the same. Police training officers are responsible for providing efficient and high quality training to meet the needs of a contemporary professional police department. His role goes beyond that of merely overseeing the training function. It includes the concerns of motivation, individual and group performance, and the overall departmental goals and objectives.

The police training officer should assume the position of role model among his fellow officers. Both his personal habits and career background, expertise and behavior must be of the highest moral and ethical standards.

His role should be looked upon within the agency as a position that is respected and envied. A training assignment should be used to develop an outstanding officer into a highly efficient, dedicated and specialized resource.[20]

If these standards are not currently met within an agency, efforts to reach them must be pursued. They will only be met through the dedication and hard work of an agency's current training officer or the individual having training responsibilities. Those striving for such objectives may meet with frustration. The pursuit of excellence is rarely a simply task.

REASONS FOR PROGRAM FAILURE

The fact that training development may be a low priority within your agency can be rationalized by many managerial arguments. The most common objections include the lack of funds necessary for training, the difficulty in evaluating and documenting training results, and the problem of manpower shortages.

Each of the aforementioned misconceptions have a degree of truth, but they all ignore some basic principles related to training development. For training to grow from a good idea to an excellent, productive program requires careful administrative reasoning.

The concerned reasoning pertains to the purpose of the training function; the scope of your agency's overall training goals; and the relationship of training to other segments of administration within your agency.

Often, the failure of training is associated with misconceptions and ignorance. There are nine major reasons why training programs may fail. These are:

1. Failure to focus your agency's resources efficiently.
2. Failure to train those who need it the most.
3. Failure to allow those officers being trained to voice their opinions concerning the issue.
4. Failure to provide practical and realistic programs.
5. Failure to simulate realism to its fullest extent.
6. Failure to develop training programs that "tell it like it is."
7. Failure to conduct a series of programs that reinforce your overall goals and objectives.

8. Failure to ensure that your chief or sheriff is kept thoroughly abreast of the program's current status to ensure his support and involvement.
9. Failure to use the program to sense new problems and generate data.[21]

ACCOMMODATING THE STAGES OF A CAREER

As an officer's career continues, the years of work usually takes its toll on his spirit to perform. Those who become frustrated with the current justice system may view their careers as dead-end jobs. They can also suffer from a lack of job achievement and have low self-esteem. Such feelings are often blamed on the agency, which in turn can start a negative spiral of decreased work performance and quality.

Where does the trainer fit in? Perhaps to help the concerned officer find the proper external training resource. Perhaps a management training program would be effective. Perhaps a training program to make management aware of such natural progressions in an officer's career. This, of course, would assist both management and the officer himself.[22]

TRAINING FEMALE POLICE OFFICERS

Following the passage of amendments to change seven of the civil rights act of 1964, law enforcement realized an emergence of female police officers into its ranks. There have been, and remain, many myths and a great deal of ignorance regarding female policing in America.

Understanding many prevalent myths concerning women in law enforcement can make the trainer more effective.

Myths

1. Women expect special treatment and favors from men.
2. Women get sick every month during their menstrual cycle.
3. Female officers cannot fight.
4. Women become sexually and romantically involved with their partners.
5. Females are more likely to use deadly force in a confrontation.
6. Women are emotionally unstable; they cry a lot.

While there are partial truths to the aforementioned facts, the majority grew from ignorance. These statements are based on a total lack of understanding or concern. New female officers will need understanding and concern from their trainers. A training officer must ensure that those such as field training officers and supervisors demonstrate the same understanding as he does.

The following are suggestions for trainers regarding the training of female officers. Unlike the preceeding myths, these facts are based upon documented research.

Facts

1. Female police officers deserve to be treated as people, as opposed to women or sex objects.
2. Recognize all female officers have individual needs just as any one else. Just as any one else does, some may lack basic skills when they are first on the department.
3. All recruits feel insecure and somewhat frightened during their initial training periods. Be supportive and provide encouragement as you would for anyone.
4. While individual needs should be met, they should not be met by granting favors or providing special treatment.[23]

ANNUAL TRAINING MATERIAL REVIEW

Conducting periodic reviews of all training material is important to ensure its continued relevance and effectiveness to current police problems. This is often overlooked due to ignorance of the need, or simply procrastination. Training material review should be a continual process for both instructor and the training officer.

Because the demands on law enforcement and the nature of society are changing so rapidly, any period longer than a year between reviews will jeopardize the effectiveness of your entire training program. Lesson plans, general orders, movies, video tapes, standard operating procedures, and any other written material should be included in regular reviews.

SELECTING TRAINING AIDS

Review of the material concerning training development presented so far may bring to mind the need for training aids or equipment such as film, written material, handouts, video cassette recorders, etc. Since a previous chapter was devoted to training equipment, little consideration will be provided at this point.

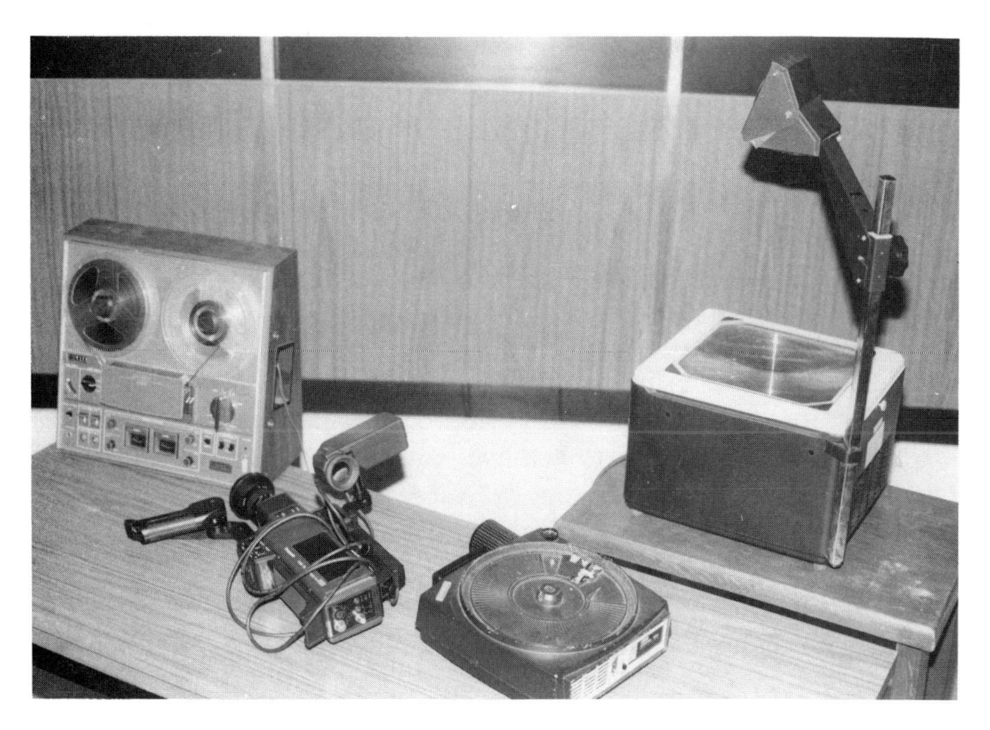

Figure 3. Training aids such as tape recorders, video cameras, slide projectors and overhead projectors are necessary instruction tools. If budget limitations hinder their purchase, fund-raising efforts must begin.

The proper selection of training aids or equipment to match the needed goals and objectives should not be underestimated: Thorough consideration to these matters should be applied during the developmental stage. Failure to do so will mean the possibility of great hardships in fulfilling your commitments during later training stages.

DEVELOPING LESSON PLANS

A training program development should begin with the overall objective to be achieved as the result of the training. This overall objective is comprised of different aspects of the training subject which must be covered to achieve the overall objective. These aspects or phases of the training subject are often referred to as "units," because they are each a separate phase of the larger course.

In developing a training program, the trainer should identify the course goals and its overall objective, the units which comprise the course, and the objectives to each one of these units. The next step is to determine the specific knowledge which must be learned to achieve the unit objectives and design a plan for learning them. This final plan of instruction is usually referred to as a "lesson plan."

A lesson plan begins with a heading and introduction which identifies the name of the course, unit, and any smaller topics. It should then identify the objective, the readings or source for the materials used during the preparation of the lesson, information concerning needed training equipment, and summary of what instruction will be conducted.

The body of a lesson plan should consist of three vertical columns. The left hand column lists the training outcomes to be achieved during the training session. The middle column describes the activities which the instructor will engage to achieve the training outcome. The right hand column is reserved for police officer/student activities which the instructor has planned for the class. Full consideration should be given to providing an interesting variety of activities to prevent boredom or loss of interest during the training. A variety of mentally stimulating activities throughout the training course should be built into the lesson plan.

Inexperienced trainers or instructors may become frustrated at the time spent in preparing a lesson plan. Generally, however, the more knowledgeable and experienced a trainer or instructor is, the more he regards the lesson plan as an absolutely essential part of his training program.[24]

The final step in the preparation of a training program is weaving units into one unified program. The lessons are reviewed and changed as necessary to provide for total achievement of the unit objectives and to ensure they are in a logical sequence. If multiple lesson plans are to be used during one in-service training course, they should be thoroughly studied and changed as necessary to meet the overall course plan and objectives. If the developmental plan has been followed closely, it is a relatively simple matter for instructors to keep their individual lesson plans in a clear relationship to the overall training program objectives and goals. Refer to the following sample lesson plan.

SAMPLE LESSON PLAN

Course. . . . . Supervisor Training Course
Unit. . . . . Human Relatons for Supervisors
Lesson . . . . Basic Psychological Needs of People
Time . . . . 8:30 am, Tuesday, January 16, 19--
Instructor . . . . B. F. Funloped
Lesson Objective. . . . . To develop in the trainees an understanding of the basic psychological needs of people which may be partially satisfied in the work situation
References. . . . . T. F. Staton, Human Relations for Supervisors, Educational Aids, 2208 Woodley Road, Montgomery, Ala., 36111
Instructional Aids. . . . . Blackboard and chalk, slide projector screen, and slides
Student Assignment . . . . None
Length of Period. . . . . 70 minutes
Plan for Conducting the Period . . . . The instructor will give a short introduction to the period, identifying the basic psychological needs of people, explaining their significance, and posing practical questions as to their relation to worker morale and production. He will then elaborate on each psychological need and will ask the class members to cite instances where this need was shown by an employee, explain what was done, and discuss the result. Major factors comprising each of the basic psychological needs, if not brought out by class members, will be identified by the instructor.

Every period of instruction should be planned. The instructor should carry a lesson plan with him into the classroom. A lesson left only in your mind is generally no lesson plan what-so-ever. It is only wishful thinking that you will be able to recall or refer to scribbled notes and conduct a thorough and competent instruction period. Do not attempt to condense your lesson plan by abbreviating it or leaving off any of the columns.

BUDGETING

Now that we have discussed how a training program can be developed, it is time to examine the training budget. The trainer needs to determine what a fully developed training program will cost and if the agency can afford it. The first step in the budgeting process is to determine all the program costs. Common cost categories will include:

- Staff
- Consultants
- Participant time
- Materials
- Audio-visual aids
- Facility
- Travel
- Food
- Advertising

All agencies have staff costs whenever an officer is assigned to work on a training program. These costs can be determined by figuring an officer's hourly rate and multiplying by the number of hours spent on the program. Failure to include these costs will result in underestimating the training budget.

Though not used on a regular basis by most agencies due to the expense involved, consultants are sometimes used to instruct training programs. They usually charge a standard daily rate which may or may not include expenses. If expenses are not included, the trainer must also add travel and per diem costs for the consultant.

Officers that are being paid while attending a training program are a cost to the department. Due to manpower restrictions, some law enforcement agencies are forced to replace an officer attending training. Training costs in this category are based on the total salary cost to the agency.

All equipment and supplies that are purchased or rented for a training program are included in the section pertaining to materials. Services such as copying charges, rental for a movie projector or training films should also be included. During budgeting decisions regarding training equipment purchase or rental, the questions of how much use of the equipment will be derived and how much availability will there be if it is rented should be asked.

Audio-visual assistance will either be produced by the agency or obtained through the purchase from another source. Audio-visual production costs should be determined only for the product, as staff time is figured under staff costs.

Agencies which do not have access to an in-house training room, or who are hosting other agencies, may need to rent a meeting room at another location. Such "away" locations have many advantages regarding seclusion from constant interruptions. Charges incurred may include rental for the meeting room, refreshments, tips, etc.

Travel costs should be determined for staff and/or participant travel that will be paid by the agency. Costs for food should include meals and lodging. Such expenses can be figured on a separate room and meal cost or on a per diem rate. Only those expenses being paid by the agency should be listed in this category.

Possible advertising costs include newspaper, television, radio, or any other direct advertising such as brochures, announcements and letters. Any expense to promote the program should be included in this budget item.

The preceding projected costs should be added for a total of the training program expense. The next step is to determine the total amount available for funding the program. Sources of funds may include the agency's budget, contributions, donations, grants, any type of governmental assistance, and tuition fees from participants.[25]

Training officers should make any changes possible to minimize costs and still meet the training objectives. The total cost of the program should be subtracted from available funds. If the program costs exceed available funds, then the trainer must re-assess all cost items or continue attempting to raise money for the program. Less expensive alternatives may also be considered. A sample program budget work sheet is provided for your convenience.

TRAINING MATERIALS

The resources used for in-service training has varied among law enforcement agencies. One method of providing such material is for the instructor to prepare his own handout material. The writing of such handouts will be exceedingly time consuming, however. As a result, most officers have found that they are not able to devote such time and effort.

The preparation for training material requires extensive research and assistance of experts in various fields. Some smaller agencies use training bulletins from other agencies. The drawback to this technique is that many training bulletins published by agencies pertain to their particular operational procedures.

Care must be taken while copying training material from books or

TABLE III
PROGRAM BUDGET WORK SHEET

Training Program: Dates:

Funds:

Available

1. From Training Agency $__________
2. From Other Agencies $__________
3. From Grants $__________
4. From Tuition Fees $__________

Total $__________

Costs:

Staff

Name	Hourly Rate	×	# of Hours	=	
__________	__________	×	__________	=	$__________
__________	__________	×	__________	=	$__________
__________	__________	×	__________	=	$__________

Sub-Total $__________

Consultants

Name	Fee	+	Travel	+	Per Diem	=	
__________	__________		__________		__________	=	$__________
__________	__________		__________		__________	=	$__________
__________	__________		__________		__________	=	$__________

Sub-Total $__________

Participate Time

# of Trainees	×	Hourly Cost	×	# of Hours	=	
__________	×	__________	×	__________	=	$__________
__________	×	__________	×	__________	=	$__________
__________	×	__________	×	__________	=	$__________

Sub-Total $__________

TABLE III Continued

Costs: (Continued)

Participate Time (Continued)

# of Staff	×	Overtime Rate	×	# of Hours	=
____	×	____	×	____	= $____
____	×	____	×	____	= $____
____	×	____	×	____	= $____

Sub-Total $____

Materials

Item	Rental Per Unit	or	Purchase Price Per Unit		# of Units	=
____	____	or	____	×	____	= $____
____	____	or	____	×	____	= $____
____	____	or	____	×	____	= $____

Sub-Total $____

Audio-Visual Aids

Aid	Rental Price Per Unit	or	Purchase Price Per Unit	×	# of Units	=
____	____		____	×	____	= #____
____	____		____	×	____	= #____
____	____		____	×	____	= #____

Sub-Total $____

Facility

Item	# of Items	×	Rate	×	# of Days	=
____	____	×	____	×	____	= $____
____	____	×	____	×	____	= $____
____	____	×	____	×	____	= $____

Sub-Total $____

Travel

Mode	Ticket Cost	or	Rate	×	Distance	=
____	____	or	____	×	____	= $____
____	____	or	____	×	____	= $____
____	____	or	____	×	____	= $____

Sub-Total $____

TABLE III Continued

Costs: (Continued)

Subsistence (Food and Lodging)

# of Persons	×	Rate	×	# of Days	=	
______	×	______	×	______	=	$______
______	×	______	×	______	=	$______
______	×	______	×	______	=	$______

Sub-Total $______

Subsistence (Continued)

Lodging	+	Meals	=	Daily Cost	×	# of Days	×	# of Persons	=	
______	+	______	=	______	×	______	×	______	=	$______
______	+	______	=	______	×	______	×	______	=	$______
______	+	______	=	______	×	______	×	______	=	$______

Sub-Total $______

Advertising

Item	Cost Per Item	×	# of Items	=	
______	______	×	______	=	$______
______	______	×	______	=	$______
______	______	×	______	=	$______

Sub-Total $______

Total $______

Total Available Funds $______

Total Program Costs $______

Balance $______

Source: Deborah Cheesebro and Gilbert H. Skinner, *Training Development For Criminal Justice Agencies*, Michigan State University, 1980.

magazines to ensure there are no copyright violations. Often, permission for such duplicating may be obtained by a letter or phone call. Many authors are willing to give permission for the use of police agencies to copy their materials. The International Association of Chiefs of Police also offers quality printed materials which can be purchased ahead of time for roll call training.

Regardless of what source is used, written materials must be accurate and up to date. Particular attention must be given to the material's clarity, accuracy, and conciseness. Attention should be given to reproducing only written material from a legitimate and/or recognized source.

RESOURCE CONSULTANTS

If you are currently a training officer, you are probably overworked, underpaid, not provided enough funding to accomplish your goals, and tend to be somewhat frustrated. Because of these things, a number of agencies are looking for resource consultants to assist them.

The process of program development can be accomplished by training officers or by retraining consultants who report to training officers.

There are many advantages to retaining an outside consultant. Most such consultants have advanced degrees in behavioral science with extensive experience in training program development and implementation. Due to this fact, your agency's top level management will be more likely to listen and agree with their proposal than they would your own.

Consultants is also more likely to be objective in their evaluation of a situation than are you. This is because they are totally removed from the internal politics and workings of the agency. In addition they are apprized of the current "state of the art" techniques and methods.

The negative aspects of hiring such consultants are that while they may be totally objective, they are also totally ignorant of the detailed structure of your agency. The informal networks and personalities which affect daily operations could take considerable time to be thoroughly understood. Furthermore, because a consultant will not work within your agency over an extended period of time on a full-time basis, it may be impossible for him to totally understand current problems as they develop. Lastly, the retaining of such a consultant can exceed your budget limitations.

While it is not practical or cost effective in every situation, the ideal solution is to hire an outside training consultant to work "hand in hand" with you or other training personnel. This will provide the best benefits with the fewest disadvantages. A consultant will bring professional experience and credibility to any project, while the insider will provide the internal skills and knowledge essential to your department's success.

If you decide to retain the services of a professional training consultant, be prepared to present the consultant with an extensive presentation of your current, past and future training situation. Failure to have this ready will waste time and money.

How do you get outside help? One effective manner is by simply reviewing the yellow pages under management or training consultation. Another way is to consult with training officers in nearby areas. A commonly overlooked manner is to contact local universities or colleges. The business department of most universities may offer very effective consultants from the ranks of their professors.

Be certain to interview the selected prospects in person. The benefit of such an inside/outside training team can quickly be negated if you and your selected consultant are personally or professionally incompatible. Any agency's training program will most likely benefit from such a consultant training program. However, if top level management has not made a full commitment, both financially and throughout the entire agency's staff personnel, the program's benefits may be drastically jeopardized.[26]

OBTAINING SUPPORT FROM MANAGEMENT

Many training officers who feel undervalued probably deserve it. They may have developed a "negative attitude" toward their responsibilities or the job itself. Any police trainer will find it beneficial, both professionally and personally, to form a habit of positive strategy in the production of training.

The positive thinking training officer not only will enjoy his career more, he will also be more productive. One of the aspects of his productivity is using his positive attitude and strategy to obtain the support of various levels of management. An organized, sequential procedure may be necessary in assisting such procurement of support.

One of the first steps to obtaining management's backing is to base all your training requests on substantiated data that demonstrates the need for such a program. Avoid promoting a program because it may simply be popular among your agency's officers. Your training documentation should let you know whether or not there is a true need for such training. Never reinvent the wheel. There may be the same training program or materials which could be borrowed by you from other agencies or resources.

Always find some way to show your appreciation to management personnel for their support. Whether it's providing additional assistance to them with particular training needs or simply a quick memorandum of appreciation, the time spent by you is usually re-paid many times over.

Lastly, consider developing a systematic approach to obtaining the support of agency management. Such a system would allow managers, at any time, to forward a written document that identifies their specific needs, describes possible responses to those needs, and suggests the outcome of such responses. Thus, by devising a form which is easily assessible to management and encouraging management to submit a completed form of this nature to you, it will foster growth and acceptance of training programs within your agency. Not only will their information and ideas usually be a benefit to you, you will automatically have their support because they will consider this as being their initial idea.[27]

GUIDELINES FOR SELECTION OF TRAINING PROGRAMS

Decide whether or not to send one or more officers away to a training school by first determining whether this training is needed. Training is not a good alternative if your internal system is what needs to be changed. To determine whether training is an appropriate solution, identify the real problem and decide what you need to change. Consider what the changed situation would be like and how it would be different from what is your current circumstance. Consider the various means you could use to make such a change and whether enrolling officer(s) in such a training program is a logical way to achieve it.

When reviewing advertising on a training workshop, seminar or conference, the major concern should be to determine whether the program will be effective. The more actively involved your officers will be in the program, the more likely they will benefit from it. Whether the officers are sent away or participate in an in-service program, those which actively involve participants will be most beneficial.

The following are characteristics of a potentially effective training program:

> There are few lectures, and practical exercises are encouraged. There is a focus on meeting the specific needs of participants, as opposed to making a general participation from which participants must apply to their own agencies. Class participation is required among all participants. The program is offered to a small group of participants as opposed to an audience which is unlimited in size.

In addition to whether or not the training seminar will be "hands on" or simply a lecture, there are other questions which should be posed. One of your most important concerns should be the competency and commitment of the organization conducting the training. Determine how long the organization has been in existence. Look for an organization that specializes in a limited number of training programs as opposed to one that offers an almost unlimited variety of subjects. Find out which instructor will actually be conducting the course and what are his qualifications. Ask whether or not officers will be provided with materials from the course. If valuable materials are included in the cost of the training, you may be able to reproduce them to expand the benefit of the program.

If you do enroll officers in a particular course, be certain they prepare a report upon completion. Such a report should evaluate and critique the course. You can easily prepare an effective evaluation for this purpose.

The obvious objective of such an evaluation process is to eliminate sending officers to schools which are not productive. It also helps to determine what organizations provide quality training programs. Future considerations regarding seminars will be made more intelligently and productively.[28]

SHIFTING CONTEXT

Shifting context is a relatively new approach to training development. The theory contends that retention and reinforcement of training may be virtually eliminated. It can result in leaving officers motivated to learn on their own any material which you would choose not to cover during training. The approach in which the positive aspects of training increase overtime rather than decrease.

While relatively new, the shifting context training approach can be extremely beneficial. Its aim is to shift or transform an officer's **point of view**. Relatively little factual information is instructed and few, if any, skills are learned. Furthermore, there is no "correct" behavior to be learned.

Instead, this training approach encourages officers to create a new "context" in which to learn and explore skills and use information. Its premise is that if officers are able to create a new context for themselves, a new and improved way of viewing themselves and their agency's purpose will result in their taking it upon themselves to do and learn most of the things required to operate within that new context.

To train officers in "shifting context," the focus shifts away from imparting facts and knowledge to instilling specific new behaviors. The goal is to lead officers to discover that their job actually consists of more than mechanical tasks they have to perform. They should begin to look at their job as ensuring that citizens receive all the benefits which a law enforcement agency can provide.

This approach to training is becoming increasingly more prevalent within the business world. The business training community has already discovered that soon after "shifting context" training, class participants already have most of the knowledge and skills necessary to perform their tasks. Participants have discovered that they both enjoy and are considerably more effective in performing their job roles. They have also learned they must practice using information, skills, and behavior that is consistent with the new context.

The use of role playing and a number of traditional training techniques can be used to accomplish these tasks. While having tremendous possible benefits, the shifting context approach is not intended to replace a major portion of traditional law enforcement training. It is, however, an avenue worth exploring as an additional means of instilling a positive sense of values and attitudes.[29]

COMPETITION AND COOPERATION

The positive effects and benefits of developing competition and/or cooperation among officers during training programs should be heavily considered. Competition can have harmful affects if "winning" is overemphasized. There are few winners and many losers when, in self-defense, officers, who are somewhat introverted, decline participation due to the competitive nature of the training. It may also be harmful when it is so intense that losing also means loss of status, or when winning at all costs overshadows other considerations.

Competition is not necessarily bad. There are many positive aspects. Research suggests that it can be positive while promoting superior performance. Training officers should, however, ensure that it stimulates greater positive output by officers, yet always be aware of its negative limitations.

DEVELOPING HOME STUDY COURSES

Home study correspondence courses can be a useful training technique even though rarely used by law enforcement agencies. Their usefulness is magnified due to the difficulty all agencies experience with manpower limitations and rotating shifts.

Developing such training programs cannot be considered as a substitute for formal and more traditional types of training. These can, however, supplement an agency's training programs and be very useful because officers may participate at their own pace. The voluntary participation by officers may also be useful in indicating an individual's initiative and perseverance for promotional consideration.

A home study program's development and administration can be costly and time consuming. The cost involves material which may be required as study guides. Such development may be time consuming if an agency plans to develop the written materials and examinations on their own.

DEVELOPMENT OF A NON IN-SERVICE TRAINING COURSE

I. **ORGANIZE AND DESIGN THE TRAINING COURSE**
   A. Select course title.
   B. Research current information.
   C. Research material for handouts.
   D. Write course agenda.

II. **INSTRUCTORS**
   A. Determine the selection procedures for speakers/instructors.
   B. Select the desired speakers/instructors.
   C. Write a letter to selected speakers/instructors inviting them to instruct.
   D. Receive response from accepting speakers/instructors.
   E. Negotiate fee with speakers/instructors.
   F. Execute the contract with the instructor.
   G. Discuss the objectives of the course with speakers.
   H. Follow-up on speaker arrangements (i.e. travel, room).
   I. Advise speaker on reimbursement procedures.
   J. Conduct a pre-course briefing for instructors.

III. **LOCATION**
   A. Determine a central location.
   B. Select a training site.

C. Establish a contact person
D. Visit site if unfamiliar with its accommodations.
E. Negotiate site rates.
F. Check guest rooms.
G. Check central training room (i.e. size, lighting, sound).

IV. **CONTRACTS**
A. Negotiate contract with speakers/instructors.
B. Write contractual agreement.
C. Obtain legal opinion on contract.
D. Revise contract based upon input (if necessary).
E. Mail contracts to instructors.
F. Obtain receipts of signed contracts.

V. **PARTICIPANT CONSIDERATIONS**
A. Establish an advertising plan.
B. Send advertising to potential participants (include a deadline response date.)
C. Organize a list confirming participants.
D. Write a letter to confirmed participants (include note of acceptance for confirmation, training description, date of training, location, cost, training agenda.)

VI. **COURSE PRESENTATION**
A. Establish course attendance log.
B. Establish seating arrangement (include name cards.)
C. Check A/V equipment.
D. Arrange for group photograph.
E. Arrange for refreshments during course.
F. Determine the timing for speaker presentation.
G. Distributes handouts (if necessary.)
H. Make opening statements and introductions.
I. Have certificates typed.

VII. **COURSE EVALUATION**
A. Prepare an evaluation tool, (if none is available).
B. Explain evaluation tool to participants.
C. Distribute evaluation tool.
D. Analyze evaluation.
E. Provide feed-back on evaluation to participants.
F. Provide feed-back to instructors based upon evaluations.
G. Revise course for subsequent presentation.

Source: Bureau of Training, Florida Police Standards and Training Commission, Florida Department of Law Enforcement.

NON-POLICE INSTRUCTORS

Training officers must give attention to the fact that some training programs should be instructed by non-police personnel. Attorneys, probation officers, psychologists and crime laboratory technicians are a few examples where civilian instructors are more proficient and qualified than police officers.

These considerations should be included during the developmental stage of any training course. Even though the benefits outweigh the drawbacks, beware that many police officers do not relate well to non-police instructors. This problem should diminish with time and be overcome through the team teaching efforts with police instructors.

The future holds many challenges. It will not be an easy task to keep an eye open for new, innovative and beneficial programs, yet not be taken in by gimmicks and publicity. We must give considerable effort to the return of basic training skills among officers.

Can we tackle controversial and relatively ignored critical issues?[30] These challenges can be met. The crucial issue will be whether or not police trainers take the initiative to grow in their capabilities and positive viewpoints. Such growth will prove to administrators across the nation that a resulting efficiency among police trainers will provide such positive results to the department that the training function can no longer be ignored.

REFERENCES

1. Thomas F. Staton, *How To Instruct Successfully,* New York: McGraw-Hill, 1960, pg. 268.
2. Thomas F. Staton, *How To Instruct Successfully,* New York: McGraw-Hill, 1960, pg. 273.
3. Elliot Eisner, *The Educational Imagination,* New York: Macmillan, 1979, Chapter 6.
4. Deborah Cheesebro and Gilbert H. Skinner, *Training Program Development For Criminal Justice Agencies,* Michigan State University, 1980, pg. 7–8.
5. Training For Development, pg. 342.
6. C. K. Klaus, *Stating Behavioral Objectives For Classroom Instruction,* New York: Macmillan. 1970, pg. 53–56.
7. Peter Franz Renner, *The Instructor's Survival Kit,* Training Associates Ltd., Vancouver, B. C., Canada, 1983, pg. 99.
8. Robert F. Mager, *Preparing Instructional Objectives,* Palo Alto, Calif:Fearon. 1962.
9. Wayne J. Foreman, A Study Of Management Techniques Used By Large Corporations, *Public Personnel Review,* 28, (Jan., 1967), pg. 31–35.
10. See bottom of table.
11. J. Robert Havlick, Recruit Training: Police Chief's Dilemma, *Public Management,* 50 (Dec., 1968), pg. 300–303.

12. Chip R. Bell, Criteria For Selecting Instructional Strategies, *Training and Development Journal,* 1977.
13. Peter Franz Renner, *The Instructor's Survival Kit,* Training Associates Ltd., Vancouver, B. C., Canada, 1983, pg. 9.
14. Thomas F. Staton, *How To Instruct Successfully,* New York: McGraw-Hill, 1960, pg. 193–194.
15. Thomas F. Staton, *How To Instruct Successfully,* New York: McGraw-Hill, 1960, pg. 201–217.
16. John Lawrie, Skills Development With A Permanent Impact, *Personnel Journal,* June 1984, pg. 39.
17. Charles E. Higginbotham, In-Service Training, *The Police Chief,* September 1980, pg. 16–19.
18. Charles W. Steinmetz and Francis R. Dunphy, The Roll Call Message, *The Police Chief,* October 1984, pg. 53–54.
19. Dean Spitzer, Misconceptions That Produce Bad Training, Training, June 1985.
20. Jack Molden, The Training Officer's Role, *Law and Order,* March 1983, pg. 10–11.
21. Larry L. Lambert, Nine Reasons That Most Training Programs Fail, *Personnel Journal,* January 1985, pg. 62–64.
22. Stephen B. Wehrenberg, Accommodating The Stages Of Career Development, *Personnel Journal,* May 1984, pg. 19–20.
23. Jack Molden, Female Police Officers.... Training Implications, *Law and Order,* June 1985.
24. Thomas F. Staton, *How To Instruct Successfully,* New York: McGraw-Hill, 1960, pg. 64.
25. Deborah Cheesebro and Gilbert H. Skinner, *Training Program Development For Criminal Justice Agencies,* Michigan State University, 1980, pg. 33–38.
26. Stephen B. Wehrenberg, Inside or Outside Resources: Which Are Best For Training? *Personnel Journal,* July 1984, pg. 23–24.
27. John Lawrie, Get Support Right Down The Line, *Personnel Journal,* April 1984, pg. 66.
28. Norton Kiritz, *Guidelines for the Selection Of Training Programs,* The Giantsmanship Center News, March 1985.
29. Morty Lefkoe, Shifting Context: A Better Approach To Training, *Training,* February 1985.
30. Jack Seitzinger, Police Training, *The Police Chief,* September 1980, pg. 20–21.

2.

THE FIELD TRAINING OFFICER PROGRAM

The level of training that a police officer possesses has always been a concern. It concerns not only an agency's administration, but to the community's citizens as well. Contemporary demands placed upon the police are drastically different than a few decades ago. Stories told by senior officers which reflect "here's your badge and gun, now go out and put somebody in jail" attitudes are nothing more than memories of a time long gone.

Many officers remember a time when rookies had virtually no initial training. The field training officer concept is still relatively new. "On the job training" is entrenched within many professions, however. To become a school teacher you must usually complete an internship during the final stages of your college degree program. All states require that physicians complete an extensive internship as part of their formalized training. The armed services has a wide variety of "on the job" training programs for almost all job assignments, regardless of the training topic. All such training must be highly structured and selectively focused upon the duties and responsibilities inherent to the specific job.

Though slow in coming, the field training officer concept is one of the most valuable innovations in the history of law enforcement training. While a few progressive agencies have had a field training officer program for years, such training has only become accepted in the law enforcement community since the late 1970's. Be careful not to confuse the field training officer concept with that of field training. The concept of field training is not new. The distant past often found rookie officers indiscriminately assigned to ride with another officer for a particular period of time. It was then that the new officer was told "now forget all that stuff they taught you in the police academy, I'll show you how it's really done."[1] In most cases the rookie officer did exactly what he was told. He forgot what he had been taught in the academy and did exactly what the senior officer advised. More often than not, this included any and all negative aspects the veteran happened to have had. Selection of the veteran officer usually depended on nothing more than his seniority.

A comparison of the "state of the art" field training officer program with previous field training programs allows a true understanding of how crucial the field training officer program is to law enforcement. Instead of simply helping new officers get through their initial months on the force, we can now provide a smooth transition from theory to the realities of the streets. Many of the guidelines presented in this chapter should be modified to meet the specific needs of an agency. As an example, agency size will require modifications.

INHERENT GOALS

All FTO programs should have several inherent guidelines:

1. Allow rookie officers a period to become comfortable with their new working environment. Most employees find their initial weeks on a new job somewhat overwhelming. The demands for learning a particular agency's standard operating procedures, various regulations and policies, developing a "street sense" and applying theory to the real world is difficult to say the least. A formal training period gives him time to get used to his new world.
2. New officers are forced to face the challenge of applying academy theory to real life situations. The majority of academy training has been in classroom settings through lecture instruction. The challenge of an FTO program is to apply theory to daily real life situations.
3. Rookie officers require a great deal of guidance and direction. Faced with a variety of demands, guidance, evaluation, counseling, and monitoring will be invaluable to their personal and professional development. As discussed later in this chapter, daily evaluations provide a crucial function of the training program. Both the field training officer and the officer trainee must always know exactly where the trainee stands.
4. The training program should offer new officers a highly competent and qualified role model.[2] Researchers in developmental adult psychology now know psychological growth of adult development is influenced greatly by those advising, instructing and counseling

Figure 4. As with all in-service programs, training goals and objectives must be established for a field training officer program.

in a work setting environment.[3] The long term effect which a field training officer has on his trainee should not be underestimated.

ADVANTAGES OF THE FIELD TRAINING OFFICER PROGRAM

A well developed FTO program has numerous advantages. Understanding the advantages will be a tremendous benefit to training officers while justifying the program's implementation.

- An academy classroom environment is inherently limited in its ability to apply areas of training which require a realistic setting. The FTO program allows for a practical and realistic learning environment.
- The evaluation process will compensate for errors made in recruit selection. Daily evaluations of the trainee provides sound documentation for termination. Rotating the trainee to several FTO's

ensures fairness. This consideration becomes particularly important in light of current legalities which regulate and limit both the hiring and termination process.

- A well developed FTO program allows for knowledge acquired in the police academy to be applied under controlled situations. Failure to control a rookie officer's performance during his initial work places unnecessary safety risks upon the officer and jeopardizes the agency from a civil litigation standpoint.
- The effectiveness of an FTO program will result in more productive new officers in a far shorter time period than was previously required. This will also be accomplished in a manner consistent with current state of the art training.
- The program provides an effective manner through which agencies may instruct organizational goals, rules and regulations, city ordinances and other important aspects of employment.[1]
- An FTO program produces an indirect benefit to those selected as field training officers. As any experienced instructor knows, those required to train benefit greatly from their efforts to instruct others.

Aprofessional police officer is the result of a culmination of both personal qualities and productive training. The overwhelming advantage of an effective FTO program is that it provides the vehicle through which training can productively enhance the qualities and alter the negative traits possessed by new officers.

COMMITMENT FROM AGENCY HEAD

The first step in initiating an FTO program is to obtain a true commitment from the head of your agency. Without such a commitment, your efforts will undoubtedly be in vain.

Prior to formerly submitting your proposal, considerable preparation and research must be conducted. Be prepared to answer all questions with practical and straightforward answers. The advantages to FTO training are easily recognized and understood. What should also be considered are any concerns which may affect the overall operation of the agency.

Obtaining a commitment from your agency head should begin by providing thorough explanation of how the program will operate. Do this in a logical and sequential fashion. The advantages should follow such an overall summary.

Any administrator will be concerned with the amount of funding required for the program. Fortunately, very little funding is necessary. The only substantial expense may be that necessary for enrollment of selected field training officers in an FTO seminar.

Another concern will be manpower considerations. It may be tempting for an agency head to limit the necessary length of time a new officer takes during his training program. Uniform patrol manpower shortages are common. A lack of commitment from the chief or sheriff will result in officers having their training terminated prior to its completion. This, of course, will be devastating to the program. Most agencies have found that four months has been an adequate period of time for completion of the program.

PROGRAM SEQUENCE

Officer development is a continuous process. It continues throughout the time an officer works for his organization. Well organized FTO programs follow a generally accepted method of development. The San Jose Police Department FTO program was developed in the early 1970's. San Jose is credited for creation of the original concept which has now become so widely accepted.

Program development should begin with an orientation. Providing an orientation period during the onset of an FTO program enables the new officer to adjust more readily to his responsibilities. Officers will make fewer mistakes and experience enhanced job satisfaction as a result.

The content of an orientation program will vary from agency to agency. Instructional methods for orientation topics will also vary. Suggested topics are as follows:

1. Goals of the agency.
2. General orders or standard operating procedures.
3. Specific job duties of the new officer's position.
4. An organizational chart of the agency.
5. Identifying various departmental personnel and relating their specific job responsibilities.
6. New and/or future developments within the agency.
7. Various employee benefits.
8. Promotion procedures.
9. A tour of the physical facilities.
10. A brief tour of the geographic boundaries within your agency's jurisdictions.

11. A brief summary of duties for each division or section.
12. An explanation of how each division interacts with other divisions.

Many departments have found that developing a checklist specifically for orientation is very beneficial. The checklist can allow for the trainee's signature to properly document the concerned topics were instructed.[4]

An option for extending the initial orientation period is to arrange for new officers to train with various sections within the department before continuing with field training officers. Supervisors within the records section, the communications section, detective bureau, and traffic division or other specialized units may use outlines to conduct such training. Most agencies will find that several days is sufficient time for training with each division.

Officers are not evaluated during orientation. This allows for him to become more familiar and comfortable with his surroundings. The evaluation process begins when the officer is assigned to actual field training officers.

Following the orientation phase, training by field training officers begins. From three to five field training officers, per trainee, are used to conduct all other training topics. Each field training officer will evaluate the trainee daily. Every training officer is assigned specific topics. No trainee should continue training unless the field training officer is convinced that the trainee thoroughly understands all covered materials.

Following completion of a field training officer's instruction, the trainee rotates to a second field training officer for further training. Training continues through this process until the trainee rotates to the last field training officer.

All field training officers should use an extensive training topic outline to ensure that no areas of instruction are overlooked. Following completion of all training topics, the trainee and the field training officer must both sign the outline, attesting the concerned areas were thoroughly instructed and understood. These outlines become a permanent part of the trainee's training record.

Unlike prior field training officers, the last field training officer assumes a primary role of observer and evaluator. He has no specific training areas to cover, yet must be prepared to instruct any topic. Some departments prefer that this field training officer wear civilian clothes to encourage all questions and necessary decisions to be directed to the trainee. Any serious situations would be intervened upon by the field training officer.

Following completion of an assigned task, the trainee and final field training officer should discuss how the trainee handled the particular situation. This final step is intended to provide rookie officers with a less structured form of training before he graduates to policing by himself.

Finally, an FTO program supervisor must pay close attention to all trainee evaluations. If such evaluations indicate particular weaknesses in a trainee's performance, the supervisor is responsible to ensure that additional training and counseling is provided for in these areas. The supervisor is also responsible for conveying his opinion to the chief administrator regarding whether to terminate or recommend that the trainee be permanently assigned to a uniform shift.

RESPONSIBILITIES OF THE FIELD TRAINING OFFICER

Obviously, the field training officer is the essential ingredient to a successful program. It is he who actually translates goals and objectives into results.

The field training officer has considerably more responsibility than his counterparts in uniform patrol. Not only must he assume responsibility as a patrolman, he remains continually responsible for training and evaluating recruit personnel. A field training officer must always be capable of carrying out the responsibility of a variety of roles.

1. **Human Relations** — It's important that a field training officer have the ability to apply proper human relation skills. Having the ability to assess the need for training in the work environment by analyzing an organization and the job skills necessary to perform efficiently are also necessary. "On the job" training, simulation training, special courses, and retraining will become crucial ingredients in the effective development of human relation skills within new officers.

   Leadership personality traits which perpetuate corporation and positive human relations will also be an important factor. The importance of good human relations should not be underestimated. The degree of effectiveness the field training officer will have communicating with the recruit will be influenced greatly by their personal relationship.

2. **Role Model**—The field training officer will act as a trainer, counselor, and supervisor for the new officer. As a result of their constant contact, he will become a role model. The importance of this relationship must be realized. It will be vital for developing traits such as sincerity, loyalty, honesty, respect, and dedication.[5]
3. **Counseling Techniques**—The counseling process which develops between the recruit and his field training officer may be extremely beneficial. It is important that field training officers have the ability to apply basic counseling techniques. Such skills will be of assistance in the solution of a variety of problems and adjustments. The counseling strategies commonly used are: emphasizing, suggesting, referring, reviewing, motivating, clarifying, informing and interpreting. The traits of friendliness, sincerity and warmth must be conveyed to the recruit on a daily basis. Assisting the new officer with a variety of professional and personal problems dealing with adjustment, problem solving, and making choices and/or decisions are typical. Assistance and encouragement must be conveyed by the field training officer no matter what situation arises.
4. **Motivation**—Field training officers must thoroughly understand the effect motivation may have on the new recruit. Motivation strategies which enhance the successful performance officers must be developed and used regularly.

   Emphasis should be placed on the significance of enhancing an officer's work environment and the relationship that those improvements will have on motivation. A positive and supportive atmosphere must prevail during all field training officer aspects.
5. **Communication Techniques**—It is crucial that a field training officer be effective in communicating with new officers. Reading, writing, listening, and speaking are skills he must possess and ensure the trainee does also.

   Being able to make constructive criticisms, disagree ascertively, be an effective listener, summarize your message, and confirm a final decision are all important traits for a field training officer. The new officer must thoroughly understand the importance of communication skills in law enforcement.
6. **Teaching Techniques**—A field training officer must possess the knowledge necessary to instruct the trainee in matters pertaining to his department needs. He should also be able to fairly and efficiently evaluate the new officers' abilities and skills. The psychological

factors involved in adult instruction should be understood. Concentration, reaction, comprehension, and repetition are important aspects of adult instruction. Employing these and a variety of other teaching and coaching skills will greatly effect the degree of a field training officer's effectiveness.

7. **Evaluation Responsibilities** —A field training officer must accept the challenges and responsibilities associated with documenting and correcting improper behavior. He must identify and evaluate performance on a daily basis. This process should be communicated to the recruit officer as it occurs. It should be documented in writing for possible future action.
8. **Knowledge Source** —Staying knowledgeable is essential for the field training officer's effectiveness. A thorough knowledge of departmental regulations and procedures, local ordinances, traffic regulations, state statutes, and various training information must be conveyed continually. Furthermore, the lack of knowledge on the part of the field training officer is likely to act in a discrediting manner to the recruit. If situations arise when the answer to a particular question is not known, the field training officer should find the answer.

In summary, a field training officer assumes a tremendous amount of responsibility. He is responsible for preparing a new officer for patrol by instructing, demonstrating, monitoring and evaluating the trainee's progress. Crucial to these tasks are maintaining open communications and setting a proper role model. The field training officer also has a great deal of responsibility for his agency. His department becomes dependent upon him to ensure that a high level of training is afforded new officers. The long term effects of his efforts will become apparent with time.

Lastly, all field training officers are responsible to themselves for ensuring that their training efforts will benefit all within the department. Any benefit for the department will in turn be a benefit of self-satisfaction, advancement, pride, prestige, and personal betterment for a competent field training officer.

SELECTION AND RETENTION OF FIELD TRAINING OFFICERS

All agencies should establish guidelines for the selection of field training officers. Extreme care must be exercised in the selection process. Standardized guidelines will ensure a selection process capable of identifying qualified field training officers.

Entry requirements for field training officers are to be of the highest standards. Previously appointed field training officers who meet these standards must have constantly demonstrated an ability consistent with the rank of supervisor. This, of course, is in keeping with the fact that field training officers are the first line supervisors of new officers. The selection process should consider that not only will training be the foremost responsibility, supervising and evaluating are crucial as well.

Any candidate for a field training officer position should be nominated by his or her supervisor. Departmental guidelines must note the factors to be considered by the nominating supervisor:

A. Knowledge of teaching techniques
B. Skill in verbal presentation
C. Skill in personal relationships
D. Understanding and knowledge of training procedures
E. Past and current job performance

The constructive input from supervisors is beneficial to the selection process. Supervisors must be constantly looking for the qualities inherent in individuals who may become field training officers. Departmental guidelines must establish a procedure to formerly encourage and accept their input.

While standards should not be lowered, the selection process may not be as complex in a smaller agency. Larger agencies must rely upon the observation of candidate's supervisors to identify the most qualified personnel. No matter what size the department, ascertaining the opinion of officers on the candidates own shift will provide an important insight as to their skills, qualifications, and attitudes.

It is recommended that the following qualifications be formerly established in agency selection guidelines:

A. Candidates must have exceptional past performance evaluations.
B. Candidates length of time on the department should be heavily considered.

C. Any prior formal training relating to instruction, counseling, evaluation, stress management, technical techniques, and field training officer programs should be considered.

D. A candidate's overall attitude as to his anticipated devotion and dedication to the principles of the field training officer should be considered.

The final phase of selection should be an oral review board. Prior to the board, candidates should submit a memorandum detailing their qualifications and aspirations for the position. The board should be comprised of a current field training officer, the training officer and a line supervisor.

Following the appointment of field training officers, emphasis should be placed upon development. Regular in-service training meetings will promote efficiency and effectiveness. Topics to be considered for each meeting may include teaching techniques, evaluation procedures, program curriculum, training philosophy, stress management, counseling, role playing, guest lecturers, and ethics and professionalism.

Many quality field training officer seminars and training programs are now offered throughout the nation. Be certain to take advantage of what they have to offer. Trainers are now selecting officers which possess the greatest personal qualities compatable to the field training officer's position and offer the highest degree of potential for success. Be certain to use "long range" planning regarding which training seminars potential field training officers attend.

The selection process should have identified and chosen motivated and dedicated field training officers. As time goes on, however, even the most devoted officers may become weary of their added responsibilities without any monetary reward. Providing a financial incentive will benefit the agency as well as the individual field training officer. Improved incentive, morale, motivation, and demonstration that management really is supportive of the program will be seen. It will also add support when demanding high quality performance from field training officers. Payment may take place in the form of an annual bonus, salary percentage increase, extra vacation days off or a bonus for every officer they train.[6]

THE TRAINEE EVALUATION PROCESS

Field training officers mold raw recruits into productive, skillful and knowledgeable officers. Their guidance to a rookie officer is the key to a successful program. No function is more critical than evaluation. Its importance lies not only in providing an evaluation of the new officer, but in providing an evaluation of the program itself.

Written evaluations begin as instruction with field training officers start. Field training officers write daily evaluations of the trainee's performance and submit additional documentation as required. As mentioned previously, the initial training phase does not include evaluations so the recruit can become familiar with his new surroundings without the stress of daily written critiques.

The evaluation process actually begins before the evaluations start. New officers should be told from the very beginning exactly where they stand and what is expected of them. Considerations which should be explained initially include:

A. Explain to the trainee exactly what is expected of him.
B. Advise trainees that field training officers will be candid and specific in their evaluations.
C. Explain to trainees exactly how specific procedures should be accomplished.
D. Set standards of acceptable and unacceptable performance.
E. Field training officers are to keep records of both favorable and unfavorable performance.
F. Field training officers will judge performance not personality.
G. Field training officers should deal with specific incidences, as opposed to generalities, during evaluations.
H. Field training officers will critique the handling of all calls and incidences.
I. Field training officers must emphasize the importance of evaluations to the trainee's future career.
J. Field training officers must evaluate the trainee in his presence, explaining all written comments.

One effective method of evaluation is group assessment and evaluation conducted during field training officer meetings. Training officers should take advantage of meetings to assess and discuss the training performance and status of all trainees.

Group interaction and candid constructive criticism of trainees may provide new insights and perceptions regarding particular evaluation problems. As recruits progress through the program, the decision to provide unique specialized training or termination is made only after the opinion of field training officers have been voiced.

THE SAN JOSE POLICE DEPARTMENT EVALUATION PROCESS

The San Jose Police Department performance criteria evolved from an analysis of the narrative comments of field training officers. The analysis concerned present and previous recruit officer performance. After an extensive study of these narrative comments, the San Jose Psychological Services Unit determined thirty-one performance criteria most commonly given. These criteria were given numerical scores. Upon analysis of these scores, it was determined there were common evaluation references among all field training officers. This resulted in the development of specific scores for specific behavior in each of the described performance criteria.

To promote standarization of the evaluative process, the undefined reference points needed to be articulated and documented. In other words, the common reference points used in the evaluative process needed to be articulated in order to explain the rationale behind a numerical score of "1," "4," or "7" in each of the thirty-one performance criteria.

To accomplish this task and promote standardization of the evaluative process, an extensive study of the evaluation process was launched. More specifically, the Field Training and Evaluation Program Curriculum Committee, through a well-designed questionnaire, identified and analyzed the specific behavior criteria employed by seventy past and present field training officers. These seventy FTO's were requested to "put into words" the exact behavioral criteria they were referring to when they have a numerical rating of 1, 4, etc. The result of the study was the establishment of specific criteria to be used in the evaluation of recruit performance in any of thirty-one areas.

Because law enforcement, like so many other professions, has a wide variety of techniques and procedures, it becomes very important that standardization of performance evaluation take place. Evaluation without standardization is not possible.

Perhaps the most difficult task facing the rater is applying the numerical rating which represents the behavior he is evaluating. The following explanations should clarify the issue of rating and philosophy and ease the concern of the field training officer and the trainee.

The first principle of value application is that each of us has different perceptions on nearly all of life's experiences. While a standardization of ratings is a necessity, an attempt to standardize perceptions is doomed to failure. For example, FTO "A," based on a prior negative experience of his own, sees recruit's exposure of his weapon to a suspect as worth a "1" rating (Officer Safety-Suspects/Suspicious Persons/Prisoners) while FTO "B" may see the same behavior as worth a "3." As long as both officers see the performance as "Unacceptable," no serious problem will exist. A serious problem does, if a lack of standardization is created by one FTO viewing the performance as unacceptable scale values 1, 2, or 3 and the other seeing the same behavior as acceptable scale values 4, 5, 6, or 7. In summary, it is acceptable for there to be differences in officers' perceptions unless these perceptional differences vary between unacceptable and acceptable ratings for the same behavior.

Another important principle concerns the value assigned to the performance of remedial training when the recruit is not responding to training. A trainee who performs at a less than acceptable level might be evaluated at a level of 1, 2, or 3. The field training officer is under an obligation to correct the trainee and assess the recruit's performance at a less than acceptable level. The following is an example of a daily evaluation form, followed by detailed descriptions of standardized evaluation guidelines.

FIELD TRAINING AND EVALUATION PROGRAM

Standardized Evaluation Guidelines

The following "1," "4" and "7" scale value definitions are to be used when rating a recruit officer's behavior in each of the performance categories. It is through the use of these guidelines that program standardization and rating consistency is achieved.

FIELD TRAINING PROGRAM DAILY EVALUATION

RATING INSTRUCTIONS: Rate observed behavior according to the scale below. Specific narrative comments are required on any rating of "2" or less and of "6" or more. Comments are also required on most acceptable and least acceptable performance for this tour of duty. If category is not observed, indicate "N/O." If trainee fails to respond to training, indicate "NRT" and comment.

______________________ Trainee/Recruit

______________________ Field Training Officer

CATEGORY	RATING SCALE								
APPEARANCE/EQUIPMENT									
1- General appearance; condition of equipment	NRT	1	2	3	4	5	6	7	N/O
ATTITUDE									
2- Acceptance of feed-back; verbal and behavior	NRT	1	2	3	4	5	6	7	N/O
3- Attitude toward police work	NRT	1	2	3	4	5	6	7	N/O
KNOWLEDGE									
4- Knowledge of policies and procedures	NRT	1	2	3	4	5	6	7	N/O
5- Knowledge of state statutes and city ordinances	NRT	1	2	3	4	5	6	7	N/O
6- Knowledge of Florida Traffic Code	NRT	1	2	3	4	5	6	7	N/O
7- Knowledge reflected by verbal/written test	NRT	1	2	3	4	5	6	7	N/O
8- Knowledge reflected by field performance	NRT	1	2	3	4	5	6	7	N/O
PERFORMANCE									
9- Driving skill: normal conditions	NRT	1	2	3	4	5	6	7	N/O
10- Driving skill: stress conditions	NRT	1	2	3	4	5	6	7	N/O
11- Use of city map; orientation; response time	NRT	1	2	3	4	5	6	7	N/O
12- Report writing: accuracy and completeness	NRT	1	2	3	4	5	6	7	N/O
13- Report writing: organization and details	NRT	1	2	3	4	5	6	7	N/O
14- Report writing: grammar, spelling, and neatness	NRT	1	2	3	4	5	6	7	N/O
15- Report writing: use of time	NRT	1	2	3	4	5	6	7	N/O
16- Field performance: normal conditions	NRT	1	2	3	4	5	6	7	N/O
17- Field performance: stress conditions	NRT	1	2	3	4	5	6	7	N/O
18- Self initiated field activity	NRT	1	2	3	4	5	6	7	N/O
19- Officer safety: general	NRT	1	2	3	4	5	6	7	N/O
20- Officer safety: suspects and prisoners	NRT	1	2	3	4	5	6	7	N/O
21- Control of conflict: voice command	NRT	1	2	3	4	5	6	7	N/O
22- Control of conflict: physical skills	NRT	1	2	3	4	5	6	7	N/O
23- Use of common sense and good judgement	NRT	1	2	3	4	5	6	7	N/O
24- Radio: use of proper codes	NRT	1	2	3	4	5	6	7	N/O
25- Radio: listens to and comprehends transmissions	NRT	1	2	3	4	5	6	7	N/O
26- Radio: articulation of transmissions	NRT	1	2	3	4	5	6	7	N/O
RELATIONSHIPS									
27- Citizens generally	NRT	1	2	3	4	5	6	7	N/O
28- Ethnic groups other than his/her own	NRT	1	2	3	4	5	6	7	N/O
29- Superior officers	NRT	1	2	3	4	5	6	7	N/O
30- Other officers	NRT	1	2	3	4	5	6	7	N/O

A rating of NRT (not responding to training) is extremely unacceptable; ratings of 1, 2, or 3 are not acceptable by the program standards; a rating of 4 is the acceptable level; ratings of 5, 6, or 7 are superior by the program standards.

Source: The San Jose, California Police Department.

APPEARANCE

(1) **GENERAL APPEARANCE** – Evaluates physical appearance, dress, demeanor and basic issued equipment.

1. Overweight, dirty shoes, dirty and wrinkled uniform. Uniform fits poorly or is improperly worn. Hair ungroomed

NARRATIVE COMMENTS

Most acceptable performance: ______________________________

____

____

____

____

____

____

Least acceptable performance: ______________________________

____

____

____

____

____

____

Additional comments: ______________________________

____

____

____

____

____

____

____

____

______________________ ______________________
Trainee/Recruit Signature Training Officer Signature

Date: ____/____/_____ Squad:_________ Hours:_______ to _______

TRAINING OFFICER: FORWARD COMPLETED FORM TO OPERATIONS COMMANDER

and/or in violation of department regulation. Dirty weapon, equipment. Required equipment often missing or inoperative. Offense body odor and/or bad breath.

4. Uniform neat, clean. Uniform fits and is worn properly. Weapon, leather, equipment is clean and operative. Hair within regulations, shoes are shined. Rarely without required equipment.
7. Uniform neat, clean and tailored. Leather is shined, shoes are

spit-shined. Hair and/or moustache within regulation, never without required equipment. Equipment always clean and operative.

ATTITUDE

(2) **ACCEPTANCE OF FEED-BACK** – Evaluates the way recruit accepts trainer's criticism and how that feed-back is used to further the learning process and improve performance.

1. Rationalizes mistakes, denies that errors were made, is argumentative, refuses to, or does not attempt to make corrections. Considers criticism as personal attack.
4. Accepts criticism in a positive manner and applies it to improve performance and further learning.
7. Actively solicits criticism/feed-back in order to further learning and improve performance. Does not argue or blame others for errors.

(3) **ATTITUDE TOWARD POLICE WORK** – Evaluates how recruit views new career in terms of personal motivation, goals and acceptance of the responsibilities of the job.

1. Sees career only as a job, uses job to boost ego, abuses authority, demonstrates little dedication to the principles of the profession.
4. Demonstrates an active interest in new career and in police responsibilities.
7. Utilizes off duty time to further professional knowledge, actively soliciting assistance from others to increase knowledge and improve skills. Demonstrates concern for the fair and equitable enforcement of the law, maintaining high ideals in terms of professional responsibilities.

KNOWLEDGE

(4) **KNOWLEDGE OF DEPARTMENT POLICIES AND PROCEDURES**

1. Unacceptable: Has no knowledge of department policies and procedures and makes no attempt to learn.
4. Acceptable: Familiar with most commonly applied departmental policies and procedures.

7. Superior: Exceptional working knowledge of departmental policies and procedures.

(5) **KNOWLEDGE OF THE FLORIDA STATE STATUTES/CITY ORDINANCES**

1. Unacceptable: Does not know elements of basic section, not able to learn, no attempt at improvement.
4. Acceptable: Working knowledge of commonly used sections, relates elements to observed criminal activity.
7. Superior: Outstanding knowledge of Penal Code and ability to apply it to both normal and unusual criminal activity.

(6) **KNOWLEDGE OF THE FLORIDA TRAFFIC CODE**

1. Unacceptable: Does not know elements of basic sections, not able to learn, no attempt at improvement.
4. Acceptable: Working knowledge of commonly used sections, related elements to observed traffic related activity.
7. Superior: Outstanding knowledge of commonly used sections, relates it and applies it to both normal and unusual traffic related situations.

(7) **KNOWLEDGE REFLECTED IN VERBAL OR WRITTEN TESTS**

1. Unacceptable: Consistently scores below average (70%) on written test. Consistently unable to answer FTO's questions.
4. Acceptable: Scores 70–90% on tests. Answers most of FTO's questions.
7. Superior: Scores above 90% on all tests, answers all of FTO's questions.

(8) **KNOWLEDGE REFLECTED IN FIELD-PERFORMANCE TESTS**

1. Unacceptable: After receiving training, unable to apply training to practical situations.
4. Acceptable: After the FTO instructs in proper procedure, recruit is usually able to apply instruction.
7. Superior: After training, always applies the proper procedures as instructed.

PERFORMANCE

(9) **DRIVING SKILL: NORMAL CONDITIONS**—Evaluates recruit's skill in the operation of the police vehicle under routine or normal driving conditions.

1. Frequently violates traffic laws. Involved in chargeable acci-

dent(s). Fails to maintain control of the vehicle or displays poor manipulative skills in vehicle operation.

4. Obeys traffic laws when appropriate. Maintains control of the vehicle. Performs vehicle operation while maintaining an alertness to surrounding activity. Drives defensively.
7. Sets an example for lawful, courteous driving. Maintains complete control of the vehicle while operating radio, checking BOLOS, etc. Is a superior defensive driver.

(10) **DRIVING SKILL: MODERATE AND STRESS CONDITIONS**—Evaluates recruit's skill in vehicle operation under immediate or emergency response situations and in situations calling for other than usual driving skill.

1. Involved in chargeable accident(s). Uses blue lights and siren unnecessarily or improperly. Drives too fast or too slow for the situation. Loses control of the vehicle. Does not exercise defensive driving techniques.
4. Maintains control of vehicle and evaluates driving situations properly. Exercises good judgement in speed, use of blue lights and siren. Exercises defensive driving techniques.
7. Displays high degree of reflex ability and driving competence. Anticipates driving situations in advance and acts accordingly. Practices excellent defensive techniques. Responds very well relative to the degree of stress present.

(11) **USE OF THE CITY MAP BOOK: ORIENTATION/RESPONSE TIME TO CALLS**—Evaluates recruit's awareness of surroundings, ability to find locations and arrive at destination within an acceptable period of time.

1. Unaware of location while on patrol. Does not properly use map book. Unable to relate location to destination. Gets lost. Expends too much time getting to destination by using improper routes.
4. Is aware of location while on patrol. Properly uses the map. Can relate location to destination. Arrives within reasonable amount of time.
7. Remembers locations from previous visits and does not need the map to get there. Is aware of shortcuts and utilizes them to save time. High level of orientation to the sector and city.

(12) **ROUTINE FORMS: ACCURACY/COMPLETENESS**—Evaluates

recruit's ability to properly utilize departmental forms necessary to job accomplishment.

1. Is unaware that a form must be completed and/or is unable to complete the proper form for the given situation. Forms are incomplete, inaccurate or improperly used.
4. Knows the commonly used forms and understands their use. Completes them with reasonable accuracy and thoroughness.
7. Consistently makes accurate form selection and rapidly completes detailed form without assistance. Displays high degree of accuracy.

(13) **REPORT WRITING: ORGANIZATION/DETAILS**—Evaluates the recruit's ability to prepare reports that accurately reflect the situation and in a detailed, organized manner.

1. Unable to organize information and to reduce it to writing. Leaves out pertinent details in report.
4. Completes reports, organizing information in a logical manner. Reports contain the required information and details.
7. Reports are a complete and detailed accounting of events from beginning to end, written and organized so that any reader understands what occured.

(14) **REPORT WRITING: GRAMMAR/SPELLING/NEATNESS**—Evaluates the recruit's ability to use proper English; to follow the rules for spelling and to write neatly.

1. Reports are illegible. Reports contain excessive number of misspelled words. Sentence structure or word usage is improper or incomplete.
4. Reports are legible and grammar is at an acceptable level. Spelling is acceptable and errors are rare. Errors, if present, do not impair an understanding of the report.
7. Reports are very neat and legible. Contain no spelling or grammatical errors.

(15) **REPORT WRITING: APPROPRIATE TIME USED**—Evaluates the recruit's efficiency relative to the amount of time taken to write a report.

1. Requires an excessive amount of time to complete a report. Takes three or more times the amount of time a non-probationary officer would take to complete the report.
4. Completes reports within a reasonable amount of time.

7. Completes reports very quickly, as quickly as a skilled veteran officer.

(16) **FIELD PERFORMANCE: NON-STRESS CONDITIONS**—Evaluates the recruit's ability to perform routine, non-stress police activities.

1. When confronted with a routine task, becomes confused and disoriented. Unable to determine course of action or takes wrong course of action. Avoids taking action.
4. Properly assesses routine situations, determines appropriate action and takes same.
7. Properly assesses situations including unusual or complex ones. Determines appropriate course of action and takes same.

(17) **FIELD PERFORMANCE: STRESS CONDITIONS**—Evaluates the recruit's ability to perform in moderate to high stress situations.

1. Becomes emotional, is panic stricken, cannot function, holds back, loses temper or displays cowardice. Overreacts.
4. Maintains calm and self-control, determines proper course of action and takes it. Does not allow the situation to further deteriorate.
7. Maintains calm and self-control in even the most extreme situations. Quickly restores control in the situation and takes command. Determines best course of action and takes it.

(18) **SELF-INITIATED FIELD ACTIVITY**—Evaluates the recruit's interest and ability to initiate police-related activity, to view same and to act on even low-priority situations.

1. Does not see or avoids activity. Does not follow up on situations. Rationalizes suspicious circumstances. Does not have a broad orientation to the job.
4. Recognizes and identifies police-related activity. Has a broad orientation to the job including low priority activity. Develops cases from observed activity. Displays inquisitiveness.
7. Seldom misses observable activity. Maintains lookouts and information given at briefing and uses that information as "probable cause." Makes good quality arrests and/or proper dispositions from observed activity. Thinks well "on his feet."

(19) **OFFICER SAFETY: GENERAL**—Evaluates the recruit's ability to perform police tasks without injuring self or others or exposing self to others to unnecessary danger/risks.

1. Fails to follow accepted safety procedures or to exercise officer safety, i.e.
   A) Exposes weapons to suspect (baton, mace, handgun, etc.).
   B) Fails to keep gun hand free during enforcement situations.
   C) Stands in front of violator's car door.
   D) Fails to control suspect's movements.
   E) Does not keep suspect/violator in sight.
   F) Fails to use illumination when necessary or uses it improperly.
   G) Fails to advise dispatcher when leaving police vehicle.
   H) Fails to maintain good physical condition.
   I) Fails to utilize or maintain personal safety equipment.
   J) Does not anticipate potentially dangerous situations.
   K) Stands too close to passing vehicular traffic.
   L) Is careless with gun and other weapons.
   M) Stands in front of doors when knocking.
   N) Makes poor choice of which weapon to use and when to use it.
   O) Fails to cover other officers.
   P) Stands between police and violator's vehicle on car stop.
   Q) Fails to search police vehicle prior to duty and after transporting suspect.
4. Follows accepted safety procedures. Understands and applies them.
7. Always works safely. Foresees dangerous situations and prepares for them. Keeps partner informed and determines the best position for self and partner. Is not over-confident. Is in good physical condition.

(20) **OFFICER SAFETY: SUSPECTS, SUSPICIOUS PERSONS AND PRISONERS**—Evaluates the recruit's ability to perform police tasks in a safe manner while dealing with suspects, suspicious persons or prisoners.

1. Violates officer safety principles outlined in (19) above. Additionally, fails to "pat search" when appropriate, confronts people while seated in the patrol vehicle, fails to handcuff when appropriate. Conducts poor searches and fails to maintain a position of advantage to prevent attack or escape.
4. Follows accepted safety procedures with suspects, suspicious persons and prisoners.

7. Foresees potential danger and eliminates or controls it. Maintains position of advantage in even the most demanding situations. Is alert to changing situations and prevents opportunities for danger from developing.

(21) **CONTROL OF CONFLICT: VOICE COMMAND** – Evaluates the recruit's ability to gain and maintain control of situations through verbal command and instruction.

1. Speaks too softly or timidly, speaks too loudly, confuses or angers listeners by what is said and/or how it is said. Fails to use voice when appropriate or speaks when inappropriate.
4. Speaks with authority in a calm, clear voice. Proper selection of words and knowledge of when and how to use them.
7. Completely controls situations with voice tone, word selection, inflection, and the bearing which accompanies what is said. Restores order in even the most trying situations through use of voice.

(22) **CONTROL OF CONFLICT: PHYSICAL SKILL** – Evaluates the recruit's ability to use proper level of force for the given situation.

1. Uses too little or too much force for the give situation. Is physically unable to perform the task. Does not use proper restraints.
4. Obtains and maintains control through use of the proper amounts of techniques of force application.
7. Excellent knowledge and ability in the use of restraints. Selects the right amount of force for the given situation. Is in superior physical condition.

(23) **USE OF COMMON SENSE AND GOOD JUDGEMENT** – Evaluates the recruit's performance in terms of ability to perceive, form valid conclusion and arrive at sound judgements.

1. Acts without thought or good reason. Is indecisive, naive. Is unable to reason through a problem and come to a conclusion. Cannot recall previous solutions and apply them in like situations.
4. Able to reason through a problem and come to an acceptable conclusion in routine situations. Makes reasonable decisions based on information available. Perceives situations as they really are. Makes decisions without assistance.
7. Able to reason through even the most complex situations and is able to make appropriate conclusions. Has excellent per-

ception. Anticipates problems and prepares resolutions in advance. Relates past solutions to present situations.

(24) **RADIO: APPROPRIATE USE OF THE RADIO CODES**—Evaluates the recruit's ability to use the police radio in accordance with department policy and procedure.

1. Violates policy concerning use of radio. Does not follow procedures or follows wrong procedure. Does not understand or use proper codes.
4. Follows policy and accepted procedures. Has good working knowledge of most often used sections of the codes.
7. Uses the codes with ease in all sending-receiving situations. Does not unnecessarily take up air time; is conversant with policy and procedures and follows same.

(25) **RADIO: LISTENS AND COMPREHENDS**—Evaluates the recruit's ability to pay attention to radio traffic and to understand the information transmitted.

1. Repeatedly misses own call number and is unaware of police activity in adjoining districts. Requires dispatcher to repeat radio transmissions or does not accurately comprehend transmission.
4. Copies own radio transmissions and is generally aware of radio traffic directed to adjoining beats.
7. Is aware of own radio traffic and traffic in the surrounding beats. Is aware of traffic in other parts of the city and uses previously transmitted information to advantage.

(26) **RADIO: ARTICULATION OF TRANSMISSIONS**—Evaluates the recruit's ability to communicate with others via the police radio.

1. Does not plan his transmissions. Over or undermodulates. Cuts message off through improper use of the microphone. Speaks too fast or too slowly. Cuts off other units, violates 10-33 traffic.
4. Uses proper procedures with clear, concise and complete transmissions. Observes 10-33 procedures and exercises proper radio courtesy.
7. Transmits clearly, calmly, concisely and completely in even the most stressful situations. Transmissions are well thought out and do not have to be repeated.

RELATIONSHIPS

(27) **WITH CITIZENS: GENERAL**—Evaluates the recruit's ability to interact with citizens (including suspects) in an appropriate, efficient manner.

1. Abrupt, belligerent, overbearing, arrogant, uncommunicative. Overlooks or avoids "service" aspect of the job. Introverted, insensitive and/or uncaring.
4. Courteous, friendly and empathetic. Communicates in a professional, unbiased manner. Is service oriented.
7. Is very much at ease with citizen contacts. Quickly establishes rapport and leaves people with feeling that the officer was interested in serving them. Is objective in all contacts.

(28) **WITH ETHNIC GROUPS OTHER THAN HIS OWN**—Evaluates the recruit's ability to interact with members of ethnic or racial groups other than own, in an appropriate, efficient manner.

1. Is hostile or overly sympathetic. Is prejudicial, subjective or biased. Treats members in this grouping differently than members of own ethnic or racial group would be treated.
4. Is at ease with members of other ethnic/racial groups. Serves their needs objectively and with concern. Does not feel threatened when in their presence.
7. Understands the various cultural differences and uses this understanding to competently resolve situations and problems. Is totally objective and communicates in a manner that furthers mutual understanding.

(29) **WITH FTO, SUPERVISORS AND COMMAND OFFICERS**—Evaluates the recruit's ability to effectively interact with training officer and in other supervisory/subordinate relationships.

1. Patronizes FTO superiors or is antagonistic toward them. Gossips. Is insubordinate, argumentative, sarcastic. Resists instructions.
4. Adheres to the chain of command and accepts role in the organization. Respects authority. Follows instructions and behavior. Is not disruptive.
7. Is at ease in contacts with superiors. Understands superiors' responsibilities, respects and supports their position.

(30) **WITH OTHER OFFICERS**—Evaluates recruit's ability to effectively interact with fellow officers.

1. Considers himself/herself superior. Gossips. Belittles others. Is not a team worker and does not associate with fellow officers.
4. Good peer relationships and is accepted as a group member.
7. Peer group leader. Actively assists others.

COMMON PROBLEMS ENCOUNTERED

All field training officer programs encounter difficulties at times. The best counteractive measure begins with recognizing the problem exists. It is easy to remain so comfortable with your program that you do not recognize its weaknesses.

One common weakness is the lack of training for interpersonal skills. Some agencies place extreme concentration on technical skills, while neglecting those that deal with personal relationships. A greater emphasis on attitudes and relationships both inside and outside the department is very worthwhile.

The evaluation process can present occasional problems. While one of the purposes of the FTO program is to week out incompetent officers, programs must find a balance between evaluation and training. Some frequent errors in evaluation include:

A. The tendency to evaluate on the basis of one factor rather than each trait.
B. Consistently too hard or easy.
C. The failure to evaluate at either extreme of a rating scale.
D. The tendency to be lenient due to a friendship developed during the field training officer period.
E. Inadvertent preference or prejudice.
F. The tendency to allow one recent situation to override the entire evaluation.
G. The failure by a field training officer to thoroughly understand evaluation standards.
H. Allowing one very low or high trait to influence the evaluation of other areas.
I. Emphasizing evaluation to the extent that training suffers.

The Houston Police Department concluded that training was not compatible with the evaluation process and altered their FTO program. Now, a new recruit spends the first section of the program being trained, then concludes with a different FTO for the evaluation process. The

Houston Police Department believes this process enables both the recruit and the field training officer to train in a more relaxed and productive environment before evaluation begins.[8]

Perhaps it is merely human nature, yet the tendency of field training officers to convey personal opinions among themselves regarding recruits can be detrimental. Such judgements and opinions create an image in other field training officers' minds that are unfair and unwarranted. By the time the recruit reaches additional field training officers they have formed an opinion as to how he should be evaluated.

Supervisors may sometimes interfere with the field training process by requesting a new recruit handle assignments himself due to manpower problems. This is particularly prevalent in smaller departments where uniform shifts are substantially effected by sickness or vacations. Training officers must have a strong commitment from the agency's head administrator, to prevent this.

Finally, while not a frequent occurence, field training officers sometimes become lackadaisical in their training efforts. Seasoned field training officers may occasionally need to be reminded of the importance of their function. Apathy can be a natural tendency after an extended period of time. The departmental training officer must be constantly alert to prevent it.

THE TERMINATION PROCESS

During the final phase of the field training officer process, emphasis is placed on observation and evaluation. As previously noted, the final field training officer is not required to train from a specific training area checklist. Instead, he concentrates on observation, counseling and evaluation.

At the conclusion of the final training phase a decision should be made whether to terminate or certify the officer as having passed the program. If a trainee's performance has been unsatisfactory, written evaluations should reflect this. The responsibility for corrective specialized training rests with both field training officers and the departmental training officer.

In cases where performance is unsatisfactory to the extent that termination is considered, the training officer should obtain written memorandums of overall evaluation and opinion for termination from all field training officers. These memorandums along with all daily evaluations form the basis for a full consultation with the recruit. His attitude and response during this interview should also be considered.

Figure 5. Regular field training officer meetings are beneficial for field training officers and the program administrator. Discussing trainee's evaluating field training officer performance, critiquing various training topics and striving for improvement of typical agenda items.

All memorandums should be submitted through the chain of command to the Chief of Police or the Sheriff. Following a thorough review of this information, the Chief of Police or the Sheriff will make the final termination decision. If the decision to terminate is made, the termination process will be conducted as usual. Irregardless of whether a recruit is terminated, all written evaluations should be permanently documented.

EVALUATION OF THE FIELD TRAINING OFFICER

As with any endeavor, the field training officer program should continually strive for improvement. Self-evaluation is an effective tool. Regular field training officer meetings should always allow a portion of time to be devoted to constructive self-criticism.

Another effective manner of improvement requires the program supervisor conduct confidential "exit interviews" with trainees completing the program. While the possibility of personality conflicts or unjustified evaluations must be considered, the value of such criticism far outweighs the negative aspects. Trainee opinions may provide the program supervisor with insights and views he may not otherwise learn.

In addition, the program supervisor may wish to draft an evaluation form to be completed by trainees as they complete their training. An example of such a form appears below.

FIELD TRAINING OFFICER EVALUATION FORM

RETURN TO TRAINING OFFICER

THE PURPOSE OF THIS EVALUATION IS TO PROVIDE A STRUCTURED MANNER OF CONTINUED EVALUATION AND SUBSEQUENT IMPROVEMENT. HAVING COMPLETED THE FIELD TRAINING OFFICER PROGRAM, YOU ARE IN AN IDEAL POSITION TO BE OF ASSISTANCE. PLEASE BE VERY CANDID AND STRAIGHTFORWARD IN ANSWERING. USE A SEPARATE EVALUATION FORM FOR EACH F.T.O. YOU NEED NOT PROVIDE YOUR NAME UNLESS YOU WISH TO.

F.T.O. NAME______________________________

DID THE F.T.O. MEET YOUR NEEDS (EXPLAIN)____________

____

____

____

DID YOU FEEL THE F.T.O. WAS SINCERE________________

____

PLEASE COMMENT ON THE F.T.O.'S METHOD OF INSTRUCTION____________________________

____

____

____

____

CAN YOU OFFER ANY SUGGESTIONS FOR THE F.T.O.'S IMPROVEMENT

____

____

____

____

WHAT ARE THE F.T.O.'S STRONG POINTS________________

____

____

WHAT IS YOUR OPINION OF THE F.T.O. PROGRAM OVERALL (YOU ONLY NEED TO ANSWER THIS ONCE)____________

____

____

____

____

To prevent unnecessary hard feelings, the program supervisor must inform each concerned field training officer of the opinions provided by the trainees without allowing them to see the actual complete form. Ensuring the confidentiality of trainees identity will be crucial to obtaining candid evaluations. Saving the forms until several evaluations can be read at one time will provide additional confidentiality.

A FINAL TRAINING PROCEDURE

It is possible that recruits could complete the field training officer program with performance weaknesses. To ensure this does not occur, an additional training step should be added.

The additional procedure requires a training officer or other member of the training staff to ride a few days with the new officer approximately six months following the completion of the FTO program. A performance weakness which may not have been noted could be identified through this relatively easy safeguard.

SUPERVISION FTO PROGRAM

A need exists for supervisors to receive supervision training immediately after their promotion. The majority of the departments across the nation offer no organized method of in-service training for new supervisors.

The lack of training for supervisors becomes more critical when you consider that new supervisors are usually transferred to the patrol division even though they may have been out of patrol for an extended period of time prior to their promotion. Providing reorientation to changes and/or new departmental procedures is vital. Recently promoted sergeants are sometimes too embarrassed to ask questions. The result is considerable ineffective and inept supervision.

The organization of a supervisor field training officer program is essentially the same as for a standard FTO program. The San Jose California Police Department's Bureau of Field Operations provides new sergeants with a 40 hour course upon their promotion. In addition, they ride with a training officer of the same rank for a minimum of one week.

A supervisor's manual is provided to new supervisors as well. The manual contains updated information on rules and procedures, training checklists, and a variety of reference material. The manual is completed from the prospective that some new supervisors will be required to supervise officers who have had more tactical training on new procedures than they have had. The San Jose Police Department is convinced that the effort required for such a program is repaid many times over by the benefits produced for these new supervisors.[9]

REFERENCES

1. Paul D. Walker, Jr., Effective Field Training, *Law and Order,* March 1981, pg. 32.
2. Jack Molden, The Role of The Field Training Officer, *Law and Order,* March 1984, pg. 16.
3. A. Burton, The Mentoring Dynamic in Therapeutic Transformation, *The American Journal of Psychoanalysis,* vol. 37, 1977, pg. 115–122.
4. Zane K. Quible, *Administrative Office Management,* Winthrop, 1984, pg. 202–203.
5. Jack Molden, The Role of The Field Training Officer, *Law and Order,* March 1984, pg. 74.
6. Paul D. Walker, Jr., Effective Field Training, *Law and Order,* March 1981, pg. 34.
7. M. Roberts and R. Allen, *The Field Training Officer Program,* San Jose Police Department, San Jose, California.
8. M. Michael Fagan and Kenneth Ayers, Jr., Professors of the Street—Police Mentors, *F.B.I. Law Enforcement Bulletin,* January 1985, pg. 8–12.
9. San Jose Police Expand Nationally Acclaimed Training Programs For Field Officers, *Training Aids Digest,* May 1984, pg. 3.

3.

SUPERVISION TRAINING

Almost without exception, police supervisors began their careers as rookie patrolmen. All experienced officers have received a wide variety of street experiences which they continually call upon for supervisory decisions. The majority of their remaining supervision traits are usually based upon interactions with other supervisors.

Unfortunately, the law enforcement profession has rarely provided staff officers with quality supervision training. A new sergeant is typically faced with a "sink or swim" dilemma. He relies upon his own untrained opinion which may be severely limited in scope and/or improper. All agencies provide supervisors with the authority and responsibility to carry out their tasks. Few agencies provide them with the mental tools or knowledge necessary to carry out their responsibilities.

PRESUPERVISORY TRAINING

Contrary to popular opinion, the best way to provide supervisory training is to ensure that it is an ongoing process throughout the department. Thus, even before particular officers are promoted, they will possess a basic understanding of quality supervisory functions.

There are several ways to approach presupervisory training. One choice is to provide such training for all those within the department who wish to participate. The advantage of this strategy is that it will assist to ensure that officers with high supervisory potential are not overlooked. Examinations taken during the program may serve to assist management and promotion decisions.

Another approach is to select officers for management courses based upon a variety of considerations. Written examinations concerning competence and adaptability may be used in the selection process. If examinations are given, they should not be weighed as heavily as an officer's previous overall performance.

Presupervisory training has several major benefits:

1. As a result of the training program, officers may decide they no longer wish to be considered for supervisory promotions.
2. Presupervisory training provides information which may be considered during the promotional process.
3. Such training will develop a qualified group of supervisory candidates from which administration may choose.[1]

SUPERVISION TRAINING DEVELOPMENT

American law enforcement has neglected supervision training. Well organized in-service training programs for supervisors are rare. This is ironic since the quality of supervision is frequently a weakness within the law enforcement community.

Due to the time, effort and expertise required to develop an in-service supervision training program, the majority of supervision training is conducted by sources from outside an agency. Such training courses tend to have a relatively "short lived effect," because they are not customized to a department's particular needs. There is no continual reinforcement of knowledge learned after the course has concluded.

SUPERVISORY NEEDS ASSESSMENT

The first phase in developing a supervisory training program is to determine your agency's supervisory training needs. A review and analysis of departmental goals and objectives pertaining to supervisors must first be accomplished. A job task analysis will be invaluable in conducting a thorough assessment. The analysis is achieved by having supervisors complete a detailed questionnaire which ascertains exactly what jobs and tasks your supervisors perform.

Conducting personal interviews with all supervisors is another beneficial method of determining supervisory training needs. Interviews should be done independently and in private. They should focus on each particular supervisor's opinion of his supervisory difficulties, strengths and problem areas.[2]

The effectiveness of evaluation and assessment interviews will largely depend upon the preplanning and organization of the interviews. Their effectiveness will be greatly enhanced if the following areas of evaluation are stressed. One simple and productive interview technique is to ask every supervisor his view concerning each topic and provide examples of how he applied such principles to real life situations.

Loyalty—Loyalty is essential to any organization. It is crucial that supervisors have the loyalty of their subordinates and that all employees are loyal to the organization itself.

Integrity—Honesty and truthfulness are character traits which must be present within any supervisor. Supervisors must set examples of integrity for others to follow.

Self-Discipline—Self-discipline in an employment setting means having the perseverance to adhere to departmental regulations and general orders.

Professional Competence—Attaining professional competence is a task earned only by hard work and discipline. The lack of professional competence by a supervisor will result in the supervisor losing the respect of his subordinates.

Courage—Courage is the mental and physical ability to control yourself in the presence of danger. Whether you are setting an example by leading fellow officers into a dangerous situation or following through with an unpopular yet fair supervisory decision, a supervisor must always possess the courage to do the right thing.

Physical Fitness—Contemporary American law enforcement has become very aware of the responsibility and benefits of physical fitness. Supervisors will find little disagreement that fitness is important, yet, they will find considerable resistance to the effort required for officers to stay physically fit. Supervisors must be encouraging, inspiring and set an example for all to follow.

Command Presence—Command presence results from self-confidence, dignity, self-control, high self-image and fairness. The ability to take control of a situation and set an example for others to follow is vital to leadership.

Fairness—Fairness is generally considered the most important quality a supervisor can possess. Fairness will only result from a thorough understanding of both others and yourself. Supervisors

> must not jump to conclusions or base decisions on biased, prejudiced or superficial examinations of a situation. They must be constantly aware that a reputation for fairness can take years to build, but may be destroyed in a matter of minutes.[3]

ON-THE-JOB TRAINING

Few law enforcement agencies provide "on-the-job" supervisory training regularly. When supervisors do receive training, it is sporatic at best. It is usually provided in the form of sending one or more staff member to a supervisory skills training seminar.

While supervisory seminars and workshops are valuable, what an agency really needs is a quality in-service supervision training program. The need for supervision training is widely recognized. The lack of proficient supervision remains a devastating problem within many law enforcement agencies.

As previously noted, the cornerstone of any effective in-service training program is evaluation and needs assessment. Following evaluation, a trainer can work to improve his agency's particular problem areas.

Irregardless of whether supervisors have had formal supervision courses, the majority of supervision training should take place within the department. Thus, the primary concern is whether supervisors will learn proper supervision techniques or outlooks and habits from supervisors who may have become lazy and cynical. Ensuring supervisors learn proper lessons from "on-the-job" experiences can require as much work and dedication as developing any other quality training program.

Any "on-the-job" supervision training program should have certain elements necessary to ensure an efficient and productive outcome. These ingredients include:

A. Guided practice of management theory.
B. Observation by experienced and effective supervisors.
C. A schedule establishing the types of experiences to be included in the program.
D. Established goals and objectives.
E. One or more supervisors assigned to guide the experiences of those supervisors participating in the program.[4]

SUPERVISION FIELD TRAINING OFFICER PROGRAM

Many agencies across the nation consider the field training officer program to be one of the most beneficial projects they have ever undertaken. A new officer is provided with an extensive and effective in-service training program. Field training officers build upon the basic knowledge he received in the police academy to ensure his capabilities are adequate.

There remains no reason why the same efficient and productive training principles cannot be applied to new supervisors. Establishing a thorough and confident field training officer program for supervisors is no more difficult than developing a basic field training officer program.

Applying the same principles and guidelines used to establish the basic field training officer program will enable you to develop a productive field training officer program for supervisors. Special developmental emphasis should be placed on the following areas:

A. Sound support from your chief administrator.
B. A thorough training outline.
C. Selection of a competent FTO supervisor.
D. Constructive criticism, feed-back and evaluation.

The following is a recommended Field Training Officer outline for your supervision program. It should be customized to include your agency's particular policies and standard operating procedures.

IN-SERVICE CLASSROOM TRAINING

The benefit of providing short in-service supervision training courses on a regular basis should not be overlooked. Management theory, leadership skills, supervision concepts, management strategy and a variety of structured supervision training can be effectively provided for all supervisors.

One important advantage of a classroom setting over an FTO program is the capability to use various forms of media instruction. Unlike the realism and practicality of the field training officer setting, a classroom environment enables the instructor or trainer to use movies, video tape training, slides, overhead projector, opague projector or any other form of instructional aid to assist in conveying instruction. The trainer will find the classroom setting beneficial for training concepts and theory.

TABLE IV
SUPERVISION FIELD TRAINING OFFICER PROGRAM OUTLINE

Training Topic	*Date Instruction Completed*
I. *The Supervisor's Role*	
A) The Supervisor's Position	______
B) Basic Supervisory Responsiblities Line Function	______
II. *The Supervisor's Function in Organization, Administration, and Management*	
A) The Supervisor's administrative functions	______
B) Work Assignments	______
C) Unity of Command	______
D) Span of Control	______
E) Delegation of Work	______
F) Personnel Developmment	______
G) Completed Staff Work	______
H) Budgeting	______
I) Planning	______
III. *Distribution and Deployment of Field Forces*	
A) Fixed Post Positions	______
B) Patrol allotments	______
C) Assignments Based on Proportionate Need	______
D) Overlapping of Shifts	______
IV. *The Essentials of Communicating*	
A) The Processes of Communications	______
B) Barriers to Effective Communications	______
C) Overcoming Communications Barriers	______
D) Written Communications	______
E) Briefing	______
F) Typical Deficiencies in Writing	______

TABLE IV Continued

Training Topic	*Date Instruction Completed*
V. *Elements of Leadership, Supervision and Command Presence*	
A) Types of Leaders	________
B) Elements of Leadership	________
C) Self-Appraisal	________
D) Leadership Characteristics	________
E) Personality of the Leader	________
F) Human Relations and Leadership	________
G) Commending and Praising Others	________
H) Know Your Subordinates	________
I) Reprimanding	
J) Order Giving and Communications	________
K) Decision-Making	________
L) Drawing Conclusions	________
M) Moderation in Supervision	________
N) Setting an Example	________
O) Female Employees	________
P) Symptoms of Leadership Failure	________
Q) Consistency	________
R) Self-Control	
S) Keep Promises	
T) Professional Knowledge	
U) Avoid Favoritism	________
V) Praise Good Work	________
VI. *The Training Function: Problems & Approaches*	
A) The Importance of Training	________
B) Instructing as a Supervisory Responsibility	________
C) Constant Need for Training	________
D) Principles of Learning	________
E) Teaching Techniques	________

TABLE IV Continued

Training Topic	*Date Instruction Completed*
VII. *Principles of Interviewing*	
A) Preparing for the Interview	______
B) Attitude of Interviewer	______
C) Eliminating Bias	______
D) Confidential Agreements	______
E) Psychological Reactions	______
F) Recording Results	______
G) Causes of Failure	
VIII. *Personnel Evaluation Systems*	
A) Objectives of Rating System	______
B) Causes for Rating System Failures	______
C) Gathering & Recording Performance Data	______
D) Setting Standards of Performance	______
E) Documentation	______
IX. *Performance Rating Standards & Methods*	
A) Rating Standards	______
B) Common Rating Errors	______
C) Evaluation Period	______
D) Discussion of Rating With Employee	______
E) Written Notification of Rating	______
X. *Principles of Discipline*	
A) Forms of Discipline	______
B) Discipline by Example	______
C) The Relationship Between Discipline, Morale and Esprit de Corps	______
XI. *Discipline: Policies and Practices*	
A) Results of Unsustained Disciplinary Actions	______
B) Complaint Investigation Policy	______

TABLE IV Continued

Training Topic	*Date Instruction Completed*
XII. *Personnel Complaint Investigation Procedures and Techniques*	
A) Case Preparation: General S.O.P. Procedures	________
B) Sources of Complaints	________
C) Observed Infractions	________
D) Recording Complaints	________
E) Complaint Investigation	________
F) Reporting Procedures	________
G) Notifications to Complainant	________
H) Notifications to Accused Employee	________
I) Administering Penalty	________
J) Disciplinary Failures	________
XIII. *Psychological Aspects of Supervision*	
A) Drives, Satisfactions and Needs	________
B) Increasing Motivation	________
C) The Supervisor and the Frustrated Employee	________
D) The Nature of Frustration	________
E) Some Common Reactions to Frustrations	________
F) Preventing Frustration	________
XIV. *General Policies*	
A) Standard Operating Procedures	________
B) Civil Service Regulations	________
C) City Ordinances	________
D) State Statutes	________

In addition to theoretical prospectives, a job task analysis will suggest a variety of demanding supervisory responsibilities be covered. Suggested topics include discipline, morale, grievances, enforcing rules and regulations, training subordinates, shift assignment, care of equipment, accident prevention, evaluation, communicating with subordinates and higher management, and stress management.

Providing training areas which are practical and can be related to on a daily basis will meet with considerably more favoritism than those of a more theoretical nature. It is vital that classroom instruction provide not only more popular topics but those which will convey a theoretical framework upon which supervisors may test practical occurences on a daily basis.

Acquiring professional supervision ability is a continual training process. It necessitates not only "on-the-job" field training but theoretical and conceptional learning as well. This fact must be sincerely believed for supervisors to appreciate the advantages of supervision training. The nucleus for such an attitude to grow among all supervisors is the chief administrator and top level management.

The trainer must instill upon all supervisors that theoretical concepts of supervision are not intended to provide solutions. He must convey that their purpose is to provide a framework upon which supervisors may apply actual situations to determine answers.[5]

THE SUPERVISORY TRAINING OBJECTIVE

Supervision theory and concepts are not intended to provide direct answers for management personnel. Instead, their purpose is to provide guidelines which may be directly related to specific, practical supervisory problems. Supervisors should be instructed how to apply theoretical concepts to current daily problems.

The basic objectives of the theoretical phase of supervisory training are:

A. Instill the theoretical knowledge which provides a framework capable of being applied to daily situations.
B. To provide new supervisory theories which may be compared with those presently being applied.
C. To create an atmosphere of constant learning and growing among staff members. Many trainers will meet resistance to supervisory training from supervisors themselves. Trainers should be aware of this and prepare to deal with it accordingly. Many experienced supervisors resent being told they are not handling their responsibilities and duties in the most productive manner. They may interpret the reasons for such training as a personal criticism toward them. They may also interpret such instructions as though they are being "talked down to."

The solution to this dilemma is to illustrate the relevance of intellectual growth to managerial competence.[6] A 1950 management development study conducted by the National Industrial Conference Board reached this conclusion when they concluded:

> Few companies enter upon a program of executive training without misgivings. The testimony of these same companies later showed their fears were largely ungrounded. Executives do the training. Executives can learn and grow perpetually within their jobs. The more proficient a supervisor is, the more he will recognize the value of training, and will subsequently desire it. It is the inept and unproductive supervisor who will be most likely to resist the idea of training.[7]

It is the trainer and/or his staff of supervision instructors who must change the view of any supervisors who have negative feelings toward supervision training. Trainers must inspire motivation and a thirst for learning. They must help those with negative attitudes overcome their personal faults for the good of the department. In summary, they must lead those who supervise to a positive, optimistic view of supervision and leadership.

THE SUPERVISION INSTRUCTOR

The selection of those who instruct a supervision course will be crucial to its success. Veteran law enforcement officers tend to be somewhat critical and cynical. Supervisors participating in training may tend to be critical of the program's instructors. For this reason, they must have a respectable background and exceptional instruction ability.

It is permissable to use an instructor from within your own agency if the concerned individual enjoys an unusually high degree of professional respect among his peers. If you do not have a supervisor possessing the expertise and instruction ability to provide exceptional training, look elsewhere. If you do select your instructors from outside the department, whether he is a college professor, management consultant or businessman, his background will be a significant factor to your program's success.

An instructor from outside your agency must thoroughly understand your specific needs and wishes before developing his curriculum. The development of his instruction should meet with your ongoing input and approval. Give special consideration to the curriculum having realistic and practical significance.

Should the instructor be a staff member from within your department, be assured that a quality program is ascertainable. He should emphasis to his peers that the information presented by him is "state of the art" information or supervision techniques, rather than merely his own personal opinion. He should frequently cite references and background information regarding his various instruction sources. He should emphasis that his presentation is open to question and invite discussion for differing viewpoints.

Regardless of any difficulties or reactions to the classroom phase of the training program, never lose sight of the fact that your objectives more than justify your time and effort. Those objectives are:

A. Assist the supervisor in growing intellectually.
B. Teach the supervisor how to apply sound, theoretical knowledge to practical specific situations.
C. To broaden his overall professional knowledge.[8]

TRAINING METHODS

A wide variety of training programs currently exist to assist the trainer in developing productive supervision training. While the previously discussed methods of supervision field training and the historical classroom setting deserve particular recognition, there remains a wide variety of productive and effective methods from which the trainer may choose.

Book Reviews—There are numerous management books currently on the market which excel at providing the reader with a clear and precise understanding of supervision. "State of the art" techniques and concepts are presented in clearly defined terms.

One innovative and very practical technique that may be applied to law enforcement supervision training is to purchase books such as **Megetrends** or **In Pursuit of Excellence.** These publications can be issued to supervisors for them to read within a designated length of time. Following the time period a class may be held for an instructor to conduct a book review.

The book review seminar will serve to discuss concepts of the book and initiate productive group discussion. You may wish to assign supervisors to write a book review to be due at the beginning of the seminar. This will ensure thoroughness in reading the concerned book.

Another technique is to assign a separate chapter or section of the book to each supervisor. Supervisors will be responsible for making a short presentation to the class on his particular chapter or section. This technique ensures assignments are carried out and creates an interesting and productive classroom experience.

Simulation Training Exercise – Simulation training exercises involve the use of a model of your city or section of your jurisdiction. The model will be a near duplication of streets and buildings which enables supervisors to "act out" their duties and responsibilities during the simulation of an occurance.

The construction of a model duplicate of your jurisdiction can be extremely time consuming. A model can be made to any size or scale you wish, however, most models are slightly smaller than the average desk top. This will enable it to be placed on the top of a desk while supervisors take a circular position surrounding the desk. Lakes and streets may be painted on a piece of plywood. Buildings may be cut from Styrofoam or purchased at a toy or hobby shop.

Such simulation exercises are virtually limitless in scope. The trainer must write a script of a simulated situation for each exercise. He may select particular supervisors to play the roles of first supervisor on the scene, shift commander, watch commander, detective bureau commander, swat team commander, etc. After a 15 minute period during which time participates reflect upon his anticipated actions, each supervisor will be called upon to present his course of action. The supervision model simulation exercise will conclude with a group discussion and critique. The benefits of practicality and realism are obvious. Simulation exercises have met with positive response from supervisors.

Management Training Games – The use of management training games are a fairly recent addition to the list of training methods which may be used to effectively promote quality supervision training. Training games are usually just as the name implies. They are usually board games designed to reinforce specific training theories. Learning Managerial techniques, providing supervisors with the opportunity to make decisions, increasing factual knowledge and applying and reinforcing learned knowledge to realistic situations are typical benefits.

Management Training Games have a unique added advantage over most training environments: They can be a lot of fun. Creating a fun training atmosphere will usually promote increased incentive and motivation to learn. Trainers may find supervisors looking anxiously towards attending a training class as opposed to an often uncommitted attitude.

An example of a supervision training game is **The Situational Leadership Game** developed by Paul Hersey and Ken Blanchard. This game presents numerous situations which require the supervisor to take some sort of action. Supervisors will divide into teams. The first team to complete a circuit around the board wins the game. Training games are designed to allow supervisors to experience some of the frustrations of real life while participating in realistic and practical situations. Games tend to be useful because they generate active participation. Those who would normally sit through a lecture without making a single comment may actively participate in and enjoy supervision games.

Sources for additional information and material are:

A. Psychology Today Games
P.O. box 60279, Terminal Annex
Los Angeles, California 90080

The Game Group
9728 Byeforde Road
Kensington, Maryland 20895

Institute For International Research
4423 East Trainridge
Bloomington, Indiana 40401

Abt Associates Incorporated
55 Wheeler Street
Cambridge, Massachusetts 02138

Role Playing — The role playing technique is a widely used variation of the formal conference method. Typically, the trainer will present a situation involving several different participants. Each supervisor plays the role of a particular participant. The situation is described by the trainer, setting the stage for group interaction to follow. Following supervisors playing various roles, a group discussion and critical analyzation of attitudes and actions of the players should conclude the session.

Job Rotation — Job rotation is a time proven supervision training method. Supervisors are assigned for limited periods of time to different divisions or sections within the department. After completion of the designated period he rotates to another division. The intent of job rotation is to provide a variety of experiences and allow the designated supervisor to become familiar with the inter-working of each department.[10] One disadvantage of job rotation is the loss of expertise to the division when supervisors are transfered.

ENCOURAGING SUPERVISORS TO TRAIN

Training is one of the most productive and cost efficient activities a supervisor can undertake. If a supervisor found that training benefited himself, he will usually view it as a productive method of improving the job performance of his subordinates. He will also be more likely to take the initiative to arrange roll call or midnight shift training. The departmental trainer is responsible for explaining the departmental and personal benefits of training to supervisors. Private conversations with supervisors may alleviate negative attitudes.

Supervisors may understand the performance and significance of training easier if the trainer presents an example of how performance increase can result from training. An example such as a shift supervisor who has decided to conduct three, one hour training classes for his shift may be used. The total number of hours expended by the shift sergeant during the training project totaled 12 hours. If the sergeant had a 5 man shift, they would work approximately ten thousand hours during the next year. If the supervisor's training efforts resulted in a 1 percent improvement in his subordinate's work performance, his agency would gain the equivalent of one hundred work hours as a result of his twelve hours of preparation and instruction.

Effective training can be produced by any knowledgeable and competent instructor. There is one particular reason an immediate supervisor may be the best individual to instruct his subordinates, however. Training should be conducted by an individual who represents a qualified and suitable role model. Instructors other than a subordinate's own supervisor may not assume that role no matter how well versed or knowledgeable he may be. The instructor must be seen as believeable, qualified, confident and respected role model.[11]

COMMUNICATIONS TRAINING FOR SUPERVISORS

Courses designed to assist supervisors in developing effective communication skills are frequently taught at universities or within corporate organizations. Because most employees spend a great deal of time communicating, many believe their communication skills are already effective. While this assumption is widespread, most supervisors would find it beneficial to participate in formal communication training.

Effective communication often depends on mutual trust between supervisor and subordinate. Communication within this relationship is often jeopardized because a supervisor fails to show empathy or concern for his subordinate.

Another common fault among supervisors is the habit of exhibiting a defensive attitude. If a good relationship exists between a supervisor and his subordinate, the subordinate may sometimes make statements which result in the supervisor becoming defensive. Such difficulties can be overcome by role playing within a classroom setting.

Formal in-service training should also emphasis communication barriers. Bias, prejudice or the tendency for a message to become distorted in meaning as it is relayed from person to person are common. A supervisor can strengthen the communication process by using discretion while communicating. A direct or indirect communication approach may often produce different results. Training will illustrate these differences and assist supervisors in deciding which situations require particular approaches.

THE SUPERVISOR'S INDIRECT TRAINING FUNCTION

Supervisors play an important role in the training function. These roles may often be indirect in nature. As an example, a supervisor may frequently select and recommend personnel who would benefit most from an upcoming training course.

Supervisors are obviously responsible for their subordinates complying with departmental regulations and policies. Applying this responsibility to training is exemplified by the supervisory review of distributed training bulletins. The role call period is an ideal opportunity for supervisors to review and explain issued memorandums.

Providing encouragement for subordinates to participate in self-development seminars is also a duty of supervisors. Opportunity such as specialized units, training programs, and professional associations will be beneficial both to the individual and the overall organization. The supervisor himself must be careful not to neglect his self-development as well.

Lastly, regardless of the method, staff members must solicit, gather and analyze information to assist in evaluating the degree training attains its objectives. While the scope of his feed-back will be limited to one particular shift, valuable assistance may be provided to the trainer by the collective results of supervisors monitoring and evaluating shift performance relative to training.

SIMULATION EXERCISES

As with any type of training, the application of theories, concepts and policies to realistic and practical situations is a vital ingredient of thorough understanding. Supervision training can be greatly enhanced by simulation exercises which provide practical situations upon which knowledge can be applied. Virtually endless simulations may be developed. Be certain to take advantage of your agency's own particular circumstances, locations and uniqueness. The following are examples of simulation situations.

A. **Interview With Troubled Officer** —This simulation exercise focuses on the role of Sergeant John Benson. Sergeant Bensons's current task is to interview subordinate officer, William Johnson. Officer Johnson's performance had recently become inadequate. In addition, he developed a negative attitude toward fellow officers, creating friction and discontent. Another supervisor assumes the role of Officer Johnson.

B. **In-Basket Exercise** —This simulation exercise places a supervisor in the position of handling an assortment of administrative duties. Seated at a desk before the class, the officer assumes the role of a shift sergeant who must process a number of letters, memos and miscellaneous administrative matters that have accumulated. The supervisor shall read the various tasks aloud then present what actions he will take based upon the considerations he deems valuable.

C. **Evaluation Simulation Exercise** —All officers participating in this supervisory task are provided with an identical evaluation script which presents a narrative depicting the overall performance and productivity of a hypothetical subordinate. After studying the script for several minutes, supervisors are given identical evaluation forms to evaluate the hypothetical subordinate. A short break is taken following the evaluations. This gives the instructor an opportunity to prepare a synopsis of the supervisor's evaluations. The instructor then leads the classroom discussion concerning the need for standardization of evaluations. This exercise may be repeated several times in one classroom setting.

TRAINING OF EXECUTIVES

Though seemingly ironic on a national scale, the law enforcement profession requires virtually no standard of continual professionalization for Chiefs of Police or Sheriffs. Chief administrators across the nation are usually not required to undergo continual executive development.

Law enforcement executives, for the most part, have acquired sufficient knowledge of their particular departments to cope with its daily operations. Specialized programs for the development of executive proficiency, however, are rare. This is indeed unfortunate. Keeping pace with society's complex managerial responsibilities through regular executive workshops and seminars should no longer be considered a luxury.

The sophisticated and complex problems of civil liability, labor/management issues and budgetary considerations require contemporary, sophisticated solutions. Police executives can not afford to simply react. Instead, they must anticipate, prevent, research and plan.

Should any law enforcement agency obtain professionalism, its leaders must actively engage society's contemporary managerial concepts. Many jurisdictions assume their agency's chief executive's ability will automatically improve with time. This, of course, is far from the answer. Now, more than ever, police executives must keep pace with ever changing administrative problems and practices.

State of the art executive enrichment and development seminars exist across the nation. If not within your law enforcement community, certainly your business sector can provide quality managerial development. Whether a Chief of Police or Sheriff takes advantage of the opportunities is a different matter. A trainer is responsible for determining where such opportunities exist, notifying his Sheriff or Chief of Police and providing encouragement to participate.

TEACHING SUPERVISORS HOW TO CONDUCT A MEETING

Due to the nature of their duties and responsibilities, supervisors will attend meetings. They may also be responsible for presiding over meetings from time to time. In either case, the effectiveness and productivity which results will largely depend upon the meeting's organization and pre-planning.

Many meetings have a tendency to drag on beyond their reasonable limits. They veer from their chartered course or become platforms for a single speaker delivering a pep talk. Others have a propensity to be dull and monotonous. These reasons cause some staff members to resent or dread attending them.

If trainers teach supervisors to restore meaning to their meetings, increased productivity will result. Several measures may be taken to help streamline meetings. Steps which should be portrayed as crucial for any successful meeting are:

- Decide what the goals are prior to the meeting.
- Inform those attending what topics will be addressed and encourage them to prepare.
- Start on time.
- Prepare introductory comments to set the tone of the meeting.
- Provide agendas informing participants of the meeting plan.
- Take steps to ensure the meeting is not dominated by one or two people. This can be accomplished by distributing the agenda in advance and allowing time for others to prepare responses.
- Keep discussion moving quickly towards the conclusion without squelching creativity.
- End on time.

SUPERVISORS MOST FREQUENT PROBLEM AREAS

Training officers will find short in-service courses on frequent supervision problem areas to be useful. The focus of such courses should be that there are no gimmicks or shortcuts to successful supervising. The essence of good supervision is to respect and like those who work for you. A supervisor's job is not only to serve his organization but his men as well, by providing guidance and leadership. A variety of problems arise when supervisors neglect this guideline.

If trainers determine not to organize in-service courses on supervision techniques, it may be beneficial to provide similar information in training bulletins. Ten minute presentations at staff meetings could also prove useful. No matter what mode the trainer selects, topics such as these below should be expounded upon. These are intended for line supervisors.

1. Do not allow yourself to do too much of your officers' work.
2. Don't refuse to pitch in and help when the situation warrants it.
3. Avoid making too many major changes immediately following being transferred to a new shift or division.
4. Avoid being considered as "one of the boys."
5. Be careful not to leave the impression that you are overly impressed with yourself.
6. Be certain to maintain a balance of loyalty between top level management and your subordinates.[12]

TRAINING SUPERVISORS TO DISCIPLINE

It is all too often assumed that line supervisors understand how to manage the discipline process. The fact remains, however, that many line supervisors do not know how to properly discipline because they have never been trained. Interdepartmental inconsistencies, variations of policy interpretations and regulations which are open to dispute, require standardization of action by all supervisors within an agency.

One of the first considerations for the training of discipline or any other administrative topic is the set of departmental policies which govern discipline. Before a supervisor can be taught to deal with disciplinary problems, he or she must first understand the organization's regulations.

If regulations or standard operating procedures need to be changed, the trainer should take it upon himself to initiate them. Any changes in departmental policies should be communicated to all supervisors in writing and/or special training sessions. It should not be assumed that supervisors will automatically become aware of what occurs without such notification.

One of the first concepts to be considered by a trainer should be to verify that supervisors view carrying out established policies and procedures as their obligation. They must sincerely believe that it is not their role to create organizational policies, unless so designated. The failure to enforce a rule because particular supervisors do not agree with it can be devastating to the overall effectiveness of the agency.

The demoralizing result of supervisors following their own individual policies instead of established policies must be stressed. The effect of such improper action is an uneven application of regulations which undoubtedly will result in disciplinary problems. Trainers must stress the importance of supervisors remaining cool, calm and collected. Fairness during disciplinary matters is extremely important. Unfair or inconsistent supervisors will earn a reputation they will never be without and always regret.

The role of documentation in the discipline process should be impressed during any in-service training dealing with discipline. Topics such as investigating an occurence, obtaining proven facts, and making objective decisions should be included. Supervisors who use a factual approach gain the reputation of being fair and just. Discipline is a necessary and crucial ingredient to any law enforcement agency. The disciplinary process must follow sound disciplinary theory and concepts.[13]

SUPERVISION EXCHANGE PROGRAM

A supervision exchange program is an extremely cost effective way of enhancing law enforcement managerial capabilities. The purpose of the program is to upgrade supervision skills by broadening the career experiences of those personnel participating. Length of the exchange is usually six to ten weeks.

Two or more agencies exchanging staff members for a given length of time may greatly broaden the administrative outlook of the entire agency. An exchange program is valuable not only among law enforcement agencies but the private sector as well.

Training officers should realize that problems confronting the managerial staffs of private corporations and industries are very similar to those in a police department. The purpose of the organization may be different, but supervision techniques remains the same. Because the training process in the private sector is greatly advanced over that in law enforcement, trainers should look toward their counterparts in the business world for ideas and assistance.[14]

SUPERVISION TRAINING: THE FUTURE

The effective training of law enforcement supervisors will be a critical issue in coming years. Police trainers must take the initiative to develop productive in-service supervision training if their agency is to stay abreast with managerial complexities. The wisest move a trainer can make is to look toward the private training sector for guidance in future supervision training.

The personnel management consulting firm of Human Resources Associates, Westport, Connecticut, recently conducted a survey to predict the future trends of corporate management training. The survey concluded that companies currently rely more heavily on internally developed management training programs than the use of ready made packaged supervision programs purchased from external sources.

The survey, which focused on large corporations across the country, concluded that future management training will focus on interpersonal communication skills, general management skills, human performance management, productivity improvement and new information technology involving data networks and computers. Current budgetary restraints indicate more emphasis on supervision in-service training programs tailored to meet the unique combinations of needs within individual agencies both in law enforcement and the private sector. Formal, written policies regarding needs analysis and goals and objectives will become more prevalent as the knowledge of their benefits become more widespread.[15]

REFERENCES

1. Margaret Bahniuk, *Training and Education – The Training of Supervisors,* Office Administration and Automation, March 1984, pg. 77.
2. Thomas C. Younce, Management Development, *The Police Chief,* July 1981, pg. 14.
3. George E. Galvan, Supervision Versus Leadership, *Law and Order,* May 1981, pg. 32–33.
4. Margaret Bahniuk, *Training and Education, On and Off the Job Training,* Office Administration and Automation, January 1985, pg. 84.
5. I. L. Heckmann and S. G. Humeryager, *Management of the Personnel Function,* Charles E. Merrill, 1962, pg. 300–305.
6. I. L. Heckmann and S. G. Humeryager, *Management of the Personnel Function,* Charles E. Merrill, 1962, pg. 305–206.
7. Stephen Habbe, *Company Programs of Executive Development,* Studies in Personnel Policy No. 107 (New York, National Industrial Conference Board, 1950) pg. 6.
8. I.L. Heckman and S. G. Humeryager, *Management of the Personnel Function,* Charles E. Merrill, 1962, pg. 307–308.
9. Stephen B. Wehrenberg, Management Training Games: The Play's The Thing, *Personnel Journal,* March 1985, pg. 88–91.
10. Dale Yoder, *Personnel Management and Industrial Relations,* Englewood Cliffs, New Jersey: Prentice-Hall, Inc., 1962, pg. 402.
11. Andrew S. Grove, Why Training is the Boss's Job, *Fortune Magazine,* January 23, 1984, pg. 93–95.

12. Jack B. Molden, Pitfalls of the New Supervisor, *Law and Order,* December 1982, pg. 42–46.
13. Marcia Ann Pulich, Train First-Line Supervisors to Handle Discipline, *Personnel Journal,* December 1983, pg. 980–985.
14. Thomas C. Younce, Management Development, *The Police Chief,* July 1981, 14–17.
15. Industrial Report, Training Magazine, June 1985.

4.

VIDEO TRAINING

The use of video tape training among law enforcement agencies has become widespread. It has flourished because training officers find it to be productive, realistic, practical and cost effective. In summary, it's a solution to a variety of problems which have plagued police training for decades.

With a relatively small investment any agency can purchase a video cassette recorder and television set. These basic pieces of equipment will enable officers to view video training tapes 24 hours a day, 7 days a week. It will enable virtually limitless training techniques and methods which until now have been unreachable.

Video is not so much a means of delivering new services as it is a method of delivering traditional ones in a more effective, colorful and economical way. The advantages are overwhelming:

- Video offers standardization of training by assuring all officers receive the same application.
- Video training provides excellent documentation by enabling the trainer to reproduce the exact training in question.
- Video allows instructors to refine their techniques by reviewing their own instruction.
- Video training offers a solution to manpower shortages in uniform patrol by allowing any number of officers to receive training at any particular time.
- The production of your own video tapes allow for "custom made training."
- Producing your own training tapes cost merely a fraction of mass produced training movies or tapes.
- Video tapes offer a greater impact than written interdepartmental memorandums.
- As video training becomes more prevalent, tapes may be borrowed or copied by neighboring agencies.

- Training realism is easily enhanced by producing video tapes on location within your jurisdiction.
- The burden of training all officers assigned to different working schedules is resolved by the use of the video 24 hour a day operation.
- A basic video cassette recording system including a camera for the production of training tapes can be purchased for the relatively inexpensive sum of a few thousand dollars.

The versatility of video for application to law enforcement training is virtually limitless. The preceding list of video training benefits will be useful for a trainer who is justifying the expenditure of funds for purchasing video equipment. Take advantage of video training. The advantages are too great for any competent trainer to ignore.

VIDEO EQUIPMENT

All trainers need to understand how video equipment operates. If your agency hasn't acquired a video training system, your need will focus on intelligently purchasing the system most suitable to your needs. If your department already has a video system, acquiring a thorough understanding of how the equipment works will allow you to receive more productive use of what you have.

Video Cassettes—Unlike movies which record chemically on film, a video system will record electromagnetically on video tape. Thus, film and video tape are totally different. Instructors will not need to thread the video tape like they did when showing a movie. Splicing will become a thing of the past because video tapes are edited electronically.

Unlike its counterpart, video tape doesn't have to be processed chemically before viewing. It offers the benefits of immediate playback without being developed. Furthermore, video tape may easily be erased or a previous segment may be taped over.

Video cassettes are produced according to tape width. The most prevalent tape is one half inch in width. Quarter inch tapes and 3 inch tapes are also produced. Quarter inch and ½ inch are usually sold for home use. Three quarter inch tape is generally used for commercial recording, such as that used by television stations.

Which size video cassette you use will of course depend upon which is used in your video cassette recorder. Three quarter inch tape will provide better quality than ½ inch. Half inch tape produces better quality than ¼ inch.

Figure 6. Building a video cassette library does not need to be expensive. Many fine quality training topics can be produced without cost by acquiring the assistance of local attorneys, crime lab personnel, management specialists, medical experts and other instructors.

Video cassettes are purchased by length of recording time, from 30 minutes to 6 hours. Many video cassette recorders are equipped with multiply speed settings. These settings allow for the length of time a cassette will record and play to be extended up to the 6 hour limit. Every video cassette recorder format is equipped with a standard speed to provide the highest quality picture. The faster the speed at which the tape runs, the better quality of picture and sound it will produce. When tapes are recorded and played at slower speeds to allow for a longer length of playback, picture and sound quality is sacrificed.[1]

Video Cassette Recorder — When connected to a television set via a cable, a video cassette recorder will allow for the playing of video cassettes. One half inch video cassette recorders will play only ½ inch video tapes, while ¾ inch models must be used to play ¾ inch tapes.

There is another difference between ½ inch VCR's. The VHS model is a ½ inch video tape format produced by the manufacturing corporation of JVC. VHS means the Video Home System. The second predominate ½ inch video cassette recorder is known as BETA. The BETA video tape format was developed by the SONY Corporation.

Selection of a VHS or BETA format, as well as ½ inch or ¾ inch models, should largely depend upon which models are most prevalently used by other agencies in your area. Selecting the same type VCR as surrounding departments use will allow for a frequent exchange of video tapes. Exchanging and copying video cassettes, as long as you are not in violation of copyright laws, is a tremendous asset.

Another important consideration is the benefit of selecting a portable video cassette recorder. As opposed to a table top model, a portable unit will allow the taping of training segments on location through the use of a chargeable battery. When not used on location, the system is equipped with an AC adaptor. Due to its versatility in producing training segments, a portable unit is highly recommended, even if you do not currently have a video camera.

Video Camera—Acquiring a video camera for your video training system will greatly enhance training effectiveness. Obviously, the ability to produce your own training tapes is a tremendous asset. A video camera is connected to the video cassette recorder through the use of a cable. Understanding the basic operations of a camera will allow you to select one suitable to your needs and use it to its fullest capabilities.

One of the most important features of a camera is the view finder. The view finder is actually a small black and white TV screen you may view to see exactly what is being recorded. You will find the electronic view finder to be invaluable. The ability to instantly replay what you have recorded is extremely valuable.

Another important feature is the camera lens. Having a zoom lens will allow the operator a variable focal link as he zooms in from a telephoto setting to a wide angle setting. The benefits of a zoom lens over that of a fixed lens is well worth the extra expense at time of purchase.

Other features you should have explained at the time of purchase are considerations such as auto/manual aperture control, automatic fade, macro focus, white balance, camera microphone, the hand grip, and additional rechargeable batteries.

The purchase of a quality tripod is essential to effective video production. Attempting to constantly hold a camera by hand will result in uneasy shakiness and a great deal of frustration from having to tape scenes over. The head of the tripod is its most crucial part. I recommend you invest a few extra dollars and buy at least a medium quality head. An inexpensive tripod will always result in jerky and/or shaky movements. Additionally, the purchase of a dolly allows the camera and tripod to move smoothly across the floor while taping a scene.

Telecine Converter—A telecine converter is a piece of equipment which enables the user to transfer slides or movies to video tape. It is a fairly simple device and produces good quality copying. A telecine converter is very easy to use. It is available at most quality video equipment stores.

Industrial Video Systems—Trainers may find the use of industrial video equipment more suitable to their requirements than commercial systems. The superior performance of most industrial video cassette recorders and cameras are well worth the relatively small increase in purchase price. The extra time spent locating industrial systems will be repaid by the quality of your productions. Your local phone book yellow pages will indicate nearby industrial and broadcast outlets you may contact.

Industrial systems are available in both 3/4 inch and 1/2 inch models. VHS and BETA models can be obtained. Half inch video cassette recorders are produced, for the most part, by JVC, Sony, and Panasonic Manufacturers. There are numerous beneficial considerations to purchasing an industrial model for your agency.

- Warranties for industrial video systems are generally much longer than are consumer warranties.
- Portable industrial video equipment is manufactured to "hold up better" during rough field operations.
- Industrial models accept a wider range of accessories.
- Industrial color video cameras are manufactured to allow for many interchangeable features.
- Industrial color video cameras have an advanced vidicon tube.
- Industrial video systems often deliver a picture that is superior to typical home systems.
- Industrial models cost relatively little more than home systems.[2]

JUSTIFYING THE VIDEO SYSTEM PURCHASE

No one needs to explain to a training officer that he must departmentally justify any sizeable purchase. We live in a cost-conscience environment where the expenditure of municipal or county funds is reviewed closely. Convincing immediate supervisors and elected officials that an expenditure is worth the total sum requested will depend upon how well you justify the request.

Your success or failure in justifying the expenditure will depend on several factors. The overriding consideration was eluded to previously—the need. Written and/or oral presentations intended to justify the purchase must convey a crucial need. Your sincerity while explaining the need should be conveyed throughout the presentation. Be thorough, yet concise in describing the variety of reasons your video cassette recording system is desperately needed.[3]

After stressing how crucial the need for a video system is, your focus should turn to the proposal's cost effectiveness. A sound cost effective proposal may be presented by a multiple justification approach. This approach strategy presents a variety of benefits. The total of these benefits should vastly outweigh the relatively small cost of purchasing the unit. Examples of typical benefits include:

A. A video system will assist in reducing overtime funding for training because the production of training tapes offers training 24 hours a day, 7 days a week.

B. Video training program allows a given amount of in-service training for considerably less money due to all officers receiving training while on duty.

C. Video training will reduce the amount of man power lost for training since officers may be trained individually, or as an entire shift during roll call.

D. Effectiveness of investigating crime scenes will be enhanced by video taping scenes for evidential purposes.

E. Convictions of driving while intoxicated offenses should drastically increase by video taping offenders.

F. Overtime expenses, as well as man power, will be saved because many DWI offenders will plead guilty before trial.

G. Detective Bureau procedures will improve through the video taping of interrogations.

H. Video offers proof of exactly what training took place, if a civil liability issue arises.
I. By reviewing their instruction, departmental in-service training instructors can refine their techniques.
J. Video training offers a practical solution for training all those on shift rotations.
K. Video taping in-service training courses enables anyone missing a particular course to view it on a later date.

VIDEO TRAINING TOPICS

Organization and planning should determine the topics of video training tapes your agency produces. There are two major considerations to take into account as your video library grows. First, special emphasis should be placed on the high liability areas of firearms, driving, first aid, use of force and survival training. Second, the production and purchasing of video tapes should be based upon a needs assessment of your agency.

The results of a training needs assessment should be considered during the initial planning of a video cassette library. Assessment techniques such as a job task analysis, departmental examinations, review of performance evaluations, in-depth interviews with line supervisors, and needs assessment surveys will provide invaluable assistance in determining where to focus your video production efforts.

Planning for video training is no different than planning for the overall training effort. Strong consideration must be given to the highest liability areas. Fortunately, the areas of first aid, firearms, driving and defensive tactics can be demonstrated through video taping simulations and demonstrations.

These suggestions are intended as general guidelines for the organization of a video cassette production and purchasing sequence. Obviously, you should never ignore the opportunity to obtain a high quality video cassette. As with most endeavors, opportunity may only knock once.

VIDEO PRODUCTION

The primary consideration when planning the actual production of a video tape is your production capability. If production of the concerned training tape will require additional expense, budgeting must first be considered. The availability of man power must be considered for production needs, actors and instructors. Needed visual aids and video equipment must be provided for at the onset.

Following these initial stages, a basic script must be written based upon a thorough lesson plan. If actors are required, rehearsals should be conducted. Some trainers have a tendency to pass over these preparation stages. Those who are not thorough often regret the lack of preparation following completion of the concerned video tape. Take the time to do it right.

If a studio will be used, it must be large, well equipped, brightly colored and have proper lighting. Without these necessary ingredients, good color balance will be difficult to achieve. A bright and cheerful background will assist in holding the attention of viewers.

Obtaining a portable video cassette recorder allows considerable versatility during tape production. Virtually any training topic will be most effectively instructed through demonstrations and realistic simulation exercises. Add realism to video productions by going "on location" whenever possible. More reality occurs when demonstrations and events are taped in their natural environment. While manufactured background noise may be added later, it has always been best to use real sounds whenever possible.[4]

VIDEO PRODUCTION EFFECTIVENESS

As America became accustomed to the amazing creativity of movie producers such as Steven Spielberg or the high tech excitement of contemporary television, we've come to expect a degree of entertainment in television viewing. Contemporary commercial television and Hollywood film makers are experts at holding an audience captive with imaginative and spectacular programs. The viewer of a law enforcement training tape now subconsciously expects the same spectacular effects and creativity.

The dull and less effective black and white movies of yesterday are no longer accepted by today's police officer. Yet, do not become frustrated. There are simple and productive steps which will result in productive and interesting video tapes at a fraction of what commercially produced tapes cost.

The first step in achieving maximum effectiveness is to design the video tape to be appropriate for its application. There are a variety of

Figure 7. While not essential for some basic video tape production, many larger departments now have elaborate production equipment.

methods which convey particular messages. Each method can be very effective in a particular situation.

For example, if your goal is to introduce a new traffic accident report system, several methods may be effective. You can simulate proper use of the new reporting system by taping an officer handling a mock traffic accident. This sequence would be followed by him properly completing the subsequent reporting forms. A panel or well developed lecture illustrating each specific part of the new forms may be used.

Once you've selected a method, be confident and optimistic during production. The power of positive thinking should not be underestimated.

True, you may not be capable of producing a Steven Spielberg block buster, yet if you select one of several effective production methods the tape will probably be a success.

There are no mysteries to the production of effective training tapes. The basics are no more complicated than keeping your camera centered on your subject matter, proper focusing, proper lighting and noise level, holding the shot long enough for the audience to comprehend your instructional point and producing your program in a logical sequence.

In summary, the 3 basic phases of production essential to production are:

1. Picking a concept
2. Writing a script
3. Producing the video tape

The overriding theme upon which video tapes must be produced is for them to instruct the intended information in a simple, clearly understood and logical fashion. Essential instructional points should be provided during each of 3 distinctly separate phases of the tape: The introduction; the body of the video tape; a concise summary.[5]

VIDEO FACTS AND MYTHS

A well planned audio-visual message has greater impact than conventional classroom dialogues – FACT – The conciseness that video technology can provide, along with the realism of natural sights and sounds provide a far superior medium than conventional instructional techniques. The classic lecture can now "come alive" with demonstrations, simulations and a host of practicality which greatly enhances any instruction.[6]

Humor is an essential ingredient to video effectiveness – MYTH – Contrary to popular belief, there is no substantial evidence that learning is enhanced by the use of humor. Humor can be effective in particular situations; but the situations must be selective. Using humor for the wrong topic or wrong audience will be antiproductive. Unfortunately, it is sometimes used by trainers to compensate for their lack of knowledge in the proper methods of video production.[7]

Production time rather than preparation and research will comprise the vast majority of time and effort necessary to produce video tapes – MYTH – The research and preparation of video tapes should include approximately 80 percent research and 20 percent production time. Conducting thorough research is crucial to the formation of objectives and identification of major instructional points. Though the benefits are not quickly realized, research and preparation are vital to a quality product.[8]

You should not encourage note taking during the viewing of a video training tape—TRUE—Unless the video program specifically provides time for note taking, it is most likely to interfere with the intended learning. The taking of notes can distract from the audio and visual effectiveness of the training tape. An alternative to note taking is to provide a summary of the tape's highlights following the conclusion of the viewing.[7]

One of the benefits of video training is that it virtually eliminates the need for written documentation and administrative paperwork—MYTH—While it is true that a video training tape is ideal documentation to combat the claim of negligent training, it does not eliminate the need for written documentation. The research and written preparation material produced during the production of training tapes should be permanently stored. Producing such research may be required at a later time to disprove allegations of negligence regarding the quality of video instruction. Furthermore, written documentation is essential to document the identity and time that officers viewed concerned training tapes. Administrative duties such as ordering tapes, labeling and indexing tapes and devising a system of accountability for loaning tapes will be necessary.

Video training is most useful for acquiring knowledge rather than skills or attitudes—FACT—The most effective way to use video training is by allowing instructors to teach specific skills and attitudes following a transfer of knowledge through the use of video. Considerable information must be learned by officers before they will benefit by improved performance of skills or enhanced interpersonal relationships based upon revised attitudes.[6]

Trainers should limit the number of officers watching a video training tape—MYTH—Unlike traditional lecture instruction, video training does not require a small class of students. Instructional video training is equally effective with small or large viewing groups. Trainers should be concerned with the viewer's ability to see the screen and physical comfort, yet large classes do not interfere with the learning process itself.[7]

Trainers should create a luxurious theater viewing environment—MYTH—While trainers should be concerned with viewers' basic comfort and seating arrangements, creating a very comfortable environment will have drawbacks. When officers find a theater environment comprised of a darkened room, conference chairs and extremely relaxed atmosphere, they expect to be entertained as opposed to trained. A fully illuminated training or conference room with desks, chairs, pens and writing paper at each seat is an atmosphere more conducive to learning than entertaining.[9]

Repetition and subtitles are useful video training tools—FACT—While both can be overused, the use of repetition and subtitles are very effective training techniques. Subtitles enhance the learning process. Repetition will reinforce the most vital training points.[7]

When buying video equipment it is always best to shop around and take the lowest price—MYTH—A sizeable savings in purchase price can be obtained by taking time to compare equipment and prices. However, equipment purchased at a bargain price is of little value if it soon breaks. The smartest way to shop is to consider your personal situation, in addition to the equipment and price. If your agency is near a variety of repair facilities, consultant technicians and rental equipment, it will probably be wise to take the lower price. If you live in a rural or an area isolated from quality repair services, buying from a reputable dealer who can ensure quality repairs is the wisest route.[10]

You should be careful not to violate copyright restrictions when using music in the production of training tapes—FACT—Music is frequently used during the introduction and conclusion of law enforcement video tapes. It is illegal to use copyrighted music in this fashion without first obtaining a copyright release. To comply with copyright restrictions, arrangements may be made and records can be purchased from a supplier. A payment, usually in the sum of less than ten dollars, will be made to the supplier.[8]

INTERACTIVE VIDEO INSTRUCTION

Interactive video instruction combines the benefits of computer and video disk players to provide the user with "state of the art" training. Interactive video will provide several practical learning capabilities:

1. Officers can control video functions such as scanning, slow motion, and freeze frame.
2. A computer allows a video disk to be programmed so an officer can respond to programs on a numerical keypad.
3. Instruction is controlled by a computer and compatible, programmed software.

Computer assisted interactive video offers several forms of interaction to create a variety of effective instruction. One form, sometimes referred to as reactive design, limits the user to the programmed instructional

Figure 8. A video tape system must be constantly accessible to officers. Having a system located in the roll call room will enable uniform supervisors to show 10 minute training tapes during roll call.

content and structure. Students simply react to presented material in a manner designed. Responding to questions with answers is the most typical of these designs.

The second form of interaction is sometimes referred to as a co-active design. This form will allow officers to assist in making decisions regarding presented instructional materials.

Lastly, a proactive design form allows the user to design his own instructional program. Many other courses are limited because a specific format must be followed.[11] Officers may find proactive design more interesting due to the ability to create their own design.

Recent advancements in technology have expanded the abilities of interactive video training to include a new form of interaction; transactive. In addition to the previously mentioned capabilities of interactive video, transactive design allows for the following features:

A. The ability for visual and auditory feed-back of performance.
B. The ability for word processing and decision analysis.

C. Access to literature searches, encyclopedias, image collections and library collections.

Such new developments in video/computer technology provides almost unlimited capability for high tech training design. The design, programming and implementation of computer assisted interactive systems are drastically lacking in the law enforcement community. Trainers must take the initiative to provide the enhancement and effectiveness such instructional developments provide.[11]

REFERENCES

1. Bruce Apar and Henry B. Cohen, *The Home Video Book,* New York: Amphoto Books, 1982, pg. 25–27.
2. Bruce Apar and Henry B. Cohen, *The Home Video Book,* New York: Amphoto Books, 1982, pg. 45–48.
3. Reinhardt Krause, Making A Video Unit Pay, *Law Enforcement Technology,* October/November 1985, pg. 17.
4. Jack Walsh and Ronald T. Foote, Ohio Officer's Benefit From a Videotape Training Program, *The Police Chief,* July 1981, pg. 24–26.
5. Peter R. Schleger, For Effectiveness Sake, *Training and Development Journal,* December 1985, pg. 48–49.
6. John Fakler, The Value of Instructional Television, *The Police Chief,* October 1984, pg. 51.
7. David R. Torrence, How Video Can Help, *Training and Development Journal,* December 1985, pg. 51.
8. Noel Day, Using Video Programs For Roll Call Training, *The Police Chief,* 1981, pg. 30.
9. Peter Martin, Training By Video: How To Shoot Yourself In The Foot, *Training,* April 1985.
10. Peter R. Schleger, Crash Course In Teaching A Video Crash Course, *Training and Development Journal,* October 1985, pg. 81–84.
11. Dent Rhodes and Janet White Azbell, Designing Interactive Video Instruction Professionally, *Training and Development Journal,* December 1985, pg. 31–32.

5.

COMPUTER TRAINING

A law enforcement training officer does not need to become an expert on computers to effectively maintain a computerized training system. A certain amount of understanding and familiarization of computers is necessary, however. This chapter will furnish the trainer with a portion of the knowledge necessary to confidently and intelligently implement and maintain a productive computer training program.

COMPUTERS—HOW THEY WORK

For the majority of police training divisions, a microcomputer will be used. A microcomputer is the least expensive and the smallest of the four basic computer types. It will usually provide an adequate computing ability and be considerably easier to obtain and use.

All computers process data in basically the same manner. The difference in basic computer types is determined by what techniques are used for input and output of data, how many devices can be connected to the computer without overworking it and how quickly the devices work.

Simply put, the computer has four basic parts:

1. The central processing unit.
2. One or more storage devices to store information of programs.
3. One or more input devices to input data into the computer.
4. One or more output devices to provide data from the computer.[1]

The central processing unit is comprised of several interrelated systems:

- **An Operating System** which stores data and programs in the proper memory areas, keeps track of available space, sorts, displays messages and routes information back and forth between devices.
- **A User Program** which instructs the user exactly how he should operate the computer.
- **The Main Memory System** which determines the level of complexity of the program which can be accomplished.

- **Data** which consists of numbers, names, dates, etc. which have significance to the user.

If various information and instructions must be routed back and forth between the external memory devices in the central processing unit, a longer period of time will be required to accomplish a particular task. Computers which have a larger main memory capacity are generally more expensive.[2]

Disk Drives

Disk drives are devices that write and read information. The information is stored on flat, thin magnetic coated plates referred to as diskettes. Commonly referred to as floppies, they can store more than a million characters of data. Disks are simply stacks of diskettes inside a sealed case.

Input Devices

Input devices allow for instructions and data to be transmitted into the central processing unit. There are a variety of input devices.

- Optical scanners are used to describe items such as closing dates, amount due and account numbers.
- Bar code scanners are scanners which can read imprinted bar codes such as those used in supermarket checkout counters.
- Attaching a typewriter keyboard will allow almost all computers to accept direct input via the keyboard.

Output Devices

Computer output devices deliver the final product of the computers processing function. There are a variety of means to accomplish this task.

- **Microfilm and microfiche**—Computers can develop images that are recorded on microfiche or microfilm at speeds of approximately 3200 lines per minute.
- **Printers**—Entire lines of information or one character after another can be printed by computer printers.

- **Voice Synthesizers** — Computer generated data is converted into words of synthetic speech.
- **Video Display Terminals** — Can be purchased in all shapes and sizes. This is the most common way for computer processing to be delivered.[4]

The intricate operational details and capabilities of small computers may be overwhelming for the first time buyer or user. The limitations of a personal microcomputer generally involve less storage capabilities and reduced operating speeds than larger computers. There are many quality seminars and workshops available across the nation pertaining to computers. If you are unable to locate a seminar dealing with law enforcement computer use, do not hesitate to contact nearby corporations to ascertain the availability of computer seminars. The time devoted to attend a school for basic computer operation use will be worthwhile.

PURCHASING A COMPUTER

Computer use has become common in the business world. Many corporations have literally thrown away their first computer system. Other businesses have spent substantial amounts after their initial purchase to derive the benefits they thought they would have to begin with.

Purchasing a computer is not easy. To survive the experience you must first understand what you are doing. There are several essential steps to a successful purchase of a computer. Follow them and your chances of being satisfied will be dramatically increased.

A. Before you make a final purchase decision, make certain whatever data which needs to be entered in the computer system is organized. A computer will not organize a system which is based upon disorganized procedures.

B. Choose a quality company to deal with. A good computer vendor can provide the hardware, software, installation, training, procedures and long range assistance and maintenance essential to a successful operation.

C. Be alert to common purchasing pitfalls. Even respected computer vendors may sometimes be inept at providing quality sales and service. Most common purchasing complaints are:

1. System costs exceeds the anticipated figures.
2. Necessary equipment arrives late.

3. The vendor did not furnish promised software.
4. Installation of the equipment was delayed.
5. The system proposed by the vendor was not large enough to handle the work load.

D. Following selection of the vendor, the next consideration is the contract. A properly drawn contract clearly states the obligations of all concerned parties. Make certain that it is clear who is responsible for what. A quality contract provides responsible remedies in the event of failures to "live up" to obligations.[5]

The suggestions and guidelines regarding the methods, purchase and use of the computers for training are merely a superficial explanation of a complicated subject. Be thorough and organized while purchasing and implementing a computer system. The potential benefits more than justify the time and effort required to be thorough.

DOCUMENTATION PURPOSES

Using computers for training documentation will provide "state of the art" record keeping. Virtually anything recordable by hand can be stored, indexed and cross-referenced electronically by computer. What is done with a computer file is virtually no different than what is done with a paper file. How you do it will be different, since the task is accomplished via a computer keyboard instead of a filing cabinet.

Many tasks remain the same. You still have to learn the files and perform routine correcting and purging duties. Prefile sorting responsibilities and retrieval procedures may be different, but the task is still required and the result will still be the same.

In an age where elementary school students use computers on a daily basis, it isn't difficult to comprehend how beneficial a computer is. Sooner or later, virtually all police departments will depend on computers for various types of documentation. As the newness wears off, the availability and the lowering of prices will make their access to smaller departments more realistic. If your department is like most agencies, it can benefit substantially from a computer. If so, you undoubtedly will be installing one. If you don't purchase one now, you will sooner or later.

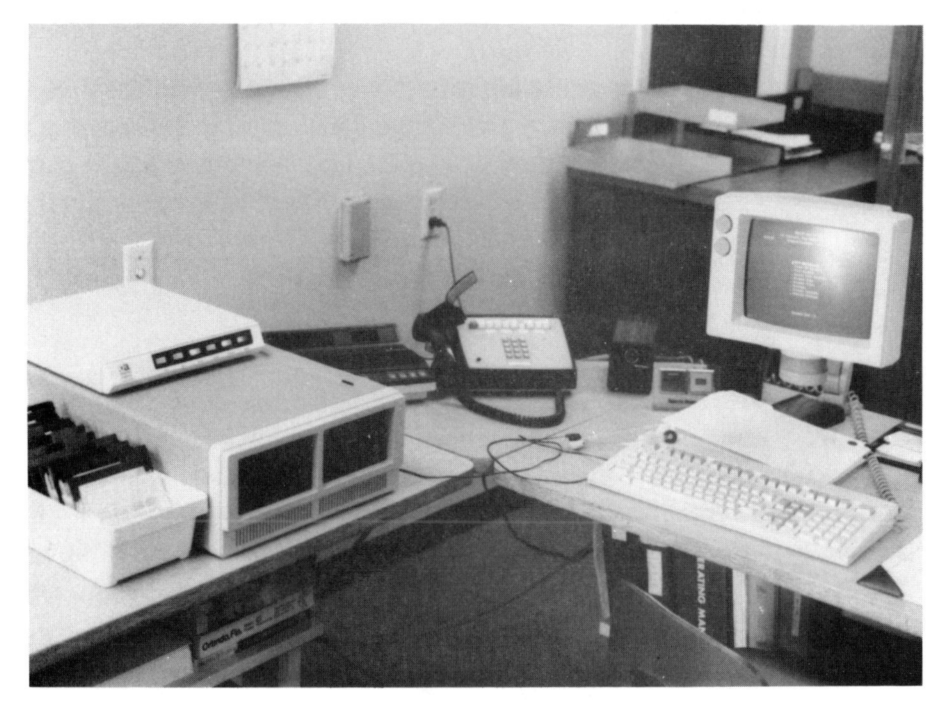

Figure 9. Training documentation has become more essential due to the potential of civil suits. Using computers for record keeping purposes is a tremendous benefit.

COMPUTERIZED EDUCATION

It's no secret that computers are now everywhere. You find them at the checkout counter of your grocery store. You find them at the walk-up teller where you bank. You even find them in the bedrooms of your neighbor's children.

Twenty years ago, computers were a rarity in the United States school system. Some school systems acquired large and expensive mainframe computers a decade ago to assist in maintaining student records and the scheduling of classes. Mainframe computers dominated the educational system until the latter 1970's when they started being replaced by less expensive smaller and more effective microcomputers.

As the market for computers grew, so did their usefulness and popularity. You now find thousands of Texas Instrument, Apple and Commodore microcomputers operating each day in classrooms across America. In 1983, there were 150,000 computers within American schools.

This figure computes to one computer for every 400 American school children.[6]

All indications suggest the tremendous growth of computer useage will only continue at a faster pace. Local school boards now use computers in a variety of effective and innovative ways. The law enforcement community can no longer wait on the sidelines. Trainers must have the initiative to take advantage of the vast benefits offered by electronic training.

ELECTRONIC TRAINING

Learning through computers is certainly not limited to a classroom setting. Most educational computer systems, used throughout the United States school systems, are available for business and home use.

Not only is there immediate availability, the quality is substantially better. Many of the early systems installed in classrooms were not designed by trainers or educators. As a result, they lacked an efficient design and were not based on sound educational principles. As an example, negative reinforcement was used by advising the student that he or she was "a dummy" if they missed a particular question.

Before long, educators and trainers sought to convey the excitement and stimulation of arcade computer games to an education or training computer system. Contemporary game rooms are usually thriving businesses.

When used to its fullest extent, a computer will be a multi-beneficial training device. An example is the variety of interaction opportunities computers yield. The more a trainer becomes knowledgeable and confident with the abilities of his computer, the more benefit he will derive.

Computers are excellent training tools because they are available 24 hours a day, 7 days a week. In addition, they furnish immediate, positive feed-back to the user.[7]

COMPUTER TRAINING METHODOLOGY

The use of instructional computers can be separated into two basic categories:

1. **Computer-Managed Instruction** — The process of training administration, documentation, scheduling of assignments and grading is referred to as Computer-Manager Instruction (CMI).

2. **Computer-Assisted Instruction**—The actual training of skills and knowledge is commonly referred to as Computer-Assisted Instruction (CAI). Computer-Assisted Instruction may take many forms. Probably the most common form is drill-and-practice. It is usually referred to in educational circles as D & P. A computer uses the drill and practice method to patiently reinforce basic concepts. A series of questions and answers are provided to the officer. If a wrong answer is given, the officer is advised it was incorrect and given a chance to try again. Tutorials are another common form of Computer-Assisted Instruction. These programs are created to train an officer by leading him, step by step, through an organized and logical method of instruction. Tutorial programs are available on a variety of training topics. They are usually most beneficial to introduce new concepts, and allow for officers to learn at their own pace and/or be repeated whenever necessary. The simulation form of Computer-Assisted Instruction has become very popular. Its practicality and realism is effective to simulate real life situations without the risk of devastating consequences. Increased interest, not having to tie up expensive and needed equipment and making training fun are a few of the positive benefits of simulation computer training. Graphic computer simulations interface with video cassette recordings, written materials and a variety of demonstration type training to provide an exciting and motivating training experience.[8]

EDUCATIONAL COMPUTER PROGRAMS

The following is a list of private concerns where programs intended to teach the use of previously purchased software may be obtained.

- Courseware, Incorporated
  10075 Carroll
  Canyon Road
  San Diego, California 92131
  619-578-1700
  Features: This program offers instruction concerning data management, communications, spread sheets, graphics, word processing, etc.

- Scholastic Wizware
  1290 Wall Street, West
  Lyndhurst, New Jersey 07071-9986
  1-800-651-1575
  Computer: VIC 20
  Features: Instruction on graphics, sound, keyboard and basic programming are offered in this package.

- CDEX
  5050 El Camino Real
  Los Altos, California 94022
  415-964-7600
  Computer: IBM, Apple, DEC Rainbow, Texas Instrument Professional, Tandy 2000
  Features: An assortment of disk based tutorials for programs such as Lotus 1-2-3, Easy Rider, Word Star, BPI Accounting, etc.

- American Training International
  Suite 201A
  3770 Highland Avenue
  Manhattan Beach, California 90266
  213-546-5579
  Computer: IBM, MS–DOS, Apple 2e, CP/M-86, CP/M
  Features: Instructional packages for specific business programs, programming language and operating systems.

- Comprehensive Software
  Post Office Box 90833
  Los Angeles, California 90009
  213-318-2561
  Computer: IBM
  Features: Instructional program termed pal, intended for the beginner in need of explanations regarding procedures in spread sheets, word processing, keyboard, and basic programming. The instructional package is similar to a user's manual on disk that acts as a tutorial regarding the PC's disk operating system.

- Knoware, Incorporated
  301 Vassar Street
  Cambridge, Maryland 02139
  Computer: IBM, Apple

Features: An instructional package that teaches via a series of games through which the user learns about word processing and data base management, graphics, spread sheets, basic programming, etc.[9]

SELECTING TRAINING SOFTWARE

For many training officers, the selecting and purchasing of training/educational software programs will be bewildering. To make an already difficult task worse, you may need to make a selection through the use of catalogs. Whenever possible, attempt to purchase software programs in person. This will allow you to examine the program first hand and ask the appropriate questions of a sales representative.

Obviously, the ability to ask intelligent purchasing related questions may ultimately mean the difference between a successful or unsuccessful training program. The initial concern should be to determine whether the program is compatible to your computer system. The following checklist is intended to ensure a software program's compatibility. Take it with you while shopping for programs.

When comparing software programs, briefly read through instructional manuals. Keep in mind it is not necessary that a manual be complex and lengthy. Training/educational software should be clear and understood, as opposed to confusing and difficult.[10]

Do not be afraid to ask questions. The failure to do so may result in a very costly mistake. It's also a good idea to have a friend who is knowledgeable with computer use to go with you.

DISADVANTAGES OF COMPUTER INSTRUCTION

Without a doubt, there are a multitude of advantages to computer based training. Many advantages are discussed within this chapter. A thorough examination, however, is not complete without reviewing disadvantages, as well.

Some potential problem areas regarding computer based instruction are:

1. Software can be inadequate in terms of reliability and system-response time. A close scrutiny before purchasing software packages is essential.
2. Insufficient time for developing and implementing software training programs.

TABLE V
COMPUTER SOFTWARE PROGRAMS CHECKLIST

1. Make note of your computer make and model number ________
2. Ensure concerned software specifically states it is compatible to your system ________
3. Name of software vendor ________
4. Title of program ________
5. Contact person ________
6. Address and phone ________
7. Purchase price ________
8. Program's objectives ________
9. Program's description ________
10. Type of program ________
    Drill and practice ________
    Demonstration ________
    Tutorial ________
    Game ________
    Simulation ________
    Problem solving ________
    Word processing ________
    Enrichment ________
    Teaching ________
    Classroom ________
    Management ________
    Other ________
11. Documentation
    Instructional manual ________
    Student guide ________
    Instructions on screen ________
    Tests ________
    Teacher's guide ________
    Workbook ________
    Student work sheets ________
    Or none ________
12. Ease of use
    Sound can be turned on or off ________
    Screen is easy to read ________
    Student can control speed of program ________
    Instruction manual is clear ________

TABLE V Continued

13. Content	
Good use of graphics	________
Good use of feed-back	________
Good difficulty level	________
Supplements classroom study	________
Objectives clearly stated	________
Objectives are met	________
Program can be modified for flexibility of teaching	________
Information within program is correct	________
Program is interesting to officer	________
14. Design	
Format is well organized	________
Program is innovative	________
Presentation is professional	________
15. Major Benefits	
Weaknesses of program	________
Additional comments	________

3. Studies indicate some people learn best when exposed to the knowledge and mistakes of other people. Individual computer training restricts such benefits.
4. As with most forms of law enforcement training, scheduling of officers may be a problem if only one computer terminal is available.[11]

The majority of those knowledgeable in the computer industry agree computer based training will play a significant role in future law enforcement training. The merits of a computer training system far out weigh its disadvantages.

JUSTIFICATION OF YOUR COMPUTER TRAINING SYSTEM

Computer training can be extremely effective and productive. This, of course, presumes you purchase a quality system and implement it wisely. Computer training requires standardization and a devotion to organizational planning. The result will be very cost effective.

A computer training program's potential is meaningless if you are unable to convince your agency's top level management to purchase it. The justification for such a purchase does not need to be difficult. After all, computer training is a tremendous asset. Computers are fast and accurate. They have virtually unlimited memories and don't become frustrated or tired as instructors do.

As with all training functions, management must look upon training expenses as an intricate part of the departmental budget. Training officers are at fault to allow training to be viewed as a separate item, rather than a crucial function within the agency's overall operations. It remains the training officer's job to provide proper training. It remains the organization's responsibility to furnish resources necessary to accomplish that process.

Training officers must receive total managerial commitment to training. It must be viewed as a necessity, rather than a luxury. Furthermore, it's a function requiring professionally trained trainers. Today's law enforcement trainer should confront management with a careful assessment of his agency's training needs. He must seek a budget which enables him to provide "state of the art" technology to accomplish those needs. Lastly, the question of whether or not his organization is willing to commit necessary resources to quality training, should be looked upon as an investment in the future.[12]

Interviews and conversations with management concerning computer training justification must be thoroughly prepared for. Written documentation should be organized, innovative and resourceful. All that is necessary is for you to be adequately informed as to the benefits, then present them in a clear and precise manner.

IMPROVED REPORT WRITING VIA COMPUTER INSTRUCTION

Most training officers consider report writing an internal problem area. All agencies have officers in need of improved writing skills. Unfortunately, many officers' writing difficulties have developed over years of inadequate childhood education.

Officers are frequently hired who lack the basic english skills necessary to write a series of paragraphs. As a result, several computer software companies have developed software programs to assist trainers in approving writing skills.

Some software packages are designed to assist individuals in learning to edit and analyze the quality of their writing. Such programs provide information on principles of writing style, spelling, sentence structure and punctuation. Improvement in writing skills will be identified and documented.

An officer participating in this type of program would complete his writing assignment first. After entering it into the computer, the program would provide an analysis and offer suggestions for rewriting. Following a review of the analysis and conducting an edit, the officer then reenters his lesson in the computer. After the reentry, the final copy is graded.

Computer training is a probable solution to your report writing problems. Officers receive assistance while they are writing, rather than after they have turned in an assignment. The computer will become a 24 hour a day, 7 day a week instructor. This will allow you to devote time to other matters.

Using technology for english/report writing development is still in the developmental stage. Most experts agree, however, the use of computers to train and improve writing skills will be an intricate part of future training efforts.[13]

Sources which may provide additional information concerning the use of computers for improved report writing are:

- **A writer's tool: The Computer and Composition Instruction.**
  University of Wisconsin Center at Marinette
  Edited by William Wresch
- **Computers and Composition Instruction**
  An International Council for Computers and Education
  University of Oregon
- **Computers and Composition**
  Michigan Technological University
  Colorado State University
  Kathleen Kiefer

COMPUTERIZED LEGAL TRAINING

Recently, several companies have developed a computerized legal training system. One such program is the electronic legal bulletin service provided by the Police Law Institute, Hollywood, Florida.

The electronic legal bulletin is a perpetual service. Computer disks containing lessons on contemporary Federal and State case decisions are delivered monthly. New State and Federal legislation is also included. Lessons review the most recent legal changes affecting police operations and procedures. Subject areas include arrest, search, seizure, interrogation, use of force and contraband forfeiture, etc.

After all officers have completed their computer lessons, they are returned to the company for grading. A written competency report on each officer is then returned to the department. Every officer will receive a written outline of the material for future reference.

The system includes a computer, computerized lessons, written outlines of lessons, scoring of results of the examinations for each officer and written reports of competency on each officer.[14]

The aforementioned legal training service is merely an example of the current state of the art training available. It furnishes not only effective and productive training, but excellent documentation as well.

COMPUTER/VIDEO DISK TRAINING MATERIAL

Computer/video disk training combines the effectiveness of computer training with the realism of video. A typical training session could require an officer to view video scenerio, then participate in a computerized training session regarding what was viewed. Officers receive superb training through the interaction of video and computer technology.

Relatively little has been written on computer/video disk interactive training. However, available material indicates this system is most appropriate when:

A. Software security is desired.
B. Excellent visual material would be useful for motivation purposes.
C. Realism is essential for understanding the process.
D. An application involves a very large data base.
E. Fast scanning of training materials is beneficial.
F. A long term demanding use of material is expected.

Trainers should note that interactive training can be extremely sophisticated. A great deal of knowledge and expertise is required in developing, purchasing and/or implementing such a program. Most trainers would be foolish to undertake such a project without knowledgeable assistance.[14]

FUTURE TRENDS IN COMPUTER TRAINING

Evidence exists that the following future computer training trends will occur. These changes may drastically effect the use of technological based training. Thus, it is wise for the professional trainer to be aware these changes are evident.

Computer use for training employees will continue to increase. The current overwhelming positive reaction to computers should continue to spiral their widespread popularity. Within the next 15 years, approximately half of all industrial training will be computerized. The software business should continue to expand at phenomenal rates.

Law enforcement training will benefit greatly by the computer explosion. An extremely advantageous "all in one" software package will become available. This new software enables trainers to use a variety of different programs within the one software package.

The growth of computers shall increase at an even greater rate. Microcomputers will become common within all facets of American life. Home use is going to be commonplace.

Competition throughout the computer industry should result in a sharp decrease in prices. Nearly all facets of the industry will be directly affected by the intense competition.

Technological advancements should alter the size and shapes of computers themselves. Portable machines as small as a loose-leaf binder will be frequently used. Flat video terminals will replace current bulky ones. Computers capable of responding to voice commands will become common.[15]

APPLICATION OF COMPUTER TRAINING TO LAW ENFORCEMENT

In 1969, the Los Angeles Police Department and the Coast Community College District began a joint project for the application of development, implementation and evaluation of computer assisted instruction to law enforcement. The project was the result of a grant from the Law Enforcement Assistance Administration.

There were two primary goals of the project. First, to evaluate the effectiveness of computer assisted training. Second, to develop a computer assisted training system in the area of search and seizure.

The following procedures were developed to serve as organization guidelines:

1. Training objectives for search and seizure and rules of evidence were written.
2. An examination was developed.
3. Study materials were prepared.

4. Case problems simulated through computer instruction were devised.
5. Computer training was conducted at the Golden West College. Conventional Classroom training was held at the Los Angeles Police Academy. In both cases, the training sources were identical.
6. An examination was administered to cadets in both the Golden West Academy and the Los Angeles Police Academy. Test results were compared to determine if computer assisted instruction techniques were more or less effective than conventional classroom instruction.
7. Comparison of examination results indicated those cadets instructed through the use of computer technology scored significantly higher than those instructed by conventional methods.[16]

COMPUTER RELATED RESOURCES

1. **Computers in the Classroom**
   Magazine
   Carlaw Avenue
   Toronto, Canada M4M2R6
   416-461-9206

2. **AEDS Journal and Monitor**
   Magazine
   Association or Educational Data Systems
   1201 16th Street, Northwest
   Washington, D. C. 20036
   202-822-7845

3. **Educational Technology**
   Magazine
   140 Sylvan Avenue
   Engelwood Cliffs, New Jersey 07632
   201-871-4007

4. **Electronic Education**
   Magazine
   Electronic Communications
   Post Office Box 20221
   Tallahassee, Florida 32316
   904-878-4178

5. **Interface: The Computer Education Quarterly**
   Magazine
   116 Royal Oak
   Santa Cruz, California 95066
   408-438-5018

6. **Microcomputer Course Ware/Materials Report**
   Magazine
   EPIE Institute
   Box 813
   Watermill, New Jersey 11976
   516-283-4922

7. **Microcomputer Digest**
   Magazine
   103 Bridge Avenue
   Bay Head, New Jersey 08742
   201-679-1877

8. **Microcomputer in Education**
   Magazine
   Queue
   Five Chapel Hill Drive
   Fairfield, Connecticut 06432
   203-335-0908

9. **Teaching in Computers**
   Magazine
   Scholastic, Incorporated
   1290 Wall Street, West
   Lindhurst, New Jersey 07071
   201-939-8050

10. **Cambridge Science Directory**
    Cambridge Development Laboratory
    100 5th Avenue
    Waltham, Massachusetts 02154
    617-890-8076
    Free

11. **Conduit**
    100 Linquist Center
    Post Office Box 338

University of Iowa
319-353-5789
Free[17]

Computerization is a challenge to all law enforcement trainers. Because of their effectiveness, computers will continue to infiltrate law enforcement. Trainers with initiative and motivation will wait no longer to take advantage of a computer's increased productivity. Those remaining will continue to procrastinate and simply fall further behind the rest.

REFERENCES

1. Edward M. Cross, *How to Buy a Business Computer and Get It Right the First time,* Reston Publishing Company, Incorporated, 1983, pg. 9.
2. Gary Meyer, What Every Personnel Manager Should Know About Computers, *Personnel Journal,* August 1984.
3. Gary Meyer, What Every Personnel Manager Should Know About Computers, *Personnel Journal,* August 1984, pg. 59.
4. Gary Meyer, What Every Personnel Manager Should Know About Computers. *Personnel Journal,* August 1984, pg. 59–61.
5. Edward M. Cross, *How to Buy a Business Computer and Get It Right the First Time,* Reston Publishing Company, Incorporated, 1983, pg. 5.
6. Peter Stoler, *The Computer Generation,* Haddon, 1984, pg. 54–57.
7. Jan Owen, *Getting the Most From Your Computer,* New York: McGraw-Hill, 1985, pg. 118–119.
8. Peter Stoler, *The Computer Generation,* Haddon, 1984, pg. 60–68.
9. Jan Owen, *Getting the Most From Your Computer,* New York: McGraw-Hill, 1985, pg. 130–134.
10. Jan Owen, *Getting the Most From Your Computer,* New York: McGraw-Hill, Inc., 1985, pg. 135–139.
11. Dr. Margaret Bahniuk, The Value In Computer-Based Training, *Office Administration and Automation,* August 1984, pg. 85.
12. Gerald L. Hershey, High Tech Training Is A Necessity, *Office Administration and Automation,* September 1984, pg. 78.
13. Margaret Bahnuik, Using Technology To Improve Writing Skills, *Office Administration and Automation,* June 1984, pg. 83.
14. William A. DuPerron and Russell Sawchuck, Functional Specifications Analysis For A Computer-Based Multi-Media Training System, *The Police Chief,* October 1984, pg. 47–50.
15. Gary Meyer, What Every Personnel Manager Should Know About Computers, *Personnel Journal,* August 1984, pg. 58–62.
16. Richard W. Brightman, *Computer Assisted Instruction Program for Police Training,* U. S. Department of Justice, National Institute of Law Enforcement and Criminal Justice, pg. 1–2.
17. Jan Owen, *Getting the Most From Your Computer,* New York: McGraw-Hill, 1985, pg. 130–139.

6.

FIRST AID TRAINING

Emergency first aid training among law enforcement agencies varies greatly throughout the nation. Some departments have developed an extensive training program to include cardiopulmonary resuscitation training for all officers, basic first aid, basic life support and segments of first responder and emergency medical technician training. Many agencies, however, have virtually no emergency medical training.

Irregardless of the level of training currently provided there are many considerations. Lack of funding, manpower restrictions, failure to thoroughly understand the need, lack of specialized instructional equipment and qualified instructors are a few common reasons a program has not been implemented. No matter what justification is furnished, it remains ethically, professionally, morally and legally unacceptable not to provide effective and continual training in basic first aid and life support.

The emergency medical services system within America is a multifaceted operation. Thousands of lives are saved annually due to the training of emergency room nurses, police officers, ambulance attendants, fire fighters, physicians and rescue squad personnel. Working together, each of these occupations become an important componant of the EMS system.

THE NEED FOR FIRST AID TRAINING

While training officers assume tremendous responsibility for ensuring that personnel receive proper first aid training, they are not alone. Top level management must be fully supportive of first aid training for it to be successful. A serious difference exists between this and most other forms of police training; someone's life may depend upon how well an officer has been trained.

Whether a citizen is severely injured in an automobile accident or a fellow officer has been shot, an office knowing the proper medical treatment may make the difference between life and death. Our society has recognized that proper initial emergency treatment is the most critical aspect of emergency medical care. The medical profession also recognizes the lack of proficiency by those who first reach the injured person is the weakest aspect of emergency medical services. Organizations such as The American Heart Association, The American Medical Association, and The American Red Cross may furnish law enforcement agencies with training assistance. Trainers should contact these organizations for assistance whenever possible.

It is vital that trainers instill within officers attending first aid training, an urgency and need to become proficient in administering emergency first aid. An instructor must motivate officers to sincerely want to learn.

LEGAL CONSIDERATIONS

Training in itself can not eliminate or drastically reduce the number of civil suits brought against law enforcement agencies. It can, however, greatly reduce the potential for awarding large financial damages by developing, implementing, reviewing and evaluating quality training programs. An agency's training philosophy can easily make the difference between failure and success in defending against civil actions. If a stagnate and lackadaisical attitude prevails throughout the training function, the result will probably mean financial disaster to the department when civil litigation is brought.

Training is a highly vulnerable area of civil liability. Police administrators assume a responsibility to train officers they employ. Administrators may be held liable when a negligent breach of duty which causes an injury to the plaintiff has occurred. The negligent failure to train involves a breach of executive duty and imposes the same liability upon the administrator as if the administrator had participated in the concerned act.

Great legal liability may occur if law enforcement agencies do not train officers in a manner adequate to prepare them for their responsibilities. One of the most prevalent areas for civil litigation against law enforcement agencies is medical aid. The failure to provide proper emergency medical assistance by officers arriving at a scene first should be of utmost concern to both administrators and trainers. If a civil suit is brought before the courts, it will examine whether sufficient first aid training existed, and if so the quality of such training.

Training officers should explain to officers, their personal civil liability pertaining to emergency medical care. These regulations require a certain standard of care be provided. Should an individual perform improperly or take acts which are not equal to this standard of care, they may be held civilly accountable. Officers performing emergency first aid must be instructed not to take actions above and beyond the level of training they have been provided.

The standard of care theory will allow an officer to be judged by a fair expectation of ability which someone with the concerned officer's training and experience should possess. Officers must also be instructed not to allow merely a potential of civil liability to prevent them from taking action at an emergency scene. Officers may also be held liable for failure to provide basic first aid in a life threatening medical emergency.

Except for Wisconsin, all states have passed good samaritan laws. Such laws provide a certain amount of immunity from civil liability to those who act as "good samaritans" at the scene of a medical emergency. The scope of good samaritan laws varies greatly throughout the nation. While some laws specify a particular "standard of care," others require the concerned individuals to act with "due care" or in "good faith." In general, the scope of protection provided consists of immunity from liability for ordinary negligence in providing medical assistance.[1]

An examination of previous civil suits brought against police departments for negligent emergency medical aid may assist the trainer in a further understanding. In Smith vs. City of Washington Courthouse, 124m.e.2nd 794 (cm. pl. Ohio 1955) the court held in favor of the police department. The case concerned officers who had failed to provide medical treatment to the victim of a heart attack.

In another case, however, the court held that the concerned officer did not take due care and act with substantial reason by not recognizing or treating the victim who was suffering massive hemorrhaging. The case of Spivy vs. City of Miami, 280southern2nd 419 (Florida. 1973) held that the city was liable. The lack of proper training provided officers in recognizing serious injuries requiring immediate medical attention was a key issue.

INITIAL RESPONSIBILITY

First and utmost, officers must be taught their first responsibility as the initial officer at a scene is the victim. Until more qualified medical help arrives, aid given a seriously injured person must be the first

TABLE VI
COMPARING GOOD SAMARITAN LAWS

	Alabama	*Alaska*	*Arizona*	*Arkansas*	*California*	*Colorado*	*Connecticut*	*Delaware*	*Dist. Columbia*	*Florida*
Date of act or last amendment	1981	1976	1978	1979	1963	1975	1978	1974	1977	1978
Covers "any person"		•	•	•		•		•	•	•
Covers in-state nurses only					•			•		
Includes out-of-state nurses in coverage	•		•			•	•	•	•	
Requires acts in good faith	•		•	•	•	•		•	•	•
Covers only gratuitous services	•	•	•	•		•	•	•	•	•
Covers aid at scene of emergency, accident, disaster	•	•	•	•	•	•	•	•	•	•
Covers only roadside accidents										
Covers emergencies outside place of employment, course of employment					•		•			
Covers emergencies outside of hospital, doctor's office, or other places having medical equipment									•	•
Protects against failure to provide or arrange for further medical treatment	•	•	•					•		•
Covers transportation from the scene of the emergency to a destination for further medical treatment										
Specifically mentions that acts of gross negligence or willful or wanton misconduct are not covered		•	•	•	•		•	•	•	

TABLE VI Continued

	Georgia	*Hawaii*	*Idaho*	*Illinois*	*Indiana*	*Iowa*	*Kansas*	*Kentucky*	*Louisiana*	*Maine*	*Maryland*
Date of act or last amendment	1962	1979	1980	1980	1973	1969	1977	1980	1964	1977	1977
Covers "any person"	•	•	•		•	•	•		•	•	
Covers in-state nurses only								•			
Includes out-of-state nurses in coverage				•			•		•		•
Requires acts in good faith	•	•	•	•	•	•			•		
Covers only gratuitous services	•	•		•	•	•	•	•	•	•	•
Covers aid at scene of emergency, accident, disaster	•	•	•	•	•	•	•	•	•	•	•
Covers only roadside accidents											
Covers emergencies outside place of employment, course of employment											
Covers emergencies outside of hospital, doctor's office, or other places having medical equipment											
Protects against failure to provide or arrange for further medical treatment	•				•				•		
Covers transportation from the scene of the emergency to a destination for further medical treatment			•								•
Specifically mentions that acts of gross negligence or willful or wanton misconduct are not covered		•	•	•	•	•	•	•	•	•	•

TABLE VI Continued

	Massachusetts	*Michigan*	*Minnesota*	*Mississippi*	*Missouri*	*Montana*	*Nebraska*	*Nevada*	*New Hampshire*	*New Jersey*
Date of act or last amendment	1969	1978	1978	1979	1979	1970	1971	1975	1977	1968
Covers "any person"			•		•	•	•	•	•	•
Covers in-state nurses only									•	
Includes out-of-state nurses in coverage	•	•		•	•			•	•	•
Requires acts in good faith	•		•	•	•	•		•	•	•
Covers only gratuitous services	•				•	•	•	•		
Covers aid at scene of emergency, accident, disaster	•	•	•	•	•	•	•	•	•	•
Covers only roadside accidents										
Covers emergencies outside place of employment, course of employment									•	
Covers emergencies outside of hospital, doctor's office, or other places having medical equipment			•							
Protects against failure to provide or arrange for further medical treatment	•						•	•	•	
Covers transportation from the scene of the emergency to a destination for further medical treatment			•	•						
Specifically mentions that acts of gross negligence or willful or wanton misconduct are not covered		•		•	•	•	•	•		

TABLE VI Continued

	New Mexico	*New York*	*North Carolina*	*North Dakota*	*Ohio*	*Oklahoma*	*Oregon*	*Pennsylvania*	*Rhode Island*	*South Carolina*
Date of act or last amendment	1972	1975	1975	1977	1981	1979	1981	1978	1969	1964
Covers "any person"	•		•	•	•	•				•
Covers in-state nurses only				•						
Includes out-of-state nurses in coverage		•				•	•	•	•	
Requires acts in good faith	•			•		•		•		•
Covers only gratuitous services	•	•			•	•	•		•	•
Covers aid at scene of emergency, accident, disaster	•	•	•	•	•	•	•	•	•	•
Covers only roadside accidents			•							
Covers emergencies outside place of employment, course of employment										
Covers emergencies outside of hospital, doctor's office, or other places having medical equipment		•			•			•	•	
Protects against failure to provide or arrange for further medical treatment										•
Covers transportation from the scene of the emergency to a destination for further medical treatment										
Specifically mentions that acts of gross negligence or willful or wanton misconduct are not covered	•	•	•		•	•	•	•	•	•

TABLE VI Continued

	South Dakota	*Tennessee*	*Texas*	*Utah*	*Vermont*	*Virginia*	*Washington*	*West Virginia*	*Wisconsin*	*Wyoming*
Date of act or last amendment	1976	1976	1977	1979	1968	1980	1975	1967	NO GOOD SAMARITAN ACT	1977
Covers "any person"		•	•		•	•	•	•		•
Covers in-state nurses only			•							
Includes out-of-state nurses in coverage	•									
Requires acts in good faith	•	•		•		•	•	•		•
Covers only gratuitous services		•	•		•	•	•	•		•
Covers aid at scene of emergency, accident, disaster	•	•	•	•	•	•	•	•		•
Covers only roadside accidents										
Covers emergencies outside place of employment, course of employment			•							
Covers emergencies outside of hospital, doctor's office, or other places having medical equipment										
Protects against failure to provide or arrange for further medical treatment		•								
Covers transportation from the scene of the emergency to a destination for further medical treatment						•	•			
Specifically mentions that acts of gross negligence or willful or wanton misconduct are not covered		•	•		•		•			•

Source: Nurses Reference Library, *Emergencies*, Springhouse Corporation, Springhouse, Pennsylvania, 1985, pages 32–36.

priority. Officers should understand they have 4 main responsibilities in such a situation:

1. Reach the victim as quickly as possible, while using the necessary care.

2. Determine what is wrong with the victim and provide emergency medical care.
3. If the situation requires the victim be moved, do so without causing additional injury.
4. When more qualified emergency personnel arrive at the scene, professionally transfer responsibility of the patient to them along with any additional information which has been learned.[2]

The first officer(s) at a serious medical emergency must remain calm and collected even though all others may be panicking. It is essential that he or she take charge and ensure that critical actions immediately take place. Additional forms of assistance will probably need to be requested. Immediate first aid will need to be administered. Multiple victims may be found at the scene. Witnesses and/or evidence of a crime must be dealt with. Training must emphasis that an officer cannot afford the luxury of becoming emotional during such a situation.

MEDICAL EMERGENCY ASSESSMENT

Officers should be instructed that making the initial assessment of an injured person must include more than an examination of an obvious injury. The initial assessment must include:

A. His own observations.
B. Possible causes of the injuries (weapons).
C. Statements of any present witnesses.
D. Statements of the victim.

The assessment of a medical emergency requires great organization, forethought and training. Officers will not have the time to thoroughly consider all available information. They will have to act quickly and effectively. The following are phases of assessment which enable an officer to assess the situation as effectively as possible.

The first phase of evaluation should focus on what is commonly referred to as life threatening situations. The lack of circulation and/or breathing should be of the utmost concern. Administering first aid for severe bleeding and shock should follow. After stabilizing these functions, obvious needs such as open wounds, burns or fractures should be dealt with.

The second phase of assessment must focus on the patient's major injuries which are difficult to detect and the concern of preventing further injury by improper first aid procedures. This secondary assessment of the victim should begin at the victim's head and literally progress down the body to the victim's feet. Close attention to such signs as swelling, discoloration, tenderness or lumps must be given.[3]

Lastly, officers must understand that the victim's care is their responsibility until additional help arrives. They should continue to observe and assess the victim's condition; as it is subject to change from moment to moment.

If a victim is unable to speak, the officer should interview him to obtain information pertinent to his injury. The victim can be calmed by officers making statements such as "relax" or "everything is going to be alright." The following questions should be asked during the secondary assessment stage:

1. Ask the victim(s) his or her name.
2. If the victim is a child, determine his or her name along with age and how to contact parents.
3. Ask what is wrong and how they feel.
4. Ask how they were injured.
5. If it is an illness rather than an obvious accident, ask if they have ever experienced it previously.
6. Ask if they are now under a doctor's care.
7. Ask if they are currently taking medications.
8. Ask if they are allergic to any medications or have any allergies.[4]

Officers must learn that interviews should be conducted only after an assessment for any life threatening condition. Medical aid for life threatening emergencies must continue even if the interview is never conducted.

During a medical assessment officers may observe medical identification cards or emblems. A card from the American Medical Association may identify special health problems. A Medic Alert emblem worn as a necklace or bracelet should alert the officer to critical information. The Medic Alert emblem has identification and phone numbers on the rear which can furnish immediate, crucial information. A tragedy may be averted by quick response to the information given on medical identification cards.

LIFE THREATENING MEDICAL EMERGENCIES

Law enforcement first aid training must focus on life threatening medical emergencies. These situations involve breathing difficulty, the circulatory system, severe bleeding and shock. Emergency first aid should be given in this order:

A. Ensure a clear air passage.
B. Ensure breathing and heart beats.
C. Stop severe bleeding.
D. Provide treatment for shock.

Ensure air passage—After determining a victim is not breathing, immediately place him on his back. He should be lying on a hard surface. Place one hand under his neck and the other on his forehead. Tilt the victim's head back so the chin points upward.

Look in the victim's mouth to determine if an obstruction exists. If so, turn the victim on his side, tilt his head down and wipe out the obstruction with 2 fingers. After the obstruction has been cleared, roll the victim on his back and tilt his head up to establish a clear airway.

A further check for breathing can be made by placing your ear near his mouth and nose. Listen quietly for several seconds. Try to hear and feel his breaths. Officers should continue to observe his chest for signs of breathing movement.

Artificial respiration—Artificial respiration should be initiated by resuming the head tilt position as previously explained. An air tight seal must be made over the victim's mouth by the officer placing his mouth upon the victim's. The officer should breathe deeply in the victim's mouth until his chest rises.

When giving artificial respiration to a child, officers must cover the child's mouth and nose with their own mouth. Breaths should be smaller for a child and even smaller for an infant. They should be given at a rate of 20 per minute for a child or infant.

Artificial respiration is administered to an adult at a rate of 12 breaths per minute. Deep, full breaths should be given to an adult victim. When breathing begins, continue to keep the head tilted back. Artificial respiration must continue until independent breathing stabilizes, you are relieved by another assistant or you are physically exhausted and unable to continue.

CARDIOPULMONARY RESUSCITATION

While artificial respiration restores breathing to the victim, cardiopulmonary resuscitation (CPR) should be applied when there is no breathing or heartbeat. Mouth to mouth resuscitation and chest heart massage are applied to this life threatening situation. If administered improperly, CPR may create additional complications.

Injuries such as broken ribs which puncture the lungs, stomach or liver may occur during CPR. However, the possibility of causing injuries should never deter an officer from performing CPR when needed. Instruction must include techniques to prevent mistaking choking, fainting or some other condition for heart and breathing stoppage. Officers may easily learn to check for lack of heartbeats by taking the victim's pulse.

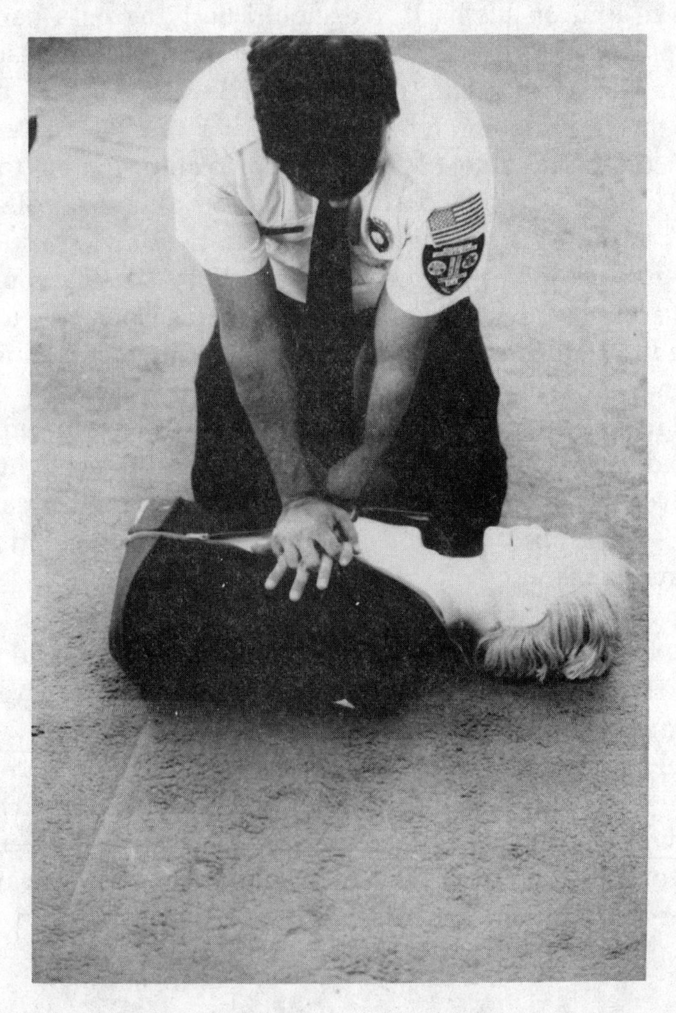

Figure 10. First aid training is a frequently overlooked training area. It is also an area of high civil liability to law enforcement agencies.

CPR INSTRUCTIONAL STEPS

1. After first determining CPR is an appropriate measure, lay the victim on his back and tilt the head back in the same manner used for artificial respiration.

2. Locate the lower tip of the victim's breast bone. Find a point the width of 3 fingers above the tip. Keep one finger at this point while positioning the heel of the second hand next to the finger. The heel of the first hand should then be placed upon the second, with fingers from both hands intertwined and off the chest.
3. Using quick thrusts, push down with the weight of the upper portion of the body. The lower portion of the victim's breast bone should be depressed one and one half to two inches. Repeat the compression every second for a total of 60 compressions per minute. Compressions will compress the heart and continue to pump blood throughout the body.
4. While heart compressions continue to circulate blood throughout the body, oxygen must be supplied to the blood. This is accomplished by providing mouth-to-mouth breathing in connection with heart compressions. If an officer is administering aid alone, 2 deep mouth-to-mouth breaths, followed by 15 chest compressions should be provided. This cycle should be repeated until additional assistance arrives. When the officer has an assistant, one deep breath should be administered by one rescuer after every 5 compressions by the second rescuer. The officer conducting chest compressions should not stop chest compressions during the moment breaths are administered. This requires the officer providing breaths to administer them immediately after the fifth compression, yet, before the next compression.
5. CPR must continue until the victim begins breathing on his own. Trainers should instruct officers to prepare for extreme physical fatigue if they must continue CPR for an extended period of time. Officers must also learn not to give up after a few minutes. It is possible for life to be sustained through CPR for at least an hour.[6]

CHOKING—THE HEIMLICH MANUEVER

Choking is the leading cause of death in the home for infants under 1 year of age. It is the sixth leading cause of accidental death for all Americans. Often being referred to as the "cafe coronary," choking on a piece of food frequently takes place in restaurants. For these reasons, officers must become proficient in life saving measures for choking.

The Heimlich Manuever is commonly referred to as an effective technique for choking. More than 20 states have passed legislation requiring a description of the method be posted in restaurants. Because death will occur 4 minutes after the victim begins to choke, there is no room for hesitation or improper application of the technique.

Diagnosis

1. Ninety-eight percent of all individuals who die in a restaurant or while dining are choking victims. The universal sign from a person choking is their hand to the front of their throat.
2. A choking victim's face will begin to turn blue as a result of the lack of oxygen.
3. The victim may soon become unconscious due to the lack of oxygen.

Performing the Heimlich Manuever

1. Stand behind the victim.
2. Wrap your arms around his or her waist.
3. Make a fist with one hand so the thumb side is against the victim's abdomen. The fist should be just below the rib cage and just above the naval.
4. Grab the fist with your other hand and forcefully press into the victim's abdomen with an upward thrust. Quickly repeat several times if necessary. It is important that officers learn to press their fists into the victim's abdomen by bending their arms at the elbow. They must know not to squeeze the chest. Squeezing the chest may cause serious injuries. If officers place their arms and fists too high, squeezing the rib cage may break ribs, causing fatal internal injuries.[7] The Heimlich Manuever is a relatively simple and effective procedure. Air is forced out the throat by compressing the lungs. The obstruction (usually a piece of food) should simply pop out with the flow of air.

SEVERE NECK AND HEAD INJURIES

Instruction for neck and head injuries must stress they be taken as a life threatening situation. An unconscious victim should be treated for a neck or head injury until more highly trained personnel assumes control. These injuries are critical due to the likelihood of spinal cord or brain damage.

Head and Neck Injury Treatment

1. Immediately check for an open airway. Extreme care must be taken, as the victim may have a broken neck.
2. If the victim is not breathing, conduct artificial respiration.
3. Do not move the victim more than is absolutely necessary.
4. Do not elevate any part of the victim's body if his face is pale.
5. Control any bleeding from the scalp by direct pressure to the injured portion.
6. Keep the victim warm.
7. Never give the victim anything by mouth.
8. Thoroughly understand that any movement of the head can result in permanent paralysis or death.
9. Use extreme care not to move the head.[8]

SEVERE BLEEDING

Bleeding victims are frequently encountered by uniform officers. Bleeding may vary greatly in severity. Bleeding from capillaries produces only small amounts of blood. That which comes from a vein produces slow blood flow and is dark red in color. Bleeding from an artery is bright red and may often spurt in large amounts. While arterial bleeding is relatively uncommon, it must be considered a life threatening situation.

There are many basic steps instruction should focus upon.

Step 1—Apply pressure—Applying pressure with a clean cloth or steril bandage will promote bleeding control. Keep pressure on the wound until bleeding stops. If bleeding continues, add additional material and continue applying pressure.

Step 2—Elevate bleeding location—Unless prevented by a broken limb, elevate the injured area higher than the heart. This will assist in slowing the rate of bleeding.

Step 3—Do not apply antiseptics on the bleeding location.

Step 4—After approximately five minutes, if bleeding has not slowed, apply pressure to one of the body's pressure points.

A. **The Subclavian Artery**—Located in the groove behind the color bone, pressure applied with a thumb may be used for bleeding from the armpit, shoulder or chest.
B. **Facial Artery**—A face wound should be treated with pressure to the artery midway along the jaw between the chin and the ear.

C. **Carotid Artery** – Located on the side of the neck below the jaw, just before the wind pipe, this pressure point is used for neck and head bleeding.
D. **Femoral Artery** – This pressure point is located on the inner thigh near the groin. Pressure should be applied with the heal of your hand for a wound to the leg.
E. **Temporal Artery** – The temporal artery pressure point is located on the side of the head, just in front of the ear. It may be used for a scalp wound.
F. **Brachial Artery** – The brachial artery pressure point is found inside of the arm, between the armpit and elbow. It is useful to stop the bleeding from an injury on the arm.

Even severe bleeding can be controlled by the use of direct pressure to a wound and indirect pressure to a designated pressure point. Officers should learn not to allow the psychological effect of severe bleeding to interfere with their ability to administer proper medical aid. Pressure should be released from the designated pressure point after bleeding stops.[9]

SHOCK

Shock occurs when the circulatory system does not provide sufficient blood throughout the body. Understanding shock treatment is important for officers, due to the likelihood that they will encounter shock victims in a variety of medical emergencies. A strong probability exists that death will occur if a victim of shock does not receive proper care.

Officers usually come in contact with victims having elapsed into shock as a result of injury. Many of the body's functions are seriously threatened by insufficient blood and/or oxygen. Instruction regarding symptoms to look for are essential.

Symptoms of Shock

- Patients show signs of restlessness and fear
- Thirst
- Vomiting
- Weakness
- Moist and/or clammy skin
- Rapid and weak pulse
- Pale and cool skin

- Unresponsiveness
- Possible unconsciousness if shock is severe
- A combination of any or all of the above symptoms

Steps to Prevent and Treat Shock

- Have the victim lay down and relax
- After checking for possible neck injuries, keep an airway open for tilting the head slightly backward.
- Treat the cause of shock
- Cover the victim with a light blanket or sheet
- If the victim has an obvious loss of blood, clammy skin and pale face, elevate the feet approximately ten inches.
- If the victim has a red face, chest pain and breathing problems, elevate the head and shoulders lightly to assist in breathing. Do not elevate the feet.
- Sustain constant observation of victim
- Provide reassurance and understanding[10]

ANAPHYLACTIC SHOCK

Anaphylactic shock occurs as a result of a victim coming in contact with something to which he is allergic. Instruction must stress this is a true life threatening situation. Death may be a certain result if treatment is not immediately provided.

A variety of situations result in anaphylactic shock. An allergic reaction to the following stimuli may result in such a medical emergency.

- Drugs
- Food
- Inhaled substances
- Chemicals
- Insect stings and bites

Symptoms of Anaphylactic Shock

- Victim may be fearful or restless
- Breathing and/or chest pains are evident
- Pulse may be extremely weak
- Face and tongue may be swollen

- Face may turn blue
- Victim's skin may itch, burn or break out in hives
- Victim may faint

Treatment for Anaphylactic Shock

Individuals who experience extreme allergic reactions may be wearing a medic alert emblem or have a medical identification card in their wallet. Officers should quickly look for these. Treatment for anaphylactic shock should be the same as for other types of shock.[11]

ELECTROCUTION

Officers responding to an accidental electrocution face unusual danger. The danger of the officer himself being electrocuted is ever present. Instruction must stress officers not directly touch the victim until the electricity no longer contacts the victim. Touching the victim before the source of electricity is eliminated will probably result in the officer being electrocuted. Victims struck by lightning do not pose this threat.

Officers should remove the victim from the source of electrocution by:

1. First, when appropriate, turn off the electric current by flipping the main electric box switch. If the victim is in contact with an outside power line, immediately contact the electric company to have the line turned off.
2. Use extreme care if it is necessary to remove the victim from contact with a live wire. Officers must ensure they stand on something totally dry and are wearing dry gloves if possible.
3. The victim should be pulled off the wire with rope or pushed off with a stick or board. Officers should never use anything wet or metallic. Above all, officers must never touch a victim until he is free from the source of electrocution.

   Following removal from the source of electrocution, officers are to immediately start cardiopulmonary resuscitation. Cardiopulmonary resuscitation should continue until reaching a hospital or relieved by more qualified medical personnel.[12]

BANDAGING

It is important that officers understand the basics of bandaging. Due to the frequency of contact with wound victims, the ability to apply basic dressing and bandaging is helpful.

One of the first principles officers should understand is that there is a difference between dressing and bandaging. A dressing is a material used to cover a wound to prevent additional infection and control bleeding. A bandage is the material used to hold the dressing in place.

All police cars should be equipped with emergency medical equipment. Reference to the identity of such equipment is made later in this chapter. Sterile dressing and bandages are basic ingredients to a first aid kit. Dressings come in a variety of shapes and sizes. The most common size is a 4 inch square. Officers may encounter some emergency situations where no sterile dressing or bandaging material is available. In such cases where bleeding is severe, use whatever clean material is immediately available. Examples are clean sheets, towels, handkerchiefs or various types of clothing. Such materials may not be ideal for that purpose, however. When an individual may be bleeding to death, officers must be instructed to improvise.

The following guidelines are intended to aid instruction of first aid dressing.

- Applying any type of dressing will do little good if it does not control bleeding. Bleeding must be stopped by applying a dressing along with pressure.
- Avoid touching the portion of dressing which will contact the wound. This will assist in controlling contamination from an officer's hands.
- The entire wound area should be covered with a dressing larger than the wound itself.
- Once a dressing has been applied, it should not be removed. Should blood soak through the dressing, simply apply additional dressing on top.

The following guidelines are to assist with instruction of bandaging:

- While bandaging, should firmly hold dressing in place, be careful not to bandage so tightly that it will restrict blood flow.
- Bandaging must be applied firmly enough to ensure the dressing or bandage will not move from the wound.
- Bandaging cannot be done so that loose ends are left dangling. The ends may become entangled on objects further injuring the wound.

- All the victim's fingers and toes should be left unbandaged. This is because fingers and toes must be observed to detect any change in skin color. If skin should turn blue, the bandage must be loosened.[13]

FIRST AID EQUIPMENT

A great deal of expensive equipment is not needed for officers to be prepared to administer emergency medical aid. However, an adequate first aid box should be placed in every law enforcement vehicle. The following is recommended as a minimum for adequate first aid supplies:

- Various sizes of dressings/gauze pads
- Roller-type bandages
- Triangular bandages
- Adhesive tape
- Scissors
- Pillow
- Blanket

A common problem officers may encounter is keeping first aid kits fully equipped. Various supplies may be used without being replaced. This, of course, results in officers not having needed items in an emergency. A simple, yet effective system to prevent this occurance is placing a piece of evidence tape over the lid of the first aid kit. Officers can easily notice the broken seal while checking contents of the vehicle before a tour of duty.

REALISTIC AND PRACTICAL INSTRUCTION

The key to successful first aid training is realism and practicality. Fortunately, virtually all topics of first aid instruction can be easily demonstrated. Take advantage of the benefits which demonstrations, field exercises and active participation have to offer. In addition to officers performing and practicing virtually every skill included in a lecture, the following exercises are suggested:

- Practical demonstrations are useful to instruct a wide assortment of emergency first aid situations.
- Role playing may be helpful for topics such as determining vital signs, treatment of shock and bandaging techniques.
- A medical instruction mannequin should be obtained for cardiopulmonary resuscitation exercises.

- Field exercises dealing with techniques to stop bleeding should be conducted.
- Surprise field exercises involving mock scenes will add tremendous realistic benefits.
- Video taping various participation exercises followed by a class critique is very beneficial.

REFERENCES

1. Diana Odell Potter, *Nurse's Reference Library,* Emergencies, Springhouse Corporation, 1985, pg. 30.
2. J. David Bergeron, First Responder, Englewood Cliffs, New Jersey: Prentice-Hall, 1982, pg. 3.
3. Jeffrey Weiss, *The Peoples Emergency Guide,* New York: St. Martins Press, 1980, pg. 16.
4. J. David Bergeron, First Responder, Englewood Cliffs, New Jersey, Prentice-Hall, 1982, pg. 26–28.
5. Jeffrey Weiss, *The Peoples Emergency Guide,* St. Martin Press, 1980, pg. 18.
6. Henry J. Heimlich, *Emergency Medical Situations,* New York: Simon and Schuster, 1980, pg. 52–54.
7. Henry J. Heimlich, *Emergency Medical Situations,* New York: Simon and Schuster, 1980, pg. 40–44.
8. Gail Anderson, and Christine Haycock, and Stanley Zydlo, *The American Medical Association's Handbook of First Aid and Emergency Care,* New York: Random House, 1980, pg. 24–26.
9. Charles Mosher, *Emergency First Aid,* Publications International, 1978, pg. 29–34.
10. Gail Anderson, Christine Haycock, and Stanley Zydlo, *American Medical Association's Handbook of First Aid and Emergency Care,* New York: Random House, 1980, pg. 204–206.
11. J. David Bergeron, *First Responder,* Englewood Cliffs, New Jersey: Prentice-Hall, 1982, pg. 109–110.
12. Gail Anderson, Christine Haycock, and Stanley Zydlo, *American Medical Association's Handbook of First Aid and Emergency Care,* New York: Random House, 1980, pg. 21–22.
13. J. David Bergeron, *First Responder,* Englewood Cliffs, New Jersey: Prentice-Hall, 1982, pg. 126–128.

VII

STREET SURVIVAL TRAINING THE PROPER PERSPECTIVE

Obviously, survival training is important. Like all subject matter, the degree of priority it should receive within the scope of in-service training is a matter of opinion. It is my belief that training necessary to provide officers with the capability to protect themselves must receive the utmost of priorities. Improved survival training is desperately needed in American law enforcement. Historically, law enforcement agencies and/or trainers have neglected their responsibility to do so.

An example of law enforcement training's ineptness is illustrated by examining the history of police firearms training in America. For decades virtually all agencies conducted firearms training at distances between 21 feet and 150 feet. The 7, 15, 25 and 50 yard line were typical firing distances throughout the nation. Only in recent years have we realized that most firearm related officer murders occur within 15 feet. Thus, while we have been training officers at distances between 21 and 150 feet, most officers have been dying within 15 feet of their perpetrator.

Another example is daylight firearms training. Almost without exception, most agencies usually conduct firearms training during daylight hours. Few nighttime courses are held because it is simply easier to train during the day. We now know the majority of police shoot-outs occur during hours of darkness. If the truth be known, most agencies still don't conduct the majority of their firearms training at night because it is more of a "hastle" for firearms instructors.

Still more evidence is found in the practice of training at a single silhouette target. Until recently, very few agencies trained with multiple targets on a regular basis. We now know many police shoot-outs occur when an officer is facing more than one armed perpetrator. Using a single, non-moving, silhouette target continued for decades. It is still practiced among many agencies.

Firearms training is but one aspect of survival training. Deficiencies such as those previously described are riddled throughout many aspects of common street procedure. Perhaps it's unfortunate that when an officer is murdered in the line of duty we refer to him as a hero, irregardless of what he did to have caused his death. Following most police funerals, the fact remains that more hours were used in preparation of the burial than the officer had received in training which may have kept him alive.

Improvement of survival training is needed within virtually all law enforcement agencies. The initial step is to properly develop and organize in-service courses. Don't allow yourself to provide training simply for the sake of being popular or building impressive statistics. The stakes are much too high to not be thorough and effective in your training product. The degree of initial planning and forethought may ultimately make the difference in an officer's living or dieing on the street.

Figure 11. Demonstrations and practical exercises which illustrate both correct and improper survival techniques are important. Basic mistakes such as standing in front of a door, as this officer is demonstrating, can be a deadly mistake.

DEVELOPMENT OF IN-SERVICE SURVIVAL TRAINING

As with all in-service training programs, survival training must be supported by top level management. Considerable time and effort is required to produce a realistic and effective survival course. While the vast majority of survival training is relatively simple, creative and frequent training is crucial.

Trainers must understand that no survival training can provide all the answers. The variety of possible street situations is so immense that it is virtually impossible to train for every occurrence.

The best survival training approach is one that combines several components:

1. Firearms proficiency
2. Survival related knowledge
3. Survival tactics
4. Survival attitude
5. Physical ability

FIREARMS PROFICIENCY

The effective use of firearms is, of course, a crucial component for survival training. Firearms training imposes tremendous responsibility on both the agency and training officer. The agency and trainer must accept their obligation to train in a meaningful, practical, realistic and effective manner. Officers must accept their responsibility to apply themselves totally to such training.

This text does not concern itself with the fundamentals of firearms training. Academy training should ensure officers receive a level of knowledge and skill adequate for initial employment. Instead, the concern will focus upon using in-service training to develop the street skill and expertise which results in the greatest probability for survival. This level of proficiency demands a considerably higher degree of skill than an academy provides.

A separate chapter is devoted to a discussion of "state of the art" firearms training procedures. Certainly an examination of survival training is insufficient without a thorough firearms consideration.

SURVIVAL KNOWLEDGE

An effective approach to the development of survival training begins with providing officers relevant survival knowledge. Preparation of a statistical based lecture may initially appear merely theoretical. However, in addition to dispelling certain myths, such data should build a foundation upon which demonstrations, practical exercises and realistic stress training may follow. An example of such data follows.

Officer killed data—Officers learn how, when and where most law enforcement officers are murdered. The American Law Enforcement Officer Killed Summary—January through August 1985, documents:

- Fifty-five local, county, state and federal law enforcement officers were murdered.
- Twenty-five officers were killed in Southern states.
- Eleven officers were killed in Mid-Western states.
- Seven were killed in Western states.
- Seven were killed in Northeaster states.
- Four were killed in Puerto Rico.
- One officer was killed in Mexico.
- Fifteen officers were murdered in arrest situations.
- Five were killed handling robbery situations.
- Four were killed responding to burglaries.
- Four were murdered during drug related situations.
- Two were slain attempting arrests for crimes other than robbery, burglary or drugs.
- Ten officers were slain while enforcing traffic laws.
- Eleven officers were murdered answering disturbance calls.
- Ten were murdered investigating suspicious persons or circumstances.
- Eleven were killed in ambush attacks.
- Four were killed while handling prisoners.

Of the 55 officers murdered during the first half of 1985: Forty-eight officers were killed by firearms.

Of the 48 murders, 38 officers were killed with handguns.

Four officers were killed through the use of vehicles.

Two officers were murdered by blunt objects.

Seven officers were killed through the use of knives.

Fifty-one of the 35 murders have been cleared by law enforcement authorities by the latter half of 1985.[1]

Beginning in 1972, the United States Department of Justice Uniform Crime Reporting Program began issuing annual reports regarding law enforcement officers killed and assaulted. The purpose of these publications and the following tables is to provide data regarding previous police murders so future tragedies may be prevented. Furnishing officers with the following data will better prepare them to survive similar acts. The following series of tables pertain to statistics collected over the 10 year period from 1974 to 1983. Topics are worthwhile, practical information:

Number of law enforcement officers killed
Type of weapons used
Type and size of firearm used
Distance between victim/officer and offender
Location of fatal wounds suffered by victim/officer
Time of day
Month of occurrence
Day of week
Type of assignment
Profile of victim/officer
Profile of perpetrator
Circumstances of officers accidentally killed

SURVIVAL TACTICS

An often overlooked ingredient of survival training is instilling a comprehension among officers as to the overwhelming odds against their survival of a shoot-out. The disadvantages come from every angle, size, shape and form. The cards have been stacked against an officer even before he is "sworn-in." His upbringing taught him to live by a standard of morals and ethics which preclude the unprovoked viciousness that will be directed toward him without warning. On the other hand, the typical police assailant has lived in an environment of violence and aggression. Using violence and intimidation to satisfy his needs have been a way of life.

Many other disadvantages await officers on the street. Trainers must not neglect their examination during survival training.

TABLE VII
LAW ENFORCEMENT OFFICERS FELONIOUSLY KILLED, 1974-1983
BY REGION, DIVISION AND STATE

Area	*Total*	*1974*	*1975*	*1976*	*1977*	*1978*	*1979*	*1980*	*1981*	*1982*	*1983*
Total	1,031	132	129	111	93	93	106	104	91	92	80
Northeast	132	14	19	15	11	12	13	23	13	7	5
New England											
Connecticut	3	–	–	–	1	–	–	1	1	–	–
Maine	1	–	–	–	–	1	–	–	–	–	–
Massachusetts	9	1	3	–	–	1	–	2	1	–	1
New Hampshire	1	–	–	1	–	–	–	–	–	–	–
Rhode Island	–	–	–	–	–	–	–	–	–	–	–
Vermont	1	–	–	–	–	1	–	–	–	–	–
Middle Atlantic											
New Jersey	20	1	3	5	–	1	5	2	3	–	–
New York	67	9	8	4	9	5	7	11	6	7	1
Pennsylvania	30	3	5	5	1	3	1	7	2	–	3
North Central	198	37	25	24	19	10	16	15	18	21	13
East North Central											
Illinois	38	11	4	5	3	–	4	2	1	6	2
Indiana	21	5	3	1	–	–	2	4	4	–	2
Michigan	30	11	4	3	2	1	1	1	–	4	3
Ohio	34	5	5	6	1	2	6	1	3	3	2
Wisconsin	14	2	4	–	2	2	–	–	2	2	–
West North Central											
Iowa	6	–	–	1	2	–	–	1	2	–	–
Kansas	9	1	1	1	–	1	1	1	1	2	–
Minnesota	11	–	–	1	2	2	–	1	2	3	–
Missouri	24	1	2	5	4	2	2	3	3	–	2
Nebraska	5	1	–	–	3	–	–	1	–	–	–
North Dakota	2	–	–	–	–	–	–	–	–	–	2
South Dakota	4	–	2	1	–	–	–	–	–	1	–

TABLE VII Continued

Area	*Total*	*1974*	*1975*	*1976*	*1977*	*1978*	*1979*	*1980*	*1981*	*1982*	*1983*
South	478	57	54	57	47	47	49	45	43	42	37
South Atlantic											
Delaware	–	–	–	–	–	–	–	–	–	–	–
District of Columbia	7	1	–	1	1	1	–	1	–	2	–
Florida	59	9	4	7	4	5	4	7	6	7	6
Georgia	40	6	5	6	3	3	5	9	1	1	1
Maryland	25	5	3	3	2	2	3	1	2	1	3
North Carolina	31	5	4	3	6	1	5	2	3	2	–
South Carolina	22	7	3	2	2	–	4	–	–	2	2
Virginia	19	2	1	3	2	2	1	1	3	2	2
West Virginia	17	–	3	4	4	1	1	–	3	1	–
East South Central											
Alabama	32	3	5	2	2	2	5	3	4	4	2
Kentucky	18	–	2	3	1	1	5	3	1	–	2
Mississippi	30	3	2	3	2	5	4	2	6	1	2
Tennessee	32	1	6	2	4	5	1	1	5	4	3
West South Central											
Arkansas	20	1	2	4	4	–	–	3	3	2	1
Louisiana	23	2	2	2	3	6	2	2	1	3	–
Oklahoma	16	3	1	–	3	4	1	1	–	1	1
Texas	87	9	11	12	4	9	8	9	5	9	11
West											
Mountain											
Arizona	16	4	3	–	–	–	2	–	–	4	3
Colorado	13	–	5	–	–	–	–	2	3	2	1
Idaho	3	–	–	1	–	–	–	–	2	–	–
Montana	3	2	–	–	–	1	–	–	–	–	–
Nevada	7	–	2	–	1	1	3	–	–	–	–
New Mexico	12	–	–	–	2	1	3	3	1	1	1
Utah	4	1	–	1	–	1	–	–	–	1	–
Wyoming	2	–	–	–	–	1	–	–	–	–	1

TABLE VII Continued

Area	*Total*	*1974*	*1975*	*1976*	*1977*	*1978*	*1979*	*1980*	*1981*	*1982*	*1983*
Pacific											
Alaska	7	2	1	–	–	–	2	–	–	1	1
California	88	9	11	5	10	12	10	7	8	7	9
Hawaii	2	–	–	1	–	–	–	–	–	–	1
Oregon	7	1	1	1	–	–	2	1	–	1	–
Washington	10	1	–	1	1	3	1	1	–	1	1
U.S. Territories											
America Samoa	1	–	–	–	–	–	–	–	1	–	–
Guam	4	–	1	–	–	–	2	–	–	–	1
Mariana Islands	2	–	–	–	–	–	–	–	–	1	1
Puerto Rico	38	4	6	4	1	4	3	6	2	3	5
Virgin Islands	3	–	1	–	1	–	–	1	–	–	–
Foreign	1	–	–	1	–	–	–	–	–	–	–

Source: U.S. Department of Justice
Federal Bureau of Investigation
Uniform Crime Reports: Law Enforcement Officers Killed and Assaulted

- Potential perpetrators may remain virtually unseen or undetected, while an officer's uniform and patrol vehicle make him a highly visible target.
- The length of time required by a perpetrator to fire his already cocked and aimed firearm is less than a half second.[2]
- The quickest that an officer can draw, point and shoot a firearm is more than twice the time noted above.
- An officer must consider the legalities of his act.
- An officer must consider the presence of innocent bystanders.
- Officers are usually forced to react after the perpetrator has begun his assault.
- The time it takes an officer to draw, aim and shoot his firearm is several times as long as it takes the assailant to fire his already aimed firearm.
- Lastly, most police officers are inadequately trained in survival tactics.

Even though the aforementioned facts substantiate overwhelming odds against the survival of an armed attack, contemporary survival training

TABLE VIII
LAW ENFORCEMENT OFFICERS FELONIOUSLY KILLED, 1974-1983
BY TYPE OF WEAPON

Year	*Grand Total*	*Handgun*	*Rifle*	*Shotgun*	*Total Firearm*	*Knife*	*Bomb*	*Personal Weapons*	*Other*
Total	1,031	708	143	109	960	19	5	4	43
1974	132	95	12	21	128	1	–	–	3
1975	129	93	21	13	127	–	–	–	2
1976	111	66	12	16	94	5	4	–	8
1977	93	59	13	11	83	–	–	1	9
1978	93	67	13	11	91	–	–	1	1
1979	106	76	18	6	100	4	1	–	1
1980	104	69	13	13	95	3	–	–	6
1981	91	69	12	5	86	1	–	–	4
1982	92	60	17	5	82	3	–	2	5
1983	80	54	12	8	74	2	–	–	4

Source: U.S. Department of Justice
Federal Bureau of Investigation
Uniform Crime Reports: Law Enforcement Officers Killed and Assaulted

makes the chances of survival better than they have ever been. As an example, the stated disadvantages do not consider training which can lessen the probability of officers being caught off guard. Further training will engrave techniques of preparation and anticipation of danger. Training that allows for repetition of survival techniques in a realistic environment will sharpen skills essential for survival. As every experienced trainer knows, under the stress of a real crisis officers will revert to however they have been trained.

The fact remains that many officers killed in shoot-outs would probably have lived if they had:

A. Understood the dynamics of shoot-outs.
B. Been properly trained on how to evaluate the situation they were facing.
C. Anticipated the situation by planning what steps to take if it did occur.
D. Master appropriate survival tactics through repeated practice.[3]

TABLE IX
LAW ENFORCEMENT OFFICERS FELONIOUSLY KILLED, 1983
TYPE AND SIZE OF FIREARM

		Type of Firearm		
Size of Firearm	*Handgun*	*Officer's Own Weapon*	*Rifle*	*Shotgun*
Total	54	12*	12	8
Handgun Size				
.22 Caliber	5			
.25 Caliber	4			
.32 Caliber	3			
9 Millimeter	3			
.357 Magnum	11	5		
.38 Caliber	24	6		
.44 Magnum	2			
.45 Caliber	1			
Caliber not reported	1			
Rifle Size				
.22 Caliber			1	
.223 Caliber			6	
.270 Caliber			1	
.30 Caliber			1	
.30-30 Caliber			2	
.45 Caliber Submachinegun			1	
Shotgun Size				
16 Gauge				1
12 Gauge		1		7

*Included in appropriate firearm category

Source: U.S. Department of Justice
Federal Bureau of Investigation
Uniform Crime Reports: Law Enforcement Officers Killed and Assaulted

TABLE X
LAW ENFORCEMENT OFFICERS FELONIOUSLY KILLED BY FIREARMS, 1974-1983
DISTANCE BETWEEN VICTIM OFFICER AND OFFENDER

Feet	*Total*	*1974*	*1975*	*1976*	*1977*	*1978*	*1979*	*1980*	*1981*	*1982*	*1983*
Total	960	128	127	94	83	91	100	95	86	82	74
0–5	494	71	62	53	41	37	50	60	46	39	35
6–10	192	28	24	17	19	20	19	15	17	15	18
11–20	152	14	18	14	9	24	17	11	16	16	13
21–50	66	9	14	4	8	5	5	5	4	8	4
Over 50	56	6	9	6	6	5	9	4	3	4	4

Source: U.S. Department of Justice
Federal Bureau of Investigation
Uniform Crime Reports: Law Enforcement Officers Killed and Assaulted

TABLE XI
LAW ENFORCEMENT OFFICERS FELONIOUSLY KILLED BY FIREARMS, 1974-1983
LOCATION OF FATAL WOUNDS SUFFERED BY VICTIM OFFICER

Point of Entry	*Total*	*1974*	*1975*	*1976*	*1977*	*1978*	*1979*	*1980*	*1981*	*1982*	*1983*
Total	960	128	127	94	83	91	100	95	86	82	74
Front Head	309	45	43	26	26	40	36	26	24	20	23
Rear Head	61	9	6	4	6	5	2	7	12	4	6
Front Upper Torso	451	57	54	48	42	32	53	48	40	44	33
Rear Upper Torso	77	8	9	8	3	5	6	10	7	12	9
Front Below Waist	58	8	15	8	6	9	2	3	3	1	3
Rear Below Waist	4	1	–	–	–	–	1	1	–	1	–

Source: U.S. Department of Justice
Federal Bureau of Investigation
Uniform Crime Reports: Law Enforcement Officers Killed and Assaulted

Tactics

The use of survival tactics comprise ongoing mental and physical processes. A superficial definition of the term survival tactic is an officer's response to a life threatening situation.

A more indepth examination reveals this definition does not include how frequently survival tactics prevent life threatening situations from

TABLE XII
LAW ENFORCEMENT OFFICERS FELONIOUSLY KILLED, 1974–1983
BY TIME OF DAY

Time of Day	*Total*	*1974*	*1975*	*1976*	*1977*	*1978*	*1979*	*1980*	*1981*	*1982*	*1983*
Total	1,031	132	129	111	93	93	106	104	91	92	80
A.M.											
12:01–2:00	125	19	14	9	13	13	15	9	12	12	9
2:01–4:00	108	18	15	10	13	9	8	13	9	8	5
4:01–6:00	44	7	5	7	5	2	2	8	6	–	2
6:01–8:00	24	3	5	4	3	–	2	1	2	1	3
8:01–10:00	46	4	7	6	3	8	5	4	4	3	2
10:01–Noon	73	9	9	9	6	8	9	4	5	7	7
P.M.											
12:01–2:00	77	14	13	4	9	4	8	7	8	4	6
2:01–4:00	80	7	9	5	8	11	5	11	8	11	5
4:01–6:00	66	6	6	6	3	3	10	8	8	6	10
6:01–8:00	104	12	10	14	5	10	13	11	7	11	11
8:01–10:00	139	17	18	15	12	11	16	14	5	20	11
10:01–Midnight	145	16	18	22	13	14	13	14	17	9	9

Source: U.S. Department of Justice
Federal Bureau of Investigation
Uniform Crime Reports: Law Enforcement Officers Killed and Assaulted

occurring. Thus, the proper explanation is that survival tactics are the perpetual mental and physical responses to all street situations, which result in less potential for harm to an officer.

Historically, there was a lengthy era when survival training was virtually non-existent. Officers were literally handed a badge, nightstick and gun, then told to go out and put somebody in jail. Tactics now include training in the use of nightsticks, firearms, hand-to-hand combat, PR24 batons, chemical agents, electronic weapons and other accessories intended to reduce the risk of harm to offenders and officers.

Contemporary American way of life is considerably different than that of the past, however. Training officers must ensure that some street tactics employed by officers in the past are no longer used. Several reasons for this exist:

TABLE XIII
LAW ENFORCEMENT OFFICERS FELONIOUSLY KILLED, 1974-1983
BY MONTH

Month	*Total*	*1974*	*1975*	*1976*	*1977*	*1978*	*1979*	*1980*	*1981*	*1982*	*1983*
Total	1,031	132	129	111	93	93	106	104	91	92	80
January	89	8	12	13	7	4	5	8	11	9	12
February	81	13	10	11	3	6	6	8	6	11	7
March	65	8	9	13	2	2	10	1	8	5	7
April	91	10	8	12	11	16	8	12	3	5	6
May	93	12	13	3	8	10	16	9	11	5	6
June	88	10	12	7	4	10	12	12	10	4	7
July	87	16	9	9	11	6	8	6	5	9	8
August	95	13	12	9	13	10	11	5	6	10	6
September	77	6	10	7	12	6	7	8	4	12	5
October	81	11	10	11	8	4	6	7	10	10	4
November	82	12	9	10	8	7	8	12	5	5	6
December	102	13	15	6	6	12	9	16	12	7	6

Source: U.S. Department of Justice
Federal Bureau of Investigation
Uniform Crime Reports: Law Enforcement Officers Killed and Assaulted

1. Criminals of a previous era tended to react submissively to the mere presence of police officers. This resulted in less need for police aggression.
2. Unlike the previous era, contemporary America is eager to file law suits. Municipal law enforcement agencies are now nicknamed within the legal community as "deep pockets," because of the ease at which large settlements and judgements are obtained.
3. The criminal element of previous times were not as heavily armed as those of today.
4. Today's general population is more likely to criticize and demand improvement of police training and policies when police abuse or negligence occur.
5. Officers are no longer satisfied with inadequate or improper training. Some officers have directed their wills to file suit against their agency for the lack of training if they are killed in the line of duty.

TABLE XIV
LAW ENFORCEMENT OFFICERS FELONIOUSLY KILLED, 1974–1983
BY DAY OF WEEK

Day of Week	*Total*	*1974*	*1975*	*1976*	*1977*	*1978*	*1979*	*1980*	*1981*	*1982*	*1983*
Total	1,031	132	129	111	93	93	106	104	91	92	80
Monday	133	22	17	11	16	13	10	10	13	12	9
Tuesday	150	11	17	22	15	11	18	9	13	15	19
Wednesday	139	15	15	11	10	16	18	17	11	14	12
Thursday	175	24	17	17	12	15	25	25	12	23	5
Friday	152	23	23	18	13	18	11	11	16	6	13
Saturday	168	25	19	16	20	11	15	20	16	13	13
Sunday	114	12	21	16	7	9	9	12	10	9	9

Source: U.S. Department of Justice
Federal Bureau of Investigation
Uniform Crime Reports: Law Enforcement Officers Killed and Assaulted

6. Efforts to professionalize have increased dramatically within the law enforcement profession. Never in the history of American law enforcement has there been such an emphasis on training.[4]

Improper execution of survival tactics lead to serious injury or death. Officers may acquire the appropriate knowledge and skills, yet fail to properly execute the lifesaving techniques on the street. There are many faults that officers having been seriously injured or killed seem to have in common such as:

- The failure to conduct a proper search of suspect(s).
- Improper care, cleaning and maintenance of firearm.
- Apathetic and or careless attitude.
- False courage.
- Failure to anticipate danger.
- Improper use of handcuffs.
- Failure to observe suspect's hands.
- Lack of proper arrest techniques.
- Assuming an improper tactical position.

ANTICIPATING DANGER

One of the most effective tactics for surviving on the street is anticipating danger. This should not be confused with being unjustly scared or afraid. Anticipating danger means taking full advantage of your senses

TABLE XV
LAW ENFORCEMENT OFFICERS FELONIOUSLY KILLED, 1974-1983
CIRCUMSTANCES BY TYPE OF ASSIGNMENT

			Type of Assignment						
			1 Officer Vehicle		*Foot Patrol*		*Det., Spec. Assignment*		
Circumstances at Scene of Incident	*Total*	*2-officer vehicle*	*Alone*	*Assisted*	*Alone*	*Assisted*	*Alone*	*Assisted*	*Off Duty*
Total	1,031	196	322	150	12	5	61	155	130
Disturbance Calls	182	55	43	44	2	–	2	18	18
Bar Fights, Man With Gun	126	40	28	28	2	–	2	10	16
Family Quarrels	56	15	15	16	–	–	–	8	2
Arrest Situations	456	68	104	63	4	5	30	104	78
Burglaries in Progress or Pursuing Burglary Suspects	65	14	26	11	1	–	6	2	5
Robberies in Progress or Pursuing Robbery Suspects	174	22	40	19	1	2	13	16	61
Drug-Related Matters	58	3	1	2	–	1	5	45	1
Attempting Other Arrests	159	29	37	31	2	2	6	41	11
Civil Disorders (mass disobedience, riot, etc.)	1	–	–	–	–	–	–	1	–
Handling, Transporting, Custody of Prisoners	41	10	6	4	–	–	10	10	1
Investigating Suspicious Persons or Circumstances	106	18	49	10	4	–	4	9	12
Ambush Situations	93	15	27	9	2	–	13	9	18
Entrapment and Premediation	53	10	12	7	–	–	5	8	11
Unprovoked Attack	40	5	15	2	2	–	8	1	7
Mentally Deranged	23	4	6	8	–	–	1	3	1
Traffic Pursuits and Stops	129	26	87	12	–	–	1	1	2

Source: U.S. Department of Justice
Federal Bureau of Investigation
Uniform Crime Reports: Law Enforcement Officers Killed and Assaulted

to prepare yourself in advance of an assault. Anticipating danger and planning for the unexpected is a basic ingredient for staying alive.

TABLE XVI
PROFILE OF VICTIM OFFICERS, 1974–1983

Victim Officers	
Total	1,031
Under 25 Years of Age	116
From 25 through 30 Years of Age	303
From 31 through 40 Years of Age	369
Over 40 Years of Age	243
Male	1,022
Female	9
White	907
Black	113
Other Race	11
Hispanic Ethnicity (Data not available prior to 1980)	28
Non-Hispanic Ethnicity (Data not available prior to 1980)	338
Average Years of Service	8
Less than 1 Year of Service	53
From 1 to 5 Years of Service	350
From 5 to 10 Years of Service	346
Over 10 Years of Service	268
Average height	5′ 11″
In uniform	738
Wearing protective body armor (Data not available prior to 1980)	59

Source: U.S. Department of Justice
Federal Bureau of Investigation
Uniform Crime Reports: Law Enforcement Officers Killed and Assaulted

Trainers must furnish techniques and examples which illustrate how officers can anticipate danger on a daily basis:

1. Never become too comfortable on the street.
2. Develop a survival "state of mind" and use it wherever you go.
3. Do not patrol the same way every day.
4. When answering any call, always anticipate a dangerous situation.
5. Handle calls as if they could be an ambush.
6. Use all of your senses to their maximum.

TABLE XVII
PROFILE OF PERSONS IDENTIFIED IN THE FELONIOUS KILLING OF LAW ENFORCEMENT OFFICERS, 1974-1983

Persons Identified	
Total	1,394
Under 18 Years of Age	103
From 18 to 30 Years of Age	810
Male	1,338
Female	56
White	768
Black	595
Other Race	31
Hispanic Ethnicity (Data not available prior to 1980)	83
Non-Hispanic Ethnicity (Data not available prior to 1980)	428
Prior Criminal Arrest	963
Convicted on Prior Criminal Charge	699
Prior Arrest for Crime of Violence	478
Convicted on criminal charges—Granted Leniency	563
On parole or probation at time of killing	285
Prior arrest for murder	71
Prior arrest for drug law violation	257
Prior arrest for assaulting an officer or resisting arrest	101
Prior arrest for weapons violation	382

Source: U.S. Department of Justice
Federal Bureau of Investigation
Uniform Crime Reports: Law Enforcement Officers Killed and Assaulted

7. Be constantly alert to any signs of danger.
8. Think and plan ahead.
9. Plan your survival tactics based upon the circumstances.
10. Be prepared to carry out your survival plan instantly.

The following are survival tips to be employed by all police officers. Trainers should remind officers of their obligation to their family to stay alive. Learning and practicing self-preservation measures should become second nature.

TABLE XVIII
LAW ENFORCEMENT OFFICERS ACCIDENTALLY KILLED, 1974–1983
CIRCUMSTANCES AT SCENE OF INCIDENT

Circumstances	*Total*	*1974*	*1975*	*1976*	*1977*	*1978*	*1979*	*1980*	*1981*	*1982*	*1983*
Total	545	47	56	29	32	52	58	61	66	72	72
Automobile Accidents	204	15	19	14	11	18	20	35	21	24	27
Motorcycle Accidents	36	2	1	2	2	1	8	2	3	6	9
Aircraft Accidents	74	11	5	1	4	6	9	6	11	11	10
Struck by Vehicles (traffic stops, road-blocks, etc.)	67	5	6	3	3	8	6	6	12	10	8
Struck by Vehicles (directing traffic, assisting motorists, etc.)	73	4	10	2	6	8	5	6	11	11	10
Accidental Shootings (crossfires, mistaken identity, firearm mishaps)	42	6	10	4	–	5	6	4	3	3	1
Accidental Shootings (training sessions)	7	–	–	–	2	–	1	–	–	1	3
Accidental Shootings (self-inflicted)	15	1	3	–	1	2	2	1	3	1	1
Other (falls, drownings, etc.)	27	3	2	3	3	4	1	1	2	5	3

Source: U.S. Department of Justice
Federal Bureau of Investigation
Uniform Crime Reports: Law Enforcement Officers Killed and Assaulted

1. Always expect the unexpected to happen.
2. Be suspicious.
3. In combat, take the high ground.
4. Don't move unless totally necessary in a combat situation.
5. Select your next position before moving when in combat.
6. If you must move during combat, do so by short bursts.
7. Never advertise your presence.
8. Approach all traffic stops as dangerous situations.
9. Develop self-confidence by being professional.
10. Never give up your gun.
11. Practice reloading in the dark.

Figure 12. Lecturing on street survival is important, but where officers really learn what they need is through realistic and practical exercises. This exercise deals with building approaches.

12. Don't look around the corner at eye level.
13. If attacked, don't freeze; react with every ounce of power you have.
14. In a combat situation, beware of "bouncing bullets." that skim along a surface.
15. Practice counting your shots.
16. Reduce your target size.
17. Never stand in front of a window.
18. Never stand in front of a door.
19. Drive through an ambush.
20. Be alert for a secondary ambush.
21. Always wait for a backup unit on a felony stop or whenever you face an uncertain situation.
22. When looking around corners, be careful not to look around at the same level in succession.
23. Hold your flashlight to the front and side of your body.
24. Be careful not to silhouette yourself with light behind you.

25. Stay in top physical shape.
26. Practice loading and reloading with your weak hand.
27. Keep all issued equipment in top condition.
28. If permitted by departmental policy, keep a "backup" firearm.
29. Always use light to YOUR advantage.
30. Always carry an extra, concealed handcuff key.
31. Keep a quarter in your handcuff case to use a pay phone in an emergency.
32. Always use the words "police, freeze."
33. Always remember to LOOK UP.
34. Always open doors fully before entering a room.
35. Always take your car keys with you.
36. It is crucial to know your exact location at all times.
37. If two officers are present, one officer should search while the other covers the first officer.
38. Allow time for your eyes to adjust after entering a dark location from a bright location.
39. Be certain you understand and always remember the difference between concealment and cover.
40. Take charge of street situations with a loud and authoritarian tone of voice.[5]

APPROACHES

There is no such thing as a "routine call." Many officers have been murdered responding to "routine calls." Assuming an assignment is routine, then approaching the area with that frame of mind is the trait of an untrained and unprofessional officer.

Trainers assume the responsibility for training how to approach a variety of situations. Basic tactics such as never approaching a situation as routine are crucial. Officers must learn how to take advantage of the precious moments before the arrival at a location. These moments are what make the difference between life and death. The moment he begins to make the approach, even if that should be miles away, he must begin to anticipate possible danger and form a survival plan. He must learn to look ahead and plan every step of the way.

Training how to anticipate the unexpected is challenging, to say the least. An effective in-service program will use role playing to illustrate a variety of responses to an assortment of situations and calls. Examples such as "if this happens I'll do this... ; if this should occur I'll respond this say.... ;" will be productive. Creating a survival habit places officers in the best possible positions if an attack should come. It also prevents carelessness, apathy, over-confidence and thoughtless approaches.

Training officers to always approach any situation as though an armed confrontation will take place is important. While no one standard approach will prevent injury or death in every situation, performing survival tactics will greatly increase the chance of survival.

The following survival techniques are intended to assist trainers in providing adequate instruction for a variety of common situations. They are not intended to be applied in every situation. No set of rules will fit the virtually endless array of possible circumstances. They are, however, sound guidelines for instruction. They may be condensed or expanded upon to suit your specific needs.[6]

Response to the Scene

Departmental policies dictate when and how officers use emergency lights and siren. They will also control driving within an agency. The following information will assist trainers with instructions of response to in-progress calls. They should be alerted to fit a specific situation or general order.

A. Officers must have a thorough understanding of an act according to departmental guidelines regarding vehicular response.

B. The selection of a response route should be thoroughly and quickly analyzed. The following factors are to be taken into consideration:
- The location of any other responding units.
- The direction of perpetrator's travel.
- Traffic congestion.
- Severity of situation.
- Any roadway obstructions.
- Distance to be travelled.

C. Notify other responding unit(s) of your route of travel to the scene.

D. If the situation involves a serious assault in progress, to stop the perpetrator from continuing the assault, use the siren to scare the perpetrator away. Generally, the siren should not be used for in-progress calls, however. Instruct officers that a siren may be heard at distances considerably further away than they may believe. Alerting perpetrators creates extreme danger. Demonstration of this point should be included in instruction.

E. Reduce speed when nearing the scene to avoid noise which may alert perpetrator.
F. Plan where to stop your vehicle. Instructors must emphasize the location must be out of sight of the scene.
G. If nighttime, turn all lights off when entering the immediate area.
H. Turn radio down.
I. Request dispatchers to "pinpoint" the exact location if you are unfamiliar with the address.
J. Don't "overshoot" the location.
K. Coast to a stop.
L. Communicate with other responding units so that you arrive at the same time.

Building Approaches

Hundreds of officers have met death while approaching buildings during in-progress calls. Whether it's an armed residential disturbance, possible robbery or a burglary in progress, guidelines should reduce the risk of harm to officers.

Any experienced trainer can recall seeing fellow officers respond to an in-progress call by driving up directly in front of the scene. The overwhelming point to stress during instruction is that OFFICERS MUST REMAIN UNSEEN TO THE PERPETRATORS. This process began with the controlled use of the siren, planning ahead and coasting to a stop. After arrival, the same frame of mind prevails. Common sense should dictate an officer's actions fit a particular geographic environment.

Even though the location chosen to park is beyond eyesight of the scene, officers can never assume a "look out" is not within firing range. Officers should:

- Pause to observe the surrounding area before exiting the vehicle.
- Look for anything out of the ordinary or that is suspicious.
- Take advantage of proper positioning of the vehicle.

- The vehicle should be positioned to afford the officer cover upon exiting his vehicle. This will reduce the likelihood of officers being immediately shot as he exits his vehicle.
- Close the vehicle door quietly.
- Place keys and other loose objects which may make noise in pockets.
- Immediately begin looking for cover and take advantage of it.
- When possible, walk or run on grass as opposed to sidewalk. This will cause less noise.
- Radio communication should be held to a minimum; request emergency communications when needed.
- Only one officer should issue commands at the scene. This will avoid unnecessary confusion. If two or more officers have arrived, each should take positions at diagonal corners of the building.

Officers should conduct the following procedures during a preliminary visual and physical search of the exterior of a building.

A. Always use concealment and cover whenever possible.
B. Never stand or walk in front of windows.
C. Use walls for protection.
D. Check nearby vehicles for warm engines or persons hiding.
E. If vehicular or pedestrian traffic poses a danger, instruct additional officers to redirect traffic.
F. After checking the interior of the building from the corner of a window, cross under the window.

Robbery in Progress Calls

Answering a robbery call is extremely dangerous. Instructors must convey the extent of danger. Of the 1,031 American law enforcement officers killed from 1974 through 1983, 174 of them were killed answering robbery calls.[7] The majority of these deaths could have been avoided. There are 2 major reasons that contributed greatly to these tragedies. First, officers rarely received adequate survival training. Second, officers become complacent after answering a large number of unfounded robbery alarms.

Trainers are charged with the responsibility of training survival tactics to safeguard officers' lives. The following guidelines are intended as an easy reference for instructors. While the guidelines may be used for immediate instruction, uniform supervisors must be alerted to their responsibilities. Supervisors must continually verify the considered in-service training is followed.

A. If departmental policies require sirens to be used in response to a robbery in-progress call, they should be turned off at least six blocks from the scene.
B. Park out of sight of concerned scene.
C. Wait for backup units to arrive.
D. Make thorough examination of area for consideration of cross fire, pedestrians or vehicles in the line of fire, possible accomplices to the crime and location of concealment or cover.
E. Only one or two units should respond to the scene: Additional units should respond to major intersections and await a perpetrator description. If determined that the perpetrator is still within the building, the on-scene supervisor should deploy additional units at his discretion.
F. All officers must treat every robbery alarm as if it is an actual robbery.
G. Plain clothes officers responding to the scene should advise their response before arrival.
H. Ideally, community relations and/or crime prevention officers will conduct robbery training seminars with bank employees and other businesses in the community. These seminars should include a briefing on the communications section, telephoning the concerned business to determine if there is trouble inside. Using a predetermined and coordinated code name will be extremely beneficial. A police dispatcher should speak with someone in a particular division, such as personnel. The dispatcher should identify himself and ask if everything is ok. If a particular statement is used in response, the dispatcher will know a robbery is in progress at the business.
I. Officers must continue to evaluate their position to ensure the safety of innocent bystanders.
J. When encountering perpetrators at the scene, wait until they exit before challenging them.
K. During any challenge, officers should shout "police, freeze." Ordinarily, the perpetrators should be able to see only the officer's shotgun barrel and a portion of the officer's eye.

L. Officers must be instructed if a hostage is taken and if they are ordered to give up their firearm, under no circumstances do they ever relinquish their weapon.[8]

Disturbance Calls

Disturbance calls are one of the most frequently handled and potentially dangerous types of situation. From a survival standpoint, it is crucial that officers are instructed how to quickly analyze and defuse a disturbance. The failure to properly execute tactical procedures can result in officer injuries or deaths.

Classroom instruction and discussion will furnish officers with tactics to safely resolve disturbance crisis situations. Role playing and other practical exercises may be used to learn how to apply classroom information.

The following guidelines should assist instructors in conveying pertinent and practical knowledge.

Guidelines for Handling Disturbance Calls

A. If not provided by dispatcher, ask for crucial information such as if the disturbance is in progress or whether parties are armed.
B. If it is a "hot" call, ask the dispatcher to pinpoint the house.
C. Attempt to recall any past information you may know concerning the parties involved.
D. Plan your approach.
E. If it is a "hot" disturbance, coordinate your approach with additional responding units.
F. Park away from the home or business.
G. Park so that your vehicle is between you and the location of the disturbance.
H. While exiting your vehicle, observe your surroundings for signs of danger.
I. As you begin to walk towards the location, continue to observe all doors and windows. Be alert for anyone watching you. Stay alert for any signs of weapons.
J. Pay close attention to anything which may be used as cover in case you come under attack.
K. As you near the building, do not walk in front of windows.
L. As you near the door attempt to listen for sounds or voices from within. Do not stand in front of a door.

M. If 2 officers respond, each officer should stand to the side of the door.
N. Using the non-gun hand, one officer should knock on the door with a nightstick or a PR24 baton. Use extreme caution while entering the residence or business.
O. Continue to use extreme caution after you enter. If an assault is in progress, use only the force necessary to subdue the combatants.
P. Your demeanor should be firm, sincere and professional.
Q. Their is no room for complacency or apathy.
R. Separate the disputing parties.
S. Be alert for objects which may be used as weapons.
T. Always maintain a visual contact with your partner.
U. Allow for disputing parties to release their frustrations while you are present.
V. Don't fall victim to false, macho courage; admit to yourself that disturbance calls are extremely dangerous situations.
W. Use all your senses to anticipate danger.
X. Statistically, the most dangerous moment of a disturbance call is the point of arrest.
Y. Of the 1,031 officers murdered in the line of duty between 1974 and 1983, 182 of them were killed while handling disturbance calls. Of this figure, 56 of them were killed during family quarrels while 126 were murdered during bar fights or reports of a man armed with a gun.[7]

Response to Burglary in Progress Calls

Safe and professional response to a burglary in-progress call requires many of the same tactics used for robbery and disturbance in-progress calls. Obtaining needed information from the dispatcher, approaching safely and parking the proper distance from the location are required. There are several crucial differences, however. The exterior of the building and its surrounding area should be examined for accomplices, ladders, burglary tools, suspect vehicles and signs of forced entry.

Extreme caution must always be used. Walking quietly within shadows and using hand signals are beneficial. "Covering" each other as you search the exterior is vital. Officers should be instructed to make use of an available helicopter or the fire department's ladders if the situation dictates.

Extreme care must also be used when inspecting the roof. Officers must cover the officer climbing to the roof. All officers at the scene should be notified when an officer is climbing onto the roof. Any logical place of concealment should be inspected. Skylights and air vents seem to be frequent points of entry.

Due to man power limitations, many agencies may find it difficult to establish a perimeter and conduct an adequate search of the building simultaneously. The number of officers available will dictate what can be accomplished. Instructors should advise that decisions concerning deployment of man power are based upon that which provides the most safety.

If circumstances indicate that perpetrators may be in the building, someone with a key to the premises should be notified and requested to respond. Information concerning the building's layout should be gathered. Routes of escape, possible hiding location, light switches, electrical power box, locations of any weapons, type of ceiling and other possible hazards should be determined before entering.

Before entering the building, attempt to observe the interior. Never choose a logical location to look into a window. Always peak in a window at the corner. Don't continue to look in a window in the same spot.

Entry

The entry of any building where perpetrators may be present, should be made with the assumption that they are present and armed. Several considerations are important:

1. Use of K-9 unit.
2. What method of entry should be made. (Obtaining a key, entering through the perpetrator's point of entry, breaking a door, etc.)
3. Select a location of entry the suspects would not expect you to choose.
4. The use of distractions such as making a telephone call into the building, breaking a window at the opposite location you intend to enter or banging on a rear door just before you enter the opposite side of the building.
5. Should you wait for additional man power before entering?

Figure 13. Doorway entry must be trained thoroughly. Building searches are often neglected during in-service training.

The entry team should consist of between two to four officers. A plan must be developed so all officers combine their efforts into a coordinated plan of action. The team will always stay together. Instructors may illustrate proper tactical movement of a three man entry team through the use of guidelines provided below.

1. Before entering through a doorway, 2 officers should be on one side of the door while the remaining 1 is on the opposite side.
2. One of the officers should open the door then quickly jump back for cover.
3. While 1 officer is opening the door, the remaining officers should have firearms aimed inside the building at areas opposite their positions. This should allow for overlapping fields of view and fire. One should be lying prone, while the other officer is in a crouch position.
4. Arrangements be made among team leaders as to the sequence which officers will move inside the door. Timing of movement sequence will be coordinated by hand or leg signals.

5. Upon the signal to move, each member moves in to their side of the interior wall. All three officers should come to rest with their back against the wall facing the center of the considered room.
6. Little or no voice communications should be made among team members. After searching each room, close it off, turn on the lights and leave them on.
7. Be certain to open doors fully before entering a room.
8. Stay next to the wall when walking on a staircase. This will create less noise and provide better vision.
9. Take short steps to avoid losing balance or stumbling over an unseen object.
10. When searching a multi story building, search 1 floor at a time. The search should be conducted from the lowest level to the highest level.
11. Avoid a cross fire situation by searching abreast each other.
12. Ceilings, escalators, elevators and any other similar locations must be searched thoroughly.
13. If a suspect is located, he should be cuffed, searched, guarded and interrogated regarding additional accomplices.[5]

Of the 1,031 officers killed in the line of duty between 1974 and 1983, 65 of them were murdered while answering burglaries in-progress or pursuing burglary suspects.[7]

USE OF LIGHT

How, when and where officers use light during life threatening situations can literally mean life or death to the officer. Used properly, great advantages will be gained by the officers. Used improperly, being silhouetted or illuminated could result in their death.

The Federal Bureau of Investigation verifies year after year that hours of darkness are the most dangerous to police officers. When the sun goes down, the percentage of police officers murdered in America goes up. A 10 year study concluded the most dangerous 2 hour period is from 10 pm until midnight. The next most deadly time is from 8 pm until 10 pm. Midnight to 2 am is the next most dangerous period. Two am until 4 am is the fourth most deadly time span. More than 2/3 of all police murders occur between 6 pm and 6 am.[9]

As previously eluded to, darkness does not have to be your enemy. While the improper use of darkness and light can lead to tragedy, instructors must emphasize that proper use can provide an additional blanket of safety. Just as concealment will provide the advantage of remaining unseen, darkness can do the same. The key is to acquire needed knowledge, then anticipate danger and plan your actions before it's too late.

Flashlight

There are several basic guidelines for the use of flashlights. These are not complicated. They are not difficult to learn or use. Failure to do so can lead to disaster.

The most basic of all flashlight survival tactics is how to hold the flashlight. Instructors will find a brief description and demonstration of this technique to be very effective.

The flashlight should be held in an officer's non-gun hand. One of the most common mistakes of flashlight use is failure to control backlighting. Backlighting is the dim light projected to the sides and slightly backwards of the beam of the flashlight. If officers hold the flashlight directly to the side, they will be unknowingly illuminated. For this reason, the flashlight must be held to the side and well in front of his body. Most perpetrators will shoot directly at the light, as opposed to the officer.

How to hold the flashlight is important. When to use the flashlight is equally important. Unfortunately, many officers have not been taught when to turn the flashlight on. It is frequently turned on and left on until a search is over. This technique places an officer in needless jeopardy. All officers should be equipped with flashlights which have a temporary push button and a permanent on/off switch.

The most effective technique for searching without the benefit of cover is termed "flash and go." In other words, momentarily flash a beam of light then continue to move under the cover of darkness. This technique is repeated throughout the search.

One frequently used technique is useful when coming around corners or through doorways. Whether in darkness or daylight, officers should crouch to a height the perpetrator would not expect him to come around. Holding a flashlight well above your head and to the front of your body will give the appearance of standing instead of crouching. This is another technique which is easily and effectively demonstrated. The effectiveness of the demonstration will be lessened if done in a room which is not dark.

If 2 officers are in a doorway, one technique offers a great tactical advantage. Often referred to as the "flashlight roll," it is used after officers are in a crouch position on each side of the doorway. One officer points his flashlight inside the concerned room, turns the switch on, then rolls it over to the other officer. Placement of a flashlight in the doorway must be forward enough so that officers are not illuminated. After the second officer catches the flashlight, he simply rolls it back to the first. Each officer takes advantage of observing illuminated, overlapping views of the room.

Officers must be given the opportunity to practice the tactical use of a flashlight. A variety of easily prepared exercises can be conducted. During the initial stage of these exercises, trainers should warn against too frequent a use of a flashlight. Do not use a flashlight when natural lighting will suffice. The reason is that a flashlight use will destroy an officer's night vision. His ability to see immediately after turning the flashlight off will be greatly impaired.

Vehicle Lights

The use of vehicle lights is based upon a simple, yet effective tactic; blind the suspect. Most officers learned the values of using vehicle headlights and spotlights during a staged traffic stop at the basic academy. This remains an extremely effective survival tool. The only fallacy is that many officers fail to use it. This is an example of where complacency kills.

All general orders should include traffic stops and the use of vehicle lights. It should be mandatory that all officers stopping a vehicle during the night turn on both headlights and spotlight at the vehicle. Common sense explains how blinding the perpetrator will be if he should turn around to attack the approaching officer.

Though not used frequently, blinding the suspects with vehicle lights then moving away from the vehicle, is effective. This can save your life if a shootout should ensue. It must be done properly, however. Officers must run to locations behind and to the side of their vehicle. Running only sideways will unknowingly illuminate officers. This tactic should not be used if nearby cover is unavailable.[10]

Pedestrian Approaches

A pedestrian is a person travelling on foot. How you approach and confront pedestrians is important. Once more, trainers have an obligation to train the most effective survival tactics.

Deciding who an officer stops may be more complicated than it first appears. The selection of a pedestrian for stopping should be based on several factors:

- Departmental guidelines and/or standard operating procedures may dictate when and where individuals may be stopped.
- "Stop and frisk" decisions have provided officers with a regulation allowing them to stop and frisk an individual who may be posing an immediate danger to them. A smooth, continuous feel of the exterior of the suspect's clothing should be conducted for hard objects which appear to be weapons. This type of search is advised over a "pat down," which increases the possibility of missing a weapon within his clothing.
- Instructors must emphasize and encourage the use of an officer's "Sixth Sense." It is extremely difficult to describe how you "simply know something is wrong." Such intuition has saved more than one life.
- A subject's appearance.
- The area which he is located.
- The time of day.
- The officer's personal knowledge of the subject.
- The subject being identified in connection with a warrant, teletype or some form of bolo.
- Information concerning the subject obtained from an informant.

Several considerations are important when selecting the location of a pedestrian stop. Instructors should note that many officers simply stop a subject wherever they happen to be. This does not take into account that innocent bystanders may be in the area if a shoot-out or other form of attack occurs. The likelihood of a citizen being taken hostage increases as the number of citizens in the area increases. Attempting to eliminate obvious escape routes should also be considered when selecting the location.

Before approaching a subject, a number of actions should be considered and taken:

1. Request a backup unit if the circumstances warrant it.
2. Notify the dispatcher of a description of the subject and location of the stop.
3. Observe the subject for a few minutes before approaching him.
4. Make continued observations of the subject's clothing and hands.
5. Always remain alert.
6. Develop a survival plan and be ready to initiate it at a moments notice if you come under attack.
7. Extreme care must always be used as you approach a pedestrian.
8. Stopping a pedestrian should never be considered routine. The approach should be made from the rear. Ideally, it should be made from his right rear. This will allow the officer to keep a constant view of his right side and right hand.

The following guidelines should be used to assist further instruction concerning pedestrian approaches:

1. The officer should use a firm yet professional tone of voice to state "police, don't move!"
2. If the subject's hands are not in view, ask him to remove them from his pockets and keep them down by his side and in open view.
3. Tell him to slowly turn around and face you.
4. Assume a position with your body at an angle; gun side away. You should be half way between his right side and in front of him at a distance of approximately three and a half feet.
5. If your agency carries the PR24 baton, the position of interrogation should be assumed.
6. The distance between the officer and subject should place the officer out of his arm reach yet he is within reach of the baton or nightstick.
7. Advise subject the reason for stopping him.
8. If circumstances warrant a stop and frisk, have the suspect turn

around, interlace his fingers on the back of his head, spread his feet and begin to lean forward. Conduct the search with one hand while firmly grasping his fingers with the other.

9. As a field interrogation continues, always watch the subject's hands.
10. Request a backup if one is not already coming.
11. **Never** turn your back on a subject or allow him to come close to your firearm.
12. If there are two officers and one subject, the secondary officer should assume a position to the subject's rear and left. This position should be beyond the subject's peripheral vision while talking to the initial officer, yet not so far to the rear that he would be in cross fire if there is a shoot-out.
13. If two officers were present, they should develop a plan to use hand signals or a particular phrase to coordinate their actions. This is particularly useful to coordinate and effect an arrest.
14. If there are two officers and two or more subjects, the secondary officer should assume a position at the rear of the subjects. The initial officer should assume the basic position of interrogation.
15. If an officer determines he has stopped the wrong individual, he should apologize and provide an explanation.

Trainers have ample opportunity to provide demonstrations and participation exercises concerning pedestrian approaches. They should include the correct method for approaching a pedestrian while on the sidewalk and a demonstration of the entire field interrogation. Role playing will be an effective technique.

VOICE COMMANDS

The "unsung hero" of street survival tactics is the use of your voice. Proper voice commands can be astoundingly effective. Improper voice tactics can be devastating.

In a crisis, officers must overcome timidness to accomplish effective voice commands. Instructors can demonstrate examples such as drawing a weapon and giving the command of "police, freeze." The proper use of voice is so uncommon that perhaps instructors will be unfamiliar with the technique. Officers should not simply say "police, freeze" in a loud voice. In a crisis, officers are to shout at the top of their voice, POLICE–

FREEZE. Their voices should be so loud that anyone in the immediate area should literally jump with surprise.

Using your voice this way is a form of intimidation. You are teaching officers to control a suspect during the moment of crisis. Unlike most situations, this form of intimidation is extremely beneficial. Officers will shock the suspect into pausing for a moment.

At a time when fractions of a second may save lives, this momentary pause will be very important. An additional benefit of shouting "police, freeze" while drawing your firearm is that it alerts innocent bystanders in the immediate area of the crisis. In real life, innocent bystanders will scatter like ants as a result.

The topic of voice control in life threatening situations can begin with a demonstration of how to take control in a crisis by using a loud, intimidating tone. Demonstrating "police, freeze" without warning will have an impact that officers will not soon forget. This technique is unnatural to most individuals. A practical exercise provides officers the opportunity to participate in practicing the technique.

TRAFFIC STOPS

More than a tenth of all police officers murdered died while performing a traffic stop. To be exact, 129 officers out of 1,031 officers killed between 1974 and 1983 met their death during traffic stops or traffic pursuits.[7]

Such statistics assume a more realistic meaning when the circumstances of one death is examined:

> "The Metro City Police Department reported that Officer Scott, a patrolman, white male, 27 years of age, was shot and killed after he stopped a motorist for a traffic violation. The subject, a wanted parole violator, was later apprehended and charged with his murder. A few days after the funeral, the detective who investigated the Scott shooting told what had really taken place. As usual, the story was only discussed privately. There is no question Officer Scott had been careless with the subject. After stopping the car he did not, as was required, advise the dispatcher of his location and license number of the vehicle.
>
> Officer Scott had been warned repeatedly of his failure to follow this and similar procedures. He had failed to see the colored plastic tape on the stolen vehicle's license plate, converting a 7 to a 1 and an 8 to a 3.

He was shot in the back while writing a citation on the hood of his patrol vehicle."[11]

As with virtually all law enforcement funerals, Officer Scott was hailed as a hero who gave his life for the betterment of his community. Any officer killed in the line of duty is a hero. Yet, in another sense, Officer Scott, and many others, made needless and unnecessary judgements in error. These mistakes, not an heroic act, is what caused their deaths.

Many of the survival tactics instructed to officers regarding traffic stops have been taught to them before. Most basic recruit academies are proficient in providing basic techniques of vehicle stops. Then why do officers no longer follow those survival guidelines as years pass? The answer is complacency. Conducting traffic stops happens so frequently officers no longer feel the sense of danger that was present during a recruit academy training exercise. Conducting a traffic stop hundreds of times without incident naturally leads to apathy.

Stimulating in-service training is the answer to this deadly problem.

Figure 14. Vehicle approaches should be trained by lecture, demonstration, practical exercises then critique and review.

Training officers must meet the challenge of providing meaningful survival training pertaining not only to traffic stops but all forms of life preserving tactics. Training traffic stop procedures, like all other survival training must focus on practicality and realism. The impact of such training must impress officers until additional training can reinforce it again.

There is a fundamental concept instructors must drill into officers' minds. This concept should be repeated so often officers will subconsciously comply with it. It is; staying alive on the street is a matter of developing a survival state of mind. Everything you do evolves around this SUBCONSCIOUS, LIFESAVING ATTITUDE.

The following guidelines are offered to assist trainers and instructors in traffic stop instruction. They are presented in a logical sequence to promote an effective learning process. Instruction should be conveyed through a mixture of lecture, class discussion, demonstration and plenty of "hands on" practical exercises.

A. No traffic stop is ever routine. It's impossible to predetermine what type of individual is being stopped for a minor traffic infraction.

B. Conducting sound survival tactics during vehicle stops can be accomplished with a professional and pleasant demeanor.

C. The patrol vehicle should come to a stop approximately fifteen feet to the rear and three feet to the left of the violator's vehicle. This location provides a good view of the perpetrator and added protection from vehicles approaching from the rear. Be certain to call in a full description of the vehicle and location before exiting your vehicle.

D. Keep a constant view of the occupant's actions.

E. If the vehicle stop is at night, use your vehicle headlights and spotlight to their fullest advantage.

F. As you begin to approach the vehicle, develop and use all of your senses to detect any unusual circumstances.

G. When you reach the trunk of the vehicle, touch it to make sure it's secure.

H. Never carry anything in your gun hand.

I. Stop just behind the driver's door.

J. If the vehicle is still running, ask the driver to turn off the ignition.
K. If you decide to write a citation, back away from the driver's door while watching the occupant's.
L. Move to a location behind the right front door of the patrol vehicle.
M. Write a citation while standing upright, facing the stopped car. Do not write a citation bending over the patrol vehicle. Use your peripheral vision to watch the occupants while you continue writing the citation.
N. Keep the right side front door of your patrol vehicle unlocked with the window rolled down. This will leave easy access to your shotgun and/or vehicle radio.
O. If the driver exits his vehicle, request that he stand with you off of the roadway.
P. Never allow him on your gun side.
Q. If any other occupants of the vehicle exit, tell them to reenter and stay in the vehicle.
R. Return to the stopped vehicle using the same caution and alertness.

FELONY STOPS

Felony stops should be initiated when a known or suspected felony vehicle is observed. Most of these situations occur when an officer observes a vehicle matching the description of a bolo. The organization of a felony stop should be coordinated with nearby units. An officer's safety should never be sacrificed for public relation purposes.

A. After observing the concerned vehicle, advise headquarters and nearby officers of the circumstances. Request assistance in conducting the felony stop.
B. Begin thinking of a possible location for the stop. Considerations should focus on determining an area free of innocent bystanders, businesses or residences.
C. Coordinate your organizational plans with the responding unit.
D. Use your emergency lights and sirens to stop the vehicle at a predetermined location.
E. After the vehicle comes to a complete stop, pull in directly behind it. You should stop approximately twenty-five feet to the rear. If at

night, use your highbeam headlights and spotlight to illuminate and blind the perpetrators.

F. Your assisting patrol car should stop alongside the driver's side of your vehicle. Approximately three to four feet should be left between the 2 patrol cars.

G. Do not approach the suspect's vehicle.

H. All officers should remain in their vehicle immediately aiming firearms and/or shotguns at the suspect's vehicle. This is accomplished by opening the patrol car door then positioning yourself so your back leans against the doorpost for support. This will provide cover from within the vehicle.

I. Shouting in a loud authoritative manner is preferred over using the loud speaker. Holding the microphone will prevent the officer from properly holding his firearm.

J. The following commands should be shouted: "Everyone in the vehicle! Look straight ahead. Put your hands behind your heads. Interlace your fingers. Driver, turn the engine off! Put the keys in your pocket! Driver—reach outside the door and open it from the outside! Face the other direction! Interlace your fingers behind your head and walk backwards to the patrol cars!"

K. The driver should be immediately handcuffed, searched and relieved of the keys to his vehicle.

L. After placing the driver in the caged patrol vehicle, remove any other occupants of the vehicle in the same manner. If several occupants are present, remove the ones in the front seat first. All occupants should be removed through the open driver's door.

HIGH-RISK INCIDENT TRAINING

Training for a high-risk incidence is crucial. Recent years have seen a tremendous move toward developing thorough and competent in-service training. Law enforcement agencies are becoming more professional in the handling of life threatening situations. Incidences such as narcotic raids, terrorism, hostage situations, barricaded individuals, and suicide situations are of grave concern. Effective strategies coupled with perpetual in-service training have begun to produce very effective and successful results.

Lieutenant James W. Koleas, Milwaukee Police Department, surveyed 200 law enforcement agencies regarding high-risk incident training. One hundred and forty-eight of the 200 agencies returned the 121 item questionnaire. Three distinct training implications can be determined:

1. Law enforcement agencies wish to enhance high-risk incident management capabilities. A great interest for the improvement of such training now exists among the law enforcement community.
2. Budgetary restraints are resulting in agencies desiring to develop more cost-effective crisis training. A general belief exists that in-service training and self evaluation will lead to more cost effectiveness.
3. Just less than 75 percent of all agencies responding to the questionnaire requested additional training:
   mentally ill individuals—78.6 percent
   armed suicide situations—77.1 percent
   high-risk incidents inside automobiles—75.7 percent
   barricaded incidents—74.3 percent
   terrorists situations—73.6 percent
   domestic incidents—73.6 percent
   trapped criminals—70 percent
   narcotics raids—60 percent[12]

REFERENCES

1. Federal Bureau of Investigation, Law Enforcement Officers Killed Summary January–August 1985, *FCIC Teletype*, 9-19-85.
2. J. C. Muirhead, Some Comments on the Hostage Situation, *The Police Chief*, February 1978.
3. Ronald Adams, Thomas McTernan, Charles Remsberg, *Street Survival*, Evanston, Illinois: Calibre Press, 1980, pg. 6.
4. Robert W. Wennerholm, Officer Survival Recommendations—New Civil Liability Concerns, *The Police Chief*, June 1984, pg. 59.
5. Orange County Sheriffs Department, *Officer Survival Course*, Orange County, Florida.
6. Ronald Adams, Thomas McTernan, Charles Remsberg, *Street Survival*, Calibre Press, Evanston, Illinois, 1980, pg. 46–47.
7. U.S. Department of Justice, *Uniform Crime Reports: Law Enforcement Officers Killed and Assaulted*, Federal Bureau of Investigation, 1983, pg. 18.
8. Andrew P. Sutor, *Police Operations—Tactical Approaches to Crimes in Progress*, St. Paul, Minnesota: West, 1976, pg. 304–305.
9. U.S. Department of Justice, *Uniform Crime Reports: Law Enforcement Officers Killed and Assaulted*, Federal Bureau of Investigation, 1983, pg. 14.
10. Ronald Adams, Thomas McTernan, Charles Remsberg, *Street Survival*, Evanston, Illinois: Calibre Press, 1980, pg. 101–106.
11. Pierce Brooks, *Officer Down, Code Three*, Motorola Teleprograms, 1975, pg. 2–3.

8.

FIREARMS TRAINING

Firearms training is one of the most critical responsibilities of a training officer. The only individual within our society who has the lawful right and immediate capability of taking another individual's life is a law enforcement officer. The professional consideration surrounding that deadly moment is extremely complex. Law enforcement trainers are charged with the responsibility of providing officers with training so proficient that he is able to instantly analyze and conclude his decision whether to use deadly force based upon legal, moral, interdepartmental and personal considerations.

Training programs must be developed which prepare officers both physically and mentally to make proper decisions at a moments notice. All programs must be based upon not only sound instructional theory, but an agency's written directives regarding deadly force as well.

USE OF DEADLY FORCE—WRITTEN POLICY

The failure to have a sound, written policy controlling the use of deadly force rids a training officer of the nucleus of his firearms training program. Trainers must take the initiative to ensure written policies are not ignored. The department's failure to have adequate policies may result in professional and financial devastation to the department. In addition, in-service firearms training must be conducted according to such policies.

The International Association of Chiefs of Police has thoroughly researched the use of deadly force. They have identified 5 phases which must be included within an effective use of deadly force written policy. These areas are:

1. Firearms training standards.
2. When to shoot.
3. The shooting review procedure.

4. The investigation of a shooting.
5. Firearm equipment standards.

Agencies should consider including statements regarding the following points in written policies:

1. A legal disclaimer advising that the written policy is for interdepartmental use only and does not pertain to any civil or criminal proceeding.
2. A definition of the term "deadly force."
3. A statement pertaining to the requiring of all officers to have any weapon carried on or off duty be inspected and registered by departmental personnel.
4. A statement of policy regarding the carrying of weapons off duty.
5. A statement pertaining to the use of deadly force against juveniles.
6. A statement that the protection of any human life is the utmost concern.
7. A statement that officers may use deadly force to protect themselves or others from the immediate threat of death or severe harm.
8. A statement prohibiting the use of deadly force at or from a moving vehicle except when the officer is being fired upon from a moving vehicle or in self-defense from the vehicle itself.
9. A statement prohibiting the use of firearms when an individual may be injured.
10. A statement prohibiting the use of warning shots.
11. A statement requiring all on duty officers to be armed with a firearm inspected, registered and approved by the department.
12. A statement controlling the use of secondary weapons.[1]

INITIAL FIREARMS TRAINING CONSIDERATIONS

Deadly force is the amount of force used by an officer having the potential to cause death. In-service firearms training must broaden its focus over that of previous years. The familiar statement "ready on the right, ready on the left, ready on the firing line" definitely has its place. We now know, however, the benefits of street practicality and realism are too important to ignore.

This text will not concern itself with the basic instruction of firearm training. The recruit academy class is responsible for providing the fundamentals of firearm instruction. Certainly there will be instances when officers need additional training in breath control, sight alignment, squeezing the trigger or other fundamentals. Training officers and firearms instructors must be constantly alert to such needs and correct them as they develop. While virtually all types of in-service firearms training provide sufficient practice of shooting fundamentals, an extremely effective technique to detect deficiencies is video taping officers. Instant replay allows both instructor and officer to determine problem areas which would otherwise remain undetected.

Deadly Force Considerations

In-service firearms training often neglects the topic of deadly force. Some agencies have no written policies regarding deadly force. Other agencies have a written policy, yet do not provide officers with training pursuant to it. Still, other departments have a written policy and provide officers with a brief classroom session prior to every range training. Topics such as the department's deadly force policy, are covered. The last training example is unfortunately the least frequent.

Officers must learn what to consider when determining whether to use deadly force. Instructional topics should include:

1. The immediate extent of threat to concerned individuals.
2. Type of crime.
3. The current law.
4. The departmental policy.
5. Circumstances surrounding the suspect.
6. Capability of suspect to carry out the threat.
7. Possibility of officer's actions injurying innocent bystanders.

Instruction must also include circumstances which may prevent officers from acting appropriately in a crisis situation. Because the life or death of an officer or bystander may rest on a fraction of a second, any possibility that officers may unnecessarily hesitate should be examined. A lack of absolute firearm competence or confidence should be examined. Having self-control in a life threatening situation is an issue to be confronted ahead of time. Still another concern is the possibility an officer may momentarily panic in a crisis.

Physiological Changes Due to Stress

One detrimental factor is caused by physiological reactions to extreme stress. Most officers have never received instruction concerning these uncontrollable reactions. Instruction should include the fact many physiological reactions instantly occur when individuals are placed in situations of severe stress.

One of the first physiological changes to occur is the constriction of blood vessels. This constriction prevents the normal flow of blood throughout the body. A lessening of blood flow results in less oxygen reaching the brain. Because the brain has insufficient oxygen, a series of additional physiological reactions occur. These reactions include:

1. Increased frequency and degree of heartbeat.
2. Increased frequency and degree of breathing.
3. Decreased ability to think due to a lessened supply of oxygen.
4. Increased flow of adrenaline.

It is this hindrance of the thinking process which is of tremendous concern to firearms training. Most officers are totally unfamiliar with this phenomenon. They may easily relate to it by recalling moments in high school or college when they were called upon to answer a question. The moment they were under pressure, their mind went blank, even though they knew the answer. The common saying, "If you hadn't asked me I could have told you" is more than just a saying. Its truth is based upon the physiological reaction to stress. The brain simply cannot function as well due to the lack of oxygen.

There are additional areas of concern which can cause an officer to inappropriately hesitate during a shooting situation. Like those previously addressed, these should be confronted and dealt with in a classroom setting.

1. The moral issue of taking another individual's life.
2. Professional issues associated with deadly force.
3. The officer's concern of civil liability.
4. Interdepartmental disciplinary concerns.
5. Concerns of being charged with homicide.

Figure 15. Creating a mental and physical stress through physical exertion will help to simulate the realism officers feel during actual shoot-outs. Requiring officers to exercise immediately prior to firing will allow them to experience an increased heart and breathing rate while shooting.

STATE OF THE ART

Contemporary firearms training has become quite sophisticated. It has not always been that way, however. There have been many glaring deficiencies in previous training practices. For example, virtually all law enforcement agencies previously trained at distances between twenty-one feet and one hundred-fifty feet. The 7, 15, 25 and 50 yard line were standard firing distances. We now know that the vast majority of shoot-outs in which officers are murdered occur at distances within fifteen feet.

Another unfortunate fact is that most agencies trained at single silhouette targets. Studies have now determined that approximately 40 percent of the time when officers are in shoot-outs they will be facing more than one gunman.

Another problem area has been the failure to have frequent firearms training in darkness or low light conditions. Many agencies neglect to hold firearms training other than in daylight. Research has determined the majority of shoot-outs occur in hours of darkness. Many firearms instructors simply find it more convenient to conduct the range during the day.

A variety of research has been conducted on firearms training during the last decade. The ineptness of past decades has given way to a virtually endless number of contemporary firearms products and techniques. Properly conducted research has afforded the knowledge to develop effective, practical and realistic firearms training. The concern of civil liability has made law enforcement firearms training "big business." This has afforded police much improved equipment.

Any experienced training officer or firearms instructor has noticed the recent flood of advertising pertaining to new and innovative firearms training programs. All of course, claim to be the best: firearms stress courses, various shooting simulator courses, turning targets, moving targets, cinematic target shooting, laser firearms training and tactical exertion courses. There are so many products on the market it is easy to become bewildered when deciding which one will suit your agency's needs. Do not become so preoccupied with today's "toys" that you forget to stick to the basics of practical and realistic in-service training. A review of the chapter on survival training should serve as a guide to the priorities of staying alive on the street.

Training officers must ensure their agency has not been lulled into complacency and train with ineffective and outdated techniques. Regular nighttime firing, realism, multiple target systems and close range firing should be a regular part of any agency's in-service firearms training. At the same time, they can't fall prey to a training "toy" which may not only be ineffective but soon not working.

FIREARMS TRAINING STAFF

The size of your agency will usually dictate the size of your firearms training staff. Small agencies may need only one firearms instructor. Larger departments may have dozens of certified instructors. The training officer should always have an adequate number of firearms instructors.

The number of instructors is irrelevant when compared to their quality. Whether you serve as the single firearms instructor or you supervise an extensive staff, all must be professionally qualified. Their selection is based on personal firearms expertise, dedication, instructional ability and a conscientious loyalty to excellence.

As with any professional group, firearms instructors must constantly strive for their own improvement. Organizations such as the National Rifle Association or the Federal Bureau of Investigation offer firearm instructor schools. Taking advantage of advanced training offers numerous benefits. The quality of instruction will remain high, personal expertise and qualifications are advanced with each seminar. The department is also better prepared to fight civil litigation based upon improved qualifications. Information concerning enrollment in such classes can be obtained from your local Federal Bureau of Investigation office or the National Rifle Association Headquarters, 1600 Rhode Island Avenue, Northwest, Washington, D.C. 20036.

There are many other ways that firearms instructors may keep themselves "up-to-date." Subscribing to several law enforcement firearms related magazines will help instructors stay abreast of the latest firearm innovations and techniques. Constant contact with firearms instructors in nearby communities will assist in an exchange of valuable information and innovative thinking.

Staying thoroughly familiar with all weapons and ammunition within your own agency is a responsibility sometimes neglected by many instructors. Quality mean a constant refining of lessen plans, instruction techniques and training aids. Training officers who are not firearms trainers themselves are still responsible for maintaining other instructors' high level of expertise and performance.

PLANNING

An initial step to the development of a sound firearms training program is planning. Firearms training should not be conducted because someone realized it's been a long time since training was held. Planning an organization schedule should be an annual event. A year round program of in-service training and qualification enable those within the department to reach their highest level of proficiency.

Long range planning also assists in developing a program's potential. Sitting down with a calendar for an hour or so is all that is needed to think through the year's activities. Organization will greatly ease the burden of ensuring an effective variety of firearms training is conducted, the proper frequency is held and a high level of proficiency is obtained.

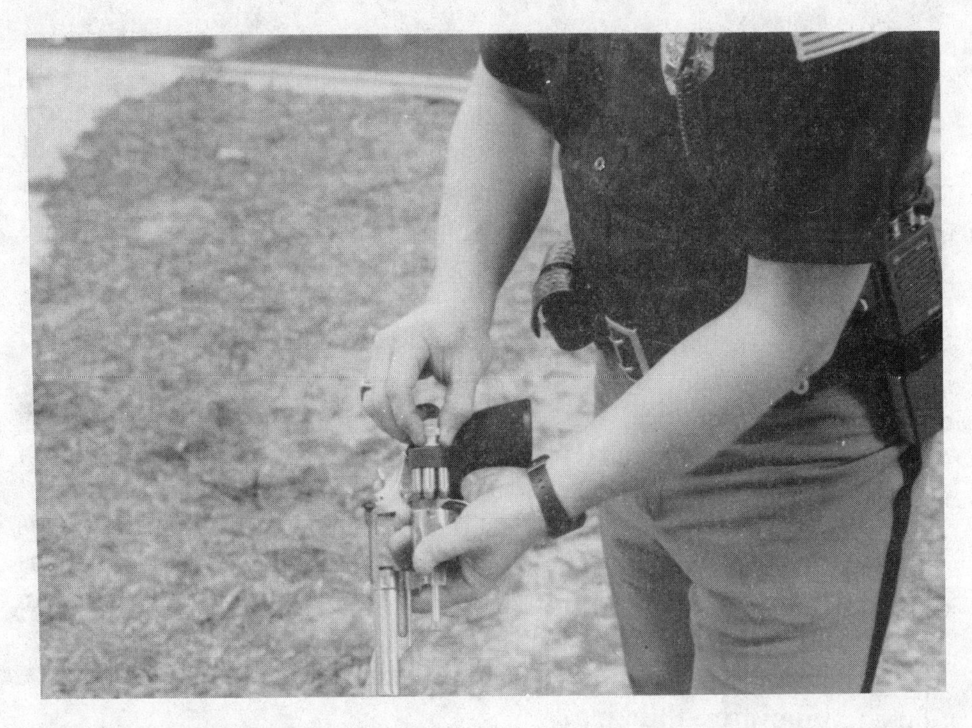

Figure 16. Firearms instructors must be highly qualified. Constant instructor retraining and certification of particular expertise is necessary.

The following considerations are recommended to be included in an annual firearms planning schedule:

1. A minimum frequency of firing four times a year is desirable.
2. Firearms training should not be conducted in the same manner every time. Trainers and instructors must plan to offer a variety of situations in a realistic and stressful environment. This will develop officers' abilities to perform in a crisis.
3. Those officers who do poorly at the range must be provided with extra training. Unfortunately, every agency has officers who perform unsatisfactorily at the range. Few agencies, however, furnish these officers with the additional training needed to increase their proficiency. Furthermore, the same officers usually continue to be assigned where there is a reasonable expectation they may have to use their firearm. Remedial instruction must be mandatory in such instances. The use of video to record and play back their performance is recommended.
4. Trainers should also develop plans for regular shotgun training.

5. Planning must also include the frequently neglected areas of nighttime firing, close range shooting, multiple target firing and implementing stress and physical exertion as part of regular firearms training courses.

As with any form of training, adequate record keeping procedures must be developed. Constant documentation is an effective method of determining where weaknesses within a program lie. Essential information such as who attended, when and where training was held, and how officers performed is mandatory. While conscientious trainers would maintain adequate records if they weren't mandatory, civil liability considerations make sound documentation crucial.[2]

FIREARMS SAFETY TRAINING

Firearms safety training is frequently viewed as unpopular and unnecessary. This attitude often results in safety being virtually neglected. Firearms instructors must evaluate their professional viewpoint and previous performance regarding safety. There is substantial justification professionally, ethically and morally to provide such training. Tragic deaths among officers and their families occur annually due to negligent handling of their service weapons. In addition to personal tragedies, the civil liability incurred by the failure to address this issue is tremendous. The following should serve as minimum guidelines:

A. **General Safety Guidelines**
- Treat every firearm as if it were loaded.
- When handing a firearm to another person, always ensure that it is uncocked, unloaded, and the muzzle of a firearm is not pointing at anyone.
- Never point the muzzle of a firearm, even if it is unloaded, at anyone.
- Unloaded guns kill.
- Keep your triger finger out of the trigger guard until you are ready to fire.
- Never train with firearms alone.
- Never handle a firearm if you've been drinking.
- Take care of and maintain your firearm as if your life depended on it.

B. **Range Safety Rules**

- Immediately follow all instructions of the firearms instructor.
- If a firearm failed to fire immediately, notify the range officer in charge of the firing line.
- If holding a firearm while on the firing line, never turn around.
- Do not load your weapon until instructed to do so by the firearms instructor.
- Never dry fire if anyone is in front of you.
- Always wear eye and ear protection at the range.

C. Drawing Techniques

- Remove strap.
- Grasp stock with finger outside trigger guard.
- Pull firearm up and away from leg.
- Point handgun in direction of target.

D. Unloading Procedures

- Activate cylinder release with thumb and immediately obtain a resupply of ammunition.
- Use thumb to eject casing directly to the ground. Do not attempt to catch empty casings.
- Use whatever cover is available while reloading.
- Move strong foot to rear to assist keeping barrel toward target during unloading and reloading.
- Stay constantly alert; anticipate your future actions.

E. Loading Procedures

- If loading cartridges without "speed loaders," turn the cylinder with thumb. There is no need to turn the cylinder if speed loaders are being used. Speed loaders are recommended.
- Close firearm cylinder with barrel down range, while grip is re-assumed.

F. Instruction For The Principles Of Firing A Firearm

- Safety guidelines.
- Stance.
- Grip.
- Sight alignment.
- Trigger control.
- Loading/unloading procedures.
- Drawing the firearm.

G. Firearms Safety While Not On The Range

- Departmental guidelines must be thoroughly understood and continually adhered to.

- Never stand so any citizen will be on your "gun side."
- Do not practice dry firing anywhere other than the range.
- When at home, all firearms should be unloaded and safely stored away.
- Ammunition should be kept in a separate location than firearm.

H. **Cleaning A Firearm**

- Treat the weapon as if it were loaded.
- Always keep muzzle directed in a safe direction.
- Open the cylinder.
- Inspect firearm for properly functioning parts.
- Thoroughly clean and lubricate using proper cleaning equipment.

SUGGESTIONS FOR DEMONSTRATIONS AND PRACTICAL EXERCISES

Firearms training is an ideal topic for the use of demonstrations. While listening to a lecture or watching a demonstration is beneficial, the most effective way of learning is by doing. Practical exercises which allow officers to practice techniques demonstrated by instructors should be done whenever possible. The following guidelines should serve as minimum guidelines for participation exercises:

- Safety remains a very neglected area of firearms training. Instructor demonstration followed by officer participation in loading and unloading service handguns should be conducted.
- Develop demonstrations which are followed by officer participation in the proper methods of firearms cleaning.
- Officer participation in the proper drawing of firearms is recommended.
- A variety of survival firing stances should be demonstrated by instructors.
- Demonstrations should be followed by repetitive practical exercises.
- The proper techniques of cover should be demonstrated. A variety of practical exercises must follow.
- Instructors should demonstrate the proper technique of cleaning a firearm. Officer participation and cleaning suggestions should follow.
- Demonstration and officer participation in sight alignment is suggested.

Figure 17. Occasional retraining in basic firearm positions and stances must be conducted.

- Demonstration and officer participation in trigger control is recommended.
- Officer participation in assuming proper grip is suggested. Instructor demonstration of survival tactics regarding the use of light should be conducted. Practical exercises using a variety of light sources during firing situations should be furnished.
- Firearms training immediately after and during physical exertion should be implemented. Exercises simulating situations, such as an officer in a foot pursuit immediately prior to a shooting situation, is recommended.
- Realistic training exercises involving building searches should be part of the overall firearms training program.
- Exercises which include the use of sirens, blue and red flashing lights, realistic loud tape recordings, yelling or shouting and a variety of other stimulators of stress should be conducted.

SHOTGUN TRAINING

The use of a shotgun in law enforcement has usually been surrounded by some degree of controversy. With a few exceptions, it is the dealiest of all firearms used by the police. Due to this firepower, some police administrators do not equip patrol officers with shotguns. Others establish guidelines which strictly limit their use. Still others order shotguns be locked in a vehicle shotgun rack and seldom taken out.

These strict regulations are based upon the fear that innocent individuals will be harmed by the degree of firepower capable of a shotgun. Street officers, however, know the firepower is needed. They fully realize the necessity for meeting firepower with equal or greater firepower. They have seen the psychological advantage of a shotgun lessen a potential shoot-out threat.

In some communities, police administrators remain on one side while street officers stand on the other. What is the answer to the controversy? The solution is proper training. It is not difficult to understand the view of administrators. They, like everyone, have heard the horror stories of multimillion dollar law suits stemming from the improper use of firearms. Since the lack of adequate training was a key ingredient in those suits, training can greatly lessen an agency's civil liability.

Unfortunately, shotgun training in some departments is virtually non-existent. The most frequent reason is complacency by training officers and firearms instructors. Some trainers feel basic shotgun training in the academy is sufficient. This, combined with the thought that almost everyone can hit their target with a shotgun, makes training easy to ignore. Such an unprofessional attitude creates extreme liability, increases the possibility an innocent person will be harmed and staggers sincere efforts for professionalism.[3]

Shotgun use in law enforcement began after the end of the civil war. By the end of the 1870's, it was frequently used by state coast guards and western law enforcement officers. The pump action and self-loading shotguns had been introduced by the early 1900's.

Contemporary firearms instructors consider the shotgun the most versatile firearm available to law enforcement. While its training is often neglected, shotgun proficiency is more easily accomplished than with most weapons.

Training guidelines and suggestions are presented below:

A. Identification of major parts
   - Stock

- Barrel
- Magazine
- Slide-Pump
- Chamber
- Trigger
- Sight
- Muzzle
- Safety devices
- Heel

B. Appropriate safety guidelines should be instructed.

C. Firearms instructors should demonstrate the proper stance for firing a shotgun. Verifying officers use it through observation of practical exercises is important. The recommended stance is heel of the shotgun to shoulder. Additional support is provided by opposite hand and cheek to shotgun stock.

D. Adherence to basic firearms principles must be assured. Instructors should make observations during practical exercises for the proper adherence to the principles of:
- Shotgun safety guidelines
- Stance
- Sighting
- Breath control
- Loading and unloading

E. Officer's knowledge of the firepower capable of shotguns is usually very limited. Most officers have never fired a shotgun at anything except a paper target. This results in most agencies being extremely negligent. Failing to furnish training of this type may cause an officer to fire in a seemingly safe location only to kill an innocent bystander on the other side of the wall. An elaborate demonstration is not required. Building a series of mock walls out of 2 × 4's and plasterboards, then placing them several yards apart will be adequate. The demonstration should be conducted with the same ammunition used by your agency.

F. Separate demonstrations which illustrate the spread of buckshot should be conducted. The recommended maximum range of firing 00 buckshot for law enforcement is 40 yards. At 40 yards, 8 of the 9 pellets will remain within a thirty inch circle. Instructors must convey that the further a distance is to the perpetrator the more likely an innocent bystander will be injured. The probable shot spread, distance to perpetrator, innocent citizens present, type of construction nearby and occupancy of anyone within the building must be considered in shoot-out situations.[4]

The shotgun is a practical, realistic and useful law enforcement tool. Many needless deaths and serious injuries may be prevented by its effective and proper use. As with most police tools, effective and proper use is dependent upon training. The operation of a shotgun is not difficult. Training is relatively easy.

The major reason most agencies have not conducted more shotgun training is complacency. An improved, conscientious and professional training attitude will provide greater safety to the officer and allow him to better protect those he serves.

FIREARMS TRAINING FACILITIES

No single type of firearms range is best for every law enforcement agency. A number of factors should be considered when planning, constructing, or rennovating range facilities. The particularities involved in each agency's unique situation can be very complex. Only general guidelines may be presented. Even the generalities will usually need to be modified.

Recent technical advances in firearms training equipment have been astounding. Do not assume, however, that such improvements require an agency to have complex range facilities to provide adequate training. Firearms safety, realistic training, and productivity and efficiency can be achieved through knowledge and hard work.

A wide difference of opinion prevails regarding the benefits and disadvantages of an indoor versus outdoor ranges. Everything considered, most agencies would be better served by an indoor range. Having both an indoor and outdoor range is ideal, yet, of course beyond the finances of virtually all of us. The major benefits of an indoor range are:

1. The ability to simulate nighttime firing anytime.
2. Not being hampered by poor weather conditions.
3. Not having to spend time driving to less populated areas where most ranges are located.
4. The ability to fire at any time of day.

5. The ability to simulate more realistic "street conditions" via the use of lights, sirens, tape recordings, etc.

Figure 18. The key to meaningful firearms training is realism. This includes short distance firing, nighttime firing, multiple targets, use of emergency lights and siren and realistic targets during the majority of range training.

A serious deficiency plaguing firearms training facilities is the neglect of trainers to use them to their fullest benefit. Many ranges have been used to furnish only basic and remedial training. If adequate space allows, an endless variety of realistic, survival oriented in-service training sessions are possible. Relatively minor renovations such as installing a patrol vehicle's emergency lights and siren bar to create higher levels of realism and stress are beneficial. Another suggestion is install loud speakers through which tape recordings may be played to create "street situations.[5]"

PERCEPTUAL DISTORTIONS AND FIREARMS TRAINING

A study by the Salt Lake City Police Department concerned various information pertaining to the law enforcement shooting incidents. Of particular concern is the finding that a high percentage of officers involved in shootings experienced significant distortions of their perceptual facilities.

More than three fourths of all officers surveyed reported one or more types of distortions during their combat situation. The most frequent distortion was described as experiencing the incident in slow motion. The second most common distortion was the narrowing of visual field, often referred to as "tunnel vision." The failure to hear is still another perceptual distortion, even though reported less frequently.

Additional findings of the Salt Lake City study are important to training. Of the 254 agencies surveyed, 47.2 percent stated they did not conduct survival training. Of those departments which did conduct survival training, only 30 percent did so after the basic academy. Of this remaining 30 percent, more than half used outside resources in conducting the training.

In-service firearms training can not ignore the phenomenon of perceptual distortion as an intricate element of its in-service program. Instruction providing information on the phenomena should be an initial phase of training. Lectures must stress how the reduction of mental ability will limit an officer's effectiveness and ability in a crisis.

The only logical way to recreate the phenomena is to develop extremely realistic and stressful training exercises. Unfortunately, as the previous statistics indicate, few departments provide such training. Take the initiative to recreate survival phenomena such as perceptual distortion.[6]

NIGHTTIME FIREARMS TRAINING

As repeatedly referred to, firearms training must emphasize realism. The fact that the majority of police shoot-outs occur during darkness, yet the majority of firearms training is conducted in daylight, is shameful. Many officers' lives have been lost, in part, due to the failure to provide adequate, realistic, nighttime survival training.

The time worn adage, "as different as night and day," is never more relevant than for firearms training. In-service training must first emphasize the practical differences between a daytime and nighttime shoot-out.

Sufficient opportunity for officers to train in conditions of darkness must follow. The lecture phase should focus upon the following:

1. The physiological response of eyes when coming into darkness from a bright area can be deadly. The common example of walking into a dark warehouse or other structure from bright sunlight can illustrate this phenomenon. The simple, yet effective, technique of turning all the lights off on either an outdoor or indoor range can simulate many hazardous nighttime situations.
2. The proper use of flashlights should be demonstrated. Participation exercises which involve firing in darkness while using a flashlight should be conducted.
3. Instruction and demonstration of the effects of a muzzle flash in darkness is vital. Ammunition actually carried on the street must be used. The expense of using live ammunition as opposed to wad cutters is well worth it, even if additional fund-raising efforts must achieve this capability.
4. Proficiency and accuracy usually decrease during nighttime firing. This is even more complicated due to the difficulty in seeing officers' mistakes. Correction of basic difficulties will usually mean there needs to be more time devoted to correcting the problem. One innovative approach is to use nighttime surveillance equipment to observe officers' firing procedures. An even more elaborate training technique involves a "night scope" attached to the camera lense of a video cassette recorder.
5. Training officers should keep the instructor/shooter ratio much smaller during nighttime firing. A one-on-one training ratio is preferred.
6. Additional concern for overall safety should be instilled prior to every nighttime firing exercise.
7. Every effort should be made to ensure firearms instructors receive specialized training in conducting nighttime classes.

FIREARMS TRAINING REALISM

As eluded to frequently, realism is an essential ingredient for effective training. The merits of realism have become widely known in recent years. The difference between life and death may rest on how effective training has been in developing it.

The benefits of providing realistic firearms training has become so prevalent that the law enforcement training community has been deluged with offers from police product companies to furnish an assortment of training courses and devices. Whether you purchase an already developed firearms-stress course of develop your own, never forget the main objective is to keep officers alive. Flashing lights, sirens, and tape recordings have already been mentioned as simple and effective methods of implementing realism. Additional techniques include scenerios which place officers in common, yet, stressful crisis situations. Lights and sirens are turned on at predetermined times. Tape recordings are synchronized to fit particular moments in each scenerio. Physical exertion such as running or doing deep knee bends prior to participating in firearms training is extremely beneficial. The physiological response of increased heartbeat and breathing rate will create the feeling of an officer having been in foot pursuit or a fight before a shoot-out.

One often overlooked responsibility of training officers and firearms instructors is to teach officers how to cope with such stress. Departmental

Figure 19. Portable windows, walls and assorted obstacles can be inexpensively built. All will add considerable realism.

psychologists or counselors may be of assistance in designing this aspect of a program. If an agency does not have such assistance readily available they should seek it from a nearby university or college. The benefits of learning how to cope with stress are great. Any crisis will be more easily handled once officers learn stress management.

COMBAT EVALUATION

Training officers should not miss the opportunity to evaluate training programs through the investigation of shooting incidents. Trainers should, as soon as practical, interview the officer(s) involved in a shooting. The purpose is to determine any possible weakness in the departmental firearms training program. The interview cannot interfere with an internal investigation, however. Guidelines which may be made into an evaluation form are presented below:

Officer's name____________ Interview Date & Time______________
Date & Time of Incident________________________________
Location of Incident__________________________________
Type of assignment at time of incident____________________
Basic facts known to officer immediately prior to incident
____
____
Description of perpetrator(s)___________________________
____
Brief synopsis of incident______________________________
____
____
Distance from perpetrator______________________________
Number of rounds exchanged by all parties________________
Movement of perpetrator(s)_____________________________
Description of noise and or sound(s)_____________________
____
Description of any available cover_______________________
____
Description of any wounds inflicted______________________
____
Any training recommendations by officer(s) involved
____
____

DEADLY FORCE DECISION MAKING

On March 27, 1985 the United States Supreme Court declared Tennessee's "Fleeing Felon Law" unconstitutional. As a result, some states which permitted the use of deadly force to prevent the escape of fleeing felons simply because they could not be caught have now decided to enact revisions. Training which will assist in making split second deadly force decisions is crucial.

Figure 20. An indoor firearms range offers many advantages. The ease of creating realism is invaluable.

In most areas, the major elements which justified the use of deadly force were the capability of the perpetrator, the opportunity of the perpetrator and the amount of jeopardy conveyed. The failure for any of these elements to be present meant deadly force was not justifiable. Unfortunately, many officers do not receive any deadly force decision making instruction after the basic academy.

The International Association of Law Enforcement Firearms Instructors has an excess of 600 members. The Association has recommended that firearms training be broadened to include the instruction of reasonable force in threatening situations. The use of reasonable force also depends on written departmental policy. Instruction may be provided by a firearms instructor or local attorney. No matter who teaches, it's the training officer's responsibility to see the officers learn it.

FIREARMS TRAINING TIPS

1. Trainers should remember that more than a third of all police shoot-outs involve more than one perpetrator. Training should be conducted so a third to one half of the situations have more than one target.
2. Virtually no shoot-out begins with an officer standing in the "ready position" like some instructors conduct range. Typically, an officer may have a ticket book in one hand or be reaching for an object when he is fired upon. Trainers should train to simulate these situations.
3. Officers should practice drawing and firing their weapon in approximately a second. Perpetrators of police shoot-outs usually initiate the incident, forcing officers to respond instantly.
4. Officers must be required to reload from ammo pouches or speed loaders they use on the street. Never allow extra rounds or any condition which is unrealistic on the range.
5. Some form of incentive should be developed within in-service firearms training. Whether it's a vacation day off or a small bonus pay, those who perform exceptionally well should be rewarded. Incentive and recognition is important to encourage and motivate officers.
6. Regular inspection **prior** to firearms training must always be held. Officers having unclean firearms must be disciplined. The fact that inspection is held prior to training will assist in motivating officers to clean their firearms on a regular basis.[7]

REFERENCES

1. Kenneth J. Matulia, The Use Of Deadly Force: A Need For Written Directives and Training, *The Police Chief,* May 1983, pg. 30–32.
2. National Rifle Association, *NRA Police Firearms Instructor's Manual,* National Rifle Association of America, 1968, pg. 16–18.
3. Bill McLennan, The Shotgun In Police Work, *Law and Order,* September 1982, pg. 16–18.

4. National Rifle Association, *NRA Police Firearms Instructor's Manual: Shotguns and Ammunition*, 1968, pg. 5–6.
5. G. A. Zeiss, Shooting Range Recommendations, *Law and Order*, October 1979, pg. 44–46.
6. Eric Nielsen and Deen Eskridge, Police Shooting Incidents: Implications For Training, *Law and Order*, March 1982, pg. 16–18.
7. J. D. Weller, Firearms Training: Path To Survival, *Law and Order*, October 1982, pg. 24–27.

9.

DRIVING TRAINING

PUTTING THINGS IN PROSPECTIVE

Officer John R. Davis was enroute to "backup" a fellow officer assigned to a shoplifting in-progress at a local shopping center. Officer Davis was a good officer. Though young and fairly inexperienced, he was dedicated, intelligent and had everything it took to do well on the street.

Half way to the shopping center he heard his fellow officer was in foot pursuit of 2 male shoplifters. The emergency lights and sirens were turned on and the speedometer started climbing. That was John's partner and friend out there. He wasn't going to let his partner down. Though traffic was heavy in the business district, he was soon reaching speeds of 60 miles per hour. The speed limit was 30 miles per hour.

With only 2 blocks to the shopping center, John's partner advised that he had lost the suspects. Having only 2 blocks to go, John continued to brake intersections and keep his speed at 60 miles per hour. He'd be there in a second.

Dick Harrison, his wife Ruth and their 2 small sons were approaching the last cross street before the shopping center. Having a green light, the Harrisons entered the intersection. The air conditioner was on, windows rolled up and the radio playing. At the last moment Mr. Harrison heard Officer Davis's emergency siren. It was too late. The patrol vehicle hit the Harrison vehicle at a speed estimated to be forty-five miles per hour. The impact killed Dick Harrison instantly. His wife was left crippled and one of their sons received permanent brain damage.

Nine months after the accident, the Harrison family filed a civil suit. They were ultimately awarded 1.8 million dollars in an out of court settlement. The lack of driving training for Officer Davis was a critical issue of the litigation. In-service driving training for Officer Davis and his fellow officers was non-existent. It was an area of training that had always been neglected. The department had always intended to develop a driving program, yet never quite got around to it.

The story you have just read is fictional. While it did not happen, there are hundreds of similar situations each year. In every instance, the degree of driver training received by the concerned officer becomes the key issue. How will you justify your driving program when such an incident happens in your agency?

The Public Safety Officers' Benefit Program is a federally funded program that authorizes the payment of $50,000 to the survivors of a local or state public safety officer who is killed in the line of duty. A study was conducted from September of 1976 until April, 1983 to analyze different circumstances surrounding the deaths of public safety officers. Two thirds of these officers were law enforcement officials, while the remainder were fire fighters and a few other isolated criminal justice personnel.

As the following table illustrates, 39 percent of the total of 1,365 individuals died as the result of gunshot wounds. The surprising figure, however, is that almost one third of the total number of officers killed died as a result of vehicle use.[1] These statistics are a surprise to most people. Whether the deceased are police officers or not, an incident simply receives more publicity if those involved died from a shoot-out than if their death was caused by an automobile accident.

The law enforcement profession has almost totally neglected the area of driving training. Just as an officer buckles on his gun belt each day, his vehicle can be just as lethal. In the hands of an unskilled driver, a patrol car may become a 4,000 pound projectile. The National Highway Transportation Safety Agency's National Center For Statistics and Analysis report stated there were 54,650 traffic fatalities in 1983. Of this figure, 243 deaths resulted from high speed pursuits with the police.[2]

EXTENT OF POLICE DRIVING TRAINING

The widespread void of driving training is not without reason. Locally, the lack of driving facilities, financial restrictions and manpower shortages are common obstacles. Many administrators feel they just don't have the resources necessary to conduct driving in-service programs. Another frequent problem is the availability of qualified driving instructors. The lack of a suitable location to conduct courses and the expense of vehicle maintenance can be difficult to overcome.

A relatively recent survey was conducted among members of the National Association of State Directors of Law Enforcement Training.

TABLE XIX
LAW ENFORCEMENT OFFICER DEATHS IN LINE OF DUTY
BY OCCUPATION

			Law Enforcement Officers						
Sept. 1976– April 1983	*Total Number*	*Percent*	*All law Enforcement*	*Police*	*Trooper*	*Sheriff*	*Fire Fighter*	*Corrections*	*Other*
Total	1,365	100.0	903	616	106	181	391	47	24
Cause of Death									
Gunshots	535	39.2	512	367	47	98	5	11	7
Vehicle related	444	32.5	324	198	57	69	108	3	9
Fire scene	228	16.7	0	0	0	0	226	0	2
Other	158	11.6	21	5	2	14	52	33	6
Marital Status									
Married	1,248	91.4	822	551	102	169	360	43	23
Divorced	65	5.2	49	37	3	9	14	2	0
Single	52	3.8	32	28	1	3	17	2	1
Sex									
Male	1,352	99.0	892	607	105	180	390	46	24
Female	13	1.0	11	9	1	1	1	1	0
Average Age	37.1		35.7	35.6	39.1	34.9	44.1	37.1	42.4

Source: U.S. Department of Justice

This nationwide survey places the extent of law enforcement driver training in perspective. The survey indicated:

1. **None** of the responding 30 states require any retraining or requalification of officers for **any** form of driving training.
2. Five of the 30 states had absolutely no driver training requirements of any form.
3. Recruit academy driving training averaged 19.5 hours, with a low of 1 hour and a high of 56 hours.
4. Almost half of those participating in the survey felt pursuit driving training in American law enforcement was virtually "non-existent."[3]

In June of 1985, **The Washington Crime News Services**, through their publications, **The Crime Control Digest, Criminal Justice Digest**, and **Training Aids Digest**, combined forces with the National Association of State Directors of Law Enforcement Training. The purpose of this united effort was to conduct a nationwide study of the extent of law enforcement driving training. Unlike the aforementioned survey, this study focused

Figure 21. Driving training is one of the most needed, yet, neglected in-service training areas.

on separate agencies as opposed to state requirements. Response to the study was tremendous. Agencies throughout 25 states, having an average number of 354 sworn personnel, participated. Twenty-seven percent of those responding represented state agencies, 7 percent were county agencies and 66 percent were local departments. Twenty percent of the agencies participating in the study used a community college for driving training. Twenty-four percent used a state training facility. The remaining 34 percent provided training within their own agency.

Results of the study substantiated the claim that law enforcement was in desperate need of driver training improvement.

1. Ninety percent stated they were dissatisfied with the pursuit driver training within their agency.
2. Thirty-one percent advised their department did have some form of annual retraining or requalification in defensive driving. Twenty-four percent offered annual retraining for emergency driving, while 17 percent provided it for pursuit driving.
3. Ninety-five percent of the agencies stated the police academy in their area provided some form of driver training.

4. Approximately half advised their area academy training included emergency driving, pursuit driving and defensive driving. The other half noted their academy did not provide pursuit driving, but did include emergency and defense driving.
5. Approximately 75 percent of the agencies stated they had achieved some degree of emergency and defense driving training within their department.
6. Only 40 percent of the participating departments advised they had achieved proficiency in the area of pursuit driver training.[4]

It would appear to be a safe assumption that the agencies which responded to the study tend to be leaders within the field of driving training. It also appears logical that departments which provide driving training would be most likely to reply to such a study. If this conclusion is correct, law enforcement driving training in America may be considerably worse than the study indicates.

IS DRIVING TRAINING DIFFICULT TO ACCOMPLISH?

There is no doubt that we as a profession, fail to adequately train the skill of driving. No other profession requires that an employee risk his or her life in a vehicular pursuit. In addition, the potential for danger is present whether the situation is a pursuit or routine, daily driving.

Training officers can no longer ignore the lack of driving training. We owe it to our profession, our fellow officers and ourselves to develop effective in-service programs. When that task is accomplished, most will find it was surprisingly simple.

Justifying Your Program

One initial concern in developing a driving program is in obtaining approval and support from administrators. Information provided thus far certainly establishes the need for such training. Careful preparation and planning should be a prelude to any written or oral presentation. All topics of concern must be addressed.

The area of most concern to many administrators is the cost of the program. Administrators and trainers may be surprised to know driving training can be very cost effective—so much so that trainers should use the prospect of financial gain as a major justification point. For ease of preparation, an outline of justification points is presented below:

1. The primary reason to develop an effective police driving program is that it save lives. Whether the lives saved are law enforcement officers or innocent citizens, training is essential to the protection of life.
2. As previously noted by various statistical data, the training of driving skills has been terribly neglected.
3. Insurance premiums can be substantially reduced by the implementation of driving training.
4. The potential of civil liability without regular driving training is astronomical. A single traffic accident may result in a multi-million dollar judgement against the agency and its governmental body.
5. A law enforcement agency has a moral responsibility to train for dangerous situations.
6. The cost of damage to vehicles or other property resulting from traffic accidents is often substantial.
7. The loss of officers' wages due to injuries resulting from traffic accidents can be substantial.
8. Loss of man power due to traffic accident injuries are detrimental to an agency.
9. Officers want to be professional. Providing quality training that had been neglected will result in improved morale.

Obtaining interdepartmental approvals and authorizations to implement the program can be extremely frustrating. Training officers must be optimistic and persevering. If you are determined not to give up, the likelihood of success is great.

DRIVING TRAINING EXPENSES

The extent to which agencies allocate funds for driving training usually depends upon available funding. While large agencies may have the necessary funds to build an elaborate driving track, these situations are rare. The vast majority of law enforcement agencies in America have less than 15 officers. Most agencies will never be able to afford such an undertaking.

For all practical purposes, this chapter will assume virtually no funding is available for driving training. It remains a fairly safe assumption that if a trainer can implement an effective driving program without needing substantial funding, the program will be approved. The following are examples which demonstrate how the development of a program can be virtually cost free.

- Building a $500,000 driving course is fine if the money is available, yet you don't need to spend a penny. Almost all jurisdictions have locations which may be used. Acquiring approval for a large parking lot, airport facility, privately owned race track or other large paved areas will serve the purpose.
  Acquiring a location for high speed driving should be sought, yet is not essential. A "skid pan" area will allow officers to experience handling high speed skids even though they are only travelling at 10 miles per hour. A skid pan is merely a hard surface which has water, oil or some other slippery substance.
- If a large parking lot has been acquired, the use of cones can afford an endless array of driving courses. A beneficial selection of courses will be examined further in this chapter.
- One initial phase of training can be accomplished with virtually no equipment. A lecture covering departmental policy, state statutes, or other restrictions and guidelines pertaining to driving, should be instructed. Topics of personal liability, driving physics and techniques of driving cannot be overlooked.
- Because the majority of driving training is "hands-on experience," an instructor/student ratio no larger than 1 to 3 is necessary. This is not necessarily bad because it often allows training to be conducted while officers are on duty. Manpower restrictions are acceptable as a result.
- The frequent administrative concern of overtime expenses is of little concern because training is held while officers are on duty.
- No agency needs to purchase a vehicle solely for driving training. Simply select a used patrol vehicle which was about to be sold. Ideally, the vehicle should be equipped with a roll bar and heavy duty steel rims. Seat belts with a shoulder harness and safety helmets must always be worn. Heavy duty steel enforced rims are also recommended.[5]
  Determining the exact expense required for driving training is difficult. A great deal depends on how successful trainers and instructors are at obtaining the aforementioned equipment. Developing

Figure 22. While various expenses often prohibit driving training, they can be overcome. As an example, the lack of a driving track can be solved through the use of large, local parking lots.

and implementing a high stress/low speed program, as opposed to a high speed program will mean less vehicle repairs and maintenance. Additional ideas include a publicity oriented fund-raising drive and combining the efforts of several local agencies to develop one driving training facility which they may all use.

DEVELOPING A DRIVING PROGRAM

An in-service driving program should train officers to be capable of avoiding vehicular accidents. It should also introduce them to a variety of driving concepts which will develop driving skills. Implementing a series of practical exercises designed to train officers to use vehicles in the most efficient manner must be stressed. A developmental design allowing for the instruction of accident avoidance techniques and the acquisition of efficient vehicular operation skills must be of utmost importance.

Instructor Selection

The selection of driving instructors should be an initial consideration. Following selection, a substantial length of time may be needed to have instructors undergo extensive training at a driving instructor certification school. While driving instructor training is not offered in many communities, it can always be located. An easy source of reference is your area police academy. Academy instructors can provide you with details regarding their own training.

The selection of instructors within your agency will be crucial to the program's success. They must possess not only teaching abilities, but be skilled in driving as well. Those who lack creditability and a high reputation among their peers should not be selected. Sound communication skills, intelligence, and maturity are important qualities.

PUTTING CLASSROOM TRAINING IN PERSPECTIVE

Most trainers view in-service driving training as a "behind the wheel" program designed to afford officers with knowledge and skills sufficient to safeguard themselves and others. There is no doubt that active student participation is the best way to learn virtually any topic. In addition, the actual driving is what officers look forward to and expect from the course. This view can prove to be a deadly assumption.

Basic firearms instruction involves hours of actual handgun firing. While this is proper, vital classroom training preceded the "hands-on" practice. Just as with firearms, officers can't be assigned to the driving track without an understanding of what they should do. There are many important issues to be addressed.

Among the topics applicable to a classroom setting are:

- the importance and need for driving training
- what is expected of officers during the course
- an explanation of the course agenda
- administering a pretest
- instruction on state statutes pertaining to police driving
- a discussion of pertinent departmental standard operating procedures
- conducting a vehicle operation inspection
- basic driving techniques
- the psychology of pursuit
- accident avoidance

Most instructors will find the aforementioned topics require approximately eight hours of classroom time. The decision to select 1 full day, 2 four hour sessions or another allocation of time is a matter of discretion. As with any lecture, a 15 minute break should be allowed each hour.

TRAINING AIDS

Organization, pre-planning and preparedness are key ingredients when developing any training program. Giving attention to the effective use of training aids during the initial stages of development is a sign of professionalism. Though most agencies are forced to use whatever facilities are available, ensuring a comfortable and quiet setting is essential.

Basic instructional aids such as a chalkboard, opaque projector, overhead projector and 16 mm projector must be available. Visual aids enhance the effectiveness of teaching. Learning is made easier by using visual examples of verbal instruction. Many quality movies and video cassettes regarding police driving are available. Several major media producers offer media on a "trial rental basis" for very nominal fees. Trainers may be surprised to know that the insurance carrier which covers their vehicular liability would probably purchase them driving training films or video tapes, if asked to.

Another form of pre-planning is the preparation of handouts. Officers should be furnished with copies of departmental standard operating procedures, state statutes pertaining to police driving, diagrams of upcoming driving tracks, a variety of case law and a glossary of driving related terms.

COURSE INTRODUCTION

Development of a course introduction must be included in the course opening. It is particularly important if the course is new and officers are unsure of what to expect. Forty-five minutes is usually sufficient time to convey a thorough orientation of the program.

The introduction should begin with a presentation of the current "state of the art" of police driving training. Facts and figures must adequately impress upon officers that a desperate need for training exists. A synopsis of the civil and criminal legal consequences to officers for the failure of safe driving must be stressed. A course agenda should be distributed and explained. Attendance should be documented and any other administrative paperwork completed.

PRETEST

The value of administering a pretest prior to instruction of a training course is often underestimated by training officers. The failure to administer such tests are frequently the result of not understanding their value and appreciating the benefits. All trainers are concerned with the effectiveness of their training programs. In practical terms, it is virtually impossible to determine the benefits of a program if you don't know the degree of knowledge and/or skill possessed by officers prior to the course.

Thorough documentation is essential for contemporary law enforcement training. Record keeping of driving training is no exception. What may seem insignificant to you now, could be invaluable next year. Administering a pretest at the beginning of a course, followed by a similar test at its conclusion, will document officers learned vital knowledge and skills. Without doing so there is no way to know how much they learned. There will be little you can do to prove during future civil proceedings that a particular officer learned anything during his in-service training.

A pretest is not difficult to develop and is easy to administer. Review the lesson plan you have developed. Write a series of true/false or multiple choice questions which adequately cover all essential topic areas. Do not provide officers with answers to the pretest until completion of the course. Doing so may jeopardize the creditability of the final examination. The same test may be used for both pretest and the final examination. After grading both examinations, distribute both pretest and the final examination to officers. Conduct a thorough explanation of the test to allow them to see their improvement. This technique should also assist to inspire, motivate and provide a feeling that the course was worthwhile.

DRIVING REGULATIONS

It is the trainer's responsibility to see that officers learn what authority and regulations govern the operation of emergency vehicles. State statutes and interdepartmental general orders or standard operating procedures must be thoroughly comprehended. There are 3 types of regulations to be instructed:

1. State statutes regulating the use of motor vehicles.
2. Local ordinances.
3. Departmental policy.

State statutes regarding law enforcement driving regulations vary. Of particular interest to officers are the exemptions pertaining to emergency vehicle operators and when emergency operation is allowed. Generally, emergencies exist when there is significant potential for property loss and/or high probability of severe injury or death. Instruction must stress that departmental superiors and any possible judicial proceedings will judge whether a situation was a true emergency and if due regard was displayed for the safety of others.

Instruction must emphasize that law enforcement agencies are being sued for careless or improper driving more than at any time in our nation's history. The last few decades have seen a steady erosion of the doctrine of sovereign immunity, which prohibited suits against governmental entities. In addition, a United States Supreme Court ruling now allows citizens to file suit against local governments for violations of civil rights. The number of civil litigations brought against police departments for negligent actions has been rising steadily in state court.

In March 1983, a federal district court awarded Alvin B. Biscoe, Jr. and his wife, 5 million dollars in compensatory damages. The case concerned a high speed pursuit in Washington, D.C. during September of 1979. Mr. Biscoe lost both his legs when hit by a car involved in the high speed chase. He had been waiting to cross a street in downtown Washington.

While the case of Biscoe versus Arlington County resulted in the largest monetary award in history against a police department for actions concerning a high speed pursuit, the feeling that police departments are "easy game" for civil suits is now prevalent. If officers used negligence during pursuits twenty or thirty years ago, there were usually no repercussions. Contemporary law enforcement finds itself under close scrutiny for any property damage or bodily injury resulting from the operation of a vehicle.[6] As always, officers must understand and respect the legal climate in which their profession exists.

Classroom instruction must not only discuss how to use a motor vehicle, but when to engage in high speed driving as well. Police pursuit driving is rapidly becoming rare. Departmental policy should dictate that it be allowed only in extreme situations. Standard operating procedures must also specify when high speed driving should be cut off. There are few situations which justify driving at excessive rates of speed. In the Biscoe versus Arlington County case, for instance, a police helicopter was also engaged in the pursuit. If the police vehicle had pulled off, the helicopter could have continued, thus lessening the danger to innocent bystanders.

Richard H. Turner, founder and chairman of the National Academy For Professional Driving states "Police pursuit is a dinosaur. Ninety percent of the time, the pursuit is not undertaken for any kind of hard crime. Nine out of ten pursuits are for a traffic violation of one sort or another. What we have here is a situation where the state of the art for apprehension has to improve."

Training officers must take the initiative to see that proper driving policies are implemented. Training based on sound driving techniques and departmental policy must be regular, consistent, and thorough. Confront officers with whether they had ever continued a pursuit because of the "he ain't going to get away from me attitude." Take advantage of the classroom setting for re-evaluation of previous ways of thinking and implementing new, improved attitudes.

VEHICLE INSPECTION

The importance of officers thoroughly understanding the assortment of vehicle equipment must be stressed. They should be able to properly operate all equipment and comprehend its importance to the vehicle's safe operation. A patrol vehicle is to be inspected prior to every tour of duty. The inspection should include observing all sides of the vehicle for physical damage, brief observations under the vehicle and inside the hood and various equipment. Noticing how it operates while in motion is also important.

Determining when and if a vehicle is unsafe is the responsibility of the officer about to use it. Inspections to be completed before and during a patrol vehicle's operation include:

1. Check the windows, mirrors and windshield for adequate cleaniness.
2. Check the windshield wipers for proper working condition.

3. Check the brakes for proper operation.
4. Check the siren, emergency lights and horn for proper operation.
5. Check all lighting equipment.
6. Check the shotgun for proper operating preparedness.
7. Check the trunk for proper emergency equipment.
8. Check the rear seat area for any weapons which may have been left by a prisoner prior to your tour of duty.

BASIC DRIVING TECHNIQUES

The various factors which influence vehicle operation and control are usually taken for granted by officers. Understanding the wide array of factors affecting vehicular operation will result in a more knowledgeable and effective driver. The most influential forces controlling a vehicle are centrifugal force, inertia, momentum and friction. Instructors should explain how each of these can affect the operation of a vehicle.

The related topics of proper acceleration, braking, weight transfer and hydroplaning should also be explained. Such phenomena is important to understand prior to vehicle operation. Failure to comprehend them can result in a collision. The driving procedures that most frequently result in collisions are right of way violations, parking, turning left and backing.

The daily operation of a vehicle can become very routine and uneventful. Driving can become so complacent that little thought is given to proper technique. Some common mistakes which result in collisions include:

1. Changing directions too quickly.
2. Accelerating too fast.
3. Improper braking.
4. Driving faster than proper road, weather, or tire conditions permit.
5. Driving too fast around a curve.

Nighttime driving presents unique and often dangerous driving conditions. Officers must appreciate the dangers involved. The overriding point to be stressed by the instructor is that a higher level of caution must be carried out during hours of darkness. Some of the more dangerous aspects of nighttime driving include:

1. The presence of an increased number of drunk drivers.
2. Lessened visibility.
3. Presence of an increased number of tired drivers.

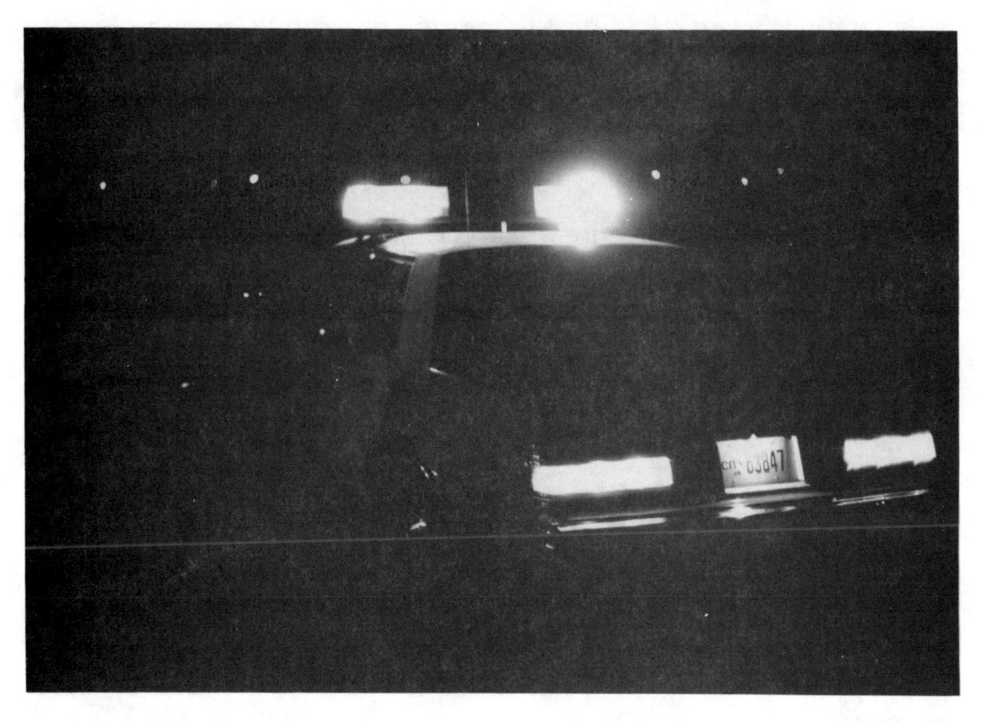

Figure 23. In-service driving training remains scarce. Nighttime driving training is even rarer, yet, the need remains high.

Pursuit Driving Techniques

All officers understand what a vehicular pursuit is. Yet, it's ironic that the belief that they "understand," is what so often results in tragedy. The fact is; most police officers don't understand the multifaceted concepts of vehicular pursuits. This is demonstrated by the simple fact that if they did, there would not be so many of them.

The mentality of the past has been very simple; if the vehicle tries to get away, you catch it. At first glance this appears to be a very unprofessional, ignorant and immature attitude. The truth is, that's exactly what it is. Yet, officers themselves are not the only ones at fault. The law enforcement training community has also been unprofessional. Training, for the most part, has simply ignored the area of driving. If an officer has never received in-service driving training, how can we expect him to act in a professional manner?

A professional manner includes a quick examination of numerous considerations when deciding whether to engage in a pursuit. Such an examination provides officers with the proper answer as opposed to the "he ain't getting away from me" type of logic. For the process to be effective, training must also be effective. Officers must be trained to the extent they will automatically consider the following factors:

- The severity of the offense which occupants of the vehicle are wanted for.
- The amount of evidence on the occupants of the vehicle which committed the offense.
- The likelihood that the occupants can be apprehended at a later date.
- The amount of traffic.
- The amount of pedestrian traffic.
- The weather conditions.
- Condition and type of roadway.
- The officer's driving skill.
- Condition of the police vehicle.
- The likelihood of the perpetrators being apprehended by other police units.
- Speed and danger involved in the pursuit.
- State statutes.
- Application of aforementioned considerations to your agency's pursuit driving policy.[7]

A series of actions must immediately be carried out if a pursuit is engaged. These immediate actions include acknowledging to shift supervisors, fellow officers and the communications section you are in pursuit. Extreme care must be taken, as this is done while engaged in the pursuit. This initial information will help to ensure the officer's safety in the event of his injury. It will also be helpful to the shift supervisor while he decides whether to terminate the pursuit. The initial information should include:

1. Acknowledgement of being in pursuit.
2. Location and direction of travel.
3. Description of vehicle.
4. Reason for pursuit.
5. Description or other information regarding occupants.

There are many techniques to be employed by officers in pursuit. They should be instructed in a classroom and demonstrated, when practical, on the driving range. While the following guidelines will be useful for developing a lesson plan, reviewing them in class will generate group discussion. Such guidelines include:

1. Immediately roll your window up. Failure to do this may prevent other officers from understanding your radio transmissions due to your sirens.
2. No more than two police vehicles should become involved in the actual pursuit.
3. All other officers should be instructed to stay abreast of the pursuit's progress.
4. Dispatchers must be instructed to keep surrounding law enforcement agencies informed of the pursuit in the event it travels into their jurisdiction.
5. Pursuing officers should not attempt to overtake the fleeing vehicle. Instead, their purpose is to keep the suspect's vehicle in sight until it voluntarily stops.
6. Officers should be instructed to never shoot from a moving vehicle.
7. Instruction should include not to ram the fleeing vehicle with a police vehicle.[8]
8. Headlights, emergency lights and sirens must be operating any time an officer is in pursuit.
9. Officers should be trained for the unexpected actions of unaware citizens in vehicles and pedestrians.
10. Officers must expect the unexpected.
11. Circumstances which justify a vehicular pursuit are rare. Even when a pursuit is warranted, the officer's safety and that of innocent citizens must always be compared with the need to apprehend the violator.
12. When travelling at excessive speeds during a pursuit, the pursuing police vehicle should remain several hundred feet behind the fleeing vehicle.
13. All braking when "taking a curve" should be done prior to entry into the curve.
14. If, while taking a curve, the rear wheels begin to slide, it is best to steer in the direction of the slide and accelerate slightly to regain traction.[9]

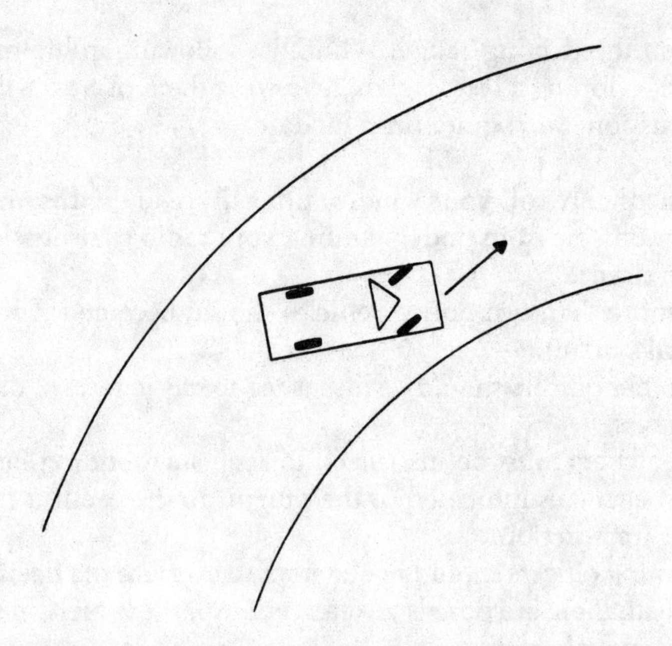

Figure 24. This illustration shows a vehicle starting to slide sideways. Officers must learn to discontinue breaking and turn the front wheels in the direction you want to go.

THE PSYCHOLOGY OF PURSUIT

Pursuit driving creates both mental and physiological reactions within an officer. Understanding them will be a tremendous asset for the officer. A lack of understanding will result in an increased probability he will make errors in judgement.

Instruction should include the physiological aspects to high levels of stress. Engaging in pursuit creates a series of automatic physiological changes. One of the first reactions is a constriction of blood vessels. This constriction results in a lessening of blood flow to the brain. A restricted blood flow results in less oxygen provided to the brain. The brain signals the heart and lungs to work harder in their efforts to provide blood flow and oxygen.

The heart beating stronger and faster, along with deeper breaths are obvious reactions to stress. A much less noticeable, yet much more dangerous, physiological reaction is the lessened ability of the brain to function. The decrease in oxygen to the brain will hamper the ability to think. An obvious example of this phenomena is when a person faints

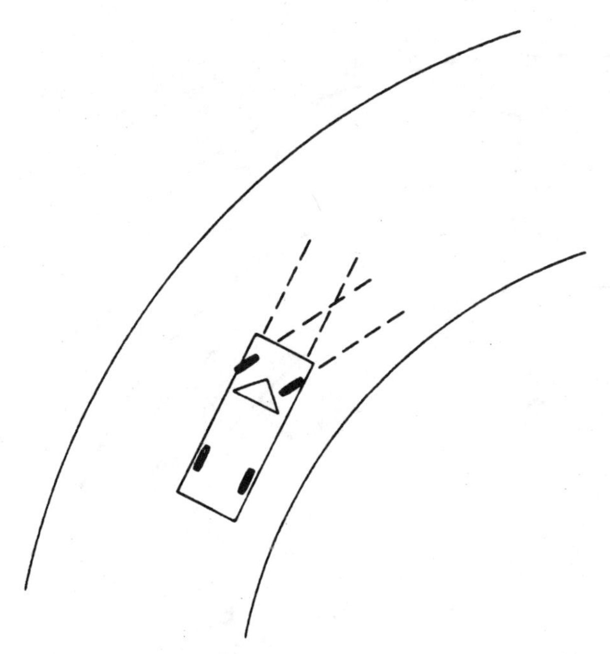

Figure 25. Though the front wheels of this vehicle are turned, the momentum is greater than the wheel's traction. Thus, the vehicle begins to slide.

during a crisis. Officers must understand this is a natural reaction and compensate by remaining as calm as possible.

Lastly, the fact that some officers allow a pursuit to become a personal vendetta must cease. This is significant enough to warrant additional reinforcement. Officers must be cautioned against allowing their ego to do battle with their logic. They must forget their personal feelings and think about all aspects of the pursuit. If an officer feels he is driving in excess of his capabilities he should simply slow down. No pursuit is worth his life.[10]

Accident Avoidance

The highest priority during a pursuit is the preservation of life. All other considerations are secondary. Where serious injury or death resulted from a police pursuit, this fact usually became secondary to another consideration or it was simply forgotten. An officer can not afford the luxury of allowing his emotions to override his intelligence.

When in pursuit, officers should follow the fleeing vehicle at a distance of five to seven car lengths. Staying two and a half to three feet to

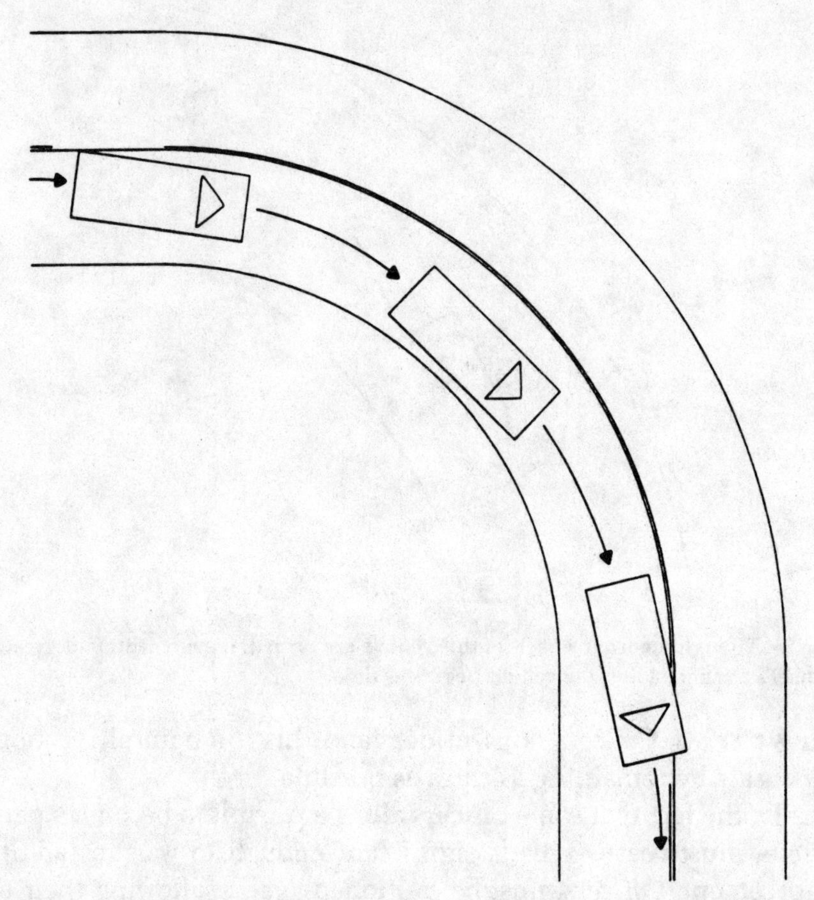

Figure 26. Train officers to take a curve in a single, smooth motion. If they are travelling too fast, braking must be done before turning begins.

the left of center behind the fleeing vehicle will provide several advantages:

1. This position allows the officer to see all 4 tires. Because reaction times of fractions of a second may make the difference between life and death, seeing the front tires turn give the officer a few moments of extra notice.
2. This position provides a clearer view of the road ahead.
3. This position will furnish oncoming traffic with more notice that a pursuit is headed their direction.
4. More effectively alerting oncoming traffic should result in the officer having more room to drive and reduce the danger to all concerned.

Obviously, of utmost concern is the avoidance of an accident. The key factor in avoiding an accident is to steer through the situation, rather than to "slam" on the brakes. There's a greater chance of success through steering control than skidding. In addition, if an accident does occur, there is a greater probability of injury if the driver is applying the brakes. Such a driver's body is rigid, thus absorbing the entire force of the crash.

The most deadly type of accident is a head-on collision. When a head-on accident occurs the force from both vehicles are directly transmitted in a straight line to the occupants. A very high percentage of deaths occur in head-on collisions. If a serious collision appears eminent, lie down on the seat, turn the steering wheel left and grab the bottom of the seat. This will expose the right front corner to the oncoming vehicle and provide the greatest amount of safety to the officer.

Whether the approaching object is an oncoming vehicle or a stationary structure, time will usually permit an officer to take defensive action to prevent a head-on collision. The most affective action is to change the direction of impact from head-on to a glancing blow. This is relatively simple if the object is stationary, such as a wall. If the object is an oncoming vehicle, keep in mind that most drivers will instinctively turn to the right. Finally, classroom instruction should include the effects of various surfaces on driving. Concrete is very rigid and will not give under the weight of a vehicle. It is very stable, predictable, and the easiest to drive on. Asphalt, on the other hand, never completely hardens. Nearly all asphalt surfaces are slippery shortly after it starts to rain. This is caused by oil floating on the water.

A very dangerous phenomena known as hydoplaning should also be taught. The phenomena occurs when a tire, travelling at a relatively high rate of speed, does not have time to push away water that has accumulated on the roadway. Instead, the rain is trapped under and immediately ahead of the tire. Thus, the tire is actually riding on a thin layer of water as opposed to the roadway. The probability of hydroplaning increases with the amount of tread exposed to the water at the point of contact, the total width of the tire tread and the speed of the vehicle.[11]

THE DRIVING COURSE

The final phase of the classroom instruction should be a brief summary of what officers can expect on the driving range. They should be advised that the objective of their participation is to develop an ability to

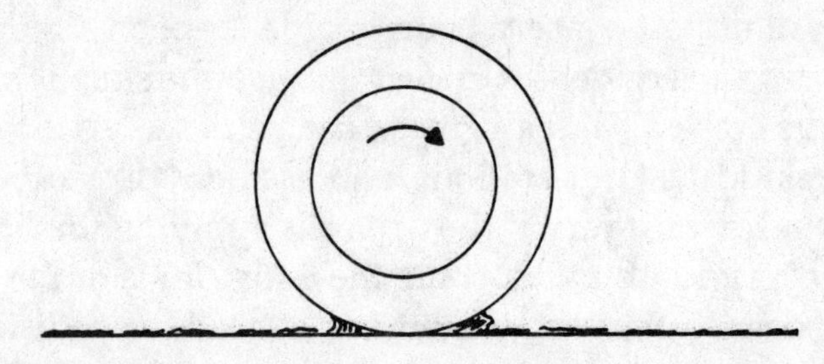

Figure 27. Asphalt roadways are extremely slippery after rain first starts. This is due to a mixture of water and oil forming on the surface. As a tire rolls across water, the water is moved out of the way.

Figure 28. This picture illustrates how a fast moving tire actually leaves the roadway and travels on a thin layer of water. The phenomenon is referred to as hydroplaning.

operate the vehicle safely and effectively. Emphasis will be placed on alertness, driving smoothness, and control of the vehicle. Principles learned in the classroom setting will be applied to the driving track. The techniques of acceleration, road position, braking, steering, turning, backing, low speed versus high speed driving, and practicing quick reaction will be applied.

Rigid safety rules must be developed and explained to participants, then strictly enforced. A minimum set of rules should include:

1. No "kidding around" will be allowed at any time.
2. Any occupant of a vehicle must wear seat belts.
3. Any vehicle that malfunctions must be immediately reported to the instructor.
4. Do not take any action unless instructed to do so by the instructor.

The recommended length of the course is 8 hours. Even though the instructor's certification course will have adequately prepared your driving instructors to proficiently carry out this phase, the following tips should assist him.

The following exercises should maximize the affectiveness of your program. Instructors are cautioned to "set up" the exercises in advance so they may test them. Failure to do so may result in the instructor being unable to pass the exercise, thus discrediting the entire program.

Slalom

The slalom exercise provides training in proper steering techniques and cornering. It demonstrates the importance of smoothness of hand movements, weight positioning and body restraints.

Skid Pan

The skid pan is an area covered with a slippery surface. It provides the opportunity for officers to practice skid control and hydroplaning. The simulation of high speed steering techniques may be accomplished while driving at slow speeds.

Backing Exercise

A backing exercise is very important since many police accidents occur while backing. An exercise which includes turning within a confined area at slow and high speeds is most beneficial. The limitations in steering and braking control during backing should be illustrated.

Emergency Lane Change

The emergency lane change exercise is intended to develop skills needed for avoiding collisions with unexpected objects. Steering, braking, acceleration, quickness of reaction, road position, turning, and judgement are emphasized.

Curve Negotiation Exercise

This exercise teaches proper braking, vehicle control, curve approach and negotiation.

Control Braking Exercise

This exercise is intended to train officers in the proper principles of controlled braking.[12]

REFERENCES

1. Annesley K. Schmidt, *Deaths In The Line Of Duty,* National Institute of Justice, U. S. Department of Justice, January 1985, pg. 6–7.
2. G. Patrick Gallagher, Lethal Force On Wheels: What Can Trainers Do, *Training Aids Digest,* Washington Crime News Service, October 1985, pg. 2.
3. G. Patrick Gallagher, Lethal Force On Wheels: What Can Trainers Do, *Training Aids Digest,* Washington Crime News Service, October 1985, pg. 3.
4. G. Patrick Gallagher, In Pursuit Of Pursuit Driver Training: What Our Survey Found, *Training Aids Digest,* Washington Crime News Services, September 1985, pg. 2.
5. James J. Barron and Steven L. Aurilio, Driver Training For Your Department? *F.B.I. Law Enforcement Bulletin,* October 1981, pg. 1–5.
6. Emily Couric, Police Use of Cars, Firearms. Spark Suits, Reprinted from the *National Law Journal,* The Thin Blue Line, September 1985, pg. 20.
7. E. W. Jones, *Police Pursuit Driving,* North Carolina Department of Motor Vehicles, 1967, pg. 11–35.
8. Lively Police Academy, *Student Training Manual,* Lively Area Vo-Tech, Florida, 1983.
9. E. W. Jones, *Police Pursuit Driving,* North Carolina Department of Motor Vehicles, 1967, pg. 20–35.
10. Richard H. Turner and Carl R. Headen, *Mental and Physical Aspects of Tactical Police Driving,* National Academy For Police Driving, 1976, pg. 11–14.
11. Richard H. Turner and Carl R. Headon, *Mental and Physical Aspects of Tactical Police Driving,* National Academy For Police Driving, 1976, pg. 38–49.
12. Central Florida Criminal Justice Regional Training Center, *Collision Avoidance Training Manual,* Orange County Sheriff's Office, Orlando, Florida.

10.

STRESS MANAGEMENT TRAINING

To exclaim that law enforcement is stressful is nothing new. Virtually all training officers agree that many aspects of police work create harmful stress. Numerous studies have indicated most officers work within a stressful environment. Unfortunately, many officers are abandoned by their agencies when it comes to coping with the effects of stress. In-service stress management programs are relatively rare. When an agency doesn't furnish officers with the tools necessary to cope, the agency is negligent—both professionally and morally. Bullets are not the only thing that can kill an officer.

POLICE STRESS

Any veteran officer has seen fellow officers incapacitated by health problems. Alcoholism, heart attacks, suicide, mental depression, back problems, ulcers, headaches, and a variety of stress related difficulties take a heavy toll each year. Most officers agree that the effects of job related stress can put their health in jeopardy.

The negative effects of stress seem ironic. Almost all departments have medical and fitness related employment standards. Compared to other occupations, police hiring standards are high. These requirements for employment result in newly appointed officers being healthy and fit. The irony is that these same officers are often riddled with health problems as their career ends. Year after year of job related stress gradually takes its toll.

Statistics indicate career police officers die younger than most occupational groups. They also suffer particularly high instances of health difficulty. Researchers of occupational hazards continually conclude stress is the fundamental debilitation factor in law enforcement.[1]

CAUSE OF STRESS

Police officers experience stress for the same reasons the rest of society does. Life's daily activities always seem to go astray; traffic is at its worst when you're in a hurry, unexpected bills always pile up, personality conflicts get you down, and there just aren't enough hours in the day to get everything done. No one ever said life was going to be fair, yet, life's endless problems create tremendous stress.

Day to day frustrations and irritations can gradually become a major source of stress. In addition, traumatic events such as the death of a loved one, divorce, or serious financial troubles may become overwhelming.

Detrimental situations like those previously referred to are what most people consider the causes of stress. Though not frequently associated with stress, positive events may also be a cause. Moving into a new home, a marriage, changing jobs, being promoted, or even receiving a high honor will create pressure within the concerned individual.

The very nature of law enforcement places officers in stressful situations. While the typical citizen only has to deal with life's daily irritations, an officer must also contend with the pressure of the street. Responding to traffic accidents with injuries, fights in progress, various medical emergencies, robbery or burglary alarms, and the vast assortment of other "hot calls" take a high toll. The frustration of the criminal justice system's inadequacies must be faced as well. Only an officer sees the victims of brutal crimes. Only the officer feels the frustration as the offenders of those crimes are repeatedly set free.

THE EFFECTS OF STRESS

If officers are not taught how to effectively manage stress, the effects of stress will manage them. It may severly effect their attitude, performance, mental health, and physical ability. The intensity of the effects depend upon a variety of factors. Teaching them how to control their response to stress, enhance problem solving techniques, and reduce stress levels can combat harmful stress.

Headaches, nausea, back problems, high blood pressure, ulcers, muscle tension, and a variety of other physical symptoms are frequently linked to stress. Emotional reactions such as anger, depression, anxiety, irrational fears, loss of sleep, difficulty in concentrating, and relating to others are common. Unusual eating habits, sexual promiscuity, alcoholism, drug abuse, self-defeatist attitude, abnormal eating habits, and withdrawing from people are occasional symptoms.[2] The effects of stress are difficult to accurately determine because so many officers refuse to acknowledge they are having a problem. Some facts can be determined, however. In 1976, 1,500 of New York City's 25,000 officers were officially examined by a psychiatrist, alcoholism counselor or psychologist. Two thirds of those examined were forced to do so. All showed signs of emotional difficulty.[3]

Most officers who experience even mild effects of stress do not perform to the best of their capabilities. Low morale, high absenteeism, decreased productivity, and a variety of disciplinary problems often result. Police agencies face losses not only in productivity but higher medical insurance rates, increased civil litigation, increased overtime pay, and a decline in community relations. An unusually high rate of suicide, alcoholism, and divorce among law enforcement is well documented.

RECOGNITION THAT STRESS EXISTS

Prior to the 70's, there was relatively little recognition of stress or its affects. Only in recent years have law enforcement agencies come to realize its importance. Even today, many officers refuse to accept that stress management is a necessary tool.

Those who ignore the effects of stress are becoming a minority. The last decade has seen an increased willingness to shed the superficial macho image and recognize the emotional pressures of policing.

A large percentage of the increased stress recognition has resulted from sociological, psychiatric, and psychological research. The increase of interest among researchers and their improvement in detection and measurement techniques has played an important role in the recognition. A considerable amount of attention has been directed toward the detrimental effects of stress as a result of research notoriety.

Increased recognition and attention has also resulted from the recognition that employee productivity is negatively affected. Both the corporate world and law enforcement has been stunned to learn how detrimental stress can be. Increased absenteeism, decreased productivity, emotional disturbances, increased civil liability, and low morale are typical results of stress. An urgent plea for the development of a stress management program is now frequently heard.[2]

BASIC STRESS MANAGEMENT

The recommended procedure for establishing a stress management program is to retain the services of a psychiatrist, psychologist or qualified psychotherapist and/or counselor. The ability of a highly educated individual will permit a variety of useful in-service training programs. Trainers are cautioned against attempting any form of counseling or psychotherapy themselves.

No matter what his or her credentials, a departmental counselor can provide an agency with 2 crucial ingredients: stress management training and confidential counseling of employees. Developing this 2 pronged approach to stress management will provide a very stable foundation on which a program may be erected.

Training is generally considered as the first and most important step in stress management.[4] To be effective, it must encompass a variety of prospectives. The most frequent approach is to concentrate on teaching officers to recognize symptoms and dangers. A less common but equally important responsibility is to focus on the internal organization and supervisory practices which may create stress among employees.

Trainers themselves must understand the basic physiological responses to stress. Management programs should concentrate on both short term and long term stress. The average citizen may experience a handful of high stress situations in a lifetime. A police officer, however, can encounter situations such as a pursuit, fight, or other high stress situations several times a week. The body will undergo many physiological reactions during these incidents.

Long term stress can result from a single unresolved high stress incident or a continuous series of relatively minor pressures. Left without proper management, the affects of long term stress are likely to become serious. The need for treatment of a single traumatic incident is relatively obvious. The need for treatment of less obvious daily pressures may go undetected without proper training. Training should emphasize both procedures to recognize various forms of negative stress and techniques for properly managing it.

STRESS RECOGNITION TRAINING

Training to recognize the warning signs of stress and the impact which may result from ignoring them must not be ignored. Officers should learn how to examine their personal life-styles and job environment for signs. If officers are not afforded the opportunity of stress recognition training, this is impossible.

Knowing the early warning signs is important for not only individual officers, but supervisors as well. Quick detection of stress symptoms permit the easiest and most effective treatment.

The term "stressor" typically refers to anything which may produce stress. Situations which frequently become stressors are listed below:

Career Stressors

A. Insufficient training
B. Lack of or no equipment
C. Low salary
D. Insufficient community resources
E. Low opinion of police by community
F. Leniency of judicial system
G. Frustration from waiting for judicial proceedings
H. Rotating shifts
I. Fear
J. Heavy work load
K. Need to act "macho"
L. Failure of administration to support rank and file
M. Inept supervision
N. Lack of future career opportunities
O. Lack of reward for hard work
P. Lack of financial support from city or county government

Personal Stressors

A. Parenting difficulties
B. Financial problems
C. Attending college in spare time
D. The death of a close friend or relative
E. Divorce
F. Relationships with the opposite sex
G. Difficulties involving a friendship
H. Need to achieve a high status in community

STRESS WARNING SIGNS

Virtually anyone will react to stress. Recognizing common warning signs will help to reduce the frequency of more serious reactions. Common methods used to cope with stress include:

A. Cursing
B. Laughing
C. Anxiety
D. Crying
E. Headaches
F. Increased smoking
G. Irritability
H. Erratic behavior
I. Daydreaming
J. Being hard to get along with
K. Fatigue
L. Sudden change in behavior
M. Unnecessary worrying
N. Sexual promiscuity
O. Manipulation of friends and relatives
P. Depression
Q. Alcoholism
R. Drug Abuse
S. Low self-esteem

DEVELOPMENT OF A STRESS MANAGEMENT TRAINING PROGRAM

Developing a stress management program is a new experience for most law enforcement trainers. Professional guidance is recommended. Since the majority of police agencies do not have the financial resources necessary to retain a full time counseling staff, it is usually necessary to begin a selection process. A series of personal interviews after receiving written proposals is recommended.

Several considerations must be utmost in the mind of trainers during the selection process. First, ensure that considered psychologist/counselors are qualified. Close inspection of formal education and practical experience is necessary. Second, whoever is selected must have a personality and demeanor which will easily gain acceptance by officers. Some resistance from the rank and file is natural. A counselor has to overcome this resistance.

Never lose sight of the fact that the ultimate objective is to provide officers with the knowledge and skills necessary to cope with the negative aspects of stress. Written proposals should include an assortment of training areas. One successful training program was implemented by Chief Charles Kilgore, Delray Beach Police Department, Delray Beach, Florida. The Delray training program consisted of 1, 60 minute training session per week, for 20 weeks.

Week 1	–1. Introduction (goals of the program, role of the psychologist) 2. Introduction Part II—The "Ideal" Officer 3. Hazards of Police Work (frustration, etc.) 4. Stress Management Part I (individual questionnaires, types, definition) 5. Stress Management Part II (long or short term planning, nutrition and exercise) 6. Stress Management Part III (work stressors, anxiety, letting go)
Week 7	Stress Management Part IV (relaxation techniques)
Week 8	Communication Part I (listening and enhancing communication)
Week 9	Communication Part II (listening to others, role playing)
Week 10	Hostility Part I (how to defuse, role playing, acknowledge emotion)
Week 11	Hostility Part II (recognizing your own hostility, coping)
Week 12	Assertiveness Part I (definition, differences between assertion and aggression)
Week 13	Assertiveness Part II (role playing, car stop, etc.)
Week 14	Assertiveness Part III (role playing, fights, domestics)
Week 15	Racial Tension Part I (introduction, group discussion)
Week 16	Racial Tension Part II (experience prejudice)
Week 17	Racial Tension Part III (role playing, case history)
Week 18	Racial Tension Part IV (role playing, small group discussions)
Week 19	Cultural Differences (ethnic, religion, homosexuality)
Week 20	Police Community Relations (a practical approach)[5]

It should be noted that the training program for the Delray Police

Department emphasized training which would provide a better understanding of area minority groups. Trainers can customize stress management training to receive maximum benefit toward particular internal problems within their own agency. Training may emphasize the improvement of relationships with minority groups, interdepartmental relationship difficulties, marital problems, substance abuse or any other problem area.

STRESS MANAGEMENT TRAINING FOR SUPERVISORS

As with most aspects of an agency, staff personnel will have a substantial effect upon the success of stress management—so much so that a separate training program should be developed for supervisors. Since the active support of staff personnel is crucial to the overall success of stress management, it is suggested that the supervision training program be conducted initially.

The Dallas Police Department provides an excellent stress management training outline for supervisors.

A. Introduction
   1. Background of psychological services
   2. Stress awareness
   3. Explanation of video tapes and films to be used during training
B. Video tapes and films
   1. Officer stress awareness
   2. Officer stress awareness: externalization
   3. Officer stress awareness: internalization
C. Break
D. Discussion
   1. Stress warning signs
   2. Stress reduction
   3. How to approach and refer officers to psychological services
   4. Methods of entry into the program
E. Question and Answer Period.[6]

STRESS MANAGEMENT/COUNSELING PROGRAM

The Winter Park Police Department, Winter Park, Florida, offers departmental guidelines regarding their stress management/counseling program.

The Winter Park program emphasizes indepth departmental stress management training and confidentiality within counseling procedures.

TRAUMATIC INCIDENT PROGRAM

Purpose

To provide an employee program which will offer assistance to the employee in resolving those stress related problems that might affect his/her well-being, health and employment.

Definition

A traumatic incident is any police incident or action which may result in emotional or psychological anguish. A traumatic incident includes, but is not limited to the following; police shooting incidents which result in injury or fatality, situations in which officers are fired upon, police vehicle accidents involving death or serious personal injury, etc.

Procedure

When a traumatic incident occurs; an officer shall notify his supervisor that he will contact the departmental counselor within forty-eight hours of the traumatic incident; it shall be mandatory that the officer contact the departmental counselor within forty-eight hours of the incident.

Shift or Unit Supervisor

The supervisor shall ensure that the officer involved in the traumatic incident contacts the departmental counselor within forty-eight hours.

Departmental Counselor

Assists the concerned officer to understand the impact of traumatic incidents; ensure that the concerned officer has resolved any problems which may have resulted from the traumatic incident; ensure that all conversation with the concerned officer remains **confidential.**

Procedure

Stress Management/Counseling Program

The Department will provide a Stress Management and Counseling program for all members of the Department. This shall include full time officers, reserve officers, and civilian members. Furthermore, immediate family members and/or the fiancee of a member of the department is eligible for the program.

The program will consist of:

A. General training seminars in stress.
B. Training seminars for supervisors.
C. Training seminars for family members.
D. An advisement resource for supervisors.
E. Information material for employees.
F. Individual sessions with employees and/or the immediate family members.
G. Twenty-four hour, seven days a week availability for counseling.

Confidentiality

All communications of clients in the counseling program are to be the property of the client and may **not** be released, in any form, to others without the written consent of the client. The only exception to this rule is a circumstance in which the counselor perceives severe, immediate danger to the client or others. This danger must be of such severity that it meets the requirements of judicial mandates for the mentally ill. If this should occur, the Chief of Police shall be notified by the departmental counselor.

An individual eligible for the counseling program can contact the department counselor via the phone numbers provided to the Communications Division. No authorization need be requested. The Counselor's office shall not be located in Winter Park.

All supervisors have the authority to recommend to an officer under his command that the officer seek counseling; however, the officer **cannot** be ordered to participate. The program is strictly **voluntary.** The concerned supervisor shall not inquire later as to whether the officer is participating. Recommendations or referrals to this program **will not** be used as a substitute for normal disciplinary processes.

Recognizing that this is a highly sensitive and confidential service, files and records of the counseling program will be kept under lock and key by **only** the departmental counselor. The concerned records maintained by the counselor **cannot** be inspected by anyone other than the counselor and client.

ALCOHOL AND DRUG ABUSE PROGRAMS

The Los Angeles County Sheriff's Office, under the direction of Sheriff Peter J. Pitchess, has developed a very effective alcoholism program. The purpose of their program is to furnish employees with an avenue for treating abuse. It was established through the combined efforts of the departmental psychologist, the administration, and several recovered alcoholic officers.

From an administrative standpoint, the unacceptable level of work performance associated with alcoholism was a major reason for establishing the program. Though concern for employee welfare is extremely important, the basic responsibility of the department is to ensure that job performance is adhered to in a confident manner. When personal problems affect an officer's work, departmental intervention should return the officer to his most competent level of performance.

The development of an alcoholism program should always result from the combined efforts of the entire department. Initial input, at all levels, is important to develop a quality program and win its acceptance. If the program is to experience high levels of success, certain essential elements must be present. The Los Angeles program identified these essential aspects as:

A. Supervisory training pertaining to operations of the program and appropriate methods of supervision.
B. Confidentiality for anyone seeking assistance from the program.
C. Employee awareness of the program.
D. Instruction regarding the aspects of alcohol.

Source: Stress Management Program, Winter Park Police Department, Winter Park, Florida 32789

E. Recovered alcoholic officers are available 24 hours a day to assist other officers.
F. Meetings are held once a week at a location other than the department building.
G. Group members publish regular news letters which contain information and articles of support and reassurance.[7]

The Chicago Police Department has established general orders governing the organization and operation of their alcohol and drug assistance program. They include:

1. The alcohol and drug assistance unit shall be administered by a unit commander, under the direct supervision of the administrator, professional counseling service. Specially selected department members shall staff the unit as trained counselors.
2. Any department member or member of his/her family is urged to contact a counselor of the unit for assistance. Unit phone numbers are distributed throughout the department.
3. The administrator of the professional counseling service assumes responsibility for maintaining all records of the alcohol and drug assistance unit. Records containing statistical information will be submitted monthly to the deputy superintendent, bureau of administrative services. Confidential records will be destroyed 3 months after termination from the counseling. Any record pertaining to counseling will be considered strictly confidential.
4. An officer's participation or lack of participation in the alcohol and drug assistance program will not delay the initiation of disciplinary action or completion of an internal investigation.[8]

PEER COUNSELING PROGRAMS

One extremely effective approach to stress management is peer counseling. Its value lies in the fact that many troubled officers will submit to counseling from a fellow officer, but absolutely refuse to see a psychiatrist or "outside" counselor. Quite often the mistrust of external counselors is never overcome.

While many people view a peer counseling program as a directly opposite approach to stress management, the combination of peer counseling and counseling from a mental health professional is another option. This approach affords officers with the services of a formally educated counselor, while those who are mistrusting have the comfort of a fellow officer.

Agencies may find several aspects of peer counseling programs appealing:

1. The obvious ability to reach officers who would normally not become involved due to the lack of trust.
2. Peer counseling programs can be conducted at virtually any location. This establishes a greater degree of creditability and confidentiality. A program requiring officers to undergo counseling at the department will find little participation unless forced to attend.
3. Peer counseling programs are substantially less expensive due to counselors being volunteer officers.
4. Troubled officers can often be helped without losing self-esteem because peer counselors assist without being judgemental.
5. Peer counselors can relate to officers more effectively than a formally educated counselor having never been "on the street."

One of the most successful peer counseling programs in the nation is the Boston Police Stress Program. Under the direction of veteran Boston police officer, Edward C. Donovan, Boston's program has always adhered to the principle of officers helping each other. The Boston program was created because officers needed to relate their difficulties to other officers. A feeling of distrust and lack of ability for outsiders to understand their problems had prevailed prior to the establishment of the program.

The Boston Police Stress Program was created in the early 1950's as an informal alcoholism counseling group. It had been patterned after alcoholics anonymous. In 1973, officers Edward Donovan and Joe Rovino expanded the program to include its services for any personal problem, regardless of magnitude.

Today, peer counselors undergo a week long training program which instructs how to listen and guide counseling sessions. The basic skills of counseling are taught. Experience has shown that peer counselors already have the essential elements of counseling through practical experience. Counselor training refines these qualities. It molds their raw abilities into an organized and productive peer counseling program.

The Boston Program ensures that a peer counselor is available 24 hours a day, 7 days a week. Counselors will meet officers virtually any time. The biggest obstacle is having an officer arrange for the initial meeting. The single biggest step a troubled officer can take is seeking help to begin with.[9]

POST-SHOOTING TRAUMA

One terribly neglected aspect of stress management is the trauma resulting from shoot-outs. After surviving a shoot-out, officers are likely to suffer severe stress. Common post-shooting trauma symptoms include:

1. Loss of sleep
2. Inability to concentrate
3. Nightmares
4. Irritability and difficulty with personal relationships
5. Sexual disfunction
6. Lack of confidence
7. Desire for isolation from other people

Keith J. Bettinger, a nationally recognized authority of post-shooting trauma, notes several methods of treatment useful to those suffering from such stress. The department, the concerned officer's family, and his fellow officers must work together to assist in his recovery. These 3 groups comprise the support necessary for recuperation. Understanding, compassion and thoughtfulness should be conveyed whenever possible.

Using peer counseling programs can also be a valuable tool.[10] Counseling from a psychiatrist, psychotherapist or other qualified counselors should be available. It is recommended that mandatory guidelines be implemented requiring officers to undergo some form of counseling following a shooting.

As with any form of stress management, training is the first step in developing a successful program. Officers should be taught the skills necessary to cope with an assortment of stress related difficulties. Supervisors, peer counselors, family members and field training officers must learn stress management and counseling techniques. Stress management training is crucial to thoroughly understanding the complexity of our profession.

REFERENCES

1. Carl Googin, from his opening remarks of the symposium. "*Job Stress and the Police Officer: Identifying Stress Reduction Techniques.*" Cincinnati, Ohio, May 1975.

2. F. Barry Schreiber and Jack Seitzinger, from the article, *The Stress Pressure Cooker: A Comprehensive Model of Stress Management.*
3. Georgette Bennett-Sandler and Earl Ubell, *Time Bombs in Blue,* August 1977, pg. 55.
4. Katherine W. Ellison, John P. Cross, John L. Genz, Training in Stress Management, *The Police Chief,* September 1980, pg. 27.
5. Charles Kilgore, Human Relations and Stress Training in a Small Police Department: An Evaluation, *The Florida Police Chief,* Volume 10, Number 1, pg. 33–34.
6. Psychological Services, *Unit, Stress Management Seminar for Police Supervisors,* Dallas Police Department, Dallas, Texas.
7. John G. Stratton, Alcoholism Programs for Police, Part *II, Law and Order,* October 1980, pg. 18–22.
8. General Order 80-4, *Alcohol and Drug Assistance Unit,* Chicago Police Department, Chicago, Illinois, November 22, 1980.
9. Edward C. Donovan, *The Boston Police Stress Program,* Boston Police Department.
10. Keith J. Bettinger, After the Gun Goes Off, *Police Product News,* April 1985.

11.

PHYSICAL FITNESS TRAINING

THE NEED FOR FITNESS

The last decade has seen fitness sweep America off its feet. Jogging, bicycling, aerobics, and staying in shape have proven to be more than a fad. Fitness has become an enduring and significant national pastime. It's now a multifaceted, multimillion dollar business, with millions of participants actively involved.

It hasn't always been this way, however. Prior to the 1970's, fitness, wellness and stress related programs were rare. Any corporate related fitness program usually consisted of a company softball or bowling team. In those days you didn't even talk about the effects of stress.

Attitudes and opinions started to change in the 1970's. Businesses began to sponsor formal physical fitness programs and corporate athletic facilities such as swimming pools, gymnasiums, exercise rooms, and jogging tracks. Many employees were beginning to think about running during their lunch hour or working out in the exercise room before they went home at the end of the day. Lifestyles were beginning to change for the better.

By 1980, employer sponsored fitness programs began to include physical assessment. Lifestyle surveys, stress tests and personally prescribed dietary and athletic prescriptions were beginning to take hold. Soon a broader definition of fitness was conceived. Concepts such as individual responsibility, corporate wellness and mental, spiritual and physical health were merged into the overall topic of wellness. Sought after benefits like improved moral, decreased absenteeism, lower insurance rates, increased productivity, and generally happier employees helped to fuel the spread of fitness throughout the business world.

The fitness boom has now gone far beyond the employer/employee relationship. On any given day in America, millions of Americans will perform some type of exercise. There are currently millions of regular joggers, body builders and dieting Americans. Thousands of health food stores and fitness trails have been built. Organized sports such as softball, bowling, and basketball are popular as ever.

Without a doubt, virtually the entire country has come to realize that you feel better and look better when you're in shape. Setting the personal reasons aside, few professions have more of a need for excellent physical conditioning than does law enforcement. All you have to do to put this in prospective is imagine being in foot pursuit of a 17 year old fleeing felon jumping fences through the back yards of a residential area. Now imagine yourself weighing 265 pounds at a height of 5 feet 10 inches. Anyone who doesn't believe that physical fitness is crucial for a law enforcement officer is only fooling himself. An out of shape officer will not be able to carry out fundamental law enforcement duties. All officers have an obligation to remain physically capable of providing protection to those citizens within his community.

Though law enforcement is primarily a sedentary occupation, officers can be called upon to put forth extraordinary physical exertion for short periods of time. An unfit individual risks serious injury during sudden participation of strenuous activity. If these haven't been reasons enough, try explaining to a fellow officer, who has been fighting two men by himself because his partner couldn't keep up with the foot pursuit, that fitness isn't important.[1]

THE STATUS OF POLICE FITNESS

While fitness for most of America has become virtually a national pastime, law enforcement trainers find themselves struggling with a variety of fitness related problems. Several issues make the development of successful police fitness programs difficult. The obstacles that any trainer must confront and overcome include:

1. The inherent pessimism and cynicism that many officers seem to develop. The same fitness program which is perceived by employees of a major corporation as a great company benefit may be viewed by veteran police officers as being "dumped on" because they are asked to exercise and get in shape.
2. Getting an officer's entire family involved in fitness to improve the officer's lifestyle.
3. That physical fitness tests are fair and valid.

4. That sincere support from the agency's chief of police or sheriff is obtained.
5. Support from local government administrators.
6. Developing fitness standards that are job related and validated.

Doctor Kenneth Cooper's Aerobics Institute in Dallas, Texas is recognized as a world wide leader in the administration of physical fitness programs. The Institute's training of those who will manage and supervise fitness programs, along with expert advice has been extremely beneficial to both governmental agencies and the private sector. Providing assistance to law enforcement agencies has played a major role within the Aerobics Institute for more than a decade.

A national survey on law enforcement fitness was conducted by the International Association of Chiefs of Police and Doctor Cooper's Aerobics Institute in 1975. The survey concluded that police officers were less physically fit than the main stream of society. The study also determined that only 14 percent of local, state or federal agencies had formal fitness programs.

Another important conclusion drawn from the survey concerned the health of officers. Lower back pain and cardiovascular disease were determined to be the most serious health risk.

Following the survey, the Institute developed a training program to prepare fitness instructors for developing, implementing and managing a law enforcement training program. The "certificate of proficiency training course" has now trained more than eight hundred law enforcement officers representing 100 police agencies.[2]

The International Association of Chiefs of Police, Federal Bureau of Investigation, Doctor Kenneth Cooper's Aerobics Institute, the U.S. Secret Service and numerous other well respected organizations provide their expertise and assistance to local agencies developing fitness programs. Just as law enforcement's efforts to professionalize have met many obstacles and difficult times, so have the efforts to promote police fitness. Allegations of discrimination in the administration of fitness programs, an assortment of legal obstacles, and the need to prove that fitness is beneficial, have hampered the development of fitness within law enforcement. Relatively few police agencies have organized physical fitness programs. Only those trainers with ample foresight and initiative have been successful in overcoming the difficulties. We continue to compromise a profession that may have more reason to be physically fit than any other in America. The police are not even as fit as most Americans. This must change. The only way it will happen is through the perseverance and hard work of training officers.

FITNESS PROGRAM DEVELOPMENT

The justification, development, implementation and continued administration of a departmental fitness program is something new to most trainers. As with any new endeavor, a lack of knowledge may result in hesitation or uncertainty. This section will examine and present easy to understand methods of program development.

Justification – Preceding sections of this chapter dealt with the benefits of providing a physical fitness program. The two primary benefits of fitness programs remain improved health to the officer and financial savings to the agency. These aspects of justification must be greatly stressed.

The various health benefits and departmental needs previously examined should be used during any oral or written justification presentation. They are of tremendous importance and should make a lasting impression upon those from whom approval is sought. A more subtle, yet equally effective approach, is to emphasize the positive financial benefits.

Many direct and indirect cost savings are derived as a result of a productive and effective fitness program.

1. Evidence exists to indicate that a decrease in employee absenteeism will result.[3]
2. A lowering in employee turnover may also be derived.[4]
3. There is evidence that regular participation within fitness programs have reduced direct health care costs within industry by approximately $85 per employee per year.[5]
4. Evidence also indicates that employees will be involved in fewer accidents as a result of fitness programs.[6]

Health costs for employers now staggers the imagination. Doctors Herbert, Montgomery and Wetzler in their report **PLANNING A FITNESS PROGRAM FOR INDUSTRY**, have documented that American health care now costs hundreds of billions of dollars annually.[7] The New York Times reported on March 28, 1982 that the total health care expenditure for America in 1971 was 27 billion dollars. This had risen to 270 billion dollars in 1980 and is anticipated to be 800 billion dollars by 1990.

Contacting the personnel officer of your city or county may provide you with the total health care expenditures within your agency. The insurance carrier for your department may also provide similar figures to justify a fitness program. Do not underestimate the impact such financial justification may derive. The adage, "money talks," is certainly true within local government.

Fitness program development actually starts during the justification stage. You must be prepared to explain the basic components and concepts of your fitness program. Failure to do so will likely result in the failure of administration to support and endorse your efforts. Should this happen, your efforts are doomed to failure.

One very effective developmental strategy is to establish a fitness "support group." The support group is comprised of one officer from every shift and/or division within the department. The officers within the group become "fitness trainers." As such, their primary purpose is to promote fitness throughout the department through motivation, encouragement and inspiration for fellow officers to become fit and stay fit.

As the departmental training officer, you must select fitness trainers very carefully. The utmost qualification is the ability to motivate and inspire others. The second most important quality is that they sustain a high level of fitness themselves. Leading by example is crucial to the program's creditability.

Once fitness trainers are selected, the next step is to train them. The most practical solution is to seek the assistance of a local university or college. Many institutions of higher learning have an exercise physiology department. Fitness officers may be enrolled in a variety of fitness and nutrition courses or a custom designed program of instruction may be developed for your department. Another option is to seek the educational assistance of local physicians. Sports physicians, in particular, can provide lectures and seminars on a variety of important topics.

How and what material is instructed to your fitness trainers is obviously of great importance. How the material will be instructed should not be a concern if a professor or physician is acquired. What is to be instructed is a more complex issue.

Frank D. Rohter, Ph. D, is a professor of exercise physiology, co-director of the Institute of Exercise Physiology and Health, University of Central Florida, and co-director, Florida Heart Group Wellness Center, Orlando, Florida. Doctor Rohter is a highly respected and nationally recognized expert in the field of exercise physiology. Having completed the Iron

Man Triathalon several times, Dr. Rohter is not only knowledgeable but practices what he preaches. He provides the following instructional components of an effective training program for fitness trainers. They should be viewed as guidelines for developing your training program.

CONCEPT I

An Optimal Physical Activity Program

Concept I is a motivational presentation manifesting the physiological potential of man's tolerance to an exercise stress. Also, this presentation identifies the realistic components of an optimal exercise program and the most meaningful approach to starting and sustaining an effectively active lifestyle. This presentation will answer the following questions:

- How long can a middle-aged person exercise without endangering the body?
- What is a realistic exercise starting point after being inactive for several years?
- Is a stress test essential before starting an exercise program?
- What are the most beneficial types of physical activities—dual, team, or individual sports?
- Is walking just as beneficial as jogging?
- What are the beneficial differences between aerobic (long-slow distance exercises) and anaerobic (short-fast moving exercises)?
- Is "prereceived exertion" a better exercise stress monitor than the palpated pulse rate?
- How does one prevent injuries, drop out, and boredom?
- What is the significance of quantifying and quantitating an exercise regimen?
- What is the effect of intrinsic and extrinsic motivation on sustaining an effective exercise program?
- What are the beneficial differences between strength training and cardiovascular training?
- What is the relationship between resistance training and osteoporosis, lower back pain, structural support for long distance exercise, and self-image?

CONCEPT II

Coronary Heart Disease And Exercise Intervention

CONCEPT I is a presentation of the objective research evidencing the relationship between the prevention of coronary heart disease (CHD) and exercise intervention. It includes a series of cited research publications that reveals the cause and development of coronary heart disease, and the recommended lifestyles for its prevention. This presentation will include the following topics:

- The significance of coronary heart disease on the mortality rate.
- Your chances of dying from coronary heart disease.
- The "risk factors" associated with coronary heart disease.
- Total serum cholesterol as a poor predictor of coronary heart disease.
- High density lipoprotein-cholesterol (HDL–C) as an independent and powerful predictor of coronary heart disease.
- The physiology of why high density lipoprotein-cholesterol is a "good" fraction and low density lipoprotein-cholesterol (LDL–C) is a "bad" fraction, of the total cholesterol (TC) constituency.
- Factors that raise the HDL–C (the "good" fraction).
- Factors that raise the LDL–C (the "bad" fraction).
- Established norms for using the total cholesterol (TC): high density lipoprotein-cholesterol (HDL–C) ratio as predictor of coronary heart disease.
- The scientific evidence that demonstrates the significance of exercise intervention to the management of an anti-atherogenic serium cholesterol fraction profile.

CONCEPT III

Weight Management and Exercise Intervention

Concept III is a presentation of scientific studies revealing the significance of exercise to control obesity. It reports the research that compares the beneficial effects of exercise to the superficial effects of diet on the maintenance of ideal body weight. It addresses the following questions:

- Are the Metropolitan or Fogerty Height/Weight Norms realistic?
- Are percent body fat measurements (Hydrostatic weighing or fat calipers) more valid than standard height/weight tables for evaluating optimal weight?
- What is the difference between lean body mass (muscle and bone) and body fat?
- What are the norms for percent body fat?
- What is the difference between storage fat and essential fat?
- What are the recommended essential fat percentages for men and women?
- What is the effect of dieting on lean body mass (muscle)?
- What are the comparative effects of diet and exercise on the BMR (Basil Metabolic Rate)?
- Do lean people eat more or less than obese people?
- Will walking a mile burn the same amount of calories as running a mile?
- Will aerobic (slow) exercise burn more fat than anaerobic (fast) exercise?
- What is the effect of obesity on sex appeal?
- Is obesity a strong predictor of coronary heart disease?
- Are the number of fat cells determined during the early years?
- Can the number of fat cells be reduced in number or only in size?
- What is the "set point" theory and how does it relate to diet and exercise?
- What is the recommended weekly weight loss?

CONCEPT IV

Nutrition

Concept IV is a synthesis of an extensive review of the literature relating to healthy nutritional practices. This presentation identifies the good foods as well as those to be avoided. It includes the following propositions.

- Simple sugars and the production of hypoglycemia (low blood sugar and fatigue).
- Identifying the simple sugars.

- The difference between simple sugars (they are carbohydrates), and the complex carbohydrates.
- The relationship between salt intake and hypertension (high blood pressure).
- The RDA (Recommended Daily Allowance) for salt.
- The foods which are high/low in salt.
- The RDA for protein and the essential amino acids.
- The nutritional differences between various proteins.
- The hazards of fat.
- The difference between saturated and unsaturated fats.
- The value of complex carbohydrates.
- Carbohydrates storage and the prevention of fatigue.
- Fiber (a complex carbohydrate), "regularity" and the prevention of diverticulitus and colon cancer.
- Vitamins, minerals, additives and processed foods.
- Comparative diets: Average American; Heart Association; Pritkin; Atkins; Cambridge; Stillwell and others.
- Recommended eating schedules—time and size—as related to exercise, fatigue and maximal metabolism (caloric burning).
- Food labeling and evaluation.
- Negative aspects of reducing diets.
- Calcium, iron and select vitamins and other possible nutritional deficiencies.

CONCEPT V

Resistance Exercise

Resistance exercise is a system to develop muscle strength through an overload movement of a specific body part. This component will manifest the following topics.

- Comparative evaluation of strength training equipment.
- Recommended strength training regimens.
- Recommended strength training protocols.
- Fast twitch vs. slow twitch muscle fibers.
- Concentric, eccentric, isometric, isotomic, isokinetic, sustained and rhythmic contractions.

- Huxley's sliding filament theory.
- Overload principles.
- Neurological vs. muscle fiber strengths.
- Muscle fiber tissue breakdown and regeneration.
- Strength training hazards, injuries and cardiovascular stress.
- Muscle atrophy, hypertrophy and hyperplasma.
- Warm-up; cool-down.
- Strength training vs. cardiovascular training.
- Capillary occlusion theory.
- Major vessel compression theory.
- Starting and sustaining a meaningful strength and training program.
- Cultural support group.
- Osteoporosis.
- Lower back pain.
- Self-image.
- Posture.

IMPLEMENTATION

The creation of a well trained and highly motivated fitness trainer support group will lay a solid foundation for your fitness program. You must now mold the fitness trainers into a nucleus from which a desire for fitness will spread throughout the department. Shaping the fitness trainers into a tight knit group may take time. If you picked your officers wisely, their inherent personalities should be optimistic, motivated and enthusiastic. These qualities will need only your direction and organization to reach the group's full productiveness.

You must teach the trainers that they are now disciples for fitness, nutrition and a healthy lifestyle. Like yourself, they must constantly provide positive and encouraging reinforcement to their shifts and divisions. Negative feed-back and criticism toward anyone's fitness efforts is absolutely prohibited. A fitness trainer's primary purpose will always be to encourage fitness through instruction and positive reinforcement.

Your role as the overall departmental training officer will usually allow sufficient time to adequately manage the entire fitness program. This will, of course, be largely dependent upon the size of your agency. Should sufficient time be a problem, an alternative solution is to select one of the fitness trainers as a "fitness leader." The leader's function is to provide managerial assistance. Documentation of various fitness programs, organization of special events, and motivating the fitness trainers are his primary responsibility.

Ensuring that the fitness trainers stay motivated is essential to the overall success of the program. One method of ensuring this is to hold regular fitness trainer meetings. The meetings will derive a variety of benefits:

1. Continued instruction for fitness trainers may be provided by guests lecturers.
2. Discussion of new ideas may take place.
3. Discussion and resolution of problems are possible.
4. Involving all fitness trainers in decision making processes will instill a meaningful cohesiveness.
5. Many issues are more effectively resolved through the collective thinking of a group.
6. The delegation and distribution of work assignments is easily accomplished.

Medical examinations—A thorough medical examination for every employee participating in the program should be given annually. The initial medical examination should be provided in the initial stages of implementation. All health risks must be detected early, before exercise could endanger an officer. It's possible for anyone to have serious undetected medical problems which would be aggravated by physical exertion.

Primary concern of the medical examination should be that it is thorough. While financial restraints may limit the examinations, certain aspects must not be jeopardized. Minimum requirements for the examination should include:

1. The examination be conducted by qualified medical personnel.
2. Submission of a thorough medical questionnaire.
3. A blood analysis to include a body chemistry profile and a cardiac risk profile.
4. Measurements of blood pressure, respiration, resting heart rate, height and weight.
5. A physical inspection of various body parts to include eye, ear, nose, throat, joints, limbs, heart sounds, lung sounds, and detection of any abnormalities.
6. An EKG test.
7. A chest x-ray.

The health history questionnaire and medical examination must be combined by the physician to provide training officers with a health hazard appraisal. The appraisal must be written. It should attest to each officer's capability to safely participate in an exercise program. The physician should state in writing, whether or not each officer is fit or unfit to participate. Any officer having a serious risk factor, or for any reason deemed unfit by the physician, is prohibited from the exercise portion of the fitness program. Such written forms are to be permanently documented.

If finances allow, a treadmill stress test should also be performed. This stress test will examine the performance of the heart under stress. The treadmill stress test is relatively expensive. It is recommended that several proposals be obtained for comparison of price and thoroughness of examination.

Medical examinations should be treated with confidentiality. Documenting the extent of health necessary to participate in the fitness program is achieved through obtaining the written "fit or unfit for participation" form. This form is the only paperwork a trainer needs to receive. The concerned officer is to be the sole recipient of more detailed results of his medical examination.

MAKING FITNESS FUN

As with the general public, a large percentage of police officers find physical exercise distasteful. An important function of any fitness program is implementing various ways to make fitness fun. This of course, goes hand in hand with encouraging and motivating officers to change their lifestyles for the better.

Fitness trainers must impart knowledge to officers within their division or shift. This should always be done in a positive manner. There is no such thing as an easy and simple way of getting in shape. It takes dedication, tenacity and hard work. Cardiovascular improvement requires a sustained elevation of heart rate. Muscles need to be stressed and strengthened. Joints throughout the body must work through their entire range of motion. Thus, to see improvement, fitness programs should be sustained and vigorous.

Anyone who has worked hard to get into shape knows it isn't easy. There are many ways to make it easier, however. Some people even believe there are ways to make it fun and enjoyable. One popular way is

Figure 29. Canoe races which match an agency's shifts and divisions against each other promote both fitness and fun.

to exercise in a group. Exercising alone is much more difficult from a psychological standpoint. The companionship and social atmosphere that a group provides can be very motivating. Examples of group participation activities which may be organized include:

1. Softball
2. Group jogging
3. Basketball games
4. Bowling teams
5. Racquetball competitions
6. Group aerobics
7. Touch or flag football
8. Canoe races
9. Tennis matches
10. Volleyball games

A more elaborate example of group participation is the organizing of a fitness competition day. Developed very similar to popular TV shows, a series of fitness games are prepared which competes shifts and divisions

Figure 30. The fitness program can sponsor special events such as this white water rafting trip. Soon officers will relate having fun with fitness.

against each other. Events such as tug-of-war, obstacle course, a mile relay run, frisbee accuracy throw, a canoe race, a bicycle race and a softball dunking machine are examples of events which may be used. Points are given for first, second and place teams. The overall winner can be awarded a cash prize or trophy. Second and third place overall winners may receive similar awards. Fitness trainers may assume various responsibilities for making "fitness day" a big success. The benefits of creating such an event can be far reaching.

MOTIVATION

The significance of motivation has been referred to several times in this chapter. The absence of motivation will likely resort in a stagnant and slowly dying fitness program. In addition, motivation is one ingredient that makes fitness fun to be involved with. There are numerous techniques to motivate and encourage fitness.

Appointing fitness trainers will automatically structure your program to promote motivation and encouragement. One of a fitness trainer's main responsibilities is to motivate. Organizing a variety of group participation events, especially if they include prizes, trophies or other awards are the giant steps toward a successful program.

As the fitness program continues to prompt officers to participate, personal achievements and triumphs will be accomplished. Giving officers needed recognition for their efforts is crucial. An easy yet effective method of providing recognition is to distribute memorandums whenever individuals accomplish a personal fitness goal. One way to organize this technique is in naming a fitness officer of the month. Included in the memorandum is a short paragraph describing the officer's fitness efforts and accomplishments. The selection of the fitness officer of the month should be based upon an officer's efforts more than his accomplishments.

FITNESS NEWSLETTER

Newsletter—Still another effective motivational strategy is publishing your own departmental fitness and nutrition newsletter. Each month a different fitness trainer can write the newsletter. A mixture of fitness, nutrition or sports related articles can be included within the publication. Numerous short stories may appear regarding how various individuals or shifts are getting into shape. Upcoming events, the fitness officer of the month, new ideas and even diet suggestions can be included. Mailing the newsletter to officers' homes will make it even more effective because it will get spouses and families involved.

Goal setting—Fitness trainers should keep a separate folder for each officer in their division. Personal data such as height, weight, fitness test results, interests and any fitness problems must be documented. Keeping a "fitness profile" for each officer will assist in developing their capabilities. Each profile should include a section on the setting of goals. Fitness trainers should discuss with each of their officers what goals may be realistically strived for. Goals must be well within the reach of the individual's capabilities, yet challenging. They should be customized to fit every officer's personal interest and abilities. Frequent conversations by fitness trainers will help to ensure the meeting of goals. As they are reached, new goals should be established.

FUND-RAISING

Fund-raising may be necessary for many departments to obtain necessary fitness equipment. Training officers should include budgetary requests for such equipment every year. If additional funds are needed, fund-raising should not be ignored.

There are surprizing benefits to fund-raising which may be unexpected by most trainers. The benefits of increased comradeship, fellowship and morale will usually be derived as a group works together for a common cause. Like virtually all aspects of fitness, fund-raising should be organized so that it is fun.

The Winter Park, Florida, Police Department has provided examples where fund-raising is both profitable and fitness oriented. A basketball game placing police officers against a local professional football team was organized. This not only raised money for needed exercise equipment, but initiated the forming of a basketball team as well.

The Winter Park Police developed another innovative idea by staging a fitness cross Florida run. Fourteen officers volunteered to participate in a run from one coast of Florida to the other. A great deal of publicity via radio, television and the newspaper resulted in approximately $2,500 in donations. These funds were used to purchase various exercise equipment for the police department. In addition, the trip developed considerable togetherness and fellowship along the way.

FITNESS EXAMINATIONS

The development and implementation of a physical fitness examination is essential to ensure that a minimum level of fitness, consistent with the standards needed to carry out an officer's duties, is maintained. Examinations are needed to measure the progress achieved for both individuals and the overall program. Such evaluation must be made mandatory for all officers. If examinations are voluntary, the officers who need an improved fitness level the most will be the ones who do not take the examination.

Medical exemptions—As previously referred to, any officer who is deemed unfit to participate by the fitness program physician must receive an exemption from participation. The exemption process must be organized through a standard medical exemption form. High blood pressure, heart ailments, fractures, etc., will be identified and treated on an indi-

Figure 31. These officers literally ran across Florida in a fund-raising effort for their department fitness program. Alot of fun and comradeship was a welcome benefit.

vidual basis. Many medical impairments such as sprains, fractures, or the common flu should receive temporary exemptions until a later date. Allowing excessive and unjustified exemptions can produce a lack of creditability.

Physical efficiency examination — In 1975, the University of Washington Police Department began administering the Police Officer Physical Efficiency Battery examination to in-service officers. The examination consists of a body diameter measurement to estimate percent of body fat, an isometric push/pull test to estimate one's arm and shoulder strength, and a step test to measure an individual's cardiovascular efficiency level and an agility run to determine the individual's agility and speed and coordination.

Assistant Chief of Police, Roger Serra, states, "If physical fitness is to be encouraged for police officers, it is only appropriate that some means of evaluation be conducted. Effectiveness of the overall program and the fitness profile of departmental personnel cannot be determined without some form of evaluation." The University of Washington Police Department has seen two significant improvements since the implementation of in-service fitness testing. The first has been a cardiovascular efficiency improvement. The second has been a reduction in body fat percentage.

Fitness examinations have become an accepted occurence within the University of Washington Police Department. Doing well on the examination has become a strong consideration for the transfer of assignments, a means of insurance against liability suits, a step toward improved public confidence and a source of personal gratification. Participating officers have been neither formally rewarded for passing or disciplined for failing the examination. Personal achievement and peer pressure have been the only motivator.[8]

Physical fitness examination — An example of a physical fitness program which includes a mandatory fitness examination twice a year is found at the Winter Park Police Department, Winter Park, Florida. Initiated in 1984, the fitness examinations are held every spring and fall. They are administered by fitness trainers each morning and afternoon for three consecutive days. There are three separate phases of the examination: push-ups, sit-ups and a one mile run.

Push-ups

1. Assume a standard push-up position. Ensure that your body is totally straight.
2. Lower body to within three inches of ground. The body must be kept totally straight for push-ups to be accepted during the test.
3. Arms are placed at a width equal to your shoulders.
4. Raise body until arms are totally straight.
5. Do as many as you can do within two minutes.

Sit-ups

1. Do as many as you can do within two minutes without stopping.
2. Lie flat on your back with knees bent, feet held on the floor by partner.
3. With arms straight out raise forward until your elbows reach your knees.
4. Lower yourself back.
5. If you stop for more than a second, the test is terminated.

One mile run

Any combination of running and/or walking is permitted to achieve your best time. The one mile run is comprised of four laps around a standard quarter mile track. The following fitness examination rating table is used to compute scores for not only the run but sit-ups and push-ups as well.

As with most decisions concerning the fitness program, fitness training officers voted to establish a policy of publishing fitness test results after each examination. As a result, test results are published within a glass enclosed bulletin board following each examination. Any officer has the right to prohibit the publishing of his or her results. The Winter Park Police Department has found that publishing test results increases motivation, incentive and positive competition among officers.

Winter Park implemented its fitness exam several years ago. They purposely developed a rating scale that was relatively easy. Officers who had been working hard to increase their fitness level were encouraged by their test results. Raising the rating standards to a more difficult level is always a future option. Those trainers seeking a more difficult scoring system may contact the Doctor Kenneth Cooper Fitness Institute in Dallas, Texas.

Decisions regarding mandatory fitness examinations should also address what actions will be taken if officers should refuse to participate or fail the examination. Any officer refusing to participate in the fitness program without justification should be subject to normal disciplinary action for failure to comply with a mandatory order. Officers who fail an established passing grade should be assigned additional instruction to increase his/or her level of fitness to appropriate standards. Any negative reinforcement of participants should be a last resort.

SAFETY CONSIDERATIONS

As mentioned previously, establishing a high quality, annual medical examination is crucial for all fitness participants. It is essential for the protection of officers' safety and well being. No fitness program should be undertaken without it. Safety considerations should not stop after the implementation of an annual medical exam; it should be a continual process.

Fitness trainers must be well versed on the hazards and potential dangers of exercise physiology. They, in turn, must provide department wide instruction as to the same issues. Departmental training officers assume responsibility for ensuring continual emphasis is placed upon

TABLE XX
PHYSICAL FITNESS RATING TABLE

Under 25

1 Mile		Sit-Ups		Push-Ups	
Superior		Superior		Superior	
Time	Score	Reps	Score	Reps	Score
8.02	100	50	100	40	100
8.04	98	49	98	39	98
8.10	96	48	96	38	96
8.14	94	47	94	37	94
8.18	92	46	92	36	92
Above Average		Above Average		Above Average	
8.22	90	45	90	35	90
8.43	88	44	88	34	88
8.46	86	43	86	33	86
8.50	84	42	84	32	84
8.54	82	41	82	31	82
Average		Average		Average	
8.58	80	40	80	30	80
9.03	78	39	78	29	78
9.22	76	38	76	28	76
9.27	74	37	74	27	74
9.30	72	36	72	26	72
Below Average		Below Average		Below Average	
9.35	70	35	70	25	70
9.39	68	34	68	24	68
9.43	66	33	66	23	66
10.03	64	32	64	22	64
10.07	62	31	62	21	62

25–29

1 Mile		Sit-Ups		Push-Ups	
Superior		Superior		Superior	
Time	Score	Reps	Score	Reps	Score
8.22	100	48	100	37	100
8.25	98	47	98	36	98
8.30	96	46	96	35	96
8.34	94	45	94	34	94
8.38	92	44	92	33	92

TABLE XX Continued

25–29 Continued

Above Average		Above Average		Above Average	
8.42	90	43	90	32	90
9.03	88	42	88	31	88
9.06	86	41	86	30	86
9.10	84	40	84	29	84
9.14	82	39	82	28	82
Average		Average		Average	
9.18	80	38	80	27	80
9.23	78	37	78	26	78
9.42	76	36	76	25	76
9.47	74	35	74	24	74
9.50	72	34	72	23	72
Below Average		Below Average		Below Average	
9.55	70	33	70	22	70
9.59	68	32	68	21	68
10.03	66	31	66	20	66

30–34

1 Mile		Sit-Ups		Push-Ups	
Superior		Superior		Superior	
Time	Score	Reps	Score	Reps	Score
8.43	100	45	100	34	100
8.47	98	44	98	33	98
8.50	96	43	96	32	96
8.55	94	42	94	31	94
8.59	92	41	92	30	90
Above Average		Above Average		Above Average	
9.03	90	40	90	29	87
9.23	88	39	88	28	84
9.27	86	38	86	27	81
9.31	84	37	84	26	78
9.35	82	36	82		
Average		Average		Average	
9.39	80	35	80	25	75
9.43	78	34	78	24	72
10.03	76	33	76	23	69
10.07	74	32	74	22	66
10.11	72	31	72		

TABLE XX Continued

30–34 Continued

Below Average		Below Average		Below Average	
10.15	70	30	70	21	63
10.19	68	29	68	20	60
10.22	66	28	66	19	57
10.43	64	27	64		
10.47	62				

35–39

1 Mile		Sit-Ups		Push-Ups	
Superior		Superior		Superior	
Time	Score	Reps	Score	Reps	Score
9.03	100	42	100	30	100
9.07	98	41	98	29	98
9.10	96	40	96	28	96
9.15	94	39	94	27	94
9.19	92	38	92	26	90
Above Average		Above Average		Above Average	
9.23	90	37	90	25	87
9.43	88	36	88	24	84
9.47	86	35	86	23	81
9.51	84	34	84	22	78
9.55	82	33	82		
Average		Average		Average	
9.59	80	32	80	21	75
10.03	78	31	78	20	72
10.23	76	30	76	19	69
10.27	74	29	74	18	66
10.31	72	28	72		
Below Average		Below Average		Below Average	
10.35	70	27	70	17	63
10.39	68	26	68	16	60
10.42	66	25	66	15	57
11.02	64	24	62		
11.06	62				

TABLE XX Continued

40–44

1 Mile		Sit-Ups		Push-Ups	
Superior		Superior		Superior	
Time	Score	Reps	Score	Reps	Score
9.25	100	34	100	26	100
9.27	98	33	98	25	97
9.31	96	32	96	24	94
9.35	94	31	94	23	91
9.39	92	30	90		
Above Average		Above Average		Above Average	
9.43	90	29	87	22	88
10.03	88	28	84	21	84
10.07	86	27	81	20	80
10.11	84	26	78	19	76
10.15	82				
Average		Average		Average	
10.19	80	25	75	18	72
10.23	78	24	72	17	68
10.43	76	23	69	16	64
10.47	74	22	66	15	60
10.51	72				
Below Average		Below Average		Below Average	
10.55	70	21	63	14	56
10.59	68	20	60	13	52
11.03	66	19	57	12	48
11.23	64	18	54	11	44

45–49

1 Mile		Sit-Ups		Push-Ups	
Superior		Superior		Superior	
Time	Score	Reps	Score	Reps	Score
9.43	100	32	100	24	100
9.47	98	31	98	23	97
9.51	96	30	96	22	94
9.55	94	29	94	21	91
9.59	92	28	90		

TABLE XX Continued

45–49 Continued

Above Average		Above Average		Above Average	
10.03	90	27	87	20	88
10.23	88	26	84	19	84
10.27	86	25	81	18	80
10.31	84	24	78	17	76
10.35	82				
Average		Average		Average	
10.39	80	23	75	16	72
10.43	78	22	72	15	68
11.03	76	21	69	14	64
11.07	74	20	66	13	60
11.11	72				
Below Average		Below Average		Below Average	
11.15	70	19	63	12	56
11.19	68	18	60	11	52
11.23	66	17	57	10	48
11.43	64	16	54	9	44

Over 50

1 Mile		Sit-Ups		Push-Ups	
Superior		Superior		Superior	
Time	Score	Reps	Score	Reps	Score
10.03	100	30	100	22	100
10.07	98	29	98	21	98
10.11	96	28	96	19	94
10.15	94	27	94	18	91
10.19	92	26	90		
Above Average		Above Average		Above Average	
10.22	90	25	87	17	88
10.43	88	24	84	16	84
10.47	86	23	81	15	80
10.51	84	22	78	14	76
10.55	82				
Average		Average		Average	
10.59	80	21	75	13	72
11.03	78	20	72	12	68
11.23	76	19	69	11	64
11.28	74	18	66		
11.31	72				

TABLE XX Continued

Over 50 Continued					
Below Average		Below Average		Below Average	
11.35	70	17	63	10	50
11.40	68	16	60	9	47
11.44	66	15	57	8	45
12.04	64	14	54		
12.08	62				

Source: Winter Park Police Department
Winter Park, Florida

the prevention of injuries and treatment of emergency situations. Areas of particular concern include:

1. Instruction concerning the prevention of exercise related injury.
2. The identification of potentially dangerous situations.
3. Safety demonstrations and instruction regarding the use of any fitness equipment.
4. The treatment and response to essential emergency situations.
5. The prevention and treatment of running related injuries.
6. The establishment of a policy governing the reporting of fitness related injuries.

THE DEPARTMENTAL TRAINING OFFICER'S ROLE

From a national perspective, law enforcement fitness programs remain relatively uncommon. Many of those currently in existence are struggling due to the tendancy for interest and motivation to lessen as time goes on.

The key to preventing stagnation rests with the department's training officer. It is he, through principles of sound leadership, who must continue to inject the program with motivation and enthusiasm. Should he ever start to view the program as capable of "running itself" the beginning of the end is near.

REFERENCES

1. Roger C. Serra, Police Officer Physical Efficiency Battery, *The Police Chief,* January 1984, pg. 45.
2. Thomas Collingwood, Get Fit-Fitness For Cops, *World Police and Fire Games Magazine,* Summer 1984, pg. 23.
3. M. H. Cox and R. J. Shepard: Employee Fitness, Absenteeism and Work Performance, *Med-Sci Sports,* 11(1):105 (abstract), 1979.
4. G. F. Shea, Profiting From Wellness Training, *Training and Development Journal,* October 1981, pg. 32–37.
5. R. J. Shepard, P. Corey and P. Remland, The Influence of An Employee Fitness and Lifestyle Modification Program Upon Medical Care Costs, *Journal Public Health,* 73, 1982, pg. 259–263.
6. V. Pravosvdov, The Effects of Physical Exercise On Health and Economic Efficiency, in *Physical Activity and Human Well-Being,* Volume 1, F. Landry and W R Orlan, Miami, Florida, Symposia Specialists, pg. 261–271
7. Henry Herbert, Leslie Montgomery, Harry Wetzler, *Planning A Fitness Program for Industry,* Uniformed Services University of The Health Sciences, Bethesda, Maryland.
8. Roger C. Serra, Police Officer Physical Efficiency Battery, *The Police Chief,* January 1984, pg. 45–46.

INDEX

V

Elements of Linear Algebra

SECOND EDITION

Elements of Linear Algebra

Lowell J. Paige
University of California, Los Angeles

J. Dean Swift
University of California, Los Angeles

Thomas A. Slobko
Occidental College

Xerox College Publishing, Lexington, Massachusetts/Toronto

ISBN: 0–536–00820–5
Library of Congress Catalog Card Number: 73–82137
Printed in the United States of America.

Preface

This book is a complete revision of *Elements of Linear Algebra*, by L. J. Paige and J. D. Swift (Ginn and Company, Boston, Massachusetts, 1961).

At the time the original edition was written, linear algebra was just beginning to find a standard place in the undergraduate curricula of mathematics and science students. That position is now firmly established, but there is still a lack of complete agreement on the timing and the manner of its presentation. Although a substantial argument can be made for integration of the subject matter with the teaching of multivariable calculus, many teachers prefer to give a unified course in linear algebra, or to present a minimum amount during a calculus sequence and return to a fuller development later. The aim of this book is to satisfy the requirements of either type of independent course in linear algebra.

This edition, then, is intended for much the same audience as the first: undergraduate students without any background in linear algebra, but with the mathematical maturity normally acquired in one year of a good calculus course. There is more in the text than can conveniently be covered in a single quarter or semester. Students who have had an introduction to linear algebra during or before their calculus sequence could begin with selected topics from, or a review of, Chapters 3, 4, and 5, and go on from there.

In order to minimize the number of new concepts required at the outset of a course in linear algebra, we have concentrated on R^n until complex numbers are required in the canonical form theory. However, care has been taken to state the essential elements in such a way that generalization to spaces over abstract fields is readily accomplished.

At the time the original text was written, there was no general agreement on a customary order of writing a matrix and a vector on which it acts. The method of putting the vector on the left has some conceptual advantages and was utilized as the standard in the first edition. It has since become general practice to follow the functional notation $f(x)$, and thus to write the operator on the left. The notation in this edition has been changed to agree with this convention.

Another major change is the omission of a separate, essentially independent, chapter on Euclidean n-dimensional geometry and the addition of a chapter on applications of linear algebra, including a discussion of linear programs and the simplex method. Although the geometrical orientation of the earlier edition was noted favorably, the additional chapter was rarely utilized, and the provision of applications is considered more important.

A third major change has been effected by placing the introduction of linear transformations and their matrix representations immediately after the introduction of vector spaces. This order emphasizes the importance of the concept of mappings between spaces.

In a large number of cases, it has been possible to simplify or clarify proofs and discussions. The authors are grateful to many users of the text for helpful suggestions for such improvements. Also, additional exercises have been provided at the end of a number of sections.

Illustrative examples are used abundantly throughout the text. The exercises are problems that either supplement the examples or carry out the simpler and more direct portions of the theory. No attempt has been made to provide a large number of abstractly identical drill problems. With a few exceptions, where provision for some practice is clearly necessary, each problem covers a distinct point. A reasonably large percentage of the problems should be solved by the student. A few exceptionally difficult problems have been starred, as have some sections on which the remainder of the text does not depend.

Answers are provided for those problems whose answers are unique or for which a particular answer will not create confusion even though it may differ from the one found by the student.

The new edition, like the first, has benefited from several thoughtful reviews. The authors wish to thank particularly Professor Larry Dornhoff of the University of Illinois for his careful and detailed criticism. Finally, we wish to express our appreciation to Mrs. Elaine Barth, who prepared the typescript of this edition as well as that of the original one.

L. J. P.
J. D. S.
T. A. S.

Contents

1 Introduction

The students using this text will, in all probability, have had various preparatory courses. The purpose of this chapter is to establish a common background of notation and terminology that we shall use throughout the text. In doing this, we shall review the concept of a function and properties of the real numbers and indicate some of the types of proof that may be found later. These introductory remarks should be particularly valuable to those students whose previous courses in algebra have been primarily computational in nature. The concept of a set of elements, the Cartesian product of sets, the extension of the idea of a function on the real numbers to mappings of arbitrary sets, the notion of groups and fields, and a knowledge of the nature of various proofs are fundamental to all higher courses in mathematics.

1.1 Set Notation

We will have many occasions throughout this book to consider an aggregate or collection of objects. These objects will vary considerably both as to description and as to the properties possessed by the individual objects. We shall refer to such an aggregate or collection as a *set of elements.* The individual objects are elements (or members) of the set. For example, 3 is an element of the set of all positive integers; the letter p is an element of the set of letters of the alphabet; the set of all integers t such that $t^3 = 11$ contains no elements.

In view of the last example, we see that a set, defined as consisting of those elements that have certain properties, may, in fact, contain no elements. We call such a set an *empty* set.

EQUALITY OF SETS. The sets A and B are equal if every element of A is an element of B and every element of B is an element of A.

We write $A = B$ for equal sets and note that A and B contain the same elements. Thus, in particular, any two empty sets are equal. The empty set will be denoted by $\emptyset$.

We write $s \in S$ to denote that s is an element of S; the contrary case is written $s \notin S$. If A and B are two sets and each element of A is an element of B, we write $A \subseteq B$ and say that A is *contained in* B or A is a *subset* of B or B *contains* A. If $A \subseteq B$ and $B \subseteq A$, $A = B$ by the definition of equality of sets. If $A \subseteq B$ and $A \neq B$, we say that A is a proper subset of B and write $A \subset B$. The notations $B \supseteq A$ and $B \supset A$ are also used with the same meanings as $A \subseteq B$ and $A \subset B$, respectively. Note that the empty set is a subset of every set.

Occasionally, to avoid difficulties of logic, a distinction must be made between an element $a \in A$ and the subset of A whose only element is a. The latter is written $\{a\}$, and we have $\{a\} \subseteq A$. More generally, we often denote a set or subset by specifying each element. For example, $S = \{a, b, x, y, z\}$ or $S = \{1, 2, 3, 4, 5, 6\}$.

The *intersection* of two sets A and B is the set of all elements belonging simultaneously to both A and B; it is written $A \cap B$. The brief notation

$$A \cap B = \{x \mid x \in A \quad \text{and} \quad x \in B\}$$

illustrates the convention to be adopted for sets defined by specifying properties shared by all elements of the set. The symbol $\{x \mid \ldots\}$ is to be read "the set of all elements x such that ...."

If two sets have no elements in common their intersection is the empty set $\emptyset$. In this case we say that A and B are *disjoint*.

The *union* of two sets A and B is the set of all elements belonging either to A or to B or to both A and B. It is denoted by $A \cup B$; by way of illustration,

$$A \cup B = \{x \mid x \in A \quad \text{or} \quad x \in B\}.$$

Example 1. We illustrate many of our definitions with sets of points in a plane. For example, let the sets A, B, C be the points of a plane bounded by the three circles a, b, c, respectively, as in Figure 1.1. The shaded portion is the set $A \cap (B \cap C) = (A \cap B) \cap C$. This relation is valid for arbitrary sets, and the proof is typical of arguments demonstrating the equality of sets.

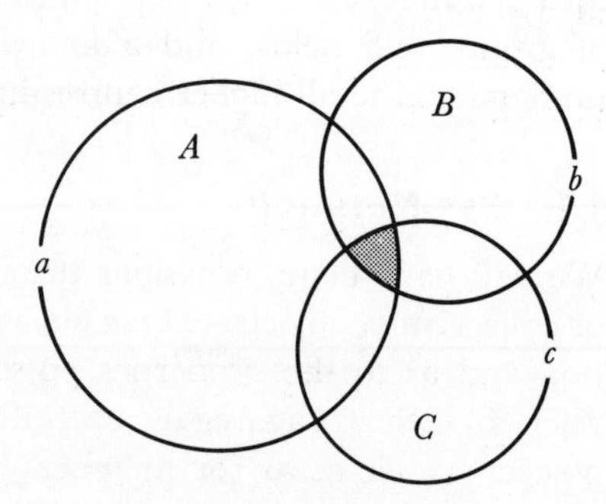

FIGURE 1.1

PROOF. Let x be an arbitrary element of $(A \cap B) \cap C$. Then, because of the definition of intersections, $x \in (A \cap B)$ and $x \in C$. Similarly, $x \in A \cap B$ implies $x \in A$ and $x \in B$. On the other hand, $x \in B$ and $x \in C$ means $x \in B \cap C$. Moreover, $x \in A$ and $x \in B \cap C$ means $x \in A \cap (B \cap C)$. Therefore an arbitrary element x of $(A \cap B) \cap C$ is an element of $A \cap (B \cap C)$ or

$$(A \cap B) \cap C \subseteq A \cap (B \cap C).$$

We now essentially repeat the arguments, beginning with an arbitrary element y of $A \cap (B \cap C)$ to show that

$$A \cap (B \cap C) \subseteq (A \cap B) \cap C,$$

and consequently we have the equality of the sets as desired.

Note that no reference to Figure 1.1 has been made in the proof so that the relation $(A \cap B) \cap C = A \cap (B \cap C)$ is valid for arbitrary sets. Therefore the parentheses are unnecessary and the set may be denoted unambiguously by $A \cap B \cap C$. A similar result is true for unions. These facts are expressed by saying that the operations of set union and set intersection are *associative.*

Example 2. Let P denote the set of positive integers and let

$$\begin{aligned} A &= \{x \in P \mid x \text{ is divisible by } 2\}, \\ B &= \{x \in P \mid x \text{ is divisible by } 3\}, \\ C &= \{x \in P \mid x \text{ is not divisible by } 2\}. \end{aligned}$$

It is easy to see that $A \cap C = \emptyset$ (the empty set), $A \cup C = P$, and

$$A \cap B = \{x \in P \mid x \text{ is divisible by } 6\}.$$

The concepts of sets, subsets, set intersections, and set unions are the basis of a language for mathematics. However, the simple process of forming new sets different from $A \cap B$ and $A \cup B$ or subsets thereof will require additional definitions. One of the simplest ways of forming a new set from the sets A and B is to construct the set of all *ordered pairs* of elements (a, b), where $a \in A$, $b \in B$. This set will be denoted by $A \times B$ and it is called the *Cartesian product* of the sets A and B; notationally,

$$A \times B = \{(a, b) \mid a \in A, \quad b \in B\}.$$

It should be clear that the concept of Cartesian product can be extended to any finite number of sets $A, B, C, \ldots$ with the elements $(a, b, c, \ldots)$.

Example 3. Let A be the set consisting of the letters of the alphabet, $B = \{1, 2, 3\}$, and C the set of letters of the Greek alphabet. Then typical elements of the Cartesian product $A \times B \times C$ will be

$$(\text{d}, 2, \alpha), (\text{x}, 1, \beta), (\text{p}, 3, \mu), (\text{z}, 2, \gamma).$$

Exercises

1. Let I denote the set of all integers, positive, negative, and zero. What integers are identified in the following sets?
   (a) $S = \{x \in I \mid x^2 = 4\}$,
   (b) $S = \{x \in I \mid (x + 1)/x \geq 1\}$,
   (c) $S = \{x \in I \mid x \text{ divides } 24\}$.
2. In Example 1, indicate the following sets by cross-hatching a redrawing of Figure 1.1 in each case:
   (a) $A \cap B$, (b) $B \cap C$, (c) $(A \cap B) \cup C$,
   (d) $A \cap (B \cup C)$, (e) $(A \cup B) \cap C$, (f) $(A \cap B) \cup (A \cap C)$.
3. In Example 2, describe the following sets:
   (a) $B \cap C$, (b) $A \cup B$, (c) $(A \cup B) \cap C$, (d) $A \cup (B \cap C)$.
4. Let $A = \{1, 2, 3, 4\}$ and $B = \{2, 4, 6, 8\}$. Which of the following elements are in the Cartesian product $A \times B$?
   (a) (2, 3), (3, 2), (8, 1), (1, 6).
   (b) How many elements are in $A \times B$?

5. Let $A = \{1, 2, 3\}$. List eight subsets of A. Determine a relation between the number of elements of a set with n elements and the number of subsets.
6. Prove that $A \cup (B \cup C) = (A \cup B) \cup C$ for arbitrary sets A, B, C.
7. Prove that $(A \cap B) \cup C \supseteq A \cap (B \cup C)$ for arbitrary sets A, B, C. Note that these sets are unequal in both Example 1 and Example 2. The inequalities indicate the necessity for caution in dealing with parentheses.
8. Prove that equality will always occur in the relation of Exercise 7 if $C \subseteq A$. Illustrate by a diagram.
9. Prove that $(A \cup B) \cap C = (A \cap C) \cup (B \cap C)$ for arbitrary sets A, B, C.
10. Is there any necessary set-subset relation between $(A \cup B) \cap C$ and $A \cup (B \cap C)$ for arbitrary sets A, B, C? Illustrate possible equality with a diagram.

*11. Let S be a finite set and let $P_1, P_2, \ldots, P_n$ be properties possessed by the elements of S. For each property P_i, form the set

$$S_i = \{x \in S \mid x \text{ has property } P_i\}.$$

Denote by $n(S)$ the number of elements in S and similarly let $n(S_i)$ denote the number of elements in S_i.

(a) Show that the number of elements having properties P_1 and P_2 is

$$n(S_1) + n(S_2) - n(S_1 \cap S_2).$$

(b) Show that the number of elements *not* having properties P_1, P_2, or P_3 is

$$n(S) - n(S_1) - n(S_2) - n(S_3) + n(S_1 \cap S_2) + n(S_1 \cap S_3) + n(S_2 \cap S_3) - n(S_1 \cap S_2 \cap S_3).$$

(c) Generalize (a) and (b) to any number of properties $P_1, P_2, \ldots, P_r$.

(d) Solve the old lady's question of Clara in Knot X of "A Tangled Tale," by Lewis Carroll.

1.2 Mappings

The concept of a function which has occurred in the student's earlier courses in mathematics will be reformulated to provide the notation and terminology of current mathematical usage. The student is probably most familiar with functions that involve two subsets, X and Y, of the real numbers and are given by a rule assigning to each element $x \in X$ a particular element $y \in Y$. For example, let

$$X = \{x \mid -1 \leq x \leq 1\},$$
$$Y = \{y \mid \ 0 \leq y \leq 1\},$$

and let the rule be $y = \sqrt{1 - x^2}$; that is, to each $x \in X$ we assign the real number $\sqrt{1 - x^2} \in Y$.

There are three components in the definition of a function: a *domain* (of definition) *set* X, a *range set* Y, and a rule that assigns to each element $x \in X$ a unique element $y \in Y$. The type of functions first described, in which X and Y are restricted to be subsets of the real numbers, is a special case of what we shall call mappings.

DEFINITION 1.1. Let X and Y be two arbitrary sets. Let T be a rule that assigns to each element $x \in X$ a unique element $y \in Y$. Then T is called a MAPPING of (from) the set X to the set Y.

The set X is called the *domain* of the mapping T and the set Y is called the *range* of T. The element $y \in Y$ assigned by T to x, denoted by $y = \mathrm{T}(x)$, is called the *image* of the element x.

The set $\mathrm{T}(X)$ consisting of all those elements of X which are images of elements X is called the *image* of X; notationally,

$$\mathrm{T}(X) = \{y \in Y \mid y = \mathrm{T}(x) \text{ for some } x \in X\}.$$

Example 1. Let X be the set consisting of an ordinary deck of playing cards (joker excluded). Let Y consist of the three-element set of colors {red, black, yellow}. The obvious rule that assigns to each card the color of its marking is a mapping of X to Y. For example,

$$\begin{aligned} \mathrm{T}(\text{jack of diamonds}) &= \text{red}; \\ \mathrm{T}(\text{ace of spades}) &= \text{black}; \end{aligned}$$

and, of course, yellow is not the image of any card in X.

Example 2. Let X and Y be two sets and for suggestive, heuristic reasons picture X and Y as line segments in a plane with the Cartesian product $X \times Y$ being the rectangle illustrated in Figure 1.2. If T is a mapping from X to Y, the elements $(x,\mathrm{T}(x))$ are elements of the Cartesian product $X \times Y$. The set of all elements $(x,\mathrm{T}(x))$ is a subset of $X \times Y$.

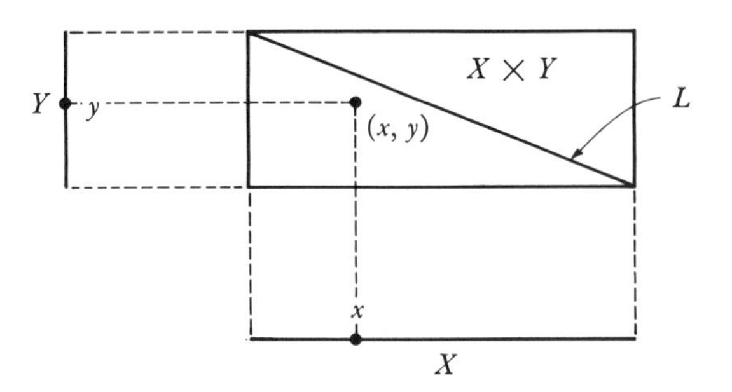

FIGURE 1.2

A subset of $X \times Y$ consisting of those points lying on a line L might represent the elements $(x,\mathrm{T}(x))$ for a particular mapping T. On the other hand, there are mappings T for which a simple interpretation would be inappropriate (see Exercise 8).

We shall use the notations

$$\mathrm{T}: X \to Y, \qquad f: X \to Y, \qquad \theta: X \to Y;$$

or, equivalently,

$$X \xrightarrow{T} Y, \qquad X \xrightarrow{f} Y, \qquad X \xrightarrow{\theta} Y,$$

to indicate that we are considering mappings T, f, and θ with domain X and range Y.

If $\mathrm{T}: X \to Y$, it is certainly possible for the image $\mathrm{T}(X)$ to be a proper subset of Y (Example 1). However, when $\mathrm{T}(X) = Y$, we say that T is a mapping of X *onto* Y or that T is an onto (surjective) mapping. In every case, T is a mapping of X *onto* $\mathrm{T}(X)$.

Example 3. Let I denote the set of integers and let X denote $I \times I$, $Y = I$. The rule T that assigns to the element $(a, b) \in X$ the element $a + b \in Y$ is a mapping of X to Y. Note that the mapping is a mapping of the Cartesian product $I \times I$ onto I. Why is the mapping *onto*?

DEFINITION 1.2. Let $\mathrm{T}: X \to Y$. *The mapping* T *is called a one-to-one (injective) mapping if* $\mathrm{T}(x_1) = \mathrm{T}(x_2)$ *implies* $x_1 = x_2$.

We note for one-to-one mappings that distinct elements in X have distinct images in Y. A mapping that is at the same time both one-to-one and onto is called a *biunique* (bijective) mapping of X to Y.

The following diagrams may be useful in clarifying these definitions. To simplify matters, we let X and Y denote sets of points in the plane. The mapping T is indicated by drawing an arrow from the element $x \in X$ to the element $y \in Y$ to represent the relationship $y = \mathrm{T}(x)$. See Figure 1.3.

The entire mapping of X by T might be indicated by Figure 1.4. Somewhat crudely, if the image set $\mathrm{T}(X)$ covers all of Y, the mapping T is *onto* Y. Again we point out that the mapping T is always *onto* $\mathrm{T}(X)$.

The situation illustrated in Figure 1.5 can *never* occur for a mapping; that is, a unique y is assigned to each $x \in X$. However, we can have the situation illustrated in Figure 1.6 for a mapping. This would merely indicate that the mapping T is *not* one-to-one. Thus in agreement with Definition 1.2, in order to prove that a mapping T is one-to-one it is necessary to show that $x_1 = x_2$ if $\mathrm{T}(x_1) = \mathrm{T}(x_2)$.

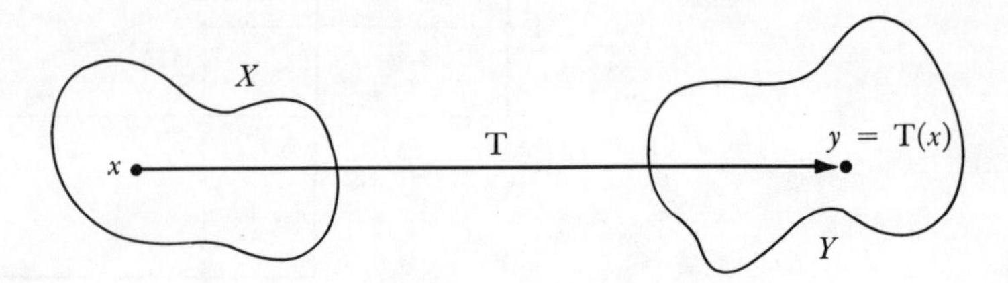

FIGURE 1.3

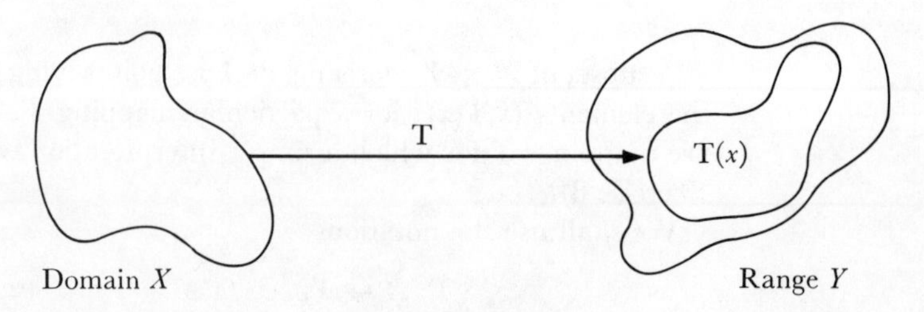

FIGURE 1.4

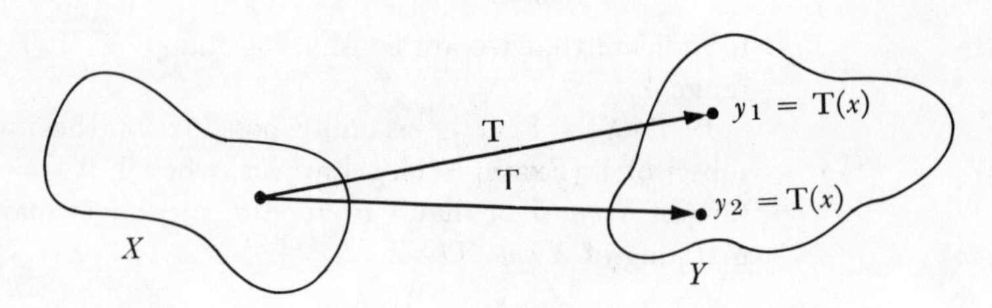

FIGURE 1.5

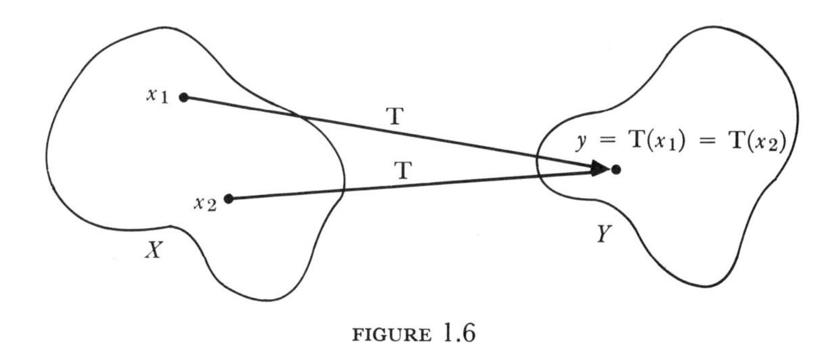

FIGURE 1.6

Example 4. Let A be the set whose elements are triangles in a plane. Let B consist of the positive real numbers. A rule T assigns to each triangle the area of this triangle. T is a mapping of A onto B. Clearly T is not a one-to-one mapping since many different triangles have the same area.

Even when one is considering mappings of a set to itself, a suggestive diagram can be made by merely repeating the set; thus we might have the situation shown in Figure 1.7, and again $T(a)$ is in A.

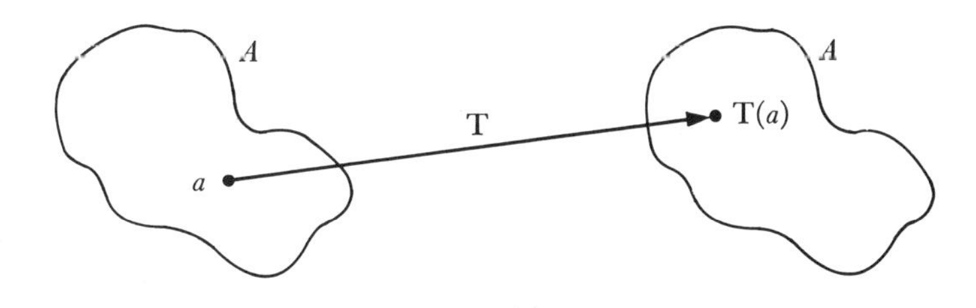

FIGURE 1.7

The *equality* of two mappings is defined for mappings having the same domain X and the same range Y in precisely the manner one would expect. If $F: X \to Y$ and $G: X \to Y$, then we say that the mappings F and G are equal, written $F = G$, if $F(x) = G(x)$ for all $x \in X$.

Example 5. Let D be the set of all differentiable functions defined on the interval $0 \leq x \leq 1$. Let E be the set of all functions defined on $0 \leq x \leq 1$. The rule T that assigns to each function $f \in D$ its derivative df/dx is a mapping of D to E. The mapping T is not one-to-one. (Why?) Is the mapping T onto? (No)

Example 6. Let P be the set of all positive integers and Q the set of all rational numbers. The rule F that assigns to each element $(a, b) \in P \times P$ the element $a/b \in Q$ is a mapping of $P \times P$ to Q. Let G be the rule that assigns to each element $(a, b) \in P \times P$ the element $(a^2 + ab)/(b^2 + ab) \in Q$. We note that F and G are equal mappings. (Why?) Is the mapping onto Q?

Let A, B, C be arbitrary sets. If $F: A \to B$ and $G: B \to C$, it is possible to define a mapping from A to C in terms of the mappings F and G in a rather natural way. To do so, let us start with an element $a \in A$ and determine its image $F(a) \in B$ and then the element $G(F(a)) \in C$. Pictorially, we would have the situation in Figure 1.8; the assignment of the unique element $G(F(a)) \in C$ to the element $a \in A$ provides the rule for a mapping from A to C.

The mapping we have described from A to C is called the *composition* of F and G and is denoted by $G \circ F$. Symbolically,

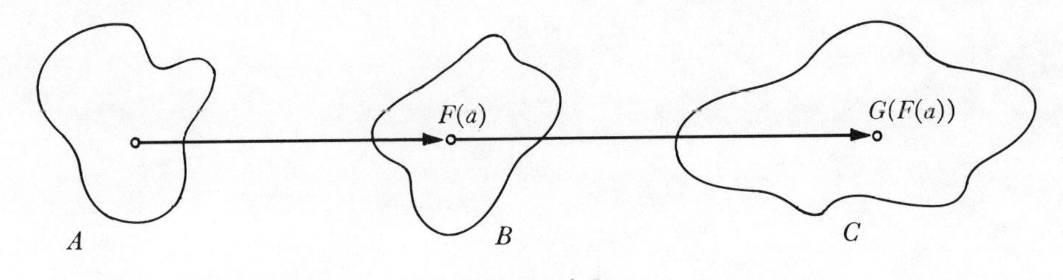

FIGURE 1.8

$$G \circ F: A \to C;$$

for the individual elements of A,

$$(G \circ F)(a) = G(F(a)).$$

The definition of $G \circ F$ requires a slight distortion in habit. Although reading normally proceeds from left to right, it is to be remembered that $(G \circ F)(a)$ requires one to first apply the mapping F to a and then G to $F(a)$.

Example 7. The simplest examples are given by functions defined on subsets of the reals. Let A, B, C all be the set of positive real numbers. Let F be the mapping $x \to x^2$; G, the mapping $x \to 1/x$; H, the mapping $x \to x + 3$. Then $G \circ F = F \circ G$ is the mapping $x \to 1/x^2$. $H \circ F$ is the mapping $x \to x^2 + 3$ while $F \circ H$ is the mapping $x \to x^2 + 6x + 9$. What are $G \circ H$ and $H \circ G$?

The composition of mappings for which the sets $A = B = C$ will be of particular interest. In this case F, G, and $G \circ F$ (or $F \circ G$) are mappings from A to A. In the following exercises we ask the student to verify some elementary properties for these mappings.

Exercises

1. Let the set X consist of the people listed in a telephone directory. Let $Y = \{0, 1, 2, \ldots, 9\}$. Define a mapping of X onto Y.
2. Let P denote the set of positive integers. Let T be the rule that assigns to n the number n^2. Describe the situation in the terminology of this section.
3. Let A be the finite set of integers $1, 2, \ldots, n$. Let T be a mapping of A onto A. Prove that T must be a one-to-one mapping.
4. Let P be the set of positive integers and let E be the set of positive even integers. Let θ assign to n the value $2n$. Is θ a one-to-one mapping? Consider the fact that $E \subseteq P$. When is such a one-to-one mapping of a set onto a proper subset possible?
5. Let P be the set of positive integers. Let T be a rule that assigns the value n in P to the odd integer $2n - 1$ and also the value n to the even integer $2n$. Is T a mapping of P onto P? Is it one-to-one? Compare with Exercise 3.
6. How many different one-to-one mappings of the set $\{1, 2, 3\}$ onto itself are there? Generalize to the set of Exercise 3.
7. Let I be the set of integers. To an element $(a, b) \in I \times I$ let f assign the element $a^2 + b^2 \in I$. Is f a one-to-one mapping of $I \times I$ to I? Is the mapping onto I?
8. Let P denote the positive integers. In a manner similar to Example 2,

think of $P \times P$ as the lattice points of the first quadrant. Let T be the rule that assigns to each integer $n \in P$ the largest integer k such that $k^2 \leq n$. Do the points $(x,\mathrm{T}(x))$ lie on a line L in $P \times P$?

9. Many texts define a mapping of the set X to the set Y to be a subset T of the Cartesian product $X \times Y$ with the property that for each $x \in X$ there is precisely one element $(x, y) \in \mathrm{T}$. Compare this definition of a mapping with the one given in this text.
10. Let $A = \{1, 2, 3, 4\}$ and consider the mappings

$$\mathrm{F}: \begin{cases} 1 \to 2 \\ 2 \to 3 \\ 3 \to 1 \\ 4 \to 4 \end{cases} \quad \text{and} \quad \mathrm{G}: \begin{cases} 1 \to 3 \\ 2 \to 4 \\ 3 \to 2 \\ 4 \to 1 \end{cases}$$

of A to itself.
(a) Compute $(\mathrm{F} \circ \mathrm{G})(2)$, $(\mathrm{G} \circ \mathrm{F})(2)$, and show that $\mathrm{F} \circ \mathrm{G} \neq \mathrm{G} \circ \mathrm{F}$.
(b) Compute the mappings $\mathrm{F} \circ \mathrm{F}$, $\mathrm{G} \circ \mathrm{G}$, $\mathrm{F} \circ (\mathrm{F} \circ \mathrm{G})$, $(\mathrm{F} \circ \mathrm{F}) \circ \mathrm{G}$.
11. A biunique mapping of a set A to itself is often called a *permutation* of A. Show for permutations F, G, and H of the set A that composition is associative; that is,

$$(\mathrm{F} \circ \mathrm{G}) \circ \mathrm{H} = \mathrm{F} \circ (\mathrm{G} \circ \mathrm{H}).$$

Is the composition of arbitrary mappings of a set A to itself associative?

*12. If T is a biunique mapping of the set A to the set B, define the *inverse* mapping T^{-1} to be the mapping from B to A that assigns to an element $b \in B$ the element $a \in A$ for which $\mathrm{T}(a) = b$; that is, if $\mathrm{T}(a) = b$, then $\mathrm{T}^{-1}(b) = a$. Show for the compositions $\mathrm{T} \circ \mathrm{T}^{-1}$ and $\mathrm{T}^{-1} \circ \mathrm{T}$ that

$$(\mathrm{T} \circ \mathrm{T}^{-1})(b) = b \qquad \text{for all } b \in B,$$
$$(\mathrm{T}^{-1} \circ \mathrm{T})(a) = a \qquad \text{for all } a \in A.$$

*13. Let $\mathrm{T}: A \to B$ be a biunique mapping. Let the mapping E_A be defined on A by the relation $\mathrm{E}_A(a) = a$ for all $a \in A$. Similarly, let $\mathrm{E}_B(b) = b$ define a mapping for B.
(a) Prove that $\mathrm{E}_B \circ \mathrm{T} = \mathrm{T}$.
(b) Prove that $\mathrm{T} \circ \mathrm{E}_A = \mathrm{T}$.

*14. Prove that

$$\sum_{k=0}^{m-1} (-1)^k (m - k)^m C_k^m = m!,$$

where $\sum$ is the usual summation symbol and C_k^m is the usual combinatorial symbol for $m!$ divided by $k!(m - k)!$. *Hint:* Consider the set of all mappings of $\{1, 2, 3, \ldots, m\}$ to itself and denote by P_k the property that a particular mapping T maps the m elements on at most $m - k$ elements. Determine the number of mappings having property P_k and use the result of Exercise 11(c) in Section 1.1 to obtain the number of mappings without property $P_1, P_2, \ldots, P_{m-1}$. Now compare with the generalization in Exercise 6 above.

1.3 Fields, Groups

The student is undoubtedly familiar with the basic properties of the set of real numbers R, and with those of some of its subsets such as the rational numbers and the integers: for example, the associative property for the addition of real numbers

$$a + (b + c) = (a + b) + c.$$

We have seen that a similar property is valid for set intersection

$$A \cap (B \cap C) = (A \cap B) \cap C,$$

and, in the preceding exercises, for the composition of mappings

$$\mathrm{F} \circ (\mathrm{G} \circ \mathrm{H}) = (\mathrm{F} \circ \mathrm{G}) \circ \mathrm{H}.$$

Other properties of the real numbers will have analogous applications to sets we shall consider in this text.

It would be possible to list a few basic properties of the natural numbers 1, 2, 3, . . . and, on the basis of these alone, to construct the systems of the integers (positive, negative, and zero), the rationals (numbers of the form p/q, where p and q are integers), and the real numbers in turn. In doing so, we would determine properties of the real numbers of interest to us. This is done, for example, in the book *Foundations of Analysis*, by E. Landau (New York: Chelsea Publishing Company, 1960). Such a procedure, while admittedly a logical choice, would carry us too far from our goal. We shall confine ourselves primarily to a rephrasing of some of the properties of real numbers in the terminology of the preceding sections, to preparing a short catalog of laws possibly satisfied by the elements of a set S, and to a few side remarks.

First, we note that the usual addition and multiplication of real numbers assigns to each ordered pair (a, b) of real numbers the real numbers $a + b$ and $a \cdot b$. This assignment provides the rules for two mappings from the Cartesian product $R \times R$ to R; specifically,

$$+ : (a, b) \to a + b \in R,$$

$$\cdot : (a, b) \to a \cdot b \in R,$$

for all $(a, b) \in R \times R$.

DEFINITION 1.3. Let S be an arbitrary set. A mapping from the Cartesian product $S \times S$ to S is called a binary operation defined on S.

A "binary operation" operates on ordered pairs of elements of S to produce elements of S. Quite correctly, we could indicate the situation as follows:

$$\mathrm{T}: S \times S \to S$$

and $\mathrm{T}((a, b)) \in S$. More often than not, we are interested primarily in the behavior of the images $\mathrm{T}((a, b)) \in S$ for a binary operation, for example, in the sum $a + b$ or product $a \cdot b$ of real numbers. Therefore it has become customary to denote a binary operation by some symbol such as $+$, $\cdot$, $\times$, $*$, and to simply denote the image of the ordered pair (a, b) by $a + b$, $a \cdot b$, $a \times b$, $a * b$.

Example 1. Let A be an arbitrary set and let $S = \{f \mid f: A \to A\}$. If f, g are two elements of S, then we have seen that the composition $g \circ f$ is again a mapping of A to A. Thus $g \circ f \in S$ and consequently $\circ$ is a binary operation defined on S.

Example 2. A simple way to exhibit a binary operation for a finite set is to prepare a table of the following type:

$*$	a	b	c
a	b	c	a
b	a	b	b
c	c	c	a

$\circ$	a	b	c
a	a	b	c
b	c	a	b
c	b	c	a

Here the symbol for the binary operation on the set $\{a, b, c\}$ is indicated in the upper left, and the images $a * b$ or $a \circ b$ are to be found at the intersection of the row and column headed by a and b. Thus, $c * b = c$, $b * a = a$, $b * c = b$, $a \circ c = c$, $b \circ b = a$, etc.

Let us now suppose we have a set S. For the elements of S suppose further that we have two binary operations defined: one an "addition" of elements denoted by $+$, and the other a "multiplication" of elements denoted by $\cdot$ or simply by juxtaposition. We shall assume for the elements of S that one or more of the following laws are valid:

A1. If $a \in S$, $b \in S$, then $a + b \in S$.
A2. If $a \in S$, $b \in S$, $c \in S$, then

$$(a + b) + c = a + (b + c). \qquad \textit{(associative law)}$$

A3. There is an element $0 \in S$ such that

$$a + 0 = 0 + a = a \qquad \text{for every } a \in S.$$

A4. For every $a \in S$ there is an element $-a \in S$ such that

$$a + (-a) = (-a) + a = 0.$$

A5. If $a \in S$, $b \in S$, $a + b = b + a$. *(commutative law)*
M1. If $a \in S$, $b \in S$, then $a \cdot b \in S$.
M2. If $a \in S$, $b \in S$, $c \in S$, then

$$(a \cdot b) \cdot c = a \cdot (b \cdot c). \qquad \textit{(associative law)}$$

M3. There is an element $1 \in S$ such that $1 \neq 0$ and

$$a \cdot 1 = 1 \cdot a = a \qquad \text{for every } a \in S.$$

M4. For every $a \in S$ such that $a \neq 0$, there is an element $a^{-1} \in S$ such that

$$a \cdot a^{-1} = a^{-1} \cdot a = 1.$$

M5. If $a \in S$, $b \in S$, $a \cdot b = b \cdot a$. *(commutative law)*
D1. If $a \in S$, $b \in S$, $c \in S$,

$$a \cdot (b + c) = a \cdot b + a \cdot c; \qquad \textit{(left distributive law)}$$

$$(b + c) \cdot a = b \cdot a + c \cdot a \qquad \textit{(right distributive law)}.$$

If we choose S to be the set of all real numbers R (or the set of all rational numbers Q) together with the usual addition and multiplication of numbers, then all of the laws listed above are satisfied by the elements of R (or Q).

DEFINITION 1.4. A set S for which an "addition" and a "multiplication" of elements are defined satisfying the laws A1–A5, M1–M5 *and* D1 *is called a field.*

In addition to the *real field R* and the *rational field Q*, the student is probably familiar with the *complex field C*. The latter field can be described as consisting of numbers of the form $a + bi$, where $a, b \in R$ and equality, addition, and multiplication are defined by the rules

$$a + bi = c + di \quad \text{if and only if} \quad a = c, \quad b = d;$$

$$(a + bi) + (c + di) = (a + c) + (b + d)i,$$

$$(a + bi)(c + di) = (ac - bd) + (ad + bc)i.$$

It is a perfectly straightforward, but by no means brief, exercise to show that all of the laws for a field are satisfied by the elements of C. We leave this task for the student.

There are many other examples of fields, some of which we have deferred to the exercises. At this time there are several remarks worthy of note concerning the laws defining a field.

REMARK 1. Since we shall be using these laws individually or in small groups, no attempt was made to use the results of one law in stating another. For example, if M5 is assumed, the right distributive law in D1 would follow from the left distributive law and vice versa. However, in Chapter 6 we shall have occasion to consider sets where M5 does not apply but D1 does.

REMARK 2. The statement $1 \neq 0$ in M3 is inserted to prevent the set consisting of the number 0 alone from being a field. If this set were a field it would make a number of our statements awkward. Without the requirement $1 \neq 0$, the student can easily verify that the set $\{0\}$ would logically satisfy all eleven laws.

REMARK 3. The laws A3 and M3 are distinguished from the rest in that they call two particular elements, 0 and 1, to our attention. These elements appear again in A4 and M4, where they are used to define the *negative* $-a$ and the *inverse* a^{-1}, respectively. In terms of the negative and inverse elements we may in turn define the familiar processes of *subtraction* and *division* by the formulas $a - b = a + (-b)$ and $a/b = ab^{-1}$.

REMARK 4. The laws selected for our catalog were not chosen by whim nor even on strictly utilitarian grounds for our needs in the remainder of the book. The assumption of various subsets of these laws for the elements of S is the basis of practically all areas of study in algebra. Moreover, properties of the real numbers that depend only upon addition and multiplication are direct consequences of these laws, and similar results are consequently valid for any field. For example, let us prove that $a \cdot 0 = 0$ for any real number a. Now, $0 + 0 = 0$ by A3; to this equality we apply the left distributive law after multiplying by a,

$$a \cdot (0 + 0) = a \cdot 0,$$

$$a \cdot 0 + a \cdot 0 = a \cdot 0.$$

Now to both sides add $-(a \cdot 0)$, whose existence is ensured by A4. Then,

$$[(a \cdot 0) + (a \cdot 0)] + [-(a \cdot 0)] = a \cdot 0 + [-(a \cdot 0)].$$

An application of A2 to the left member and A4 to the right member of the previous equation yields $a \cdot 0 + \{(a \cdot 0) + [-(a \cdot 0)]\} = 0$; then $a \cdot 0 + 0 = 0$ by A4. Finally $a \cdot 0 = 0$ by A3.

No property of real numbers other than those listed has been used in this proof. Therefore $a \cdot 0 = 0$ is valid for any field.

The properties of a field listed thus far are not sufficient to identify the real field R. For one thing, we have no properties that justify our saying 6 is larger than $\sqrt{2}$. Since our arguments will, on occasion, involve this type of statement, we shall remedy this shortcoming with four more laws concerning order.

Let the set of elements S considered previously have defined for its elements a relation "greater than," written $>$, holding between pairs of elements. Then we consider the applicability of the following laws to S:

O1. If $a \in S,\ b \in S$, precisely one of the following three possibilities is true: $a > b,\ a = b,\ b > a$.
O2. If $a \in S,\ b \in S,\ c \in S$ and $a > b,\ b > c$, then $a > c$.
O3. If $a \in S,\ b \in S,\ c \in S$ and $a > b$, then $a + c > b + c$.
O4. If $a \in S,\ b \in S,\ c \in S$ and $a > b,\ c > 0$, then $ac > bc$.

If all fifteen laws so far written apply to S, S is called an *ordered field.* The real field R and the rational field Q are ordered fields. The complex field C is not an ordered field (Exercise 9).

In terms of an order relation for a set S, we could define positive elements $(a > c)$, negative elements $(a < 0)$, and the absolute value $|a|$ for elements of $S\,(|a| = a$ if $a \geq 0$ and $|a| = -a$ if $a < 0)$. Actually, we will be concerned primarily with the laws defining a field as illustrated by the real field R, and the order relation $>$ in R will play a minor role. Hence we shall assume that the student's knowledge of order and absolute value for the real field R is sufficient for our purpose. (Exercises 7 and 8 are designed primarily to refresh the student's memory.)

If our concern throughout the remainder of the text were to be limited to the real field R, it would be proper to identify R uniquely (if possible). The laws presented so far do not do this because the rational field Q is also an ordered field; there are other ordered fields. The one remaining property needed to identify the real field among all ordered fields is that of least upper bounds. However, this property is more a topic for an analysis course and affects the subject matter of this book only in our need for a particular relationship between the real field R and the set of points of a line. We shall assume the relationship when needed and pursue the question of least upper bounds no further.

Remark 5. The similarity of laws A1–A5 to M1–M5, except for the restrictions $1 \neq 0$ in M3 and $a \neq 0$ in M4, may have been noticed by the student. Sets for which only one binary operation is defined (or is of immediate interest) occur frequently in mathematics. The operation on the elements of S may take various forms which we may wish to call addition, multiplication, or composition of mappings, etc., depending upon the circumstances. We can encompass all of these alternatives by indicating the binary operation by $*$. The laws of interest to us then take the form

(i) If $a \in S,\ b \in S$, then $a * b \in S$.

(ii) If $a \in S,\ b \in S,\ c \in S$, then $(a * b) * c = a * (b * c)$.

(iii) There is a unique element $e \in S$ such that, for all elements $a \in S$,

$$a * e = e * a = a.$$

(iv) For every $a \in S$ there exists a unique element $a^{-1} \in S$ such that

$$a * a^{-1} = a^{-1} * a = e.$$

(v) If $a \in S,\ b \in S$, then

$$a * b = b * a.$$

(1.3)

A set S with a binary operation $*$ satisfying the laws listed above is called an *Abelian group* (relative to the operation $*$). When requirement (v) is omitted, the set S is called a *group*.

The integers (positive, negative, and zero) form an Abelian group under addition. All even integers form an Abelian group under addition. The set of all nonzero rationals forms an Abelian group under ordinary multiplication. We have not illustrated, as yet, an example of a group that is not Abelian. However, such examples will be given in the exercises.

Exercises

1. Two binary operations on the set $\{a, b, c\}$ are given in the following tables:

+	a	b	c
a	a	b	c
b	b	c	a
c	c	a	b

·	a	b	c
a	a	a	a
b	a	b	c
c	a	c	b

(a) Determine $a + c$, $b + b$, $c + b$.
(b) Determine $a \cdot c$, $b \cdot b$, $c \cdot b$.
(c) Is $a + b = b + a$?
(d) Is $(a + b) \cdot b = a \cdot b + b \cdot b$?

2. Let I be the set of integers. For every ordered pair (a, b), $b \neq 0$, it is possible to find unique integers q and r such that $a = bq + r$, where $0 \leq r < |b|$ (the usual division process). Denote r by $a * b$.
(a) Is the mapping $(a, b) \to a * b$ a binary operation defined on I?
(b) Is $7 * 13 = 13 * 7$?
(c) Is $(a * b) * c = a * (b * c)$ valid for all choices of $a, b, c \in I$? Are there choices of a, b, and c for which the associative law is valid?

3. How many of the fifteen basic laws for an ordered field are satisfied by:
(a) The positive integers?
(b) The integers?
(c) The subset of the reals consisting of numbers of the form $a + b\sqrt{2}$, where a and b are rational?

4. Prove that the right distributive law follows from the other laws of a field. Justify each step.

5. Prove: If a and b are elements of a field S such that $a \neq 0$ and $ab = 0$, then $b = 0$.

6. Prove that $(-a)(-b) = ab$ by associating in two ways the expression $ab + a(-b) + (-a)(-b)$.

7. Let S be an ordered field. Prove the following:
(a) If $a > b$ and $ab > 0$, then $1/b > 1/a$.
(b) If $a > b$ and $c > d$, then $a + c > b + d$.
(c) If $a > b > 0$ and $c > d > 0$, then $ac > bd$.

8. Let $|a|$ denote the absolute value for the real field R. Prove:
(a) $|ab| = |a|\,|b|$;
(b) $|a + b| \leq |a| + |b|$.

9. For the complex number i, show that neither $i > 0$ nor $-i > 0$ by

using property O4 after assuming either case. Now show that the complex field is not ordered.

10. Consider the set $S = \{a, b\}$ with addition and multiplication defined by

$$a + a = b + b = a, \qquad a + b = b + a = b;$$

$$aa = ab = ba = a, \qquad bb = b.$$

How many of the first eleven laws are satisfied by S? Is S a field?

11. (a) In Exercise 1, how many separate cases would be necessary to verify that $(a + b) + c = a + (b + c)$?
   (b) How many separate cases are necessary to verify that both distributive laws are valid?

   Actually, the "addition" and "multiplication" of the distinct elements a, b, c in Exercise 1 are those of a three-element field.
   (c) Which element plays the role of 0? 1?
   (d) Which element is b^{-1}? $(-b)$?

12. There are six biunique mappings of the set $\{1, 2, 3\}$ to itself. Let us denote these by

$$\text{I}: \begin{cases} 1 \to 1 \\ 2 \to 2 \\ 3 \to 3 \end{cases} \quad \text{A}: \begin{cases} 1 \to 2 \\ 2 \to 3 \\ 3 \to 1 \end{cases} \quad \text{B}: \begin{cases} 1 \to 3 \\ 2 \to 1 \\ 3 \to 2 \end{cases}$$

$$\text{C}: \begin{cases} 1 \to 1 \\ 2 \to 3 \\ 3 \to 2 \end{cases} \quad \text{D}: \begin{cases} 1 \to 3 \\ 2 \to 2 \\ 3 \to 1 \end{cases} \quad \text{E}: \begin{cases} 1 \to 2 \\ 2 \to 1 \\ 3 \to 3 \end{cases}$$

Determine the various compositions of mappings to complete the following table:

$\circ$	I	A	B	C	D	E
I	I					E
A		B			C	
B			A	D		
C	C	D	E	I		
D	D	E	C		I	
E	E	C	D			I

   (a) What is the "inverse" (see Exercise 12, Section 1.2) of A? B? C?
   (b) Is it true that $\text{A} \circ \text{A}^{-1} = \text{I}$?
   (c) Is the set of biunique mappings of the set $\{1, 2, 3\}$ to itself a group (relative to $\circ$)? An Abelian group?

*13. Show that the set of all permutations (see Exercise 11, Section 1.2) of a set A forms a group under composition of mappings $\circ$ (see Exercises 11, 12, 13, Section 1.2).

1.4 Proofs

As a final introductory topic we will make a few comments on some of the methods of proof used in mathematics. It is clear from the exercises of the preceding sections that we have assumed that the student already has a basic understanding of the meaning of mathematical proof as a logical process of reaching a definite conclusion from definite assumptions. Therefore, it is not our purpose to engage in a lengthy discussion of logic or truth tables but merely to provide a guide from the student's intuitive concepts of logic to some typical types of mathematical arguments which frequently cause difficulty for those inexperienced in rigorous mathematics.

The statement of a problem requiring a proof will provide the student with certain assumptions that may be used. A proof based on these, without further assumptions, will be called a *direct proof.* Let us illustrate a direct proof by considering Exercise 5 of the preceding section:

Prove: If a and b are elements of a field S such that $a \neq 0$ and $ab = 0$, then $b = 0$.

Here the permitted assumptions may be divided into four simple statements:

(i) a is an element of S;
(ii) b is an element of S;
(iii) $a \neq 0$;
(iv) $ab = 0$.

The desired conclusion to be obtained is that $b = 0$.

If we study the assumptions, we see that (i) and (ii) simply tell us what elements we are dealing with and what rules we may use: A1–A5, M1–M5, and D1. Statements (iii) and (iv) offer specific evidence to work with. Indeed, we recall that (iii) guarantees the existence of an inverse, a^{-1}, such that $a^{-1}a = 1$ (M4).

We begin our proof by multiplying both sides of (iv) by a^{-1} to obtain

$$(a^{-1} \cdot a) \cdot b = a^{-1} \cdot 0.$$

Now, we can simplify matters to obtain

$$1 \cdot b = a^{-1} \cdot 0 \qquad \text{or} \qquad b = 0,$$

where the latter equation has involved (M3) and the result $a \cdot 0 = 0$ proved in Remark 4 of Section 1.3.

The detailed justification for each step in the preceding proof may be suppressed for economy of words, but a student must be prepared to defend his argument. There are, of course, other satisfactory solutions. We might, for example, decide to investigate what would result if all the assumptions held and the conclusion $b = 0$ were false. That is, suppose a and b are elements of S, $a \neq 0$, $ab = 0$ *and* $b \neq 0$. Since we would know that b^{-1} exists, we could argue

$$(ab)b^{-1} = 0 \cdot b^{-1}, \qquad a \cdot 1 = 0 \cdot b^{-1} \qquad \text{or} \qquad a = 0.$$

This contradicts the assumption that $a \neq 0$. Thus we see that if we assume $a \neq 0$, $ab = 0$, we cannot simultaneously have $b \neq 0$. Hence we must conclude that $b = 0$.

Mathematical Induction

A common method of proof throughout mathematics is that of *mathematical induction.* In those theorems or problems where one finds this method to be effective, we usually have a statement that involves an integer n and is to be verified for all such integers—for example,

$$1 + 2 + \cdots + n = n(n + 1)/2,$$

or,

Prove that the number of biunique mappings of the set $\{1, 2, \ldots, n\}$ to itself is $n!$

These are really two variations to the method of proof by induction. In either case the statement is shown to be true for $n = 1$. In the first variation, the statement is next proved for $n = k$ on the assumption that it is true for $n = k - 1$. In the second variation, the statement is proved for $n = k$ on the "stronger" assumption that it is true for *all* integers less than k. When, in either case, the two parts are successively (and successfully) concluded, we assert that the statement is true for all positive integers.

The justification for the last assertion rests on a postulate or law concerning the positive integers:

WELL-ORDERING PRINCIPLE. Any nonempty set of positive integers contains a least element.

Let us indicate precisely how this property of the positive integers provides the basis for proofs by induction. We have a statement $P(n)$ that depends upon n and we denote the set of integers for which the statement is false by F; that is,

$$F = \{x \mid P(x) \text{ is false}\}.$$

If F is the empty set $\emptyset$, the statement $P(n)$ is true for all n. We proceed with a proof by assuming that F is not empty and let k be the least integer in F (applying here the well-ordering principle). We know $k \neq 1$ since we prove the statement $P(1)$ is true. Hence there are positive integers x smaller than k for *all* of which $P(x)$ is true. But in one form of induction we prove that if $P(k - 1)$ is true, then $P(k)$ is true; in the other form we prove that if $P(x)$ is true for all $x < k$, then $P(k)$ is true. In either case, the statement $P(k)$ is true. This is a contradiction. Hence F is empty.

Example 1. We shall illustrate proofs by induction by showing that the number of biunique mappings of the set $\{1, 2, \ldots, n\}$ to itself is $n!$

We find it easier to do a more general problem—one suggested by the observation made earlier in this section. Let A be the set $\{a_1, a_2, \ldots, a_n\}$ and let $B = \{b_1, b_2, \ldots, b_n\}$. We only need to prove that the number of mappings of A onto B is $n!$ since Exercise 3 of Section 1.2 provides the one-to-oneness.

First, for $n = 1$, it is obvious that the only single-valued mapping of $\{a_1\}$ onto $\{b_1\}$ is that given by the correspondence $a_1 \to b_1$.

Now, assume that the number of single-valued mappings of any set of $k - 1$ elements onto another set of the same number of elements is $(k - 1)!$ and consider the possible mappings of $\{a_1, a_2, \ldots, a_k\}$ upon $\{b_1, b_2, \ldots, b_k\}$. We may take the image of a_1 to be any of the k elements $b_1, b_2, \ldots, b_k$; having made a choice, it is left to determine a single-valued mapping of the subset $\{a_2, \ldots, a_k\}$ upon the set of the remaining $k - 1$ elements of B. By assumption there are $(k - 1)!$ such mappings. Hence the total number is $k \cdot (k - 1)! = k!$.

It might be instructive to provide the student with an illustration of a statement to show that both parts of a proof by induction are necessary. For example, let $P(n)$ be the statement

$$1 + 2 + \cdots + n = n(n + 1)/2 + 31.$$

If we assume that $P(k - 1)$ is true, then

$$1 + 2 + \cdots + k - 1 = (k - 1)k/2 + 31.$$

Now add k to both sides to obtain

$$1 + 2 + \cdots + k - 1 + k = (k - 1)k/2 + k + 31 = k(k + 1)/2 + 31.$$

Hence we see that *if* $P(k - 1)$ is true, then $P(k)$ is true. However $P(1)$ is not true! We have not completed and *cannot* complete the proof.

The student should provide a statement $P(n)$ that is true for $n = 1$ and for which the validity of $P(k - 1)$ does not imply that $P(k)$ is true.

Exercises

1. In the argument given on the validity of the induction method, state specifically what the hypothesis, or basic assumptions, was and the conclusion was. Was the proof direct or indirect? If indirect, how was the conclusion assumed false and what contradiction resulted?
2. Give a direct proof by induction of the generalized statement that any single-valued mapping of a set with n elements onto another such set is a one-to-one mapping. Could such a proof be given for the original statement of Exercise 4, Section 1.3?
3. Why was it easier in the induction proof illustrated in the text to prove the more general statement?
4. Prove by induction:

   (a) $1 + 2 + \cdots + n = n(n + 1)/2$,

   (b) $\binom{n}{k-1} + \binom{n}{k} = \binom{n+1}{k}$, where $\binom{n}{k} = \dfrac{n!}{k!\,(n-k)!}$.
5. Using the well-ordering principle, prove that there is no integer between 0 and 1. *Hint:* If m is an integer such that $0 < m < 1$, $0 < m^2 < m < 1$.
6. What is wrong with the following "proof" that all elements of any finite nonempty set are identical?

   First, the statement is certainly true for any set with just one element. Now suppose the statement true for any set with $k - 1$ elements and consider a set $A = \{a_1, a_2, \ldots, a_k\}$. If we remove the first element, a_1, of A, the rest are the same by assumption. If we remove the last, a_k, the rest are again the same. That is, $a_2 = a_3 = \cdots = a_k$ and $a_1 = a_2 = \cdots = a_{k-1}$. Combining the two sets of equalities, $a_1 = a_2 = \cdots = a_k$.
7. Prove by induction that the number of subsets of a set with n elements is 2^n.
8. If A and B are finite sets with m and n elements, respectively, prove that the number of single-valued mappings of A into B is n^m. Show how Exercise 7 may be obtained as a special case of this exercise.
9. Let P and Q stand for two statements. Suppose that the compound statement, "if P, then Q" is true. Prove that the compound statement, "if not Q, then not P" is true.
10. Many texts use the form "a necessary and sufficient condition for P to be true is that Q be true" where we use the form "P is true if and only if Q is true." Does "necessary" correspond to "if" or "only if"?

Vectors and Vector Spaces

The purpose of this chapter is to introduce vector spaces, the basic mathematical structures to be studied in this text. We begin by studying the vector space structure of ordinary two- and three-dimensional Euclidean spaces in order to build an intuitive base for the study of more abstract spaces. In fact, two- and three-dimensional spaces will be the fundamental examples throughout this chapter, and we shall make every effort to relate each new concept to these familiar spaces.

2.1 Coordinate Systems in Space

Coordinate systems are introduced in geometry to permit precise statements of relative position and orientation and to facilitate the use of algebraic language and manipulations. The reader is certainly aware that many geometrical results are capable of being stated and proved much more easily in coordinate language (in analytic geometry rather than in synthetic geometry). On the other hand, the reader should be aware of the fact that there are examples where the reverse is true.

The disadvantage of coordinate notation lies in the arbitrary choices required. Different choices may give different results. For example, in former times, the map makers of each country assigned their own capital the position on the 0-meridian of longitude. Thus when latitude and longitude coordinates of a point were given, it was necessary to specify in whose coordinate system they were stated. Similarly, students who have worked problems in physics or measurement, where they have had to set up their own coordinates, may have been chagrined to discover how much easier the problem was for someone who had made a better choice of coordinates.

When it is at all convenient, then, there is reason to state geometric facts in terms that do not depend upon coordinates (in coordinate-free language). Frequently, however, we shall be directly concerned with statements that depend essentially on the coordinate systems involved. For example, relationships between different coordinate systems will be discussed in detail. Thus, while reasonable preference will be given to coordinate-free expression, it should be kept in mind that actual calculation normally involves coordinate systems and we must be ready to use them.

Let us remind ourselves of exactly what is meant by coordinate systems on a line, in a plane, and in space. We shall emphasize the characteristics of the systems important to future development and take the opportunity to introduce a generalization of the usual Cartesian systems.

To begin with, we assume that the reader has certain valid intuitions about familiar Euclidean space. Inherent in this assumption is the concept of the distance between two points.

We first coordinatize a line L; all of our coordinate systems will depend directly on this coordinatization. For a line L_1 choose a point P_0 as the origin. Choose a sense of direction and, at a unit distance from P_0 in the direction chosen, make a point P_1. See Figure 2.1. The chosen direction will be called the *positive direction*. Now, if P is any point on L, let its distance from P_0 be a. Then the coordinate of P is a if P_0 does not lie between P_1 and P; otherwise, the coordinate of P is $-a$. Note that P_0 has coordinate 0 and P_1 has coordinate 1.

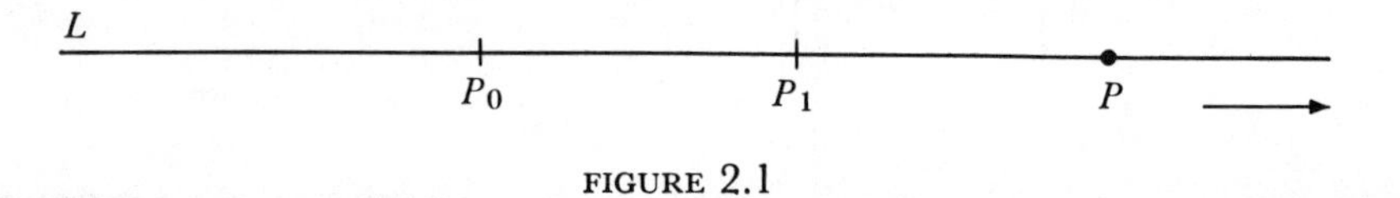

FIGURE 2.1

A slightly different definition may be given as follows: Choose P_0 as before and then choose P_1 as any point on L distinct from P_0. If P is any point on L, let a be the ratio of the distance from P_0 to P to that from P_0 to P_1. Assign the coordinate a or $-a$ to P by the same role as before. Note that again P_0 has coordinate 0 and P_1 has coordinate 1. The difference between the two systems is that, in the first, we assume a basic, preexisting unit of distance. In the second, we establish a unit of distance (and the positive direction) by the arbitrary choice of P_1. We shall use the first formulation when we define *Cartesian* systems. The second will be used for the more general *linear* systems.

In either case the essential property of the construction is the establishment of a one-to-one mapping from the points of L onto the real numbers R. The one-to-one condition follows from the axiom of Euclidean distance, which postulates that the distance between two points is zero if and only if the points are identical. The "onto" property—that every real number is the coordinate of some point—is called the *axiom of continuity*. It is the mapping $\mathrm{T}: L \to R$, where $\mathrm{T}(P)$ is the coordinate of P, which *is* the *coordinate system* for L.

If we have a plane π, *a Cartesian coordinate system* for π is established as follows: Pick a point P_0 as the origin and a line L through P_0. On L_1, with P_0 as origin, establish a Cartesian coordinate system T_1. Let L_2 be the line through P_0 that is perpendicular to L_1. Establish a Cartesian coordinate system T_2 on L_2 using the same unit of distance and P_0 as origin. Now if P is a point on L_1 with T_1 coordinate a, assign to P the coordinates $(a, 0)$. If P is on L_2 with T_2 coordinate b, assign to P the coordinates $(0, b)$. If P is on neither line, suppose that the line through P parallel to L_2 intersects L_1 in a point having T_1 coordinate x, and the line through P parallel to L_1 intersects L_2 in a point having T_2 coordinate y; then assign to P the coordinates (x, y). See Figure 2.2.

A linear system for π is defined similarly except that no condition is made on the choice of L_2 except that it pass through P_0 and be distinct from L_1. Note

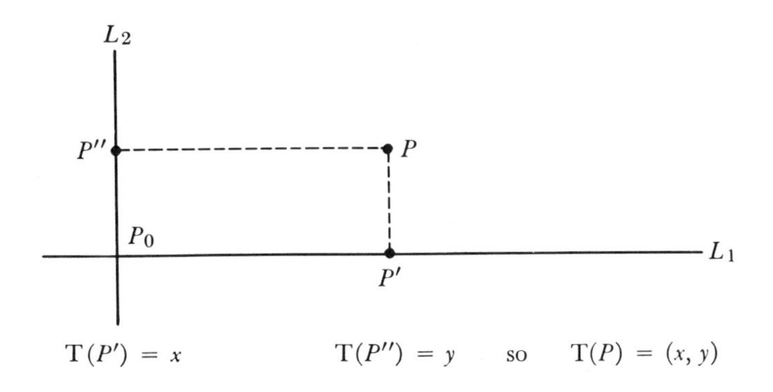

FIGURE 2.2

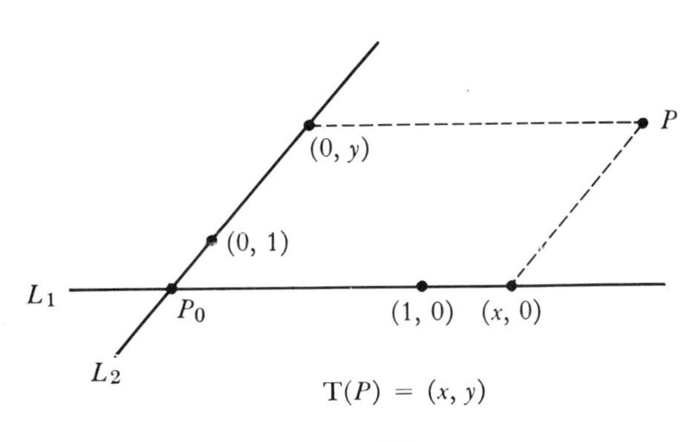

FIGURE 2.3

also that we do not require the units of distance on L_1 and L_2 to be the same. See Figure 2.3.

In either case a one-to-one map is established from the points of π onto $R \times R$. It is this mapping $T: \pi \to R \times R$ which we call the coordinate system of π.

Finally, consider three-dimensional Euclidean space. Take a point P_0 for origin, and three mutually perpendicular lines L_1, L_2, L_3 through P_0. (See Figure 2.4.) On them establish Cartesian coordinate systems T_1, T_2, T_3, respectively. Let the pairs of lines L_2L_3, L_1L_3, and L_1L_2 determine the planes

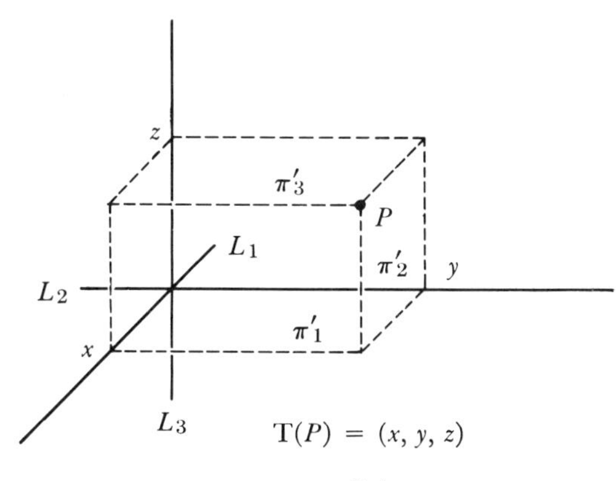

FIGURE 2.4

π_1, π_2, and π_3, respectively (two intersecting lines determine a unique plane). For any point P in space, let π_1' be the plane through P either parallel to or coinciding with π_1 (through any point not in a given plane, there is a unique plane parallel to the given plane). Define π_2' and π_3' similarly. Suppose that π_1' intersects L_1 in a point with T_1 coordinate x, π_2' intersects L_2 in a point with T_2 coordinate y, and π_3' intersects L_3 in a point with T_3 coordinate z. Then assign to P the coordinates (x, y, z).

For the more general linear coordinate system of space, we only require that L_1, L_2, L_3 are three distinct lines and that L_3 is not in the plane determined by L_1 and L_2. Also we use the general point determination for unit distances. Note that π_1' will still intersect L_1 in a unique point since it cannot be parallel to or contain L_1.

In either case we have a mapping from space S to $R \times R \times R$; $T: S \to R \times R \times R$ which is one-to-one and onto. Again no new assumptions are necessary.

The reader may have noticed the close similarity between the Cartesian and the linear coordinate systems. Either or both of two questions may have occurred to him: Why have I never seen generalized linear systems before? Why bother generalizing Cartesian systems?

To the first question, the simplest answer is the great advantage in distance and angular formulas which the Cartesian systems offer with their fixed units and angular relationships. For example, what is the distance between two points with Cartesian coordinates (x_1, y_1, z_1) and (x_2, y_2, z_2)? Two applications of the Pythagorean theorem yield that the distance is

$$\sqrt{(x_2 - x_1)^2 + (y_2 - y_1)^2 + (z_2 - z_1)^2}.$$

In the general linear case there is no correspondingly simple formula. The distance depends on the relative sizes of the units of distance chosen and on the angles between the coordinate lines.

The answer to the second question will become more clear as the theory is developed. We will find that in many problems the ideas of perpendicularity and a fixed distance are not involved. In these cases the general linear formulation allows us a great deal of freedom in our choice of coordinates. It is in this freedom that the advantage of general linear systems lies.

Example 1. Consider a linear system in the plane. Let the plane be coordinatized by a Cartesian system determined by L_1, L_2, P_1, and P_1'. For the generalized linear system use L_1 and P_1 again but let L_2' be defined by P_0 and the point P_1'' whose Cartesian coordinates are $(1, 1)$. Let the point $(1, 1)$ be the "unit point" on L_2'. See Figure 2.5. Note that P_1'' has Cartesian coordinates $(1, 1)$ while its linear coordinates are $(0, 1)$ and the point P_1 has coordinates $(1, 0)$ in both systems. What is the linear coordinate system designation of P_1'? Draw the lines parallel to L_2' and L_1 through P_1'. They intersect L_2' and L_1, respectively, at points having linear coordinates 1 and -1. Thus the answer is $(-1, 1)$.

What are the Cartesian coordinates of the point P whose linear coordinates are $(1, 2)$? Points whose first coordinate is 1 lie on a line parallel to L_2' and intersecting L_1 at P_1. Points whose second coordinate is 2 lie on a line parallel to L_1 and intersecting L_2' at a point twice as far from P_0 as P_1''; i.e., at a point whose Cartesian coordinates are $(2, 2)$. Thus P has Cartesian coordinates $(3, 2)$.

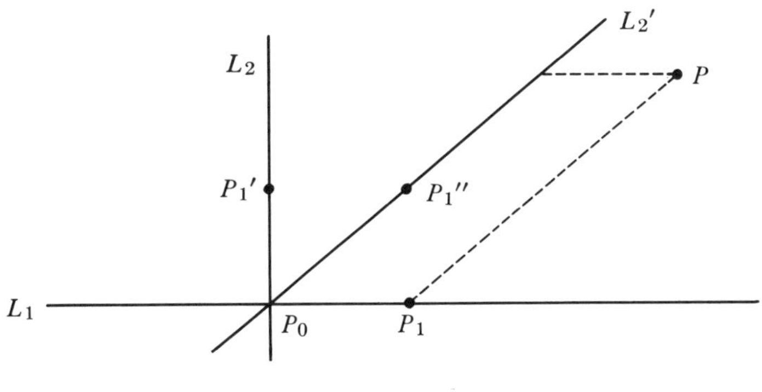

FIGURE 2.5

Exercises

1. Let a new coordinate system be assigned to an existing coordinate system on a line by taking the point whose coordinate is -3 to be P_0 and the point whose coordinate is $+5$ to be P_1.
   (a) Determine the new coordinates of the points whose old coordinates are: (i) -3; (ii) 5; (iii) 2; (iv) 16; (v) -24; (vi) $\frac{3}{7}$.
   (b) Determine the former coordinates of the points whose new coordinates are: (i) 0; (ii) 1; (iii) $\frac{3}{8}$; (iv) 8; (v) -2.
2. In Exercise 1, if x is the old coordinate of a point P, and x' the new coordinate of P, find an equation expressing x' in terms of x.
3. Use the linear system of Example 1 of this section.
   (a) Find the linear coordinates of points whose Cartesian coordinates are (0, 2), (1, 2), (2, 1), and (3, 3).
   (b) Find Cartesian coordinates of points whose linear coordinates are (1, 1), (0, 3), (3, 0), and (2, 3).
   (c) Find a rule that changes Cartesian coordinates to linear coordinates.
4. Let a line L have two coordinate systems with the same choice for P_0 and different choices for P_1. Prove that only one point has the same coordinates in both systems.
5. Extend the result of Exercise 4 to show that two different coordinate systems yield the same coordinate for at most one point.
6. The definition of the coordinates for a plane was given by means of three cases (point on L_1, point on L_2, neither). Give a definition that eliminates this case breakdown.
7. Give a definition of coordinates of a point P in space in terms of lines through P parallel to the coordinate axes. Can you eliminate a breakdown by cases? Can you give a similar definition for the general linear case?
8. Find a distance formula for the linear system of Example 1. That is, given two points with linear coordinates (x_1, y_1) and (x_2, y_2) find a formula for the length of the line segment joining them.
9. Assuming that the coordinatization of a line is a one-to-one onto map, prove that any coordinatization of the plane is a one-to-one map from the plane onto $R \times R$.

2.2 Line Segments in Space

In any coordinate system a line segment will be determined by giving the coordinates of the endpoints. In those cases where attention is to be drawn to the order of presenting the endpoints, the line segment will be called a *directed line segment*, the direction being from the endpoint first presented to the second. Thus XY will be used to indicate the directed line segment from X to Y. We shall also use XY to denote the length of the line segment from X to Y. The meaning should be clear from the context of the discussion. In a diagram, where it is desirable to emphasize the direction of a line segment, an arrowhead will be indicated on the terminal (second) point of the segment.

No essential importance attaches to the use of the letters x, y, z in the first, second, and third places of the coordinate triples. Any letters will serve as well, and, to prepare for future generalizations, we will customarily use notations of the type (x_1, x_2, x_3).

In this section we shall make no use of perpendicularity or specific distance formulas and can, therefore, use a general linear system. We wish to obtain some basic information about the relationship between lines and line segments and the coordinate system.

We begin with a line L, assumed not to be parallel to any of the planes π_1, π_2, π_3 defined by pairs of the lines L_1, L_2, L_3 (Figure 2.6). Let X and Y be two fixed points on L and let R be another arbitrary point on L.

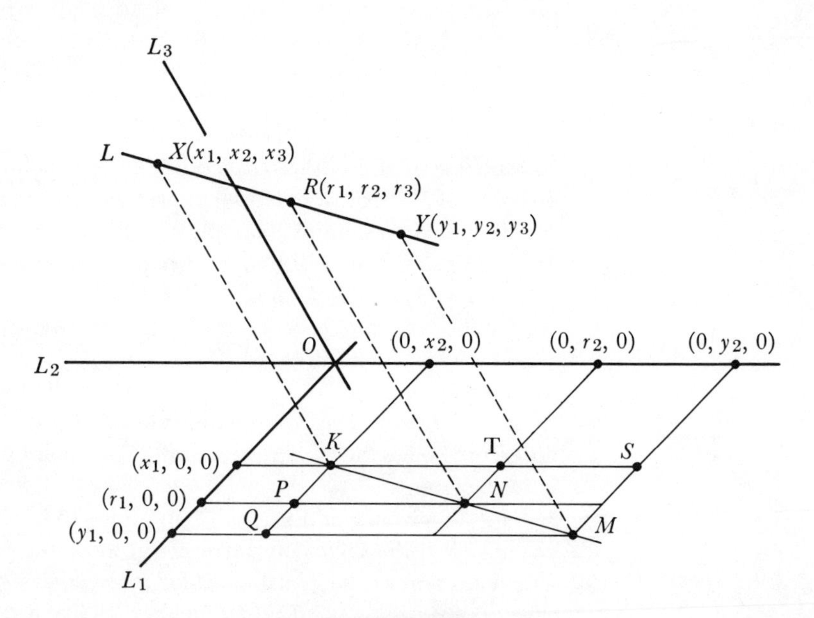

FIGURE 2.6

Through X, Y, and R we pass lines parallel to L_3 intersecting the plane determined by L_1 and L_2 at K, M, and N. The lines through K, M, N parallel to L_1, and L_2 intersect the coordinate lines as indicated. The similarity of the triangles KPN to KQM and KTN to KSM implies

$$\frac{KP}{KQ} = \frac{KN}{KM} = \frac{KT}{KS} \quad \text{or} \quad \frac{r_1 - x_1}{y_1 - x_1} = \frac{r_2 - x_2}{y_2 - x_2}.$$

A similar consideration in the plane determined by L_2 and L_3, combined with the result above, yields the following relations for the coordinates of the points X, Y, and R:

$$\frac{r_1 - x_1}{y_1 - x_1} = \frac{r_2 - x_2}{y_2 - x_2} = \frac{r_3 - x_3}{y_3 - x_3}. \tag{2.1}$$

If the common ratio in (2.1) is denoted by t, these relations may be expressed by the equations

$$\begin{aligned} r_1 &= x_1 + t(y_1 - x_1), \\ r_2 &= x_2 + t(y_2 - x_2), \\ r_3 &= x_3 + t(y_3 - x_3). \end{aligned} \tag{2.2}$$

The value of t depends upon the position of R with respect to X and Y; t is positive if R and Y are on the same side of X; $t = 0$ if R coincides with X; and t is negative if X separates R and Y. The absolute value of t is the ratio of the lengths XR and XY.

Even if L is parallel to one or two of the planes π_1, π_2, π_3 and thus one or two of the quantities in the parentheses are zero, Equations (2.2) are still valid, although Equations (2.1) are not. The proof of this statement is left as an exercise. We see that the coordinates of any point on a line are given in terms of the coordinates of a fixed point X, a triple of real numbers

$$[y_1 - x_1, y_2 - x_2, y_3 - x_3]$$

determined by a directed segment XY on the line, and a real number t. The function of these various quantities may be summarized as follows:

1. The assignment of the triple $[y_1 - x_1, y_2 - x_2, y_3 - x_3]$ to the directed line segment from $X(x_1, x_2, x_3)$ to $Y(y_1, y_2, y_3)$ determines a mapping from the set of directed line segments in space to the set of triples of real numbers. For example, if the coordinates of X and Y are $(3, 1, 1)$ and $(2, -1, 3)$, the triple $[-1, -2, 2]$ is assigned to XY and $[1, 2, -2]$ is assigned to YX. We shall say that the directed segment XY is *associated with* the triple $[-1, -2, 2]$. YX is associated with the triple $[1, 2, -2]$.

2. The mapping just indicated is *not* one-to-one. If P and Q have coordinates $(1, 4, 2)$ and $(0, 2, 4)$, the triple assigned to PQ is again $[-1, -2, 2]$. It is intuitively clear that PQ is parallel to and equal in length to XY. In fact it may be shown that if two segments are associated with the same triple they are equal in length and either collinear or parallel. The student is urged to devise a formal proof of this fact. Every triple of real numbers $[a_1, a_2, a_3]$ is associated with at least one segment (in fact, an infinite number of segments) except that the triple $[0, 0, 0]$ has no associated segment. The triple $[a_1, a_2, a_3]$ is, for example, associated with the segment OA where A has coordinates (a_1, a_2, a_3) and O is the origin.

3. If $X'(x'_1, x'_2, x'_3)$ and $Y'(y'_1, y'_2, y'_3)$ are points on the line XY, the corresponding elements of the triples associated with $X'Y'$ and XY are proportional. To see this, apply (2.2) to the points Y' and X':

$$\begin{aligned} y'_1 &= x_1 + t_1(y_1 - x_1), & x'_1 &= x_1 + t_2(y_1 - x_1), \\ y'_2 &= x_2 + t_1(y_2 - x_2), & x'_2 &= x_2 + t_2(y_2 - x_2), \\ y'_3 &= x_3 + t_1(y_3 - x_3), & x'_3 &= x_3 + t_2(y_3 - x_3). \end{aligned} \tag{2.3}$$

Now subtract the two sets of equations, and let $t_3 = t_1 - t_2$:

$$\begin{aligned} y'_1 - x'_1 &= t_3(y_1 - x_1), \\ y'_2 - x'_2 &= t_3(y_2 - x_2), \\ y'_3 - x'_3 &= t_3(y_3 - x_3). \end{aligned} \tag{2.4}$$

4. If $X(x_1, x_2, x_3)$, $Y(y_1, y_2, y_3)$, and $Z(z_1, z_2, z_3)$ are any three points in space, the triple associated with XZ can be obtained by *adding* the corresponding elements of the triples associated with XY and YZ. That is,

$$\begin{aligned} z_1 - x_1 &= (z_1 - y_1) + (y_1 - x_1), \\ z_2 - x_2 &= (z_2 - y_2) + (y_2 - x_2), \\ z_3 - x_3 &= (z_3 - y_3) + (z_3 - x_3). \end{aligned} \tag{2.5}$$

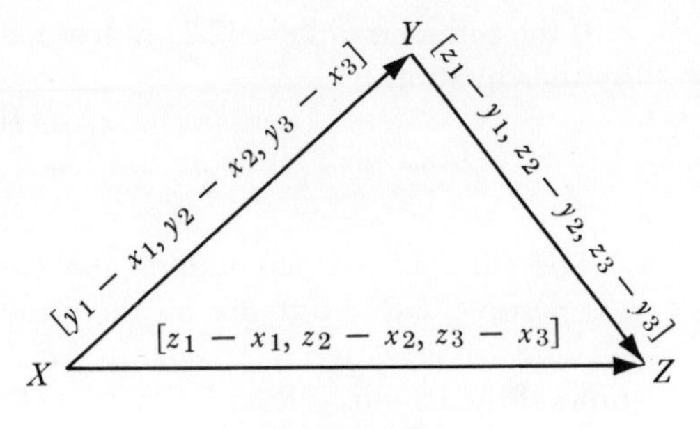

FIGURE 2.7

In Figure 2.7 the associated triples are indicated beside the corresponding segments.

Exercises

In these problems, assume that space has been coordinatized by some fixed coordinate system.

1. Find equations for a point $R(r_1, r_2, r_3)$ on the line joining (1, 1, 1) and (2, −1, 3). What is the triple associated with the line segment OR? With the line segment RO?
2. Find equations for a point $R(r_1, r_2, r_3)$ on the line joining (2, 3, −4) and (5, −2, 0). What is the triple associated with the line segment from (2, 3, −4) to R? With the line segment from R to (2, 3, −4)?
3. Find coordinates of a point P on the line joining $X(1, -2, 3)$ and $Y(2, 4, -1)$ which is
   (a) The midpoint of XY.
   (b) Such that $XP/PY = \frac{1}{3}$.
   (c) Such that Y is the midpoint of XP.
   (d) Such that X is the midpoint of PY.
4. Let X, Y, Z be points whose coordinates are (1, −1, 2), (3, 1, 4), (2, 0, 2) respectively. Find the triples associated with the directed line segments XY, YZ, XZ. Verify that the relations corresponding to (2.5) are satisfied.
5. Show that the points $P(1, -1, 4)$ and $Q(5, 3, 0)$ are collinear with the points $X(2, 0, 3)$ and $Y(-2, -4, 7)$.
6. Give a complete proof for the statement: If XY and $X'Y'$ are segments associated with the same triple, either XY is collinear with $X'Y'$ or the segments are parallel. In either case, the segments are equal in length.
7. Prove that Equations (2.2) are valid when L is parallel to one or two of the planes π_1, π_2, π_3 determined by pairs of L_1, L_2, L_3.

2.3 Translations and Vectors

The concept of a directed line segment and its association with a triple of real numbers in the presence of a coordinate system has been developed and shown to have geometric applications. In this section we will extend this usefulness by developing an algebra of these quantities.

First, is there a meaningful way to "add" two directed line segments? A hint of an answer is given in remark 4 on page 25. The answer may also be found by thinking of applications involving directed line segments with which the reader is familiar. If the reader has studied elementary physics he will have

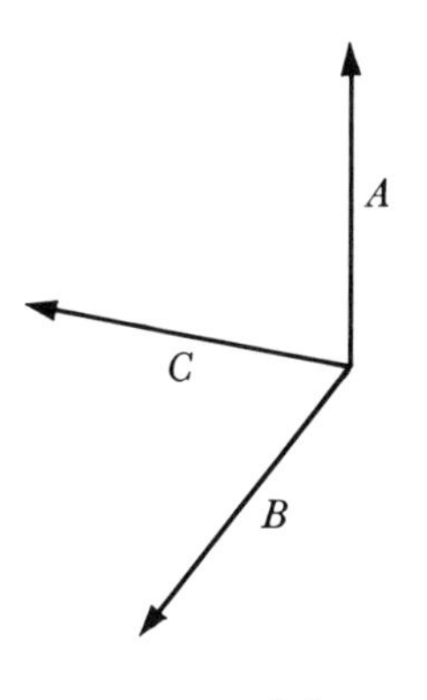

FIGURE 2.8

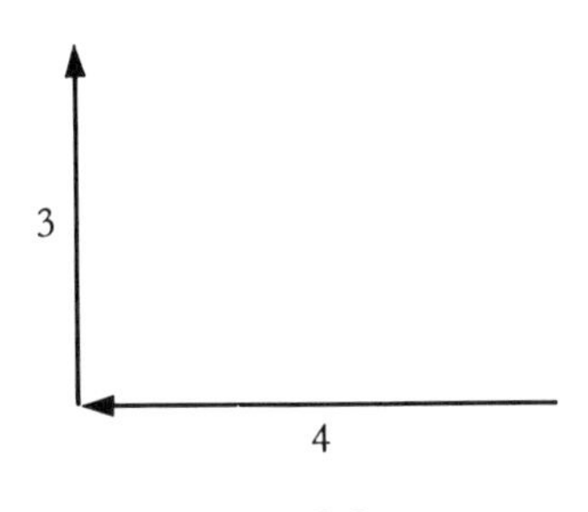

FIGURE 2.9

seen directed line segments used to depict forces acting on a body. Suppose two forces, A and B, act as shown in Figure 2.8. What is the resulting or total force C?

Another application where directed line segments are naturally "added" involves displacements. Suppose I walk 4 miles west and then 3 miles north; how far and in which direction have I traveled? (Figure 2.9.)

Answers to the questions raised above are usually phrased in terms of a parallelogram law. A more precise answer which is also more amenable to generalization can be given in terms of another set of objects that correspond to directed line segments: translations.

Given a directed line segment OP, we associate a mapping, F, carrying points of space to other points as follows: If X is a point, $\mathrm{F}(X)$ is the point Y such that XY has the same length and direction as OP. That is, Y is the point in space such that $OXYP$ is a parallelogram. (Figure 2.10.) Note that, if a coordinate system is given, XY and OP will be associated with the same real number triple.

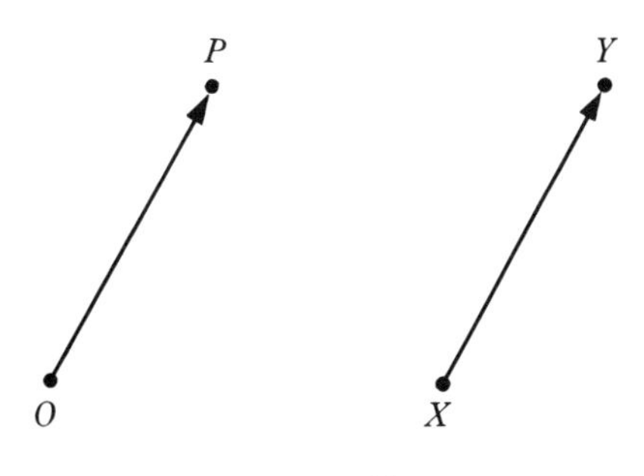

FIGURE 2.10

We call such a mapping F a *translation* of space or simply a translation. It is clear that any directed line segment parallel to OP and of the same length will define the same translation. Let us examine some of the properties of translations. Translations are biunique (reversing the arrow will show that they are both one-to-one and onto). Since they all have the same domain and range, they can be composed; in fact, if F and G are translations, then the composite $F \circ G$ is also a translation. This is easily seen if any one of F, G, or $F \circ G$ is the identity map. Otherwise, let G be associated with OP, Q be the image of P under F, X be any point, and Z be $F(G(X))$. We assert that $OXZQ$ is a parallelogram, which means that $F \circ G$ is the translation associated with the directed line segment OQ (see Figure 2.11). $OXYP$ is a parallelogram because G is a translation, and similarly $PYZQ$ is a parallelogram. Thus $QZ = PY = OX$ in length and the segments QZ, PY, and OX are parallel, giving us that $OXZQ$ is a parallelogram.

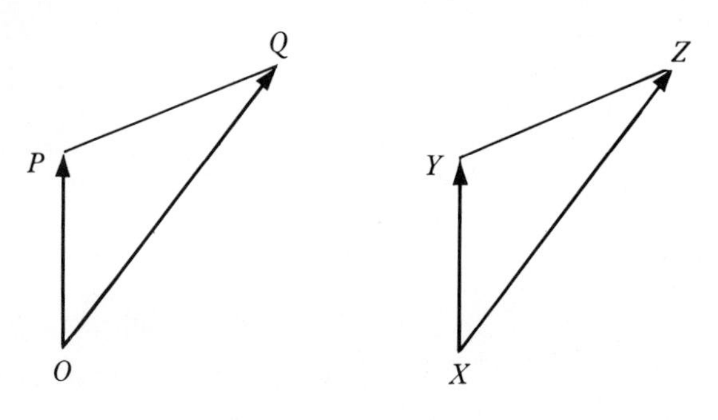

FIGURE 2.11

By a similar argument one can see that $F(G(X)) = G(F(X))$ for every X, $F \circ G = G \circ F$. Finally, remember that composition of maps is associative whenever it is defined and thus $F \circ (G \circ H) = (F \circ G) \circ H$. Putting this all together we have shown that:

THEOREM 2.1. *Translations of space form an Abelian group under composition.*

Let us write composition of translations additively, replacing $F \circ G$ with $F + G$. Note that, since a given translation is associated with many directed line segments (all those parallel to and of the same length as a given one), composition defines not a sum of two directed line segments, but rather the sum of two classes of segments as another class of segments. In the example of physical forces this situation corresponds to the usual statement that two forces are equal if they have the same magnitude and direction; and thus our composition does indeed correspond to adding two forces to obtain a new force, the sum.

What does our sum look like in the presence of a coordinate system? First, observe that while a given translation corresponds to many directed line segments, these segments are of equal length and in the same direction; thus a given translation will correspond to a unique triple of real numbers. So, if we are given two translations F and G corresponding to $[x_1, x_2, x_3]$ and $[y_1, y_2, y_3]$, we can ask, "which triple corresponds to $F + G$?" Remark 4 of the previous section shows that $F + G$ corresponds to $[x_1 + y_1, x_2 + y_2, x_3 + y_3]$.

There is another operation on translations which arises naturally. It is called a *scale shift* or, more commonly, *scalar multiplication*. Let F be the translation associated with the directed line segment OP, and let t be any real number. We define a new translation tF as follows: If $t > 0$, tF is the translation associated with the segment OR, in the same direction as OP but such that the ratio of lengths OR/OP equals t. If $t < 0$, the associated segment OR is in the opposite direction with ratio of lengths OR/OP equal to $|t|$. If $t = 0$, tF is the identity translation.

If we have a coordinate system defined, what is the relationship between the triples associated with F and tF? Recall the discussion of the previous section which shows that, if F is associated with the triple $[x_1, x_2, x_3]$, then tF is associated with $[tx_1, tx_2, tx_3]$.

Scalar multiplication is easily seen to have the following properties, where s, t are any real numbers, and F, G are any two translations:

$$\begin{aligned} &(1) \quad (st)\mathrm{F} = s(t\mathrm{F}),\\ &(2) \quad (s + t)\mathrm{F} = s\mathrm{F} + t\mathrm{F},\\ &(3) \quad s(\mathrm{F} + \mathrm{G}) = s\mathrm{F} + s\mathrm{G},\\ &(4) \quad 1\mathrm{F} = \mathrm{F}. \end{aligned} \tag{2.6}$$

If we think just about triples of numbers, we see that we could have forgotten about the underlying transformations and simply *defined* our operations on triples as

$$\begin{aligned} &\text{(a)} \quad [x_1, x_2, x_3] + [y_1, y_2, y_3] = [x_1 + y_1, x_2 + y_2, x_3 + y_3],\\ &\text{(b)} \quad t[x_1, x_2, x_3] = [tx_1, tx_2, tx_3]. \end{aligned}$$

With these definitions we see that $R \times R \times R$ is an Abelian group satisfying the four laws (2.6) (taking F, G as triples). Why then did we state our definitions and properties in the coordinate-free way? For two reasons: first to show the physical motivation of the definitions, and second, so that we can be sure that our definitions do not depend on the particular choice of coordinate system involved. We want the resultant of two forces to be the same regardless of whether the origin is the earth or the sun.

Nonetheless, the observation that triples of reals satisfy the same axioms (or have the same algebra) as the set of translations is important. We will soon encounter other, more general, examples of systems with this same algebraic structure.

Exercises

1. Perform the indicated operations:
   (a) $[1, 3, -1] + [1, 0, 2] = ?$
   (b) $4[1, 0, -2] - 3[1, -1, -3] = ?$
   (c) $a[1, 2, -1] + b[1, 3, 1] = ?$
2. Choose two sides XY and XZ of a triangle XYZ as the coordinate lines in a linear coordinate system and let the unit point on each line be chosen at a vertex; take the third coordinate line as any line through X not in the plane of the triangle. What is the triple associated with YZ? What is the triple associated with the segment from the origin to midpoint of YZ?
3. Do the points

   $$(3, 7, -2),\ (5, 5, 1),\ (4, 0, -1), \text{ and } (6, -2, 2)$$

   form the vertices of a parallelogram?
4. What is the triple associated with the line segment OR, where R is a point $\frac{1}{3}$ of the distance from $(2, 6, -4)$ to $(5, 3, -1)$?

5. Prove that the sum (composition) of two translations is a translation by using the coordinate notation.
6. Prove that addition (composition) of translations is commutative by using the coordinate notation.

2.4 R^n

In the last section we noted that two different systems, one of ordered triples, the other of translations, had natural algebraic structures that were the same. Whenever we encounter systems of the same type in the future the elements of the set involved will be called *vectors*. The vectors of this section are a simple generalization of number triples; namely, ordered real n-tuples, where n is some fixed positive integer. The set of all n-tuples of real numbers will be denoted by R^n. Of course, the cases $n = 2$ and $n = 3$ are included, and the reader should keep these in mind as examples throughout this section.

The reader will have noted that we used square brackets [] to distinguish the triples associated with directed line segments from the triples that were being used as coordinates of points. Since we are now interested in the structure of R^n which corresponds to the structure of directed line segments, we will use the square bracket notation for elements (vectors) of R^n. Thus we will write $\mathbf{X} = [x_1, x_2, \ldots, x_n]$ for a vector in R^n. We begin by giving a definition that serves to establish the distinct elements of R^n.

DEFINITION 2.1. If

$$\mathbf{X} = [x_1, x_2, x_n] \quad \textit{and} \quad \mathbf{Y} = [y_1, y_2, \ldots, y_n],$$

then $\mathbf{X} = \mathbf{Y}$ *means* $x_i = y_i$ *for every* i. *Thus* $[\frac{1}{2}, 2, 3, -1] = [\frac{4}{8}, \sqrt{4}, 3, \log_{10}(\frac{1}{10})]$, *but* $[1, 2, 3] \neq [1, 3, 2]$.

Just as n-tuples are natural generalizations of triples, we see that the addition and scalar multiplication of vectors in space have the following generalizations to n-tuples.

DEFINITION 2.2. (Addition of vectors in R^n.) *If*

$$\mathbf{X} = [x_1, x_2, \ldots, x_n] \quad \textit{and} \quad \mathbf{Y} = [y_1, y_2, \ldots, y_n],$$

then

$$\mathbf{X} + \mathbf{Y} = [x_1 + y_1, x_2 + y_2, \ldots, x_n + y_n].$$

DEFINITION 2.3. (Scalar multiplication in R^n.) *If* t *is any real number and* $\mathbf{X} = [x_1, x_2, \ldots, x_n]$, *then* $t\mathbf{X} = [tx_1, tx_2, \ldots, tx_n]$.

Note that we have only defined the addition of two vectors of the same size; that is, one adds an n-tuple $\mathbf{X}$ to an m-tuple $\mathbf{Y}$ *only* when $m = n$. It is to be emphasized that in a given situation the n in R^n is fixed.

Example 1. Let $\mathbf{X} = [0, -1, 2, 3]$ and $\mathbf{Y} = [5, 1, 2, -3]$; then

$$\mathbf{X} + \mathbf{Y} = [0 + 5, -1 + 1, 2 + 2, 3 + (-3)] = [5, 0, 4, 0]$$

and

$$3\mathbf{X} = 3[0, -1, 2, 3] = [3 \cdot 0, 3(-1), 3 \cdot 2, 3 \cdot 3] = [0, -3, 6, 9].$$

The zero vector $[0, 0, \ldots, 0]$ of R^n will be denoted by $\mathbf{0}$. Note that

$$\begin{aligned}[x_1, x_2, \ldots, x_n] + [0, 0, \ldots, 0] &= [x_1 + 0, x_2 + 0, \ldots, x_n + 0] \\ &= [x_1, x_2, \ldots, x_n]\end{aligned}$$

or $\mathbf{X} + \mathbf{0} = \mathbf{X}$ for all $\mathbf{X}$ in R^n. Similarly $\mathbf{0} + \mathbf{X} = \mathbf{X}$. We are really using the symbol $\mathbf{0}$ for many different vectors: sometimes for $[0, 0]$, sometimes for $[0, 0, 0, 0, 0]$, etc. However, as we noted above, in any given context the n in R^n will be fixed and thus the meaning of $\mathbf{0}$ will be clear.

The negative $-\mathbf{X}$ of a given vector $\mathbf{X} = [x_1, x_2, \ldots, x_n]$ is the vector $[-x_1, -x_2, \ldots, -x_n]$; thus $\mathbf{X} + (-\mathbf{X}) = -\mathbf{X} + \mathbf{X} = \mathbf{0}$ for all $\mathbf{X}$. Using the notation suggested by the real numbers we will write $\mathbf{X} - \mathbf{Y}$ for $\mathbf{X} + (-\mathbf{Y})$.

Example 2. Let $\mathbf{X} = [1, 2, 3, -4, 5]$ and $\mathbf{Y} = [1, 1, 2, -1, 3]$; then

$$\begin{aligned}\mathbf{X} - \mathbf{Y} &= [1, 2, 3, -4, 5] + [-1, -1, -2, -(-1), -3] \\ &= [1 - 1, 2 - 1, 3 - 2, -4 + 1, 5 - 3] \\ &= [0, 1, 1, -3, 2].\end{aligned}$$

The fact that $\mathbf{X} + \mathbf{Y} = \mathbf{Y} + \mathbf{X}$ for any $\mathbf{X}$, $\mathbf{Y}$ in R^n is readily established, and thus we have shown that R^n together with its addition has the same algebraic structure as translations with their addition (i.e., R^n with $+$ is an Abelian group). It is also important to note that the scalar multiplication of R^n satisfies the rules (2.6). By way of illustration we establish the analog of (2.6) (1), which says that $(st)\mathbf{X} = s(t\mathbf{X})$ for any reals s, t and any vector $\mathbf{X}$. Say $\mathbf{X} = [x_1, x_2, \ldots, x_n]$; then by Definition 2.3,

$$(st)\mathbf{X} = [(st)x_1, (st)x_2, \ldots, (st)x_n]$$

and

$$s(t\mathbf{X}) = s[tx_1, tx_2, \ldots, tx_n] = [s(tx_1), s(tx_2), \ldots, s(tx_n)].$$

Now notice that, for each i, $(st)x_i$ and $s(tx_i)$ are just products of real numbers and are equal by the associative law of the reals. From this we conclude that $(st)\mathbf{X} = s(t\mathbf{X})$ by Definition 2.1.

The notation and algebra of vectors that we have been developing serves to simplify many geometric statements. For example, consider the equations for a line (2.2). If we set

$$\mathbf{R} = [r_1, r_2, r_3], \quad \mathbf{X} = [x_1, x_2, x_3] \quad \text{and} \quad \mathbf{Y} = [y_1, y_2, y_3],$$

these three equations can be written $\mathbf{R} = \mathbf{X} + t(\mathbf{Y} - \mathbf{X})$ or $\mathbf{R} = (1 - t)\mathbf{X} + t\mathbf{Y}$. From these equations we see that the vector associated with OR can be given in terms of the vectors associated with OX and XY or in terms of the vectors associated with OX and OY.

Example 3. The vector equation of the line through $(1, 2, -2)$ and $(2, 3, 1)$ is

$$\mathbf{R} = (1 - t)[1, 2, -2] + t[2, 3, 1].$$

If $t = \frac{1}{2}$, $\quad \mathbf{R} = \frac{1}{2}[1, 2, -2] + \frac{1}{2}[2, 3, 1] = [\frac{3}{2}, \frac{5}{2}, -\frac{1}{2}]$.

If the vector $\mathbf{R}$ is interpreted as being associated with the line segment OR, we see that the point $(\frac{3}{2}, \frac{5}{2}, -\frac{1}{2})$ is the midpoint of the line segment from $(1, 2, -2)$ to $(2, 3, 1)$. Here, we have associated the vectors $[1, 2, -2]$ and $[2, 3, 1]$ with the line segments from the origin to the points $(1, 2, -2)$ and $(2, 3, 1)$.

Exercises

1. Let $\mathbf{X} = [2, 3, -1, 5]$ and $\mathbf{Y} = [1, 2, 0, -1]$. Compute the following:
   (a) $\mathbf{X} + 2\mathbf{Y}$; (b) $3\mathbf{X} - \mathbf{Y}$; (c) $a\mathbf{X} + b\mathbf{Y}$.
2. Let $\mathbf{X} = [2, i, -1, 2i]$ and $\mathbf{Y} = [i, 0, 2i, 1]$ be elements of C^4. Compute the following:
   (a) $\mathbf{X} - i\mathbf{Y}$; (b) $3\mathbf{X} + i\mathbf{Y}$; (c) $a\mathbf{X} + b\mathbf{Y}$.
3. How many distinct vectors are there in F^4, where F is the finite field of Exercise 1, Section 1.3?
4. Show that the scalar multiplication of R^n satisfies the properties (2.6).
5. What are the vector equations of the lines joining the following pairs of points?
   (a) $(2, 3, -4), (5, -2, 0)$;
   (b) $(1, 1, 1), (2, -1, 3)$;
   (c) $(1, -2, 3), (2, 4, -1)$.
6. Choose two sides XY and XZ of a triangle XYZ as the coordinate lines in a linear coordinate system and let the unit point on each line be chosen at a vertex. Take the third coordinate line as any line through X not in the plane of the triangle. What is the vector associated with YZ? What is the vector associated with the line segment from the origin to the midpoint of YZ?
7. What is the vector associated with the line segment OR, where R is a point $\frac{1}{3}$ of the distance from $(2, 6, -4)$ to $(5, 3, -1)$?

2.5 Vector Spaces

In the preceding sections we have seen several mathematical systems all having the same algebraic structure. In this section we shall give a precise, complete list of these properties, discuss some of the implications, and give examples to show the diversity of applications for the resulting theory.

As in the preceding examples we start with a set of elements V and a field F. (So far, with the exception of some exercises, F has always been the real numbers. This will be true in most of this book.) We shall always have two operations defined; one a binary operation (that is, a mapping from $V \times V$ into V) called *addition*, with the notation $\mathbf{X} + \mathbf{Y}$ for the image of $(\mathbf{X}, \mathbf{Y})$ under the prescribed mapping. The second operation, called *scalar multiplication*, is a mapping from $F \times V$ into V with the image of $(a, \mathbf{X})$ being denoted simply by $a\mathbf{X}$.

DEFINITION 2.4. A VECTOR SPACE *over a field F is a set V with a binary operation + and a scalar multiplication satisfying the following rules.*

(1) *V is an Abelian group with respect to addition; that is,*
   A1. $(\mathbf{X} + \mathbf{Y}) + \mathbf{Z} = \mathbf{X} + (\mathbf{Y} + \mathbf{Z})$ *for all* $\mathbf{X}, \mathbf{Y}, \mathbf{Z}$ *in* V.
   A2. *There is an element* $\mathbf{0} \in V$ *such that* $\mathbf{0} + \mathbf{X} = \mathbf{X} + \mathbf{0} = \mathbf{X}$ *for all* $\mathbf{X} \in V$.
   A3. *To each* $\mathbf{X}$ *in* V *there corresponds an element* $-\mathbf{X}$ *in* V *with* $\mathbf{X} + (-\mathbf{X}) = -\mathbf{X} + \mathbf{X} = 0$.
   A4. $\mathbf{X} + \mathbf{Y} = \mathbf{Y} + \mathbf{X}$ *for every* $\mathbf{X}$ *and* $\mathbf{Y}$ *in* V.

(2) *For all* $a, b \in F$, $\mathbf{X}, \mathbf{Y} \in V$ *the scalar multiplication satisfies the rules for all* $a, b \in F$ *and* $\mathbf{X}, \mathbf{Y} \in V$:
   S1. $(ab)\mathbf{X} = a(b\mathbf{X})$.
   S2. $(a + b)\mathbf{X} = a\mathbf{X} + b\mathbf{X}$.
   S3. $a(\mathbf{X} + \mathbf{Y}) = a\mathbf{X} + a\mathbf{Y}$.
   S4. $1\mathbf{X} = \mathbf{X}$.

DEFINITION 2.5. A VECTOR *is an element of a vector space V.*

This definition may appear circular at first glance. However, the situation is not at all unusual. It is the same as defining a Boy Scout to be any member of the Boy Scouts. What we have, then, is an answer to the question, "What is a vector? Is it an arrow, a triple, a translation mapping, or what?" Our answer is simply, "Any, all, or none of these; a vector is an element of any vector space."

The basic example of a vector space throughout this book will be R^n; however, there are many other important vector spaces and we shall present some of them at this time.

Example 1. Let V be the set of all polynomials of degree less than or equal to n (n some *fixed* positive integer) with real coefficients; that is, our vectors are formal sums of the form $p(x) = a_0 + a_1x + \cdots + a_nx^n$ where each a_i is a real number. Addition and scalar multiplication are defined as usual for polynomials:

$$(a_0 + a_1x + \cdots + a_nx^n) + (b_0 + b_1x + \cdots + b_nx^n) = (a_0 + b_0) + (a_1 + b_1)x + \cdots + (a_n + b_n)x^n$$

and

$$a(a_0 + a_1x + \cdots + a_nx^n) = aa_0 + aa_1x + \cdots + aa_nx^n.$$

It is an easy (if somewhat lengthy) process to verify that these operations define a vector space for the given set.

Example 2. Let V consist of all real-valued functions defined on the interval $0 \leq x \leq 1$. We define addition and scalar multiplication of these vectors (functions) to be the usual addition of functions and multiplication of a function by a real number. To see that this process defines a vector space, one must check that rules A1–A4 and S1–S4 are satisfied. For example, the zero vector of this space is the function $\mathbf{0}$ defined by $\mathbf{0}(x) = 0$ for all x, $0 \leq x \leq 1$. We have

$$(\mathbf{0} + f)(x) = \mathbf{0}(x) + f(x) = 0 + f(x) = f(x) = f(x) + 0 = (f + \mathbf{0})(x)$$

for each x, or that $\mathbf{0} + f = f + \mathbf{0}$ for any f in V (A2). The reader should verify enough of the remaining rules to convince himself that this is, indeed, a vector space.

Example 3. If in Example 1 we take the coefficients (the a_i's) to be rational numbers, and we allow only scalar multiplication by rationals, the resulting set of polynomials is a vector space over the field Q of rationals.

Example 4. Let V be the set of all triples of real numbers with first coordinate zero. Our vectors are of the form $[0, x_2, x_3]$ and we define addition and scalar multiplication as before. V then becomes a vector space over R.

The situation of the last example is an important one and deserves further discussion. We took a proper subset of a vector space (R^3) and noted that, with the inherited operations, the proper subset was itself a vector space. The importance of the situation arrives from the fact that any result known about vector spaces can be applied to this proper subset. We make a formal definition, which looks less restrictive at first glance.

DEFINITION 2.6. Let W be a subset of a vector space V over a field F with the following property: If $\mathbf{X}$ and $\mathbf{Y}$ are in W and $a \in F$, then $\mathbf{X} + \mathbf{Y}$ and $a\mathbf{X}$ are in W. Then W is called a SUBSPACE *of V.*

Note that *any* subset W of a vector space (along with the inherited operations) will satisfy A1, A4, and S1–S4. Thus the two conditions of our definition guarantee that a subspace is a vector space in its own right. And we need only verify two rules to show that a subset of a vector space is a subspace.

Many subspaces occur naturally; we list a few examples.

Example 5. Fix a plane π in three-dimensional space. Let V be the vector space of all translations of space and W the set of translations that carry points of π into points of π. Note that W consists of those translations that correspond (in the sense of Section 2.3) to directed line segments parallel to W.

Example 6. Let $\mathbf{X}_1, \mathbf{X}_2, \ldots, \mathbf{X}_p$ be any p fixed vectors from a vector space V over a field F. Let W consist of all vectors of V which can be written in the form

$$\mathbf{X} = a_1\mathbf{X}_1 + \cdots + a_p\mathbf{X}_p$$

for some scalars $a_1, a_2, \ldots, a_p$ in F. Such a vector $\mathbf{X}$ will be called a *linear combination* of the vectors $\mathbf{X}_1, \mathbf{X}_2, \ldots, \mathbf{X}_p$. The reader should verify that W is a subspace and, further, that it is the *smallest* subspace of V that contains $\mathbf{X}_1, \mathbf{X}_2, \ldots, \mathbf{X}_p$ in the sense that if W' is a subspace of V containing all the $\mathbf{X}_i$'s, then $W \subseteq W'$. This situation will occur often in future work and we will call W the *subspace generated* by $\{\mathbf{X}_1, \mathbf{X}_2, \ldots, \mathbf{X}_p\}$ or the *span* of $\{\mathbf{X}_1, \ldots, \mathbf{X}_p\}$ and write $W = L\{\mathbf{X}_1, \mathbf{X}_2, \ldots, \mathbf{X}_p\}$.

Exercises

1. Determine whether the following subsets of R^4 are subspaces of R^4 and hence vector spaces over R:
   (a) the set of all vectors $[x_1, x_2, x_3, x_4]$ with $x_1 = x_4$,
   (b) the set of all vectors $[x_1, x_2, x_3, x_4]$ with $x_1 + x_2 = 0$,
   (c) the set of all vectors $[x_1, x_2, x_3, x_4]$ with $x_1x_2 = 0$.
2. Describe, as simply as possible, the smallest subspaces of R^4 containing the sets of vectors
   (a) $[0, 0, 0, 0], [1, 0, 0, 0]$,
   (b) $[1, 2, 0, 1], [2, 4, 0, 2], [0, 0, 0, 1]$,
   (c) $[a, a, 0, 0], [a, 0, 0, 0]$.
3. Using the same operations of addition and scalar multiplication as in Example 1, determine whether the set of all polynomials in x with real coefficients (without any limitation on the degrees) forms a vector space over R.
4. Let V be the space of polynomials of degree ≤ 6 with real coefficients. What is the smallest subspace containing the polynomials $1, x, x^2, x^3, x^4$, and x^5?
5. Let V be the vector space of Example 2. Determine which of the following subsets of V are subspaces of V:
   (a) the set of all functions f for which $f(1) = 0$,
   (b) the set of all functions f for which $f(0) = f(1)$,
   (c) the set of all functions f for which $f(0) + f(1) = 0$,
   (d) the set of all functions f for which $f(x) \geq 0$, for all x,
   (e) the set of all functions f for which $f(\frac{1}{2}) = [f(0) + f(1)]/2$.
6. Show that the set W in Example 5 is a subspace.

7. Consider the plane in three-dimensional space represented by the equation $2x_1 + 3x_2 - 5x_3 = 0$. If the points (x_1, x_2, x_3) of the plane are considered as vectors $[x_1, x_2, x_3]$ of R^n, do they form a subspace? The same question for the plane $2x_1 + 3x_2 - 5x_3 = 4$. In general, which equations will give rise to a subspace in this manner?
8. Consider the equation $a_1x_1 + a_2x_2 + \cdots + a_nx_n = 0$, where the a_i are fixed real numbers. If we consider a set of real numbers $\{x_1, x_2, \ldots, x_n\}$ that satisfy the equation as an n-tuple $[x_1, x_2, \ldots, x_n]$ in R^n, is the set of all such n-tuples a subspace of R^n?
9. Show that Properties A1, A4, S2, S3, and S4 hold in R^n.
10. For an arbitrary vector space V, show that $0\mathbf{X} = \mathbf{0}$ for all $\mathbf{X}$ in V, where the 0 on the left is the zero element of the underlying field and the $\mathbf{0}$ on the right is the zero of V.
11. Show that the set W of all vectors $[x_1, x_2, x_3]$ in R^3 which satisfy $x_1 = x_2$ is a subspace. Find a set of vectors in R^3 such that W is the subspace generated by your set of vectors. Can you do this with a set of three vectors? Of two? Of one?

2.6 Linear Dependence and Generators

In this section we examine the meaning of the geometric notions of segments being collinear or coplanar in the algebraic setting developed in the preceding sections. This leads naturally to several important concepts in a general vector space.

Suppose that two directed line segments in three-dimensional space are collinear and associated with the vectors (triples) $\mathbf{X}$ and $\mathbf{Y}$. What can we say about $\mathbf{X}$ and $\mathbf{Y}$? An easy calculation shows that $\mathbf{X} = t\mathbf{Y}$ for some number t (pick a coordinate system and try it). On the other hand, if we are given two vectors $\mathbf{A}$, $\mathbf{B}$ which are related by $\mathbf{A} = t\mathbf{B}$ for some nonzero t, then we can find collinear segments which are associated with $\mathbf{A}$ and $\mathbf{B}$ as follows: pick any segment associated with $\mathbf{B}$ and then, using the same initial point, take the segment on the same line with length $|t|$ and with the appropriate direction.

Briefly then: *two nonzero triples are associated with collinear segments exactly when one is a nonzero multiple of the other.*

When are triples associated with coplanar segments? The situation is illustrated in Figure 2.12. The segments AB, CD, and EF are coplanar. Initially, we assume that no two of these are parallel or collinear. Let $\mathbf{X}$ be associated with AB, $\mathbf{Y}$ with CD, and $\mathbf{Z}$ with EF. Draw BD' parallel to and equal in length to CD, and AF' parallel to and equal in length to EF. Then $\mathbf{Y}$ is also associated with BD' and Z with AF'. Next, if necessary, extend BD' or AF'

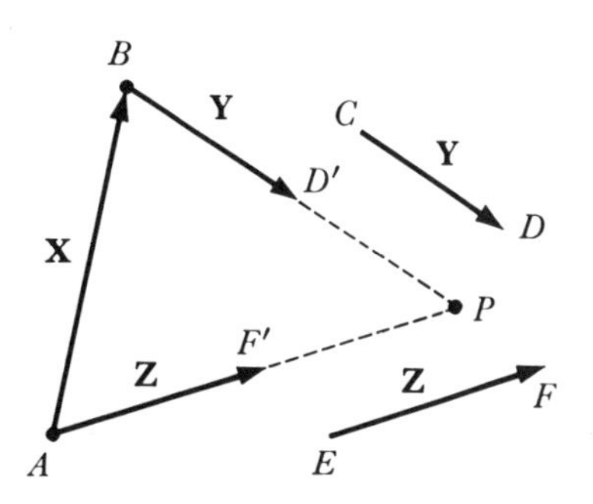

FIGURE 2.12

(or both) until the resulting lines intersect in some point P. Then there are real numbers s and t such that BP is associated with $s\mathbf{Y}$ and AP with $t\mathbf{Z}$. Finally, we have from the definition of vector addition

$$\mathbf{X} + s\mathbf{Y} = t\mathbf{Z} \qquad \text{or} \qquad \mathbf{X} = -s\mathbf{Y} + t\mathbf{Z}. \tag{2.7}$$

We can now partially remove the restrictions made on collinearity and parallelism of the segments. If AB is collinear with or parallel to CD, we can still write $\mathbf{X} = -s\mathbf{Y} + t\mathbf{Z}$, with $t = 0$, since $\mathbf{X}$ will be a multiple of $\mathbf{Y}$. If AB and EF are collinear or parallel, then s will be zero in (2.7). If CD and EF are parallel to each other and not to AB then (2.7) cannot be valid for any s and t. However, in that case $\mathbf{Y} = r\mathbf{Z}$ for some r and so we can write

$$\mathbf{Y} = r\mathbf{Z} + 0\mathbf{X}. \tag{2.7$'$}$$

If we recall the definition of a linear combination from Example 6 of Section 2.5 we can summarize the results of the preceding paragraph as:

THEOREM 2.2. If three segments are coplanar, then the vector associated with one of them is a linear combination of the vectors associated with the other two.

Conversely, if $\mathbf{X}$ is a linear combination of $\mathbf{Y}$ and $\mathbf{Z}$, then proceeding exactly as in Figure 2.12 we can construct segments associated with $\mathbf{X}$, $\mathbf{Y}$, and $\mathbf{Z}$ which form a triangle and are thus coplanar. We state this as a theorem.

THEOREM 2.3. If three vectors are related so that one is a linear combination of the other two, they can be associated with coplanar segments.

Example 1. We shall show that the points $A(1, 1, 2)$, $B(3, -2, 3)$, $C(2, -3, 5)$, and $D(4, -1, -1)$ are not coplanar.

The vectors $\mathbf{X}$, $\mathbf{Y}$, $\mathbf{Z}$ associated with the line segments AB, BC, and AD are

$$\mathbf{X} = [2, -3, 1], \qquad \mathbf{Y} = [-1, -1, 2], \qquad \mathbf{Z} = [3, -2, -3].$$

No two of the segments AB, BC, AD are collinear or parallel. Therefore, if A, B, C, D are coplanar, real numbers r, s must exist such that $\mathbf{X}$, $\mathbf{Y}$, $\mathbf{Z}$ satisfy an equation of the form

$$\mathbf{X} = r\mathbf{Y} + s\mathbf{Z},$$

or

$$\begin{aligned}[2, -3, 1] &= r[-1, -1, 2] + s[3, -2, -3] \\ &= [-r + 3s, -r - 2s, 2r - 3s].\end{aligned}$$

Hence, from the equality of vectors,

$$\begin{aligned} 2 &= -r + 3s, \\ -3 &= -r - 2s, \\ 1 &= 2r - 3s. \end{aligned} \tag{2.8}$$

The first two equations yield $r = s = 1$. These values do not satisfy the third equation and so $\mathbf{X}$ is not a linear combination of $\mathbf{Y}$ and $\mathbf{Z}$. Hence the four points are not coplanar.

If we were to replace D by the point $E(4, 1, -1)$, we could show that $\mathbf{X}$, $\mathbf{Y}$, and the vector associated with AE, $[3, 0, -3]$, satisfy the relation

$$[2, -3, 1] = 3[-1, -1, 2] + \tfrac{5}{3}[3, 0, -3].$$

Now Theorem 2.3 and a simple geometric argument prove that A, B, C, and E are coplanar.

We noticed in the proof of Theorem 2.2 that if $\mathbf{X}$, $\mathbf{Y}$, and $\mathbf{Z}$ are vectors that represent coplanar segments, it is not always possible to write a specific one of the vectors as a linear combination of the other two. We can avoid these special cases as follows:

THEOREM 2.4. *The nonzero vectors* $\mathbf{X}, \mathbf{Y}, \mathbf{Z}$ *are associated with coplanar segments if and only if real numbers* p, q, r *(not all zero) exist such that*

$$p\mathbf{X} + q\mathbf{Y} + r\mathbf{Z} = \mathbf{0}. \tag{2.9}$$

PROOF. If a relation (2.9) is satisfied, choose a nonzero coefficient, transpose and divide by the nonzero coefficients; for example, if $q \neq 0$

$$\mathbf{Y} = -\frac{p}{q}\mathbf{X} - \frac{r}{q}\mathbf{Z}. \tag{2.10}$$

This relation gives $\mathbf{Y}$ as a linear combination of $\mathbf{X}$ and $\mathbf{Z}$ and Theorem 2.3 then gives the desired coplanar segments.

The algebraic relation (2.9) is a special case of a general class of relations which are very important in linear algebra. The following definition serves to specify this class of relations.

DEFINITION 2.7. *The vectors* $\mathbf{X}_1, \mathbf{X}_2, \ldots, \mathbf{X}_r$ *of a vector space* V *are said to be* LINEARLY DEPENDENT *if there exist scalars* $a_1, a_2, \ldots, a_r$ *not all zero, such that*

$$a_1\mathbf{X}_1 + a_2\mathbf{X}_2 + \cdots + a_r\mathbf{X}_r = \mathbf{0}. \tag{2.11}$$

A relation of the form of (2.11) is called a linear relation among $\mathbf{X}_1, \ldots, \mathbf{X}_r$ and is said to be nontrivial if at least one of the a_i's is not zero. Thus $\mathbf{X}_1, \mathbf{X}_2, \ldots, \mathbf{X}_r$ are linearly dependent if there exists some nontrivial linear relation among them. If there exists no nontrivial relation among $\mathbf{X}_1, \ldots, \mathbf{X}_r$, then we say that $\mathbf{X}_1, \mathbf{X}_2, \ldots, \mathbf{X}_r$ are *linearly independent.* These concepts are so important that we give several illustrative examples.

Example 2. Let $\mathbf{X}_1 = [1, 1, 1, 0]$, $\mathbf{X}_2 = [0, 1, 1, 0]$, $\mathbf{X}_3 = [0, 1, 0, 0]$, and $\mathbf{X}_4 = [0, 0, 1, 0]$. Then

$$0\mathbf{X}_1 + 1\cdot\mathbf{X}_2 - 1\cdot\mathbf{X}_3 - 1\cdot\mathbf{X}_4 = 0,$$

so that the vectors $\mathbf{X}_1, \mathbf{X}_2, \mathbf{X}_3, \mathbf{X}_4$ are linearly dependent.

Example 3. Let

$$\mathbf{X}_1 = [1, 0, 0, 0],$$
$$\mathbf{X}_2 = [0, 1, 0, 0],$$
$$\mathbf{X}_3 = [0, 0, 1, 0].$$

If

$$a_1\mathbf{X}_1 + a_2\mathbf{X}_2 + a_3\mathbf{X}_3 = [a_1, a_2, a_3, 0] = \mathbf{0},$$

then, by the definition of equality, $a_1 = a_2 = a_3 = 0$. Hence, the vectors $\mathbf{X}_1$, $\mathbf{X}_2$, and $\mathbf{X}_3$ are linearly independent. Note that the vectors used in Examples 2 and 3 are generating sets for the space of vectors with zero fourth coordinate. One set of generators is linearly independent and the other set is linearly dependent.

Our first application of the notion of linear independence is to the problem of finding minimal sets of generators for a vector space. Let

$$\mathbf{E}_1 = [1, 0, \ldots, 0], \mathbf{E}_2 = [0, 1, 0, \ldots, 0], \ldots, \mathbf{E}_n = [0, \ldots, 0, 1].$$

Then if $\mathbf{X} = [a_1, a_2, \ldots, a_n]$ is any vector in R^n, we have $\mathbf{X} = a_1\mathbf{E}_1 + \cdots + a_n\mathbf{E}_n$. Hence $R^n = L\{\mathbf{E}_1, \ldots, \mathbf{E}_n\}$ or $\mathbf{E}_1, \ldots, \mathbf{E}_n$ are a set of generators for R^n. But notice that if $\mathbf{Y}_1, \ldots, \mathbf{Y}_r$ are any vectors whatever from R^n, then $\mathbf{E}_1, \ldots, \mathbf{E}_n, \mathbf{Y}_1, \ldots, \mathbf{Y}_r$ also generates R^n. (Why?) Thus a given set of generators may have proper subsets that also generate. So we are naturally led to the following questions:

1. Given a set of generators for a vector space V, which subsets will also serve as generators?
2. Do any two minimal sets of generators for V have the same number of vectors?

To answer these questions, we begin by proving a technical theorem.

THEOREM 2.5. The nonzero vectors $\mathbf{X}_1, \ldots, \mathbf{X}_n$ of a vector space V are linearly dependent if and only if some $\mathbf{X}_k$ with $2 \leq k$ is a linear combination of the preceding $\mathbf{X}_i$'s, that is, $\mathbf{X}_1, \mathbf{X}_2, \ldots, \mathbf{X}_{k-1}$.

PROOF. Let the vector $\mathbf{X}_k$ be a linear combination of the preceding $\mathbf{X}_i$'s. Then

$$\mathbf{X}_k = a_1\mathbf{X}_1 + \cdots + a_{k-1}\mathbf{X}_{k-1}$$

or

$$a_1\mathbf{X}_1 + a_2\mathbf{X}_2 + \cdots + a_{k-1}\mathbf{X}_{k-1} - 1\mathbf{X}_k + 0 \cdot \mathbf{X}_{k+1} + \cdots + 0 \cdot \mathbf{X}_n = \mathbf{0}$$

and, consequently, $\mathbf{X}_1, \ldots, \mathbf{X}_n$ are linearly dependent because the coefficient -1 is certainly not zero.

In order to prove the "only if" part we assume that the vectors $\mathbf{X}_1, \mathbf{X}_2, \ldots, \mathbf{X}_n$ are linearly dependent. Hence,

$$a_1\mathbf{X}_1 + \cdots + a_n\mathbf{X}_n = \mathbf{0}$$

with not all of the coefficients being zero. Let a_k be the last nonzero coefficient. Then

$$\mathbf{X}_k = -\frac{a_1}{a_k}\mathbf{X}_1 - \frac{a_2}{a_k}\mathbf{X}_2 - \cdots - \frac{a_{k-1}}{a_k}\mathbf{X}_{k-1}$$

and the conditions of the theorem are fulfilled as k cannot be 1 since $\mathbf{X}_1 \neq \mathbf{0}$.

Returning to the problem of determining minimal generating sets, let $V = L\{\mathbf{X}_1, \ldots, \mathbf{X}_r\}$. Two situations may occur:

1. The vectors $\mathbf{X}_1, \mathbf{X}_2, \ldots, \mathbf{X}_r$ are linearly independent. In this case, if any vector $\mathbf{X}_i$ is removed, the remaining vectors will not generate V. For we know $\mathbf{X}_i \in V$, and if the remaining vectors generate V, then

$$\mathbf{X}_i = a_1\mathbf{X}_1 + \cdots + a_{i-1}\mathbf{X}_{i-1} + a_{i+1}\mathbf{X}_{i+1} + \cdots + a_r\mathbf{X}_r$$

for scalars $a_1, \ldots, a_{i-1}, a_{i+1}, \ldots, a_r$, or

$$a_1\mathbf{X}_1 + \cdots + (-1)\mathbf{X}_i + \cdots + a_r\mathbf{X}_r = \mathbf{0},$$

contradicting our assumption that $\mathbf{X}_1, \ldots, \mathbf{X}_r$ are linearly independent. Consequently, no proper subset of $\mathbf{X}_1, \ldots, \mathbf{X}_r$ will generate V.

2. The vectors $\mathbf{X}_1, \ldots, \mathbf{X}_r$ are linearly dependent. In this case consider the vectors

$$\{\mathbf{X}_1, \ldots, \mathbf{X}_r\}$$

and beginning with $\mathbf{X}_2$ remove a vector if it can be written as a linear combination of the preceding vectors. (We can assume $\mathbf{X}_1 \neq \mathbf{0}$; otherwise, we could remove it.) There remains after this process, by virtue of Theorem 2.5, a set of linearly independent vectors

$$\{\mathbf{X}_1, \mathbf{X}_{i_2}, \ldots, \mathbf{X}_{i_k}\}, \tag{2.12}$$

where $i_2, i_3, \ldots, i_k$ are a subset of $2, 3, \ldots, r$.

Certainly $\mathbf{X}_1, \mathbf{X}_{i_2}, \ldots, \mathbf{X}_{i_k}$ generate V, since for every $\mathbf{X}$ in V

$$\mathbf{X} = a_1\mathbf{X}_1 + \cdots + a_r\mathbf{X}_r$$

and if $\mathbf{X}_i$ is not among the vectors (2.12) it may be replaced by a linear combination of vectors from the set (2.12) which preceded it.

Thus we have the following partial answer to question 1.

THEOREM 2.6. *If $\mathbf{X}_1, \ldots, \mathbf{X}_r$ generate a vector space V, then there is a linearly independent subset of these vectors which generates V.*

We are now in a position to give complete answers to questions 1 and 2.

THEOREM 2.7. *Let*

$$V = L\{\mathbf{X}_1, \mathbf{X}_2, \ldots, \mathbf{X}_r\},$$

where $\mathbf{X}_1, \mathbf{X}_2, \ldots, \mathbf{X}_r$ are linearly independent. If $\mathbf{Y}_1, \mathbf{Y}_2, \ldots, \mathbf{Y}_s$ are a set of linearly independent vectors of V, then $r \geq s$.

COROLLARY 1. *Let*

$$V = L\{\mathbf{X}_1, \ldots, \mathbf{X}_r\} = L\{\mathbf{Y}_1, \ldots, \mathbf{Y}_s\},$$

where both $\mathbf{X}_1, \ldots, \mathbf{X}_r$ and $\mathbf{Y}_1, \ldots, \mathbf{Y}_s$ are linearly independent. Then $r = s$.

COROLLARY 2. *If $V = L\{\mathbf{X}_1, \ldots, \mathbf{X}_n\}$, then the maximum number of linearly independent vectors in V is n. Stated otherwise, every $n + 1$ vectors of V are linearly dependent.*

Note that in the special case $V = R^n$, Corollary 2 says that at most n vectors are linearly independent in R^n.

PROOF OF THEOREM 2.7. We know that $\mathbf{Y}_s \in V$, and that

$$\mathbf{Y}_s = a_1\mathbf{X}_1 + a_2\mathbf{X}_2 + \cdots + a_r\mathbf{X}_r$$

or

$$(-1)\mathbf{Y}_s + a_1\mathbf{X}_1 + \cdots + a_r\mathbf{X}_r = \mathbf{0}.$$

Thus the vectors $\mathbf{Y}_s, \mathbf{X}_1, \ldots, \mathbf{X}_r$ are linearly dependent because the coefficient (-1) of $\mathbf{Y}_s$ is not zero.

We consider $V = L\{\mathbf{Y}_s, \mathbf{X}_1, \ldots, \mathbf{X}_r\}$ and reduce the generators to a set of linearly independent generators by removing a vector $\mathbf{X}_i$ if it can be written as a linear combination of preceding vectors $\mathbf{Y}_s, \mathbf{X}_1, \ldots, \mathbf{X}_{i-1}$. Certainly $\mathbf{Y}_s$

will be retained (why?) and at least one vector $\mathbf{X}_i$ will be removed. Let us assume that $\mathbf{X}_i$ is the first vector removed so that

$$\mathbf{X}_i = a_1\mathbf{Y}_s + a_2\mathbf{X}_1 + \cdots + a_i\mathbf{X}_{i-1},$$

and $a_1 \neq 0$ for otherwise the vectors $\mathbf{X}_1, \ldots, \mathbf{X}_i$ would be linearly dependent. Then

$$V = L\{\mathbf{Y}_s, \mathbf{X}_1, \ldots, \mathbf{X}_{i-1}, \mathbf{X}_{i+1}, \ldots, \mathbf{X}_n\}.$$

Now repeat the process:

$$V = L\{\mathbf{Y}_{s-1}, \mathbf{Y}_s, \mathbf{X}_1, \ldots, \mathbf{X}_{i-1}, \mathbf{X}_{i+1}, \ldots, \mathbf{X}_n\},$$

and these vectors must be linearly dependent by the same argument used to show that the vectors $\{\mathbf{Y}_s, \mathbf{X}_1, \ldots, \mathbf{X}_n\}$ were dependent. Then again we may remove at least one vector which is a linear combination of the preceding ones. This vector must be an $\mathbf{X}_j$ since it cannot be $\mathbf{Y}_{s-1}$ or $\mathbf{Y}_s$ because the vectors $\{\mathbf{Y}_i\}$ are independent.

Continue in this way: at each step one $\mathbf{Y}$ vector is introduced and an $\mathbf{X}$ vector removed. Now it follows that $r \geq s$ since there must be an $\mathbf{X}$ vector to remove each time a $\mathbf{Y}$ vector is added. If the $\mathbf{X}$ vectors were exhausted, the $\mathbf{Y}$ vectors would be linearly dependent since each time the new $\mathbf{Y}$ vector is added the set becomes dependent.

Corollary 1 now follows immediately from the theorem. We first consider the linearly independent vectors $\mathbf{Y}_1, \ldots, \mathbf{Y}_s$ of $L\{\mathbf{X}_1, \ldots, \mathbf{X}_r\}$ and conclude $r \geq s$. Now consider $\mathbf{X}_1, \ldots, \mathbf{X}_r$ as linearly independent vectors of $L\{\mathbf{Y}_1, \ldots, \mathbf{Y}_s\}$; then $s \geq r$. Hence $r = s$.

In order to verify Corollary 2, first reduce $\mathbf{X}_1, \ldots, \mathbf{X}_n$ to a linearly independent set as in Case 2 of Theorem 2.6. Now, if $\mathbf{Y}_1, \ldots, \mathbf{Y}_{n+1}$ were linearly independent in V we would have by Theorem 2.7 that $n + 1 \leq n$, a clear contradiction.

In light of Theorem 2.6 we now have that $\mathbf{X}_1, \ldots, \mathbf{X}_n$ is a minimal generating set for V if and only if $X_1, \ldots, X_n$ are linearly independent. Corollary 1 then gives that any two minimal generating sets have the same number of elements. Thus we have given complete answers to our questions.

Another question suggests itself at this point. Does there exist at least one set of linearly independent generators for a given vector space V? The complete answer to this question is beyond the scope of this text; however, note that it is easy to give an example of a vector space that has no finite set of generators. Let U be the set of all real polynomials in one indeterminate, x. If there were a finite set of generators, there would be among these generators a polynomial of highest degree. Let this degree be n. How would we write the polynomial x^{n+1} in terms of the generators? We couldn't.

In this text we shall only consider vector spaces that have a finite set of generators and we therefore add the following assumption to those of Definition 2.4 for a vector space V over a field F:

F. FINITENESS. *There exists a finite set of vectors* $\mathbf{X}_1, \mathbf{X}_2, \ldots, \mathbf{X}_m$ *of* V *such that every vector* $\mathbf{X}$ *of* V *may be expressed in the form*

$$\mathbf{X} = a_1\mathbf{X}_1 + \cdots + a_m\mathbf{X}_m,$$

where $a_1, \ldots, a_m$ *are elements of* F.

We have already shown that R^n has a finite set of generators, and we can also show that every subspace V of R^n has a finite, linearly independent set of generators. Consider V and choose a vector $\mathbf{X}_1 \neq \mathbf{0}$ of V. If $V = L\{\mathbf{X}_1\}$, we are through. Otherwise, let $\mathbf{X}_2$ be a vector of V not in $L\{\mathbf{X}_1\}$. Then $\mathbf{X}_1$, $\mathbf{X}_2$ are linearly independent, for otherwise $\mathbf{X}_2$ would be a multiple of $\mathbf{X}_1$ and would be contained in $L\{\mathbf{X}_1\}$. If $V = L\{\mathbf{X}_1, \mathbf{X}_2\}$, we are through. If $V \neq L\{\mathbf{X}_1, \mathbf{X}_2\}$, choose $\mathbf{X}_3 \in V$ and not in $L\{\mathbf{X}_1, \mathbf{X}_2\}$. Again $\mathbf{X}_1, \mathbf{X}_2, \mathbf{X}_3$ are linearly independent and, continuing in this manner, we reach a point where

$$V = L\{\mathbf{X}_1, \ldots, \mathbf{X}_k\}.$$

We know the process must end with $k \leq n$ because Corollary 2 of Theorem 2.7 states that there is no set of $n + 1$ linearly independent vectors in R^n.

Example 4. We illustrate a method for determining whether a given set of vectors is linearly dependent. Actually we do much more; namely, we determine a linearly independent set of generators for the subspace generated by the given vectors. Consider $V = L\{\mathbf{X}_1, \mathbf{X}_2, \mathbf{X}_3, \mathbf{X}_4\}$, where

$$\mathbf{X}_1 = [1, 1, 2, -1], \qquad \mathbf{X}_2 = [0, 1, -1, -1],$$
$$\mathbf{X}_3 = [1, 0, 3, 0], \qquad \mathbf{X}_4 = [2, 3, 3, -3].$$

We first use $\mathbf{X}_1$ to reduce the first coordinates of the other vectors to zero; that is, we form four new vectors by

$$\mathbf{Y}_1 = \mathbf{X}_1 = [1, 1, 2, -1],$$
$$\mathbf{Y}_2 = \mathbf{X}_2 - \frac{0}{1}\mathbf{X}_1 = [0, 1, -1, -1],$$
$$\mathbf{Y}_3 = \mathbf{X}_3 - \frac{1}{1}\mathbf{X}_1 = [0, -1, 1, 1],$$
$$\mathbf{Y}_4 = \mathbf{X}_4 - \frac{2}{1}\mathbf{X}_1 = [0, 1, -1, -1].$$

Since the $\mathbf{Y}_i$'s are linear combinations of the $\mathbf{X}_i$'s it is clear that $L\{\mathbf{Y}_1, \mathbf{Y}_2, \mathbf{Y}_3, \mathbf{Y}_4\} \subseteq V$, but since $\mathbf{X}_1 = \mathbf{Y}_1$ and $\mathbf{X}_i = \mathbf{Y}_i + c_i\mathbf{Y}_1$ for some c_i and each $i \geq 2$, it is also clear that $V \subseteq L\{\mathbf{Y}_1, \mathbf{Y}_2, \mathbf{Y}_3, \mathbf{Y}_4\}$.

We now repeat the process with the last three vectors, trying to make all second coordinates save one equal to zero. (In our case, $\mathbf{Y}_2$ has nonzero second coordinate; if not we would just find one of the three vectors with nonzero second coordinate and relabel it so that it was $\mathbf{Y}_2$. If all three vectors have zero in their second coordinate, proceed to the third coordinate.)

$$\mathbf{Z}_1 = \mathbf{Y}_1 = [1, 1, 2, -1],$$
$$\mathbf{Z}_2 = \mathbf{Y}_2 = [0, 1, -1, -1],$$
$$\mathbf{Z}_3 = \mathbf{Y}_3 - \frac{-1}{1}\mathbf{Y}_2 = [0, 0, 0, 0],$$
$$\mathbf{Z}_4 = \mathbf{Y}_4 - \frac{1}{1}\mathbf{Y}_2 = [0, 0, 0, 0].$$

Again

$$L\{\mathbf{Z}_1, \mathbf{Z}_2, \mathbf{Z}_3, \mathbf{Z}_4\} = L\{\mathbf{Y}_1, \mathbf{Y}_2, \mathbf{Y}_3, \mathbf{Y}_4\} = V.$$

But it is immediate that

$$L\{\mathbf{Z}_1, \mathbf{Z}_2, \mathbf{Z}_3, \mathbf{Z}_4\} = L\{\mathbf{Z}_1, \mathbf{Z}_2\}$$

and that $\mathbf{Z}_1, \mathbf{Z}_2$ are linearly independent, so Corollary 1 gives that $\mathbf{X}_1, \mathbf{X}_2, \mathbf{X}_3, \mathbf{X}_4$ are linearly dependent.

To further illustrate the method we determine a linearly independent set of generators for

$$L\{[0, -1, 1, 2], [2, 1, -1, 1], [1, 3, 1, 1], [1, 2, 1, 2]\}.$$

We cannot pick the first vector as $\mathbf{X}_1$ since it has nonzero first coordinate; to avoid fractions we avoid the second vector. Thus we relabel the vectors as

$$\begin{aligned}\mathbf{X}_1 &= [1, 3, 1, 1],\\ \mathbf{X}_2 &= [0, -1, 1, 2],\\ \mathbf{X}_3 &= [2, 1, -1, 1],\\ \mathbf{X}_4 &= [1, 2, 1, 2].\end{aligned}$$

We apply the method,

$$\begin{aligned}\mathbf{Y}_1 &= \mathbf{X}_1 = [1, 3, 1, 1],\\ \mathbf{Y}_2 &= \mathbf{X}_2 - \frac{0}{1}\mathbf{X}_1 = [0, -1, 1, 2],\\ \mathbf{Y}_3 &= \mathbf{X}_3 - \frac{2}{1}\mathbf{X}_1 = [0, -5, -3, -1],\\ \mathbf{Y}_4 &= \mathbf{X}_4 - \frac{1}{1}\mathbf{X}_1 = [0, -1, 0, 1];\end{aligned}$$

$$\begin{aligned}\mathbf{Z}_1 &= \mathbf{Y}_1,\\ \mathbf{Z}_2 &= \mathbf{Y}_2,\\ \mathbf{Z}_3 &= \mathbf{Y}_3 - \frac{-5}{-1}\mathbf{Y}_2 = [0, 0, -8, -11],\\ \mathbf{Z}_4 &= \mathbf{Y}_4 - \frac{-1}{-1}\mathbf{Y}_2 = [0, 0, -1, -1];\end{aligned}$$

$$\begin{aligned}\mathbf{W}_1 &= \mathbf{Z}_1 = [1, 3, 1, 1],\\ \mathbf{W}_2 &= \mathbf{Z}_2 = [0, -1, 1, 2],\\ \mathbf{W}_3 &= \mathbf{Z}_3 = [0, 0, -8, -11],\\ \mathbf{W}_4 &= \mathbf{Z}_4 - \frac{-1}{-8}\mathbf{Z}_3 = [0, 0, 0, \tfrac{3}{8}];\end{aligned}$$

clearly $\mathbf{W}_1$, $\mathbf{W}_2$, $\mathbf{W}_3$, $\mathbf{W}_4$ are linearly independent and since at each stage the space generated was unchanged, we have the conclusion that our original four vectors must be linearly independent.

Exercises

1. Are the points $(1, 1, -1)$, $(2, 1, 1)$, $(3, -1, 2)$, $(0, 3, -2)$ coplanar?
2. Can one vector be linearly dependent?
3. Determine whether the following vectors are linearly independent. If not, express A_3 as a linear combination of A_1 and A_2.
   (a) $A_1 = [1, 2, -1]$, $A_2 = [2, 1, 4]$, $A_3 = [-1, 7, -17]$;
   (b) $A_1 = [2, 1]$, $A_2 = [1, 1]$, $A_3 = [4, 5]$;
   (c) $A_1 = [3, 1, 0, 1]$, $A_2 = [1, 4, -1, 0]$, $A_3 = [0, 1, -1, 0]$.
4. Consider the vectors

$$\begin{aligned}\mathbf{X}_1 &= 2x^3 - x^2 + 4,\\ \mathbf{X}_2 &= x^3 - 2x + 6,\\ \mathbf{X}_3 &= x + 1,\\ \mathbf{X}_4 &= x^4\end{aligned}$$

in the space of polynomials with real coefficients. Are $\mathbf{X}_1, \mathbf{X}_2, \mathbf{X}_3, \mathbf{X}_4$ linearly independent?

5. (a) Determine an independent generating set of

$$L\{[1, -1, 0, 1, 1], [2, 1, 0, 1, -1], [1, 1, 1, 1, 1], [2, -1, -1, 1, -1], [0, 2, 1, 0, 0]\}.$$

   (b) By tracing the work in part (a), give a subset of the original set which is an independent generating set.

6. Determine a value of k which makes the following vectors linearly dependent:

$$[1, 2, k], [0, 1, k - 1], [3, 4, 3].$$

7. Let $V = L\{\mathbf{X}_1, \mathbf{X}_2, \ldots, \mathbf{X}_k\}$, where $\mathbf{X}_1, \ldots, \mathbf{X}_k$ are linearly independent vectors. Show that if

$$\mathbf{X} = a_1\mathbf{X}_1 + a_2\mathbf{X}_2 + \cdots + a_k\mathbf{X}_k = b_1\mathbf{X}_1 + b_2\mathbf{X}_2 + \cdots + b_k\mathbf{X}_k,$$

then $a_1 = b_1, a_2 = b_2, \ldots, a_k = b_k$.

2.7 Bases and Dimension of Vector Spaces

It is time to draw together several threads of previous discussions. In particular, we would like to make precise the central place which R^n occupies among vector spaces over R. We have seen that R^n has a simple linearly independent generating set $\mathbf{E}_1, \mathbf{E}_2, \ldots, \mathbf{E}_n$, and that every subspace has a finite independent generating set. What is the relation of other spaces over R which satisfy F to R^n? Why was R^n called "the basic example" in Section 2.5?

In order to answer these questions we must make precise our notion of what it means for two vector spaces to be algebraically indistinguishable. The following definition serves that purpose:

DEFINITION 2.8. *Two vector spaces V and W (over the same field F) are said to be* ISOMORPHIC *if there exists a one-to-one mapping* T *from V onto W which satisfies*

(1) $\mathrm{T}(\mathbf{X} + \mathbf{Y}) = \mathrm{T}(\mathbf{X}) + \mathrm{T}(\mathbf{Y})$ *for all* $\mathbf{X}, \mathbf{Y} \in V$.
(2) $\mathrm{T}(a\mathbf{X}) = a\mathrm{T}(\mathbf{X})$ *for all* $a \in F$ *and* $\mathbf{X} \in V$.

The mapping T *is called an* ISOMORPHISM *and as it is one-to-one it has an inverse function* T^{-1}. T^{-1} *is an isomorphism from W to V.*

Note that the last statement of the definition is actually an assertion requiring proof; this is left as an exercise.

Note that an isomorphism along with its inverse is a two-way street between V and W. It permits us to do calculations that originate in one vector space in another space and then take the answers back to the original space. Somewhat surprisingly the sequence (1) T, (2) calculation in $\mathrm{T}(V)$, (3) T^{-1}, can be more economical in some cases than simply doing the calculations in V to begin with.

Example 1. We saw earlier that $L\{1, x, x^2, \ldots, x^{n-1}\} = P^n$, the space of polynomials of degree less than n. The student may have noticed that this set of generators behaves exactly like the $\mathbf{E}_i$'s in R^n. This suggests the mapping T defined by

$$\mathrm{T}(a_1 + a_2x + \cdots + a_nx^{n-1}) = [a_1, a_2, \ldots, a_n].$$

In particular,

$$\mathrm{T}(1) = \mathbf{E}_1, \quad \mathrm{T}(x) = \mathbf{E}_2, \ldots, \mathrm{T}(x^{n-1}) = \mathbf{E}_n.$$

It is easily verified that T satisfies (1) and (2) and that it is one-to-one and onto.

Example 2. Let $W = L\{\mathbf{X}_1, \mathbf{X}_2, \ldots, \mathbf{X}_n\}$ with $\mathbf{X}_1, \mathbf{X}_2, \ldots, \mathbf{X}_n$ linearly independent. For any vector $\mathbf{A} \in R^n$, $\mathbf{A} = [a_1, a_2, \ldots, a_n]$, we define

$$\mathrm{T}(\mathbf{A}) = a_1\mathbf{X}_1 + a_2\mathbf{X}_2 + \cdots + a_n\mathbf{X}_n.$$

Then T is an isomorphism of R^n onto W.

Now, if W is a space satisfying condition F with say $\mathbf{Y}_1, \mathbf{Y}_2, \ldots, \mathbf{Y}_m$ spanning W, then using the process of the previous section we may reduce the set $\{\mathbf{Y}_1, \ldots, \mathbf{Y}_m\}$ to a set of linearly independent vectors that generate W. If we renumber the resulting set $\{\mathbf{Y}_1, \mathbf{Y}_2, \ldots, \mathbf{Y}_n\}$, then by Corollary 2 of the previous section, no set of independent vectors of W can have more than n elements. More is true: *every* set of n independent vectors of W spans W. To see this, let $\mathbf{Z}_1, \ldots, \mathbf{Z}_n$ be linearly independent in W and suppose that some $\mathbf{Z} \in W$ is not in the span of $\mathbf{Z}_1, \ldots, \mathbf{Z}_n$. Then $\mathbf{Z}_1, \ldots, \mathbf{Z}_n, \mathbf{Z}$ are linearly independent. (Why?) But this is impossible since W has no set of $n + 1$ independent vectors.

Further, if V is any other space spanned by n linearly independent vectors $\mathbf{X}_1, \ldots, \mathbf{X}_n$, then we can define an isomorphism from W to V by

$$\mathrm{T}(a_1\mathbf{Y}_1 + a_2\mathbf{Y}_2 + \cdots + a_n\mathbf{Y}_n) = a_1\mathbf{X}_1 + a_2\mathbf{X}_2 + \cdots + a_n\mathbf{X}_n.$$

These results may be summarized by:

THEOREM 2.8. Every vector space, V, satisfying condition F *has an associated number n with the following properties:*

(1) *V is generated by a set of n independent vectors.*
(2) *Every set of n independent vectors generates V.*
(3) *No set of independent vectors in V has more than n elements.*
(4) *V is isomorphic to all other vector spaces with n independent generators.*

From this theorem it is clear that n plays an important role. In fact, from condition (4) one can almost say that the essential thing about V is n. When we know n, we at once know one space with n independent generators, R^n, and thus we know *all* such spaces in the sense that results depending directly on the postulates for vector spaces can be obtained for R^n and applied at once to any isomorphic space. Hence we give names to n and to sets of independent generators.

DEFINITION 2.9. A set of linearly independent vectors that generate a vector space V is called a BASIS *of V.*

DEFINITION 2.10. The number of vectors of a basis of V is the DIMENSION *of V.*

How does one find a basis for a particular space V? One way is to start with any nonzero vector $\mathbf{Y}_1$ in V. If $V \neq L\{\mathbf{Y}_1\}$, there is a vector $\mathbf{Y}_2$ in V but not in $L\{\mathbf{Y}_1\}$; $\mathbf{Y}_1, \mathbf{Y}_2$ are linearly independent. If $V \neq L\{\mathbf{Y}_1, \mathbf{Y}_2\}$, pick $\mathbf{Y}_3 \in V$, $\mathbf{Y}_3 \notin L\{\mathbf{Y}_1, \mathbf{Y}_2\}$, and $\mathbf{Y}_1, \mathbf{Y}_2, \mathbf{Y}_3$ will be independent. The next theorem tells us that this process never leads to a blind alley. Regardless of what vectors we choose for $\mathbf{Y}_1, \ldots, \mathbf{Y}_k$ we will eventually attain a basis for V.

THEOREM 2.9. If $\mathbf{Y}_1, \mathbf{Y}_2, \ldots, \mathbf{Y}_k$ are linearly independent vectors of a vector space V of dimension n, then vectors $\mathbf{X}_{k+1}, \mathbf{X}_{k+2}, \ldots, \mathbf{X}_n$ may be found so that $\mathbf{Y}_1, \ldots, \mathbf{Y}_k, \mathbf{X}_{k+1}, \ldots, \mathbf{X}_n$ is a basis for V.

PROOF. Let $\mathbf{X}_1^*, \mathbf{X}_2^*, \ldots, \mathbf{X}_n^*$ be some basis for V. Consider the vectors $\mathbf{Y}_1, \mathbf{Y}_2, \ldots, \mathbf{Y}_k, \mathbf{X}_1^*, \ldots, \mathbf{X}_n^*$. This is obviously a generating set. Reduce it to a basis by removing one vector at a time, each time removing a vector that is dependent on preceding ones. No $\mathbf{Y}_i$ will be removed. (Why?) The result will be a linearly independent generating set, that is, a basis, containing all the $\mathbf{Y}_i$'s.

The reader may object that in explaining how to get a basis we have assumed a basis. But the theorem does not promise a method for deciding if any basis exists; rather it shows how to find a special kind of basis once it is known that at least one basis exists (in the statement of the theorem, the assumption that V is of dimension n is just the assumption that some basis of n elements exists).

Theorem 2.9 is often paraphrased by saying that any linearly independent set may be extended to a basis. The theorem is often called the Steinitz replacement theorem.

Exercises

1. Let V be the set of all vectors $[x_1, x_2, x_3, x_4]$ of R^4 such that
$$x_1 + x_2 + x_3 + x_4 = 0.$$
   (a) Do the vectors $[1, -1, 0, 0]$, $[1, 1, -2, 0]$, $[1, 0, -1, 0]$ form a basis for V?
   (b) Do the vectors $[1, 0, 0, -1]$, $[1, 0, -1, 0]$, $[4, -1, -2, -1]$ form a basis for V?
2. Find two bases of R^4 that have no elements in common.
3. Find two bases of R^4 that have only the vectors $[0, 0, 1, 0]$ and $[0, 0, 0, 1]$ in common.
4. For what values of k will the vectors $[k, 1 - k, k]$, $[2k, 2k - 1, k + 2]$, $[-2k, k, -k]$ form a basis for R^3?
5. Find a basis for the subspace of R^5 in which $x_1 = x_2 = -x_3$. It will be necessary to make certain that your basis is complete; that is, that you actually have the maximum number of independent elements.
6. Find a basis of $L\{[1, -1, 2, 3], [1, 0, 1, 0], [3, -2, 5, 7]\}$ which includes the vector $[1, 1, 0, -1]$.
7. Extend the set $[1, 1, -1, 1]$, $[1, 0, 1, 1]$, $[1, 2, 1, 1]$ to a basis of R^4.
8. Consider the subspace V of R^4 for which a basis is $[1, -1, 0, 1]$ and $[2, 1, -1, 0]$.
   (a) What is the form of the general vector of this subspace?
   (b) In terms of your answer to the previous part indicate an isomorphic mapping of V onto R^2.
9. Prove that every subspace of R^n has no more than n linearly independent vectors. What can you conclude about the dimension of every subspace V of R^n from this fact?

2.8 Subspaces of Vector Spaces

In previous sections we have used various devices to identify subspaces of a vector space; a set of generators or, better, a basis, may be given. Also, when we are dealing with the vector space R^n, a relationship between components such as the set of vectors $[x_1, x_2, \ldots, x_n]$ of R^n for which $x_1 = x_2$ is a satisfactory definition. In this section we wish to define operations for subspaces that do not depend on the particular manner in which they are identified.

If S and T are two arbitrary subspaces of a vector space V, the *intersection* $S \cap T$ and the *union* $S \cup T$ of these spaces are defined as the *intersection* and *union* of the sets S and T. The latter is not usually a subspace in its own right.

DEFINITION 2.11. *If S and T are subspaces of a vector space V, the set of all possible sums of a vector in S with a vector in T is denoted by $S + T$ and is called the* SUM *of the subspaces S and T.*

Note that, since the zero vector at least is in both S and T, $S + T$ will include $S \cup T$. Moreover, any subspace W that includes $S \cup T$ will certainly include $S + T$.

THEOREM 2.10. *The intersection $S \cap T$ and sum $S + T$ of subspaces S and T of a vector space V are again subspaces of V.*

PROOF. If $\mathbf{X}$ and $\mathbf{Y}$ are arbitrary vectors of $S \cap T$, then $\mathbf{X}$ and $\mathbf{Y}$ are vectors of S and of T. Then $a\mathbf{X} + b\mathbf{Y}$ is a vector of both S and T so that $a\mathbf{X} + b\mathbf{Y} \in S \cap T$, where a and b are arbitrary scalars. Consequently $S \cap T$ is a subspace of S and of T as well as of V.

An arbitrary vector of $S + T$ is of the form $\mathbf{X}_1 + \mathbf{Y}_1$, where $\mathbf{X}_1 \in S$ and $\mathbf{Y}_1 \in T$. Given any two elements $\mathbf{X}_1 + \mathbf{Y}_1$ and $\mathbf{X}_2 + \mathbf{Y}_2$ of $S + T$,

$$a(\mathbf{X}_1 + \mathbf{Y}_1) + b(\mathbf{X}_2 + \mathbf{Y}_2) = (a\mathbf{X}_1 + b\mathbf{X}_2) + (a\mathbf{Y}_1 + b\mathbf{Y}_2),$$

where a and b are arbitrary scalars. Since $a\mathbf{X}_1 + b\mathbf{X}_2 \in S$, $a\mathbf{Y}_1 + b\mathbf{Y}_2 \in T$, we see that $a(\mathbf{X}_1 + \mathbf{Y}_1) + b(\mathbf{X}_2 + \mathbf{Y}_2)$ is again in $S + T$ and hence that $S + T$ is a subspace of V.

Example 1. Let $S = L\{[1, -1, 0], [1, 0, 2]\}$, $T = L\{[0, 1, 0], [0, 1, 2]\}$. We wish to determine the subspaces $S \cap T$ and $S + T$.

It is relatively easy to determine $S + T$, since

$$S + T = L\{[1, -1, 0], [1, 0, 2], [0, 1, 0], [0, 1, 2]\}.$$

The vectors $[1, 0, 2]$, $[0, 1, 2]$, and $[0, 1, 0]$ are linearly independent because a linear relation $c_1[1, 0, 2] + c_2[0, 1, 2] + c_3[0, 1, 0] = \mathbf{0}$ leads to a system of equations

$$c_1 = 0, \qquad c_2 + c_3 = 0, \qquad 2c_1 + 2c_2 = 0,$$

and the unique solution is

$$c_1 = c_2 = c_3 = 0.$$

We now apply Theorem 2.8, part 2, and have $S + T = R^3$.

In order to determine $S \cap T$, note that an arbitrary vector $\mathbf{X}$ of $S \cap T$ must have the form $a[1, -1, 0] + b[1, 0, 2]$ since it is contained in S. At the same time $\mathbf{X}$ must have the form $c[0, 1, 0] + d[0, 1, 2]$, as $\mathbf{X}$ is also a vector of T. Thus,

$$a[1, -1, 0] + b[1, 0, 2] = c[0, 1, 0] + d[0, 1, 2],$$

and this vector relation leads to the system of equations

$$\begin{aligned} a + b \qquad\qquad &= 0,\\ -a \qquad - c - d &= 0,\\ 2b \qquad - 2d &= 0. \end{aligned}$$

Consequently, for a solution, a may be arbitrary and then $b = -a$, $d = -a$, $c = 0$. Hence,

$$\mathbf{X} = a[1, -1, 0] + (-a)[1, 0, 2] = a[0, -1, -2],$$

or

$$\mathbf{X} = 0[0, 1, 0] \quad + (-a)[0, 1, 2] = a[0, -1, -2],$$

and $S \cap T = L\{[0, 1, 2]\}$.

For arbitrary subspaces S and T of a vector space V, there is an interesting relation between the dimensions of the subspaces S, T, $S \cap T$, and $S + T$.

THEOREM 2.11. If S and T are subspaces of a vector space V, then

$$\textit{dimension } S + \textit{dimension } T = \textit{dimension } (S \cap T) + \textit{dimension } (S + T).$$

PROOF. Let a basis for $S \cap T$ be $\mathbf{X}_1, \ldots, \mathbf{X}_k$. By Theorem 2.9 we may extend this linearly independent set of vectors of S to a basis for S. Then let vectors $\mathbf{S}_1, \mathbf{S}_2, \ldots, \mathbf{S}_{m-k}, \mathbf{X}_1, \mathbf{X}_2, \ldots, \mathbf{X}_k$ be a basis for S. Similarly, we may extend $\mathbf{X}_1, \mathbf{X}_2, \ldots, \mathbf{X}_k$ to a basis $\mathbf{X}_1, \ldots, \mathbf{X}_k, \mathbf{T}_1, \ldots, \mathbf{T}_{r-k}$ of T.

We will now show that the vectors

$$\mathbf{S}_1, \mathbf{S}_2, \ldots, \mathbf{S}_{m-k}, \mathbf{X}_1, \ldots, \mathbf{X}_k, \mathbf{T}_1, \mathbf{T}_2, \ldots, \mathbf{T}_{r-k} \tag{2.13}$$

form a basis for $S + T$. Certainly all the vectors of (2.13) are elements of $S + T$; furthermore, any vector of $S + T$ is the sum of a vector of S and a vector of T and may be expressed as a linear combination of the vectors (2.13); the first m are a basis for S, and the last r are a basis for T. Hence

$$S + T = L\{\mathbf{S}_1, \ldots, \mathbf{S}_{m-k}, \mathbf{X}_1, \ldots, \mathbf{X}_k, \mathbf{T}_1, \ldots, \mathbf{T}_{r-k}\}.$$

It remains to be shown that these vectors are linearly independent. Suppose there is a linear relation of the form

$$\begin{aligned} a_1\mathbf{S}_1 + a_2\mathbf{S}_2 + \cdots + a_{m-k}\mathbf{S}_{m-k} \\ + b_1\mathbf{X}_1 + \cdots + b_k\mathbf{X}_k + c_1\mathbf{T}_1 + \cdots + c_{r-k}\mathbf{T}_{r-k} = \mathbf{0}, \end{aligned} \tag{2.14}$$

where not all the a_i, b_i, c_i are 0. Indeed we may assume that not all the a_i are 0 since otherwise the vectors $\mathbf{X}_1, \ldots, \mathbf{X}_k, \mathbf{T}_1, \ldots, \mathbf{T}_{r-k}$ would be dependent, contrary to the assumption that they are a basis of T.

Transposing, we have

$$\begin{aligned} a_1\mathbf{S}_1 + \cdots + a_{m-k}\mathbf{S}_{m-k} \\ = -(b_1\mathbf{X}_1 + \cdots + b_k\mathbf{X}_k + c_1\mathbf{T}_1 + \cdots + c_{r-k}\mathbf{T}_{r-k}). \end{aligned} \tag{2.15}$$

Now Equation (2.15) implies that $a_1\mathbf{S}_1 + \cdots + a_{m-k}\mathbf{S}_{m-k}$ is in T and hence in $S \cap T$. Then it may be expressed as a linear combination of the $\mathbf{X}_i$,

$$a_1\mathbf{S}_1 + \cdots + a_{m-k}\mathbf{S}_{m-k} = d_1\mathbf{X}_1 + d_2\mathbf{X}_2 + \cdots + d_k\mathbf{X}_k.$$

This is impossible unless all a_i and d_i are 0 because $\mathbf{S}_1, \ldots, \mathbf{S}_{m-k}, \mathbf{X}_1, \ldots, \mathbf{X}_k$ are linearly independent. Since the a_i are not all zero we have a contradiction, and the vectors of (2.13) are linearly independent.

Now the theorem results when we note that dimension $S = m$, dimension $T = r$, dimension $S \cap T = k$, and dimension $S + T = m + r - k$.

Example 2. Every pair S, T of two-dimensional subspaces of R^3 has a nonzero intersection. To prove this, we note that $S + T$ has dimension at most 3 (and at least 2). Then the equation of the theorem reads:

$$4 = \text{dimension } (S + T) + \text{dimension } (S \cap T),$$

or

$$4 - \text{dimension } (S + T) = \text{dimension } (S \cap T).$$

Hence dimension $(S \cap T)$ is either 1 or 2.

Geometrically, this has a simple interpretation in space. With S, since it is generated by two linearly independent vectors, we can associate a plane passing through the origin. All line segments in this plane will be associated with linear combinations of the two generating vectors. Similarly T can be associated with another plane passing through the origin. These planes will either be identical or intersect in a line. In the latter case, a vector $\mathbf{X}$ associated with a segment of the line of intersection will lie in both S and T and hence be in $S \cap T$. Moreover, $S \cap T = L\{\mathbf{X}\}$ will be one-dimensional.

If S and T are subspaces of a vector space V, we have seen that $S + T$ is a subspace W of V. Let us now change our point of view. Starting with a subspace W of the vector space V, is it possible to express W as the sum of two other subspaces S and T? We let

$$W = L\{\mathbf{X}_1, \mathbf{X}_2, \ldots, \mathbf{X}_k\}$$

be a subspace of dimension $r > 1$ (where, of course, $k \geq r$). Now by letting

$$S = L\{\mathbf{X}_1, \ldots, \mathbf{X}_t\},$$
$$T = L\{\mathbf{X}_{t+1}, \ldots, \mathbf{X}_k\}$$

for $1 \leq t \leq k - 1$ we obtain a *decomposition* of W into the sum of subspaces S and T; that is, $W = S + T$. It should be clear that W can be expressed as the sum of subspaces in many ways. If the vectors we have used to generate W are linearly independent, then $S \cap T = \mathbf{0}$ and every $\mathbf{X}$ of W can be expressed uniquely in the form

$$\mathbf{X} = \mathbf{Y} + \mathbf{Z}, \tag{2.16}$$

where $\mathbf{Y} \in S$, $\mathbf{Z} \in T$. Otherwise the vectors $\mathbf{X}_1, \ldots, \mathbf{X}_k$ would be linearly dependent. (Why?)

Conversely, if $W = S + T$ and every vector $\mathbf{X}$ of W can be written uniquely in the form (2.16), $S \cap T = \mathbf{0}$. We see this because the assumption that $S \cap T \neq \mathbf{0}$ means that the vectors of this intersection can be expressed as elements either of S or of T and hence not uniquely.

A decomposition of a vector space V into the sum of subspaces $S + T$, where $S \cap T = \mathbf{0}$, will be of importance in the next section.

DEFINITION 2.12. If $W = S + T$, where S and T are subspaces of a vector space W and $S \cap T = \mathbf{0}$, we write $W = S \oplus T$ and say that W is the DIRECT SUM *of the subspaces S and T.*

The concept of a direct sum decomposition has a simple geometric interpretation in space. We let W be the vector space R^3 and associate the vector $[x_1, x_2, x_3]$ of R^3 with the line segment OX. Let S be a two-dimensional subspace of R^3 generated by the vectors $\mathbf{Y} = [y_1, y_2, y_3]$ and $\mathbf{Z} = [z_1, z_2, z_3]$. Associate with S the plane π containing the line segments OY and OZ (Figure 2.13). Now if $R^3 = S \oplus T$, and T is generated by $\mathbf{X} = [x_1, x_2, x_3]$, the line

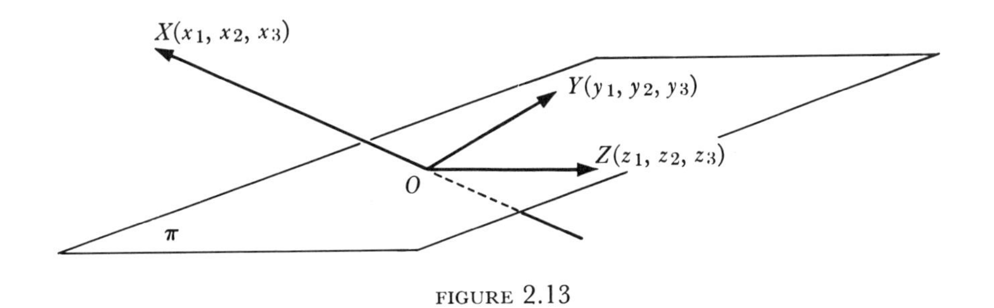

FIGURE 2.13

segment OX cannot lie in the plane π, for then $\mathbf{X}$ would be a linear combination of $\mathbf{Y}$ and $\mathbf{Z}$, and $\mathbf{X}$ would be contained in S contrary to the direct sum requirement. Hence T is associated with a line intersecting π. Now it should be clear that *any* line intersecting π at O could be used to determine a subspace T, such that $R^3 = S \oplus T$. Hence a direct sum decomposition is not unique even when S is kept fixed.

We also see why T cannot be two-dimensional. In that case T would be associated with a plane π^*, and the planes π and π^* would have at least a line of intersection so that $S \cap T \neq \mathbf{0}$.

Example 3. Let

$$V = L\{[1, 0, 1, 0], [1, 0, 1, 1], [1, 0, 0, 0]\}.$$

Then

$$V = L\{[1, 0, 1, 0], [1, 0, 1, 1]\} \oplus L\{[1, 0, 0, 0]\};$$

or

$$V = L\{[1, 0, 1, 0], [1, 0, 1, 1]\} \oplus L\{[3, 0, 2, 1]\}.$$

We note that even though S is the same, T is different for the two decompositions. We have merely selected the first two elements of a basis for V as the basis for S. The second basis for T is the sum of the basis vectors of V as originally presented.

Exercises

1. Find the intersection and sum of the subspaces

$$S = L\{[1, 0, 1], [1, 1, 0]\} \quad \text{and} \quad T = L\{[1, 2, 3], [0, 0, 1]\}.$$

2. In R^4 let

$$S = L\{[2, 2, -1, 2], [1, 1, 1, -2], [0, 0, 2, -4]\},$$

and

$$T = L\{[2, -1, 1, 1], [-2, 1, 3, 3], [3, -6, 0, 0]\}.$$

Determine the dimensions of S, T, $S \cap T$, $S + T$ and verify the relation of Theorem 2.11.

3. Prove that every pair of k-dimensional subspaces of a $(2k - 1)$-dimensional vector space must have a nonzero intersection.
4. Let

$$S = L\{[1, 0, 2], [-1, 1, 0]\}$$

and find two subspaces T such that $R^3 = S \oplus T$.

5. If $V = S \oplus T$, and $\mathbf{X}$ is a vector of V such that $\mathbf{X} = \mathbf{Y} + \mathbf{Z}$, where $\mathbf{Y} \in S$, $\mathbf{Z} \in T$; then $\mathbf{Y}$ is called the projection of $\mathbf{X}$ on S, $\mathbf{Z}$ the projection of $\mathbf{X}$ on T. Let

$$V = L\{[1, 2, -1], [1, -1, 0]\} \oplus L\{[1, 0, 1]\}$$

(i.e., $V = S \oplus T$); find the projection of $\mathbf{X} = [4, 1, -3]$ on S and on T. Interpret this result geometrically in space.
6. If $V = S \oplus T$, under what conditions will the projection of a vector $\mathbf{X}$ of V on S be $\mathbf{0}$? The projection of $\mathbf{X}$ on T be $\mathbf{0}$?
7. In Exercise 1, show that $S \cup T$ is not a subspace. For a vector space V give sufficient conditions on subspaces S and T so that $S \cup T$ is a subspace.
8. In R^4, let S be the subspace of those vectors $[x_1, x_2, x_3, x_4]$ such that $x_1 - 2x_3 = 0$, and let T consist of vectors such that $x_2 = x_4$. Describe $S + T$, $S \cap T$.
9. If $W = L\{\mathbf{X}_1, \mathbf{X}_2, \ldots, \mathbf{X}_k\}$ is a subspace of a vector space V, show that W may also be considered as the intersection of all subspaces of V that contain the vectors $\mathbf{X}_1, \mathbf{X}_2, \ldots, \mathbf{X}_k$.

2.9 Inner Products

Assume that we have coordinatized ordinary three-space with a Cartesian coordinate system and consider a vector $\mathbf{Z}$ associated with the directed line segment from (x_1, x_2, x_3) to (y_1, y_2, y_3). Application of the Pythagorean theorem yields that the length of this line segment is given by

$$\sqrt{(y_1 - x_1)^2 + (y_2 - x_2)^2 + (y_3 - x_3)^2}.$$

Notice that

$$\mathbf{Z} = [y_1 - x_1, y_2 - x_2, y_3 - x_3].$$

Thus for any vector $\mathbf{A} = [a_1, a_2, a_3]$ we are led to defining the length of $\mathbf{A}$ as the number $\sqrt{a_1^2 + a_2^2 + a_3^2}$, denoted by $|\mathbf{A}|$.

Now if $\mathbf{A} = [a_1, a_2, a_3]$, $\mathbf{B} = [b_1, b_2, b_3]$ are any two vectors, associate them with the directed line segments from the origin to the points (a_1, a_2, a_3) and (b_1, b_2, b_3), respectively, and consider the angle θ between the two segments OA and OB. (See Figure 2.14.) We assume that θ is chosen between 0 and π. We would like to relate the angle θ to the triples of numbers $[a_1, a_2, a_3]$ and $[b_1, b_2, b_3]$. Applying the law of cosines to the triangle OAB we obtain

$$(b_1 - a_1)^2 + (b_2 - a_2)^2 + (b_3 - a_3)^2 = |\mathbf{A}|^2 + |\mathbf{B}|^2 - 2|\mathbf{A}|\,|\mathbf{B}| \cos \theta.$$

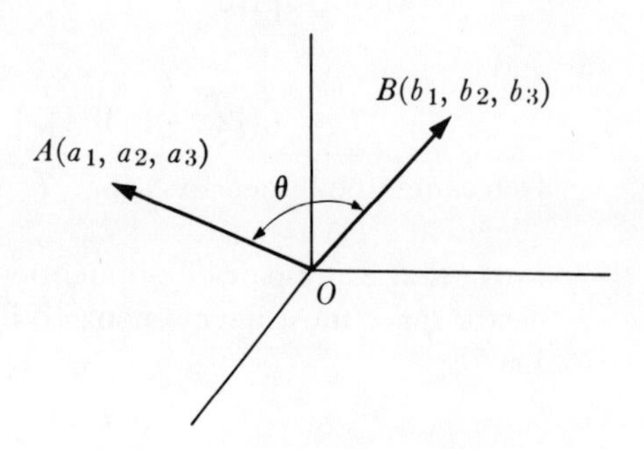

FIGURE 2.14

Expansion of the left side yields

$$|\mathbf{A}|^2 + |\mathbf{B}|^2 - 2(a_1b_1 + a_2b_2 + a_3b_3) = |\mathbf{A}|^2 + |\mathbf{B}|^2 - 2|\mathbf{A}|\,|\mathbf{B}| \cos\theta,$$

or

$$\cos\theta = \frac{a_1b_2 + a_2b_2 + a_3b_3}{|\mathbf{A}|\,|\mathbf{B}|}.$$

Let us denote the number $a_1b_1 + a_2b_2 + a_3b_3$ that is associated with the vectors $\mathbf{A} = [a_1, a_2, a_3]$ and $\mathbf{B} = [b_1, b_2, b_3]$ by $(\mathbf{A}, \mathbf{B})$. We have seen that this number arises naturally in two ways: first, the length of any segment associated with $\mathbf{A}$ is given by $|\mathbf{A}| = (\mathbf{A}, \mathbf{A})^{1/2}$, and second, the cosine of the angle between line segments associated with $\mathbf{A}$ and $\mathbf{B}$ is given by

$$\cos\theta = (\mathbf{A}, \mathbf{B})/|\mathbf{A}|\,|\mathbf{B}|.$$

The geometric arguments above motivate the following definitions.

DEFINITION 2.13. *The* INNER *(or scalar)* PRODUCT $(\mathbf{X}, \mathbf{Y})$ *of vectors* $\mathbf{X} = [x_1, x_2, \ldots, x_n]$ *and* $\mathbf{Y} = [y_1, y_2, \ldots, y_n]$ *is given by*

$$(\mathbf{X}, \mathbf{Y}) = x_1y_1 + x_2y_2 + \cdots + x_ny_n.$$

DEFINITION 2.14. *The* LENGTH *of a vector* $\mathbf{X} = [x_1, x_2, \ldots, x_n]$ *is defined to be*

$$|\mathbf{X}| = (\mathbf{X}, \mathbf{X})^{1/2}.$$

The following properties of the inner product $(\mathbf{X}, \mathbf{Y})$ are immediate consequences of the definition:

$$\left.\begin{array}{ll} \text{(i)} & (a\mathbf{X} + b\mathbf{Y}, \mathbf{Z}) = a(\mathbf{X}, \mathbf{Z}) + b(\mathbf{Y}, \mathbf{Z}) \text{ for any choice of} \\ & \mathbf{X}, \mathbf{Y}, \mathbf{Z} \text{ in } R^n \text{ and real numbers } a, b. \\ \text{(ii)} & (\mathbf{X}, \mathbf{Y}) = (\mathbf{Y}, \mathbf{X}). \\ \text{(iii)} & (\mathbf{X}, \mathbf{X}) > 0 \quad \text{if and only if} \quad \mathbf{X} \neq \mathbf{0}. \end{array}\right\} \qquad (2.17)$$

To prove (i), let

$$\begin{aligned} \mathbf{X} &= [x_1, x_2, \ldots, x_n], \\ \mathbf{Y} &= [y_1, y_2, \ldots, y_n] \\ \mathbf{Z} &= [z_1, z_2, \ldots, z_n]; \end{aligned}$$

then

$$\begin{aligned} &(a\mathbf{X} + b\mathbf{Y}, \mathbf{Z}) \\ &\quad = ([ax_1 + by_1, ax_2 + by_2, \ldots, ax_n + by_n], [z_1, z_2, \ldots, z_n]) \\ &\quad = (ax_1 + by_1)z_1 + (ax_2 + by_2)z_2 + \cdots + (ax_n + by_n)z_n \\ &\quad = (ax_1z_1 + ax_2z_2 + \cdots + ax_nz_n) + (by_1z_1 + by_2z_2 + \cdots + by_nz_n) \\ &\quad = a(x_1z_1 + x_2z_2 + \cdots + x_nz_n) + b(y_1z_1 + y_2z_2 + \cdots + y_nz_n) \\ &\quad = a(\mathbf{X}, \mathbf{Z}) + b(\mathbf{Y}, \mathbf{Z}). \end{aligned}$$

Properties (ii) and (iii) are verified similarly.

Our derivation of $\cos\theta = (\mathbf{A}, \mathbf{B})/|\mathbf{A}|\,|\mathbf{B}|$ in three-space motivates the following:

DEFINITION 2.15. *Two vectors* $\mathbf{X}$ *and* $\mathbf{Y}$ *are called* ORTHOGONAL *if* $(\mathbf{X}, \mathbf{Y}) = 0$.

DEFINITION 2.16. *A set of vectors* $\mathbf{X}_1, \ldots, \mathbf{X}_n$ *is said to be an* ORTHOGONAL SET OF VECTORS *if* $(\mathbf{X}_i, \mathbf{X}_j) = 0$ *whenever* $i \neq j$.

DEFINITION 2.17. *Two subspaces* S *and* T *of* R^n *are called* ORTHOGONAL SUBSPACES *if* $(\mathbf{X}, \mathbf{Y}) = 0$ *for all vectors* $\mathbf{X}$ *of* S *and* $\mathbf{Y}$ *of* T.

Example 1. Let us find all vectors orthogonal to $[1, -1, 2]$. If $\mathbf{X} = [x_1, x_2, x_3]$ is such a vector, then

$$([1, -1, 2], [x_1, x_2, x_3]) = x_1 - x_2 + 2x_3 = 0.$$

Thus the set of vectors required will be given by the set of solutions of the homogeneous equation $x_1 - x_2 + 2x_3 = 0$. It is apparent that this solution space has dimension 2 and that a basis is $[1, 1, 0]$, $[2, 0, -1]$. The answer then is $L\{[1, 1, 0], [2, 0, -1]\}$.

The example is just a special case of this following theorem:

THEOREM 2.12. *The set of all vectors orthogonal to vectors* $\mathbf{X}_1, \ldots, \mathbf{X}_k$ *is a vector subspace of* R^n.

The proof of Theorem 2.12 is a simple extension of the arguments of Example 1 and will be left as an exercise for the student. Moreover it is easy to show that the subspace in Theorem 2.12 is orthogonal to all of $L\{\mathbf{X}_1, \mathbf{X}_2, \ldots, \mathbf{X}_k\}$.

Orthogonal Bases—the Gram-Schmidt Process

Suppose a subspace V of R^n is given; can we find an orthogonal basis for it? That is, we want a basis consisting of orthogonal vectors. The question and its affirmative answer are important in a number of applications. We take any basis of V and choose one of the vectors, $\mathbf{X}_1$, of this basis as the first member $\mathbf{Y}_1$ of the orthogonal basis. Then we find the second member $\mathbf{Y}_2$ by determining a vector orthogonal to $\mathbf{Y}_1$ which is a linear combination of $\mathbf{X}_2$ and $\mathbf{Y}_1$; that is, $\mathbf{Y}_2$ is an element of $L\{\mathbf{Y}_1, \mathbf{X}_2\} = L\{\mathbf{X}_1, \mathbf{X}_2\}$. We proceed in this way to get successive vectors $\mathbf{Y}_i$ orthogonal to all the previous ones and belonging to the space V. The whole process may be summarized in the proof of the following theorem:

THEOREM 2.13. *Every subspace* V *of* R^n *possesses an orthogonal set of vectors as a basis for* V.

PROOF (THE GRAM-SCHMIDT PROCESS.) Let $\mathbf{X}_1, \mathbf{X}_2, \ldots, \mathbf{X}_r$ be a basis for V. We will modify the vectors of this basis in a systematic manner to obtain an orthogonal basis for V. First, let $\mathbf{Y}_1 = \mathbf{X}_1$ and then successively:

$$\mathbf{Y}_i = \mathbf{X}_i - \left\{\frac{(\mathbf{X}_i, \mathbf{Y}_{i-1})}{(\mathbf{Y}_{i-1}, \mathbf{Y}_{i-1})}\right\} \mathbf{Y}_{i-1} - \cdots - \left\{\frac{(\mathbf{X}_i, \mathbf{Y}_1)}{(\mathbf{Y}_1, \mathbf{Y}_1)}\right\} \mathbf{Y}_1 \qquad (2.18)$$

for $2 \leq i \leq r$.

The remainder of the proof will now follow by induction. We assume the following properties to be valid for $j < i$:

(i) $L\{\mathbf{Y}_1, \ldots, \mathbf{Y}_j\} = L\{\mathbf{X}_1, \ldots, \mathbf{X}_j\}$.
(ii) $\mathbf{Y}_1, \mathbf{Y}_2, \ldots, \mathbf{Y}_j$ form an orthogonal set of vectors.

We are using strong induction and it is clear that properties (i) and (ii) are valid for $j = 1$. The next step is to show that properties (i) and (ii) are valid for $j = i$ under the assumptions above.

First, $\mathbf{Y}_i \neq \mathbf{0}$ or it would follow from (2.18) and the induction assumptions that $\mathbf{X}_1, \ldots, \mathbf{X}_i$ would be linearly dependent. (Why?)

If $j < i$, we take the inner product of both sides of (2.18) with $\mathbf{Y}_j$ and use the induction assumption that $\mathbf{Y}_j$ is orthogonal to all the $\mathbf{Y}_k$ $(k < i; k \neq j)$. Then,

$$(\mathbf{Y}_i, \mathbf{Y}_j) = (\mathbf{X}_i, \mathbf{Y}_j) - \left\{\frac{(\mathbf{X}_i, \mathbf{Y}_j)}{(\mathbf{Y}_j, \mathbf{Y}_j)}\right\}(\mathbf{Y}_j, \mathbf{Y}_j) = 0.$$

Hence $\mathbf{Y}_1, \mathbf{Y}_2, \ldots, \mathbf{Y}_i$ are mutually orthogonal.

We see from (2.18) and the induction assumption that

$$L\{\mathbf{Y}_1, \ldots, \mathbf{Y}_i\} \subseteq L\{\mathbf{X}_1, \ldots, \mathbf{X}_i\}.$$

Moreover, $\mathbf{X}_i \in L\{\mathbf{Y}_1, \ldots, \mathbf{Y}_i\}$ and $L\{\mathbf{Y}_1, \ldots, \mathbf{Y}_{i-1}\} = L\{\mathbf{X}_1, \ldots, \mathbf{X}_{i-1}\}$ by the induction assumption so that

$$L\{\mathbf{Y}_1, \ldots, \mathbf{Y}_i\} \supseteq L\{\mathbf{X}_1, \ldots, \mathbf{X}_i\}.$$

Hence we have $L\{\mathbf{Y}_1, \ldots, \mathbf{Y}_i\} = L\{\mathbf{X}_1, \ldots, \mathbf{X}_i\}$, and our induction proof is complete.

Example 2. Let $V = L\{[1, 0, 1, 0], [1, 1, 3, 0], [0, 2, 0, 1]\}$ and find an orthogonal basis for V.

Set

$$\mathbf{Y}_1 = [1, 0, 1, 0].$$

Then

$$\mathbf{Y}_2 = [1, 1, 3, 0] - \frac{([1, 1, 3, 0], [1, 0, 1, 0])}{([1, 0, 1, 0], [1, 0, 1, 0])}[1, 0, 1, 0]$$

or

$$\mathbf{Y}_2 = [1, 1, 3, 0] - 2[1, 0, 1, 0] = [-1, 1, 1, 0].$$

Finally,

$$\mathbf{Y}_3 = [0, 2, 0, 1] - \frac{([0, 2, 0, 1], [-1, 1, 1, 0])}{([-1, 1, 1, 0], [-1, 1, 1, 0])}[-1, 1, 1, 0]$$
$$- \frac{([0, 2, 0, 1], [1, 0, 1, 0])}{([1, 0, 1, 0], [1, 0, 1, 0])}[1, 0, 1, 0]$$

or

$$\mathbf{Y}_3 = [0, 2, 0, 1] - \tfrac{2}{3}[-1, 1, 1, 0] - 0[1, 0, 1, 0] = [\tfrac{2}{3}, \tfrac{4}{3}, -\tfrac{2}{3}, 1].$$

It is easily checked that $(\mathbf{Y}_1, \mathbf{Y}_2) = (\mathbf{Y}_1, \mathbf{Y}_3) = (\mathbf{Y}_2, \mathbf{Y}_3) = 0$.

The vectors of R^n whose length is 1 are called *unit vectors*. If $\mathbf{X}$ is any nonzero vector, then $\mathbf{Y} = \mathbf{X}/(\mathbf{X}, \mathbf{X})^{1/2}$ is a unit vector since

$$(\mathbf{Y}, \mathbf{Y}) = \left(\frac{\mathbf{X}}{(\mathbf{X}, \mathbf{X})^{1/2}}, \frac{\mathbf{X}}{(\mathbf{X}, \mathbf{X})^{1/2}}\right) = \frac{1}{(\mathbf{X}, \mathbf{X})}(\mathbf{X}, \mathbf{X}) = 1.$$

The process of replacing a vector by the corresponding unit vector in a computation is called *normalization*. When it is applied to an orthogonal basis the result is termed an *orthonormal* basis.

In actual calculations there are two ways to find an orthonormal basis. The first is to follow the method of Example 2 and then to divide each $\mathbf{Y}_i$ by $(\mathbf{Y}_i, \mathbf{Y}_i)^{1/2}$. The second is to normalize at each step (including the first); in this case the denominators in the Gram-Schmidt process may be ignored. (Why?) The student may choose whichever method he prefers; we merely offer the observation that in machine calculation the second method is preferable since fewer divisions are involved. The second method may be illustrated by its application to the problem of Example 2.

$$\mathbf{Y}_1 = \left[\frac{1}{\sqrt{2}}, 0, \frac{1}{\sqrt{2}}, 0\right].$$

$$\mathbf{Y}_2' = [1, 1, 3, 0] - \left([1, 1, 3, 0], \left[\frac{1}{\sqrt{2}}, 0, \frac{1}{\sqrt{2}}, 0\right]\right)\left[\frac{1}{\sqrt{2}}, 0, \frac{1}{\sqrt{2}}, 0\right]$$
$$= [1, 1, 3, 0] - [2, 0, 2, 0] = [-1, 1, 1, 0];$$

$$\mathbf{Y}_2 = \left[-\frac{1}{\sqrt{3}}, \frac{1}{\sqrt{3}}, \frac{1}{\sqrt{3}}, 0\right].$$

$$\mathbf{Y}_3' = [0, 2, 0, 1] - \left([0, 2, 0, 1], \left[-\frac{1}{\sqrt{3}}, \frac{1}{\sqrt{3}}, \frac{1}{\sqrt{3}}, 0\right]\right)\left[-\frac{1}{\sqrt{3}}, \frac{1}{\sqrt{3}}, \frac{1}{\sqrt{3}}, 0\right]$$
$$- \left([0, 2, 0, 1], \left[\frac{1}{\sqrt{3}}, 0, \frac{1}{\sqrt{2}}, 0\right]\right)\left[\frac{1}{\sqrt{2}}, 0, \frac{1}{\sqrt{2}}, 0\right]$$
$$= [0, 2, 0, 1] - \left[-\frac{2}{3}, \frac{2}{3}, \frac{2}{3}, 0\right] - 0\left[\frac{1}{\sqrt{2}}, 0, \frac{1}{\sqrt{2}}, 0\right] = \left[\frac{2}{3}, \frac{4}{3}, -\frac{2}{3}, 1\right];$$

$$\mathbf{Y}_3 = \left[\frac{2}{\sqrt{33}}, \frac{4}{\sqrt{33}}, \frac{-2}{\sqrt{33}}, \frac{3}{\sqrt{33}}\right].$$

Orthogonal Complements

At the present time, we shall content ourselves with an application of orthogonal vectors in the identification of subspaces of R^n. We shall first prove that for any subspace V of R^n there exists an orthogonal subspace W such that R^n is the direct sum of the subspaces V and W; that is, $R^n = V \oplus W$. Example 3 will illustrate the proof to follow.

Example 3. We seek to find a subspace W of R^4 orthogonal to $V = L\{[1, 0, 1, 0], [1, 1, 3, 0]\}$ and such that $V \oplus W = R^4$.

We know from Theorem 2.9 that the vectors [1, 0, 1, 0], [1, 1, 3, 0] can be extended to a basis of R^4. This may be done in many ways; we choose

$$[1, 0, 1, 0], [1, 1, 3, 0], [0, 1, 0, 0], [0, 0, 0, 1].$$

Now we apply the Gram-Schmidt process to obtain an orthogonal basis.

$$\mathbf{Y}_1 = [1, 0, 1, 0];$$
$\mathbf{Y}_2 = [-1, 1, 1, 0]$ from Example 2;
$$\mathbf{Y}_3 = [0, 1, 0, 0] - \frac{([0, 1, 0, 0], [-1, 1, 1, 0])}{([-1, 1, 1, 0], [-1, 1, 1, 0])}[-1, 1, 1, 0]$$
$$= [\tfrac{1}{3}, \tfrac{2}{3}, -\tfrac{1}{3}, 0];$$
$$\mathbf{Y}_4 = [0, 0, 0, 1].$$

It is clear that

$$V = L\{[1, 0, 1, 0], [-1, 1, 1, 0]\}$$

and

$$W = L\{[\tfrac{1}{3}, \tfrac{2}{3}, -\tfrac{1}{3}, 0], [0, 0, 0, 1]\}$$

are orthogonal subspaces of R^4. Moreover, $V \cap W = \mathbf{0}$, so that $R^4 = V \oplus W$.

THEOREM 2.14. If V is a subspace of R^n, there exists a unique subspace W of R^n orthogonal to V such that $R^n = V \oplus W$.

PROOF. Let $\{\mathbf{X}_1, \mathbf{X}_2, \ldots, \mathbf{X}_k\}$ be a basis for V. Extend this set of vectors to a basis for R^n. Thus,

$$R^n = L\{\mathbf{X}_1, \ldots, \mathbf{X}_k, \mathbf{Z}_{k+1}, \ldots, \mathbf{Z}_n\}.$$

Now apply the Gram-Schmidt process to this basis to obtain an orthogonal basis for R^n. Thus,

$$R^n = L\{\mathbf{Y}_1, \mathbf{Y}_2, \ldots, \mathbf{Y}_k, \mathbf{Y}_{k+1}, \ldots, \mathbf{Y}_n\},$$

and we know from the Gram-Schmidt procedure that

$$L\{\mathbf{X}_1, \ldots, \mathbf{X}_k\} = L\{\mathbf{Y}_1, \ldots, \mathbf{Y}_k\}.$$

Set $W = L\{\mathbf{Y}_{k+1}, \ldots, \mathbf{Y}_n\}$. Then $R^n = V \oplus W$, and W is a subspace orthogonal to V.

We must still prove that if W_1 is any subspace orthogonal to V such that $R^n = V \oplus W_1$, then $W_1 = W$. This is left as an exercise (Exercise 10).

The subspace W of Theorem 2.14 is called the *orthogonal complement* of V in R^n.

The concept of orthogonal complement provides another method of describing subspaces of R^n. Let V be a subspace of R^n and let W be the orthogonal complement of V. Suppose W has a basis

$$\begin{aligned}
\mathbf{A}_1 &= [a_{11}, a_{12}, \ldots, a_{1n}],\\
\mathbf{A}_2 &= [a_{21}, a_{22}, \ldots, a_{2n}],\\
&\vdots\\
\mathbf{A}_k &= [a_{k1}, a_{k2}, \ldots, a_{kn}].
\end{aligned}$$

Every vector $\mathbf{X}$ of V satisfies the conditions $(\mathbf{X}, \mathbf{A}_1) = (\mathbf{X}, \mathbf{A}_2) = \cdots = (\mathbf{X}, \mathbf{A}_k) = 0$. If we write $\mathbf{X} = [x_1, x_2, \ldots, x_n]$, these conditions are equivalent to

$$\begin{aligned}
a_{11}x_1 + a_{12}x_2 + \cdots + a_{1n}x_n &= 0\\
a_{21}x_1 + a_{22}x_2 + \cdots + a_{2n}x_n &= 0\\
&\vdots\\
a_{k1}x_1 + a_{k2}x_2 + \cdots + a_{kn}x_n &= 0,
\end{aligned} \tag{2.19}$$

so that the components of every vector of V satisfy the homogeneous equations (2.19). On the other hand, if $[x_1, x_2, \ldots, x_n]$ is any element of the solution space of the system (2.19), it is orthogonal to all members of W. This together with Exercise 10 shows that every solution to (2.19) is in V. Thus the subspaces of R^n are precisely the solution sets of linear homogeneous equations.

General Inner Products

The inner product we defined on R^n may be viewed as a function taking ordered pairs of elements of R^n to real numbers. If V is any vector space over the reals and T is a function, T: $V \times V \to R$ which satisfies

$$\begin{aligned}
&\text{(i)} \quad \mathrm{T}(a\mathbf{X} + b\mathbf{Y}, \mathbf{Z}) = a\mathrm{T}(\mathbf{X}, \mathbf{Z}) + b\mathrm{T}(\mathbf{Y}, \mathbf{Z}), \\
&\text{(ii)} \quad \mathrm{T}(\mathbf{X}, \mathbf{Y}) = \mathrm{T}(\mathbf{Y}, \mathbf{X}), \\
&\text{(iii)} \quad \mathrm{T}(\mathbf{X}, \mathbf{X}) > 0 \text{ if and only if } \mathbf{X} \neq \mathbf{0} \text{ for all } \mathbf{X}, \mathbf{Y}, \mathbf{Z} \text{ in } V \text{ and all scalars } a, b,
\end{aligned} \tag{2.20}$$

then T is called a (real) inner product on V. A vector space along with such an inner product is called a real inner product space.

Example 4. Let V be the set of all continuous real-valued functions on the closed interval $0 \leq x \leq 1$ and define

$$\mathrm{T}(f, g) = \int_0^1 f(x)g(x)\, dx.$$

This defines an inner product on V.

If V is a vector space over the complex numbers, a complex inner product is a function T: $V \times V \to \mathbf{C}$ satisfying (2.20) except that (ii) is replaced by

$$\text{(ii}') \quad \mathrm{T}(\mathbf{X}, \mathbf{Y}) = \overline{\mathrm{T}(\mathbf{Y}, \mathbf{X})},$$

where the bar denotes complex conjugation.

Example 5. The standard complex inner product on C^n is given by

$$\mathrm{T}([z_1, \ldots, z_n], [w_1, \ldots, w_n]) = z_1\overline{w}_1 + z_2\overline{w}_2 + \cdots + z_n\overline{w}_n.$$

The student should verify that this function satisfies (i), (ii′), and (iii).

Exercises

1. Find the value of $(\mathbf{X}, \mathbf{Y})$ for the vectors
   (a) $\mathbf{X} = [1, 2, 3, -1, 2]$, $\mathbf{Y} = [0, 1, 2, 1, -4]$;
   (b) $\mathbf{X} = [1, 2, -1, 3]$, $\mathbf{Y} = [4, -1, -1, -1]$.
2. Determine the values of x for which the following vectors are orthogonal:
   $$[x, x - 1, x, -1], [2x, x, 3, 1].$$
3. Using the Gram-Schmidt process, obtain a basis of orthogonal vectors for the vector space
   $$V = L\{[1, 2, -1, 0], [1, 0, -2, 1], [0, 1, 1, 0]\}.$$
4. Prove that any set of nonzero orthogonal vectors is a linearly independent set.
5. Prove that the intersection, $S \cap T$, of two orthogonal spaces S and T consists of the zero vector only.
6. What is the geometrical interpretation of the Gram-Schmidt process in the plane and in space?
7. Prove the Schwarz inequality
   $$(\mathbf{X}, \mathbf{Y}) \leq |\mathbf{X}|\,|\mathbf{Y}|.$$
   Hint: Consider the vector $a\mathbf{X} + \mathbf{Y}$ and determine a condition necessary

for $(a\mathbf{X} + \mathbf{Y}, a\mathbf{X} + \mathbf{Y}) \geq 0$.

8. Let $R^n = V \oplus W$, where V and W are orthogonal subspaces. Then for any vector $\mathbf{X}$, $\mathbf{X} = \mathbf{Y} + \mathbf{Z}$, where $\mathbf{Y} \in V$, $\mathbf{Z} \in W$. We call $\mathbf{Y}$ the orthogonal projection of $\mathbf{X}$ on V, $\mathbf{Z}$ the orthogonal projection of $\mathbf{X}$ on W (see Exercise 5, Section 2.8). Find the orthogonal projection of $\mathbf{X} = [1, -2, 3, 0]$ on the subspace $L\{[0, 1, -2, 0], [1, 2, 1, 0]\}$.
9. What is the geometric interpretation of the orthogonal projection of a vector on a subspace V in the plane and in space?
10. If V and W are subspaces of R^n such that $R^n = V \oplus W$ and W is orthogonal to V, show that any vector $\mathbf{X}$ orthogonal to all members of V is in W. Hence show that the orthogonal complement of V may be uniquely defined as the set of all vectors orthogonal to all members of V. *Hint:* Certainly $\mathbf{X} = \mathbf{Y} + \mathbf{Z}$, $\mathbf{Y} \in V$, $\mathbf{Z} \in W$. Now show $\mathbf{Y} = \mathbf{0}$.
11. Show that the Gram-Schmidt process provides an effective way to determine whether or not the vectors $\mathbf{X}_1, \ldots, \mathbf{X}_k$ are dependent. If they are dependent, one of the $\mathbf{Y}_i$ must be zero.
12. Verify that the function of Example 4 defines an inner product.
13. Let V be the space of polynomials in x with real coefficients of degree less than 5, and define

$$(f, g) = \int_0^1 f(x)g(x)\, dx.$$

Use the Gram-Schmidt process to find an orthogonal basis for this inner product space.
14. Explain why it is necessary to alter (ii) to (ii′) for complex vector spaces. *Hint:* What would be the length of the vector $[1, i]$ in $\mathbf{C}^2$ if the standard definition of inner product were followed?

2.10 Dual Spaces

We have seen several examples of spaces of functions. In this section we consider a space that is very important to advanced work in vector spaces; namely we consider the linear functions from a vector space to its underlying field. Since we can define addition and scalar multiplication in the usual pointwise manner, this set of functions will be a vector space, and because we consider only linear functions, properties of the underlying space will often carry over into the function space.

DEFINITION 2.18. If V is a vector space over a field F, then the dual space V^* is the set of all functions f from V to F which satisfy

(1) $f(\mathbf{X}_1 + \mathbf{X}_2) = f(\mathbf{X}_1) + f(\mathbf{X}_2)$,
(2) $f(a\mathbf{X}_1) = af(\mathbf{X}_1)$,

for all $\mathbf{X}_1$, $\mathbf{X}_2$ in V and $a \in F$.

In the definition we are tacitly assuming that the set of functions defined is, in fact, a vector space. To establish this property, we recall that the usual way to add two functions f and g is to define $(f + g)(\mathbf{X}) = f(\mathbf{X}) + g(\mathbf{X})$ and to multiply f by a scalar a, we define $(af)(\mathbf{X}) = a(f(\mathbf{X}))$. We must now check all the axioms of a vector space to verify that V^* is actually a vector space when endowed with these operations. Let us check that $f + g$ is linear, i.e., that V^* is closed under the addition we have defined:

$$\begin{aligned}(f+g)(\mathbf{X}+\mathbf{Y}) &= f(\mathbf{X}+\mathbf{Y}) + g(\mathbf{X}+\mathbf{Y}) && \text{by the definition,}\\ &= f(\mathbf{X}) + f(\mathbf{Y}) + g(\mathbf{X}) + g(\mathbf{Y}) && \text{since } f, g \in V^*,\\ &= f(\mathbf{X}) + g(\mathbf{X}) + f(\mathbf{Y}) + g(\mathbf{Y}) && \text{since } F \text{ is a field,}\\ &= (f+g)(\mathbf{X}) + (f+g)(\mathbf{Y}) && \text{again, by the definition.}\end{aligned}$$

Also

$$\begin{aligned}(f+g)(a\mathbf{X}) &= f(a\mathbf{X}) + g(a\mathbf{X})\\ &= af(\mathbf{X}) + ag(\mathbf{X})\\ &= a(f(\mathbf{X}) + g(\mathbf{X}))\\ &= a((f+g)(\mathbf{X})).\end{aligned}$$

The other properties of a vector space may be easily verified: the zero vector is the function that takes every vector of V to the zero of F; the additive inverse of f is the function $-f$ defined by $(-f)(\mathbf{X}) = -f(\mathbf{X})$; and the various associative and commutative laws follow directly.

Once we are convinced that V^* is a vector space, several questions arise naturally. If V satisfies condition F, does V^*? Can we find a simple basis for V^*?

First, we adopt a new notation to remind ourselves that the functions under consideration are also vectors. We shall use boldface lowercase letters for the functions in the dual space, and we will adopt the usual convention of calling them *linear functionals*.

We also need to observe that a linear functional is determined by its values on a basis. More precisely, let $\{\mathbf{X}_1, \mathbf{X}_2, \ldots, \mathbf{X}_n\}$ be a basis of V and $\mathbf{f}$ an element of V^*. Then if $\mathbf{X} \in V$, it can be written

$$\mathbf{X} = a_1\mathbf{X}_1 + a_2\mathbf{X}_2 + \cdots + a_n\mathbf{X}_n$$

so

$$\mathbf{f}(\mathbf{X}) = \mathbf{f}(a_1\mathbf{X}_1 + \cdots + a_n\mathbf{X}_n) = a_1\mathbf{f}(\mathbf{X}_1) + \cdots + a_n\mathbf{f}(\mathbf{X}_n).$$

Since the a_i's depend on $\mathbf{X}$, not on $\mathbf{f}$, we see that the $\mathbf{f}(\mathbf{X}_i)$'s determine $\mathbf{f}$.

We now define some very natural linear functionals called projections. We define $\mathbf{f}_1, \mathbf{f}_2, \ldots, \mathbf{f}_n$ by $\mathbf{f}_i(\mathbf{X}_j) = 1$ if $i = j$ and by $\mathbf{f}_i(\mathbf{X}_j) = 0$ if $i \neq j$. If we consider the special case $V = R^3$ with the standard basis as an example, then $\mathbf{f}_1$ is just projection onto the x-axis. The student should examine $\mathbf{f}_2$ and $\mathbf{f}_3$ to familiarize himself with these projections.

Now suppose $\mathbf{g}$ is an element of V^* such that

$$\mathbf{g}(\mathbf{X}_1) = b_1, \qquad \mathbf{g}(\mathbf{X}_2) = b_2, \ldots, \mathbf{g}(\mathbf{X}_n) = b_n.$$

Then, if $\mathbf{X} = a_1\mathbf{X}_1 + \cdots + a_n\mathbf{X}_n$, we have

$$\begin{aligned}\mathbf{g}(\mathbf{X}) &= \mathbf{g}(a_1\mathbf{X}_1 + \cdots + a_n\mathbf{X}_n)\\ &= a_1\mathbf{g}(\mathbf{X}_1) + \cdots + a_n\mathbf{g}(\mathbf{X}_n)\\ &= a_1b_1 + \cdots + a_nb_n;\end{aligned}$$

notice that $\mathbf{f}_i(\mathbf{X}) = a_i$ for each i, so

$$\mathbf{g}(\mathbf{X}) = b_1\mathbf{f}_1(\mathbf{X}) + b_2\mathbf{f}_2(\mathbf{X}) + \cdots + b_n\mathbf{f}_n(\mathbf{X})$$

for *every* $\mathbf{X}$ in V. Thus this rather easy calculation shows that $\{\mathbf{f}_1, \ldots, \mathbf{f}_n\}$

span V^*. But are these functions linearly independent? If $\{a_1, \ldots, a_n\}$ is a set of scalars such that

$$a_1\mathbf{f}_1 + a_2\mathbf{f}_2 + \cdots + a_n\mathbf{f}_n = \mathbf{0},$$

then

$$a_1\mathbf{f}_1(\mathbf{X}) + \cdots + a_n\mathbf{f}_n(\mathbf{X}) = 0$$

for *every* $\mathbf{X}$ in V. By taking $\mathbf{X} = \mathbf{X}_1$ we have

$$a_1\mathbf{f}_1(\mathbf{X}_1) + \cdots + a_n\mathbf{f}_n(\mathbf{X}_1) = 0,$$

but all the terms are zero except the first, so we have

$$a_1 \cdot 1 + a_2 \cdot 0 + \cdots + a_n \cdot 0 = 0$$

or $a_1 = 0$. For any i, taking $\mathbf{X} = \mathbf{X}_i$ will yield $a_i = 0$ in exactly the same way, and thus $\mathbf{f}_1, \ldots, \mathbf{f}_n$ are linearly independent. We have just proved that if V is n-dimensional then V^* is also n-dimensional by actually exhibiting a basis for V^*. We summarize our results in the following theorem.

THEOREM 2.15. *If V is an n-dimensional vector space, then its dual, V^*, is also n-dimensional.*

Example 1. In light of the work in Section 2.7, the previous discussion says that a finite-dimensional space and its dual are isomorphic as vector spaces (mathematicians would say "finite dimensional spaces are self-dual"). However, when V is an inner product space we can give a concrete description of V^* as follows. For a fixed element $\mathbf{X}_0$ in V, define $\mathbf{f}\colon V \to F$ by $\mathbf{f}(\mathbf{X}) = (\mathbf{X}, \mathbf{X}_0)$ (F in this discussion is R or $\mathbf{C}$, depending on whether V is real or a complex inner product space; $(\,,)$ denotes the inner product on V). Then $\mathbf{f}$ is easily seen to be a linear functional on V, that is, an element of V^*. If $\mathbf{X}_1, \mathbf{X}_2, \ldots, \mathbf{X}_n$ is a basis for V and $\mathbf{f}_1, \mathbf{f}_2, \ldots, \mathbf{f}_n$ are the corresponding linear functionals $f_i(\mathbf{X}) = (\mathbf{X}, \mathbf{X}_i)$, then the $\mathbf{f}_i$'s are linearly independent and hence a basis for V^* by Theorem 2.15. But even more can be said; if $\mathbf{f}$ is any element whatever of V^*, then it can be written as some combination of the $\mathbf{f}_i$'s, say, $\mathbf{f} = a_1\mathbf{f}_1 + \cdots + a_n\mathbf{f}_n$. Now note that

$$\begin{aligned}
\mathbf{f}(\mathbf{X}) &= a_1\mathbf{f}_1(\mathbf{X}) + \cdots + a_n\mathbf{f}_n(\mathbf{X}) \\
&= a_1(\mathbf{X}, \mathbf{X}_1) + \cdots + a_n(\mathbf{X}, \mathbf{X}_n) \\
&= (\mathbf{X}, \bar{a}_1\mathbf{X}_1) + \cdots + (\mathbf{X}, \bar{a}_n\mathbf{X}_n) \\
&= (\mathbf{X}, \bar{a}_1\mathbf{X}_1 + \cdots + \bar{a}_n\mathbf{X}_n)
\end{aligned}$$

(the bars above the a_i's are unnecessary if V is a real inner product space). Thus $\mathbf{f}$ corresponds to the vector $\bar{a}_1\mathbf{X}_1 + \cdots + \bar{a}_n\mathbf{X}_n$, and we see that our natural way of defining functionals, in fact, gives rise to *all* of the elements of V^*.

Exercises

1. Verify the statement of Example 1 that if $\mathbf{X}_1, \ldots, \mathbf{X}_n$ is a basis for an inner product space, then the corresponding functionals are linearly independent.
2. Exhibit a basis for $(R^n)^*$ by
   (a) the method of the proof of Theorem 2.15,
   (b) the method of Example 1.
   Use the standard basis of R^n in both cases.

3. Let $\mathbf{X}_1$, $\mathbf{X}_2$ be any two distinct elements of a vector space V. Show that there is a linear functional, $\mathbf{f}$, on V such that $\mathbf{f}(\mathbf{X}_1) \neq \mathbf{f}(\mathbf{X}_2)$.

In Exercises 4–6 P^n is the space of polynomials with real coefficients of degree less than n.

4. If a is a fixed real number show that the function on P^n defined by $\mathbf{f}(p(x)) = p(a)$ is a linear functional.
5. Let $a_1, a_2, \ldots, a_n$ be fixed, distinct real numbers and define linear functionals on P^n by $f_i(p(x)) = p(a_i)$ as in Exercise 4. Show that $\mathbf{f}_1, \ldots, \mathbf{f}_n$ are linearly independent, and thus actually are a basis for the dual of P^n. *Hint:* If

$$\mathbf{f} = b_1\mathbf{f}_1 + b_2\mathbf{f}_2 + \cdots + b_n\mathbf{f}_n = \mathbf{0},$$

consider the values of $\mathbf{f}$ at the n polynomials

$$q_i(x) = \prod_{k \neq i} (x - a_k), \qquad \text{where } i = 1, 2, \ldots, n.$$

6. Show that if $p(x)$ and $q(x)$ are two elements of P^n which agree at n distinct real numbers, then $p(x) = q(x)$. Use Exercises 3 and 5.

3 Linear Transformations and Matrices

In recent years, mathematicians interested in algebra have come more and more to the realization that algebraic structures such as vector spaces are never profitably studied alone. There are, more or less automatically, mappings from one structure to another called homomorphisms or, recently, simply morphisms, which preserve and illuminate the basic properties of the structures. For vector spaces these morphisms are linear transformations.

In this chapter we shall study the algebra of linear transformations and the representation of these mappings by matrices. In a very definite sense, this chapter is the heart of the book. In both theory and applications, it is not so much the vector spaces but their mappings which are of importance. There is an analogy here to the previous experience of the reader. Although it is necessary to develop a full understanding of the real number system, real functions are far more important mathematically than the number system by itself.

3.1 Linear Transformations

The concept of an isomorphism between vector spaces was mentioned briefly in Section 2.7. Since we wish to investigate functions that generalize this concept, let us recall the notion of an isomorphism.

If T is a one-to-one mapping from a vector space V onto a vector space W such that, for any two vectors $\mathbf{X}$ and $\mathbf{Y}$ of V and any scalar r:

(i) $\mathrm{T}(\mathbf{X} + \mathbf{Y}) = \mathrm{T}(\mathbf{X}) + \mathrm{T}(\mathbf{Y})$,
(ii) $\mathrm{T}(r\mathbf{X}) = r\mathrm{T}(\mathbf{Y})$,

then T is called an isomorphism of V onto W.

Example 1. A simple class of isomorphisms of R^2 onto itself may be obtained by considering the rotations of the plane. Specifically, let a vector $[x_1, x_2]$ be associated with the directed line segment from the origin O to the point

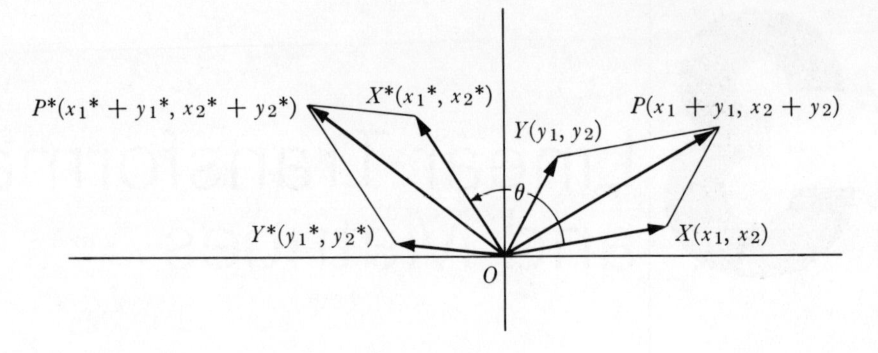

FIGURE 3.1

$X(x_1, x_2)$ in a Cartesian coordinate system for the plane. The rotation through the angle θ about the origin will take the point $X(x_1, x_2)$ to the point $X^*(x_1^*, x_2^*)$ and the segment OX to the segment OX^* (see Figure 3.1).

The corresponding mapping of R^2 to R^2 may be denoted by T_θ and defined by assigning to $[x_1, x_2]$ the image $[x_1^*, x_2^*]$, or

$$\mathrm{T}_\theta([x_1, x_2]) = [x_1^*, x_2^*].$$

This is a one-to-one mapping since for any segment OY^* there is precisely one segment, OY, which is taken to OY^* by T_θ.

It remains to show that if

$$\mathrm{T}_\theta([x_1, x_2]) = [x_1^*, x_2^*] \quad \text{and} \quad \mathrm{T}_\theta([y_1, y_2]) = [y_1^*, y_2^*],$$

then

$$\mathrm{T}_\theta([x_1, x_2] + [y_1, y_2]) = [x_1^*, x_2^*] + [y_1^*, y_2^*]$$

and

$$\mathrm{T}_\theta(r[x_1, x_2]) = r[x_1^*, x_2^*].$$

Figure 3.1 illustrates the first part; the segment OP associated with $[x_1, x_2] + [y_1, y_2]$ is the diagonal of the parallelogram $OXPY$. Under the rotation this parallelogram is rotated to $OX^*P^*Y^*$ and OP goes to OP^*. Since OP^* is the diagonal of $OX^*P^*Y^*$, the coordinates of P^* are $(x_1^* + y_1^*, x_2^* + y_2^*)$. That is,

$$\mathrm{T}_\theta([x_1, x_2] + [y_1, y_2]) = [x_1^* + y_1^*, x_2^* + y_2^*] = [x_1^*, x_2^*] + [y_1^*, y_2^*].$$

The relation

$$\mathrm{T}_\theta(r[x_1, x_2]) = r\mathrm{T}_\theta([x_1, x_2])$$

may be seen in the same geometric fashion.

Isomorphisms are useful tools to investigate vector spaces, but even more can be learned using a larger class of mappings, namely those which arise when the conditions that the mapping be one-to-one and onto are dropped.

DEFINITION 3.1. *A mapping* T *from a real vector space* V *to a real vector space* W *is called a* LINEAR TRANSFORMATION *if for all vectors* $\mathbf{X}$, $\mathbf{Y}$ *of* V *and all real numbers* r, T *satisfies*

$$\left.\begin{array}{ll}\text{(i)} & \mathrm{T}(\mathbf{X} + \mathbf{Y}) = \mathrm{T}(\mathbf{X}) + \mathrm{T}(\mathbf{Y}), \\ \text{(ii)} & \mathrm{T}(r\mathbf{X}) = r\mathrm{T}(\mathbf{X}).\end{array}\right\} \tag{3.1}$$

Note that it is *not* required that V and W be distinct. The isomorphisms of Example 1 are special cases of linear transformations. If V, W are spaces over a field F, linear transformations from V to W are defined similarly, with real numbers replaced by elements of F.

The reader may have noticed that we have used uppercase letters to denote linear transformations rather than the lowercase letters we have used for unspecified functions. We will adopt this convention and we will often drop the parentheses, writing $\mathrm{T}\mathbf{X}$ for $\mathrm{T}(\mathbf{X})$, whenever it is convenient and unambiguous.

It will be of considerable value in the remainder of the book that the reader have a stock of examples of linear transformations which he can use for geometrical intuition. We first list a number of examples involving ordinary two- and three-dimensional space along with a capsule description of the geometric effect of each.

(1) $[x_1, x_2] \to [x_2, x_1]$ reflection about the line $x_1 = x_2$,
(2) $[x_1, x_2] \to [x_1 + x_2, x_2]$ 45° shear,
(3) $[x_1, x_2, x_3] \to [x_1, x_2]$ projection on the x_1, x_2 plane,
(4) $[x_1, x_2] \to [x_1, x_2, x_2]$ injection onto the plane $x_2 = x_3$,
(5) $[x_1, x_2, x_3] \to [2x_1, 2x_2, 2x_3]$ a dilation.

Some of the geometrical terms may be new to the reader. They will be discussed in the following. The reader should verify that each of the maps is indeed a linear transformation, decide which are isomorphisms, and, most important, check the effect of each on simple geometric objects such as straight lines and circles. As an example we do this for (2).

Example 2. Consider the function S defined by

$$\mathrm{S}[x_1, x_2] = [x_1 + x_2, x_2].$$

This 45° shear can easily be seen to be an isomorphism by writing

$$[x_1^*, x_2^*] = \mathrm{S}[x_1, x_2].$$

Then

$$\begin{aligned} x_1^* &= x_1 + x_2, \\ x_2^* &= x_2; \end{aligned}$$

solving for x_1, x_2 we obtain

$$\begin{aligned} x_1 &= x_1^* - x_2^*, \\ x_2 &= x_2^*. \end{aligned}$$

These last two equations make it clear that each point in the plane has one and only one preimage under S.

What happens to the "y-axis," $x_1 = 0$, under S? Since $\mathrm{S}[0, x_2] = [x_2, x_2]$, points on the line $x_1 = 0$ are mapped to points on the line $x_1^* = x_2^*$.

What happens to the line $x_1 = x_2$? If $x_1 = x_2$, then $x_1^* - x_2^* = x_2^*$ or $x_1^* = 2x_2^*$.

What is the effect of S on the circle $x_1^2 + x_2^2 = 1$? We have $(x_1^* - x_2^*)^2 + (x_2^*)^2 = 1$; plotting points will convince one that this is the equation of an ellipse with its axis tilted. The results are sketched in Figure 3.2.

In general, any linear transformation of the type $[x_1, x_2] \to [x_1 + ax_2, x_2]$ is called a *shear*. In a shear the x_2-axis is transformed to the line through the

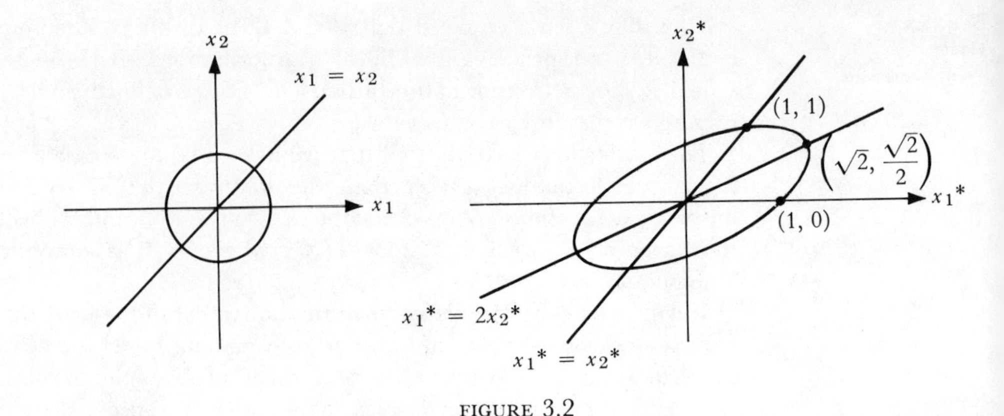

FIGURE 3.2

origin of slope $1/a$. A line through the origin with slope m is taken to a line through the origin with slope

$$\frac{m}{(1 + ma)} = \frac{1}{a}\left(1 - \frac{1}{1 + ma}\right).$$

A *dilation*, illustrated in (5) above, is a transformation of the form

$$[x_1, x_2, \ldots, x_n] \to [ax_1, ax_2, \ldots, ax_n]$$

for $a > 1$. If $0 < a < 1$ the mapping is called a *contraction*. Both these transformations map lines through the origin to lines through the origin.

Example 3. Define a mapping $\mathrm{D}\colon P^4 \to P^4$ by

$$\mathrm{D}(a_0 + a_1x + a_2x^2 + a_3x^3) = a_1 + 2a_2x + 3a_3x^2.$$

D is just the differentiation operator. It is a standard fact of calculus (easily checked in this case) that D is linear. Since D takes all constant polynomials to zero, D is not one-to-one, and thus not an isomorphism.

The reader may have noticed in the above examples that lines always were transformed to lines under linear transformations. Recall that the line determined by $\mathbf{X}$ and $\mathbf{Y}$ in R^n is given by the set of $\mathbf{R}$'s which satisfy $\mathbf{R} = (1 - t)\mathbf{X} + t\mathbf{Y}$ for some number t. Then if T is any linear transformation, we have $\mathrm{T}\mathbf{R} = (1 - t)\mathrm{T}\mathbf{X} + t\mathrm{T}\mathbf{Y}$, or that $\mathrm{T}\mathbf{R}$ lies on the line determined by $\mathrm{T}\mathbf{X}$ and $\mathrm{T}\mathbf{Y}$. Of course, it is possible that $\mathrm{T}\mathbf{X} = \mathrm{T}\mathbf{Y}$, in which case $\mathrm{T}\mathbf{R} = \mathrm{T}\mathbf{X}$ and the line is mapped to a point. We have seen that any linear transformation of R^n to itself will take a line to either a line or a point; an isomorphism will take lines to lines.

Exercises

1. Show that the following are linear transformations of R^2 to itself and describe the effect of T on a line segment OX:
   (a) $\mathrm{T}[x_1, x_2] = [x_2, x_1]$,
   (b) $\mathrm{T}[x_1, x_2] = [x_1 - x_2, x_2 - x_1]$,
   (c) $\mathrm{T}[x_1, x_2] = [2x_1, x_2]$.
2. Which of the linear transformations of Exercise 1 are one-to-one? What are the image sets of those that are not one-to-one?

3. In a plane consider the line L given by $\mathbf{R} = (1 - t)[1, 1] + t[-1, 2]$.
   (a) Sketch the line, assuming a Cartesian coordinate system.
   (b) Sketch the lines into which L is taken by each of the transformations of Exercise 1.
4. If the linear transformation of Exercise 1(b) is applied to the vectors $\mathbf{R} = (1 - t)[2, 1] + t[3, 2]$, what happens to the line represented by this equation?
5. Define a mapping $\mathrm{I}: P^n \to P^{n+1}$ by $\mathrm{I}(P(x)) = \int_0^x P(t)\, dt$.

$$\mathrm{I}(a_0 + a_1 x + \cdots + a_{n-1}x^{n-1}) = a_0 x + \frac{a_1}{2}x^2 + \cdots + \frac{a_{n-1}}{n}x^n.$$

   Show that this integration operator is a linear transformation. Is it one-to-one? Onto?
6. Determine which of the following mappings are linear transformations:
   (a) $\mathrm{T}_1[x_1, x_2] = [x_1 + 1, x_2]$,
   (b) $\mathrm{T}_2[x_1, x_2, x_3] = [x_3, x_1 + x_2, -x_2]$,
   (c) $\mathrm{T}_3[x_1, x_2, x_3] = [0, 0, 0, 0]$,
   (d) $\mathrm{T}_4[x_1, x_2] = [x_1 + x_2, x_1 - x_2, 2x_1, x_2, x_1]$,
   (e) $\mathrm{T}_5[x_1, x_2] = [x_1 x_2, x_2]$.
7. (a) In Example 1 show that $x_1^* = x_1 \cos\theta - x_2 \sin\theta$ and $x_2^* = x_1 \sin\theta + x_2 \cos\theta$.
   (b) Using the notation $\mathrm{T}_\theta[x_1, x_2] = [x_1^*, x_2^*]$, prove algebraically that T_θ is a linear transformation.
8. Which of examples 1–3 on page 63 are isomorphisms? Are there any that are one-to-one but not onto? Onto but not one-to-one? Find one that carries a line to a point. Which line?
9. In R^3, consider the mapping that takes a point X to point X^*, where XX^* is a line segment parallel to the x_3-axis whose midpoint lies on the x_1, x_2 coordinate plane. Describe this mapping in vector language as a mapping from R^3 to R^3 by the customary associations and determine whether the mapping is a linear transformation.
10. Let V be a vector space with the direct sum decomposition $V = S \oplus W$. Let T be a mapping that takes any vector $\mathbf{X}$ of V into its projection on S (see Exercise 5, Section 2.8). Prove that T is a linear transformation from V to S. The transformation T is called the *projection* of V onto S along W.

3.2 Elementary Properties of Linear Transformations

The defining properties of a linear transformation have many important implications. In this section we discuss some of the immediate ones. For example, if we set $a = 0$ in the property

$$\mathrm{T}(a\mathbf{X}) = a\mathrm{T}(\mathbf{X}),$$

we obtain

$$\mathrm{T}(0\mathbf{X}) = \mathrm{T}(\mathbf{0}) = 0 \cdot \mathrm{T}(\mathbf{X}) = \mathbf{0};$$

in words, this shows that every linear transformation maps the **0** vector in its domain to the **0** vector in its range.

Calculations are often simplified by noticing that the two conditions of Definition 3.1 can be combined into a single statement

$$\mathrm{T}(a\mathbf{X} + b\mathbf{Y}) = a\mathrm{T}(\mathbf{X}) + b\mathrm{T}(\mathbf{Y}) \quad \text{for all vectors } \mathbf{X}, \mathbf{Y}, \text{ and scalars } a, b. \tag{3.2}$$

That (3.2) is equivalent to the two conditions of (3.1) can be seen by taking first $a = b = 1$ and secondly $b = 0$.

We have seen that $\mathrm{T}\mathbf{0} = \mathbf{0}$ for any linear transformation T; thus the set of vectors $\mathbf{X}$ for which $\mathrm{T}\mathbf{X} = \mathbf{0}$ is never empty. In fact, this set is always a subspace of the domain of T. To see this, let $\mathrm{T}\mathbf{X} = \mathbf{0}$ and $\mathrm{T}\mathbf{Y} = \mathbf{0}$; then

$$\mathrm{T}(\mathbf{X} + \mathbf{Y}) = \mathrm{T}\mathbf{X} + \mathrm{T}\mathbf{Y} = \mathbf{0} + \mathbf{0} = \mathbf{0}$$

and

$$\mathrm{T}(a\mathbf{X}) = a\mathrm{T}\mathbf{X} = a \cdot \mathbf{0} = \mathbf{0}.$$

This justifies the following definition.

DEFINITION 3.2. If T *is a linear transformation from V to W, the set of all vectors* $\mathbf{X}$ *of V such that* $\mathrm{T}\mathbf{X} = \mathbf{0}$ *is called the* NULL SPACE *of* T, *or the* KERNEL *of* T.

Another set of vectors naturally associated with a linear transformation T is the set of all vectors (in the range) of the form $\mathrm{T}\mathbf{X}$. This set is called the *image* of T or the *rank space* of T.

THEOREM 3.1. The image of a linear transformation is a subspace of the range.

PROOF. If T is a linear transformation from V to W, and $\mathrm{T}\mathbf{X}$, $\mathrm{T}\mathbf{Y}$ are elements of the image of T, then $\mathrm{T}(\mathbf{X} + \mathbf{Y}) = \mathrm{T}\mathbf{X} + \mathrm{T}\mathbf{Y}$ so that the image is closed under addition. Since $a\mathrm{T}\mathbf{X} = \mathrm{T}(a\mathbf{X})$ it is also closed under scalar multiplication.

The reader may have noticed that our examples of linear transformations on R^n given in the previous section were defined by their action on the coordinates of a vector. The analog of this procedure in a general setting is to pick a basis $\mathbf{X}_1, \ldots, \mathbf{X}_k$ for a space V and then for a vector $\mathbf{X} = a_1\mathbf{X}_1 + \cdots + a_k\mathbf{X}_k$ to define $\mathrm{T}\mathbf{X}$ in terms of $a_1, \ldots, a_k$. We do this by picking any k vectors $\mathbf{Y}_1, \ldots, \mathbf{Y}_k$ of a space W and then defining

$$\mathrm{T}(a_1\mathbf{X}_1 + \cdots + a_k\mathbf{X}_k) = a_1\mathbf{Y}_1 + \cdots + a_k\mathbf{Y}_k.$$

This is easily seen to be a linear transformation. Note, moreover, that if S is a linear transformation such that

$$\mathrm{S}\mathbf{X}_1 = \mathbf{Y}_1, \mathrm{S}\mathbf{X}_2 = \mathbf{Y}_2, \ldots, \mathrm{S}\mathbf{X}_k = \mathbf{Y}_k,$$

then for any vector $\mathbf{X} = b_1\mathbf{X}_1 + \cdots + b_k\mathbf{X}_k$ we have

$$\begin{aligned}\mathrm{S}\mathbf{X} &= \mathrm{S}(b_1\mathbf{X}_1 + \cdots + b_k\mathbf{X}_k)\\ &= b_1\mathrm{S}\mathbf{X}_1 + \cdots + b_k\mathrm{S}\mathbf{X}_k\\ &= b_1\mathbf{Y}_1 + \cdots + b_k\mathbf{Y}_k\\ &= \mathrm{T}\mathbf{X}.\end{aligned}$$

We state these results as a theorem.

THEOREM 3.2. If $\mathbf{X}_1, \ldots, \mathbf{X}_k$ *is a basis for a space V, and* $\mathbf{Y}_1, \ldots, \mathbf{Y}_k$ *are any k vectors whatever from a space W, then there is one and only one linear transformation* $\mathrm{T}: V \to W$ *which satisfies* $\mathrm{T}\mathbf{X}_i = \mathbf{Y}_i$ *for* $i = 1, 2, \ldots, k$.

The "only one" part of Theorem 3.2 is often paraphrased by saying that a linear transformation is completely determined by its values on any basis.

In the usual situation, the vectors $\mathbf{Y}_1, \ldots, \mathbf{Y}_k$ will themselves be given in terms of a basis $\mathbf{X}'_1, \ldots, \mathbf{X}'_m$ of W.

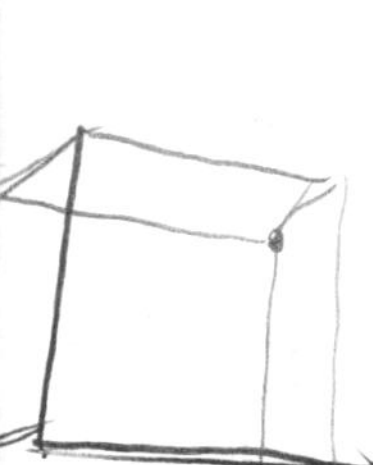

$$\begin{aligned}
\mathrm{T}\mathbf{X}_1 &= \mathbf{Y}_1 = a_{11}\mathbf{X}'_1 + a_{12}\mathbf{X}'_2 + \cdots + a_{1m}\mathbf{X}'_m,\\
\mathrm{T}\mathbf{X}_2 &= \mathbf{Y}_2 = a_{21}\mathbf{X}'_1 + a_{22}\mathbf{X}'_2 + \cdots + a_{2m}\mathbf{X}'_m,\\
&\vdots\\
\mathrm{T}\mathbf{X}_k &= \mathbf{Y}_k = a_{k1}\mathbf{X}'_1 + a_{k2}\mathbf{X}'_2 + \cdots + a_{km}\mathbf{X}'_m.
\end{aligned} \tag{3.3}$$

Thus the a_{ij}'s determine T, and any choice of a_{ij}'s will give rise to a linear transformation. Equations (3.3) will be fundamental to some of our later work, when we will say that the a_{ij}'s represent T with respect to the bases $\mathbf{X}_1, \ldots, \mathbf{X}_k$ and $\mathbf{X}'_1, \ldots, \mathbf{X}'_m$. In the future we will save space by writing $\{\mathbf{X}'_i\}$ for $\mathbf{X}'_1, \ldots, \mathbf{X}'_m$ whenever the number of vectors in the basis is clear from the context.

Example 1. We examine the differentiation operator D from P^n to P^n. The null space of D is, as every calculus student should know, the constants; for if

$$\mathrm{D}(a_0 + a_1x + \cdots + a_{n-1}x^{n-1}) = 0,$$

then

$$a_1 + 2a_2x + \cdots + (n-1)a_{n-1}x^{n-2} = 0 \qquad \text{so} \quad a_1 = a_2 = \cdots = a_{n-1} = 0.$$

What is the image space of D? Certainly it is just the polynomials of the form $a_1 + 2a_2x + \cdots + (n-1)a_{n-1}x^{n-2}$ for some $a_1, a_2, \ldots, a_{n-1}$. But this is just all polynomials of degree less than $n - 1$ (to get $b_0 + b_1x + \cdots + b_{n-2}x^{n-2}$, take the derivative of $b_0x + (b_1/2)x^2 + \cdots + [b_{n-2}/(n-1)]x^{n-1}$). Note that the dimension of the null space is 1 and the dimension of the image is $n - 1$.

Example 2. Let $\mathrm{T}: R^3 \to R^4$ be defined by

$$\begin{aligned}
\mathrm{T}[1, 0, 0] &= [0, 1, 0, 2],\\
\mathrm{T}[0, 1, 0] &= [0, 1, 1, 0],\\
\mathrm{T}[0, 0, 1] &= [0, 1, -1, 4].
\end{aligned}$$

The image of T is

$$W^* = L\{[0, 1, 0, 2], [0, 1, 1, 0], [0, 1, -1, 4]\},$$

so clearly $W^* \neq R^4$. We can determine the dimension of W^* by noting that the first two generators are linearly independent and $[0, 1, -1, 4] = 2[0, 1, 0, 2] - [0, 1, 1, 0]$. Hence the dimension of W^* is 2.

In order to determine the null space for T, we note that for any vector $[x_1, x_2, x_3]$

$$\begin{aligned}
\mathrm{T}[x_1, x_2, x_3] &= \mathrm{T}(x_1[1, 0, 0] + x_2[0, 1, 0] + x_3[0, 0, 1])\\
&= x_1\mathrm{T}[1, 0, 0] + x_2\mathrm{T}[0, 1, 0] + x_3\mathrm{T}[0, 0, 1]\\
&= x_1[0, 1, 0, 2] + x_2[0, 1, 1, 0] + x_3[0, 1, -1, 4]\\
&= [0, x_1 + x_2 + x_3, x_2 - x_3, 2x_1 + 4x_3].
\end{aligned}$$

If $[x_1, x_2, x_3]$ is in the null space of T, then $\mathrm{T}[x_1, x_2, x_3] = \mathbf{0}$; therefore from our expression for $\mathrm{T}[x_1, x_2, x_3]$ we must have

$$\begin{aligned} x_1 + x_2 + \ x_3 &= 0, \\ x_2 - \ x_3 &= 0, \\ 2x_1 \qquad + 4x_3 &= 0. \end{aligned}$$

These equations have the solution vectors $[-2a, a, a]$, where a is an arbitrary real number. Hence the null space of T is $L\{[-2, 1, 1]\}$, which is of dimension 1.

In both of these examples we see that the dimension of the null space plus the dimension of the image space equals the dimension of the domain. This is always the case.

THEOREM 3.3. *If* T *is any linear transformation* T: $V \to W$, *then*

$$\dim V = \dim (\text{null space of T}) + \dim (\text{image of T}).$$

PROOF. Let $\mathbf{X}_1, \ldots, \mathbf{X}_n$ be a basis for the null space of T and extend this to a basis $\mathbf{X}_1, \ldots, \mathbf{X}_n, \mathbf{X}'_1, \ldots, \mathbf{X}'_k$ of V. We have $\dim V = n + k$. Now the image of T, W^* is certainly given by

$$W^* = L\{\mathrm{T}\mathbf{X}_1, \ldots, \mathrm{T}\mathbf{X}_n, \mathrm{T}\mathbf{X}'_1, \ldots, \mathrm{T}\mathbf{X}'_k\},$$

but

$$\mathrm{T}\mathbf{X}_1 = \mathrm{T}\mathbf{X}_2 = \cdots = \mathrm{T}\mathbf{X}_n = \mathbf{0},$$

so

$$W^* = L\{\mathrm{T}\mathbf{X}'_1, \ldots, \mathrm{T}\mathbf{X}'_k\}.$$

If we can establish that $\mathrm{T}\mathbf{X}'_1, \ldots, \mathrm{T}\mathbf{X}'_k$ are linearly independent, we will have dim (image of T) $= k$ and the theorem will be established. If

$$a_1\mathrm{T}\mathbf{X}'_1 + \cdots + a_k\mathrm{T}\mathbf{X}'_k = \mathbf{0},$$

then

$$\mathrm{T}(a_1\mathbf{X}'_1) + \cdots + \mathrm{T}(a_k\mathbf{X}'_k) = \mathrm{T}(a_1\mathbf{X}'_1 + \cdots + a_k\mathbf{X}'_k) = \mathbf{0},$$

so $a_1\mathbf{X}'_1 + \cdots + a_k\mathbf{X}'_k$ is in the null space of T. Since $\mathbf{X}_1, \ldots, \mathbf{X}_n$ span the null space,

$$a_1\mathbf{X}'_1 + \cdots + a_k\mathbf{X}'_k = b_1\mathbf{X}_1 + \cdots + b_n\mathbf{X}_n$$

for some choice of $b_1, \ldots, b_n$. But this last equation can be written

$$-b_1\mathbf{X}_1 - \cdots - b_n\mathbf{X}_n + a_1\mathbf{X}'_1 + \cdots + a_k\mathbf{X}'_k = 0.$$

Hence, all of $a_1, a_2, \ldots, a_k, b_1, b_2, \ldots, b_n$ must be zero; thus $\mathrm{T}\mathbf{X}'_1, \ldots, \mathrm{T}\mathbf{X}'_k$ are linearly independent.

Linear transformations, like other functions, may or may not be one-to-one. However, there is a very simple condition which determines when a linear transformation is one-to-one.

THEOREM 3.4. *A linear transformation is one-to-one if and only if its null space is* **0** *alone.*

PROOF. If T is one-to-one it certainly takes only **0** to **0**; on the other hand, if T takes only **0** to **0** and $\mathrm{T}\mathbf{X} = \mathrm{T}\mathbf{Y}$, then $\mathrm{T}\mathbf{X} - \mathrm{T}\mathbf{Y} = \mathbf{0}$ so

$$\mathrm{T}(\mathbf{X} - \mathbf{Y}) = \mathrm{T}\mathbf{X} - \mathrm{T}\mathbf{Y} = \mathbf{0},$$

and thus $\mathbf{X} - \mathbf{Y} = \mathbf{0}$. But this means $\mathbf{X} = \mathbf{Y}$, or, T is one-to-one.

The special case T: $V \to V$ is important enough to be considered separately.

THEOREM 3.5. If T: $V \to V$ *is a linear transformation, then the following conditions are equivalent:*

(i) T *is one-to-one.*
(ii) *Null space of* T $= \{\mathbf{0}\}$.
(iii) T *is onto.*
(iv) *For some basis* $\{\mathbf{X}_i\}$ *of* V, $\{\mathrm{T}\mathbf{X}_i\}$ *is a basis.*
(v) *For every basis* $\{\mathbf{X}_i\}$ *of* V, $\{\mathrm{T}\mathbf{X}_i\}$ *is a basis.*

PROOF. We have already shown that the first two conditions are equivalent. If the null space of T is $\{\mathbf{0}\}$ then, by Theorem 3.3, dim $V = 0 +$ dim (image of T). Thus the image of T is a subspace of V of the same dimension as V and hence image of T $= V$, and T is onto. Similarly if T is onto, then dim (image of T) $=$ dim V and using Theorem 3.3 again we obtain dim (null space of T) $= 0$ or that T takes only $\mathbf{0}$ to $\mathbf{0}$. Thus the first three conditions are equivalent. As the linear span of $\{\mathrm{T}\mathbf{X}_i\}$ is contained in the image of T, certainly (iv) implies (iii). It is immediate that (v) implies (iv), so we need only show that any one of (i), (ii), (iii) implies (v). For any basis $\{\mathbf{X}_i\}$, if $\{\mathrm{T}\mathbf{X}_i\}$ were linearly dependent, say

$$a_1\mathrm{T}\mathbf{X}_1 + \cdots + a_n\mathrm{T}\mathbf{X}_n = \mathbf{0},$$

then

$$\mathrm{T}(a_1\mathbf{X}_1 + \cdots + a_n\mathbf{X}_n) = \mathbf{0}$$

and thus the null space of T would not be zero alone. This, of course, means that (i) implies (v).

Exercises

1. If a linear transformation T from R^3 to R^2 is given by

$$\mathrm{T}[1, 0, 0] = [2, 1],$$
$$\mathrm{T}[0, 1, 0] = [0, 1],$$
$$\mathrm{T}[0, 0, 1] = [1, 1],$$

find the image of an arbitrary vector $[x_1, x_2, x_3]$ of R^3. What is the null space of T? The image of T?

2. Define T: $R^3 \to R^3$ by

$$\mathrm{T}\mathbf{E}_1 = \mathbf{E}_1 + \mathbf{E}_2 - \mathbf{E}_3,$$
$$\mathrm{T}\mathbf{E}_2 = \mathbf{E}_1 - \mathbf{E}_2 + \mathbf{E}_3,$$
$$\mathrm{T}\mathbf{E}_3 = \mathbf{E}_1 - 3\mathbf{E}_3 + 3\mathbf{E}_3.$$

Find the image and null space of T.

3. Find the image and the null space of the integration operator defined in Exercise 5 of Section 3.1.

4. Let

$$\{\mathbf{X}_1 = [1, 1, -1], \mathbf{X}_2 = [1, 0, 1], \mathbf{X}_3 = [2, 1, -1]\}$$

be a basis for R^3 and let

$$\{\mathbf{X}'_1 = [1, 0, 1, 0], \mathbf{X}'_2 = [0, 1, 1, 0], \mathbf{X}'_3 = [1, 0, 0, 1], \mathbf{X}'_4 = [1, 1, 1, 0]\}$$

be a basis for R^4; define T from R^3 to R^4 by

$$\mathrm{T}\mathbf{X}_1 = \mathbf{X}'_1 - \mathbf{X}'_4,$$
$$\mathrm{T}\mathbf{X}_2 = \mathbf{X}'_1 + \mathbf{X}'_2 + \mathbf{X}'_3,$$
$$\mathrm{T}\mathbf{X}_3 = \mathbf{X}'_1 + 2\mathbf{X}'_2 + 2\mathbf{X}'_3 + \mathbf{X}'_4.$$

Find bases for the image and null space of T.

5. In Exercise 4, reexpress T in terms of the standard $\mathbf{E}_i$ basis vectors for both the domain and range of T.
6. Show that the linear transformation T of R^3 given by

$$\begin{aligned} \mathrm{TE}_1 &= \mathbf{E}_1 + \mathbf{E}_2, \\ \mathrm{TE}_2 &= \phantom{\mathbf{E}_1 +{}} \mathbf{E}_2 + \mathbf{E}_3, \\ \mathrm{TE}_3 &= \mathbf{E}_1 + \mathbf{E}_2 + \mathbf{E}_3, \end{aligned}$$

is a one-to-one mapping of R^3 onto R^3.
7. In Exercise 6 reexpress T in terms of the basis vectors

$$\mathbf{X}_1 = [1, 2, 0], \mathbf{X}_2 = [1, 0, -1], \mathbf{X}_3 = [0, 1, -1];$$

that is, obtain the relations

$$\mathrm{T}\mathbf{X}_i = a_{i1}\mathbf{X}_1 + a_{i2}\mathbf{X}_2 + a_{i3}\mathbf{X}_3$$

for $i = 1, 2, 3$.
8. Assume that we have a direct sum decomposition of a vector space $V = U \oplus W$ and that T is the projection of V on U along W. What is the null space of T? The image of T? (See Exercise 10, Section 3.1.)
9. Find linear transformations T_1 and T_2 on R^2 such that
   (a) R^2 = null space of $\mathrm{T}_1 \oplus$ image of T_1, both spaces on the right being one dimensional.
   (b) Null space of T_2 = image of T_2, with both spaces one dimensional.

3.3 Algebraic Operations on Linear Transformations

Let us look at the set of all linear transformations from a space V to a space W. What kinds of algebraic operations on this set arise naturally? Recall from calculus or theory of functions the "pointwise" addition of real-valued functions: $(f + g)(x) = f(x) + g(x)$. Since the functions we are considering have vectors as values, these values can always be added. Multiplying a function by a scalar will be defined similarly.

DEFINITION 3.3. *If* T, S *are linear transformations from V to W and r is any scalar, the linear transformations* T + S, rT *from V to W are defined by*

(i) $(\mathrm{T} + \mathrm{S})(\mathbf{X}) = \mathrm{T}\mathbf{X} + \mathrm{S}\mathbf{X}$,
(ii) $(r\mathrm{T})(\mathbf{X}) = r(\mathrm{T}\mathbf{X})$.

Definition 3.3 makes a claim that must be verified: that T + S and rT are actually linear transformations. To check that T + S is linear we observe that

$$(\mathrm{T} + \mathrm{S})(\mathbf{X} + \mathbf{Y}) = \mathrm{T}(\mathbf{X} + \mathbf{Y}) + \mathrm{S}(\mathbf{X} + \mathbf{Y})$$

by the definition; then, using the linearity of T and S, we obtain

$$\begin{aligned} (\mathrm{T} + \mathrm{S})(\mathbf{X} + \mathbf{Y}) &= \mathrm{T}(\mathbf{X}) + \mathrm{T}(\mathbf{Y}) + \mathrm{S}(\mathbf{X}) + \mathrm{S}(\mathbf{Y}) \\ &= \mathrm{T}(\mathbf{X}) + \mathrm{S}(\mathbf{X}) + \mathrm{T}(\mathbf{Y}) + \mathrm{S}(\mathbf{Y}) \\ &= (\mathrm{T} + \mathrm{S})(\mathbf{X}) + (\mathrm{T} + \mathrm{S})(\mathbf{Y}). \end{aligned}$$

The reader should verify that $(\mathrm{T} + \mathrm{S})(r\mathbf{X}) = r(\mathrm{T} + \mathrm{S})(\mathbf{X})$ and that rT is linear.

Thus we may add elements of our set of transformations, as well as multiply them by scalars. This raises the natural question of whether our set, with these operations, is a vector space itself. It is, and it is such an important space that we give it a name.

DEFINITION 3.4. Hom (V, W) *denotes the set of all linear transformations from* V *to* W *together with the algebraic structure provided by the definitions of addition and scalar multiplication of linear transformations.*

THEOREM 3.6. Hom (V, W) *is a vector space.*

PROOF. The eight properties of Definition 2.4 must be verified. As usual, this is simply a matter of direct checking, and the proof is left to the reader.

What is the dimension of Hom (U, V) as a vector space? If the dimension of U is m and the dimension of V is n, then the dimension of Hom (U, V) is mn. This will be apparent when we get to matrix notation, but we give an outline of the proof for the impatient. Pick bases $\mathbf{X}_1, \mathbf{X}_2, \ldots, \mathbf{X}_m$ and $\mathbf{X}'_1, \mathbf{X}'_2, \ldots, \mathbf{X}'_n$ for U and V, respectively, and define mn linear transformations by

$$\mathrm{T}_{ij}(\mathbf{X}_i) = \mathbf{X}'_j, \qquad \mathrm{T}_{ij}(\mathbf{X}_k) = \mathbf{0}$$

for $k \neq i$ (recall that the action of a linear transformation on a basis determines the transformation). These transformations can be seen to be linearly independent, and if T is any linear transformation represented by the numbers $\{a_{ij}\}$ $(i = 1, 2, \ldots, m;\ j = 1, 2, \ldots, n)$ with respect to the bases $\{\mathbf{X}_i\}$ and $\{\mathbf{X}'_j\}$ (see Equations (3.3)), then

$$\mathrm{T} = \textstyle\sum_{i,j} a_{ij}\mathrm{T}_{ij}.$$

Thus we have a basis for Hom (U, V) with mn elements.

Are there other useful or interesting algebraic operations that can be performed with linear transformations? We cannot multiply them pointwise since there is usually no multiplication of vectors defined, and in any case such a multiplication would produce nonlinear transformations.

There is, however, an operation that can be performed on certain pairs of linear transformations, that of *iteration* or *composition.* Suppose T_1 is a linear transformation from V to W_1 and T_2 is a linear transformation from W_1 to W_2. Then we can define a new linear transformation T_3 from V to W_2 by $\mathrm{T}_3\mathbf{X} = \mathrm{T}_2(\mathrm{T}_1\mathbf{X})$. As usual, we must check that T_3 is linear.

$$\begin{aligned}\mathrm{T}_3(\mathbf{X} + \mathbf{Y}) &= \mathrm{T}_2(\mathrm{T}_1(\mathbf{X} + \mathbf{Y}))\\ &= \mathrm{T}_2(\mathrm{T}_1\mathbf{X} + \mathrm{T}_1\mathbf{Y})\\ &= \mathrm{T}_2(\mathrm{T}_1\mathbf{X}) + \mathrm{T}_2(\mathrm{T}_1\mathbf{Y})\\ &= \mathrm{T}_3\mathbf{X} + \mathrm{T}_3\mathbf{Y};\end{aligned}$$

$$\begin{aligned}\mathrm{T}_3(r\mathbf{X}) = \mathrm{T}_2(\mathrm{T}_1(r\mathbf{X})) &= \mathrm{T}_2(r\mathrm{T}_1\mathbf{X})\\ &= r\mathrm{T}_2(\mathrm{T}_1\mathbf{X})\\ &= r\mathrm{T}_3\mathbf{X}.\end{aligned}$$

Next, we shall make a notational simplification and adopt a definition that is suggested by the notation. We shall drop the parentheses whenever convenient and unambiguous; that is, we shall write $\mathrm{T}_3 = \mathrm{T}_2\mathrm{T}_1$ and $\mathrm{T}_3\mathbf{X} = \mathrm{T}_2\mathrm{T}_1\mathbf{X}$.

DEFINITION 3.5. *If the domain of* T_2 *contains as a subset the image of* T_1, *so that the composite* $\mathrm{T}_3\mathbf{X} = \mathrm{T}_2(\mathrm{T}_1\mathbf{X})$ *exists,* T_3 *is called the* PRODUCT *of* T_2 *and* T_1 *and written* $\mathrm{T}_3 = \mathrm{T}_2\mathrm{T}_1$.

Note that in $\mathrm{T}_1\mathrm{T}_2$ it is T_2 that is applied first. This deviation from the normal left to right order of operations can be confusing, and in fact, many algebraists prefer to write T_2T_1 for the transformation obtained by first applying T_2 and then T_1. However, if the latter notation is used, it is most convenient to write the variable on the left: $\mathbf{X}T$ for $T(\mathbf{X})$. As the variable is written on the right almost universally, we shall conform to this convention.

Example 1. We return to the rotations T_θ considered in Example 1 of Section 3.1 to see a particularly simple illustration of the product of two linear transformations. Here all of the spaces V, W_1, W_2 are identified with R^2.

Consider T_{θ_1} and T_{θ_2}; what is $T_{\theta_2}T_{\theta_1}$? Clearly, if one rotates by θ_1 and then θ_2, one has just performed a rotation of $\theta_1 + \theta_2$, so

$$T_{\theta_2}T_{\theta_1} = T_{\theta_1+\theta_2} = T_{\theta_1}T_{\theta_2}.$$

The reader should not let Example 1 mislead him into thinking that $T_1T_2 = T_2T_1$ in general. Usually T_1T_2 and T_2T_1 will have different domains and ranges, and one may not even be defined. If $W_2 = V$, they will both be defined, but T_2T_1 is then a function from V to V while T_1T_2 is a function from W_1 to W_1. This situation is illustrated in Figure 3.3.

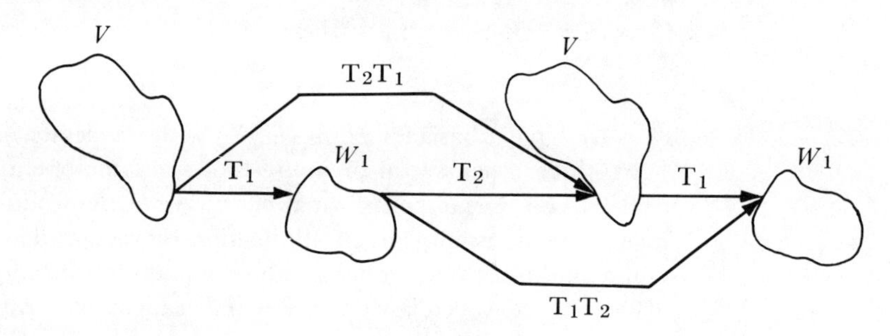

FIGURE 3.3

The next example illustrates that even if $V = W_1 = W_2$, so that T_1T_2 and T_2T_1 have the same domains, the two products may be unequal.

Example 2. Let V, W_1, W_2 be R^2. Let T_1 and T_2 be defined by

$$T_1[x_1, x_2] = [x_2, 2x_1] \quad \text{and} \quad T_2[x_1, x_2] = [x_1 + x_2, x_2].$$

It is easily verified that T_1 and T_2 are linear transformations.

$$\begin{aligned} T_2T_1[x_1, x_2] &= T_2[x_2, 2x_1] = [x_2 + 2x_1, 2x_1], \\ T_1T_2[x_1, x_2] &= T_1[x_1 + x_2, x_2] = [x_2, 2x_1 + 2x_2]. \end{aligned}$$

If the results are equal, then

$$x_2 = x_2 + 2x_1 \quad \text{and} \quad 2x_1 + 2x_2 = 2x_1$$

or $2x_1 = 0$, $2x_2 = 0$ and $x_1 = x_2 = 0$. That is, the transformation T_1T_2 agrees with the transformation T_2T_1 only at the point $[0, 0]$, where all linear transformations agree.

We next remind ourselves of a result that is true for all functions. When $f(gh)$ is defined, so is $(fg)h$ and the two are equal.

THEOREM 3.7. If T_1, T_2, T_3 *are linear transformations from* V *to* W_1, W_1 *to* W_2, W_2 *to* W_3, *respectively*, $T_3(T_2T_1)$ *and* $(T_3T_2)T_1$ *are linear transformations from* V *to* W_3 *and are equal.*

PROOF. The reader need only note that both expressions stand for the transformation obtained by first performing T_1, then T_2, and finally T_3.

THEOREM 3.8. If T_1 *is a linear transformation from* V *to* W_1 *and* T_2, T_3 *are linear transformations from* W_1 *to* W_2, *then*

$$(T_2 + T_3)T_1 = T_2T_1 + T_3T_1.$$

PROOF.

$$\begin{aligned}(T_2 + T_3)T_1\mathbf{X} &= T_2(T_1\mathbf{X}) + T_3(T_1\mathbf{X}) \\ &= (T_2T_1 + T_3T_1)(\mathbf{X}).\end{aligned}$$

THEOREM 3.9. If T_2, T_3 *are linear transformations from* V *to* W_1 *and* T_1 *is a linear transformation from* W_1 *to* W_2, $T_1(T_2 + T_3) = T_1T_2 + T_1T_3$.

These theorems may seem to lack interest since they have rather special conditions. Theorems 3.8 and 3.9 look like the distributive laws, but the hypotheses complicate the issue. There is, however, an important special case where everything works out beautifully. This is when *all* the spaces involved, V, W_1, W_2, are the same. Then we are talking about Hom (V, V).

We already know that Hom (V, V) has an additive structure because it is a vector space; it also has a multiplication (the composition of functions). Structures of this type are common in mathematics, and are called rings.

DEFINITION 3.6. A RING *is a set* **R** *with two binary relations* $+$ *and* $\cdot$ *satisfying the following laws:*

A. *R with + is an Abelian group.*
M1. *If* $a \in R$, $b \in R$, *then* $a \cdot b \in R$.
M2. *If* $a, b, c \in R$, *then*

$$(a \cdot b) \cdot c = a \cdot (b \cdot c).$$

D1. *If* $a, b, c \in R$, *then*

$$\begin{aligned}a \cdot (b + c) &= a \cdot b + a \cdot c, \\ (b + c) \cdot a &= b \cdot a + c \cdot a.\end{aligned}$$

In light of Theorems 3.7, 3.8, and 3.9 we have the following theorem.

THEOREM 3.10. Hom (V, V) *is a ring with identity when endowed with composition as multiplication; the identity map is the multiplicative identity.*

Rings that are also vector spaces are of so much importance that they have been given a special name. Somewhat confusingly, the name is *Algebra*.

DEFINITION 3.7. If V *is a ring, a vector space over* F, *and in addition satisfies*

$$a(\mathbf{X} \cdot \mathbf{Y}) = (a\mathbf{X}) \cdot \mathbf{Y} = \mathbf{X} \cdot (a\mathbf{Y}),$$

then V *is called an* ALGEBRA OVER F.

We can only advise the reader who finds the name confusing to watch for the article. *An* algebra is a special kind of ring; algebra (no article) is the study of algebraic operations on mathematical structures.

Exercises

1. Let linear transformations T_1, T_2, T_3 from $\mathbf{R}^2$ to $\mathbf{R}^2$ and $\mathbf{R}^2$ to $\mathbf{R}^3$ be defined as follows:

$$T_1[x_1, x_2] = [x_1 - x_2, x_2],$$
$$T_2[x_1, x_2] = [x_1 - x_2, x_2, x_1],$$
$$T_3[x_1, x_2] = [x_2, x_1 - x_2, x_1 + x_2].$$

   (a) Find (i) $(T_2 + T_3)[1, 0]$; (ii) $(T_2 + T_3)[0, 1]$; (iii) $T_2T_1[1, -1]$; (iv) $T_3T_1[1, -1]$; (v) $(T_2 + T_3)T_1[1, -1]$; (vi) $T_1^3[0, 1]$.
   (b) $T_2T_1[x_1, x_2] = ?$
   (c) $T_3T_1[x_1, x_2] = ?$
   (d) $(T_2 + T_3)[x_1, x_2] = ?$
   (e) $(T_2 + T_3)T_1[x_1, x_2] = ?$
2. Let linear transformations T_1, T_2, T_3 from $\mathbf{R}^3$ to $\mathbf{R}^4$ and $\mathbf{R}^3$ to $\mathbf{R}^3$ be defined by giving the effect on particular bases as follows: Let

$$\mathbf{X}_1 = [1, 0, 1], \mathbf{X}_2 = [1, -1, 1], \mathbf{X}_3 = [0, 1, 1],$$
$$\mathbf{X}_1' = [1, 0, 0, 1], \mathbf{X}_2' = [1, -1, 0, 0], \mathbf{X}_3' = [0, 1, 1, 0], \mathbf{X}_4' = [1, 0, 3, 0]$$

   and define T_1, T_2, T_3 by

$$\begin{aligned} T_1\mathbf{X}_1 &= \mathbf{X}_1' + \mathbf{X}_3', & T_2\mathbf{X}_1 &= \mathbf{X}_1' - \mathbf{X}_2' + 2\mathbf{X}_3', & T_3\mathbf{X}_1 &= \mathbf{X}_1 + \mathbf{X}_2,\\ T_1\mathbf{X}_2 &= \mathbf{X}_1' - \mathbf{X}_2', & T_2\mathbf{X}_2 &= \mathbf{X}_1' - \mathbf{X}_3' + \mathbf{X}_4', & T_3\mathbf{X}_2 &= \mathbf{X}_2 + \mathbf{X}_3,\\ T_1\mathbf{X}_3 &= \mathbf{X}_2' + \mathbf{X}_4', & T_2\mathbf{X}_3 &= \mathbf{X}_2' + \mathbf{X}_3'; & T_3\mathbf{X}_3 &= \mathbf{X}_1 + \mathbf{X}_3. \end{aligned}$$

   (a) Find T_1T_3 in terms of the same bases.
   (b) Find $T_1 + T_2$ in the same way.
   (c) Express T_1, T_2, T_3 in terms of the $\mathbf{E}_i$ bases for $\mathbf{R}^3$ and $\mathbf{R}^4$.
   (d) Find T_1T_3 in terms of the $\mathbf{E}_i$ bases.
3. For what values of $\theta_1, \theta_2, \theta_3$ is $T_{\theta_1} + T_{\theta_2} = T_{\theta_3}$ in Example 1 of Section 3.1?
4. Write T_1 of Exercise 2 as a sum of four linear transformations $T_{11}, T_{12}, T_{13}, T_{14}$ such that each T_{1i} is a linear transformation from $\mathbf{R}^3$ to $\mathbf{R}^4$ whose image is $L\{\mathbf{X}_i'\}$ for $i = 1, 2, 3, 4$.
5. Prove Theorem 3.9.
6. Suppose that, instead of restricting our attention to Hom (V, V), we considered all mappings from V to V. These functions can still be added and composed and the results will again be functions from V to V. Does this system form a ring? Which of the associative and distributive laws remain valid?
7. Prove that if T_1 and T_2 are linear transformations such that T_2T_1 is defined, the kernel of T_2T_1 contains the kernel of T_1 and the image of T_2 contains the image of T_2T_1.
8. Implicit in the discussion of the vector space property of Hom (V, W) is the idea of the relation of the negative of a linear transformation T, $-T$, to $(-1)T$. Show that $-T$ and $(-1)T$ are identical.
9. If we have a direct-sum decomposition of a vector space $V = W_1 \oplus W_2$ and if T_1 is the projection of V on W_1 along W_2 and T_2 is the projection of V on W_2 along W_1 (see Exercise 10, Section 3.1), describe the following linear transformations: (a) $T_1 + T_2$; (b) T_2T_1; (c) T_1^2; (d) T_2^2.

10. Fill in the details of the proof that the dimension of Hom (V, W) is the product of the dimensions of V and W.
11. Let T be in Hom (V, V). Prove that V = kernel of T $\oplus$ image of T if and only if kernel of T^2 = kernel of T.

3.4 Linear Transformations and Matrices

We seek now a representation for linear transformations which will simplify the calculations involved. The key lies in the set of equations (3.3) which gives the action of the linear transformation on a basis. The reader may have noticed that, in working out problems, much of the calculation could be done independently of the actual values of the bases $\{\mathbf{X}_i\}$ and $\{\mathbf{X}'_i\}$ by just keeping track of the coefficients in (3.3). Let us recall these equations and see how they may be used in calculations.

Let T be a given linear transformation from V to W. Assume that we know the values of T at the n basis elements $\mathbf{X}_1, \ldots, \mathbf{X}_n$ of V in terms of the basis elements $\mathbf{X}'_1, \ldots, \mathbf{X}'_m$ of W:

$$\begin{aligned} T\mathbf{X}_1 &= a_{11}\mathbf{X}'_1 + a_{21}\mathbf{X}'_2 + \cdots + a_{m1}\mathbf{X}'_m, \\ T\mathbf{X}_2 &= a_{12}\mathbf{X}'_1 + a_{22}\mathbf{X}'_2 + \cdots + a_{m2}\mathbf{X}'_m, \\ &\vdots \\ T\mathbf{X}_n &= a_{1n}\mathbf{X}'_1 + a_{2n}\mathbf{X}'_2 + \cdots + a_{mn}\mathbf{X}'_m. \end{aligned} \tag{3.4}$$

We have seen in Section 3.2 that the coefficients (the a_{ij}'s) completely determine T; thus we really need to save only these coefficients in order to perform calculations involving T. We write the list in the following form:

$$\begin{bmatrix} a_{11} & a_{12} & \cdots & a_{1n} \\ a_{21} & a_{22} & \cdots & a_{2n} \\ \vdots & & & \vdots \\ a_{m1} & a_{m2} & \cdots & a_{mn} \end{bmatrix}. \tag{3.5}$$

This form will be convenient for many purposes, and we give forms of this kind a name.

DEFINITION 3.8. MATRICES, EQUALITY, NOTATION. *A rectangular array of numbers (or, more generally, of elements of any selected field) of the form* (3.5) *is called an m by n* MATRIX. *Two matrices are said to be* EQUAL *if and only if the elements in corresponding positions are all equal (this automatically requires that equal matrices have the same number of rows and columns).*

For convenience we write "$m \times n$" for "m by n" and, when the size is clearly established, the notation $[a_{ij}]$ will stand for the whole array (3.5). Matrices will be denoted by capital letters.

In general, note that a_{ij} is the element in the ith row and jth column of the matrix, and an $m \times n$ matrix has m rows and n columns.*

Example 1. $A = \begin{bmatrix} 4 & 1 & -2 \\ 3 & 5 & 6 \end{bmatrix}$. A is a 2×3 matrix. $a_{12} = 1$, while $a_{21} = 3$.

* The reader may have noticed that in going from (3.4) to (3.5) we "interchanged" rows and columns. This annoyance is one of the prices we pay for writing the variable on the right in standard functional notation. In the following the reader may check that putting the variables (vectors) on the left of the linear transformation would eliminate this exchange.

Example 2. In Example 2 of Section 3.2 a linear transformation T was defined by

$$\begin{aligned} T[1, 0, 0] &= [0, 1, 0, 2], \\ T[0, 1, 0] &= [0, 1, 1, 0]. \\ T[0, 0, 1] &= [0, 1, -1, 4]. \end{aligned}$$

These equations can be rewritten:

$$\begin{aligned} T[1, 0, 0] &= 0[1, 0, 0, 0] + 1[0, 1, 0, 0] + 0[0, 0, 1, 0] + 2[0, 0, 0, 1], \\ T[0, 1, 0] &= 0[1, 0, 0, 0] + 1[0, 1, 0, 0] + 1[0, 0, 1, 0] + 0[0, 0, 0, 1], \\ T[0, 0, 1] &= 0[1, 0, 0, 0] + 1[0, 1, 0, 0] - 1[0, 0, 1, 0] + 4[0, 0, 0, 1]. \end{aligned}$$

Thus when we use the standard bases for $V = R^3$ and $W = R^4$ the matrix of T is

$$\begin{bmatrix} 0 & 0 & 0 \\ 1 & 1 & 1 \\ 0 & 1 & -1 \\ 2 & 0 & 4 \end{bmatrix}.$$

The process of passing from Equations (3.4) to the matrix (3.5), illustrated in Example 2 above, establishes a one-to-one correspondence between Hom (V, W) and the set of all $m \times n$ matrices once bases $\{\mathbf{X}_i\}$ and $\{\mathbf{X}'_i\}$ of V and W have been selected.

DEFINITION 3.9. If a linear transformation T *is defined by Equations* (3.4), *we say that the matrix* (3.5) *is* THE MATRIX OF T WITH RESPECT TO THE BASES $\{\mathbf{X}_i\}$ *and* $\{\mathbf{X}'_i\}$.

Example 3. If T is the linear transformation of Example 2 and we choose the bases

$$\begin{aligned} \{\mathbf{X}_i\} &= \{[1, 1, 0], [0, 1, 1], [0, 0, 1]\}; \\ \{\mathbf{X}'_i\} &= \{[1, 1, 0, 0], [0, 1, 1, 0], [0, 0, 1, 1], [0, 0, 0, 1]\} \end{aligned}$$

for R^3 and R^4, respectively, then we have

$$\begin{aligned} T[1, 1, 0] &= [0, 1, 0, 2] + [0, 1, 1, 0] = [0, 2, 1, 2], \\ T[0, 1, 1] &= [0, 1, 1, 0] + [0, 1, -1, 4] = [0, 2, 0, 4], \\ T[0, 0, 1] &= [0, 1, -1, 4], \end{aligned}$$

so

$$\begin{aligned} T[1, 1, 0] &= 0[1, 1, 0, 0] + 2[0, 1, 1, 0] - 1[0, 0, 1, 1] + 3[0, 0, 0, 1], \\ T[0, 1, 1] &= 0[1, 1, 0, 0] + 2[0, 1, 1, 0] - 2[0, 0, 1, 1] + 6[0, 0, 0, 1], \\ T[0, 0, 1] &= 0[1, 1, 0, 0] + 1[0, 1, 1, 0] - 2[0, 0, 1, 1] + 6[0, 0, 0, 1]. \end{aligned}$$

Thus the matrix of T with respect to the bases $\{\mathbf{X}_i\}$ and $\{\mathbf{X}'_i\}$ is

$$\begin{bmatrix} 0 & 0 & 0 \\ 2 & 2 & 1 \\ -1 & -2 & -2 \\ 3 & 6 & 6 \end{bmatrix}.$$

To see how matrices may be used to give the results of applying linear transformations, let us first consider the case where $V = R^n$, $W = R^m$, and $\{\mathbf{X}_i\}$, $\{\mathbf{X}'_i\}$ are the standard bases for R^n and R^m; i.e., $\mathbf{X}_i = \mathbf{E}_i$, $\mathbf{X}'_i = \mathbf{E}'_i$ for all applicable i and the corresponding definitions of $\mathbf{E}_i$ for the two spaces (for example, $\mathbf{X}'_2 = [0, 1, 0, \ldots, 0]$, the vector having m coordinates). A typical equation of (3.4) becomes

$$\mathrm{T}\mathbf{E}_j = a_{1j}\mathbf{E}'_1 + a_{2j}\mathbf{E}'_2 + \cdots + a_{mj}\mathbf{E}'_m = [a_{1j}, a_{2j}, \ldots, a_{mj}]. \quad (3.6)$$

The vector that is the image of $\mathbf{E}_j$ has components that correspond to the elements in the jth column of the matrix of T (see Examples 2 and 3).

Now what happens to an arbitrary vector of V? Let

$$\begin{aligned}
\mathbf{X} &= [x_1, x_2, \ldots, x_n] = x_1\mathbf{E}_1 + x_2\mathbf{E}_2 + \cdots + x_n\mathbf{E}_n,\\
\mathrm{T}\mathbf{X} &= x_1\mathrm{T}\mathbf{E}_1 + x_2\mathrm{T}\mathbf{E}_2 + \cdots + x_n\mathrm{T}\mathbf{E}_n\\
&= x_1(a_{11}\mathbf{E}'_1 + a_{21}\mathbf{E}'_2 + \cdots + a_{m1}\mathbf{E}'_m)\\
&\quad + x_2(a_{12}\mathbf{E}'_1 + a_{22}\mathbf{E}'_2 + \cdots + a_{m2}\mathbf{E}'_m)\\
&\quad \vdots\\
&\quad + x_n(a_{1n}\mathbf{E}'_1 + a_{2n}\mathbf{E}'_2 + \cdots + a_{nn}\mathbf{E}'_n)\\
&= (x_1a_{11} + x_2a_{12} + \cdots + x_na_{1n})\mathbf{E}'_1 + (x_1a_{21} + x_2a_{22} + \cdots + x_na_{2n})\mathbf{E}'_2\\
&\quad + \cdots + (x_1a_{m1} + x_2a_{m2} + \cdots + x_na_{mn})\mathbf{E}'_m.
\end{aligned}$$

Let us denote by $\mathbf{A}_i$ the vector of R^n whose components are given by the ith row of the matrix of T ($\mathbf{A}_1 = [a_{11}, a_{12}, \ldots, a_{1n}]$, etc.). Then note that

$$\mathrm{T}\mathbf{X} = (\mathbf{A}_1, \mathbf{X})\mathbf{E}'_1 + (\mathbf{A}_2, \mathbf{X})\mathbf{E}'_2 + \cdots + (\mathbf{A}_m, \mathbf{X})\mathbf{E}'_m$$

or

$$\mathrm{T}\mathbf{X} = [(\mathbf{A}_1, \mathbf{X}), (\mathbf{A}_2, \mathbf{X}), \ldots, (\mathbf{A}_m, \mathbf{X})],$$

where the notation $(\mathbf{A}_i, \mathbf{X})$ stands for the standard inner product of Chapter 2.

Already we have a use for matrices. We can readily calculate the result of a transformation on an arbitrary vector if we know its matrix with respect to the standard bases. The procedure is to take the inner product of each row with the vector to be transformed. The result of the ith product is the ith component of the image vector.

Example 4. If T is the linear transformation of Example 2, then its matrix with respect to the standard bases has been seen to be

$$\begin{bmatrix} 0 & 0 & 0\\ 1 & 1 & 1\\ 0 & 1 & -1\\ 2 & 0 & 4 \end{bmatrix}.$$

What is $\mathrm{T}[1, -2, 4]$?

$$\begin{aligned}
([0, 0, 0], [1, -2, 4]) &= 0\cdot 1 + 0(-2) + 0(4) = 0,\\
([1, 1, 1], [1, -2, 4]) &= 1\cdot 1 + 1(-2) + 1(4) = 3,\\
([0, 1, -1], [1, -2, 4]) &= 0\cdot 1 + 1(-2) + (-1)(4) = -6,\\
([2, 0, 4], [1, -2, 4]) &= 2\cdot 1 + 0(-2) + 4(4) = 18,
\end{aligned}$$

$$\mathrm{T}[1, -2, 4] = [0, 3, -6, 18].$$

Let us return to the general case where $\{\mathbf{X}_i\}$, $\{\mathbf{X}'_i\}$ are any bases for V and W. The entire procedure will be seen to carry through. Let

$$\mathbf{X} = x_1\mathbf{X}_1 + x_2\mathbf{X}_2 + \cdots + x_n\mathbf{X}_n$$

be an arbitrary vector of the domain and A be the matrix of T with respect to the given bases; again, denote by $\mathbf{A}_i$ the vector of R^n whose coordinates correspond to the ith row of A. Finally let $\mathbf{X}^*$ be the vector of R^n given by

$\mathbf{X}^* = [x_1, x_2, \ldots, x_n]$. (It is important to note that if $V = R^n$, $\mathbf{X}^*$ will not necessarily equal $\mathbf{X}$.)

If we perform the same calculations as before we obtain

THEOREM 3.11. *Under the assumptions just stated,*

$$\mathrm{T}\mathbf{X} = (\mathbf{A}_1, \mathbf{X}^*)\mathbf{X}_1' + (\mathbf{A}_2, \mathbf{X}^*)\mathbf{X}_2' + \cdots + (\mathbf{A}_m, \mathbf{X}^*)\mathbf{X}_m'.$$

Example 5. Again let T be the linear transformation of Examples 2 and 3. If we choose $\{\mathbf{X}_i\}$ and $\{\mathbf{X}_i'\}$ as in Example 3, then the matrix of T is

$$\begin{bmatrix} 0 & 0 & 0 \\ 2 & 2 & 1 \\ -1 & -2 & -2 \\ 3 & 6 & 6 \end{bmatrix}.$$

What is $\mathrm{T}(\mathbf{X}_1 + 2\mathbf{X}_2 - \mathbf{X}_3)$? $\mathbf{X}^* = [1, 2, -1]$ in this case, so we have

$$\begin{aligned}
&\mathrm{T}(\mathbf{X}_1 + 2\mathbf{X}_2 - \mathbf{X}_3) \\
&\quad = ([0, 0, 0], [1, 2, -1])\mathbf{X}_1' + ([2, 2, 1], [1, 2, -1])\mathbf{X}_2' \\
&\qquad + ([-1, -2, -2], [1, 2, -1])\mathbf{X}_3' + ([3, 6, 6], [1, 2, -1])\mathbf{X}_4' \\
&\quad = (0)\mathbf{X}_1' + (5)\mathbf{X}_2' + (-3)\mathbf{X}_3' + (9)\mathbf{X}_4'.
\end{aligned}$$

We could, of course, do this calculation without matrices:

$$\begin{aligned}
&\mathrm{T}(\mathbf{X}_1 + 2\mathbf{X}_2 - \mathbf{X}_3) \\
&\quad = \mathrm{T}\mathbf{X}_1 + 2\mathrm{T}\mathbf{X}_2 - \mathrm{T}\mathbf{X}_3 \\
&\quad = (2\mathbf{X}_2' - \mathbf{X}_3' + 3\mathbf{X}_4') + 2(2\mathbf{X}_2' - 2\mathbf{X}_3' + 6\mathbf{X}_4') - (\mathbf{X}_2' - 2\mathbf{X}_3' + 6\mathbf{X}_4') \\
&\quad = (2 + 4 - 1)\mathbf{X}_2' + (-1 - 4 + 2)\mathbf{X}_3' + (3 + 12 - 6)\mathbf{X}_4' \\
&\quad = 5\mathbf{X}_2' - 3\mathbf{X}_3' + 9\mathbf{X}_4'.
\end{aligned}$$

Thus far the matrices serve as abbreviations and as devices for arranging the numbers involved. They save us the trouble of collecting terms, as in the final step of Example 5.

The primary advantage of matrices lies in the algebra of matrices, which arises from the algebra of linear transformations. We shall proceed to develop this in the next section.

Exercises

1. Find the matrices of transformations T_1, T_2, T_3 of Exercise 1, Section 3.3 with respect to the standard bases.
2. In terms of the bases employed in Exercise 2, Section 3.3, find the matrices of T_2, T_3.
3. Find the matrices of T_1, T_2, T_3 of Exercise 2, Section 3.3 with respect to the standard bases.
4. Complete the proof of Theorem 3.11 by carrying out the calculation done in the text for the $\mathbf{E}_i$, $\mathbf{E}_i'$ bases in the general case.
5. If D is the differentiation operator on the space of polynomials of degree less than 4 with real coefficients, what is the matrix of D with respect to the bases $\{\mathbf{X}_i\}$, $\{\mathbf{X}_i'\}$ given by

$$\mathbf{X}_1 = \mathbf{X}_1' = 1, \quad \mathbf{X}_2 = \mathbf{X}_2' = x, \quad \mathbf{X}_3 = \mathbf{X}_3' = x^2, \quad \mathbf{X}_4 = \mathbf{X}_4' = x^3?$$

With respect to the bases $\{\mathbf{X}_i\}$ as above and

$$\{\mathbf{X}_i'\} = \{1, x - 1, (x - 1)^2, (x - 1)^3\}?$$

6. If, with respect to a particular basis $\mathbf{X}_1$, $\mathbf{X}_2$, $\mathbf{X}_3$ of V and $\mathbf{X}'_1$, $\mathbf{X}'_2$ of W, T has the matrix

$$\begin{bmatrix} 0 & 1 & -1 \\ 2 & 1 & 1 \end{bmatrix},$$

what is the effect of T on
(a) $\mathbf{X}_1 + 2\mathbf{X}_2 - \mathbf{X}_3$? (b) $2\mathbf{X}_1 + \mathbf{X}_3$?

3.5 Algebra of Matrices

The algebra of matrices is based directly on that of linear transformations. Let us illustrate the process with an example.

Example 1. Assume T_1, T_2 are the linear transformations on R^2 defined by

$$\begin{aligned} T_1[x_1, x_2] &= [2x_1 + x_2, x_2 - x_1], \\ T_2[x_1, x_2] &= [x_1 - x_2, 3x_1 + 2x_2]. \end{aligned}$$

Then if we choose the standard basis for both range and domain we have

$$\begin{aligned} T_1\mathbf{E}_1 &= 2\mathbf{E}_1 - \mathbf{E}_2, & T_2\mathbf{E}_1 &= \mathbf{E}_1 + 3\mathbf{E}_2, \\ T_1\mathbf{E}_2 &= \mathbf{E}_1 + \mathbf{E}_2, & T_2\mathbf{E}_2 &= -\mathbf{E}_1 + 2\mathbf{E}_2. \end{aligned}$$

Thus, with respect to the standard basis, T_1 corresponds to $\begin{bmatrix} 2 & 1 \\ -1 & 1 \end{bmatrix}$ and T_2 to $\begin{bmatrix} 1 & -1 \\ 3 & 2 \end{bmatrix}$. What is the matrix of the linear transformation $T_1 + T_2$? We have

$$\begin{aligned} (T_1 + T_2)(\mathbf{E}_1) &= (2\mathbf{E}_1 - \mathbf{E}_2) + (\mathbf{E}_1 + 3\mathbf{E}_2) = (2 + 1)\mathbf{E}_1 + (-1 + 3)\mathbf{E}_2, \\ (T_1 + T_2)(\mathbf{E}_2) &= (\mathbf{E}_1 + \mathbf{E}_2) + (-\mathbf{E}_1 + 2\mathbf{E}_2) = (1 - 1)\mathbf{E}_1 + (1 + 2)\mathbf{E}_2, \end{aligned}$$

and so $T_1 + T_2$ corresponds to $\begin{bmatrix} 3 & 0 \\ 2 & 3 \end{bmatrix}$.

Example 1 makes it reasonable to say that $\begin{bmatrix} 2 & 1 \\ -1 & 1 \end{bmatrix}$ plus $\begin{bmatrix} 1 & -1 \\ 3 & 2 \end{bmatrix}$ equals $\begin{bmatrix} 3 & 0 \\ 2 & 3 \end{bmatrix}$. Note that the components of the sum are obtained by simply adding the corresponding components of the original two matrices. This process is easily seen to apply in general.

Let T_1, T_2 be two linear transformations from V to W and $\{\mathbf{X}_i\}$, $\{\mathbf{X}'_i\}$ be bases for V and W, respectively. Assume, further, that we know the matrices $A = [a_{ij}]$ and $B = [b_{ij}]$ of T_1 and T_2. This means that

$$\begin{aligned} T_1\mathbf{X}_j &= a_{1j}\mathbf{X}'_1 + a_{2j}\mathbf{X}'_2 + \cdots + a_{mj}\mathbf{X}'_m, \\ T_2\mathbf{X}_j &= b_{1j}\mathbf{X}'_1 + a_{2j}\mathbf{X}'_2 + \cdots + a_{mj}\mathbf{X}'_m, \end{aligned} \qquad \text{for } j = 1, 2, \ldots, n. \tag{3.7}$$

What is the matrix of $T_1 + T_2$ with respect to the bases $\{\mathbf{X}_i\}$ and $\{\mathbf{X}'_j\}$?

$$\begin{aligned} (T_1 + T_2)\mathbf{X}_j &= T_1\mathbf{X}_j + T_2\mathbf{X}_j \\ &= a_{1j}\mathbf{X}'_1 + \cdots + a_{mj}\mathbf{X}'_m + b_{1j}\mathbf{X}'_1 + \cdots + b_{mj}\mathbf{X}'_m. \end{aligned}$$

Upon collecting terms we get

$$(T_1 + T_2)\mathbf{X}_j = (a_{1j} + b_{1j})\mathbf{X}'_1 + (a_{2j} + b_{2j})\mathbf{X}'_2 + \cdots + (a_{mj} + b_{mj})\mathbf{X}'_m.$$

Thus the jth column of the matrix of $T_1 + T_2$ is obtained by adding corresponding elements of the jth columns of A and B. If we call the matrix of

$T_1 + T_2$, $C = [c_{ij}]$, then in symbols $c_{ij} = a_{ij} + b_{ij}$. Having arrived so easily at this result, can we find the matrix of aT_1, where a is any scalar?

$$\begin{aligned}(aT_1)\mathbf{X}_j = a(T_1\mathbf{X}_j) &= a(a_{1j}\mathbf{X}'_1 + \cdots + a_{mj}\mathbf{X}'_m) \\ &= aa_{1j}\mathbf{X}'_1 + aa_{2j}\mathbf{X}'_2 + \cdots + aa_{mj}\mathbf{X}'_m.\end{aligned}$$

Thus to get the matrix of aT_1 simply multiply every element of A by a.

The previous discussion serves to motivate our definition of addition and scalar multiplication of matrices.

DEFINITION 3.10. If A and B are $m \times n$ matrices whose elements in the ith row and jth column are a_{ij} and b_{ij}, respectively, then the matrix $A + B$ is the $m \times n$ matrix whose element in the ith row jth column is $a_{ij} + b_{ij}$, and aA is the $m \times n$ matrix with aa_{ij} in its ith row jth column.

In Definition 3.10 the reader will probably have matrices with real numbers as entries in mind; note, however, that the definition (and the preceding discussion) is valid for matrices over any field, with a from this scalar field.

Things have gone so well that one might be tempted to guess about "multiplication" of matrices. Unfortunately we are in for a bit of ugly calculation. Consider one point: If T_1 is a linear transformation from V to W_1 and T_2 a linear transformation from W_1 to W_2, and the dimensions of V, W_1, W_2 are n, m, p, respectively, then T_1 will have an $m \times n$ matrix, T_2 will have a $p \times m$ matrix, but T_2T_1, being a transformation from V to W_2, will have a $p \times n$ matrix. Thus our definition of the "product" of two matrices will have to yield that a $p \times m$ matrix times an $m \times n$ matrix is a $p \times n$ matrix.

The only way to get the full story is to see what the matrix of T_2T_1 is in terms of the matrix of T_1 and the matrix of T_2. As before, pick bases $\{\mathbf{X}_i\}$, $\{\mathbf{X}'_i\}$, $\{\mathbf{X}''_i\}$ for V, W_1, W_2, respectively, and assume that T_1 has $A = [a_{ij}]$ as its matrix with respect to $\{\mathbf{X}_i\}$ and $\{\mathbf{X}'_i\}$, while T_2 has $B = [b_{ij}]$ as its matrix with respect to $\{\mathbf{X}'_i\}$ and $\{\mathbf{X}''_i\}$. We must calculate the effect of T_2T_1 on an arbitrary $\mathbf{X}_j$.

$$\begin{aligned}(T_2T_1)\mathbf{X}_j &= T_2(a_{1j}\mathbf{X}'_1 + a_{2j}\mathbf{X}'_2 + \cdots + a_{mj}\mathbf{X}'_m) \\ &= a_{1j}T_2\mathbf{X}'_1 + a_{2j}T_2\mathbf{X}'_2 + \cdots + a_{mj}T_2\mathbf{X}'_m \\ &= a_{1j}(b_{11}\mathbf{X}''_1 + b_{21}\mathbf{X}''_2 + \cdots + b_{p1}\mathbf{X}''_p) \\ &\quad + a_{2j}(b_{12}\mathbf{X}''_1 + b_{22}\mathbf{X}''_2 + \cdots + b_{p2}\mathbf{X}''_p) + \cdots \\ &\quad + a_{mj}(b_{1m}\mathbf{X}''_1 + b_{2m}\mathbf{X}''_2 + \cdots + b_{pm}\mathbf{X}''_p).\end{aligned}$$

Finally we need to collect the coefficients of each $\mathbf{X}''_i$.

$$\begin{aligned}(T_2T_1)\mathbf{X}_j &= (a_{1j}b_{11} + a_{2j}b_{12} + \cdots + a_{mj}b_{1m})\mathbf{X}''_1 \\ &\quad + (a_{1j}b_{21} + a_{2j}b_{22} + \cdots + a_{mj}b_{2m})\mathbf{X}''_2 + \cdots \\ &\quad + (a_{1j}b_{p1} + a_{2j}b_{p2} + \cdots + a_{mj}b_{pm})\mathbf{X}''_p.\end{aligned}$$

To summarize, the coefficient of $\mathbf{X}''_1$ is just $a_{1j}b_{i1} + a_{2j}b_{i2} + \cdots + a_{mj}b_{im}$. In practice, it is more convenient to rewrite this as

$$b_{i1}a_{1j} + b_{i2}a_{2j} + \cdots + b_{im}a_{mj}. \tag{3.8}$$

The expression (3.8) is, then, the element in the ith row and jth column of the matrix of T_2T_1. We seek another way of viewing the expression (3.8) to make it easier to remember. Note that if $\mathbf{B}_i$ denotes the ith row of B considered as an m-vector, and $\mathbf{A}^j$ (superscript, but not exponent) denotes the m-vector whose components are the elements of the jth column of A (read in descending order), then the expression (3.8) is just $(\mathbf{B}_i, \mathbf{A}^j)$.

DEFINITION 3.11. If B is a $p \times m$ matrix and A is an $m \times n$ matrix, and the m-vectors $\mathbf{B}_i$, $\mathbf{A}^j$ are defined as above, then BA is defined to be the $p \times n$ matrix whose element in the ith row and jth column is $(\mathbf{B}_i, \mathbf{A}^j)$.

NOTES:

(1) The product BA of two matrices is defined only if the number of columns of B is equal to the number of rows of A.

(2) The rule for calculating expression (3.8) is best remembered by the time-honored formula "row of the first, column of the second." That is, to get the element of a particular row and column of the product, take the corresponding row of the first and the corresponding column of the second (visualized as vectors) and take their inner product.

Example 2. Let

$$A = \begin{bmatrix} 1 & -1 & 3 \\ 2 & 0 & 1 \end{bmatrix}, \qquad B = \begin{bmatrix} 1 & -1 \\ 2 & 3 \\ 1 & 4 \end{bmatrix}.$$

Then

$$BA = \begin{bmatrix} ([1, -1], [1, 2]) & ([1, -1], [-1, 0]) & ([1, -1], [3, 1]) \\ ([2, 3], [1, 2]) & ([2, 3], [-1, 0]) & ([2, 3], [3, 1]) \\ ([1, 4], [1, 2]) & ([1, 4], [-1, 0]) & ([1, 4], [3, 1]) \end{bmatrix}$$

$$= \begin{bmatrix} -1 & -1 & 2 \\ 8 & -2 & 9 \\ 9 & -1 & 7 \end{bmatrix},$$

$$AB = \begin{bmatrix} ([1, -1, 3], [1, 2, 1]) & ([1, -1, 3], [-1, 3, 4]) \\ ([2, 0, 1], [1, 2, 1]) & ([2, 0, 1], [-1, 3, 4]) \end{bmatrix}$$

$$= \begin{bmatrix} 2 & 8 \\ 3 & 2 \end{bmatrix}.$$

Of course, in general, AB does not exist when BA does (take B to be 5×6 and A to be 6×13, for example). The sizes in the above example were selected to indicate the complete lack of commutativity even when both products exist. BA and AB in the example are not even the same size!

In this section we have established an algebra of matrices by taking a mapping from linear transformations to matrices and then defining addition, scalar multiplication, and matrix multiplication so as to make this mapping an isomorphism. Thus all the properties of linear transformations are carried over to matrices. We have the following, then:

THEOREM 3.12. The $m \times n$ matrices over a field form a vector space isomorphic to the space of all linear transformations from V to W, where V and W are spaces over F of dimension n and m, respectively.

Note that there is no *one* special isomorphism in Theorem 3.12; any choice whatever of bases for V and W will give a mapping from Hom (V, W) to the set of all $m \times n$ matrices, and this mapping will always be an isomorphism.

Theorem 3.12 can be used to see that the dimension of Hom (V, W) is mn. An obvious generating set for all $m \times n$ matrices is the set $\{\mathbf{E}_{ij}\}$, where $\mathbf{E}_{ij}$ is the matrix with a 1 in the ith row jth column position and 0's elsewhere.

Since a choice of a basis for a space V gives an isomorphism from Hom (V, V) to the set of all $n \times n$ matrices, we also have the following:

THEOREM 3.13. The set of all $n \times n$ matrices over a field F forms an algebra that is isomorphic to Hom (V, V) *for any vector space V over F of dimension n.*

Since we have many mappings from Hom (V, W) to the $m \times n$ matrices, it is natural to inquire into the relationship between matrices which are the image of the same linear transformation under different choices of bases. We will need further algebraic developments in order to tackle this problem.

Exercises

1. Find the sum of the following matrices:

$$\text{(a)} \begin{bmatrix} 1 & -1 \\ 2 & 0 \end{bmatrix} + \begin{bmatrix} -1 & 2 \\ 3 & 1 \end{bmatrix}, \qquad \text{(b)} \begin{bmatrix} 1 & 2 & -1 \\ 0 & 1 & 3 \end{bmatrix} + \begin{bmatrix} 1 & 3 & 5 \\ 2 & 4 & 6 \end{bmatrix}.$$

2. Show that the matrices $3\begin{bmatrix} 1 & 0 & -2 \\ 1 & 0 & 1 \end{bmatrix}$ and $\begin{bmatrix} 3 & 0 \\ 0 & 3 \end{bmatrix}\begin{bmatrix} 1 & 0 & -2 \\ 1 & 0 & 1 \end{bmatrix}$ are equal.
3. Generalize Exercise 2 to express the matrix $a[a_{ij}]$ as a product of two matrices.
4. Find the products listed, if they exist, among:

$$A = \begin{bmatrix} 1 & -1 \\ 2 & 3 \end{bmatrix}, \qquad B = \begin{bmatrix} 1 & 1 & 1 \\ -1 & 2 & 4 \end{bmatrix},$$

$$C = \begin{bmatrix} 1 & 0 & 0 \\ 0 & 1 & 0 \\ 0 & 1 & 1 \end{bmatrix}, \qquad D = \begin{bmatrix} 1 & 1 \\ -1 & 1 \\ 2 & 3 \end{bmatrix}.$$

(a) AD; (b) $(AB)C$; (c) $A(BC)$; (d) BD; (e) BDA; (f) ABD; (g) CB; (h) A^2.

5. Let T: $R^2 \to R^3$ and S: $R^3 \to R^2$ be the linear transformations that correspond to the matrices

$$\mathrm{T} \leftrightarrow \begin{bmatrix} 1 & 2 \\ -1 & 3 \\ 4 & 2 \end{bmatrix}; \qquad \mathrm{S} \leftrightarrow \begin{bmatrix} 0 & 6 & -2 \\ -1 & -1 & 2 \end{bmatrix}$$

with respect to the standard bases (so $\mathbf{TE}_2 = 2\mathbf{E}'_1 + 3\mathbf{E}'_2 + 2\mathbf{E}'_3$, where $\mathbf{E}_2 = [0, 1]$, $\mathbf{E}'_1 = [1, 0, 0]$, etc.). Find the matrix of ST *without* using the rule of Definition 3.10. That is, in this particular example, carry out the calculations done in the text to derive expression (3.8).

6. Let linear transformations T and S from R^3 to R^3 correspond, with respect to the standard $\{\mathbf{E}_i\}$ basis, to the matrices

$$\mathrm{T} \leftrightarrow \begin{bmatrix} 1 & 2 & -1 \\ 1 & 0 & 1 \\ 0 & 2 & 1 \end{bmatrix}; \qquad \mathrm{S} \leftrightarrow \begin{bmatrix} 1 & -1 & 1 \\ 1 & 2 & 0 \\ 1 & 1 & 0 \end{bmatrix}$$

Find:

(a) the image of $[1, -1, 0]$ under T,
(b) the image of $[-1, 1, -2]$ under S,
(c) the matrix of ST,
(d) the matrix of T + S,
(e) the image of $[1, -1, 0]$ under ST; compare your answer with the result of part (b).

7. Given $A = \begin{bmatrix} 1 & -1 \\ 2 & 1 \end{bmatrix}$, $B = \begin{bmatrix} 1 & 2 \\ 1 & 1 \end{bmatrix}$. Is $AB = BA$?

8. (a) Find all 2×2 matrices that commute with the matrix

$$\begin{bmatrix} \cos\theta & -\sin\theta \\ \sin\theta & \cos\theta \end{bmatrix}.$$

(b) Find the matrix of T_θ with respect to the standard $\{\mathbf{E}_i\}$ basis.
(c) What linear transformations commute with T_θ? Give your answer in geometric, not matrix, terms.

9. Let $(a + bi)$ be an element of the ring of complex numbers

$$(a + bi) + (c + di) = (a + c) + (b + d)i;$$
$$(a + bi)(c + di) = (ac - bd) + (ad + bc)i.$$

Show that the correspondence $a + bi \rightarrow \begin{bmatrix} a & b \\ -b & a \end{bmatrix}$ is an isomorphism of the ring of complex numbers to the set of matrices of this type.

10. Write out the details of a proof that the $\mathbf{E}_{ij}$ matrices are a linearly independent generating set for the space of all $m \times n$ matrices.

11. In the matrix product of an $m \times n$ matrix $A = [a_{ij}]$ with an $n \times p$ matrix $B = [b_{ij}]$, show that the ith row of AB is a linear combination of the rows of B. Show that the jth column of AB is a linear combination of the columns of A. We are here regarding rows and columns as vectors in the same sense as we did in the discussion of the product rule.

3.6 Systems of Linear Equations

It has previously been mentioned that matrices are very useful for "keeping things in their place"; that is, as notational devices when large arrays of numbers are involved in a calculation. In this section we digress from the study of linear transformations and discuss the solution of systems of linear equations. We will find the matrix notation very helpful, both as a computational aid and as a device to help in the visualization of the problems under consideration.

Consider the system of equations

$$\begin{aligned} a_{11}x_1 + a_{12}x_2 + \cdots + a_{1k}x_k &= 0, \\ a_{21}x_1 + a_{22}x_2 + \cdots + a_{2k}x_k &= 0, \\ &\vdots \\ a_{n1}x_1 + a_{n2}x_2 + \cdots + a_{nk}x_k &= 0. \end{aligned}$$

The a_{ij}'s are fixed numbers and the x_i's are unknowns. Such a system will be called a *linear homogeneous* system of equations; linear meaning that all unknowns occur to the first power, and homogeneous meaning that the numbers on the right-hand side of the equations are all zero. If some of these numbers are nonzero the system will be said to be *nonhomogeneous.*

We can express Equations (3.9) very simply in matrix terms. Set

$$X = \begin{bmatrix} x_1 \\ x_2 \\ \vdots \\ x_k \end{bmatrix} \tag{3.9}$$

and $A = [a_{ij}]$; then (3.9) can be written economically as

$$AX = 0; \tag{3.10}$$

the 0 on the right stands for the $n \times 1$ matrix with all zero entries. In this notation A is called the matrix of coefficients of the system (3.9).

If we let $\mathbf{A}^j = [a_{1j}, a_{2j}, \ldots, a_{nj}]$ ($\mathbf{A}^j$ is the jth column of A regarded as a vector), then (3.9) and (3.10) are equivalent to the equation

$$x_1\mathbf{A}^1 + x_2\mathbf{A}^2 + \cdots + x_k\mathbf{A}^k = \mathbf{0}. \tag{3.11}$$

By equivalent we simply mean that any k numbers, $x_1, x_2, \ldots, x_k$ that satisfy any of (3.9), (3.10), (3.11) also satisfy the others.

We note that (3.11) will have a nontrivial (at least one x_i not zero) solution exactly when the columns of A are linearly dependent. This fact is of sufficient importance to state as a theorem.

THEOREM 3.14. *The system of equations (3.9) has a nonzero solution if and only if the vectors formed from the columns of the matrix of coefficients are linearly dependent.*

Recall from the previous section that the set of all $k \times 1$ matrices forms a vector space with addition given by

$$\begin{bmatrix} a_1 \\ a_2 \\ \vdots \\ a_k \end{bmatrix} + \begin{bmatrix} b_1 \\ b_2 \\ \vdots \\ b_k \end{bmatrix} = \begin{bmatrix} a_1 + b_1 \\ a_2 + b_2 \\ \vdots \\ a_k + b_k \end{bmatrix}$$

and scalar multiplication by

$$a \begin{bmatrix} a_1 \\ a_2 \\ \vdots \\ a_k \end{bmatrix} = \begin{bmatrix} aa_1 \\ aa_2 \\ \vdots \\ aa_k \end{bmatrix}.$$

We are interested in the subset of this space consisting of the solutions to a fixed system (3.9).

THEOREM 3.15. *The set of all X that satisfy $AX = 0$ for a fixed A is a subspace of the space of all $k \times 1$ matrices.*

PROOF. If

$$X = \begin{bmatrix} x_1 \\ x_2 \\ \vdots \\ x_k \end{bmatrix} \quad \text{and} \quad Y = \begin{bmatrix} y_1 \\ y_2 \\ \vdots \\ y_k \end{bmatrix}$$

are two solutions, then $A(X + Y) = AX + AY = 0 + 0 = 0$. Thus the sum of two solutions is a solution. We also have that $A(aX) = a(AX)$ (prove!). So a constant multiple of a solution is a solution and we have shown that the set of solutions is in fact a subspace. Because of Theorem 3.15, we often refer to the "space" of solutions to a homogeneous system of equations.

What can be said about the nonhomogeneous case? If we let

$$B = \begin{bmatrix} b_1 \\ b_2 \\ \vdots \\ b_n \end{bmatrix},$$

the nonhomogeneous system may be written as

$$\begin{aligned} a_{11}x_1 + a_{12}x_2 + \cdots + a_{1k}x_k &= b_1, \\ a_{21}x_1 + a_{22}x_2 + \cdots + a_{2k}x_k &= b_2, \\ &\vdots \\ a_{n1}x_1 + a_{n2}x_2 + \cdots + a_{nk}x_k &= b_n \end{aligned} \tag{3.12}$$

or, more simply, as $AX = B$.

THEOREM 3.16. *If A, X, B are as above:*

(i) *The system $AX = B$ has a solution if and only if B is in the linear span of the vectors $A^1, A^2, \ldots, A^k$. (Remember that these column matrices are vectors in the space of all $n \times 1$ matrices.)*

(ii) *If X_0 is a fixed solution of $AX = B$, then any other solution is of the form $X_0 + Y$, where Y is a solution of $AX = 0$.*

PROOF. If we observe that (3.12) can also be written as

$$x_1A^1 + x_2A^2 + \cdots + x_kA^k = B,$$

then assertion (i) is clear.

Part (ii) is easily checked. If $AX_0 = B$ and $AY = 0$, then certainly

$$A(X_0 + Y) = AX_0 + AY = B + 0 = B.$$

Thus a solution to the nonhomogeneous system added to a solution to the corresponding homogeneous system yields another solution to the nonhomogeneous system. On the other hand, if X_1 is some other solution of $AX = B$, then note that

$$X_1 = X_0 + (X_1 - X_0)$$

and

$$A(X_1 - X_0) = AX_1 - AX_0 = B - B = 0.$$

So any solution can be written as X_0 plus a solution to the homogeneous system.

Theorems 3.15 and 3.16 give descriptions of the set of solutions to linear systems which are helpful; but how do we actually "find" all solutions to a given system? The standard technique, called Gaussian elimination or elimination of variables, is to reduce the system to an equivalent system (same solutions) for which the solutions are easily seen. The key to the technique is to note that performing any of the following three operations on a system of equations will result in an equivalent system.

1. Interchange two equations.
2. Add a multiple of one equation to another.
3. Multiply one equation by a *nonzero* constant.

It is clear that an operation of type 1 will have no effect on the set of solutions. To see that a type 2 operation has no effect let us assume that a times equation i has been added to equation j. The system (3.12) becomes

$$\begin{aligned} a_{11}x_1 + a_{12}x_2 \quad + \cdots + \quad & a_{1k}x_k = b_1, \\ &\vdots \\ (a_{j1}x_1 + aa_{i1}x_1) + \cdots + (a_{jk} + & aa_{ik})x_k = b_j + ab_i, \\ &\vdots \\ a_{n1}x_1 \quad + \cdots + \quad & a_{nk}x_k = b_n. \end{aligned} \tag{3.13}$$

It is clear that a solution to (3.12) is also a solution to (3.13) (adding equals to equals gives equals). On the other hand, if $X_0 = [a_1, a_2, \ldots, a_k]$ is a solution to (3.13), it will certainly satisfy every equation of (3.12) except possibly the jth one, but we have

$$a_{i1}a_1 + a_{i2}a_2 + \cdots + a_{ik}a_k = b_i$$

and

$$(a_{j1} + aa_{i1})a_1 + \cdots + (a_{jk} + aa_{ik})a_k = b_j + ab_j$$

since X_0 satisfies (3.13). Now if we multiply the first equation above by $-a$ and add to the second equation, we obtain

$$a_{j1}a_1 + a_{j2}a_2 + \cdots + a_{jk}a_k = b_j.$$

So X_0 satisfies every equation in (3.12).

The proof that operations of type 3 do not change the set of solutions is left to the reader.

The idea of Gaussian elimination is to eliminate one variable from all equations except the first, then eliminate a second variable from all equations except the second, and so on until this is no longer possible. The method is best seen by example.

Example 1. We seek all solutions to the system of equations:

$$\begin{aligned}
x_1 + 3x_2 - 2x_3 - x_4 + 2x_5 &= 1,\\
2x_1 + 6x_2 - 4x_3 - 2x_4 + 4x_5 &= 2,\\
x_1 + 3x_2 - 2x_3 + x_4 &= -1,\\
2x_1 + 6x_2 + x_3 - x_4 &= 4.
\end{aligned}$$

We first "eliminate" x_1 from all equations but the first by adding -2 times the first equation to the second equation, adding -1 times the first equation to the third equation, and finally adding -2 times the first equation to the fourth equation. This sequence of type 2 operations yields the system

$$\begin{aligned}
x_1 + 3x_2 - 2x_3 - x_4 + 2x_5 &= 1,\\
0 &= 0,\\
2x_4 - 2x_5 &= -2,\\
5x_3 + x_4 - 4x_5 &= 2.
\end{aligned}$$

To start the second stage we interchange the second and fourth equations, and multiply the new second equation by $\frac{1}{5}$. We then eliminate x_3 from the first equation with a type 2 operation. The result of all this is

$$\begin{aligned}
x_1 + 3x_2 - \tfrac{3}{5}x_4 + \tfrac{2}{5}x_5 &= \tfrac{9}{5},\\
x_3 + \tfrac{1}{5}x_4 - \tfrac{4}{5}x_5 &= \tfrac{2}{5},\\
2x_4 - 2x_5 &= -2,\\
0 &= 0.
\end{aligned}$$

In the third stage we multiply the third equation by $\frac{1}{2}$ and use it to eliminate x_4 from the first two equations:

$$\begin{aligned}
x_1 + 3x_2 - \tfrac{1}{5}x_5 &= \tfrac{6}{5},\\
x_3 - \tfrac{3}{5}x_5 &= \tfrac{3}{5},\\
x_4 - x_5 &= -1,\\
0 &= 0.
\end{aligned}$$

The process now terminates. It is easy to find particular solutions to the last set of equations. Pick x_5 to be any number; the third equation then determines x_4 and the second determines x_3.

Now a further choice of x_2 and the first equation will determine x_1. For example, if we choose $x_5 = 1$ and $x_2 = -1$, we have

$$x_4 = -1 + x_5 = 0,$$
$$x_3 = \tfrac{3}{5} + \tfrac{3}{5}x_5 = \tfrac{6}{5}$$

and

$$x_1 = \tfrac{6}{5} - 3x_2 + \tfrac{1}{5}x_5 = \tfrac{22}{5}.$$

Thus a particular solution is given by

$$\begin{bmatrix} \frac{22}{5} \\ -1 \\ \frac{6}{5} \\ 0 \\ 1 \end{bmatrix}.$$

In general, if $x_5 = a$ and $x_2 = b$, then

$$x_4 = -1 + a,$$
$$x_3 = \tfrac{3}{5} + \tfrac{3}{5},$$

and

$$x_1 = \tfrac{6}{5} - 3b + \tfrac{1}{5}a.$$

So the set of solutions is the set of all 5×1 matrices of the form

$$\begin{bmatrix} \frac{6}{5} + \frac{1}{5}a - 3b \\ b \\ \frac{3}{5} + \frac{3}{5}a \\ -1 + a \\ a \end{bmatrix}.$$

Solving systems of linear equations, as we have seen, involves a great deal of calculation. We can reduce the effort somewhat by noticing that there is no need to "carry" the variables along at each stage. Matrix notation facilitates this process. Given a system

$$AX = B,$$

form the matrix $[A : B]$ formed by adding the column B to the right of A. This new matrix is called the *augmented matrix* of the system $AX = B$.

Now the three operations that we use to reduce systems of equations correspond to the following operations on the augmented matrix.

(1′) Interchange two rows.
(2′) Add a multiple of one row to another row.
(3′) Multiply a row by a nonzero constant.

Example 2. The system in Example 1 has augmented matrix

$$\begin{bmatrix} 1 & 3 & -2 & -1 & 2 & : & 1 \\ 2 & 6 & -4 & -2 & 4 & : & 2 \\ 1 & 3 & -2 & 1 & 0 & : & -1 \\ 2 & 6 & 1 & -1 & 0 & : & 4 \end{bmatrix}.$$

Performing operations (1′), (2′), and (3′) just as in Example 1 yields the following sequence of matrices:

$$\begin{bmatrix} 1 & 3 & -2 & -1 & 2 & : & 1 \\ 0 & 0 & 0 & 0 & 0 & : & 0 \\ 0 & 0 & 0 & 2 & -2 & : & -2 \\ 0 & 0 & 5 & 1 & -4 & : & 2 \end{bmatrix},$$

$$\begin{bmatrix} 1 & 3 & 0 & -\frac{3}{5} & \frac{2}{5} & : & \frac{9}{5} \\ 0 & 0 & 1 & \frac{1}{5} & -\frac{4}{5} & : & \frac{2}{5} \\ 0 & 0 & 0 & 2 & -2 & : & -2 \\ 0 & 0 & 0 & 0 & 0 & : & 0 \end{bmatrix},$$

$$\begin{bmatrix} 1 & 3 & 0 & 0 & -\frac{1}{5} & : & \frac{6}{5} \\ 0 & 0 & 1 & 0 & -\frac{3}{5} & : & \frac{3}{5} \\ 0 & 0 & 0 & 1 & -1 & : & -1 \\ 0 & 0 & 0 & 0 & 0 & : & 0 \end{bmatrix}.$$

The last matrix corresponds to a system whose solutions are easily seen.

Example 3. Consider the system

$$\begin{aligned} x_1 + 2x_2 + x_3 &= 8, \\ -2x_1 - 3x_2 - x_3 &= -11, \\ x_1 + 4x_2 + 4x_3 &= 21. \end{aligned}$$

The corresponding augmented matrix is

$$\begin{bmatrix} 1 & 2 & 1 & : & 8 \\ -2 & -3 & -1 & : & -11 \\ 1 & 4 & 4 & : & 21 \end{bmatrix}.$$

Using the first row and two operations of type 2′ yields

$$\begin{bmatrix} 1 & 2 & 1 & : & 8 \\ 0 & 1 & 1 & : & 5 \\ 0 & 2 & 3 & : & 13 \end{bmatrix}.$$

Now use the second row to obtain

$$\begin{bmatrix} 1 & 0 & -1 & : & -2 \\ 0 & 1 & 1 & : & 5 \\ 0 & 0 & 1 & : & 3 \end{bmatrix}.$$

Finally, subtracting the third row from the second and adding the third row to the first yields

$$\begin{bmatrix} 1 & 0 & 0 & : & 1 \\ 0 & 1 & 0 & : & 2 \\ 0 & 0 & 1 & : & 3 \end{bmatrix},$$

which corresponds to the system

$$\begin{aligned} x_1 \quad\quad\quad &= 1, \\ x_2 \quad\quad &= 2, \\ x_3 &= 3, \end{aligned}$$

whose solutions are obvious.

We give one final example to illustrate the method.

Example 4

$$
\begin{aligned}
x_1 + 2x_2 - 2x_3 &= 13,\\
2x_1 - x_2 + x_3 &= -2,\\
x_1 + x_2 - x_3 &= 7.
\end{aligned}
\tag{3.14}
$$

The augmented matrix is

$$\begin{bmatrix} 1 & 2 & -2 & : & 13 \\ 2 & -1 & 1 & : & -2 \\ 1 & 1 & -1 & : & 7 \end{bmatrix};$$

we proceed to "reduce" it using our three operations.

$$\begin{bmatrix} 1 & 2 & -2 & : & 13 \\ 0 & -5 & 5 & : & -28 \\ 0 & -1 & 1 & : & -6 \end{bmatrix},$$

$$\begin{bmatrix} 1 & 2 & -2 & : & 13 \\ 0 & -1 & 1 & : & -6 \\ 0 & -5 & 5 & : & -28 \end{bmatrix}.$$

This last exchange of rows is not essential, but it avoids fractions.

$$\begin{bmatrix} 1 & 0 & 0 & : & 1 \\ 0 & -1 & 1 & : & -6 \\ 0 & 0 & 0 & : & 2 \end{bmatrix}.$$

This last matrix corresponds to the system

$$
\begin{aligned}
x_1 \qquad\qquad &= 1,\\
-x_2 + x_3 &= -6,\\
0 &= 2.
\end{aligned}
$$

The third equation is false, no matter what numbers one chooses for x_1, x_2, and x_3. What does this mean? Simply that (3.14) has no solutions (just as the last system). Upon reflection, this is not so surprising. Many systems have no solutions. For example,

$$
\begin{aligned}
x_1 + x_2 &= 3,\\
x_1 + x_2 &= -1.
\end{aligned}
$$

By performing operations of types 1, 2, and 3, one can transform such a system into a system that looks plausible enough, but which in fact has no solutions.

Exercises

1. Determine all solutions of the system of equations

$$
\begin{aligned}
3c_1 + 2c_2 - c_3 &= 0,\\
c_1 + 3c_2 + 2c_3 &= 0,\\
-2c_1 + c_2 + 3c_3 &= 0.
\end{aligned}
$$

2. The number of solutions of the equations of Exercise 1 determines the linear independence or dependence of a certain set of vectors in R^3 (see Theorem 3.14). List these vectors and state whether they are linearly dependent or independent.

3. Determine whether or not the following vectors are linearly independent. If not, express $\mathbf{A}_3$ as a linear combination of $\mathbf{A}_1$ and $\mathbf{A}_2$.
(a) $\mathbf{A}_1 = [1, 2, -1]$, $\mathbf{A}_2 = [2, 1, 4]$, $\mathbf{A}_3 = [-1, 7, -17]$;
(b) $\mathbf{A}_1 = [2, 1]$, $\mathbf{A}_2 = [1, 1]$, $\mathbf{A}_3 = [4, 5]$;
(c) $\mathbf{A}_1 = [3, 1, 0, 1]$, $\mathbf{A}_2 = [1, 4, -1, 0]$, $\mathbf{A}_3 = [0, 1, -1, 0]$.
4. Determine all solutions of the system of linear equations

$$\begin{aligned} c_1 + 2c_2 + c_3 + 2c_4 &= 6, \\ 2c_1 - c_2 + 3c_3 + 6c_4 &= 10, \\ 3c_1 + c_2 + 4c_3 + 8c_4 &= 16, \\ c_1 - 3c_2 + 2c_3 + 4c_4 &= 4. \end{aligned}$$

5. Is the vector $[6, 10, 16, 4]$ contained in the vector space

$$V = L\{[1, 2, 3, 1], [2, -1, 1, -3], [2, 6, 8, 4]\}?$$

6. Solve the system of linear equations

$$\begin{aligned} c_1 - 2c_2 + 3c_3 &= 0, \\ 3c_1 + 2c_2 - c_3 &= 0, \\ 2c_1 + c_2 + 5c_3 &= 0, \\ -c_1 + 4c_2 + c_3 &= 0. \end{aligned}$$

What statement can you make concerning the linear independence or linear dependence of the vectors $[1, 3, 2, -1]$, $[-2, 2, 1, 4]$, and $[3, -1, 5, 1]$ from the solution of the linear equations above?
7. Solve the system of linear equations

$$\begin{aligned} c_1 - 2c_2 + 3c_3 + c_4 &= 0, \\ -2c_1 + c_2 + c_3 - 2c_4 &= 0, \\ c_2 - c_3 + 3c_4 &= 0. \end{aligned}$$

8. Verify that performing an operation of type 3 on a system of equations does not affect the set of solutions.
9. Determine a value of k that makes the following vectors linearly dependent: $[1, 2, k]$, $[0, 1, k - 1]$, $[3, 4, 3]$.

3.7 Nonsingular Linear Transformations and Matrices

The subject of one-to-one morphisms (linear transformations) between vector spaces was discussed in Section 3.2. Here we wish to consider these mappings at some length and to examine the relationship between such transformations and their matrices. The reader would do well to review the theorems of Section 3.2, in particular Theorem 3.5, which gives several equivalent conditions for a linear transformation to be one-to-one.

In this section we will restrict our attention to linear transformations on a vector space; that is, to mappings with the same space as domain and range. Further, when discussing the matrix of a linear transformation we shall usually use the same basis in the range and domain, saying, "A is the matrix of T with respect to the basis $\{\mathbf{X}_i\}$" in this case. In particular we shall be interested in the identity transformation I, which is defined by $\mathrm{I}(\mathbf{X}) = \mathbf{X}$ for every $\mathbf{X}$. Note that if $\mathbf{X}_1, \ldots, \mathbf{X}_n$ is any basis for V, then

$$\begin{aligned} \mathrm{I}(\mathbf{X}_1) &= 1 \cdot \mathbf{X}_1 + 0 \cdot \mathbf{X}_2 + \cdots + 0 \cdot \mathbf{X}_n, \\ \mathrm{I}(\mathbf{X}_2) &= 0 \cdot \mathbf{X}_1 + 1 \cdot \mathbf{X}_2 + 0 \cdot \mathbf{X}_3 + \cdots + 0 \cdot \mathbf{X}_n, \\ &\vdots \\ \mathrm{I}(\mathbf{X}_n) &= 0 \cdot \mathbf{X}_1 + \cdots + 0 \cdot \mathbf{X}_{n-1} + 1 \cdot \mathbf{X}_n, \end{aligned}$$

and thus the matrix of I is

$$\begin{bmatrix} 1 & 0 & & & \cdots & 0 \\ 0 & 1 & 0 & & \cdots & 0 \\ 0 & 0 & 1 & 0 & \cdots & 0 \\ \vdots & \vdots & & & & \vdots \\ & & & & & 0 \\ 0 & 0 & & & \cdots & 1 \end{bmatrix}$$

with respect to *any basis whatever*. We will often refer to this as the identity matrix, and will also denote it by I.

Suppose T: $V \to V$ is a linear transformation. Under what circumstances can we find a linear transformation S: $V \to V$ such that ST $=$ I? It is clear that the kernel of T must consist of the zero vector alone, for suppose $\mathrm{T}\mathbf{X} = \mathbf{0}$ for some $\mathbf{X} \neq \mathbf{0}$. Then $\mathrm{ST}(\mathbf{X}) = \mathrm{S}(\mathbf{0}) = \mathbf{0} \neq \mathbf{X}$. But this condition is also sufficient, for it implies that T is an isomorphism. (If $\mathrm{T}(\mathbf{X}) = \mathrm{T}(\mathbf{Y})$, $\mathrm{T}(\mathbf{X} - \mathbf{Y}) = \mathbf{0}$ so $\mathbf{X} = \mathbf{Y}$.) In this case we simply define $\mathrm{S}(\mathbf{Y})$ to be the unique $\mathbf{X}$ for which $\mathrm{T}(\mathbf{X}) = \mathbf{Y}$.

Example 1. Let T be the linear transformation on R^2 defined by

$$\mathrm{T}[x_1, x_2] = [x_2, 2x_1 + x_2].$$

If $\mathrm{T}[x_1, x_2] = [0, 0]$, then $x_2 = 0$ from the first coordinate of the image and $0 = 2x_1 + x_2 = 2x_1$ from the second. Thus the kernel of T is $\{\mathbf{0}\}$. To determine S so that ST $=$ I we use the fact that $\mathrm{S}[y_1, y_2]$ is the pair $[x_1, x_2]$, which satisfies $\mathrm{T}[x_1, x_2] = [y_1, y_2]$. We solve

$$\begin{aligned} x_2 &= y_1, \\ 2x_1 + x_2 &= y_2, \end{aligned}$$

for x_1, x_2 in terms of y_1, y_2 yielding

$$x_1 = \frac{y_2 - y_1}{2}, \qquad x_2 = y_1.$$

Thus

$$\mathrm{S}[y_1, y_2] = \left[\frac{y_2 - y_1}{2}, y_1\right].$$

Note that S is actually a linear transformation, with matrix $\begin{bmatrix} -\frac{1}{2} & \frac{1}{2} \\ 1 & 0 \end{bmatrix}$ with respect to the standard basis. As the matrix of T in this basis is $\begin{bmatrix} 0 & 1 \\ 2 & 1 \end{bmatrix}$ we have

$$\begin{bmatrix} -\frac{1}{2} & \frac{1}{2} \\ 1 & 0 \end{bmatrix} \begin{bmatrix} 0 & 1 \\ 2 & 1 \end{bmatrix} = \begin{bmatrix} 1 & 0 \\ 0 & 1 \end{bmatrix}.$$

The fact that the mapping S of Example 1 turned out to be linear is not an accident; S will always be linear. In fact, much more can be said.

THEOREM 3.17. Let T *be an isomorphism on* V.

(i) *There exists one and only one mapping* S *such that* ST $=$ I.
(ii) *The mapping* S *of* (i) *is linear.*
(iii) *The mapping* S *also satisfies* TS $=$ I.

PROOF. Let us first prove (ii), that is, that any S which satisfies ST $=$ I is linear. If $\mathbf{Y}_1$, $\mathbf{Y}_2$ are any two vectors of V we can find $\mathbf{X}_1$, $\mathbf{X}_2$ such that $\mathrm{T}\mathbf{X}_1 = \mathbf{Y}_1$ and $\mathrm{T}\mathbf{X}_2 = \mathbf{Y}_2$. Since T is linear we have

$$\mathrm{T}(\mathbf{X}_1 + \mathbf{X}_2) = \mathbf{Y}_1 + \mathbf{Y}_2,$$

or

$$S(\mathbf{Y}_1 + \mathbf{Y}_2) = \mathbf{X}_1 + \mathbf{X}_2 = S\mathbf{Y}_1 + S\mathbf{Y}_2.$$

Also

$$T(a\mathbf{X}_1) = aT\mathbf{X}_1 = a\mathbf{Y}_1,$$

so

$$S(a\mathbf{Y}_1) = a\mathbf{X}_1 = aS\mathbf{Y}_1$$

and S is linear.

To prove (i), let us assume that $S_1T = I = S_2T$. Then $S_1T - S_2T = \mathbf{0}$. If $\mathbf{X}$ is any vector in V, find a $\mathbf{Y}$ such that $T\mathbf{Y} = \mathbf{X}$. Then we have

$$(S_1T - S_2T)(\mathbf{Y}) = \mathbf{0}$$

or

$$S_1T\mathbf{Y} - S_2T\mathbf{Y} = \mathbf{0}$$

and thus

$$S_1\mathbf{X} - S_2\mathbf{X} = \mathbf{0}.$$

We have shown that $S_1\mathbf{X} = S_2\mathbf{X}$ for all $\mathbf{X}$ in V.

To prove (iii), pick any element $\mathbf{Y}$ from V and consider $(TS)(\mathbf{Y}) = T(S\mathbf{Y})$. Recall that $S\mathbf{Y}$ is the unique vector $\mathbf{X}$, which satisfies $T\mathbf{X} = \mathbf{Y}$; thus $T(S\mathbf{Y}) = T\mathbf{X} = \mathbf{Y}$. So $TS(\mathbf{Y}) = \mathbf{Y}$ for every $\mathbf{Y}$ in V, or $TS = I$.

The reader should note that the proofs of parts (i) and (iii) did not require that T be linear. They are statements that are true for any one-to-one function from a set to itself.

DEFINITION 3.12. *A linear transformation from V to V is called* NONSINGULAR *if it is an isomorphism. Linear transformations on V which are not isomorphisms are said to be* SINGULAR.

DEFINITION 3.13. *An $n \times n$ matrix A is called* NONSINGULAR *if there is a matrix B that satisfies $AB = BA = I$. If no such matrix exists, A is said to be* SINGULAR.

DEFINITION 3.14. *If T is a nonsingular linear transformation, the corresponding linear transformation S that satisfies ST = TS = I will be called the* INVERSE *of T, and will usually be denoted T^{-1}. Similarly, if A is a nonsingular matrix, we will call the matrix B that satisfies $AB = BA = I$ the* INVERSE *of A and denote it by A^{-1}.*

The reader should note that if T is a nonsingular linear transformation, then all matrices associated with T (by different choices of basis) are nonsingular. For if A is the matrix of T with respect to some basis, then the matrix B of T^{-1} in this basis will satisfy $AB = BA = I$ because $TT^{-1} = T^{-1}T = I$ and the fact that the identity transformation always has the same matrix.

In the same way, all matrices associated with a singular linear transformation are singular.

Example 2. Let T be the linear transformation on R^3 defined by

$$T[x_1, x_2, x_3] = [x_1 + 2x_2 - x_3, x_1 + 2x_3, 2x_1 - x_2 + 3x_3].$$

The natural basis vectors $\mathbf{E}_1, \mathbf{E}_2, \mathbf{E}_3$ are mapped respectively into $[1, 1, 2]$, $[2, 0, -1]$, and $[-1, 2, 3]$ by T. Thus the matrix of T with respect to the natural basis is

$$\begin{bmatrix} 1 & 2 & -1 \\ 1 & 0 & 2 \\ 2 & -1 & 3 \end{bmatrix}.$$

The three vectors listed can be seen to be linearly independent, and thus T is onto, hence an isomorphism. So we say that both T and the matrix are nonsingular. How do we find T^{-1}? Let us find A^{-1}, the matrix of T^{-1} with respect to the standard basis. We are seeking a matrix $B = [b_{ij}]$ such that

$$\begin{bmatrix} b_{11} & b_{12} & b_{13} \\ b_{21} & b_{22} & b_{23} \\ b_{31} & b_{32} & b_{33} \end{bmatrix} \begin{bmatrix} 1 & 2 & -1 \\ 1 & 0 & 2 \\ 2 & -1 & 3 \end{bmatrix} = \begin{bmatrix} 1 & 0 & 0 \\ 0 & 1 & 0 \\ 0 & 0 & 1 \end{bmatrix}.$$

If we equate the rows of the matrix on the right with the corresponding rows of the product of the two matrices on the left, we will obtain three systems of equations. For example, the first row gives rise to the system

$$\begin{aligned} b_{11} + b_{12} + 2b_{13} &= 1, \\ 2b_{11} \phantom{+ b_{12}} - b_{13} &= 0, \\ -b_{11} + 2b_{12} + 3b_{13} &= 0. \end{aligned}$$

After considerable calculation, the matrix B is found to be

$$\frac{1}{5}\begin{bmatrix} 2 & -5 & 4 \\ 1 & 5 & -3 \\ -1 & 5 & 2 \end{bmatrix}.$$

Fortunately, we will discover later a more efficient method of finding the inverse of a matrix.

Exercises

1. Is the linear transformation on R^2 defined by

$$T[x_1, x_2] = [x_1 - x_2, x_1 + x_2]$$

nonsingular? If so, find its inverse.

2. Answer the question of Exercise 1 if T is defined on R^3 by

$$T[x_1, x_2, x_3] = [x_1 + x_2 + x_3, x_2 + x_3, x_3].$$

3. Write the matrix of T in Exercise 2 with respect to the $\{\mathbf{E}_i\}$ basis. Find the inverse of this matrix if it has one.

4. Show that the mapping T on R^3 defined by

$$T[x_1, x_2, x_3] = [x_1 - 2, x_2, x_1 + x_3]$$

is one-to-one but not linear. Is there a unique T^{-1}?

5. Let $A = \begin{bmatrix} 1 & 0 & 1 \\ 1 & 1 & 0 \end{bmatrix}$, $B = \begin{bmatrix} 1 & -1 \\ -1 & 2 \\ 0 & 1 \end{bmatrix}$.

   (a) Show that $AB = I$, $BA \neq I$.
   (b) Let T_1 be the linear transformation from R^3 to R^2 which has A as its matrix with respect to the $\{\mathbf{E}_i\}$ bases. Similarly let T_2 be the linear transformation from R^2 to R^3 corresponding to B. Which of T_1, T_2 is onto? One-to-one?
   (c) Find a matrix $C \neq A$ such that $CB = I$.
   (d) Find a matrix $D \neq B$ such that $AD = I$.

6. Which of the following matrices are nonsingular?

$$\begin{bmatrix} 1 & -1 & 2 \\ 1 & 1 & 3 \\ 2 & 1 & 1 \end{bmatrix}, \quad \begin{bmatrix} 1 & -1 & 2 \\ 1 & 1 & 4 \\ 1 & 3 & 6 \end{bmatrix}.$$

7. If A and B are nonsingular matrices, show that AB is nonsingular.
8. Use Exercise 8 to prove that the product of two nonsingular linear transformations is nonsingular.
9. Prove that AB is singular if either of the matrices A, B is singular. *Hint:* Consider the linear transformations associated with A, B, and AB.

3.8 Relationship Between Linear Transformations and Matrices Revisited

The first goal of this section is to clarify and simplify the operation of matrices on vectors. So far, if T: $V \to W$ was associated with the matrix A with respect to the bases $\{\mathbf{X}_i\}$ of V and $\{\mathbf{X}_i'\}$ of W, and we wished to calculate

$$\mathbf{Y} = \mathrm{T}\mathbf{X}, \ \mathbf{X} = x_1\mathbf{X}_1 + \cdots + x_n\mathbf{X}_n,$$

we used the formula

$$\mathrm{T}\mathbf{X} = (A_1, [x_1, x_2, \ldots, x_n])\mathbf{X}_1' + (A_2, [x_1, x_2, \ldots, x_n])\mathbf{X}_2' + \cdots + (A_m, [x_1, x_2, \ldots, x_n])\mathbf{X}_m'. \tag{3.15}$$

Note that if

$$\mathrm{T}\mathbf{X} = \mathbf{Y} = y_1\mathbf{X}_1' + y_2\mathbf{X}_2' + \cdots + y_m\mathbf{X}_m',$$

then using matrix notation, Equation (3.15) can be written

$$\underset{m \times n}{\begin{bmatrix} a_{11} & a_{12} & \cdots & a_{1n} \\ a_{21} & a_{22} & \cdots & a_{2n} \\ \vdots & \vdots & & \vdots \\ a_{m1} & a_{m2} & \cdots & a_{mn} \end{bmatrix}} \underset{n \times 1}{\begin{bmatrix} x_1 \\ x_2 \\ \vdots \\ x_n \end{bmatrix}} = \underset{m \times 1}{\begin{bmatrix} y_1 \\ y_2 \\ \vdots \\ y_m \end{bmatrix}}. \tag{3.16}$$

Thus, if we say that

$$\begin{bmatrix} x_1 \\ x_2 \\ \vdots \\ x_n \end{bmatrix}$$

represents $\mathbf{X}$ with respect to $\{\mathbf{X}_i\}$ and

$$\begin{bmatrix} y_1 \\ y_2 \\ \vdots \\ y_m \end{bmatrix}$$

represents $\mathbf{Y}$ relative to $\{\mathbf{X}_i'\}$, the relationship $\mathrm{T}\mathbf{X} = \mathbf{Y}$ is given in matrix terms by

$$A\begin{bmatrix} x_1 \\ x_2 \\ \vdots \\ x_n \end{bmatrix} = \begin{bmatrix} y_1 \\ y_2 \\ \vdots \\ y_m \end{bmatrix}.$$

So far, we have done nothing but express the way matrices represent linear transformations in terms of matrix multiplication instead of in terms of inner products. When the bases used are the standard $\{\mathbf{E}_i\}$ bases, our new technique works particularly well.

Example 1. Let T: $R^3 \to R^2$ have the matrix $A = \begin{bmatrix} 1 & -1 & 2 \\ 0 & 1 & 1 \end{bmatrix}$. What is the image of [2, 1, −1] under T? It is given by

$$\begin{bmatrix} 1 & -1 & 2 \\ 0 & 1 & 1 \end{bmatrix} \begin{bmatrix} 2 \\ 1 \\ -1 \end{bmatrix} = \begin{bmatrix} -1 \\ 0 \end{bmatrix}.$$

That is, T[2, 1, −1] = [−1, 0].

The simplicity of calculation illustrated in Example 1 arises because $[a_1, a_2, \ldots, a_n]$ corresponds to

$$\begin{bmatrix} a_1 \\ a_2 \\ \vdots \\ a_n \end{bmatrix}$$

relative to the standard $\{\mathbf{E}_i\}$ *basis.* If some other basis is under consideration the passage from vector to column matrix is more complicated.

Example 2. Let T be the transformation of Example 1, and endow R^3 with the basis {[1, 1, 0], [0, 1, 1], [1, 0, 1]} and R^2 with {[1, 1], [1, −1]}. The matrix of T relative to these bases is given by

$$\begin{aligned} T[1, 1, 0] &= [1, 0] + [-1, 1] = [0, 1] = \tfrac{1}{2}[1, 1] - \tfrac{1}{2}[1, -1], \\ T[0, 1, 1] &= [-1, 1] + [2, 1] = [1, 2] = \tfrac{3}{2}[1, 1] - \tfrac{1}{2}[1, -1], \\ T[1, 0, 1] &= [1, 0] + [2, 1] = [3, 1] = 2[1, 1] + 1[1, -1]. \end{aligned}$$

Thus the matrix of T relative to these bases is $\begin{bmatrix} \frac{1}{2} & \frac{3}{2} & 2 \\ -\frac{1}{2} & -\frac{1}{2} & 1 \end{bmatrix}$. Again, what is T[2, 1, −1]? If we wish to use this matrix, we must write [2, 1, −1] in terms of the new basis. Solving three equations in three unknowns, we obtain $[2, 1, -1] = 2[1, 1, 0] - 1[0, 1, 1] + 0 \cdot [1, 0, 1]$. Now

$$\begin{bmatrix} \frac{1}{2} & \frac{3}{2} & 2 \\ -\frac{1}{2} & -\frac{1}{2} & 1 \end{bmatrix} \begin{bmatrix} 2 \\ -1 \\ 0 \end{bmatrix} = \begin{bmatrix} -\frac{1}{2} \\ -\frac{1}{2} \end{bmatrix}.$$

Thus $T[2, 1, -1] = -\frac{1}{2}[1, 1] - \frac{1}{2}[1, -1]$ (*not* $[-\frac{1}{2}, -\frac{1}{2}]$), and $-\frac{1}{2}[1, 1] - \frac{1}{2}[1, -1] = [-1, 0]$. This result checks with our calculation in Example 1. Note that if, now, we wish to calculate $T([1, 1, 0] + 2[0, 1, 1] - [1, 0, 1])$ we simply write

$$\begin{bmatrix} \frac{1}{2} & \frac{3}{2} & 2 \\ -\frac{1}{2} & -\frac{1}{2} & 1 \end{bmatrix} \begin{bmatrix} 1 \\ 2 \\ -1 \end{bmatrix} = \begin{bmatrix} \frac{3}{2} \\ -\frac{5}{2} \end{bmatrix},$$

so our answer is $\frac{3}{2}[1, 1] - \frac{5}{2}[1, -1]$.

The reader may ask, "Why not always use the standard basis?" A hint of an answer is at the end of Example 2. If a problem is given in terms of some nonstandard basis, the calculations may be simpler in the given basis. A more important reason is that many of the deep and important results of linear algebra involve relationships that arise when the basis is changed. We must learn to do our calculations with any basis, and to be able to go back and forth between different bases.

In the past (e.g., Example 2) to express a given vector in R^n in terms of a different basis we solved a system of linear equations. We seek a simpler method. Matrices again provide us with the answer. Suppose we have two bases $\{\mathbf{Y}_i\}$ and $\{\mathbf{X}_i\}$ for a space V, and we are able to solve for the following relationships between the bases:

$$\begin{aligned}
\mathbf{Y}_1 &= a_{11}\mathbf{X}_1 + a_{21}\mathbf{X}_2 + \cdots + a_{n1}\mathbf{X}_n, \\
\mathbf{Y}_2 &= a_{12}\mathbf{X}_1 + a_{22}\mathbf{X}_2 + \cdots + a_{n2}\mathbf{X}_n, \\
&\vdots \\
\mathbf{Y}_n &= a_{1n}\mathbf{X}_1 + a_{2n}\mathbf{X}_2 + \cdots + a_{nn}\mathbf{X}_n.
\end{aligned} \tag{3.17}$$

If we are now given a vector in terms of the $\mathbf{Y}_i$'s, say

$$\mathbf{X} = y_1\mathbf{Y}_1 + y_2\mathbf{Y}_2 + \cdots + y_n\mathbf{Y}_n,$$

what is $\mathbf{X}$ in terms of the $\mathbf{X}_i$'s? Clearly,

$$\begin{aligned}
\mathbf{X} = y_1(a_{11}\mathbf{X}_1 + \cdots + a_{n1}\mathbf{X}_n) + y_2(a_{12}\mathbf{X}_1 + \cdots + a_{n2}\mathbf{X}_n) + \cdots \\
+ y_n(a_{1n}\mathbf{X}_1 + \cdots + a_{nn}\mathbf{X}_n);
\end{aligned}$$

rearranging terms,

$$\begin{aligned}
\mathbf{X} = {} & (y_1a_{11} + y_2a_{12} + \cdots + y_na_{1n})\mathbf{X}_1 \\
& + (y_1a_{21} + y_2a_{22} + \cdots + y_na_{2n})\mathbf{X}_2 + \cdots \\
& + (y_1a_{n1} + y_2a_{n2} + \cdots + y_na_{nn})\mathbf{X}_n.
\end{aligned}$$

If we write $\mathbf{X} = x_1\mathbf{X}_1 + x_2\mathbf{X}_2 + \cdots + x_n\mathbf{X}_n$, the last relation above can be stated as

$$\begin{bmatrix} x_1 \\ x_2 \\ \vdots \\ x_n \end{bmatrix} = \begin{bmatrix} a_{11} & a_{12} & \cdots & a_{1n} \\ a_{21} & a_{22} & \cdots & a_{2n} \\ \vdots & \vdots & & \vdots \\ a_{n1} & a_{n2} & \cdots & a_{nn} \end{bmatrix} \begin{bmatrix} y_1 \\ y_2 \\ \vdots \\ y_n \end{bmatrix}.$$

Thus, given a vector in terms of the basis $\{\mathbf{Y}_i\}$, we can write it in terms of the $\{\mathbf{X}_i\}$ basis simply by multiplying by the matrix $A = [a_{ij}]$.

DEFINITION 3.15. *Equations* (3.17) *are called the* EQUATIONS OF CHANGE OF BASIS FROM $\{\mathbf{Y}_i\}$ TO $\{\mathbf{X}_i\}$ *and the matrix A is called the* MATRIX OF CHANGE OF BASIS FROM $\{\mathbf{Y}_i\}$ TO $\{\mathbf{X}_i\}$.

Example 3. Let $\{\mathbf{X}_i\}$ and $\{\mathbf{Y}_i\}$ be the basis for R^3 given in Example 2 and the standard basis, respectively. Equations (3.17) in this case are

$$\begin{aligned}
[1, 0, 0] &= \tfrac{1}{2}[1, 1, 0] - \tfrac{1}{2}[0, 1, 1] + \tfrac{1}{2}[1, 0, 1], \\
[0, 1, 0] &= \tfrac{1}{2}[1, 1, 0] + \tfrac{1}{2}[0, 1, 1] - \tfrac{1}{2}[1, 0, 1], \\
[0, 0, 1] &= -\tfrac{1}{2}[1, 1, 0] + \tfrac{1}{2}[0, 1, 1] + \tfrac{1}{2}[1, 0, 1].
\end{aligned}$$

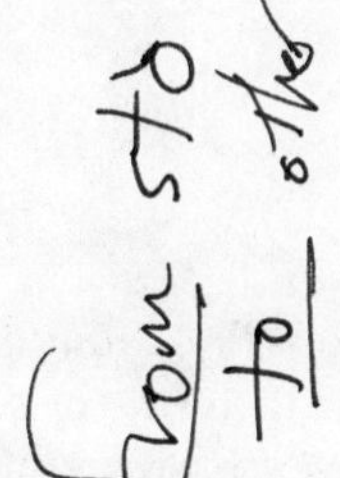

The matrix A is

$$\begin{bmatrix} \frac{1}{2} & \frac{1}{2} & -\frac{1}{2} \\ -\frac{1}{2} & \frac{1}{2} & \frac{1}{2} \\ \frac{1}{2} & -\frac{1}{2} & \frac{1}{2} \end{bmatrix} \quad \text{or} \quad \frac{1}{2}\begin{bmatrix} 1 & 1 & -1 \\ -1 & 1 & 1 \\ 1 & -1 & 1 \end{bmatrix}.$$

What is the vector $[2, 1, -1]$ in terms of the basis $\{\mathbf{X}_i\} = \{[1, 1, 0], [0, 1, 1], [1, 0, 1]\}$?

$$\frac{1}{2}\begin{bmatrix} 1 & 1 & -1 \\ -1 & 1 & 1 \\ 1 & -1 & 1 \end{bmatrix}\begin{bmatrix} 2 \\ 1 \\ -1 \end{bmatrix} = \begin{bmatrix} 2 \\ -1 \\ 0 \end{bmatrix}.$$

Thus $[2, 1, -1] = 2[1, 1, 0] - 1[0, 1, 1] + 0[1, 0, 1]$ (see Example 2). Similarly, to convert $[a, b, c]$ to the $\{\mathbf{X}_i\}$ basis,

$$\frac{1}{2}\begin{bmatrix} 1 & 1 & -1 \\ -1 & 1 & 1 \\ 1 & -1 & 1 \end{bmatrix}\begin{bmatrix} a \\ b \\ c \end{bmatrix} = \frac{1}{2}\begin{bmatrix} a + b - c \\ -a + b + c \\ a - b + c \end{bmatrix}$$

or

$$[a, b, c] = \frac{a + b - c}{2}[1, 1, 0] + \frac{-a + b + c}{2}[0, 1, 1] + \frac{a - b + c}{2}[1, 0, 1].$$

Returning to our discussion of Equations (3.17), let us define a transformation T by $\mathrm{T}(\mathbf{X}_i) = \mathbf{Y}_i$ (remember we may always define a linear transformation by giving its action on a basis). What is the matrix of T with respect to the $\{\mathbf{X}_i\}$ basis (that is, with the $\{\mathbf{X}_i\}$ basis in both range and domain)? A moment's reflection will make it clear that the matrix of T is just A.

Now, since T takes a basis to a basis it is an isomorphism, and thus it has an inverse, $\mathrm{T}^{-1}(\mathbf{Y}_i) = \mathbf{X}_i$.

$$\begin{aligned} \mathbf{X}_1 &= b_{11}\mathbf{Y}_1 + b_{21}\mathbf{Y}_2 + \cdots + b_{n1}\mathbf{Y}_n, \\ \mathbf{X}_2 &= b_{12}\mathbf{Y}_1 + b_{22}\mathbf{Y}_2 + \cdots + b_{n2}\mathbf{Y}_n, \\ &\vdots \\ \mathbf{X}_n &= b_{1n}\mathbf{Y}_1 + b_{2n}\mathbf{Y}_2 + \cdots + b_{nn}\mathbf{Y}_n. \end{aligned} \tag{3.18}$$

Thus $B = [b_{ij}]$ is the matrix of T^{-1} *with respect to the* $\{\mathbf{Y}_i\}$ *basis.* This does not imply that $AB = I$ (we know that $\mathrm{TT}^{-1} = \mathrm{I}$, which implies that if the matrix of T^{-1} *with respect to the* $\{\mathbf{X}_i\}$ *basis* is B', then $AB' = I$). Nevertheless it is true that $AB = I$! To see this, let us begin with a typical equation from (3.18),

$$\mathbf{X}_j = b_{1j}\mathbf{Y}_1 + b_{2j}\mathbf{Y}_2 + \cdots + b_{nj}\mathbf{Y}_n,$$

and substitute Equation (3.17), expressed in $\sum$ notation:

$$\mathbf{X}_j = b_{1j}\left(\sum_{k=1}^{n} a_{k1}\mathbf{X}_k\right) + b_{2j}\left(\sum_{k=1}^{n} a_{k2}\mathbf{X}_k\right) + \cdots + b_{nj}\left(\sum_{k=1}^{n} a_{kn}\mathbf{X}_k\right).$$

Collect coefficients of the $\mathbf{X}_i$'s.

$$\begin{aligned} \mathbf{X}_j = &(b_{1j}a_{11} + b_{2j}a_{12} + \cdots + b_{nj}a_{1n})\mathbf{X}_1 \\ &+ (b_{1j}a_{21} + b_{2j}a_{22} + \cdots + b_{nj}a_{2n})\mathbf{X}_2 + \cdots \\ &+ (b_{1j}a_{n1} + b_{2j}a_{n2} + \cdots + b_{nj}a_{nn})\mathbf{X}_n \\ = &(a_{11}b_{1j} + a_{12}b_{2j} + \cdots + a_{1n}b_{nj})\mathbf{X}_1 \\ &+ (a_{21}b_{1j} + a_{22}b_{2j} + \cdots + a_{2n}b_{nj})\mathbf{X}_2 + \cdots \\ &+ (a_{n1}b_{1j} + a_{n2}b_{2j} + \cdots + a_{nn}b_{nj})\mathbf{X}_n. \end{aligned}$$

These relations imply that, if $[c_{ij}] = [a_{ij}][b_{ij}]$, then

$$\mathbf{X}_j = c_{1j}\mathbf{X}_1 + c_{2j}\mathbf{X}_2 + \cdots + c_{nj}\mathbf{X}_n.$$

By the uniqueness of linear combinations of independent vectors, $c_{jj} = 1$ and all $c_{ij} = 0$, $i \neq j$. Thus $[c_{ij}] = I$ or $AB = I$.

THEOREM 3.18. The matrices of change of basis from $\{\mathbf{X}_i\}$ *to* $\{\mathbf{Y}_i\}$ *and from* $\{\mathbf{Y}_i\}$ *to* $\{\mathbf{X}_i\}$ *are inverse.*

Example 4. Returning to the setting of Example 3 we have

$$[1, 1, 0] = 1[1, 0, 0] + 1[0, 1, 0] + 0[0, 0, 1],$$
$$[0, 1, 1] = 0[1, 0, 0] + 1[0, 1, 0] + 1[0, 0, 1],$$
$$[1, 0, 1] = 1[1, 0, 0] + 0[0, 1, 0] + 1[0, 0, 1].$$

Thus $B = \begin{bmatrix} 1 & 0 & 1 \\ 1 & 1 & 0 \\ 0 & 1 & 1 \end{bmatrix}$. We already calculated A, so

$$AB = \begin{bmatrix} \frac{1}{2} & \frac{1}{2} & -\frac{1}{2} \\ -\frac{1}{2} & \frac{1}{2} & \frac{1}{2} \\ \frac{1}{2} & -\frac{1}{2} & \frac{1}{2} \end{bmatrix} \begin{bmatrix} 1 & 0 & 1 \\ 1 & 1 & 0 \\ 0 & 1 & 1 \end{bmatrix} = \begin{bmatrix} 1 & 0 & 0 \\ 0 & 1 & 0 \\ 0 & 0 & 1 \end{bmatrix}.$$

Our final item of this section concerns the *transpose* of a matrix. This notion is useful whenever orders are reversed, or when we wish to relate "column" notions to "row" notions.

DEFINITION 3.16. *The* TRANSPOSE *of an* $m \times n$ *matrix* $[a_{ij}]$ *is the* $n \times m$ *matrix* $[b_{ij}]$, *where* $b_{ij} = a_{ji}$.

Note that the transpose is obtained by interchanging rows and columns, or, if you wish, by reflecting about the main diagonal. We will denote the transpose of A by A^{T}.

Example 5. If

$$A = \begin{bmatrix} 1 & 2 & -1 \\ 3 & 1 & 5 \\ 0 & -1 & 1 \end{bmatrix}, \quad B = \begin{bmatrix} 1 & 1 \\ 0 & 1 \\ -6 & 2 \end{bmatrix}, \quad C = [1, 0, 4, -2],$$

then

$$A^{\mathsf{T}} = \begin{bmatrix} 1 & 3 & 0 \\ 2 & 1 & -1 \\ -1 & 5 & 1 \end{bmatrix}, \quad B^{\mathsf{T}} = \begin{bmatrix} 1 & 0 & -6 \\ 1 & 1 & 2 \end{bmatrix}, \quad C^{\mathsf{T}} = \begin{bmatrix} 1 \\ 0 \\ 4 \\ -2 \end{bmatrix}.$$

The notion of a transpose can be used to restate Definition 3.16 in a particularly simple form.

THEOREM 3.19. *If* T *is a linear transformation on* R^n *whose matrix is* A *relative to the* $\{\mathbf{E}_i\}$ *basis, the relation* $\mathrm{T}\mathbf{X} = \mathbf{Y}$ *is equivalent to the matrix equation* $A\mathbf{X}^{\mathsf{T}} = \mathbf{Y}^{\mathsf{T}}$. ($\mathbf{X}$ *and* $\mathbf{Y}$ *are elements of* R^n *and thus are* $1 \times n$ *matrices.*)

THEOREM 3.20. *For matrices* A *and* B *for which the operations are defined,*

(i) $(A + B)^{\mathsf{T}} = A^{\mathsf{T}} + B^{\mathsf{T}}$,
(ii) $(AB)^{\mathsf{T}} = B^{\mathsf{T}}A^{\mathsf{T}}$,
(iii) $(A^{-1})^{\mathsf{T}} = (A^{\mathsf{T}})^{-1}$.

PROOF. We prove (ii) leaving the other parts as exercises. The only hard part of the proof is to keep all the subscripts straight. Let us assume A is $m \times n$, B is $n \times p$, and write

$$A = [a_{ij}],\ B = [b_{ij}],$$
$$A^{\mathsf{T}} = [c_{ij}],\ B^{\mathsf{T}} = [d_{ij}],$$
$$AB = [r_{ij}] \quad \text{and} \quad (AB)^{\mathsf{T}} = [s_{ij}]$$

so that $s_{ij} = r_{ji}$, $c_{ij} = a_{ji}$, and $d_{ij} = b_{ji}$. Now

$$r_{ij} = \sum_{k=1}^{n} a_{ik}b_{kj} = \sum_{k=1}^{n} c_{ki}d_{jk} = \sum_{k=1}^{n} d_{jk}c_{ki}.$$

Then

$$s_{ij} = r_{ji} = \sum_{k=1}^{n} d_{ik}c_{kj},$$

but

$$B^{\mathsf{T}}A^{\mathsf{T}} = [d_{ij}][c_{ij}] = \left[\sum_{k=1}^{n} d_{ik}c_{kj}\right] = [s_{ij}],$$

or $B^{\mathsf{T}}A^{\mathsf{T}} = (AB)^{\mathsf{T}}$.

We conclude the section with an application of our new techniques to nonsingular matrices.

THEOREM 3.21. *For an $n \times n$ matrix A the following conditions are equivalent.*

(i) *A is nonsingular.*
(ii) *The columns of A are linearly independent when considered as vectors in R^n.*
(iii) *The rows of A are linearly independent when considered as vectors in R^n.*

PROOF. We note that A is nonsingular if and only if the linear transformation T, corresponding to A relative to the standard basis, is nonsingular. But, by Theorem 3.5, T is nonsingular if and only if the vectors $\mathbf{TE}_1$, $\mathbf{TE}_2, \ldots, \mathbf{TE}_n$ are linearly independent. Now what is $\mathbf{TE}_i$? By Theorem 3.20 $\mathbf{TE}_i = (\mathbf{AE}_i^{\mathsf{T}})^{\mathsf{T}}$, and this is just the ith column of A considered as a vector in R^n. Thus (i) and (ii) are equivalent. Now, by part (iii) of Theorem 3.21, if A is nonsingular, then A^{T} is nonsingular. By what we have done the columns of A^{T} are linearly independent; however, the columns of A^{T} are the rows of A. Similarly, if the rows of A are linearly independent, so are the columns of A^{T}; A^{T} is nonsingular, hence A is nonsingular. Thus (i) and (iii) are equivalent and the theorem is established.

Exercises

1. Let T be the linear transformation corresponding to $\begin{bmatrix} -1 & 1 & 2 \\ 1 & 0 & 3 \\ 0 & 1 & 1 \end{bmatrix}$ relative to the standard basis. Calculate the following:
(a) T[1, −1, 2], (b) T[0, −6, 12], (c) T[1, 0, 0], (d) T[0, 0, 1].
2. Let T be the linear transformation of Exercise 1. What is the matrix of T relative to the basis

$$\mathbf{X}_1 = [1, -1, 1],\ \mathbf{X}_2 = [1, 0, 1],\ \mathbf{X}_3 = [0, 1, 1]?$$

Calculate the following *in terms of the* $\mathbf{X}_i$'s:
(a) $\mathrm{T}(\mathbf{X}_1 - \mathbf{X}_2 + 2\mathbf{X}_3)$,
(b) $\mathrm{T}(2\mathbf{X}_1 + 2\mathbf{X}_2 - 2\mathbf{X}_3)$,
(c) $\mathrm{T}(\mathbf{X}_1 - 3\mathbf{X}_2 + 6\mathbf{X}_3)$.
3. Let $\mathbf{Y}_1 = [2, -1, 2]$, $\mathbf{Y}_2 = [1, 1, 2]$, $\mathbf{Y}_3 = [1, 0, 2]$ and $\{\mathbf{X}_i\}$ be as in Exercise 2.
(a) Find the matrices of change of basis from $\{\mathbf{X}_i\}$ to $\{\mathbf{Y}_i\}$ and $\{\mathbf{Y}_i\}$ to $\{\mathbf{X}_i\}$. Verify Theorem 3.18 for this example.
(b) If $\mathbf{Z} = \mathbf{X}_1 + 2\mathbf{X}_2 - \mathbf{X}_3$, find $\mathbf{Z}$ as a linear combination of the $\mathbf{Y}_i$ using matrix multiplication.

(c) If a subspace W of R^3 is defined by $\mathbf{Z} = c_1\mathbf{X}_1 + c_2\mathbf{X}_2 + c_3\mathbf{X}_3 \in W$ if and only if $c_1 + c_2 + c_3 = 0$, find an equivalent condition on c'_1, c'_2, c'_3 if

$$\mathbf{Z} = c'_1\mathbf{Y}_1 + c'_2\mathbf{Y}_2 + c'_3\mathbf{Y}_3.$$

4. (a) Find the matrix of change of basis from the standard basis to the basis $\{[1, 0, 2], [2, 1, 3], [-1, 3, -3]\}$.
   (b) Express the following vectors as linear combinations of the vectors in (a): $[1, 2, 3]$, $[-1, 6, 7]$, $[1, -2, -1]$, $[a, b, c]$.
5. Let $\mathbf{X}_1 = 1$, $\mathbf{X}_2 = x$, $\mathbf{X}_3 = x^2$, $\mathbf{X}_4 = x^3$, $\mathbf{Y}_1 = 1$, $\mathbf{Y}_2 = (x - 1)$, $\mathbf{Y}_3 = (x - 1)^2$, $\mathbf{Y}_4 = (x - 1)^3$.
   (a) Find the matrix of change of basis from $\{\mathbf{X}_i\}$ to $\{\mathbf{Y}_i\}$ in P^4.
   (b) Express the polynomial $3x^3 + 2x^2 - x + 4$ as a linear combination of 1, $x - 1$, $(x - 1)^2$, and $(x - 1)^3$.
6. Show that $(A + B)^{\mathsf{T}} = A^{\mathsf{T}} + B^{\mathsf{T}}$ if A and B are any two matrices of the same size.
7. Prove that $(A^{-1})^{\mathsf{T}} = (A^{\mathsf{T}})^{-1}$, and that A is nonsingular if and only if A^{T} is nonsingular.

3.9 Effect of Change of Basis on the Matrix of a Linear Transformation

The situation we wish to investigate in this section and to which we have referred several times in the past is the following: we have a linear transformation T from an n-dimensional space V to an m-dimensional space W. We have available two bases of V, $\{\mathbf{X}_i\}$ and $\{\mathbf{Y}_i\}$, $i = 1, 2, \ldots, n$, as well as two bases of W, $\{\mathbf{X}'_i\}$ and $\{\mathbf{Y}'_i\}$, $i = 1, 2, \ldots, m$. (Naturally, we make no demand that V, W; m, n; $\{\mathbf{X}_i\}, \{\mathbf{Y}_i\}$; $\{\mathbf{X}'_i\}$ $\{\mathbf{Y}'_i\}$ be distinct. Of course certain combinations of equalities will make the problem we pose very easy, but the easy cases will be contained in the general solution.)

Now T has matrices with respect to the pairs of bases $(\{\mathbf{X}_i\}, \{\mathbf{X}'_i\})$ and $(\{\mathbf{Y}_i\}, \{\mathbf{Y}'_i\})$. Denote these matrices by $A = [a_{ij}]$ and $B = [b_{ij}]$, respectively. What is the relation between A and B? This relation will clearly depend on the equations of change of basis between $\{\mathbf{X}_i\}$ and $\{\mathbf{Y}_i\}$ and between $\{\mathbf{X}'_i\}$ and $\{\mathbf{Y}'_i\}$. We then assume that $P = [p_{ij}]$ and $Q = [q_{ij}]$ are the matrices of change of basis from $\{\mathbf{X}_i\}$ to $\{\mathbf{Y}_i\}$ and from $\{\mathbf{X}'_i\}$ to $\{\mathbf{Y}'_i\}$, respectively.

We have essentially four different sets of equations of which we list the jth in each case below.

$$\mathrm{T}\mathbf{X}_j = a_{1j}\mathbf{X}'_1 + a_{2j}\mathbf{X}'_2 + \cdots + a_{mj}\mathbf{X}'_m, \qquad j = 1, 2, \ldots, n, \tag{3.19}$$

$$\mathrm{T}\mathbf{Y}_j = b_{1j}\mathbf{Y}'_1 + b_{2j}\mathbf{Y}'_2 + \cdots + b_{mj}\mathbf{Y}'_m, \qquad j = 1, 2, \ldots, n, \tag{3.20}$$

$$\mathbf{X}_j = p_{1j}\mathbf{Y}_1 + p_{2j}\mathbf{Y}_2 + \cdots + p_{nj}\mathbf{Y}_n, \qquad j = 1, 2, \ldots, n, \tag{3.21}$$

$$\mathbf{X}'_j = q_{1j}\mathbf{Y}'_1 + q_{2j}\mathbf{Y}'_2 + \cdots + q_{mj}\mathbf{Y}'_m, \qquad j = 1, 2, \ldots, m. \tag{3.22}$$

In our first and general discussion of the relation between A and B, we shall employ these four systems of equations directly. Let us begin by combining (3.19) and (3.22); that is, we write (3.22) for the special cases involved and substitute the results into (3.19). Using the $\sum$ notation, (3.22) yields, for $j = 1, 2, \ldots, m$,

$$\mathbf{X}'_1 = \sum_{k=1}^{m} q_{k1}\mathbf{Y}'_k, \ \mathbf{X}'_2 = \sum_{k=1}^{m} q_{k2}\mathbf{Y}'_k, \ldots, \mathbf{X}'_m = \sum_{k=1}^{m} q_{km}\mathbf{Y}'_k.$$

Then (3.19) becomes

$$\mathrm{T}\mathbf{X}_j = a_{1j}\sum_{k=1}^{m} q_{k1}\mathbf{Y}'_k + a_{2j}\sum_{k=1}^{m} q_{k2}\mathbf{Y}'_k + \cdots + a_{mj}\sum_{k=1}^{m} q_{km}\mathbf{Y}'_k. \tag{3.19'}$$

Next, we collect the coefficients of each $\mathbf{Y}'_i$. For example, the coefficient of $\mathbf{Y}'_1$ is

$$a_{1j}q_{11} + a_{2j}q_{12} + \cdots + a_{mj}q_{1m} = q_{11}a_{1j} + q_{12}a_{2j} + \cdots + q_{1m}a_{mj}.$$

Proceeding in this fashion, we have

$$\begin{aligned}\mathrm{T}\mathbf{X}_j = &(q_{11}a_{1j} + q_{12}a_{2j} + \cdots + q_{1m}a_{mj})\mathbf{Y}'_1\\ &+ (q_{21}a_{1j} + q_{22}a_{2j} + \cdots + q_{2m}a_{mj})\mathbf{Y}'_2 + \cdots\\ &+ (q_{m1}a_{1j} + q_{m2}a_{2j} + \cdots + q_{mm}a_{mj})\mathbf{Y}'_m.\end{aligned} \tag{3.19''}$$

That is, with respect to the bases $\{\mathbf{X}_i\}$ for V and $\{\mathbf{Y}'_i\}$ for W, T has the matrix QA. We can also find the matrix of T relative to these bases by first applying T to (3.21):

$$\mathrm{T}\mathbf{X}_j = p_{1j}\mathrm{T}\mathbf{Y}_1 + p_{2j}\mathrm{T}\mathbf{Y}_2 + \cdots + p_{nj}\mathrm{T}\mathbf{Y}_n. \tag{3.23}$$

Now, from (3.20)

$$\mathrm{T}\mathbf{Y}_1 = \sum_{k=1}^{m} b_{k1}\mathbf{Y}'_k,\ \mathrm{T}\mathbf{Y}_2 = \sum_{k=1}^{m} b_{k2}\mathbf{Y}'_k, \ldots, \mathrm{T}\mathbf{Y}_n = \sum_{k=1}^{m} b_{kn}\mathbf{Y}'_k;$$

substituting these in (3.23),

$$\mathrm{T}\mathbf{X}_j = p_{1j}\sum_{k=1}^{m} b_{k1}\mathbf{Y}'_k + p_{2j}\sum_{k=1}^{m} b_{k2}\mathbf{Y}'_k + \cdots + p_{nj}\sum_{k=1}^{m} b_{kn}\mathbf{Y}'_k. \tag{3.23'}$$

Again, we collect the coefficients of each $\mathbf{Y}'_i$. This time the coefficient of $\mathbf{Y}'_1$ is given by

$$p_{1j}b_{11} + p_{2j}b_{12} + \cdots + p_{nj}b_{1n} = b_{11}p_{1j} + b_{12}p_{2j} + \cdots + b_{1n}p_{nj}.$$

Thus

$$\begin{aligned}\mathrm{T}\mathbf{X}_j = &(b_{11}p_{1j} + b_{12}p_{2j} + \cdots + b_{1n}p_{nj})\mathbf{Y}'_1\\ &+ (b_{21}p_{1j} + b_{22}p_{2j} + \cdots + b_{2n}p_{nj})\mathbf{Y}'_2 + \cdots\\ &+ (b_{m1}p_{1j} + b_{m2}p_{2j} + \cdots + b_{mn}p_{nj})\mathbf{Y}'_m.\end{aligned} \tag{3.23''}$$

Thus T also has the matrix BP relative to the bases $\{\mathbf{X}_i\}$ and $\{\mathbf{Y}'_i\}$. But the matrix of a linear transformation (relative to *fixed* bases) is unique. Therefore,

$$\begin{aligned}BP &= QA\\ B &= QAP^{-1}.\end{aligned}$$

THEOREM 3.22. If the transformation T *from V to W has the matrix A with respect to the bases $\{\mathbf{X}_i\}$ and $\{\mathbf{X}'_i\}$ and the matrix B with respect to the bases $\{\mathbf{Y}_i\}$ and $\{\mathbf{Y}'_i\}$, then $B = QAP^{-1}$, where P and Q are the matrices of change of basis from $\{\mathbf{X}_i\}$ to $\{\mathbf{Y}_i\}$ and from $\{\mathbf{X}'_i\}$ to $\{\mathbf{Y}'_i\}$, respectively.*

Now that we have stated and proved the theorem in detail we can apply ourselves to a more direct understanding of it. Think of a vector $\mathbf{Y} \in V$ written in terms of the $\{\mathbf{Y}_i\}$. What does P^{-1} do to it? By the main result of the previous section (Theorem 3.18), P^{-1} is the matrix of change of basis from $\{\mathbf{Y}_i\}$ to $\{\mathbf{X}_i\}$. That is, P^{-1} rewrites $\mathbf{Y}$ in terms of the $\mathbf{X}_i$'s. Now A is available to act on anything written in terms of the $\mathbf{X}_i$'s, giving the result of the mapping T *in terms* of the $\mathbf{X}'_i$'s.

Thus, when AP^{-1} has acted on $\mathbf{Y}$, we have $\mathrm{T}\mathbf{Y}$ written in terms of $\{\mathbf{X}_i'\}$. But now Q is available to change from $\{\mathbf{X}_i'\}$ to $\{\mathbf{Y}_i'\}$ and the result of applying QAP^{-1} to $\mathbf{Y}$ is to get $\mathrm{T}\mathbf{Y}$ in terms of $\{\mathbf{Y}_i'\}$. But this, of course, is exactly what B does.

Figure 3.4 illustrates the process. At each corner of the rectangle we see a vector and the basis in which the vector is expressed. The arrows indicate the directions of the transformations at this point to mean that the vector $\mathbf{X}$ is given in terms of $\{\mathbf{Z}_i\}$ or changes of basis involved, and we write "$\mathbf{X}$, $\{\mathbf{Z}_i\}$."

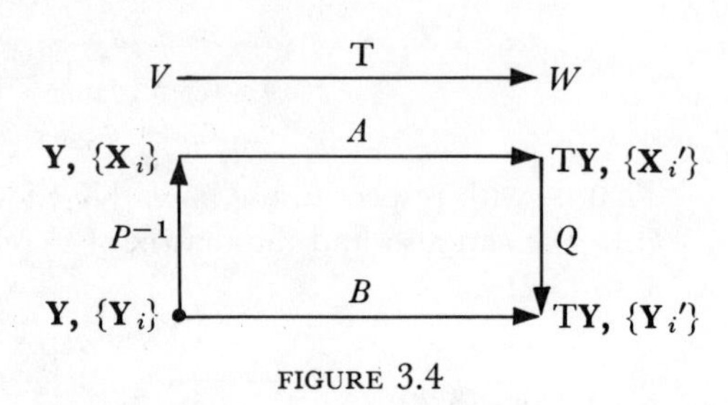

FIGURE 3.4

A similar diagram (Figure 3.5) illustrates the detailed argument used in the proof of Theorem 3.22. Here we begin at the upper left-hand corner with $\mathbf{X}_j$ written in terms of the $\{\mathbf{X}_i\}$, i.e., $\mathbf{X}_j = \mathbf{X}_j$, and proceed by two different tracks to the lower right corner, where $\mathrm{T}\mathbf{X}_j$ is given in terms of $\{\mathbf{Y}_i'\}$. Thus P followed by B, BP in functional order, gives the same result as A followed by Q, or QA. So $BP = QA$.

Question for discussion: Was the detailed proof of Theorem 3.22 with all of its subscripts and $\sum$'s really necessary, or would either of these diagrams with the accompanying brief explanations suffice?

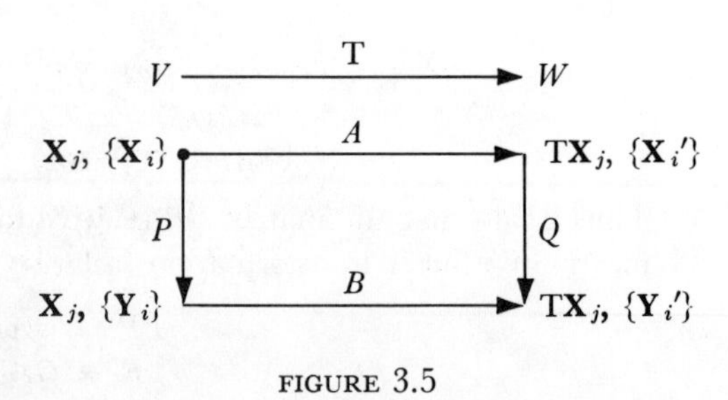

FIGURE 3.5

Example 1. Take $V = R^3$, $W = R^2$. Suppose

$$\begin{aligned} \mathbf{X}_1 &= [1, 0, 1], \\ \mathbf{X}_2 &= [1, 1, 0], \\ \mathbf{X}_3 &= [0, -1, 2], \\ \mathbf{X}_1' &= [1, 2], \\ \mathbf{X}_2' &= [2, 3]. \end{aligned}$$

Let T be defined by

$$\begin{aligned} \mathrm{T}\mathbf{X}_1 &= \mathbf{X}_1' + \mathbf{X}_2', \\ \mathrm{T}\mathbf{X}_2 &= \mathbf{X}_1' - \mathbf{X}_2', \\ \mathrm{T}\mathbf{X}_3 &= 2\mathbf{X}_1' - \mathbf{X}_2'. \end{aligned}$$

Express T as a matrix relative to the $\{\mathbf{E}_i\}$ bases of V and W.

We shall begin by doing the problem "the old way." First we find $\mathbf{E}_1, \mathbf{E}_2, \mathbf{E}_3 \in R^3$ in terms of $\mathbf{X}_1, \mathbf{X}_2, \mathbf{X}_3$. This can be done directly or by trial and error. In any case, we see that

$$\begin{aligned} \mathbf{E}_1 &= 2\mathbf{X}_1 - \mathbf{X}_2 - \mathbf{X}_3, \\ \mathbf{E}_2 &= -2\mathbf{X}_1 + 2\mathbf{X}_2 + \mathbf{X}_3, \\ \mathbf{E}_3 &= -\mathbf{X}_1 + \mathbf{X}_2 + \mathbf{X}_3. \end{aligned}$$

Hence

$$\begin{aligned} \mathrm{T}\mathbf{E}_1 &= 2(\mathbf{X}_1' + \mathbf{X}_2') - (\mathbf{X}_1' - \mathbf{X}_2') - (2\mathbf{X}_1' - \mathbf{X}_2') = [7, 10], \\ \mathrm{T}\mathbf{E}_2 &= -2(\mathbf{X}_1' + \mathbf{X}_2') + 2(\mathbf{X}_1' - \mathbf{X}_2') + (2\mathbf{X}_1' - \mathbf{X}_2') = [-8, -11], \\ \mathrm{T}\mathbf{E}_3 &= -(\mathbf{X}_1' + \mathbf{X}_2') + (\mathbf{X}_1' - \mathbf{X}_2') + (2\mathbf{X}_1' - \mathbf{X}_2') = [-4, -5]. \end{aligned}$$

The matrix B is $\begin{bmatrix} 7 & -8 & -4 \\ 10 & -11 & -5 \end{bmatrix}$.

Now, let us use matrices: From the expressions for $\mathrm{T}\mathbf{X}_1, \mathrm{T}\mathbf{X}_2, \mathrm{T}\mathbf{X}_3$,

$$A = \begin{bmatrix} 1 & 1 & 2 \\ 1 & -1 & -1 \end{bmatrix}.$$

Again, simply reading the values of $\mathbf{X}_1, \mathbf{X}_2, \mathbf{X}_3$ and writing them as column vectors,

$$P = \begin{bmatrix} 1 & 1 & 0 \\ 0 & 1 & -1 \\ 1 & 0 & 2 \end{bmatrix}.$$

In the same way

$$Q = \begin{bmatrix} 1 & 2 \\ 2 & 3 \end{bmatrix}.$$

We can find P^{-1} from the expressions for $\mathbf{E}_1, \mathbf{E}_2, \mathbf{E}_3$ above.

$$P^{-1} = \begin{bmatrix} 2 & -2 & -1 \\ -1 & 2 & 1 \\ -1 & 1 & 1 \end{bmatrix},$$

$$\begin{aligned} B = QAP^{-1} &= \begin{bmatrix} 1 & 2 \\ 2 & 3 \end{bmatrix} \begin{bmatrix} 1 & 1 & 2 \\ 1 & -1 & -1 \end{bmatrix} \begin{bmatrix} 2 & -2 & -1 \\ -1 & 2 & 1 \\ -1 & 1 & 1 \end{bmatrix} \\ &= \begin{bmatrix} 1 & 2 \\ 2 & 3 \end{bmatrix} \begin{bmatrix} -1 & 2 & 2 \\ 4 & -5 & -3 \end{bmatrix} = \begin{bmatrix} 7 & -8 & -4 \\ 10 & -11 & -5 \end{bmatrix}. \end{aligned}$$

Finally, let us follow the arrow diagram of Figure 3.4 on the vector $\mathbf{Y} = [1, -1, 2]$. First

$$P^{-1}\mathbf{Y}^{\mathrm{T}} = \begin{bmatrix} 2 & -2 & -1 \\ -1 & 2 & 1 \\ -1 & 1 & 1 \end{bmatrix} \begin{bmatrix} 1 \\ -1 \\ 2 \end{bmatrix} = \begin{bmatrix} 2 \\ -1 \\ 0 \end{bmatrix}.$$

This means that $\mathbf{Y} = 2\mathbf{X}_1 - \mathbf{X}_2$. (Check.) Applying A to $P^{-1}\mathbf{Y}^{\mathrm{T}}$:

$$\begin{bmatrix} 1 & 1 & 2 \\ 1 & -1 & -1 \end{bmatrix} \begin{bmatrix} 2 \\ -1 \\ 0 \end{bmatrix} = \begin{bmatrix} 1 \\ 3 \end{bmatrix}.$$

This gives $\mathrm{T}\mathbf{Y} = \mathbf{X}_1' + 3\mathbf{X}_2'$. The next step is to apply Q to $\begin{bmatrix} 1 \\ 3 \end{bmatrix}$:

$$\begin{bmatrix} 1 & 2 \\ 2 & 3 \end{bmatrix} \begin{bmatrix} 1 \\ 3 \end{bmatrix} = \begin{bmatrix} 7 \\ 11 \end{bmatrix},$$

which gives $\mathbf{TY} = [7, 11]$. Now that we know B, we could get the same answer from

$$\begin{bmatrix} 7 & -8 & -4 \\ 10 & -11 & -5 \end{bmatrix} \begin{bmatrix} 1 \\ -1 \\ 2 \end{bmatrix} = \begin{bmatrix} 7 \\ 11 \end{bmatrix}.$$

Example 2. This time we will avoid the $\{\mathbf{E}_i\}$ bases and the use of complete R^n spaces altogether. Let

$$V = L\{[1, -1, 0], [0, 1, 1]\}$$

and

$$W = L\{[1, 0, 1, 0], [1, 1, 0, 0], [1, -1, 0, 1]\},$$

where the vectors indicated are the $\{\mathbf{X}_i\}$ and $\{\mathbf{X}'_i\}$ bases. Let

$$\begin{aligned} \mathrm{T}[1, -1, 0] &= [1, 0, 1, 0] + 2[1, -1, 0, 1], \\ \mathrm{T}[0, 1, 1] &= 3[1, 0, 1, 0] - [1, 1, 0, 0] + [1, -1, 0, 1]. \end{aligned}$$

Thus

$$A = \begin{bmatrix} 1 & 3 \\ 0 & -1 \\ 2 & 1 \end{bmatrix}.$$

Now define new bases $\{\mathbf{Y}_i\}$ and $\{\mathbf{Y}'_i\}$:

$$\begin{aligned} \mathbf{Y}_1 &= [1, -1, 0] + [0, 1, 1] = [1, 0, 1], \\ \mathbf{Y}_2 &= [1, -1, 0] + 2[0, 1, 1] = [1, 1, 2], \\ \mathbf{Y}'_1 &= [1, 0, 1, 0] - [1, -1, 0, 1] = [0, 1, 1, -1], \\ \mathbf{Y}'_2 &= [1, 1, 0, 0] + [1, -1, 0, 1] = [2, 0, 0, 1], \\ \mathbf{Y}'_3 &= -[1, 0, 1, 0] + [1, 1, 0, 0] + [1, -1, 0, 1] = [1, 0, -1, 1]. \end{aligned}$$

(Check that the $\{\mathbf{Y}_i\}$ and $\{\mathbf{Y}'_i\}$ are bases.)

These equations are in the inverse sense of Equations (3.21) and (3.22) so that they give us P^{-1} and Q^{-1}.

$$P^{-1} = \begin{bmatrix} 1 & 1 \\ 1 & 2 \end{bmatrix}, \qquad Q^{-1} = \begin{bmatrix} 1 & 0 & -1 \\ 0 & 1 & 1 \\ -1 & 1 & 1 \end{bmatrix}.$$

We must find

$$Q = \begin{bmatrix} 0 & 1 & -1 \\ 1 & 0 & 1 \\ -1 & 1 & -1 \end{bmatrix}.$$

(Naturally, the numbers in the examples and exercises have been deliberately chosen to simplify hand calculations.) Then

$$\begin{aligned} QAP^{-1} &= \begin{bmatrix} 0 & 1 & -1 \\ 1 & 0 & 1 \\ -1 & 1 & -1 \end{bmatrix} \begin{bmatrix} 1 & 3 \\ 0 & -1 \\ 2 & 1 \end{bmatrix} \begin{bmatrix} 1 & 1 \\ 1 & 2 \end{bmatrix} \\ &= \begin{bmatrix} -2 & -2 \\ 3 & 4 \\ -3 & -5 \end{bmatrix} \begin{bmatrix} 1 & 1 \\ 1 & 2 \end{bmatrix} = \begin{bmatrix} -4 & -6 \\ 7 & 11 \\ -8 & -13 \end{bmatrix}. \end{aligned}$$

Let us take a vector $\mathbf{Z} = [2, -1, 1] \in V$, express it in the two bases, and compare results:

$$\mathbf{Z} = 2[1, -1, 0] + [0, 1, 1] = 3[1, 0, 1] - [1, 1, 2].$$

In the $\{\mathbf{X}_i\}$ form, using A,

$$\begin{bmatrix} 1 & 3 \\ 0 & -1 \\ 2 & 1 \end{bmatrix} \begin{bmatrix} 2 \\ 1 \end{bmatrix} = \begin{bmatrix} 5 \\ -1 \\ 5 \end{bmatrix}.$$

The answer is $5[1, 0, 1, 0] - [1, 1, 0, 0] + 5[1, -1, 0, 1] = [9, -6, 5, 5]$. In the $\{\mathbf{Y}_i\}$ form, using B,

$$\begin{bmatrix} -4 & -6 \\ 7 & 11 \\ -8 & -13 \end{bmatrix} \begin{bmatrix} 3 \\ -1 \end{bmatrix} = \begin{bmatrix} -6 \\ 10 \\ -11 \end{bmatrix}.$$

The answer is

$$-6[0, 1, 1, -1] + 10[2, 0, 0, 1] - 11[1, 0, -1, 1] = [9, -6, 5, 5].$$

It is important to note the results of this section in the special case when $V = W$, $\{\mathbf{X}_i\} = \{\mathbf{X}'_i\}$, $\{\mathbf{Y}_i\} = \{\mathbf{Y}'_i\}$. Then $P = Q$ and $B = PAP^{-1}$, $A = P^{-1}BP$. Figure 3.5 simplifies to Figure 3.6. Theorem 3.22 simplifies to the following corollary:

COROLLARY *If the transformation* T *on* V *has the matrix* A *with respect to the basis* $\{\mathbf{X}_i\}$ *and the matrix* B *with respect to the basis* $\{\mathbf{Y}_i\}$, *then* $B = PAP^{-1}$, *where* P *is the matrix of change of basis from* $\{\mathbf{X}_i\}$ *to* $\{\mathbf{Y}_i\}$.

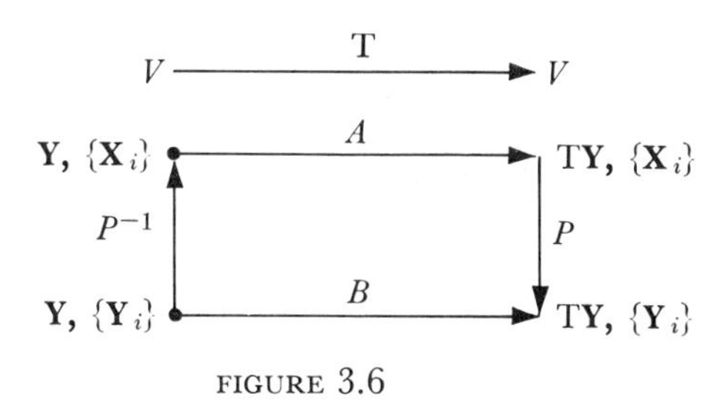

FIGURE 3.6

Exercises

In the first four problems assume the following data:

$$V = R^2;\quad \mathbf{X}_1 = [1, 1],\ \mathbf{X}_2 = [3, 2];\quad \mathbf{Y}_1 = [-1, 0],\ \mathbf{Y}_2 = [2, 1].$$
$$W = R^3;\quad \mathbf{X}'_1 = [2, 2, 3],\ \mathbf{X}'_2 = [2, -4, 1],\ \mathbf{X}'_3 = [1, 4, -2];$$
$$\mathbf{Y}'_1 = [1, 1, 0],\ \mathbf{Y}'_2 = [-1, 2, 1],\ \mathbf{Y}'_3 = [2, -1, 2].$$

T: $V \rightarrow W$ has the matrix $\begin{bmatrix} 1 & 2 \\ 2 & 1 \\ -3 & 1 \end{bmatrix}$ relative to the bases $\{\mathbf{X}_i\}$ and $\{\mathbf{X}'_i\}$.

1. Find the matrix P of the change of basis from $\{\mathbf{X}_i\}$ to $\{\mathbf{Y}_i\}$. Similarly find the matrix Q of the change of basis from $\{\mathbf{X}'_i\}$ to $\{\mathbf{Y}'_i\}$.
2. Find P^{-1} and Q^{-1} for the matrices of Exercise 1. Write the corresponding equations for the vectors $\{\mathbf{X}_i\}$ in terms of the $\{\mathbf{Y}_i\}$ and the $\{\mathbf{X}'_i\}$ in terms of the $\{\mathbf{Y}'_i\}$.
3. Find the matrix of T relative to the bases $\{\mathbf{Y}_i\}$ and $\{\mathbf{Y}'_i\}$.
4. If $\mathbf{Z} = [2, -3]$, find $\mathbf{Z}$ as a linear combination of $\mathbf{X}_1$, $\mathbf{X}_2$; of $\mathbf{Y}_1$, $\mathbf{Y}_2$. Use this result to find T$\mathbf{Z}$ in terms of the $\{\mathbf{X}'_i\}$ basis; in terms of the $\{\mathbf{Y}'_i\}$ basis. Verify that the resulting vector is the same in both cases.

5. Let $V = L\{[1, 0, 1], [1, -2, 1]\}$, $W = L\{[1, 0, 1, -1], [0, 1, -1, 0]\}$. Let T be a linear transformation from V to W whose matrix relative to the given bases of V and W is

$$\begin{bmatrix} 1 & 2 \\ -1 & 3 \end{bmatrix}.$$

Find the matrix of T relative to the bases $\{[2, -2, 2], [0, 2, 0]\}$ of V and $\{[2, 1, 1, -2], [-1, 2, -3, 1]\}$ of W.

6. Let T be a linear transformation on R^3 whose matrix relative to the natural basis $\{\mathbf{E}_i\}$ is

$$\begin{bmatrix} 1 & 0 & -1 \\ 0 & 2 & 1 \\ 1 & 0 & -1 \end{bmatrix}.$$

Find the matrix of T relative to the basis $\{[1, 1, -1], [1, 2, 0], [1, 0, 1]\}$ of R^3.

7. Let D be the differentiation operator on P^3, the space of all polynomials in x of degree ≤ 2 with real coefficients. What is the matrix A of D relative to the basis $\{1, x, x^2\}$? What is the matrix B of D relative to the basis $\{x^2, 2x, 2\}$? Find a matrix P such that $A = PBP^{-1}$.

8. Let T be a linear transformation on a space V having a basis

$$\{\mathbf{X}, \mathrm{T}\mathbf{X}, \mathrm{T}^2\mathbf{X}, \ldots, \mathrm{T}^n\mathbf{X}\}.$$

Further assume $\mathrm{T}^{n+1}\mathbf{X} = \mathbf{0}$. What is the matrix of T relative to this basis?

9. The text states that the matrix of a linear transformation changes when two vectors of the $\{\mathbf{X}_i\}$ basis arc permuted or when two vectors of the $\{\mathbf{X}_i'\}$ basis are interchanged. Precisely what are these changes when $\mathbf{X}_i$ and $\mathbf{X}_j$ are interchanged? When $\mathbf{X}_i'$ and $\mathbf{X}_j'$ are interchanged? Write the corresponding matrices P and Q and obtain Q^{-1}.

3.10 Similarity of Matrices and Equivalence Relations

In the preceding section we saw that if two matrices A and B represent the same linear transformation on a vector space V with respect to two bases $\{\mathbf{X}_i\}$ and $\{\mathbf{Y}_i\}$, then there is a nonsingular matrix P such that $B = PAP^{-1}$. In particular, P was the matrix of the change of basis from $\{\mathbf{X}_i\}$ to $\{\mathbf{Y}_i\}$. Conversely, suppose that for two $n \times n$ real matrices A, B, there exists a nonsingular matrix P such that $B = PAP^{-1}$. Then it is easy to see that there is a linear transformation T on R^n which is represented by both A and B. Let T be the transformation associated with A relative to the standard basis, and define a new basis $\{\mathbf{Y}_i\}$ by

$$\mathbf{Y}_j = P^{-1}\mathbf{E}_j^{\mathrm{T}}, \qquad j = 1, 2, \ldots, n. \tag{3.24}$$

We claim that (3.24) implies that P^{-1} is the matrix of change of basis from $\{\mathbf{Y}_i\}$ to $\{\mathbf{E}_i\}$. To see this, note that (3.24) implies that $\mathbf{Y}_i$ is just the ith column of P^{-1} considered as a vector in R^n: i.e.,

$$\mathbf{Y}_i = [q_{1i}, q_{2i}, \ldots, q_{ni}] = q_{1i}\mathbf{E}_1 + q_{2i}\mathbf{E}_2 + \cdots + q_{ni}\mathbf{E}_n,$$

where we denote P^{-1} by $[q_{ij}]$. Now compare this last equation with (3.17), the defining equations of a matrix of change of basis. Then P is the matrix of change of basis from $\{\mathbf{E}_i\}$ to $\{\mathbf{Y}_i\}$ and by the corollary at the end of the previous section, the matrix of T with respect to $\{\mathbf{Y}_i\}$ is given by $PAP^{-1} = B$. The diagram of the situation is given in Figure 3.7.

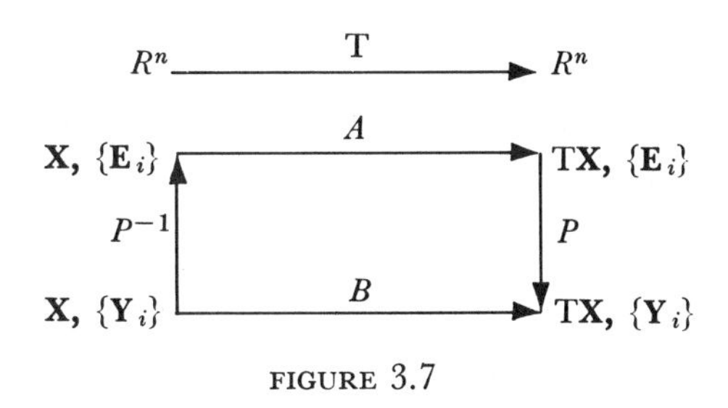

FIGURE 3.7

When two square matrices A and B are so related that they may represent the same linear transformation on a vector space V, they are said to be similar. Formally, and using only matrix language, we make the following definition:

DEFINITION 3.17. *An $n \times n$ matrix A is said to be* SIMILAR *to an $n \times n$ matrix B if there exists a nonsingular matrix R such that $B = RAR^{-1}$.*

If A is similar to B, then B is similar to A. That is, if

$$B = RAR^{-1}, \qquad BR = RA, \qquad R^{-1}BR = A,$$

and, if we write $R_1 = R^{-1}$, we have $R_1BR_1^{-1} = A$. Our informal definition of similarity of two matrices would lead one to expect this result.

The similarity of matrices is an example of a concept that is of great importance in mathematics: the notion of *equivalence*, or *equivalence relation.* In general, there are given a set S and a relation which may exist between elements of S which we denote by $\sim$ for the present. Three requirements are placed on the relation $\sim$:

(i) $x \sim x$ for all x in S (*reflexivity*).
(ii) If $x \sim y$, then $y \sim x$ (*symmetry*).
(iii) If $x \sim y$ and $y \sim z$, then $x \sim z$ (*transitivity*).

If conditions (i), (ii), and (iii) are fulfilled, then the relation denoted by $\sim$ is called an *equivalence relation.* Two elements x and y of S are said to be *equivalent* if $x \sim y$.

Some equivalence relations the student has already met are:

For numbers: equality, equality of absolute value;
For triangles: congruence, similarity;
For vectors: equality, equality of length, the property of one being a nonzero scalar multiple of the other.

The student should check these examples to see that all three properties of an equivalence relation are satisfied. It is easy to see (Exercise 1) that similarity of matrices is an equivalence relation on the set of $n \times n$ matrices.

The student has probably noticed that in the examples given the first requirement was always trivially evident. Its existence is logically necessary to ensure that an equivalence relation has the features we desire (see Exercise 6) but it is true that in most practical cases its validity is essentially automatic (see Exercise 7).

The primary use of equivalence relations on a set S is to separate the set S into convenient subsets. Let us put into one subset all the elements of S which are equivalent to a particular element a; indeed, let us repeat this process with each element of S so that we get a collection of subsets. These subsets will be called *equivalence classes*. In a vague sense, all the elements of an equivalence class have something in common. For example, under similarity of triangles, all the triangles in an equivalence class would have the same angles.

THEOREM 3.23. If equivalence classes of a set S are formed with respect to an equivalence relation denoted by $\sim$, then

(i) *Every element of S is in an equivalence class.*
(ii) *If two equivalence classes of S have an element in common, then they are identical.*

PROOF. The first assertion is trivial from the construction of equivalence classes; since $x \sim x$, x is in the class of elements equivalent to x. (This is one use of the reflexivity property of the relation $\sim$ and illustrates its necessity if we want every element of S in an equivalence class.)

To prove the second statement, let a be an element common to the equivalence classes B and C. Let B be the class of elements equivalent to b, and C the class of elements equivalent to c. If x is an arbitrary element of B, we will show $x \in C$. Now, by assumption, $x \sim b$ and $a \sim b$; hence $x \sim a$. But also $a \sim c$, since a is common to B and C. Therefore from $x \sim a$ and $a \sim c$ we conclude $x \sim c$ or $x \in C$.

Similarly, it is true that any element of C is an element of B. Hence, $B = C$.

To phrase the results of Theorem 3.23 in slightly different words, an equivalence relation on S provides a division of S into disjoint subsets. If we wish to call special attention to the fact that a particular equivalence class contains an element a, we may denote it by $E(a)$. The second part of the proof above established the fact that if $a \in E(b)$ and $a \in E(c)$, then

$$E(b) = E(a) = E(c).$$

In this notation, the equivalence classes are referred to as E-sets and we say that two E-sets are either equal or disjoint.

We may picture the situation by letting a set S be represented as a point set in the plane and dividing S into disjoint subsets representing the distinct equivalence classes.

Figure 3.8 suggests the simplest way in which an equivalence relation may be defined on a set S. We merely take a subdivision of S into disjoint subsets and then define two elements of S to be equivalent if they are contained in the same subset. The student can easily verify that properties (i), (ii), and (iii) of an equivalence relation are satisfied for this definition. Thus, an equivalence relation provides a subdivision of a set S into disjoint subsets, and conversely,

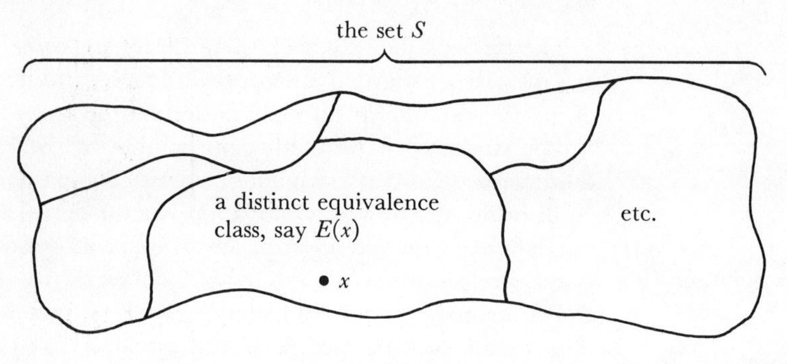

FIGURE 3.8

a subdivision of a set S into disjoint subsets provides an equivalence relation on S.

Example 1. Let S be the set of integers. Define $a \sim b$ to mean "a and b have the same parity." Thus, $5 \sim 7$, $-3 \sim -1$, $2 \sim 18$, but $6 \nsim 3$ (6 is not in relation with 3). Clearly $\sim$ is an equivalence relation. $E(1)$ consists of all the odd integers while $E(0)$ consists of all the even integers.

We may conclude that the set of $n \times n$ matrices is divided into E-sets of similar matrices under the equivalence relation of similarity of matrices. A study of these E-sets of similar matrices will constitute a considerable portion of Chapters 8 and 9 of this book. However, before we are completely prepared for this topic we will have occasion to deal with other equivalence relations in the course of the next two chapters. These examples will aid in clarifying the uses and the importance of this concept.

Exercises

1. Establish that similarity of matrices is an equivalence relation:
   (a) from the informal definition of similarity;
   (b) from Definition 3.17.
   (Here Exercise 8, Section 3.6, will be useful.)
2. Precisely where are properties (i) and (iii) of equivalence relations used in the proof of Theorem 3.23?
3. Discuss the following relations on the given sets from the standpoint of satisfying properties (i), (ii), and (iii).
   (a) Real numbers: $a > b$.
   (b) Real numbers: $a \leq b$.
   (c) People: a is a brother of b.
   (d) Male people: a is a brother of b.
   (e) Integers: $a - b$ is divisible by 3.
   (f) Real numbers: $\cos a = \cos b$.
   (g) Real numbers: $a \neq b$.
4. To decide whether B is similar to A, we must seek a matrix P such that $BP = PA$. Show that this equality leads to a system of homogeneous equations.
5. Is $\begin{bmatrix} 1 & 2 \\ 3 & 4 \end{bmatrix}$ similar to $\begin{bmatrix} 5 & 6 \\ 7 & 8 \end{bmatrix}$?
6. Consider the following relation between integers: a and b are both even. Show that this relation is symmetric and transitive but not reflexive.
7. In the light of Exercise 6, what is wrong with the following "proof" that reflexivity is a consequence of symmetry and transitivity? If $x \sim y$ then $y \sim x$, but then, from $x \sim y$ and $y \sim x$, we get $x \sim x$ by property (iii).

*8. The student may have objected that the concept of *relation* was left undefined. Consider whether the following definition will meet intuitive standards: A relation on a set S is a set of ordered pairs of elements of S. Rephrase the definition of an equivalence relation as a particular type of subset R of the set of ordered pairs of elements of S.

*9. As we have noted, essentially all of the results obtained in this chapter are applicable to matrices over *any* field, not just over the real numbers. Fields with a finite number of elements provide examples in which the number of equivalence classes and the number of matrices in each class are both finite. Consider the field of two elements 0, 1 defined by $0 + 0 = 1 + 1 = 0$, $0 + 1 = 1$, $0 \cdot 0 = 0 \cdot 1 = 0$, $1 \cdot 1 = 1$, and the commutative, associative, and distributive laws. There are sixteen 2×2 matrices over this field. Six of them are nonsingular. Find them and find the inverse of each one. Now divide the set of sixteen matrices into equivalence classes on the basis of similarity.

Sets of Linear Transformations and Matrices

In this chapter we shall consider some important sets of linear transformations and matrices. These will be applied to obtain additional information about vector spaces and their linear transformations. At the end of the chapter we shall utilize some of these special sets to introduce and study the important mathematical concept of a group.

4.1 Some Special Types of Square Matrices and Related Linear Transformations

We wish to study specific classes of square matrices which are of common occurrence or of specific use in applications. One such class, the *nonsingular matrices*, has already been utilized extensively in the preceding chapter. We have seen that a great deal of calculation is sometimes required to determine whether or not a given matrix is nonsingular.

We shall begin now with some classes whose elements are more easily recognized and which also have the property that they form a *subring* (with identity) of the ring of all $n \times n$ matrices. That is, the sum, difference, and product of two matrices in the set under consideration will again be in the set. It is easy to see that if these three conditions are satisfied (or if only the last two of them are verified) the set is a ring.

Indeed, these classes are such that a scalar multiple of a member of the class will again be in the class. They are thus *subalgebras* of the algebra of $n \times n$ matrices. This scalar multiple property will always be trivial to verify.

First we consider the *scalar* matrices. These are matrices $[a_{ij}]$ such that $a_{ij} = 0$ if $i \neq j$, and $a_{ii} = a$. That is, the off-diagonal elements are zero and the diagonal elements are all equal.

If we set up a correspondence between the real numbers and the scalar matrices such that

$$a \rightarrow \begin{bmatrix} a & 0 & \cdots & 0 \\ 0 & a & \cdots & 0 \\ \vdots & & \ddots & \vdots \\ 0 & 0 & \cdots & a \end{bmatrix}, \tag{4.1}$$

it is simple to check that

$$a+b \rightarrow \begin{bmatrix} a+b & 0 & \cdots & 0 \\ 0 & a+b & \cdots & 0 \\ \vdots & & \ddots & \vdots \\ 0 & 0 & \cdots & a+b \end{bmatrix}$$

$$= \begin{bmatrix} a & 0 & \cdots & 0 \\ 0 & a & \cdots & 0 \\ \vdots & & \ddots & \vdots \\ 0 & 0 & \cdots & a \end{bmatrix} + \begin{bmatrix} b & 0 & \cdots & 0 \\ 0 & b & \cdots & 0 \\ \vdots & & \ddots & \vdots \\ 0 & 0 & \cdots & b \end{bmatrix}$$

and

$$ab \rightarrow \begin{bmatrix} ab & 0 & \cdots & 0 \\ 0 & ab & \cdots & 0 \\ \vdots & & \ddots & \vdots \\ 0 & 0 & \cdots & ab \end{bmatrix} = \begin{bmatrix} a & 0 & \cdots & 0 \\ 0 & a & \cdots & 0 \\ \vdots & & \ddots & \vdots \\ 0 & 0 & \cdots & a \end{bmatrix} \begin{bmatrix} b & 0 & \cdots & 0 \\ 0 & b & \cdots & 0 \\ \vdots & & \ddots & \vdots \\ 0 & 0 & \cdots & b \end{bmatrix}.$$

The correspondence given in (4.1) is clearly one-to-one, and we conclude that the ring of scalar matrices is *isomorphic* to the ring (field) of real numbers.

If $\mathbf{X}$ is any vector of R^n, $\mathbf{X} = [x_1, x_2, \ldots, x_n]$, then

$$\begin{bmatrix} a & 0 & \cdots & 0 \\ 0 & a & \cdots & 0 \\ \vdots & & \ddots & \vdots \\ 0 & 0 & \cdots & a \end{bmatrix} \mathbf{X}^{\mathrm{T}} = a\mathbf{X}^{\mathrm{T}}.$$

The effect of a scalar matrix is a scalar multiplication of the vector. Such a matrix represents a linear transformation T that, in geometric language, is simply a dilation or contraction (Section 3.1). It should be clear that *any* matrix representing T is a scalar matrix.

Let us now generalize scalar matrices a bit. We keep the off-diagonal elements 0 but let the diagonal elements be arbitrary. Such a matrix is a *diagonal* matrix. For convenience we write

$$\begin{bmatrix} a_{11} & 0 & \cdots & 0 \\ 0 & a_{22} & \cdots & 0 \\ \vdots & & \ddots & \vdots \\ 0 & 0 & \cdots & a_{nn} \end{bmatrix} = \text{Diagonal } [a_{11}, a_{22}, \ldots, a_{nn}]. \tag{4.2}$$

The diagonal we have been using is called the *principal diagonal.*

It is easy to see that the sum, difference, and product of two diagonal matrices are again diagonal, while if the other diagonal is used the product is not in general in the set. Geometrically, the effect of such a matrix on a natural basis vector is an expansion or contraction while it acts on general vectors to produce the corresponding expansion or contraction in each component. Thus

$$\text{Diagonal } [a_{11}, a_{22}, \ldots, a_{nn}]\,[x_1, x_2, \ldots, x_n]^{\mathrm{T}} = [a_{11}x_1, a_{22}x_2, \ldots, a_{nn}x_n]^{\mathrm{T}}.$$

We extend our generalization still more to consider upper *triangular* matrices. Here the elements below the principal diagonal are zero; $a_{ij} = 0$ if $i > j$, but no other restriction is made. Obviously the sum and difference of two triangular matrices are again triangular. That the product has a similar property requires some proof. If we multiply

$$\begin{bmatrix} a_{11} & a_{12} & \cdots & a_{1n} \\ 0 & a_{22} & \cdots & a_{2n} \\ \vdots & & \ddots & \vdots \\ 0 & 0 & \cdots & a_{nn} \end{bmatrix} \begin{bmatrix} b_{11} & b_{12} & \cdots & b_{1n} \\ 0 & b_{22} & \cdots & b_{2n} \\ \vdots & & \ddots & \vdots \\ 0 & 0 & \cdots & b_{nn} \end{bmatrix} = [c_{ij}],$$

The general element is

$$c_{ij} = \sum_{k=1}^{n} a_{ik}b_{kj}.$$

Now we have $b_{kj} = 0$ if $k > j$ and $a_{ik} = 0$ if $i > k$. Thus, for an element of the sum to be nonzero, i.e., $a_{ik}b_{kj} \neq 0$, $k \leq j$ and $i \leq k$ or $i \leq k \leq j$. This implies $i \leq j$; thus, all summands are 0 if $i > j$ and the product is again upper triangular.

The geometric effect of a transformation represented by such a matrix is more difficult to describe than in the preceding cases. The first basis vector is merely multiplied by the scalar a_{11}. The image of the second is a linear combination of the first and the second, and, in general, if $\mathbf{X}_i$ is the ith vector of the basis under consideration, the image of $\mathbf{X}_i$ is a linear combination of $\mathbf{X}_1, \mathbf{X}_2, \ldots, \mathbf{X}_i$.

Now we consider matrices such as

$$A = \begin{bmatrix} 1 & -1 & 2 \\ -1 & 3 & 4 \\ 2 & 4 & -2 \end{bmatrix},$$

having the property that $A^{\mathsf{T}} = A$ or $a_{ij} = a_{ji}$. These are *symmetric* matrices. Clearly the sum and difference of symmetric matrices are symmetric. However, if A and B are symmetric matrices,

$$(AB)^{\mathsf{T}} = B^{\mathsf{T}}A^{\mathsf{T}} = BA,$$

which is not, in general, equal to AB so that AB need not be symmetric. Therefore the class of symmetric matrices is *not* a subring.

Of the sets of matrices considered so far, the diagonal and symmetric matrices will play the greatest role in future chapters. No simple geometric interpretation of linear transformations having symmetric matrices can be given. The importance of this set lies in other directions than the representation of linear transformations (see Chapter 8).

Several other special sets are considered in the exercises and more will be introduced with their applications in later sections of this chapter.

Exercises

1. Show that the nonsingular $n \times n$ matrices do not form a subring of the ring of all $n \times n$ matrices.
2. Define lower triangular matrices $[a_{ij}]$ by the condition $a_{ij} = 0$ if $i < j$. Show that such matrices form a subring.
3. Define *strictly* upper triangular matrices by the condition $a_{ij} = 0$ if $i \geq j$. Show that the matrices form a subring without an identity. Do the similar problem for strictly lower triangular matrices.
4. If A is a strictly upper triangular $n \times n$ matrix, show that $A^n = 0$.
5. Define a *permutation* matrix as a square matrix with precisely one nonzero element in each row and each column and such that each nonzero element is 1.
   (a) Prove that the product of two permutation matrices is a permutation matrix.
   (b) Show that, if $\mathbf{X}$ is a vector of R^n and P is an $n \times n$ permutation matrix, then $P\mathbf{X}$ is a vector whose components are a permutation of the components of $\mathbf{X}$.

6. If the condition that each nonzero element be 1 is removed from the definition in Exercise 5, the result is a definition of *monomial* matrices.
(a) Generalize part (a) of Exercise 5 to monomial matrices.
(b) Describe the effect of monomial matrices on vectors $\mathbf{X}$ of R^n.
7. Prove that $A^{\mathsf{T}}A$ is symmetric for any matrix A.
8. Prove that any square matrix is the sum of a symmetric and a *skew-symmetric* matrix, where the latter is defined by either of the relations $a_{ij} = -a_{ji}$ or $A^{\mathsf{T}} = -A$.
9. Prove that the product of two symmetric matrices A and B is a symmetric matrix if and only if $AB = BA$.
10. Prove that, for any fixed $n \times n$ matrix A, the set of all matrices which commute with A (that is, all matrices B such that $AB = BA$) forms a subring with identity.

4.2 Elementary Matrices. Inverses

In this section we shall study three special types of matrices which are grouped under the name of elementary matrices. These will be studied not in terms of their geometrical properties as representatives of transformations (which are, in fact, simple enough) but for what they do to other matrices when combined with them by matrix multiplication.

An *elementary matrix of the first kind* is a special type of $n \times n$ diagonal matrix; all the diagonal elements are 1 except for the element in the ith row, which is a real number a, $a \neq 0$. We denote this matrix by

$$D_i(a) = \text{Diagonal } [1, 1, \ldots, \underset{\substack{\uparrow \\ i\text{th position}}}{a}, 1, \ldots, 1].$$

Note that $D_i(a)$ is nonsingular and that $D_i(a)^{-1} = D_i(a^{-1})$, a matrix of the same type.

If A is an arbitrary $n \times n$ matrix, the matrix $D_i(a)A$ is identical with A except that its ith row, considered as a vector of R^n, is a times the ith row of A. All other rows are unchanged. In $AD_i(a)$, it is the ith column which is multiplied by a.

An *elementary matrix of the second kind* is a special type of permutation matrix (Exercise 5, Section 4.1). It is an $n \times n$ matrix such that every element on the principal diagonal is 1 except for the ith and jth rows. In these the diagonal element is 0, but the element in the ith row and jth column is 1 and the element in the jth row and ith column is also 1. All other off-diagonal elements are 0. We denote this matrix by

$$P_{ij} = \begin{array}{c} \\ \\ i \\ \\ j \\ \\ \\ \end{array} \begin{bmatrix} 1 & & \overset{i}{} & & \overset{j}{} & & \\ & \ddots & & & & & \\ & & 0 & \cdots & 1 & & \\ & & \vdots & \ddots & \vdots & & \\ & & 1 & \cdots & 0 & & \\ & & & & & \ddots & \\ & & & & & & 1 \end{bmatrix},$$

where the i, j above and beside the matrix indicate the corresponding columns and rows. Note that P_{ij} is nonsingular and that $P_{ij}^{-1} = P_{ij} = P_{ij}^{\mathsf{T}}$.

The matrix $P_{ij}A$ differs from A in that the ith and jth rows are exchanged. The matrix AP_{ij} has the ith and jth columns of A interchanged.

An *elementary matrix of the third kind* is a type not previously considered. All elements on the principal diagonal are 1. The only nonzero element off the principal diagonal is an a in the ith row, jth column. We denote this matrix by

$$S_{ij}(a) = \begin{array}{cc} & \begin{array}{ccccccc} & & j & & & & \end{array} \\ \begin{array}{c} \\ \\ \\ \\ i \\ \\ \\ \end{array} & \begin{bmatrix} 1 & & & & & & \\ & \ddots & & & & & \\ & & 1 & & & & \\ & & & \ddots & & & \\ & & a & & 1 & & \\ & & & & & \ddots & \\ & & & & & & 1 \end{bmatrix} \end{array}.$$

$S_{ij}(a)$ is nonsingular, and $S_{ij}(a)^{-1} = S_{ij}(-a)$, a matrix of the same type. The matrix $S_{ij}(a)A$ differs from A in having a times the jth row of A added to the ith row; $AS_{ij}(a)$ has a times the ith column of A added to the jth column.

We are going to use these elementary matrices to give a method of finding the inverse of a numerical matrix. The idea is fairly simple; we give a prescription whereby, after successive multiplications on the left (right) by elementary matrices, the original nonsingular matrix A is reduced to the identity matrix. That is, if E_i stands for an elementary matrix without regard to classification, we begin with the matrix A, then compute:

$$E_1A = A_1,\ E_2E_1A = A_2, \ldots,\ E_kE_{k-1}\cdots E_2E_1A = I.$$

Now if we multiply the equation

$$E_kE_{k-1}\cdots E_2E_1A = I \tag{4.3}$$

on the right by A^{-1}, we have

$$E_kE_{k-1}\cdots E_2E_1I = A^{-1}. \tag{4.4}$$

One interpretation of (4.3) and (4.4) is the following: If a succession of multiplications on the left by elementary matrices reduces the matrix A to I, the *same* left multiplications will change I to A^{-1}. Note particularly that we really do not have to write down the E_i; it is what they *do*, not what they *are*, that counts.

Example 1. We illustrate the preceding discussion by computing the inverse of a 3 × 3 matrix. The process is analogous to the process of elimination used for simultaneous linear equations. We begin with

$$A = \begin{bmatrix} 1 & 2 & -1 \\ 2 & 3 & 0 \\ 1 & -1 & 4 \end{bmatrix}; \qquad B = I = \begin{bmatrix} 1 & 0 & 0 \\ 0 & 1 & 0 \\ 0 & 0 & 1 \end{bmatrix}.$$

Now, whatever we do to A (multiplying on the left by E_i), we must do the same thing to B. We obtain successively:

$$A_1 = \begin{bmatrix} 1 & 2 & -1 \\ 0 & -1 & 2 \\ 1 & -1 & 4 \end{bmatrix}, \qquad B_1 = \begin{bmatrix} 1 & 0 & 0 \\ -2 & 1 & 0 \\ 0 & 0 & 1 \end{bmatrix},$$

$$A_2 = \begin{bmatrix} 1 & 2 & -1 \\ 0 & -1 & 2 \\ 0 & -3 & 5 \end{bmatrix}, \qquad B_2 = \begin{bmatrix} 1 & 0 & 0 \\ -2 & 1 & 0 \\ -1 & 0 & 1 \end{bmatrix},$$

$$A_3 = \begin{bmatrix} 1 & 2 & -1 \\ 0 & 1 & -2 \\ 0 & -3 & 5 \end{bmatrix}, \qquad B_3 = \begin{bmatrix} 1 & 0 & 0 \\ 2 & -1 & 0 \\ -1 & 0 & 1 \end{bmatrix},$$

$$A_4 = \begin{bmatrix} 1 & 2 & -1 \\ 0 & 1 & -2 \\ 0 & 0 & -1 \end{bmatrix}, \qquad B_4 = \begin{bmatrix} 1 & 0 & 0 \\ 2 & -1 & 0 \\ 5 & -3 & 1 \end{bmatrix},$$

$$A_5 = \begin{bmatrix} 1 & 2 & -1 \\ 0 & 1 & -2 \\ 0 & 0 & 1 \end{bmatrix}, \qquad B_5 = \begin{bmatrix} 1 & 0 & 0 \\ 2 & -1 & 0 \\ -5 & 3 & -1 \end{bmatrix},$$

$$A_6 = \begin{bmatrix} 1 & 2 & -1 \\ 0 & 1 & 0 \\ 0 & 0 & 1 \end{bmatrix}, \qquad B_6 = \begin{bmatrix} 1 & 0 & 0 \\ -8 & 5 & -2 \\ -5 & 3 & -1 \end{bmatrix},$$

$$A_7 = \begin{bmatrix} 1 & 2 & 0 \\ 0 & 1 & 0 \\ 0 & 0 & 1 \end{bmatrix}, \qquad B_7 = \begin{bmatrix} -4 & 3 & -1 \\ -8 & 5 & -2 \\ -5 & 3 & -1 \end{bmatrix},$$

$$A_8 = \begin{bmatrix} 1 & 0 & 0 \\ 0 & 1 & 0 \\ 0 & 0 & 1 \end{bmatrix}, \qquad B_8 = \begin{bmatrix} 12 & -7 & 3 \\ -8 & 5 & -2 \\ -5 & 3 & -1 \end{bmatrix} = A^{-1}.$$

The procedure used in Example 1 is simple and quite general: for an arbitrary nonsingular matrix A, interchange rows, if necessary, to get a nonzero element a in the first row, first column (1–1 position). Some element in the first column *must* be nonzero since A is assumed to be nonsingular. Multiply the first row by $1/a$ so that the element in the 1–1 position is now 1. Bring all other elements of the first column to zero by adding the proper multiple of the first row to each successive row (A_3 in our example).

Now interchange rows after the first to secure a nonzero element in the 2–2 position and repeat the process, using the second row to reduce all elements of the second column below the 2–2 position to zero. A nonzero element in the second column required for this step must exist since otherwise the original matrix would be singular. (See Exercise 8.)

Continue until all the elements below the principal diagonal are zero and all the diagonal elements are 1 (A_5 in our example).

Now use the last row to eliminate the elements of the last column above the last row and the next-to-the-last row for the next-to-the-last column, and so on, until all the elements above the diagonal are zero.

Each step is to be repeated on the matrix that was originally the identity matrix I.

Note in our example that the elementary matrices were not actually written down. However, they were

$$E_1 = \begin{bmatrix} 1 & 0 & 0 \\ -2 & 1 & 0 \\ 0 & 0 & 1 \end{bmatrix}, \qquad E_2 = \begin{bmatrix} 1 & 0 & 0 \\ 0 & 1 & 0 \\ -1 & 0 & 1 \end{bmatrix}, \qquad E_3 = \begin{bmatrix} 1 & 0 & 0 \\ 0 & -1 & 0 \\ 0 & 0 & 1 \end{bmatrix},$$

$$E_4 = \begin{bmatrix} 1 & 0 & 0 \\ 0 & 1 & 0 \\ 0 & 3 & 1 \end{bmatrix}, \qquad E_5 = \begin{bmatrix} 1 & 0 & 0 \\ 0 & 1 & 0 \\ 0 & 0 & -1 \end{bmatrix}, \qquad E_6 = \begin{bmatrix} 1 & 0 & 0 \\ 0 & 1 & 2 \\ 0 & 0 & 1 \end{bmatrix},$$

$$E_7 = \begin{bmatrix} 1 & 0 & 1 \\ 0 & 1 & 0 \\ 0 & 0 & 1 \end{bmatrix}, \qquad E_8 = \begin{bmatrix} 1 & -2 & 0 \\ 0 & 1 & 0 \\ 0 & 0 & 1 \end{bmatrix}.$$

In practice, a number of the steps can be condensed into a single operation. Also, what has been done by left multiplications (manipulation of the rows) could be done by right multiplications (manipulation of the columns). Do difficulties arise if we mix the two procedures?

The method illustrated and outlined above is perhaps the simplest scheme for finding the inverse of matrices larger than 3 × 3. For large numerical matrices, however, this method is subject to difficulties created by accumulation of errors generated in exact division and multiplicative roundoff. Readers are referred to texts in numerical matrix computation for other methods adapted to large-scale computation.

We leave the rigorous inductive proof of (4.3) to the student. However, if in Equation (4.3) we multiply both sides successively on the left by $E_k^{-1}, E_{k-1}^{-1}, \ldots, E_1^{-1}$, we have

$$\begin{aligned} E_{k-1} \cdots E_2 E_1 A &= E_k^{-1} \\ E_{k-2} \cdots E_2 E_1 A &= E_{k-1}^{-1} E_k^{-1} \\ &\vdots \\ E_1 A &= E_2^{-1} E_3^{-1} \cdots E_{k-1}^{-1} E_k^{-1}, \end{aligned}$$

and finally

$$A = E_1^{-1} E_2^{-1} \cdots E_k^{-1} \tag{4.5}$$

All the inverses in (4.5) are again elementary matrices, and we have the following theorem:

THEOREM 4.1. *A nonsingular matrix A can be written as the product of elementary matrices.*

Exercises

1. The following pairs of matrices satisfy matrix equations of the type $EA = B$ or $AE = B$ where E is an elementary matrix. Find E and the equation.

(a) $$A = \begin{bmatrix} 1 & 2 & 3 \\ 1 & -1 & 4 \\ 1 & 1 & 2 \end{bmatrix}, \qquad B = \begin{bmatrix} 1 & 5 & 3 \\ 1 & 3 & 4 \\ 1 & 3 & 2 \end{bmatrix}.$$

(b) $$A = \begin{bmatrix} 1 & 2 \\ -3 & 5 \\ 4 & 1 \end{bmatrix}, \qquad B = \begin{bmatrix} 1 & 2 \\ 4 & 1 \\ -3 & 5 \end{bmatrix}.$$

(c) $$A = \begin{bmatrix} 1 & -1 & 4 \\ 3 & 2 & 1 \end{bmatrix}, \qquad B = \begin{bmatrix} 2 & -1 & 4 \\ 6 & 2 & 1 \end{bmatrix}.$$

2. Write each of the following matrices as the product of elementary matrices:

(a) $\begin{bmatrix} 1 & -1 & 2 \\ 3 & 1 & 4 \\ 4 & 0 & 1 \end{bmatrix}$, (b) $\begin{bmatrix} 1 & -1 & -2 \\ 2 & 1 & 1 \\ 1 & 5 & -3 \end{bmatrix}$.

3. Find the inverses of the matrices in Exercise 2.
4. Prove that the inverse of a nonsingular (upper) triangular matrix is upper triangular.
5. Prove that a matrix is nonsingular if and only if it is the product of elementary matrices.

6. Find the inverses of the following matrices:

$$\text{(a)} \begin{bmatrix} 1 & -1 & 2 & 3 \\ 2 & 1 & -2 & 3 \\ 1 & -1 & 2 & 5 \\ 1 & -1 & 3 & 3 \end{bmatrix}, \quad \text{(b)} \begin{bmatrix} 2 & 0 & -1 & 1 \\ 1 & 1 & -2 & 0 \\ 0 & 3 & 1 & -2 \\ 0 & 6 & 4 & -1 \end{bmatrix}.$$

7. Provide a rigorous proof that the method of finding an inverse of a matrix illustrated by Example 1 and discussed in this section is valid. *Hint:* Use induction on the size of the matrix and observe that if E_i^* is an elementary $(n - 1) \times (n - 1)$ matrix, then

$$\begin{bmatrix} 1 & 0 & \cdots & 0 \\ 0 & & & \\ \vdots & & \left[\quad E_i^* \quad \right] & \\ 0 & & & \end{bmatrix}$$

is an elementary $n \times n$ matrix.

8. Let $A = [a_{ij}]$ be an $n \times n$ matrix with $a_{i1} = a_{i2} = 0$ for $i = 2, 3, \ldots, n$. Show that A is singular.

4.3 Rank of a Matrix

In this section we consider several spaces that are naturally connected with a given $m \times n$ matrix A. These are

1. The span of the columns of A when they are viewed as vectors in R^m; the *column space* of A.
2. The span of the rows of A when they are viewed as vectors in R^n; the *row space* of A.
3. The image of the transformation $\mathrm{T}: R^n \to R^m$ defined by $\mathrm{T}\mathbf{X} = A\mathbf{X}^{\mathrm{T}}$; the *image space* of A.

The dimensions of these three spaces are called the *column rank*, the *row rank*, and the *image rank* of A, respectively. The purpose of this section is to show that for a given matrix these three numbers are equal, and, along the way, demonstrate a procedure for computing this number.

Note that the image of the standard basis element $\mathbf{E}_i$ under the transformation T defined above is just the ith column of A. This means that the column space of A and the image space of A are the same. Thus it is easy to see that the column rank and the image rank are always equal. Actually, we can say slightly more.

THEOREM 4.2. *Let A be an $m \times n$ matrix, P be any invertible $m \times m$ matrix, and Q be any invertible $n \times n$ matrix. Then the column ranks of PA, AQ, and A are equal.*

PROOF. As the images of A and AQ are the same (Q is onto), we immediately conclude that A and AQ have the same column ranks. On the other hand, if S is the linear transformation associated with P and W is the image of A, then dimension (W) = dimension $(\mathrm{S}(W))$ because S is invertible. But this means that the image ranks of PA and A are the same, as the image of PA is just $\mathrm{S}(W)$. Thus the column rank of A equals the column rank of PA and the theorem is established.

Turning to the row rank, let us first consider the problem of computing the row rank of a given matrix A. Let us recall the three operations used in Section 3.6.

1. Interchange two rows.
2. Add a multiple of one row to another.
3. Multiply one row by a nonzero constant.

We note that performing any one of these operations (and hence a sequence of such operations) does not change the row rank. This is obvious for operations of type 1 or 3; for an operation of type 2 observe that the rows of the resulting matrix are sums of multiples of the rows of the original matrix, so the rank is not increased. But the operation is invertible; that is, another type 2 operation will yield A again, and thus the rank is not decreased.

As we saw in Section 3.6, a sequence of the operations will reduce A to a particularly simple matrix. We give these matrices a name.

DEFINITION 4.1. A matrix is said to be in ROW ECHELON FORM *if it has the following properties:*

1. *The first nonzero entry tn each row is* 1.
2. *Each column of A that contains the leading nonzero entry of some row has all of its other entries equal to* 0.
3. *The leading* 1 *in each nonzero row is to the right of leading ones in previous rows.*
4. *Rows consisting solely of zeros occur after all of the rows wtth one or more nonzero entries.*

We now make the observation that the row rank of a matrix in row echelon form is just the number of nonzero rows. We will leave the details of the proof as an exercise, but a quick outline is as follows: suppose a linear combination of these row vectors is $\mathbf{0}$. Let us denote the ith row of our matrix by $\mathbf{B}_i$ and assume that there are r nonzero rows. If

$$b_1\mathbf{B}_1 + b_2\mathbf{B}_2 + \cdots + b_r\mathbf{B}_r = \mathbf{0},$$

let b_k be the first nonzero b_i. Transpose and divide by b_k:

$$\mathbf{B}_k = -\frac{b_{k+1}}{b_k}\mathbf{B}_{k+1} - \cdots - \frac{b_r}{b_k}\mathbf{B}_r.$$

But this is impossible because the position of the leading 1 in $\mathbf{B}_k$ is zero in each $\mathbf{B}_i$, $i = k+1, k+2, \ldots, r$.

Example 1. Find the row echelon form and the row rank of the matrix

$$A = \begin{bmatrix} 1 & 0 & 3 & -2 & -1 & 2 \\ 2 & 0 & 6 & -4 & -2 & 4 \\ 1 & 0 & 3 & -2 & 1 & 4 \\ 2 & 0 & 6 & 1 & -1 & 0 \end{bmatrix}.$$

We first subtract twice the first row from the second and fourth rows and subtract the first row from the third:

$$\begin{bmatrix} 1 & 0 & 3 & -2 & -1 & 2 \\ 0 & 0 & 0 & 0 & 0 & 0 \\ 0 & 0 & 0 & 0 & 2 & 2 \\ 0 & 0 & 0 & 5 & 1 & -4 \end{bmatrix}.$$

We now note that first nonzero column (excluding the first row) is column four. Interchanging rows two and four and multiplying the new second row by $\frac{1}{5}$ gives

$$\begin{bmatrix} 1 & 0 & 3 & -2 & -1 & 2 \\ 0 & 0 & 0 & 1 & \frac{1}{5} & -\frac{4}{5} \\ 0 & 0 & 0 & 0 & 2 & 2 \\ 0 & 0 & 0 & 0 & 0 & 0 \end{bmatrix}.$$

We now add twice the second row to the first:

$$\begin{bmatrix} 1 & 0 & 3 & 0 & -\frac{3}{5} & \frac{2}{5} \\ 0 & 0 & 0 & 1 & \frac{1}{5} & -\frac{4}{5} \\ 0 & 0 & 0 & 0 & 2 & 2 \\ 0 & 0 & 0 & 0 & 0 & 0 \end{bmatrix}.$$

Next, multiply the third row by $\frac{1}{2}$ and subtract the appropriate multiples of it from the first two rows:

$$\begin{bmatrix} 1 & 0 & 3 & 0 & 0 & 1 \\ 0 & 0 & 0 & 1 & 0 & -1 \\ 0 & 0 & 0 & 0 & 1 & 1 \\ 0 & 0 & 0 & 0 & 0 & 0 \end{bmatrix}.$$

This matrix is in row echelon form and its row rank is clearly 3. Thus A also has row rank 3. Note that the elementary matrices corresponding to the operations we have performed are

$$E_1 = \begin{bmatrix} 1 & 0 & 0 & 0 \\ -2 & 1 & 0 & 0 \\ 0 & 0 & 1 & 0 \\ 0 & 0 & 0 & 1 \end{bmatrix}, \qquad E_2 = \begin{bmatrix} 1 & 0 & 0 & 0 \\ 0 & 1 & 0 & 0 \\ 0 & 0 & 1 & 0 \\ -2 & 0 & 0 & 1 \end{bmatrix},$$

$$E_3 = \begin{bmatrix} 1 & 0 & 0 & 0 \\ 0 & 1 & 0 & 0 \\ -1 & 0 & 1 & 0 \\ 0 & 0 & 0 & 1 \end{bmatrix}, \qquad E_4 = \begin{bmatrix} 1 & 0 & 0 & 0 \\ 0 & 0 & 0 & 1 \\ 0 & 0 & 1 & 0 \\ 0 & 1 & 0 & 0 \end{bmatrix},$$

$$E_5 = \begin{bmatrix} 1 & 0 & 0 & 0 \\ 0 & \frac{1}{5} & 0 & 0 \\ 0 & 0 & 1 & 0 \\ 0 & 0 & 0 & 1 \end{bmatrix}, \qquad E_6 = \begin{bmatrix} 1 & 2 & 0 & 0 \\ 0 & 1 & 0 & 0 \\ 0 & 0 & 1 & 0 \\ 0 & 0 & 0 & 1 \end{bmatrix},$$

$$E_7 = \begin{bmatrix} 1 & 0 & 0 & 0 \\ 0 & 1 & 0 & 0 \\ 0 & 0 & \frac{1}{2} & 0 \\ 0 & 0 & 0 & 1 \end{bmatrix}, \qquad E_8 = \begin{bmatrix} 1 & 0 & \frac{3}{5} & 0 \\ 0 & 1 & 0 & 0 \\ 0 & 0 & 1 & 0 \\ 0 & 0 & 0 & 1 \end{bmatrix},$$

$$E_9 = \begin{bmatrix} 1 & 0 & 0 & 0 \\ 0 & 1 & -\frac{1}{5} & 0 \\ 0 & 0 & 1 & 0 \\ 0 & 0 & 0 & 1 \end{bmatrix}.$$

We know then that

$$E_9 E_8 E_7 \cdots E_1 A = \begin{bmatrix} 1 & 0 & 3 & 0 & 0 & 1 \\ 0 & 0 & 0 & 1 & 0 & -1 \\ 0 & 0 & 0 & 0 & 1 & 1 \\ 0 & 0 & 0 & 0 & 0 & 0 \end{bmatrix}.$$

Using the technique just illustrated we can prove the following theorem.

THEOREM 4.3. If A is any $m \times n$ matrix, P is any invertible $m \times m$ matrix, and Q is any invertible $n \times n$ matrix, then the row ranks of A, PA, and AQ are equal.

PROOF. We noted above that performing a sequence of row operations on A does not change the row rank. Since this sequence corresponds to multiplying A on the left by a sequence of elementary matrices, we have that A and $E_1E_2 \cdots E_nA$ have the same row rank for any sequence $E_1, E_2, \ldots, E_n$ of elementary matrices. But P can be written as a product of elementary matrices by Theorem 4.1, and thus the row rank of PA is equal to the row rank of A.

To prove that the row ranks of A and AQ are equal, we note that the row rank of AQ is the column rank of $(AQ)^{\mathsf{T}} = Q^{\mathsf{T}}A^{\mathsf{T}}$. By Theorem 4.2 the column rank of $Q^{\mathsf{T}}A^{\mathsf{T}}$ is equal to the column rank of A^{T}, which is the row rank of A.

We are now in a position to put all of the pieces together and establish the main result of this section.

THEOREM 4.4. For any matrix A, the row rank, column rank, and the image rank are equal. This unique number is called the RANK *of A.*

PROOF. We need only show that the row and column ranks are equal. Let C be the row echelon form of A; thus $C = PA$, where P is a product of elementary matrices. If C has r nonzero rows, we know that the row rank of A is r by Theorem 4.3 and the statement immediately preceding Example 1. We now claim that by performing column operations on C (i.e., by multiplying on the right by elementary matrices) we can reduce it to the form $\begin{bmatrix} I_r & O \\ O & O \end{bmatrix}$.* This may be proved by induction, but we simply note that each nonzero row of C has a leading 1, which has no other nonzero elements in its column. Thus by subtracting multiples of this column from other columns we can make this leading 1 the only nonzero entry in its row, *without affecting the other rows of C.* After r such subtractions, and perhaps some interchanging of columns, we will have $PAQ = \begin{bmatrix} I_r & O \\ O & O \end{bmatrix}$, where Q is the product of elementary matrices corresponding to the operations we have performed. Now we note that this matrix clearly has column rank r, and that the column rank of PAQ equals the column rank of A by Theorem 4.2.

We illustrate the procedure outlined in the proof of Theorem 4.4 with an example.

Example 2. Let $A, E_1, E_2, \ldots, E_9$ be as in Example 1. We reduce A to the form $\begin{bmatrix} I_3 & O \\ O & O \end{bmatrix}$ by first doing the same sequence of row operations on A as in Example 1. We then do column operations on $E_9E_8 \cdots E_1A$. Subtracting the first column from the sixth and three times the first from the third yields

$$\begin{bmatrix} 1 & 0 & 0 & 0 & 0 & 0 \\ 0 & 0 & 0 & 1 & 0 & -1 \\ 0 & 0 & 0 & 0 & 1 & 1 \\ 0 & 0 & 0 & 0 & 0 & 0 \end{bmatrix}.$$

* The large zeros represent blocks of zeros.

Now add the fourth column to the sixth.

$$\begin{bmatrix} 1 & 0 & 0 & 0 & 0 & 0 \\ 0 & 0 & 0 & 1 & 0 & 0 \\ 0 & 0 & 0 & 0 & 1 & 1 \\ 0 & 0 & 0 & 0 & 0 & 0 \end{bmatrix}.$$

Next, subtract the fifth column from the sixth.

$$\begin{bmatrix} 1 & 0 & 0 & 0 & 0 & 0 \\ 0 & 0 & 0 & 1 & 0 & 0 \\ 0 & 0 & 0 & 0 & 1 & 0 \\ 0 & 0 & 0 & 0 & 0 & 0 \end{bmatrix}.$$

Now interchange columns two and four and then columns three and five.

$$\begin{bmatrix} 1 & 0 & 0 & 0 & 0 & 0 \\ 0 & 1 & 0 & 0 & 0 & 0 \\ 0 & 0 & 1 & 0 & 0 & 0 \\ 0 & 0 & 0 & 0 & 0 & 0 \end{bmatrix}.$$

The elementary matrices that correspond to the operations we have performed are

$$F_1 = \begin{bmatrix} 1 & 0 & 0 & 0 & 0 & -1 \\ 0 & 1 & 0 & 0 & 0 & 0 \\ 0 & 0 & 1 & 0 & 0 & 0 \\ 0 & 0 & 0 & 1 & 0 & 0 \\ 0 & 0 & 0 & 0 & 1 & 0 \\ 0 & 0 & 0 & 0 & 0 & 1 \end{bmatrix}, \quad F_2 = \begin{bmatrix} 1 & 0 & -3 & 0 & 0 & 0 \\ 0 & 1 & 0 & 0 & 0 & 0 \\ 0 & 0 & 1 & 0 & 0 & 0 \\ 0 & 0 & 0 & 1 & 0 & 0 \\ 0 & 0 & 0 & 0 & 1 & 0 \\ 0 & 0 & 0 & 0 & 0 & 1 \end{bmatrix},$$

$$F_3 = \begin{bmatrix} 1 & 0 & 0 & 0 & 0 & 0 \\ 0 & 1 & 0 & 0 & 0 & 0 \\ 0 & 0 & 1 & 0 & 0 & 0 \\ 0 & 0 & 0 & 1 & 0 & 1 \\ 0 & 0 & 0 & 0 & 1 & 0 \\ 0 & 0 & 0 & 0 & 0 & 1 \end{bmatrix}, \quad F_4 = \begin{bmatrix} 1 & 0 & 0 & 0 & 0 & 0 \\ 0 & 1 & 0 & 0 & 0 & 0 \\ 0 & 0 & 1 & 0 & 0 & 0 \\ 0 & 0 & 0 & 1 & 0 & 0 \\ 0 & 0 & 0 & 0 & 1 & -1 \\ 0 & 0 & 0 & 0 & 0 & 1 \end{bmatrix},$$

$$F_5 = \begin{bmatrix} 1 & 0 & 0 & 0 & 0 & 0 \\ 0 & 0 & 0 & 1 & 0 & 0 \\ 0 & 0 & 1 & 0 & 0 & 0 \\ 0 & 1 & 0 & 0 & 0 & 0 \\ 0 & 0 & 0 & 0 & 1 & 0 \\ 0 & 0 & 0 & 0 & 0 & 1 \end{bmatrix}, \quad F_6 = \begin{bmatrix} 1 & 0 & 0 & 0 & 0 & 0 \\ 0 & 1 & 0 & 0 & 0 & 0 \\ 0 & 0 & 0 & 0 & 1 & 0 \\ 0 & 0 & 0 & 1 & 0 & 0 \\ 0 & 0 & 1 & 0 & 0 & 0 \\ 0 & 0 & 0 & 0 & 0 & 1 \end{bmatrix}.$$

We now know that

$$E_9 E_8 \cdots E_1 A F_1 F_2 \cdots F_6 = \begin{bmatrix} 1 & 0 & 0 & 0 & 0 & 0 \\ 0 & 1 & 0 & 0 & 0 & 0 \\ 0 & 0 & 1 & 0 & 0 & 0 \\ 0 & 0 & 0 & 0 & 0 & 0 \end{bmatrix}.$$

As the matrix on the right has row rank = column rank = 3, we have A with column rank 3 as well as row rank 3.

Exercises

1. Reduce the following matrices to row echelon form and determine their row rank:

$$\text{(a)} \begin{bmatrix} 1 & -1 & 0 & 1 \\ 1 & 1 & 2 & 3 \\ 1 & 2 & -1 & 1 \end{bmatrix}, \qquad \text{(b)} \begin{bmatrix} 1 & -1 & 2 & 1 \\ 3 & 0 & 1 & 2 \\ 2 & 1 & -1 & 1 \end{bmatrix},$$

$$\text{(c)} \begin{bmatrix} 1 & 1 & 1 & -1 & 2 \\ 1 & -1 & 1 & 1 & 1 \\ 0 & 2 & 1 & -1 & 1 \end{bmatrix}, \qquad \text{(d)} \begin{bmatrix} 2 & -1 & 4 & 5 \\ 3 & 2 & 1 & 4 \\ 5 & -1 & 1 & 3 \end{bmatrix}.$$

2. Find the rank of the following matrix as a function of h and k:

$$\begin{bmatrix} 1 & -1 & 2 & 3 \\ 2 & 1 & h & 1 \\ 0 & -3 & k & 5 \\ 3 & 3 & 4 & -1 \end{bmatrix}.$$

3. Reduce the matrices in Exercise 1 to the form $\begin{bmatrix} I_r & O \\ O & O \end{bmatrix}$.
4. If a, b, c, d are numbers such that $a \neq 0$ and $ad - bc = 0$, find matrices P, Q that satisfy $P \begin{bmatrix} a & b \\ c & d \end{bmatrix} Q = \begin{bmatrix} 1 & 0 \\ 0 & 0 \end{bmatrix}$.
5. Prove that the rank of AB is at least as small as the smaller of the rank of A and the rank of B.
6. Let A and B be $n \times n$ matrices, and prove that rank $(A + B) \leq$ rank $A +$ rank B. Give examples of both equality and inequality.
7. Prove that the row rank of a matrix in row echelon form is the number of nonzero rows.

4.4 Applications of the Concept of Rank

We say that a matrix B is equivalent to a matrix A if there exist nonsingular matrices P and Q such that $PAQ = B$. The simple (but confusingly worded) proposition "equivalence of matrices is an equivalence relation for the set of all $m \times n$ matrices" is left as an exercise.

It is natural to ask, "When are two $m \times n$ matrices A and B equivalent?" The answer is essentially contained in our discussion of rank in the preceding section. Combining Theorems 4.3 and 4.4 we see that the ranks (we can now use the term without a modifier) of A and PAQ are equal if P and Q are invertible matrices of appropriate sizes. We have shown, then, that equivalent matrices have the same rank. We now propose to demonstrate the converse.

In the proof of Theorem 4.4 we saw that for any matrix A there exist invertible matrices P and Q such that $PAQ = \begin{bmatrix} I_r & O \\ O & O \end{bmatrix}$, where r is the rank of A. This result may be expressed formally:

THEOREM 4.5. Every $m \times n$ matrix of rank r is equivalent to precisely one matrix whose only nonzero elements are 1's occurring on the "principal diagonal" in the first r positions.

Theorem 4.5 assures us that matrices of the same rank are equivalent.

COROLLARY. Two $m \times n$ matrices are equivalent if and only if they have the same rank.

We have seen (Section 3.9) that if matrices A and B represent the same linear transformation with respect to two different choices of bases, then $B = PAQ^{-1}$ for appropriate nonsingular P and Q. Thus B is equivalent to A. Conversely, if B is equivalent to A, $B = PAQ = PA(Q^{-1})^{-1}$ so that B and A represent the same linear transformation for some choices of bases of the vector spaces R^m and R^n. Thus, the rank of a linear transformation T may be described as the rank of any matrix representing T. In particular, one such matrix is the special one described in the last theorem. This special matrix representation is an example of a general procedure by which a particular matrix (called a canonical form) is chosen to represent a set of related matrices. This topic will be discussed in detail in later chapters.

Rank of a Matrix and Linear Equations

Let us consider the system of linear equations

$$\begin{aligned} a_{11}x_1 + a_{12}x_2 + \cdots + a_{1n}x_n &= b_1, \\ a_{21}x_1 + a_{22}x_2 + \cdots + a_{2n}x_n &= b_2, \\ &\vdots \\ a_{m1}x_1 + a_{m2}x_2 + \cdots + a_{mn}x_n &= b_m \end{aligned} \tag{4.6}$$

or

$$AX = B, \tag{4.7}$$

where

$$\begin{aligned} X &= [x_1, x_2, \ldots, x_m]^{\mathsf{T}}, \\ B &= [b_1, b_2, \ldots, b_m]^{\mathsf{T}}, \end{aligned}$$

and $A = [a_{ij}]$ is the $m \times n$ matrix whose elements appear as the coefficients in (4.6). $[A : B]$ is used to denote the *augmented matrix* of A; that is, the $m \times (n + 1)$ matrix obtained by adjoining the column B to A.

THEOREM 4.6. The system of linear equations (4.6) *has solutions if and only if the rank of the augmented matrix is equal to the rank of the matrix A. If the ranks are equal to r, $n - r$ of the unknowns may be selected arbitrarily and the remaining r may be found uniquely in terms of them.*

PROOF. As we saw in Section 3.6, the system (4.6) has a solution if and only if B is in the span of the columns of A. Thus there will be a solution if and only if B is a linear combination of the column vectors of A. That is, if and only if the addition of B to the matrix A does not increase the column rank.

For the second part of the theorem, it will be helpful if we write Equations (4.6) and (4.7) in still another way, making use of the column vectors A^i of A.

$$x_1A^1 + x_2A^2 + \cdots + x_nA^n = B. \tag{4.8}$$

We know there is a largest subset of the column vectors of A that is linearly independent. For ease of notation, we shall assume that the first r columns are such a subset. This can be accomplished by renumbering the x_i's.

Under these assumptions, $\{A^1, A^2, \ldots, A^r\}$ forms a basis for the image of A; $A^{r+1}, A^{r+2}, \ldots, A^n$, B are vectors in the image of A and a linear combination of them is also in the image of A and so has a unique representation in terms of our chosen basis. Choose any selection of values for $x_{r+1}, x_{r+2}, \ldots, x_n$ and consider the vector in the image of A:

$$B - x_{r+1}A^{r+1} - x_{r+2}A^{r+2} - \cdots - x_nA^n.$$

Write this, uniquely, as a linear combination of $A^1, A^2, \ldots, A^r$, designating the coefficients by $x_1, x_2, \ldots, x_r$.

$$x_1A^1 + x_2A^2 + \cdots + x_rA^r = B - x_{r+1}A^{r+1} - x_{r+2}A^{r+2} - \cdots - x_nA^n. \quad (4.9)$$

Making the obvious transposition, (4.9) becomes (4.8). Thus $n - r$ of the x_i's have been arbitrarily assigned, resulting in a unique assignment for the other r.

Example 1. Consider the system $AX = B$, where

$$A = \begin{bmatrix} 1 & 3 & -2 & -1 & 2 \\ 2 & 6 & -4 & -2 & 4 \\ 1 & 3 & -2 & 1 & 0 \\ 2 & 6 & 1 & -1 & 0 \end{bmatrix} \quad B = \begin{bmatrix} 1 \\ 2 \\ -1 \\ 4 \end{bmatrix}.$$

This system was considered in Examples 1 and 2 of Section 3.6. Reducing the augmented matrix by elementary row operations we obtained the matrix

$$\begin{bmatrix} 1 & 3 & 0 & 0 & -\frac{1}{5} & : & \frac{6}{5} \\ 0 & 0 & 1 & 0 & -\frac{3}{5} & : & \frac{3}{5} \\ 0 & 0 & 0 & 1 & -1 & : & -1 \\ 0 & 0 & 0 & 0 & 0 & : & 0 \end{bmatrix}.$$

It is clear that columns 1, 3, and 4 of this matrix are a basis for its column space. Accordingly, x_2 and x_5 may be chosen arbitrarily and then Equation (4.9) becomes

$$(-3x_2 + \tfrac{1}{5}x_5 + \tfrac{6}{5})\begin{bmatrix} 1 \\ 2 \\ 1 \\ 2 \end{bmatrix} + \tfrac{3}{5}(x_5 + 1)\begin{bmatrix} -2 \\ -4 \\ -2 \\ 1 \end{bmatrix} + (x_5 - 1)\begin{bmatrix} -1 \\ -2 \\ 1 \\ -1 \end{bmatrix}$$

$$= \begin{bmatrix} 1 \\ 2 \\ -1 \\ 4 \end{bmatrix} - x_2\begin{bmatrix} 3 \\ 6 \\ 3 \\ 6 \end{bmatrix} - x_5\begin{bmatrix} 2 \\ 4 \\ 0 \\ 0 \end{bmatrix}.$$

This last equation is just another way of saying that all solutions are of the form

$$x_1 = -3x_2 + \tfrac{1}{5}x_5 + \tfrac{6}{5}, \qquad x_3 = \tfrac{3}{5}(x_5 + 1), \qquad x_4 = x_5 - 1,$$

x_2 and x_5 arbitrary.

Exercises

1. Reduce the following matrices to *row* echelon form and determine their rank:

(a) $\begin{bmatrix} 1 & -1 & 0 & 1 \\ 1 & 1 & 2 & 3 \\ 1 & 2 & -1 & 1 \end{bmatrix}$, (b) $\begin{bmatrix} 1 & -1 & 2 & 1 \\ 3 & 0 & 1 & 2 \\ 2 & 1 & -1 & 1 \end{bmatrix}$,

(c) $\begin{bmatrix} 1 & 1 & 1 & -1 & 2 \\ 1 & -1 & 1 & 1 & 1 \\ 0 & 2 & 1 & -1 & 1 \end{bmatrix}$, (d) $\begin{bmatrix} 2 & -1 & 4 & 5 \\ 3 & 2 & 1 & 4 \\ 5 & -1 & 1 & 3 \end{bmatrix}$.

2. Reduce the matrices in Exercise 1 to a *column* echelon form and verify your previous determination of their rank.
3. Find the rank of the following matrix as a function of h and k:

$$\begin{bmatrix} 1 & -1 & 2 & 3 \\ 2 & 1 & h & 1 \\ 0 & -3 & k & 5 \\ 3 & 3 & 4 & -1 \end{bmatrix}.$$

4. Let $D: P^5 \to P^5$ be the operator that takes a polynomial to its derivative.
   (a) Find bases for the domain and range of D such that the matrix of D is given by

$$A = \begin{bmatrix} 1 & 0 & 0 & 0 & 0 \\ 0 & 1 & 0 & 0 & 0 \\ 0 & 0 & 1 & 0 & 0 \\ 0 & 0 & 0 & 1 & 0 \\ 0 & 0 & 0 & 0 & 0 \end{bmatrix}.$$

   Note that two different bases are required.
   (b) Find matrices P, Q^{-1} such that

$$PAQ^{-1} = \begin{bmatrix} 0 & 1 & 0 & 0 & 0 \\ 0 & 0 & 2 & 0 & 0 \\ 0 & 0 & 0 & 3 & 0 \\ 0 & 0 & 0 & 0 & 4 \\ 0 & 0 & 0 & 0 & 0 \end{bmatrix}.$$

5. How many pairwise nonequivalent 4×4 matrices can be found? What about the $m \times n$ case?

4.5 Orthogonal Transformations

In Chapter 1 we introduced the concept of a *group*. We now desire to study a set of transformations that generalize the rotations T_θ discussed in Section 3.1. Since this set of transformations forms a group under multiplication, we begin by reviewing the criteria for a multiplicative group.

A set of linear transformations forms a group under multiplication if

(1) For any two elements T, S of the set, the product TS is defined and is also in the set.

(2) The identity transformation I is in the set.

(3) For any T in the set, there is an element T^{-1} in the set such that $TT^{-1} = T^{-1}T = I$.

The remaining axiom for a group (that multiplication be associative) will be automatically satisfied for any set of linear transformations.

What restrictions do these requirements impose? Statement 1 requires that the product of any two linear transformations from the set be defined; thus there must be an underlying vector space that is the range and the domain of each linear transformation from our set. Statement 3 requires that our set must consist entirely of invertible transformations.

This suggests that we consider the set of all invertible linear transformations on R^n. This set of transformations is called the *general linear group* or the *full linear group* and will be denoted by $GL(n, R)$.

Of course, if we choose a basis for R^n, then each element in $GL(n, R)$ is associated with an invertible matrix. As we saw in Chapter 3, this association preserves multiplication (in fact, all algebraic operations), and thus the set of all invertible $n \times n$ real matrices is a multiplicative group. Since the algebraic structure of this set of matrices exactly corresponds to the structure of $\mathrm{GL}(n, R)$, we shall also refer to the set of all $n \times n$ invertible real matrices as the general linear group. Note that, given any multiplicative group of linear transformations, we can always pass to an isomorphic group of matrices simply by choosing a basis.

The transformations that we wish to study in this section are defined as follows.

DEFINITION 4.2. A linear transformation T *from* R^n *to* R^n *is called an* ORTHOGONAL TRANSFORMATION *if*

$$(\mathrm{T}\mathbf{X}, \mathrm{T}\mathbf{X}) = (\mathbf{X}, \mathbf{X})$$

for all $\mathbf{X}$ *in* R^n*; that is, if* T *changes only the direction, not the length, of a vector in* R^n.

The first thing to be pointed out is that the set of all orthogonal transformations of R^n forms a subgroup of $\mathrm{GL}(n, R)$ (that is, we have a subset that forms a group under multiplication).

In order to prove the preceding statement, we may say at once that an orthogonal transformation is nonsingular. Certainly the null space of an orthogonal transformation T consists of the zero vector alone since any nonzero vector mapping onto zero would have its length changed. Hence T is nonsingular by Theorems 3.5 and 3.17, and the set of all orthogonal transformations is at least a subset of the general linear group.

Next, closure under multiplication is also evident. If neither T_1 nor T_2 changes lengths of vectors, then certainly T_1 followed by T_2 cannot change a length.

Finally, if T is an orthogonal transformation, so is T^{-1}. Suppose T^{-1} changes the length of a vector $\mathbf{X}$. Then $\mathrm{T}(\mathrm{T}^{-1}\mathbf{X})$ has the same length as $\mathrm{T}^{-1}(\mathbf{X})$, but $\mathrm{T}\mathrm{T}^{-1}\mathbf{X} = \mathrm{I}\mathbf{X} = \mathbf{X}$!

We shall call the subgroup of orthogonal transformations of the general linear group the *orthogonal group* (on R^n).

We can easily extend the idea of angle between two vectors to R^n exactly as we extended the idea of length. Recall that for vectors in R^2 or R^3 the angle θ between $\mathbf{X}$ and $\mathbf{Y}$ satisfies

$$\cos\theta = \frac{(\mathbf{X}, \mathbf{Y})}{(\mathbf{X}, \mathbf{X})^{1/2}(\mathbf{Y}, \mathbf{Y})^{1/2}}. \tag{4.10}$$

We simply use formula (4.10) to *define* the angle between $\mathbf{X}$ and $\mathbf{Y}$ for higher-dimensional spaces.

DEFINITION 4.3. The angle θ *between two vectors of* R^n *is defined by*

$$\theta = \arccos\frac{(\mathbf{X}, \mathbf{Y})}{(\mathbf{X}, \mathbf{X})^{1/2}(\mathbf{Y}, \mathbf{Y})^{1/2}},$$

the arccosine taking values between 0 *and* π.

Incidentally, the validity of this definition depends on the Schwarz inequality

$$(\mathbf{X}, \mathbf{X})(\mathbf{Y}, \mathbf{Y}) \geq (\mathbf{X}, \mathbf{Y})^2,$$

which guarantees that the fraction in the definition will lie between -1 and 1.

An important property of orthogonal transformations is expressed in the following theorem.

THEOREM 4.7. If T *is an orthogonal transformation on* R^n, *then for all vectors* **X**, **Y** *of* R^n *the angle between* **X** *and* **Y** *equals the angle between* T**X** *and* T**Y**; *that is,* T *preserves angles as well as lengths.*

PROOF. We first give an informal exposition, using the geometrical representation of vectors which is valid in ordinary two- or three-space.

Take as representatives of **X** and **Y** two segments with a common initial point. Complete the resulting triangle. The added segment represents **X** − **Y** if the direction is chosen correctly.

Now compute T**X**, T**Y**, and T(**X** − **Y**) = T**X** − T**Y**. The representative segments again form a triangle, all of whose sides are equal to the sides of the original triangle. The triangles are congruent. Hence, corresponding angles are equal. (See Figure 4.1.)

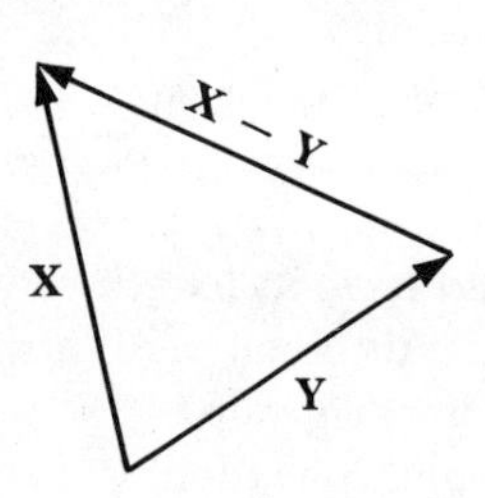

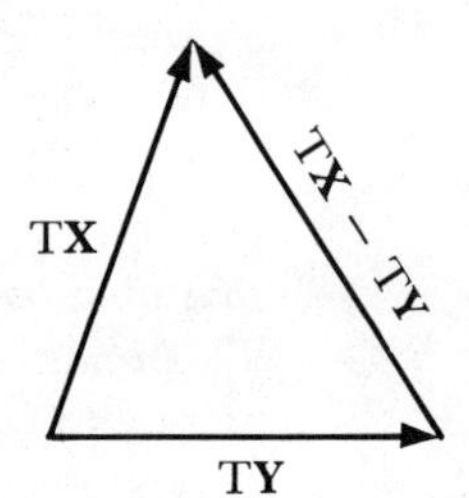

FIGURE 4.1

The formal algebraic proof follows the geometrical outline. We must prove that

$$\frac{(\mathbf{X}, \mathbf{Y})}{(\mathbf{X}, \mathbf{X})^{1/2}(\mathbf{Y}, \mathbf{Y})^{1/2}} = \frac{(\mathrm{T}\mathbf{X}, \mathrm{T}\mathbf{Y})}{(\mathrm{T}\mathbf{X}, \mathrm{T}\mathbf{X})^{1/2}(\mathrm{T}\mathbf{Y}, \mathrm{T}\mathbf{Y})^{1/2}}. \tag{4.11}$$

The denominators of (4.11) are equal by hypothesis. It then suffices to prove

$$(\mathbf{X}, \mathbf{Y}) = (\mathrm{T}\mathbf{X}, \mathrm{T}\mathbf{Y}).$$

That is, we shall prove that an orthogonal transformation leaves *all* inner products unchanged. To do this, we use **X** − **Y** as we did in the geometrical argument:

$$\begin{aligned}(\mathbf{X} - \mathbf{Y}, \mathbf{X} - \mathbf{Y}) &= (\mathrm{T}(\mathbf{X} - \mathbf{Y}), \mathrm{T}(\mathbf{X} - \mathbf{Y})) \\ &= (\mathrm{T}\mathbf{X} - \mathrm{T}\mathbf{Y}, \mathrm{T}\mathbf{X} - \mathrm{T}\mathbf{Y}).\end{aligned}$$

We expand both sides, using the linearity and commutative properties of the inner product.

$$(\mathbf{X}, \mathbf{X}) - 2(\mathbf{X}, \mathbf{Y}) + (\mathbf{Y}, \mathbf{Y}) = (\mathrm{T}\mathbf{X}, \mathrm{T}\mathbf{X}) - 2(\mathrm{T}\mathbf{X}, \mathrm{T}\mathbf{Y}) + (\mathrm{T}\mathbf{Y}, \mathrm{T}\mathbf{Y}).$$

Equating (**X**, **X**) with (T**X**, T**X**) and (**Y**, **Y**) with (T**Y**, T**Y**),

$$-2(\mathbf{X}, \mathbf{Y}) = -2(\mathrm{T}\mathbf{X}, \mathrm{T}\mathbf{Y}),$$

and the necessary equation follows.

What can we say about matrices that represent orthogonal transformations? In this generality, the answer would be rather limited, but if we limit the bases under consideration to orthonormal bases, we are able to give a characterization of an interesting set of matrices associated with orthogonal transformations.

THEOREM 4.8. If $\{\mathbf{X}_1, \mathbf{X}_2, \ldots, \mathbf{X}_n\}$ *is an orthonormal basis of* R^n *and* T *is an orthogonal transformation on* R^n *whose matrix with respect to* $\{\mathbf{X}_i\}$ *is* A, *then*

(i) *The column vectors of* A *have length* 1.
(ii) *The column vectors of* A *are mutually orthogonal.*
(iii) $A^{-1} = A^{\mathsf{T}}$, *hence* (i) *and* (ii) *are true with the word "column" replaced by "row."*

The image of $\mathbf{X}_j$ under T is given by the jth column of A; it is

$$a_{ij}\mathbf{X}_1 + a_{2j}\mathbf{X}_2 + \cdots + a_{nj}\mathbf{X}_n.$$

Now lengths and angles are preserved, or

$$(\mathrm{T}\mathbf{X}_i, \mathrm{T}\mathbf{X}_j) = (\mathbf{X}_i, \mathbf{X}_j) \begin{cases} = 0 & \text{if } i \neq j, \\ = 1 & \text{if } i = j. \end{cases}$$

But

$$(\mathrm{T}\mathbf{X}_i, \mathrm{T}\mathbf{X}_j) = ((a_{1i}\mathbf{X}_1 + a_{2i}\mathbf{X}_2 + \cdots + a_{ni}\mathbf{X}_n), (a_{1j}\mathbf{X}_1 + a_{2j}\mathbf{X}_2 + \cdots + a_{nj}\mathbf{X}_n)).$$

If we distribute the right-hand side and remember that

$$(\mathbf{X}_k, \mathbf{X}_l) = \begin{cases} 0 & \text{if } k \neq l, \\ 1 & \text{if } k = l, \end{cases}$$

the result is

$$(a_{1i}a_{1j} + a_{2i}a_{2j} + \cdots + a_{ni}a_{nj}) = (A^i, A^j).$$

Then

$$(A^i, A^j) = \begin{cases} 0 & \text{if } i \neq j, \\ 1 & \text{if } i = j, \end{cases}$$

which is the conclusion of (i) and (ii).

As for (iii), we simply compute $A^{\mathsf{T}}A$ by the product rule for matrices, "row of the first by column of the second." But the ith row of A^{T} is the ith column of A and so the element in the i, j position of the product is just $(\mathbf{A}^i, \mathbf{A}^j)$, whose value we have computed above. Thus the product has 1's on the principal diagonal and 0's everywhere else. Hence $A^{\mathsf{T}}A = I$. It follows that $A^{\mathsf{T}} = A^{-1}$ is also a matrix of an orthogonal transformation, namely T^{-1} with respect to the $\{\mathbf{X}_i\}$ basis. Thus its columns obey (i) and (ii). These columns are the rows of A.

A converse to part (iii) of Theorem 4.8 is available.

THEOREM 4.9. If A *is an* $n \times n$ *matrix such that* $A^{\mathsf{T}} = A^{-1}$, *and* $\{\mathbf{X}_i\}$ *is an orthonormal basis of* R^n, *then* A *is the matrix representation of an orthogonal transformation of* R^n *with respect to the basis* $\{\mathbf{X}_i\}$.

PROOF. Let T be the transformation that is represented by A. This means that if

$$\mathbf{X} = b_1\mathbf{X}_1 + b_2\mathbf{X}_2 + \cdots + b_n\mathbf{X}_n$$

is any vector, and

$$\mathrm{T}\mathbf{X} = c_1\mathbf{X}_1 + c_2\mathbf{X}_2 + \cdots + c_n\mathbf{X}_n,$$

then c_i is the ith component of AB, where B is the column vector whose transpose is $[b_1, b_2, \ldots, b_n]$. We must prove that $(\mathrm{T}\mathbf{X}, \mathrm{T}\mathbf{X}) = (\mathbf{X}, \mathbf{X})$.

First, note that, because of the orthonormal character of the $\{\mathbf{X}_i\}$, i.e., $(\mathbf{X}_i, \mathbf{X}_i) = 1$, $(\mathbf{X}_i, \mathbf{X}_j) = 0$ if $i \neq j$, we have

$$(\mathbf{X}, \mathbf{X}) = b_1^2 + b_2^2 + \cdots + b_n^2$$

and

$$(\mathrm{T}\mathbf{X}, \mathrm{T}\mathbf{X}) = c_1^2 + c_2^2 + \cdots + c_n^2.$$

Now

$$\begin{aligned}
c_1^2 + c_2^2 + \cdots + c_n^2 &= [c_1, c_2, \ldots, c_n]\begin{bmatrix} c_1 \\ c_2 \\ \vdots \\ c_n \end{bmatrix} \\
&= (AB)^{\mathrm{T}}AB \\
&= (B^{\mathrm{T}}A^{\mathrm{T}})AB \\
&= B^{\mathrm{T}}A^{\mathrm{T}}AB \\
&= B^{\mathrm{T}}B \\
&= [b_1, b_2, \ldots, b_n]\begin{bmatrix} b_1 \\ b_2 \\ \vdots \\ b_n \end{bmatrix} \\
&= b_1^2 + b_2^2 + \cdots + b_n^2.
\end{aligned}$$

DEFINITION 4.4. *A real matrix A such that $A^{-1} = A^{\mathrm{T}}$ is called an orthogonal matrix.*

It should be clear that the set of orthogonal matrices forms a group isomorphic to the group of orthogonal transformations and that such an isomorphism is obtained for each choice of an orthonormal basis of R^n.

If T is an orthogonal transformation on R^n which is represented by matrices A, B with respect to orthonormal bases $\{\mathbf{X}_i\}$, $\{\mathbf{Y}_i\}$, respectively, the corollary to the general theorem on change of bases tells us that $B = PAP^{-1}$, where P is the matrix of change of basis from $\{\mathbf{X}_i\}$ to $\{\mathbf{Y}_i\}$. It is left as an exercise to show that in this case P is also an orthogonal matrix.

Example 1. We consider the rotations and reflections of R^2. If T_θ is rotation counterclockwise through an angle θ, its matrix relative to the basis is

$$\begin{bmatrix} \cos\theta & -\sin\theta \\ \sin\theta & \cos\theta \end{bmatrix}.$$

The matrix of the reflection across the line that makes an angle θ with the x-axis is seen to be

$$\begin{bmatrix} \cos 2\theta & \sin 2\theta \\ \sin 2\theta & -\cos 2\theta \end{bmatrix}.$$

We claim that any orthogonal 2×2 matrix is of one of these two forms. Assume $\begin{bmatrix} a & b \\ c & d \end{bmatrix}$ is orthogonal. Then $a^2 + b^2 = c^2 + d^2 = 1$ and $ac + bd = 0$. Thus

$$(a^2 + b^2)(c^2 + d^2) - (ac + bd)^2 = 1^2 - 0^2 = 1.$$

Upon expanding the left-hand side of this equation, some cancellation results and we obtain

$$b^2c^2 + a^2d^2 - 2abcd = (ad - bc)^2 = 1.$$

If $ad - bc = +1$, we have

$$\begin{aligned} c(ac + bd) &= 0, \\ d(ad - bc) &= d. \end{aligned}$$

Adding these equations yields $ac^2 + ad^2 = d$ or $a = d$. Similarly,

$$\begin{aligned} d(ac + bd) &= 0 \\ -c(ad - bc) &= -c \\ \hline bd^2 + bc^2 &= -c \end{aligned}$$

so $b = -c$. Thus our matrix is of the form $\begin{bmatrix} a & b \\ -b & a \end{bmatrix}$. Defining θ by $\cos\theta = a$, $\sin\theta = -b$ will put the matrix in the desired form. What if $ad - bc = -1$? Repeating calculations as above yields that $a = -d$ and $b = c$. Thus our matrix is of the form $\begin{bmatrix} a & b \\ b & -a \end{bmatrix}$ and by defining θ with the equations $\sin 2\theta = b$, $\cos 2\theta = a$, we see that the matrix represents a reflection.

Exercises

1. Which of the following systems are groups? The operation in each case is matrix multiplication.
   (a) The set of all $n \times n$ upper triangular matrices.
   (b) The set of nonsingular matrices which commute with a given matrix A. (B is in the set if and only if $BA = AB$ and B is nonsingular.)
   (c) The set of 2×2 matrices of the form $\begin{bmatrix} a & b \\ -b & a \end{bmatrix}$, where a and b are real numbers.
   (d) The set of all elementary matrices of the first kind.
2. Show that the set of all $n \times n$ permutation matrices is a group under multiplication (see Exercise 5, Section 4.1).
3. Show that the transformation on R^n defined by

$$T[x_1, x_2, x_3] = \begin{bmatrix} \frac{2}{3} & \frac{2}{3} & \frac{1}{3} \\ -\frac{2}{3} & \frac{1}{3} & \frac{2}{3} \\ \frac{1}{3} & -\frac{2}{3} & \frac{2}{3} \end{bmatrix} \begin{bmatrix} x_1 \\ x_2 \\ x_3 \end{bmatrix}$$

   is an orthogonal transformation.
4. For the orthogonal transformation of Exercise 3, verify Theorem 4.7 for the vectors $[1, 2, -1]$ and $[1, 0, 3]$.
5. Determine the matrix of the orthogonal transformation of Exercise 3 relative to the orthonormal basis

$$\left\{\left[\frac{1}{\sqrt{2}}, \frac{1}{\sqrt{2}}, 0\right], \left[\frac{1}{\sqrt{2}}, -\frac{1}{\sqrt{2}}, 0\right], [0, 0, 1]\right\}.$$

6. Show that the matrix $\begin{bmatrix} 1 & 1 \\ 0 & 1 \end{bmatrix}$ cannot be the matrix of an orthogonal transformation for any basis of R^2.
7. Prove that matrices expressing a change of orthonormal basis are orthogonal. Show, conversely, that if a transformation from an orthonormal basis is expressed by an orthogonal matrix, then the new basis is orthonormal. *Hint for the first part:* If $\{\mathbf{X}_1, \mathbf{X}_2, \ldots, \mathbf{X}_n\}$ is an orthonormal basis of R^n, the matrix whose ith column is $\mathbf{X}_i$ is an orthogonal matrix.

5 Determinants

The theory of determinants that we are about to begin offers a convenient method of stating various problems and results in algebra and of proving important theorems. Its practical value is of less importance than its theoretical side. For example, in this chapter we will give an expression for the solution of a system of n linear equations in n unknowns by means of determinants. The method is rarely used in practice except when n is 2 or 3. There are other methods far less laborious, but the determinant method presents us with simple conditions for the existence and uniqueness of solutions to such systems. Throughout this chapter, then, it is more important to understand the theory than to be clever at actual calculations with determinants. We begin from a standpoint that emphasizes the theory before describing the calculations.

5.1 Definition of Determinants

It will be convenient to limit our considerations in this chapter to R^n. We will define the determinant as a function of n vectors from R^n to R. This function is to be linear in each of its arguments. That is, if we fix all the arguments except the ith, the function is a linear function in the ith argument. We shall use Δ to designate the function.

Property (i) $$\begin{aligned}\Delta(\mathbf{X}_1, \mathbf{X}_2, \ldots, \mathbf{X}_{i-1}, a\mathbf{X}_i + b\mathbf{Y}_i, \mathbf{X}_{i+1}, \ldots, \mathbf{X}_n) &= a\Delta(\mathbf{X}_1, \mathbf{X}_2, \ldots, \mathbf{X}_{i-1}, \mathbf{X}_i, \mathbf{X}_{i+1}, \ldots, \mathbf{X}_n)\\ &\quad + b\Delta(\mathbf{X}_1, \mathbf{X}_2, \ldots, \mathbf{X}_{i-1}, \mathbf{Y}_i, \mathbf{X}_{i+1}, \ldots, \mathbf{X}_n),\\ &\qquad i = 1, 2, \ldots, n.\end{aligned}$$

Next, the function is to be used to detect equality of any two arguments; in this case the value is 0.

Property (ii) $\Delta(\mathbf{X}_1, \mathbf{X}_2, \ldots, \mathbf{X}_n) = 0 \quad \text{if} \quad \mathbf{X}_i = \mathbf{X}_j, \qquad i \neq j.$

Finally, we designate a specific value for a particularly simple set of arguments.

Property (iii) $\Delta(E_1, E_2, \ldots, E_n) = 1.$

It is far from obvious that these rules define a unique mapping Δ for each n. It may seem quite possible that there might be many such functions or, on the other hand, it may not be clear that there is *any* function with these properties. In the case that $n = 2$ or 3 this last question is readily disposed of. For $n = 2$, let $\mathbf{X} = [x_1, x_2]$, $\mathbf{Y} = [y_1, y_2]$, and define $\Delta(\mathbf{X}, \mathbf{Y}) = x_1y_2 - x_2y_1$. It is a simple matter to check the three basic properties of Δ. Further, the student can readily verify that, in a Cartesian coordinate system, $|\Delta(\mathbf{X}, \mathbf{Y})|$ is the area of the parallelogram defined by segments associated with $\mathbf{X}$ and $\mathbf{Y}$ originating at the origin (Figure 5.1).

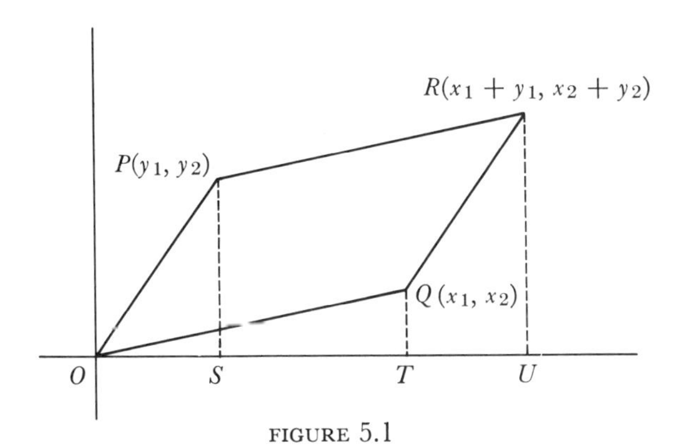

FIGURE 5.1

The proof may be most easily carried out by noting that the area $OPRQ$ is the sum of the areas OPS and $SPRU$ less the sum of the areas OQT and $TQRU$. These areas are respectively $\frac{1}{2}y_1y_2$, $\frac{1}{2}x_1(2y_2 + x_2)$, $\frac{1}{2}x_1x_2$, and $\frac{1}{2}y_1(2x_2 + y_2)$. The result now follows at once.

If $n = 3$, let

$$\mathbf{X} = [x_1, x_2, x_3], \qquad \mathbf{Y} = [y_1, y_2, y_3], \qquad \mathbf{Z} = [z_1, z_2, z_3]$$

and define $\Delta(\mathbf{X}, \mathbf{Y}, \mathbf{Z})$ as the scalar triple product

$$([\mathbf{X}, \mathbf{Y}], \mathbf{Z}) = (x_2y_3 - x_3y_2)z_1 + (x_3y_1 - x_1y_3)z_2 + (x_1y_2 - x_2y_1)z_3.$$

The three properties of Δ again can be easily verified.

In order to obtain more basic information about Δ both toward our immediate goal of establishing its uniqueness and toward eventual applications, we list some immediate consequences of the first three properties:

Property (iv) If two arguments are permuted, the value of $\Delta(\mathbf{X}_1, \mathbf{X}_2, \ldots, \mathbf{X}_n)$ is changed only in sign. That is,

$$\Delta(\mathbf{X}_1, \ldots, \mathbf{X}_i, \ldots, \mathbf{X}_j, \ldots, \mathbf{X}_n) = -\Delta(\mathbf{X}_1, \ldots, \mathbf{X}_j, \ldots, \mathbf{X}_i, \ldots, \mathbf{X}_n).$$

Property (v) If the arguments are linearly dependent,

$$\Delta(\mathbf{X}_1, \mathbf{X}_2, \ldots, \mathbf{X}_n) = 0.$$

To prove Property (iv), we observe

$$\begin{aligned} 0 &= \Delta(\mathbf{X}_1, \ldots, \underset{i\text{th position}}{\mathbf{X}_i + \mathbf{X}_j}, \ldots, \underset{j\text{th position}}{\mathbf{X}_i + \mathbf{X}_j}, \ldots, \mathbf{X}_n) && \text{[Property (ii)]} \\ &= \Delta(\mathbf{X}_1, \ldots, \mathbf{X}_i, \ldots, \mathbf{X}_i + \mathbf{X}_j, \ldots, \mathbf{X}_n) \\ &\quad + \Delta(\mathbf{X}_1, \ldots, \mathbf{X}_j, \ldots, \mathbf{X}_i + \mathbf{X}_j, \ldots, \mathbf{X}_n) && \text{[Property (i)]} \end{aligned}$$

$$= \Delta(\mathbf{X}_1, \ldots, \mathbf{X}_i, \ldots, \mathbf{X}_i, \ldots, \mathbf{X}_n) + \Delta(\mathbf{X}_1, \ldots, \mathbf{X}_i, \ldots, \mathbf{X}_j, \ldots, \mathbf{X}_n)$$
$$+ \Delta(\mathbf{X}_1, \ldots, \mathbf{X}_j, \ldots, \mathbf{X}_i, \ldots, \mathbf{X}_n) + \Delta(\mathbf{X}_1, \ldots, \mathbf{X}_j, \ldots, \mathbf{X}_j, \ldots, \mathbf{X}_n)$$
[Property (i) twice]
$$= \Delta(\mathbf{X}_1, \ldots, \mathbf{X}_i, \ldots, \mathbf{X}_j, \ldots, \mathbf{X}_n) + \Delta(\mathbf{X}_1, \ldots, \mathbf{X}_j, \ldots, \mathbf{X}_i, \ldots, \mathbf{X}_n).$$
[Property (ii) twice]

In order to prove Property (v), assume that $\mathbf{X}_1, \mathbf{X}_2, \ldots, \mathbf{X}_n$ are linearly dependent. One of them, say $\mathbf{X}_i$, is a linear combination of the preceding vectors (Section 2.6) or

$$\mathbf{X}_i = a_1\mathbf{X}_1 + a_2\mathbf{X}_2 + \cdots + a_{i-1}\mathbf{X}_{i-1}.$$

We substitute this expression for $\mathbf{X}_i$ in Δ to obtain

$$\begin{aligned}\Delta(\mathbf{X}_1, \ldots, \mathbf{X}_n) &= \Delta(\mathbf{X}_1, \ldots, \mathbf{X}_{i-1}, a_1\mathbf{X}_1 + \cdots + a_{i-1}\mathbf{X}_{i-1}, \mathbf{X}_{i+1}, \ldots, \mathbf{X}_n)\\ &= a_1\Delta(\mathbf{X}_1, \ldots, \mathbf{X}_{i-1}, \mathbf{X}_1, \ldots, \mathbf{X}_n)\\ &\quad + a_2\Delta(\mathbf{X}_1, \ldots, \mathbf{X}_{i-1}, \mathbf{X}_2, \ldots, \mathbf{X}_n) + \cdots\\ &\quad + a_{i-1}\Delta(\mathbf{X}_1, \ldots, \mathbf{X}_{i-1}, \mathbf{X}_{i-1}, \ldots, \mathbf{X}_n)\end{aligned}$$

by $i - 2$ applications of Property (i). But then all the terms in this expansion of Δ are zero by Property (ii).

Exercises

1. Show from Property (i) that

$$\Delta(\mathbf{X}_1, \ldots, a\mathbf{X}_i, \ldots, \mathbf{X}_n) = a\Delta(\mathbf{X}_1, \ldots, \mathbf{X}_i, \ldots, \mathbf{X}_n).$$

   Interpret this result in terms of area for a determinant of order 2.
2. Show that $\Delta(\mathbf{X}_1, \ldots, \mathbf{0}, \ldots, \mathbf{X}_n) = 0$.
3. Draw a figure which illustrates the linearity in the first argument of $\Delta(\mathbf{X}, \mathbf{Y}) = x_1y_2 - x_2y_1$ in terms of areas. That is, show how the area determined by $\Delta(\mathbf{X}_1 + \mathbf{X}_2, \mathbf{Y})$ is related to those determined by $\Delta(\mathbf{X}_1, \mathbf{Y})$ and $\Delta(\mathbf{X}_2, \mathbf{Y})$.

5.2 The Uniqueness of Δ for $n = 2$ and 3

We shall now show that the function Δ, as defined by Properties (i), (ii), and (iii) of Section 5.1, is unique for the cases $n = 2$ and 3.

Let

$$\begin{aligned}\mathbf{X}_1 &= [x_{11}, x_{12}] = x_{11}\mathbf{E}_1 + x_{12}\mathbf{E}_2,\\ \mathbf{X}_2 &= [x_{21}, x_{22}] = x_{21}\mathbf{E}_1 + x_{22}\mathbf{E}_2;\end{aligned}$$

then

$$\begin{aligned}\Delta(\mathbf{X}_1, \mathbf{X}_2) &= \Delta(x_{11}\mathbf{E}_1 + x_{12}\mathbf{E}_2, x_{21}\mathbf{E}_1 + x_{22}\mathbf{E}_2)\\ &= x_{11}\Delta(\mathbf{E}_1, x_{21}\mathbf{E}_1 + x_{22}\mathbf{E}_2) + x_{12}\Delta(\mathbf{E}_2, x_{21}\mathbf{E}_1 + x_{22}\mathbf{E}_2)\\ &= x_{11}x_{21}\Delta(\mathbf{E}_1, \mathbf{E}_1) + x_{11}x_{22}\Delta(\mathbf{E}_1, \mathbf{E}_2)\\ &\quad + x_{12}x_{21}\Delta(\mathbf{E}_2, \mathbf{E}_1) + x_{12}x_{22}\Delta(\mathbf{E}_2, \mathbf{E}_2)\\ &= x_{11}x_{22}\Delta(\mathbf{E}_1, \mathbf{E}_2) + x_{12}x_{21}\Delta(\mathbf{E}_2, \mathbf{E}_1),\end{aligned}$$

by successive applications of Property (i) and two applications of Property (ii). We now apply Property (iv) and Property (iii) to obtain

$$\begin{aligned}\Delta(\mathbf{X}_1, \mathbf{X}_2) &= x_{11}x_{22}\Delta(\mathbf{E}_1, \mathbf{E}_2) - x_{12}x_{21}\Delta(\mathbf{E}_1, \mathbf{E}_2),\\ \Delta(\mathbf{X}_1, \mathbf{X}_2) &= x_{11}x_{22} - x_{12}x_{21}.\end{aligned}$$

We have indicated in Section 5.1 that this expression for $\Delta(\mathbf{X}_1, \mathbf{X}_2)$ actually does satisfy Properties (i), (ii), and (iii). Hence the determinant function Δ does exist and is unique for $n = 2$.

Now let us turn to the more difficult case of $n = 3$. Let

$$\begin{aligned}\mathbf{X}_1 &= [x_{11}, x_{12}, x_{13}] = x_{11}\mathbf{E}_1 + x_{12}\mathbf{E}_2 + x_{13}\mathbf{E}_3,\\ \mathbf{X}_2 &= [x_{21}, x_{22}, x_{23}] = x_{21}\mathbf{E}_1 + x_{22}\mathbf{E}_2 + x_{23}\mathbf{E}_3,\\ \mathbf{X}_3 &= [x_{31}, x_{32}, x_{33}] = x_{31}\mathbf{E}_1 + x_{32}\mathbf{E}_2 + x_{33}\mathbf{E}_3;\end{aligned}$$

then

$$\begin{aligned}&\Delta(\mathbf{X}_1, \mathbf{X}_2, \mathbf{X}_3)\\ &\quad = \Delta(x_{11}\mathbf{E}_1 + x_{12}\mathbf{E}_2 + x_{13}\mathbf{E}_3, x_{21}\mathbf{E}_1 + x_{22}\mathbf{E}_2 + x_{23}\mathbf{E}_3, x_{31}\mathbf{E}_1 + x_{32}\mathbf{E}_2 + x_{33}\mathbf{E}_3)\end{aligned}$$

Two applications of Property (i) will yield

$$\begin{aligned}&\Delta(\mathbf{X}_1, \mathbf{X}_2, \mathbf{X}_3)\\ &\quad = x_{11}\Delta(\mathbf{E}_1, x_{21}\mathbf{E}_1 + x_{22}\mathbf{E}_2 + x_{23}\mathbf{E}_3, x_{31}\mathbf{E}_1 + x_{32}\mathbf{E}_2 + x_{33}\mathbf{E}_3)\\ &\qquad + x_{12}\Delta(\mathbf{E}_2, x_{21}\mathbf{E}_1 + x_{22}\mathbf{E}_2 + x_{23}\mathbf{E}_3, x_{31}\mathbf{E}_1 + x_{32}\mathbf{E}_2 + x_{33}\mathbf{E}_3)\\ &\qquad + x_{13}\Delta(\mathbf{E}_3, x_{21}\mathbf{E}_1 + x_{22}\mathbf{E}_2 + x_{23}\mathbf{E}_3, x_{31}\mathbf{E}_1 + x_{32}\mathbf{E}_2 + x_{33}\mathbf{E}_3).\end{aligned}$$

Repeated application of Property (i) to bring the real numbers x_{ij} outside of Δ as multipliers will ultimately lead to 27 terms involving, as arguments of Δ, only $\mathbf{E}_1$, $\mathbf{E}_2$, $\mathbf{E}_3$ in some arrangement. Of these 27 terms, the student will find that 21 will have at least two arguments equal, for example,

$$x_{11}x_{21}x_{32}\Delta(\mathbf{E}_1, \mathbf{E}_1, \mathbf{E}_2).$$

The terms having equal arguments will be zero by Property (ii). However, six terms will survive:

$$\begin{aligned}\Delta(\mathbf{X}_1, \mathbf{X}_2, \mathbf{X}_3) &= x_{11}x_{22}x_{33}\Delta(\mathbf{E}_1, \mathbf{E}_2, \mathbf{E}_3) + x_{11}x_{23}x_{32}\Delta(\mathbf{E}_1, \mathbf{E}_3, \mathbf{E}_2)\\ &\quad + x_{12}x_{21}x_{33}\Delta(\mathbf{E}_2, \mathbf{E}_1, \mathbf{E}_3) + x_{12}x_{23}x_{31}\Delta(\mathbf{E}_2, \mathbf{E}_3, \mathbf{E}_1)\\ &\quad + x_{13}x_{21}x_{32}\Delta(\mathbf{E}_3, \mathbf{E}_1, \mathbf{E}_2) + x_{13}x_{22}x_{31}\Delta(\mathbf{E}_3, \mathbf{E}_2, \mathbf{E}_1).\end{aligned}$$

Now $\Delta(\mathbf{E}_1, \mathbf{E}_2, \mathbf{E}_3) = 1$ by Property (iii); and by Properties (iv) and (iii)

$$\Delta(\mathbf{E}_1, \mathbf{E}_3, \mathbf{E}_2) = -\Delta(\mathbf{E}_1, \mathbf{E}_2, \mathbf{E}_3) = -1.$$

Similarly,

$$\begin{aligned}\Delta(\mathbf{E}_2, \mathbf{E}_1, \mathbf{E}_3) &= -\Delta(\mathbf{E}_1, \mathbf{E}_2, \mathbf{E}_3) = -1,\\ \Delta(\mathbf{E}_3, \mathbf{E}_2, \mathbf{E}_1) &= -\Delta(\mathbf{E}_1, \mathbf{E}_2, \mathbf{E}_3) = -1.\end{aligned}$$

However,

$$\Delta(\mathbf{E}_2, \mathbf{E}_3, \mathbf{E}_1) = -\Delta(\mathbf{E}_1, \mathbf{E}_3, \mathbf{E}_2) = +\Delta(\mathbf{E}_1, \mathbf{E}_2, \mathbf{E}_3) = 1$$

by two applications of Property (iv) and then Property (iii). Similarly, $\Delta(\mathbf{E}_3, \mathbf{E}_1, \mathbf{E}_2) = 1$. Thus, finally,

$$\begin{aligned}&\Delta(\mathbf{X}_1, \mathbf{X}_2, \mathbf{X}_3)\\ &\quad = x_{11}x_{22}x_{33} - x_{11}x_{23}x_{32} - x_{12}x_{21}x_{33} + x_{12}x_{23}x_{31} + x_{13}x_{21}x_{32} - x_{13}x_{22}x_{31}.\end{aligned}$$

A simple comparison reveals this result to be equivalent to the determinant of order 3 that we discussed in the last section. Hence Δ is unique for $n = 3$.

It is apparent that this procedure is, in its essentials, perfectly general for a determinant of any order. The basic method proceeds as follows:

Step 1. Beginning with $\Delta(\mathbf{X}_1, \mathbf{X}_2, \ldots, \mathbf{X}_n)$, express each vector

$$\mathbf{X}_i = [x_{i1}, x_{i2}, \ldots, x_{in}]$$

as

$$\mathbf{X}_i = x_{i1}\mathbf{E}_1 + x_{i2}\mathbf{E}_2 + \cdots + x_{in}\mathbf{E}_n$$

for $i = 1, 2, \ldots, n$ and substitute in Δ.

Step 2. Use Property (i) repeatedly to expand Δ to a sum of terms that involve only the $\mathbf{E}_i$ in various arrangements as arguments.

Step 3. Use Property (ii) to eliminate all terms that have equal arguments. The remaining terms now have each one of the $n\mathbf{E}_j$ as an argument in some arrangement. (Why?) A typical term would now look like

$$x_{1i_1}x_{2i_2}\cdots x_{ni_n}\Delta(\mathbf{E}_{i_1}, \mathbf{E}_{i_2}, \ldots, \mathbf{E}_{i_n}),$$

where $i_1, i_2, \ldots, i_n$ is some arrangement of the numbers $1, 2, \ldots, n$.

Step 4. Now apply Property (iv) and, by successive interchanges of arguments, bring $\Delta(\mathbf{E}_{i_1}, \mathbf{E}_{i_2}, \ldots, \mathbf{E}_{i_n})$ to $\pm\Delta(\mathbf{E}_1, \mathbf{E}_2, \ldots, \mathbf{E}_n)$, where the $\mathbf{E}_i$ are now in their natural order and the sign will be $+$ or $-$ according as an even or an odd number of changes was used in rearranging the $\mathbf{E}_i$.

Step 5. Apply Property (iii) to evaluate the remaining determinants.

The procedures of Steps 1, 2, and 3 should be clear and definite. We can easily see that at the conclusion of Step 2 there are n^n summands. There are n summands in breaking up $\mathbf{X}_1$, and for *each* of these, n more summands are necessary to break up $\mathbf{X}_2$, and so on. At the end of Step 3 there are $n! = n(n-1)\cdots 2\cdot 1$ summands remaining. (See Example 1 in Section 1.4.)

It is only at Step 4 that vagueness occurs. An explicit procedure for making interchanges has not been set out. Indeed, when we try it for $n > 2$, we see that there are usually many different ways in which this can be done. For example, we have shown above that

$$\Delta(\mathbf{E}_2, \mathbf{E}_3, \mathbf{E}_1) = -\Delta(\mathbf{E}_1, \mathbf{E}_3, \mathbf{E}_2) = +\Delta(\mathbf{E}_1, \mathbf{E}_2, \mathbf{E}_3);$$

however,

$$\Delta(\mathbf{E}_2, \mathbf{E}_3, \mathbf{E}_1) = -\Delta(\mathbf{E}_2, \mathbf{E}_1, \mathbf{E}_3) = +\Delta(\mathbf{E}_1, \mathbf{E}_2, \mathbf{E}_3)$$

is another possible method.

There are really two problems for determinants of order n:

(1) It must be shown that the arrangement of the arguments $\mathbf{E}_{i_1}$, $\mathbf{E}_{i_2}, \ldots, \mathbf{E}_{i_n}$ can be brought to the arrangement of arguments $\mathbf{E}_1, \mathbf{E}_2, \ldots, \mathbf{E}_n$ by successive interchanges.

(2) It must be shown that no matter how (1) is accomplished, the same value of the original Δ will arise.

In order to work out these final problems of Step 4, we must consider rearrangements of the integers $1, 2, \ldots, n$ in more detail. This will be done in Section 5.4.

Exercises

1. Find $\Delta(\mathbf{X}_1, \mathbf{X}_2)$ in the following cases:
   (a) $\mathbf{X}_1 = [1, 2]$, $\mathbf{X}_2 = [3, -1]$.
   (b) $\mathbf{X}_1 = [3, 4]$, $\mathbf{X}_2 = [-4, 1]$.
   (c) $\mathbf{X}_1 = [a, 0]$, $\mathbf{X}_2 = [0, b]$.

2. Find $\Delta(\mathbf{X}_1, \mathbf{X}_2, \mathbf{X}_3)$ in the following cases:
   (a) $\mathbf{X}_1 = [1, 2, 3]$, $\mathbf{X}_2 = [1, 0, -1]$, $\mathbf{X}_3 = [0, 0, 1]$.
   (b) $\mathbf{X}_1 = [1, 1, 1]$, $\mathbf{X}_2 = [1, 1, -1]$, $\mathbf{X}_3 = [2, 1, 0]$.
   (c) $\mathbf{X}_1 = [2, 1, -1]$, $\mathbf{X}_2 = [1, 2, 2]$, $\mathbf{X}_3 = [0, -1, -3]$.
3. Prove that $\Delta(\mathbf{X}_1 + a\mathbf{X}_2 + b\mathbf{X}_3, \mathbf{X}_2, \mathbf{X}_3) = \Delta(\mathbf{X}_1, \mathbf{X}_2, \mathbf{X}_3)$, where a and b are arbitrary real numbers.
4. What is the determinant function Δ for R^1?
5. Prove the statement that a determinant with n vector arguments has $n!$ terms in its expansion.

5.3 Cofactors and Evaluation of Determinants

For the purposes of computation with determinants a notation that exposes the components of the individual vector arguments is desirable. The standard procedure is the following: As before, let $\mathbf{X}_i = (x_{i1}, x_{i2}, \ldots, x_{in})$. Then replace $\Delta(\mathbf{X}_1, \mathbf{X}_2, \ldots, \mathbf{X}_n)$ by

$$\begin{vmatrix} x_{11} & x_{12} & \cdots & x_{1n} \\ x_{21} & x_{22} & \cdots & x_{2n} \\ \vdots & & & \vdots \\ x_{n1} & x_{n2} & \cdots & x_{nn} \end{vmatrix}.$$

Note that in this form the components are displayed as in an $n \times n$ matrix. This notation immediately suggests the idea of defining the determinant of a square matrix as the determinant of its row vectors. Given a square matrix A, we will then speak of the determinant of A and denote it by $\Delta(A)$ or det A.

The reader may now note that the expression of $\Delta(\mathbf{X}_1, \mathbf{X}_2, \mathbf{X}_3)$ in the previous section as

$$\begin{aligned} x_{11}x_{22}x_{33} &- x_{11}x_{23}x_{32} - x_{12}x_{21}x_{33} + x_{12}x_{23}x_{31} + x_{13}x_{21}x_{32} - x_{13}x_{22}x_{31} \\ &= x_{11}(x_{22}x_{33} - x_{23}x_{32}) - x_{21}(x_{12}x_{33} - x_{13}x_{32}) + x_{31}(x_{12}x_{23} - x_{13}x_{22}) \end{aligned}$$

can be written

$$\begin{vmatrix} x_{11} & x_{12} & x_{13} \\ x_{21} & x_{22} & x_{23} \\ x_{31} & x_{32} & x_{33} \end{vmatrix} = x_{11}\begin{vmatrix} x_{22} & x_{23} \\ x_{32} & x_{33} \end{vmatrix} - x_{21}\begin{vmatrix} x_{12} & x_{13} \\ x_{32} & x_{33} \end{vmatrix} + x_{31}\begin{vmatrix} x_{12} & x_{13} \\ x_{22} & x_{23} \end{vmatrix}.$$

This formula, giving the definition of Δ for $n = 3$ in terms of Δ for $n = 2$, suggests that perhaps, knowing a determinant function for 3×3 matrices, we might be able to use this to define a determinant for $n = 4$. Continuing the process, one might define a determinant function for arbitrary n (such a procedure is called an inductive definition). In this section, we shall carry out precisely such a procedure, leaving the proof that there is only one determinant function to a later section.

In the following, we assume that a determinant function Δ has been defined on the set of $(n - 1) \times (n - 1)$ matrices for some fixed $n \geq 2$. The object is to extend Δ to a determinant function on $n \times n$ matrices. We begin with a definition.

DEFINITION 5.1. If $A = [a_{ij}]$, the MINOR, $A(i;j)$, *of the element a_{ij} is the matrix obtained from A by deleting the ith row and the jth column.*

Example 1. If

$$A = \begin{bmatrix} 1 & 2 & -1 \\ 2 & 4 & -7 \\ 3 & -2 & 3 \end{bmatrix},$$

then

$$A(1;2) = \begin{bmatrix} 2 & -7 \\ 3 & 3 \end{bmatrix} \quad \text{and} \quad A(2;2) = \begin{bmatrix} 1 & -1 \\ 3 & 3 \end{bmatrix}.$$

Also notice that

$$\det A = 1 \cdot \det A(1;1) - 2 \det A(2;1) + 3 \det A(3;1).$$

THEOREM 5.1. If Δ is a determinant function defined on $(n-1) \times (n-1)$ matrices, then the function of $n \times n$ matrices defined by

$$\Delta(A) = a_{11}\Delta(A(1;1)) - a_{21}\Delta(A(2;1)) + \cdots + (-1)^{n+1}a_{n1}\Delta(A(n;1)),$$

where $A = [a_{ij}]$ is an $n \times n$ matrix, is a determinant function.

PROOF. We first verify that the function we have defined is linear in its ith coordinate (that is, in the ith row of A). If $A' = [a'_{ij}]$ is obtained from A by multiplying the ith row of A by a scalar c, then

$$\Delta(A'(j;\,1)) = c\Delta(A(j;1))$$

for $j \neq i$ and $ca_{i1} = a'_{i1}$; thus $\Delta(A') = c\Delta(A)$. Similarly, the linearity of Δ for $(n-1) \times (n-1)$ matrices implies that

$$\begin{aligned}\Delta(\mathbf{X}_1, \ldots, \mathbf{X}_{i-1}, \mathbf{X}_i + \mathbf{Y}, \mathbf{X}_{i+1}, \ldots, \mathbf{X}_n) \\ = \Delta(\mathbf{X}_1, \ldots, \mathbf{X}_n) + \Delta(\mathbf{X}_1, \ldots, \mathbf{X}_{i-1}, \mathbf{Y}, \mathbf{X}_{i+1}, \ldots, \mathbf{X}_n).\end{aligned}$$

To see that Δ satisfies Property (ii) of the definition (Section 5.1), assume that the ith and jth rows of A are equal. Then $\Delta(A(k;1)) = 0$ for all k except i and j, because $A(k;1)$ has two equal rows. Thus

$$\Delta(A) = (-1)^{i+1}a_{i1}\Delta(A(i;1)) + (-1)^{j+1}a_{j1}\Delta(A(j;1)).$$

Observe that the matrix $A(i;1)$ may be transformed into $A(j;1)$ as follows (assume $i < j$). Interchange row i with row $i+1$, then row $i+1$ with $i+2$, and so on. After $j-i-1$ such interchanges we will have transformed $A(i;1)$ into $A(j;1)$, and thus

$$\Delta(A(i;1)) = (-1)^{j-i-1}\Delta(A(j;1)),$$

and

$$\begin{aligned}\Delta(A) &= a_{i1}\Delta(A(j;1))[(-1)^{j-i-1}(-1)^{i+1} + (-1)^{j+1}] \\ &= a_{i1}\Delta(A(j;1))[(-1)^{j} + (-1)^{j+1}] = 0.\end{aligned}$$

Example 2. Calculate the determinant of the matrix

$$A = \begin{bmatrix} 0 & -3 & 2 & 1 \\ 2 & 2 & -2 & 1 \\ 3 & 1 & -1 & 2 \\ 1 & 3 & 1 & -2 \end{bmatrix}.$$

We have

$$\det A = 0 \cdot \begin{vmatrix} 2 & -2 & 1 \\ 1 & -1 & 2 \\ 3 & 1 & -2 \end{vmatrix} - 2 \begin{vmatrix} -3 & 2 & 1 \\ 1 & -1 & 2 \\ 3 & 1 & -2 \end{vmatrix} + 3 \begin{vmatrix} -3 & 2 & 1 \\ 2 & -2 & 1 \\ 3 & 1 & -2 \end{vmatrix}$$

$$- 1 \begin{vmatrix} -3 & 2 & 1 \\ 2 & -2 & 1 \\ 1 & -1 & 2 \end{vmatrix}$$

$$= 0 - 2 \cdot 20 + 3 \cdot 13 - 1 \cdot 3 = -4.$$

The process of evaluating determinants that we have developed is often referred to as *expanding* det A *by means of minors of the first column.* The reader may ask, "What is special about the first column?" The answer, naturally, is nothing whatever. For example, the expansion of det A by means of minors of the kth column is

$$(-1)^{k+1}a_{1k}\Delta(A(1;k)) + (-1)^{k+2}a_{2k}\Delta(A(2;k)) + \cdots + (-1)^{k+n}\Delta(A(n;k)).$$

One can also define the expansion of det A along the kth row as

$$(-1)^{k+1}a_{k1}\Delta(A(k;1)) + (-1)^{k+2}a_{k2}\Delta(A(k;2)) + \cdots + (-1)^{k+n}a_{kn}\Delta(A(k;n)).$$

Example 3. Expanding the determinant of the matrix of Example 2 along the second row we obtain

$$\det A = -2 \begin{vmatrix} -3 & 2 & 1 \\ 1 & -1 & 2 \\ 3 & 1 & -2 \end{vmatrix} + 2 \begin{vmatrix} 0 & 2 & 1 \\ 3 & -1 & 2 \\ 1 & 1 & -2 \end{vmatrix} + 2 \begin{vmatrix} 0 & -3 & 1 \\ 3 & 1 & 2 \\ 1 & 3 & -2 \end{vmatrix}$$

$$+ 1 \begin{vmatrix} 0 & -3 & 2 \\ 3 & 1 & -1 \\ 1 & 3 & 1 \end{vmatrix}$$

$$= -2(20) + 2(20) + 2(-16) + 28 = -4.$$

The reader may complain that it is not at all clear that all of these expansions are determinant functions, not to mention the question of their equality. Patience. The powerful techniques of the next few sections will establish all of this, and more. For the moment, we present them as tools for calculation.

The main reason for considering more than one expansion by minors is illustrated by the following example.

Example 4. Calculate the determinant of the matrix

$$A = \begin{bmatrix} 1 & -1 & 0 & -2 \\ 0 & 6 & 0 & 0 \\ 1 & 4 & 2 & 3 \\ 3 & -1 & 0 & 4 \end{bmatrix}.$$

Noting that there is but one nonzero entry in the third column, we expand along that column.

$$\det A = 0 + 0 + 2 \begin{vmatrix} 1 & -1 & -2 \\ 0 & 6 & 0 \\ 3 & -1 & 4 \end{vmatrix}.$$

Expand this 3×3 determinant along the second row.

$$\det A = 2\left(6\begin{vmatrix}1 & -2\\ 3 & 4\end{vmatrix}\right) = 12(4+6) = 120.$$

The number $(-1)^{i+j}\Delta(A(i;j))$ is called the *cofactor* of a_{ij}. The expansion of det A along a column (row) is just the sum of the numbers obtained by multiplying each element of the given column (row) by its cofactor.

Exercises

1. Let A be the 3×3 matrix $\begin{bmatrix}1 & 2 & 3\\ 4 & 5 & 6\\ 7 & 8 & 9\end{bmatrix}$. For the matrix A determine the following:
   (a) The minors of the elements 5; 6; 7.
   (b) The cofactors of the elements 5; 6; 7.
2. Evaluate the following determinants by the most economical procedure possible:

$$\text{(a)}\ \begin{vmatrix}1 & 3 & 1\\ 2 & 1 & -1\\ 1 & 0 & 1\end{vmatrix}, \quad \text{(b)}\ \begin{vmatrix}1 & -1 & 1 & -1\\ 2 & 0 & 1 & 1\\ 1 & -1 & 0 & 0\\ 1 & 1 & 1 & 1\end{vmatrix}, \quad \text{(c)}\ \begin{vmatrix}1 & 2 & 3 & -1 & 2\\ 0 & 1 & 2 & 4 & 1\\ 1 & 0 & -1 & 3 & -2\\ 2 & 0 & 1 & 0 & 1\\ 1 & 1 & -1 & 2 & 2\end{vmatrix}.$$

3. What is the value of these determinants?

$$\text{(a)}\ \begin{vmatrix}a_{11} & 0 & & \cdots & 0\\ a_{21} & a_{22} & 0 & \cdots & 0\\ \vdots & \vdots & & & \vdots\\ & & & & 0\\ a_{n1} & a_{n2} & & \cdots & a_{nn}\end{vmatrix}, \quad \text{(b)}\ \begin{vmatrix}0 & \cdots & & 0 & a_{1n}\\ 0 & & 0 & a_{2,n-1} & a_{2n}\\ \vdots & & & \vdots & \vdots\\ 0 & & & & \\ a_{n1} & \cdots & & a_{n,n-1} & a_{nn}\end{vmatrix}.$$

4. Show that

$$-\begin{vmatrix}1 & x_1 & x_1^2\\ 1 & x_2 & x_2^2\\ 1 & x_3 & x_3^2\end{vmatrix} = (x_1 - x_2)(x_1 - x_3)(x_2 - x_3).$$

5. Define $f_I(x_1, \ldots, x_n) = \prod_{i<j}(x_i - x_j)$. Generalize Exercise 4 to obtain $f_I(x_1, \ldots, x_n)$ as a determinant.
6. Let $\mathbf{X}_0 = [1, 2, 3]$, $\mathbf{X}_1 = [-1, 0, -1]$, $\mathbf{X}_2 = [4, 1, 5]$, and $\mathbf{X}_3 = [2, 0, -1]$. Show that

$$\Delta(\mathbf{X}_1 - \mathbf{X}_0, \mathbf{X}_2 - \mathbf{X}_0, \mathbf{X}_3 - \mathbf{X}_0) = -\begin{vmatrix}1 & 2 & 3 & 1\\ -1 & 0 & -1 & 1\\ 4 & 1 & 5 & 1\\ 2 & 0 & -1 & 1\end{vmatrix}.$$

7. Let $\{\mathbf{X}_i = [x_{i1}, x_{i2}, \ldots, x_{in}]\}$ for $i = 0, 1, \ldots, n$ be $n + 1$ vectors from $V_n(R)$. Show that

$$\Delta(\mathbf{X}_1 - \mathbf{X}_0, \mathbf{X}_2 - \mathbf{X}_0, \ldots, \mathbf{X}_n - \mathbf{X}_0) = (-1)^n\begin{vmatrix}x_{01} & x_{02} & \cdots & x_{0n} & 1\\ x_{11} & x_{12} & \cdots & x_{1n} & 1\\ \vdots & & & & \vdots\\ x_{n1} & x_{n2} & \cdots & x_{nn} & 1\end{vmatrix}.$$

8. Let the cofactors of x_{ij} in the $n \times n$ matrix X be denoted by C_{ij}. Show that

$$C_{ij} = \Delta(\mathbf{X}_1, \mathbf{X}_2, \ldots, \mathbf{X}_{i-1}, \mathbf{E}_j, \mathbf{X}_{i+1}, \ldots, \mathbf{X}_n),$$

where the vectors $\mathbf{X}_i$ are the rows of the matrix X.

9. Using the notation of Exercise 8, show that

$$x_{j1}C_{i1} + x_{j2}C_{i2} + \cdots + x_{jn}C_{in} = 0 \qquad \text{for } j \neq i.$$

Hint: Write $x_{jk}C_{ik} = x_{jk}\Delta(\mathbf{X}_1, \mathbf{X}_2, \ldots, \mathbf{X}_{i-1}, \mathbf{E}_k, \mathbf{X}_{i+1}, \ldots, \mathbf{X}_n)$ and sum using the linearity properties of Δ. Note now that two arguments of Δ are identical.

5.4 Permutations and the Uniqueness of Δ for Arbitrary *n*

An arrangement of the integers $1, 2, \ldots, n$ as $i_1, i_2, \ldots, i_n$ (a reordering without duplication or omission) will be called a *permutation* of the integers $1, 2, \ldots, n$. For example, 4312 is a permutation of the integers 1, 2, 3, and 4. Note that a permutation of the integers $1, 2, \ldots, n$ is a one-to-one mapping of the set of integers $1, 2, \ldots, n$ onto itself. The integer i_k is the image of the integer k, and the ordering $i_1, i_2, \ldots, i_n$ is that of the images of $1, 2, \ldots, n$.

The problem raised in Section 5.2 of bringing the arguments $\mathbf{E}_{i_1}, \mathbf{E}_{i_2}, \ldots, \mathbf{E}_{i_n}$ of Δ to the ordering $\mathbf{E}_1, \mathbf{E}_2, \ldots, \mathbf{E}_n$ by successive interchanges of arguments can be looked upon as simply passing from the permutation $i_1, i_2, \ldots, i_n$ to $1, 2, \ldots, n$ by successive interchanges of integers. As an example, consider the permutation 43512. To put this in natural order we may proceed as follows: 43512, 43152, 43125, 34125, 31425, 31245, 13245, 12345. The seven successive permutations follow a pattern: First, the last integer 5 bypasses those integers which it precedes, then the next-to-the-last integer 4 is moved into place, and so on. We can count the required number of interchanges of integers at the start. We observe that 5 precedes $\underline{2}$ numbers which it should follow (1 and 2); that 4 precedes $\underline{3}$ numbers which it should follow (3, 1, and 2); and that 3 precedes $\underline{2}$ numbers which it should follow (1 and 2). The total of the underlined numbers is the total number of interchanges of integers required, each interchange corresponding to precisely one correction of an improper order.

It is clear that the method just described may be applied to a permutation $i_1, i_2, \ldots, i_n$ of any size n to bring it into natural order $1, 2, \ldots, n$ by successive interchanges. The improper precedences counted are called *inversions;* the interchanges of two integers are referred to as *transpositions* of the integers. Hence we have:

If a permutation $i_1, i_2, \ldots, i_n$ has K inversions, it may be restored to the natural order $1, 2, \ldots, n$ by K transpositions.

Of course the method of restoring a permutation to its natural order by correcting inversions is not the only one available; the following three steps would do for the permutation of the example above: 43512, 13542, 15342, 12345. The method of inversions is useful in that it gives a definite procedure applicable to an arbitrary permutation and, more importantly, gives an easy way of counting the corresponding number of transpositions.

Example 1. The permutation 5671423 has 14 inversions. The restoring steps are: 5617423, 5614723, 5614273, 5614237, 5164237, 5146237, 5142637, 5142367, 1542367, 1452367, 1425367, 1423567, 1243567, 1234567. The student should try other methods aiming at greater economy, counting the steps in each case. Note that, however many steps are required, the number is always even.

The *invariance of parity* of a permutation (the property of a permutation always to require an even number of transpositions to bring it to $1, 2, 3, \ldots, n$ if an even number works at all, or always to require an odd number in the complementary case) must now be proved. The proof unfortunately involves an ingenious trick: a polynomial apparently designed only for this purpose is introduced, used in the proof, and then dismissed. The excuse is that other known proofs are longer and even less satisfactory.

THEOREM 5.2. If P is the permutation $i_1, i_2, \ldots, i_n$ of the integers $1, 2, \ldots, n$ and if P may be changed to the natural order $1, 2, \ldots, n$ by p and also by q transpositions, then p and q are both even or both odd integers.

PROOF. First we introduce a polynomial $f_I(x_1, x_2, \ldots, x_n)$ in n symbols $x_1, x_2, \ldots, x_n$. Here I stands for the arrangement $1, 2, \ldots, n$, and we define the polynomial as follows:

$$f_I(x_1, x_2, \ldots, x_n) = \prod_{i<j}^{n} (x_i - x_j),$$

where the right-hand side means the product of all possible factors $(x_i - x_j)$ for $i < j$ with i and j restricted to the integers $1, 2, \ldots, n$. In general, f_I has $n(n-1)/2$ factors; for $n = 4$ we have

$$f_I(x_1, x_2, x_3, x_4) = (x_1 - x_2)(x_1 - x_3)(x_1 - x_4)(x_2 - x_3)(x_2 - x_4)(x_3 - x_4).$$

The second step of the proof is to define a similar polynomial $f_P(x_1, x_2, \ldots, x_n)$ for the arbitrary permutation $P = i_1, i_2, \ldots, i_n$ as follows:

$$f_P(x_1, x_2, \ldots, x_n) = \prod_{r<s}^{n} (x_{i_r} - x_{i_s});$$

that is, in each factor of the product, the element of positive sign is the one whose subscript appears first in the permutation P. For example, if P is 2143,

$$f_P(x_1, x_2, x_3, x_4) = (x_2 - x_1)(x_2 - x_4)(x_2 - x_3)(x_1 - x_4)(x_1 - x_3)(x_4 - x_3).$$

Another way of describing $f_P(x_1, x_2, \ldots, x_n)$ is by the equation

$$f_P(x_1, x_2, \ldots, x_n) = f_I(x_{i_1}, x_{i_2}, \ldots, x_{i_n}). \tag{5.1}$$

That is, f_P is obtained from f_I by replacing x_1 by x_{i_1}, x_2 by x_{i_2}, and so on until x_n is replaced by x_{i_n}. Every factor $(x_r - x_s)$ with $r < s$ in f_I is replaced by $(x_{i_r} - x_{i_s})$. Now either $(x_{i_r} - x_{i_s})$ of f_P is in f_I or $(x_{i_s} - x_{i_r})$ is a factor of f_I. Since no two factors $(x_i - x_j)$ are identical in f_I and since the number of factors in f_I and f_P is the same, $f_P = \pm f_I$. For the particular permutation 2143, $f_P = f_I$ since precisely two terms $(x_2 - x_1)$ and $(x_4 - x_3)$ of f_P have their subscripts out of the original order in f_I.

Next, we note that, if a set of transpositions will reduce P to the natural order I, precisely the same set will transform f_P to f_I in the sense that, if integers i and j are to be interchanged in the permutations, x_i and x_j are interchanged in the polynomial. For example, 2143 may be reduced to 1234 by interchanging 1 and 2, then 3 and 4: 2143, 1243, 1234. If we interchange x_1 and x_2 in f_P, we have

$$(x_1 - x_2)(x_1 - x_4)(x_1 - x_3)(x_2 - x_4)(x_2 - x_3)(x_4 - x_3);$$

then interchanging x_3 and x_4 we obtain

$$(x_1 - x_2)(x_1 - x_3)(x_1 - x_4)(x_2 - x_3)(x_2 - x_4)(x_3 - x_4) = f_I.$$

Finally, we note what a transposition does to f_P. Suppose x_j and x_i are exchanged, what happens to the factor? There are several possibilities to examine in detail:

1. For those factors that had no x_i or x_j there is no change.
2. If there was a pair $(x_a - x_i)$ and $(x_a - x_j)$, there now is the pair $(x_a - x_j)$ and $(x_a - x_i)$; again no change in the polynomial.
3. Similarly, if a pair $(x_i - x_b)$ and $(x_j - x_b)$ existed, no overall change results.
4. If the pair was $(x_i - x_c)$, $(x_c - x_j)$, the new pair of terms reads $(x_j - x_c)$, $(x_c - x_i)$; two factors have changed sign.
5. Also for a pair of the type $(x_d - x_i)$, $(x_j - x_d)$, the result is two changes of sign.
6. The only factor involving x_i or x_j in which no pairing can be done is that which reads $(x_i - x_j)$ or $(x_j - x_i)$. The transposition changes the sign of this factor. The result can be expressed as follows: If P is transformed into Q by a transposition, $f_P = -f_Q$.

The proof is now essentially complete; for suppose the numbers p and q of the statement of the theorem were of different parity, p odd, say, and q even, then f_P, being reduced by p transpositions to f_I, is $-f_I$, while the same polynomial, being reduced to f_I by q transpositions, is $+f_I$. Hence

$$f_P = +f_I = -f_I \quad \text{or} \quad 2f_I = 0.$$

But f_I is clearly not identically zero.

The proof just completed answers the questions raised in Section 5.2 for the evaluation of $\Delta(\mathbf{X}_1, \mathbf{X}_2, \ldots, \mathbf{X}_n)$. Recall that for

$$\mathbf{X}_i = [x_{i1}, x_{i2}, \ldots, x_{in}]$$

for $i = 1, 2, \ldots, n$, $\Delta(\mathbf{X}_1, \mathbf{X}_2, \ldots, \mathbf{X}_n)$ may be expressed as the sum of $n!$ terms of the form

$$x_{1i_1}x_{2i_2}\cdots x_{ni_n}\Delta(\mathbf{E}_{i_1}, \mathbf{E}_{i_2}, \ldots, \mathbf{E}_{i_n}),$$

where $i_1, i_2, \ldots, i_n$ is a permutation of $1, 2, \ldots, n$.

The number r of transpositions used to bring the order of arguments $\mathbf{E}_{i_1}, \mathbf{E}_{i_2}, \ldots, \mathbf{E}_{i_n}$ to the order $\mathbf{E}_1, \mathbf{E}_2, \ldots, \mathbf{E}_n$ is always odd or always even. If P is the permutation $i_1, i_2, \ldots, i_n$ of $1, 2, \ldots, n$, denote by $S(P)$ the number of inversions in the permutation P. Then r and $S(P)$ are both odd or both even so that

$$\Delta(\mathbf{E}_{i_1}, \mathbf{E}_{i_2}, \ldots, \mathbf{E}_{i_n}) = (-1)^{S(P)}\Delta(\mathbf{E}_1, \mathbf{E}_2, \ldots, \mathbf{E}_n),$$

regardless of the particular transpositions used in rearranging $\mathbf{E}_{i_1}, \mathbf{E}_{i_2}, \ldots, \mathbf{E}_{i_n}$ to the order $\mathbf{E}_1, \mathbf{E}_2, \ldots, \mathbf{E}_n$. Since

$$\Delta(\mathbf{E}_1, \mathbf{E}_2, \ldots, \mathbf{E}_n) = 1,$$

the value of $\Delta(\mathbf{E}_{i_1}, \mathbf{E}_{i_2}, \ldots, \mathbf{E}_{i_n})$ is 1 if $i_1, i_2, \ldots, i_n$ results from an even number of transpositions and -1 otherwise. Thus finally,

$$\Delta(\mathbf{X}_1, \mathbf{X}_2, \ldots, \mathbf{X}_n) = \sum (-1)^{S(P)}x_{1i_1}x_{2i_2}\cdots x_{ni_n}, \tag{5.2}$$

where the sign $\sum$ indicates that a sum is to be taken of the $n!$ terms of the type indicated in (5.2) for all permutations P represented by $i_1, i_2, \ldots, i_n$ of the integers $1, 2, \ldots, n$.

As we were led to formula (5.2) using only the properties of Δ, we now know that there can be at most one determinant function. The existence of one such function was demonstrated in the previous section. While formula (5.2) is not useful for evaluating determinants, we shall see in the next section that it is useful in deriving further properties of the determinant function.

As an example of the use of formula (5.2) we show that the function which it defines satisfies Property (ii) (of course, we already have a proof of this, as we now know that the determinant defined by (5.2) equals the expansion by minors studied in Section 5.3).

Suppose $\mathbf{X}_j = \mathbf{X}_k$ for $j \neq k$ so that $x_{ji} = x_{ki}$ for $i = 1, 2, \ldots, n$. Consider any one of the expressions

$$x_{1i_1}x_{2i_2}\cdots x_{ju}\cdots x_{kv}\cdots x_{ni_n}. \tag{5.3}$$

The sign $(-1)^{S(P)}$ which is assigned to this expression to obtain one of the terms of (5.2) depends upon the parity of the permutation

$$P = i_1, i_2, \ldots, u, \ldots, v, \ldots, i_n$$

as a permutation of $1, 2, \ldots, n$. Whatever this parity may be, the permutation

$$P' = i_1, i_2, \ldots, v, \ldots, u, \ldots, i_n$$

has the opposite parity since P' arises from P by the interchange of u and v. But the parity of P' determines the sign attached to the expression

$$x_{1i_1}x_{2i_2}\cdots x_{jv}\cdots x_{ku}\cdots x_{ni_n} \tag{5.4}$$

to obtain a term of (5.2). As unsigned expressions, (5.3) and (5.4) are equal since $x_{jv} = x_{kv}$, $x_{ju} = x_{ku}$, and the remaining elements are identical. However, as terms in the evaluation of $\Delta(\mathbf{X}_1, \ldots, \mathbf{X}_n)$ by (5.2) they have opposite signs. Thus, for any term in the sum there is a term which is its negative. Hence the sum is zero and $\Delta(\mathbf{X}_1, \ldots, \mathbf{X}_n) = 0$ if $\mathbf{X}_j = \mathbf{X}_k$ with $j \neq k$.

Exercises

1. Find the number of inversions in the following permutations. Find an economical way of rearranging each permutation to the natural order. Compare the number of transpositions required by the economical and the inversion method.
   (a) 213564. (b) 1327465.
   (c) 42137865. (d) 4132.
   (e) 618975423. (f) 956742318.
   (g) 87654321. (h) 31768425.
2. Write f_P for the following permutations, determining whether $f_P = f_I$ or $f_P = -f_I$; also compute the number of inversions in P.
   (a) 4132. (b) 3142.
   (c) 4123. (d) 25413.
3. Show that precisely one half of the $n!$ permutations of order n are the result of an even number of transpositions.
4. For a determinant of order 6, what are the signs of the following expressions occurring in the evaluation of Δ?
   (a) $x_{15}x_{21}x_{32}x_{43}x_{56}x_{64}$, (b) $x_{31}x_{12}x_{63}x_{24}x_{55}x_{46}$, (c) $x_{12}x_{21}x_{34}x_{43}x_{56}x_{65}$.
   How many terms in all would there be for a determinant of order 6?

5. Find $\Delta(\mathbf{X}_1, \mathbf{X}_2, \mathbf{X}_3, \mathbf{X}_4)$ if
   (a) $\mathbf{X}_1 = [0, 1, 0, 0]$, $\mathbf{X}_2 = [0, 0, 1, 0]$,
   $\mathbf{X}_3 = [0, 0, 0, 1]$, $\mathbf{X}_4 = [2, 0, 0, 0]$.
   (b) $\mathbf{X}_1 = [0, 1, 0, -1]$, $\mathbf{X}_2 = [1, 0, 1, 0]$,
   $\mathbf{X}_3 = [0, -1, 0, 1]$, $\mathbf{X}_4 = [1, 0, -1, 0]$.
6. Prove Properties (i) and (iii) for $\Delta(\mathbf{X}_1, \mathbf{X}_2, \ldots, \mathbf{X}_n)$ from the evaluation (5.2) and thus complete a second proof of the existence of Δ.
7. Let n vectors be given by

$$\mathbf{X}_i = a_{i1}\mathbf{Y}_1 + \cdots + a_{in}\mathbf{Y}_n \qquad (i = 1, 2, \ldots, n).$$

   Show that

$$\Delta(\mathbf{X}_1, \mathbf{X}_2, \ldots, \mathbf{X}_n) = \sum (-1)^{S(P)} a_{1i_1} a_{2i_2} \cdots a_{ni_n} \Delta(\mathbf{Y}_1, \mathbf{Y}_2, \ldots, \mathbf{Y}_n),$$

   where again the sum $\sum$ is taken over all permutations P of $1, 2, \ldots, n$ and $S(P)$ is the number of inversions in the permutation P., *Hint:* Note that the $\mathbf{E}_i$ played no essential role in the derivation of (5.2) until the very last step, when we set $\Delta(\mathbf{E}_1, \mathbf{E}_2, \ldots, \mathbf{E}_n) = 1$.
8. Using the notation of Exercise 7 and letting $\mathbf{A}_i = [a_{i1}, a_{i2}, \ldots, a_{in}]$ for $i = 1, 2, \ldots, n$, show that

$$\Delta(\mathbf{X}_1, \mathbf{X}_2, \ldots, \mathbf{X}_n) = \Delta(\mathbf{A}_1, \mathbf{A}_2, \ldots, \mathbf{A}_n) \cdot \Delta(\mathbf{Y}_1, \mathbf{Y}_2, \ldots, \mathbf{Y}_n).$$

9. Occasionally there is need for a function called the *permanent* whose definition is the same as (5.2) except that $(-1)^{S(P)}$ does not occur. Which of Properties (i)–(v) for a determinant does the permanent satisfy?

5.5 Elementary Properties of Determinants

If one writes det X in the classical notation

$$\det X = \begin{vmatrix} x_{11} & x_{12} & \cdots & x_{1n} \\ x_{21} & x_{22} & \cdots & x_{2n} \\ \vdots & & & \vdots \\ x_{n1} & x_{n2} & \cdots & x_{nn} \end{vmatrix},$$

he is immediately led to questions about the effect of matrix operations on the value of det X. We begin by considering the effect of the transpose operation.

THEOREM 5.3. If X is an $n \times n$ matrix then $\det X = \det X^{\mathsf{T}}$*; or, in the classical notation*

$$\begin{vmatrix} x_{11} & x_{12} & \cdots & x_{1n} \\ x_{21} & x_{22} & \cdots & x_{2n} \\ \vdots & & & \vdots \\ x_{n1} & x_{n2} & \cdots & x_{nn} \end{vmatrix} = \begin{vmatrix} x_{11} & x_{21} & \cdots & x_{n1} \\ x_{12} & x_{22} & \cdots & x_{n2} \\ \vdots & & & \vdots \\ x_{1n} & x_{2n} & \cdots & x_{nn} \end{vmatrix}. \tag{5.5}$$

PROOF. The value of the left determinant of (5.5) is obtained from

$$\sum (-1)^{S(P)} x_{1i_1} x_{2i_2} \cdots x_{ni_n}, \tag{5.6}$$

where the sum is extended over the $n!$ permutations $P = i_1, i_2, \ldots, i_n$ of the integers $1, 2, \ldots, n$. On the other hand, the value of the right determinant of (5.5), because of the interchange of the roles of rows and columns in the matrix X^{T}, is given by

$$\sum (-1)^{S(P)} x_{i_1 1} x_{i_2 2} \cdots x_{i_n n}, \tag{5.7}$$

where the sum is extended over the same $n!$ permutations $P = i_1, i_2, \ldots, i_n$.

Apart from signs, the same terms occur in both (5.6) and (5.7) because each term involves an element x_{ij} from each row and each column. Specifically, let us consider a typical term

$$(-1)^{S(P)}x_{i_1 1}x_{i_2 2}\cdots x_{i_n n} \tag{5.8}$$

of (5.7), where P is the permutation $i_1, i_2, \ldots, i_n$ of $1, 2, \ldots, n$. Now if we rearrange the individual elements of (5.8) until the first subscripts are in ascending order, we get (ignoring the sign)

$$x_{1j_1}x_{2j_2}\cdots x_{nj_n},$$

which occurs in the term

$$(-1)^{S(P')}x_{1j_1}x_{2j_2}\cdots x_{nj_n} \tag{5.9}$$

of (5.6), where P' is the permutation $j_1, j_2, \ldots, j_n$ of $1, 2, \ldots, n$. In order to complete our proof, we must show $(-1)^{S(P)} = (-1)^{S(P')}$.

Let us interrupt the proof to illustrate our reasoning thus far for fourth-order determinants.

Example 1. For the fourth-order determinants

$$\begin{vmatrix} x_{11} & x_{12} & x_{13} & x_{14} \\ x_{21} & x_{22} & x_{23} & x_{24} \\ x_{31} & x_{32} & x_{33} & x_{34} \\ x_{41} & x_{42} & x_{43} & x_{44} \end{vmatrix} \quad \text{and} \quad \begin{vmatrix} x_{11} & x_{21} & x_{31} & x_{41} \\ x_{12} & x_{22} & x_{32} & x_{42} \\ x_{13} & x_{23} & x_{33} & x_{43} \\ x_{14} & x_{24} & x_{34} & x_{44} \end{vmatrix},$$

we have the following unsigned expression occurring in the evaluation of the right determinant:

$$x_{21}x_{42}x_{13}x_{34} \quad \text{(second subscripts in ascending order)};$$

rearranging, this becomes an unsigned expression

$$x_{13}x_{21}x_{34}x_{42} \quad \text{(first subscripts in ascending order)}$$

of the left determinant.

Note that the permutations P and P' of this illustration are 2413 and 3142, respectively. Each has three inversions so that the signs of both these expressions will be minus.

Returning to the general case, we see that our problem is to prove that $S(P)$ and $S(P')$ are both even or both odd. But the permutation P' of the second subscripts is created in the process of reducing the permutation P of the first subscripts to the natural order $1, 2, \ldots, n$. Each inversion corrected in the permutation P creates precisely one for P' since the second subscripts began in natural order and those not accompanying the integer being worked with remain in natural order. As an illustration, in Example 1 we begin with $x_{21}x_{42}x_{13}x_{34}$ and we then successively correct the inversions of 4 in the first subscripts to obtain $x_{21}x_{13}x_{42}x_{34}$; $x_{21}x_{13}x_{34}x_{42}$. Note that the three leading second subscripts 1, 3, 4 are still in natural order although the second subscripts as a whole have two inversions. Finally we have $x_{13}x_{21}x_{34}x_{42}$.

We see in this way that the number of inversions in P is precisely the same as the number in P'. This is what was needed to prove that $S(P)$ and $S(P')$ are both even or both odd, and the theorem is proved.

We can now state a general principle: *If X is an $n \times n$ matrix, the roles of rows and columns of X may be interchanged in any general prescription or result concerning the evaluation of* det X.

The relation $\Delta(\mathbf{X}_1, \mathbf{X}_2, \ldots, \mathbf{0}, \ldots, \mathbf{X}_n) = 0$ given in Exercise 2 of Section 5.1 will provide a simple illustration of this principle. We have asked the student to show that

$$\Delta(\mathbf{X}_1, \mathbf{X}_2, \ldots, \mathbf{0}, \ldots, \mathbf{X}_n) = \begin{vmatrix} x_{11} & x_{12} & \cdots & x_{1n} \\ x_{21} & x_{22} & \cdots & x_{2n} \\ \vdots & \vdots & & \vdots \\ 0 & 0 & \cdots & 0 \\ \vdots & \vdots & & \vdots \\ x_{n1} & x_{n2} & \cdots & x_{nn} \end{vmatrix} = 0.$$

Thus we have the following property for determinants:

If every number of one row of an $n \times n$ matrix X is zero, $\det X = 0$.

The principle $\det X = \det X^{\mathsf{T}}$ immediately yields

If every number of one column of an $n \times n$ matrix X is zero, $\det X = 0$.

We shall list other properties of determinants that play a role in a practical evaluation of $\Delta(\mathbf{X}_1, \mathbf{X}_2, \ldots, \mathbf{X}_n)$ if $n > 3$. The classical notation for determinants will be illustrated by giving the row (column) statement for an $n \times n$ matrix X and its consequences for $\det X$. Although explicit proofs will be omitted, we shall give references to the row statements as interpretations of properties of the function Δ. The column statements are obtained from the general principle, $\det X = \det X^{\mathsf{T}}$.

P1. If an $n \times n$ matrix B differs from an $n \times n$ matrix A only in that two rows (columns) of A have been interchanged, then $\det B = -\det A$. Classically,

$$\begin{vmatrix} a_{11} & a_{12} & \cdots & a_{1n} \\ \vdots & \vdots & & \vdots \\ a_{i1} & a_{i2} & \cdots & a_{in} \\ \vdots & \vdots & & \vdots \\ a_{j1} & a_{j2} & \cdots & a_{jn} \\ \vdots & \vdots & & \vdots \\ a_{n1} & a_{n2} & \cdots & a_{nn} \end{vmatrix} = - \begin{vmatrix} a_{11} & a_{12} & \cdots & a_{1n} \\ \vdots & \vdots & & \vdots \\ a_{j1} & a_{j2} & \cdots & a_{jn} \\ \vdots & \vdots & & \vdots \\ a_{i1} & a_{i2} & \cdots & a_{in} \\ \vdots & \vdots & & \vdots \\ a_{n1} & a_{n2} & \cdots & a_{nn} \end{vmatrix}.$$

This is an immediate consequence of Property (iv) for Δ,

$$\Delta(\mathbf{A}_1, \ldots, \mathbf{A}_i, \ldots, \mathbf{A}_j, \ldots, \mathbf{A}_n) = -\Delta(\mathbf{A}_1, \ldots, \mathbf{A}_j, \ldots, \mathbf{A}_i, \ldots, \mathbf{A}_n).$$

P2. If an $n \times n$ matrix B differs from an $n \times n$ matrix A only in that all elements of one row (column) of A are multiplied by the same number a, then $\det B = a \det A$. Again classically,

$$\begin{vmatrix} a_{11} & a_{12} & \cdots & a_{1n} \\ \vdots & \vdots & & \vdots \\ aa_{i1} & aa_{i2} & \cdots & aa_{in} \\ \vdots & \vdots & & \vdots \\ a_{n1} & a_{n2} & \cdots & a_{nn} \end{vmatrix} = a \begin{vmatrix} a_{11} & a_{12} & \cdots & a_{1n} \\ \vdots & \vdots & & \vdots \\ a_{i1} & a_{i2} & \cdots & a_{in} \\ \vdots & \vdots & & \vdots \\ a_{n1} & a_{n2} & \cdots & a_{nn} \end{vmatrix},$$

where we have indicated the change to be in the ith row of A.

This property for determinants is a consequence of choosing $b = 0$ in Property (i) for Δ.

P3. If two rows (columns) of an $n \times n$ matrix are proportional; that is, considering the ith row of A as a vector $\mathbf{A}_i$, $\mathbf{A}_i = t\mathbf{A}_j$ for $i \neq j$ (or considering the ith column of A as a vector $\mathbf{A}'_i$, $\mathbf{A}'_i = t\mathbf{A}'_j$ for $i \neq j$), then $\det A = 0$.

This is an immediate consequence of Property (v) for Δ as the vectors are linearly dependent. Why?

P4. If an $n \times n$ matrix B differs from an $n \times n$ matrix A only in that a multiple of one row of A has been added to another row of A (a multiple of one column of A has been added to another column of A), then $\det B = \det A$.

Classically,

$$\begin{vmatrix} a_{11} & a_{12} & \cdots & a_{1n} \\ \vdots & \vdots & & \vdots \\ a_{i1} & a_{i2} & \cdots & a_{in} \\ \vdots & \vdots & & \vdots \\ a_{j1} & a_{j2} & \cdots & a_{jn} \\ \vdots & \vdots & & \vdots \\ a_{n1} & a_{n2} & \cdots & a_{nn} \end{vmatrix} = \begin{vmatrix} a_{11} & a_{12} & \cdots & a_{1n} \\ \vdots & \vdots & & \vdots \\ a_{i1} & a_{i2} & \cdots & a_{in} \\ \vdots & \vdots & & \vdots \\ a_{j1} + ca_{i1} & a_{j2} + ca_{i2} & \cdots & a_{jn} + ca_{in} \\ \vdots & \vdots & & \vdots \\ a_{n1} & a_{n2} & \cdots & a_{nn} \end{vmatrix}.$$

This property follows from Property (i) for Δ with $a = c$, $b = 1$.

We shall now use Properties P1–P4 to establish an important theorem about determinants. We begin with a lemma.

PROPOSITION. *If E is an $n \times n$ elementary row matrix, and A is any $n \times n$ matrix, then* $\det EA = \det E \det A$.

PROOF. We merely verify the proposition for the three types of elementary matrices. For example, if E is the matrix obtained by interchanging the ith and jth row of the identity matrix, then $\det E = -1$ (P1). But EA is just the matrix obtained by interchanging the ith and jth rows of A, and thus $\det EA = -\det A = \det E \det A$. The proof for the remaining types of elementary matrices is left to the exercises.

COROLLARY. *If $E_1, E_2, \ldots, E_k$ are $n \times n$ elementary row matrices and A is any $n \times n$ matrix, then* $\det E_1E_2 \cdots E_kA = \det E_1 \det E_2 \cdots \det E_k \det A$.

THEOREM 5.4. *If A, B are any $n \times n$ matrices, then* $\det AB = \det A \det B$.

PROOF. We first consider the case when A is an invertible matrix. Then by Theorem 4.1 $A = E_1E_2 \cdots E_k$, where each E_i is an elementary row matrix. By the corollary above $\det A = \det E_1 \det E_2 \cdots \det E_k$. (Take the A of the corollary to be the identity matrix.) Now another application of the corollary yields

$$\begin{aligned} \det AB = \det E_1E_2 \cdots E_kB &= \det E_1 \det E_2 \cdots \det E_k \det B \\ &= \det A \det B. \end{aligned}$$

If, on the other hand, A is not invertible, then the rows of A are linearly dependent (why?) and by Property (v) $\det A = 0$. We also have that AB is not invertible (if it were, $B(AB)^{-1}$ would be the inverse of A), so $\det AB$ is also zero and the theorem follows.

Exercises

1. Determine the value of det A and det A^{T} for the following matrices A by means of Section 5.3 and verify Theorem 5.3 for these special cases:

$$\text{(a)} \begin{bmatrix} 1 & 2 \\ -1 & 1 \end{bmatrix}, \qquad \text{(b)}\ A = \begin{bmatrix} 3 & 1 \\ 2 & 0 \end{bmatrix},$$

$$\text{(c)}\ A = \begin{bmatrix} 1 & 2 & -1 \\ 3 & 1 & 0 \\ 0 & 2 & 4 \end{bmatrix}, \qquad \text{(d)}\ A = \begin{bmatrix} 2 & 1 & -1 \\ 3 & 1 & 4 \\ 1 & 0 & 2 \end{bmatrix}.$$

2. Determine the property of determinants that implies each of the following results:

$$\text{(a)} \begin{vmatrix} 1 & 2 \\ 2 & 1 \end{vmatrix} = - \begin{vmatrix} 2 & 1 \\ 1 & 2 \end{vmatrix}, \qquad \text{(b)} \begin{vmatrix} 1 & 2 & 3 \\ 1 & 0 & 1 \\ 2 & 4 & 6 \end{vmatrix} = 0,$$

$$\text{(c)} \begin{vmatrix} 4 & 1 & -1 \\ 2 & 1 & 3 \\ 1 & 2 & 1 \end{vmatrix} = \begin{vmatrix} 4 & 2 & 1 \\ 1 & 1 & 2 \\ -1 & 3 & 1 \end{vmatrix}, \qquad \text{(d)} \begin{vmatrix} 1 & 2 & 1 \\ -1 & 1 & 0 \\ 2 & 1 & 3 \end{vmatrix} = \begin{vmatrix} 1 & 2 & 1 \\ 0 & 3 & 1 \\ 2 & 1 & 3 \end{vmatrix},$$

$$\text{(e)} \begin{vmatrix} 1 & 3 & 2 \\ 2 & 4 & 4 \\ 1 & 5 & 2 \end{vmatrix} = 0.$$

3. If A is a $n \times n$ matrix of odd order such that $a_{ij} = -a_{ji}$, show that det $A = 0$.
4. By repeated application of Property P4, show that the following determinants vanish:

$$\text{(a)} \begin{vmatrix} 1 & 2 & 5 \\ 2 & 3 & -1 \\ 1 & 3 & 16 \end{vmatrix}, \qquad \text{(b)} \begin{vmatrix} a+d & 3a & b+2a & b+d \\ 2b & b+d & c-b & c-d \\ a+c & c-2d & d & a+3d \\ b-d & c-d & a+c & a+b \end{vmatrix}.$$

5. Use Property P2 to show that if E is the matrix obtained from the identity by multiplying one row by a, then det EA = det E det A for any A.
6. Use Property P4 to show that if E is the matrix obtained from the identity by adding a multiple of one row to another row, then det EA = det E det A.
7. Use Theorem 5.4 to prove that det $A^{-1} = 1/\det A$.

5.6 Applications of Determinants

We now turn to some of the applications of determinants that were indicated in the introduction to this chapter.

Dependence of Vectors

We saw in Property (v) of Section 5.1 that if the vectors $\mathbf{A}_1, \mathbf{A}_2, \ldots, \mathbf{A}_n$ were linearly dependent, then $\Delta(\mathbf{A}_1, \mathbf{A}_2, \ldots, \mathbf{A}_n) = 0$. Now we prove the converse.

THEOREM 5.5. Let

$$\mathbf{A}_1 = [a_{11}, a_{12}, \ldots, a_{1n}], \ldots, \mathbf{A}_n = [a_{n1}, a_{n2}, \ldots, a_{nn}]$$

be n vectors of R^n. If $\Delta(\mathbf{A}_1, \mathbf{A}_2, \ldots, \mathbf{A}_n) = 0$, the vectors $\mathbf{A}_1, \mathbf{A}_2, \ldots, \mathbf{A}_n$ are linearly dependent.

Proof. We seek real numbers $c_1, c_2, \ldots, c_n$ such that

$$c_1\mathbf{A}_1 + c_2\mathbf{A}_2 + \cdots + c_n\mathbf{A}_n = \mathbf{0}$$

and not all the c_i are zero. This is equivalent, when the components are collected, to finding a nonzero solution to the system of equations

$$\begin{aligned} a_{11}c_1 + a_{21}c_2 + \cdots + a_{n1}c_n &= 0 \\ a_{12}c_1 + a_{22}c_2 + \cdots + a_{n2}c_n &= 0 \\ &\vdots \\ a_{1n}c_1 + a_{2n}c_2 + \cdots + a_{nn}c_n &= 0. \end{aligned} \tag{5.10}$$

Let the largest minor of the $n \times n$ matrix

$$A = \begin{bmatrix} a_{11} & a_{12} & \cdots & a_{1n} \\ a_{21} & a_{22} & \cdots & a_{2n} \\ \vdots & & & \vdots \\ a_{n1} & a_{n2} & \cdots & a_{nn} \end{bmatrix}$$

that is not zero be of order k. (If all elements of the matrix A are zero, there is no problem since all the $\mathbf{A}_i$ are zero.) First let us assume that such a nonzero minor occurs in rows 2 through $k + 1$ and columns 1 through k. Then all determinants of the form

$$\begin{vmatrix} a_{11} & a_{12} & \cdots & a_{1k} & a_{1i} \\ a_{21} & a_{22} & \cdots & a_{2k} & a_{2i} \\ \vdots & & & & \vdots \\ a_{k+1,1} & a_{k+1,2} & \cdots & a_{k+1,k} & a_{k+1,i} \end{vmatrix} \tag{5.11}$$

for $i = 1, 2, \ldots, n$ will have the value zero, either because two columns are the same ($i = 1, 2, \ldots, k$) or because they are minors of order $k + 1$ of A ($i = k + 1, \ldots, n$).

If these determinants of (5.11) are expanded by means of minors of the last column, we have

$$a_{1i}c_1 + a_{2i}c_2 + \cdots + a_{k+1,i}c_{k+1} = 0,$$

where we have denoted the cofactor of a_{ji} by c_j. Note that $c_1 \neq 0$. Then

$$a_{1i}c_1 + a_{2i}c_2 + \cdots + a_{k+1,i}c_{k+1} + a_{k+2,i} \cdot 0 + \cdots + a_{ni} \cdot 0 = 0$$

for each $i = 1, 2, \ldots, n$. This gives a solution of the original equations (5.11) in which $c_{k+2}, \ldots, c_n = 0$ but $c_1 \neq 0$.

If the minor of order k that was used above is zero, it is necessary to take a minor of A that is not zero and adjoin the corresponding elements of a (fixed) other row and of all columns to get similar minors of order $k + 1$ as in (5.11). The essential feature is the same in any case: a solution is obtained to the original equations (5.10) with at least one nonzero c_i. The student may be interested in trying the general proof either by devising a notation to handle an arbitrary minor or by rearranging terms to move the nonzero minor into a desirable position.

Property (v) of Section 1.1 and Theorem 5.10 now yield the following result: *Vectors*

$$\mathbf{A}_1 = [a_{11}, a_{12}, \ldots, a_{1n}], \ldots, \mathbf{A}_n = [a_{n1}, a_{n2}, \ldots, a_{nn}]$$

are linearly dependent if and only if

$$\Delta(\mathbf{A}_1, \mathbf{A}_2, \ldots, \mathbf{A}_n) = \begin{vmatrix} a_{11} & a_{12} & \cdots & a_{1n} \\ a_{21} & a_{22} & \cdots & a_{2n} \\ \vdots & & & \\ a_{n1} & a_{n2} & \cdots & a_{nn} \end{vmatrix} = 0.$$

Example 1. To determine whether the vectors [1, 0, 2, −1], [3, 1, 1, −2], [−2, 1, −1, 3], and [2, 2, 2, 0] are linearly dependent, we compute

$$\begin{vmatrix} 1 & 0 & 2 & -1 \\ 3 & 1 & 1 & -2 \\ -2 & 1 & -1 & 3 \\ 2 & 2 & 2 & 0 \end{vmatrix} = \begin{vmatrix} 1 & 0 & 2 & -1 \\ 0 & 1 & -5 & 1 \\ 0 & 1 & 3 & 1 \\ 0 & 2 & -2 & 2 \end{vmatrix} = \begin{vmatrix} 1 & 0 & 2 & -1 \\ 0 & 1 & -5 & 1 \\ 0 & 0 & 8 & 0 \\ 0 & 0 & 8 & 0 \end{vmatrix} = 0.$$

Thus the vectors are known to be dependent although an explicit linear relation between them has not been obtained. A linear relation may be obtained by following the proof of Theorem 5.10 in this special case with

the nonzero minor $\begin{vmatrix} 3 & 1 & 1 \\ -2 & 1 & -1 \\ 2 & 2 & 2 \end{vmatrix}$.

Simultaneous Linear Equations

The application of determinants to the solution of simultaneous linear equations is demonstrated in this theorem:

THEOREM 5.6 (CRAMER'S RULE). If the system of equations

$$\begin{aligned} a_{11}x_1 + a_{12}x_2 + \cdots + a_{1n}x_n &= b_1 \\ a_{21}x_1 + a_{22}x_2 + \cdots + a_{2n}x_n &= b_2 \\ &\vdots \\ a_{n1}x_1 + a_{n2}x_2 + \cdots + a_{nn}x_n &= b_n \end{aligned} \tag{5.12}$$

has a unique solution, the determinant of the matrix A whose elements are a_{ij}, that is,

$$\det A = \begin{vmatrix} a_{11} & a_{12} & \cdots & a_{1n} \\ a_{21} & a_{22} & \cdots & a_{2n} \\ \vdots & & & \vdots \\ a_{n1} & a_{n2} & \cdots & a_{nn} \end{vmatrix},$$

is not zero, and the solution may be expressed in the form

$$x_i = \frac{\Delta_i}{\Delta},$$

where Δ is the determinant just given and Δ_i is obtained by substituting the vector $[b_1, b_2, \ldots, b_n]$ for $[a_{1i}, a_{2i}, \ldots, a_{ni}]$, considering the determinant as a function of the columns of A. Conversely, if $\Delta \neq 0$, the system has a unique solution of the form mentioned.

PROOF OF THEOREM 5.6. If $\Delta = 0$, $\det A^{\mathrm{T}} = 0$; and from Theorem 5.5 we know that the vectors

$$\mathbf{A}_1 = [a_{11}, a_{21}, \ldots, a_{n1}],\ \mathbf{A}_2 = [a_{12}, a_{22}, \ldots, a_{n2}], \ldots, \mathbf{A}_n = [a_{1n}, a_{2n}, \ldots, a_{nn}]$$

are linearly dependent so that there exist real numbers $c_1, c_2, \ldots, c_n$ not all zero such that

$$c_1\mathbf{A}_1 + c_2\mathbf{A}_2 + \cdots + c_n\mathbf{A}_n = \mathbf{0}.$$

Now if $x_1, x_2, \ldots, x_n$ satisfy Equations (5.12), that is, if

$$x_1\mathbf{A}_1 + x_2\mathbf{A}_2 + \cdots + x_n\mathbf{A}_n = \mathbf{B},$$

where $\mathbf{B} = [b_1, b_2, \ldots, b_n]$, then so do $x_1 + c_1, x_2 + c_2, \ldots, x_n + c_n$ since

$$\begin{aligned}(x_1 + c_1)\mathbf{A}_1 + (x_2 + c_2)\mathbf{A}_2 + \cdots + (x_n + c_n)\mathbf{A}_n \\ &= (x_1\mathbf{A}_1 + x_2\mathbf{A}_2 + \cdots + x_n\mathbf{A}_n) + c_1\mathbf{A}_1 + c_2\mathbf{A}_2 + \cdots + c_n\mathbf{A}_n \\ &= \mathbf{B} + \mathbf{0} = \mathbf{B}.\end{aligned}$$

Thus, if there is one solution, there are others, and the solution is not unique.

Next suppose $\Delta \neq 0$. Now $\mathbf{A}_1, \mathbf{A}_2, \ldots, \mathbf{A}_n$ are independent. Then these vectors form a basis for R^n. Since $\mathbf{B}$ is a vector of R^n it may be written in one and only one way as a linear combination of $\mathbf{A}_1, \mathbf{A}_2, \ldots, \mathbf{A}_n$. This means that there is precisely one set of values which satisfies the equations. It remains to show that these values are given by $x_i = \dfrac{\Delta_i}{\Delta}$.

We must show that

$$\frac{\Delta_1}{\Delta}\mathbf{A}_1 + \frac{\Delta_2}{\Delta}\mathbf{A}_2 + \cdots + \frac{\Delta_n}{\Delta}\mathbf{A}_n = \mathbf{B}$$

or

$$\Delta_1\mathbf{A}_1 + \Delta_2\mathbf{A}_2 + \cdots + \Delta_n\mathbf{A}_n - \Delta\mathbf{B} = \mathbf{0}.$$

This vector equation is equivalent to a set of scalar equations of which a typical member is

$$a_{i1}\Delta_1 + a_{i2}\Delta_2 + \cdots + a_{in}\Delta_n - b_i\Delta = 0.$$

To see that this equation is valid let us introduce a matrix D of $n + 1$ rows and consider

$$\det D = \begin{vmatrix} a_{i1} & a_{i2} & \cdots & a_{in} & b_i \\ a_{11} & a_{12} & \cdots & a_{1n} & b_1 \\ a_{21} & a_{22} & \cdots & a_{2n} & b_2 \\ \vdots & & & & \vdots \\ a_{n1} & a_{n2} & \cdots & a_{nn} & b_n \end{vmatrix}.$$

Now $\det D = 0$ because the first row is equal to a later row of D. Hence, if we expand D in cofactors of the first row we have

$$a_{i1}\begin{vmatrix} a_{12} & \cdots & a_{1n} & b_1 \\ a_{22} & \cdots & a_{2n} & b_2 \\ \vdots & & & \vdots \\ a_{n2} & \cdots & a_{nn} & b_n \end{vmatrix} + a_{i2}(-1)^1\begin{vmatrix} a_{11} & a_{13} & \cdots & a_{1n} & b_1 \\ a_{21} & a_{23} & \cdots & a_{2n} & b_2 \\ \vdots & & & & \vdots \\ a_{n1} & a_{n3} & \cdots & a_{nn} & b_n \end{vmatrix} + \cdots$$

$$+ a_{in}(-1)^{n-1}\begin{vmatrix} a_{11} & a_{12} & \cdots & a_{n1,-1} & b_1 \\ a_{21} & a_{22} & \cdots & a_{2,n-1} & b_2 \\ \vdots & & & & \vdots \\ a_{n1} & a_{n2} & \cdots & a_{n,n-1} & b_n \end{vmatrix}$$

$$+ b_i(-1)^n\begin{vmatrix} a_{11} & a_{12} & \cdots & a_{1n} \\ a_{21} & a_{22} & \cdots & a_{2n} \\ \vdots & & & \vdots \\ a_{n1} & a_{n2} & \cdots & a_{nn} \end{vmatrix} = 0.$$

Next, in the first minor above, move the column of b's to the first position without disturbing the order of the remaining $n - 1$ columns. This takes $n - 1$ interchanges and the result is Δ_1. In the second minor, move the b column to the second place; this takes $n - 2$ interchanges to give Δ_2. Continue in this way up to the last two minors, which remain as they are. In the original equation, the power of -1 associated with the coefficient a_{ik} is $k - 1$;

the number of interchanges given above is $n - k$. Thus the total is $k - 1 + n - k = n - 1$. Then

$$a_{i1}(-1)^{n-1}\Delta_1 + a_{i2}(-1)^{n-1}\Delta_2 + \cdots + a_{in}(-1)^{n-1}\Delta_n + b_i(-1)^n\Delta = 0,$$

or

$$a_{i1}\Delta_1 + a_{i2}\Delta_2 + \cdots + a_{in}\Delta_n - b_i\Delta = 0,$$

which is the desired equation.

We repeat that Cramer's rule is not being offered as a *practical* method of solving equations. The total labor involved in the Gaussian elimination method of the previous chapter is less than is required to evaluate two determinants whereas Cramer's method requires the evaluation of $n + 1$ determinants.

Cramer's rule specifies a fixed format for the solution which is available for modification as we see fit. It also gives a fixed criterion ($\Delta \neq 0$) for a unique solution to exist, which is often theoretically useful.

Exercises

1. Determine whether or not the following sets of vectors are linearly dependent by evaluating a determinant:
   (a) $[1, 2, -1]$, $[2, -1, 3]$, $[1, 7, -6]$,
   (b) $[1, 2, -1, 3]$, $[2, -4, 1, 0]$, $[0, 1, 2, -1]$, $[3, -1, 2, 2]$,
   (c) $[x, x^2, 1]$, $[-1, x, x]$, $[0, 2x^2, x^2 + 1]$.
2. The vectors $[1, -1, 0, 0]$ and $[1, -4, -3, 1]$ are contained in $L\{[2, 1, 3, -1], [1, 2, 3, -1]\}$. Show how linear expressions for $[1, -1, 0, 0]$ and $[1, -4, -3, 1]$ in terms of $[2, 1, 3, -1]$ and $[1, 2, 3, -1]$ may be obtained by finding a nonzero minor of order 2 in the determinant

$$\begin{vmatrix} 1 & -1 & 0 & 0 \\ 2 & 1 & 3 & -1 \\ 1 & 2 & 3 & -1 \\ 1 & -4 & -3 & 1 \end{vmatrix}$$

   and following the proof of Theorem 5.5 in this special case.
3. Prove: A set of k vectors of R^n is a set of linearly independent vectors if and only if one of the kth-order determinants obtained by taking k corresponding components from each vector is not zero.
4. Show that the coordinates (r_1, r_2) of any point on the line joining points $X(x_1, x_2)$ and $Y(y_1, y_2)$ of a plane with a Cartesian coordinate system satisfy the equation

$$\begin{vmatrix} r_1 & r_2 & 1 \\ x_1 & x_2 & 1 \\ y_1 & y_2 & 1 \end{vmatrix} = 0.$$

5. In the notation of Exercise 4, what does the determinant

$$\begin{vmatrix} r_1 & r_2 & 1 \\ x_1 & x_2 & 1 \\ y_1 & y_2 & 1 \end{vmatrix}$$

   represent if (r_1, r_2) does not lie on the line joining X and Y? *Hint:* Check the definition of area of a parallelogram.

6. Show that the coordinates (r_1, r_2, r_3) of any point in the plane containing the noncollinear points $X(x_1, x_2, x_3)$, $Y(y_1, y_2, y_3)$, $Z(z_1, z_2, z_3)$ of space with a Cartesian coordinate system satisfy the equation

$$\begin{vmatrix} r_1 & r_2 & r_3 & 1 \\ x_1 & x_2 & x_3 & 1 \\ y_1 & y_2 & y_3 & 1 \\ z_1 & z_2 & z_3 & 1 \end{vmatrix} = 0.$$

7. In the notation of Exercise 6, what does the determinant

$$\begin{vmatrix} r_1 & r_2 & r_3 & 1 \\ x_1 & x_2 & x_3 & 1 \\ y_1 & y_2 & y_3 & 1 \\ z_1 & z_2 & z_3 & 1 \end{vmatrix}$$

represent if (r_1, r_2, r_3) does not lie in the plane containing the points X, Y, and Z?

8. Solve the following systems of equations by Cramer's rule for the designated unknowns *only* or show that no unique solution exists.

(a) $$\begin{aligned} x + 3y - z &= 4, \\ 2x - y + z &= 1, \\ 3x + y + 2z &= 5, \end{aligned} \qquad \text{for } y.$$

(b) $$\begin{aligned} x - 2y + z - t &= 0, \\ y + t &= 1, \\ x - z &= 1, \\ x + y &= 1, \end{aligned} \qquad \text{for } z.$$

(c) $$\begin{aligned} x - y + z &= 3, \\ x + 2y + 2z &= 1, \\ x + 5y + 3z &= -1, \end{aligned} \qquad \text{for } x.$$

(d) $$\begin{aligned} x + y &= 1, \\ x - z &= 1, \\ x + t &= 1, \\ x - w &= 1, \\ x + y + z + t + w &= 1, \end{aligned} \qquad \text{for all unknowns.}$$

9. Show that a solution of the equations

$$\begin{aligned} a_{11}x_1 + a_{12}x_2 + a_{13}x_3 &= 0, \\ a_{21}x_1 + a_{22}x_2 + a_{23}x_3 &= 0, \end{aligned}$$

is given by

$$x_1 = \begin{vmatrix} a_{12} & a_{13} \\ a_{22} & a_{23} \end{vmatrix}, \qquad x_2 = \begin{vmatrix} a_{13} & a_{11} \\ a_{23} & a_{21} \end{vmatrix}, \qquad x_3 = \begin{vmatrix} a_{11} & a_{12} \\ a_{21} & a_{22} \end{vmatrix}.$$

Note that the vector $[x_1, x_2, x_3]$ is orthogonal to the vectors $[a_{11}, a_{12}, a_{13}]$ and $[a_{21}, a_{22}, a_{23}]$.

Bilinear Mappings and Quadratic Forms

6.1 Bilinear Mappings and Forms

We begin by considering the set of all ordered pairs of vectors from a real vector space V. Following the standard notation, we will denote this set by $V \times V$. Now, suppose we have a mapping or function B from $V \times V$ to R. As usual we will denote the value in R assigned to the pair (X, Y) by $\mathrm{B}(X, Y)$. The mappings that we wish to consider are those with the following properties:

$$\begin{aligned} &\text{(i)} \quad \mathrm{B}(a\mathbf{X}_1 + b\mathbf{X}_2, \mathbf{Y}) = a\mathrm{B}(\mathbf{X}_1, \mathbf{Y}) + b\mathrm{B}(\mathbf{X}_2, \mathbf{Y}), \\ &\text{(ii)} \quad \mathrm{B}(\mathbf{X}, a\mathbf{Y}_1 + b\mathbf{Y}_2) = a\mathrm{B}(\mathbf{X}, \mathbf{Y}_1) + b\mathrm{B}(\mathbf{X}, \mathbf{Y}_2), \end{aligned} \tag{6.1}$$

for all vectors $\mathbf{X}, \mathbf{X}_1, \mathbf{X}_2, \mathbf{Y}, \mathbf{Y}_1, \mathbf{Y}_2$ in V, and all real numbers a, b.

Example 1. The example that motivates this section is the standard inner product: $\mathrm{B}(\mathbf{X}, \mathbf{Y}) = (\mathbf{X}, \mathbf{Y})$.

A mapping B from $V \times V$ to R with the properties (6.1) is called a *bilinear mapping*.

Example 2. A more special example than the standard inner product is given by defining $\mathrm{B}(\mathbf{X}, \mathbf{Y}) = \Delta(\mathbf{X}, \mathbf{Y})$ for vectors in R^2, where Δ is the determinant function. Thus

$$\mathrm{B}([x_1, y_1], [x_2, y_2]) = x_1 y_2 - x_2 y_1.$$

The fact that this function is bilinear was established in Chapter 5.

Whenever we have a condition of linearity on a mapping, it is natural to express the operation in terms of a basis. In the present case, to get the generality we desire, it will be necessary to use *two* bases, one for the first element of the ordered pair, and another for the second element. Thus, if our two bases are $\{\mathbf{X}_i\}$, $\{\mathbf{Y}_i\}$ we will think of $\mathrm{B}(\mathbf{X}, \mathbf{Y})$ as

$$\mathrm{B}(x_1\mathbf{X}_1 + x_2\mathbf{X}_2 + \cdots + x_n\mathbf{X}_n, y_1\mathbf{Y}_1 + y_2\mathbf{Y}_2 + \cdots + y_n\mathbf{Y}_n),$$

where

$$\mathbf{X} = x_1\mathbf{X}_1 + x_2\mathbf{X}_2 + \cdots + x_n\mathbf{X}_n \quad \text{and} \quad \mathbf{Y} = y_1\mathbf{Y}_1 + y_2\mathbf{Y}_2 + \cdots + y_n\mathbf{Y}_n.$$

REMARK. The reader who has studied the optional Section 2.10 will see that the discussion of this section can easily be phrased in terms of dual spaces. In place of $V \times V$, think of $V^* \times V$, and $\mathrm{B}(\mathbf{X}, \mathbf{Y})$ is just the value assumed by $\mathbf{X}$ (a linear functional) at $\mathbf{Y}$ (a vector in V). Now, for example, if we take the standard bases $\{f_i\}$ for $(R^n)^*$ and $\{\mathbf{E}_i\}$ for R^n ($f_i(\mathbf{E}_j) = 0$ for $i \neq j$, 1 if $i = j$), the resulting mapping is the standard inner product in the sense that

$$\begin{aligned} B(X, Y) &= B(a_1 f_1 + \cdots + a_n f_n, b_1 E_1 + \cdots + b_1 E_n) \\ &= a_1 b_1 + a_2 b_2 + \cdots + a_n b_n. \end{aligned}$$

In this setting it is very natural to consider different bases for V^* and V. In order to avoid using the dual space in this section we are taking advantage of the isomorphism of V and V^* in the case of finite-dimensional V.

Returning to our discussion, we can use the bilinearity of B to write

$$\begin{aligned} \mathrm{B}(\mathbf{X}, \mathbf{Y}) &= \mathrm{B}(x_1\mathbf{X}_1 + x_2\mathbf{X}_2 + \cdots + x_n\mathbf{X}_n, \mathbf{Y}) \\ &= x_1\mathrm{B}(\mathbf{X}_1, \mathbf{Y}) + x_2\mathrm{B}(\mathbf{X}_2, \mathbf{Y}) + \cdots + x_n\mathrm{B}(\mathbf{X}_n, \mathbf{Y}). \end{aligned}$$

In turn, using $\mathbf{Y} = y_1\mathbf{Y}_1 + y_2\mathbf{Y}_2 + \cdots + y_n\mathbf{Y}_n$,

$$\begin{aligned} \mathrm{B}(\mathbf{X}_i, \mathbf{Y}) &= \mathrm{B}(\mathbf{X}_i, y_1\mathbf{Y}_1 + y_2\mathbf{Y}_2 + \cdots + y_n\mathbf{Y}_n) \\ &= y_1\mathrm{B}(\mathbf{X}_i, \mathbf{Y}_1) + y_2\mathrm{B}(\mathbf{X}_i, \mathbf{Y}_2) + \cdots + y_n\mathrm{B}(\mathbf{X}_i, \mathbf{Y}_n). \end{aligned}$$

Thus, in the end, the value of B at any ordered pair depends on the coefficients of the basis elements and on the particular values of the mapping B on the n^2 ordered pairs $(\mathbf{X}_i, \mathbf{Y}_j)$. For simplicity of notation, let $\mathrm{B}(\mathbf{X}_i, \mathbf{Y}_j) = a_{ij}$. Then, using the two expansions above,

$$\mathrm{B}(X, Y) = \sum_{i=1}^{n} \sum_{j=1}^{n} x_i y_j a_{ij} = \sum_{i,j=1}^{n} x_i a_{ij} y_j, \tag{6.2}$$

where the last summation extends over all n^2 possible terms. Now notice that we can simplify the notation by setting $A = [a_{ij}]$. Then formula (6.2) becomes

$$\mathrm{B}(\mathbf{X}, \mathbf{Y}) = [x_1, x_2, \ldots, x_n]A \begin{bmatrix} y_1 \\ y_2 \\ \vdots \\ y_n \end{bmatrix}. \tag{6.3}$$

Example 3. Suppose that for the case of R^3 and a particular B, formula (6.2) reads

$$\begin{aligned} \mathrm{B}(X, Y) = x_1y_1 + 2x_1y_2 + 4x_1y_3 + x_2y_1 - x_2y_2 + 3x_2y_3 \\ + 2x_3y_1 - x_3y_2 + x_3y_3. \end{aligned}$$

This formula can be written in matrix terms:

$$\mathrm{B}(\mathbf{X}, \mathbf{Y}) = [x_1, x_2, x_3] \begin{bmatrix} 1 & 2 & 4 \\ 1 & -1 & 3 \\ 2 & -1 & 1 \end{bmatrix} \begin{bmatrix} y_1 \\ y_2 \\ y_3 \end{bmatrix}.$$

The new formula is neater and at least as easy to evaluate for any particular choice of $\mathbf{X}$ and $\mathbf{Y}$.

Thus any bilinear mapping B is associated with a unique matrix A, in the presence of a pair of bases $\{\mathbf{X}_i\}$ and $\{\mathbf{Y}_i\}$. Conversely, given a pair of bases and a matrix A, formula (6.3) defines a unique bilinear mapping. The reader should verify the last statement. We sum up the discussion with a theorem.

THEOREM 6.1. *Let* $\{\mathbf{X}_1, \mathbf{X}_2, \ldots, \mathbf{X}_n\}$ and $\{\mathbf{Y}_1, \mathbf{Y}_2, \ldots, \mathbf{Y}_n\}$ *be two bases of a vector space* V. *There is a one-to-one mapping between the set of all bilinear mappings* B *of* V *and the set of all* $n \times n$ *matrices* $A = [a_{ij}]$ *such that*

$$\mathrm{B}(\mathbf{X}, \mathbf{Y}) = [x_1, x_2, \ldots, x_n]A[y_1, y_2, \ldots, y_n]^{\mathsf{T}},$$

where

$$\mathbf{X} = x_1\mathbf{X}_1 + x_2\mathbf{X}_2 + \cdots + x_n\mathbf{X}_n$$

and

$$\mathbf{Y} = y_1\mathbf{Y}_1 + y_2\mathbf{Y}_2 + \cdots + y_n\mathbf{Y}_n.$$

The matrix $A = [\mathrm{B}(\mathbf{X}_i, \mathbf{Y}_j)]$ is called *the matrix of the bilinear mapping* B (relative to the bases $\{\mathbf{X}_i\}$ and $\{\mathbf{Y}_i\}$).

An expression of the type

$$[x_1, x_2, \ldots, x_n]A[y_1, y_2, \ldots, y_n]^{\mathsf{T}} = \sum_{i,j=1}^{n} x_i a_{ij} y_j$$

with *literal elements* $x_1, x_2, \ldots, x_n; y_1, y_2, \ldots, y_n$ is called a *bilinear form.* For example,

$$[x_1, x_2]\begin{bmatrix} 1 & 2 \\ -1 & 3 \end{bmatrix}\begin{bmatrix} y_1 \\ y_2 \end{bmatrix} = x_1y_1 + 2x_1y_2 - x_2y_1 + 3x_2y_2$$

is a bilinear form. A bilinear form may be thought of as being similar to the general formula (5.2) for the expansion of a determinant; a bilinear form is a formula giving the value of a bilinear mapping when real numbers are substituted for the $\{x_i\}$ and $\{y_j\}$. Of course, a vector space V and bases $\{\mathbf{X}_i\}$ and $\{\mathbf{Y}_i\}$ must be in mind.

Example 4. If, in R^n, the bases $\{\mathbf{X}_i\}$ and $\{\mathbf{Y}_i\}$ are selected as the natural basis $\{\mathbf{E}_i\}$, then the matrix of the bilinear mapping $\mathrm{B}(\mathbf{X}, \mathbf{Y}) = (\mathbf{X}, \mathbf{Y})$ is the $n \times n$ identity matrix I and

$$\mathrm{B}(\mathbf{X}, \mathbf{Y}) = [x_1, x_2, \ldots, x_n]I[y_1, y_2, \ldots, y_n]^{\mathsf{T}},$$

where $\mathbf{X} = [x_1, x_2, \ldots, x_n]$ and $\mathbf{Y} = [y_1, y_2, \ldots, y_n]$.

Example 5. If, in R^2, we select the bases $\{\mathbf{X}_1, \mathbf{X}_2\} = \{\mathbf{Y}_1, \mathbf{Y}_2\} = \{\mathbf{E}_1, \mathbf{E}_2\}$, then the matrix of the bilinear mapping B of Example 2,

$$\mathrm{B}(\mathbf{X}, \mathbf{Y}) = \Delta(\mathbf{X}, \mathbf{Y}),$$

is $\begin{bmatrix} 0 & 1 \\ -1 & 0 \end{bmatrix}$. The bilinear form is $x_1y_2 - x_2y_1$, where $\mathbf{X} = [x_1, x_2]$ and $\mathbf{Y} = [y_1, y_2]$.

An especially simple expression of a bilinear mapping of R^n occurs when the bases $\{\mathbf{X}_i\}$ and $\{\mathbf{Y}_i\}$ are chosen as the natural basis $\{\mathbf{E}_i\}$ as in Examples 4 and 5. Here

$$\mathbf{X} = [x_1, x_2, \ldots, x_n] = x_1\mathbf{E}_1 + x_2\mathbf{E}_2 + \cdots + x_n\mathbf{E}_n,$$
$$\mathbf{Y} = [y_1, y_2, \ldots, y_n] = y_1\mathbf{E}_1 + y_2\mathbf{E}_2 + \cdots + y_n\mathbf{E}_n,$$

so that

$$\begin{aligned} \mathrm{B}(\mathbf{X}, \mathbf{Y}) &= \mathbf{X}A\mathbf{Y}^{\mathsf{T}} = \mathbf{X}(A\mathbf{Y}^{\mathsf{T}}) = (\mathbf{X}, A\mathbf{Y}^{\mathsf{T}}) \\ &= (\mathbf{X}A)\mathbf{Y}^{\mathsf{T}} = (A^{\mathsf{T}}\mathbf{X}^{\mathsf{T}})^{\mathsf{T}}\mathbf{Y}^{\mathsf{T}} = (A^{\mathsf{T}}\mathbf{X}^{\mathsf{T}}, \mathbf{Y}), \end{aligned} \tag{6.4}$$

where in the last formula in each row we use the inner product notation, although, strictly speaking, one of the vectors is a row vector and one is a column vector. We shall use this generalized notation in the sequel without comment.

Thus, in this case, the procedure of evaluating the bilinear mapping reduces to that of applying a linear transformation to one of the vectors (A to $\mathbf{Y}$ or A^{T} to $\mathbf{X}$) and then taking the standard scalar product. The generalized mapping can thus be represented as resulting from a linear transformation and the use of the special case of the inner product.

Let us summarize the ideas that have been introduced in this section.

The basic new concept is that of the *bilinear mapping*, which maps pairs of vectors to the real field and is linear with respect to both elements of the pair.

In the presence of bases of V, the bilinear mapping defines a matrix and a *bilinear form*. The latter is an algebraic formula that may be used in place of the matrix for evaluating a bilinear mapping. When bases are understood, we may use an equality:

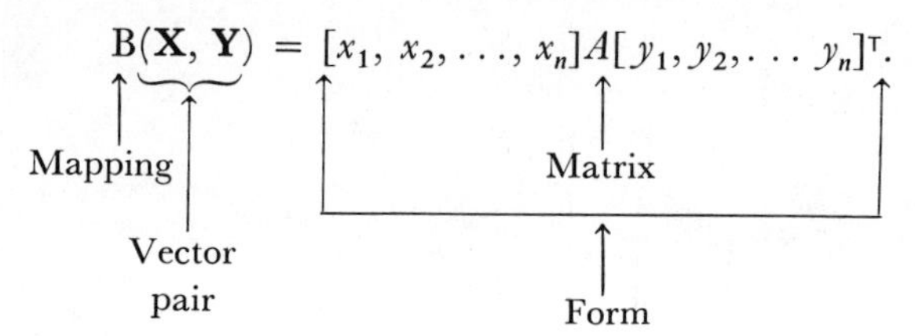

When no confusion will result, that is, when the bases $\{\mathbf{X}_i\}$ and $\{\mathbf{Y}_i\}$ are clearly specified, we will use $\mathrm{B}(\mathbf{X}, \mathbf{Y})$ to denote the form as well as the value of the mapping for the pair $(\mathbf{X}, \mathbf{Y})$.

Exercises

1. Express the following bilinear forms as matrix products $[x_1, x_2]A[y_1, y_2]^{\mathsf{T}}$ or $[x_1, x_2, x_3]A[y_1, y_2, y_3]^{\mathsf{T}}$:
   (a) $2x_1y_1 + 3x_1y_2 - 4x_2y_1 + x_2y_2$,
   (b) $5x_1y_1 - x_2y_1 + 2x_2y_2$,
   (c) $x_1y_1 + x_1y_2 - x_1y_3 + 2x_2y_1 - x_2y_3$.
2. If we write $\mathbf{X}$ and $\mathbf{Y}$ in bases other than an orthonormal basis for both vectors, the inner product cannot be computed from the coefficients of the linear combination by the standard formula. In this case the inner product itself assumes the form of a more general bilinear mapping. Find the matrix associated with the inner product in R^2 if $\mathbf{X}$ is expressed in terms of the basis $\{\mathbf{X}_1 = [1, 2], \mathbf{X}_2 = [-1, 3]\}$ and $\mathbf{Y}$ in terms of $\{\mathbf{Y}_1 = [1, -1], \mathbf{Y}_2 = [0, 1]\}$.
3. A bilinear mapping B for R^2 is defined by
$$\mathrm{B}(\mathbf{X}, \mathbf{Y}) = (\mathbf{X}, A\mathbf{Y}^{\mathsf{T}}), \qquad \text{where } A = \begin{bmatrix} 1 & 3 \\ 1 & 2 \end{bmatrix}.$$
   (a) Find $\mathrm{B}([1, -1], [2, 3])$, $\mathrm{B}([1, 4], [2, 1])$.
   (b) What is the matrix of B relative to the bases $\{\mathbf{X}_1^*, \mathbf{X}_2^*\}$ and $\{\mathbf{Y}_1^*, \mathbf{Y}_2^*\}$, where $\mathbf{X}_1^* = \mathbf{Y}_1^* = [1, -1]$ and $\mathbf{X}_2^* = \mathbf{Y}_2^* = [2, 1]$?
   (c) If P is the 2×2 matrix of change of bases from $\{\mathbf{X}_i^*\}$ to $\{\mathbf{E}_i\}$, show that the answer to (b) is given by $P^{\mathsf{T}}AP$.
4. What are necessary and sufficient conditions on the elements b_{ij} in the bilinear form
$$\sum_{i,j=1}^{n} x_i b_{ij} y_j = \mathrm{B}(\mathbf{X}, \mathbf{Y})$$
in order that $\mathrm{B}(\mathbf{X}, \mathbf{Y}) = \mathrm{B}(\mathbf{Y}, \mathbf{X})$ for all vectors $\mathbf{X}$ and $\mathbf{Y}$ of R^n?

5. If B is a bilinear mapping, show that B*, defined by

$$B^*(\mathbf{X}, \mathbf{Y}) = B(\mathbf{X}, \mathbf{Y}) + B(\mathbf{Y}, \mathbf{X}),$$

is also a bilinear mapping. Is

$$B^*(\mathbf{X}, \mathbf{Y}) = B^*(\mathbf{Y}, \mathbf{X})$$

for all pairs $\{\mathbf{X}, \mathbf{Y}\}$?

6. Generalize the definition of a bilinear function to a mapping from ordered pairs of vectors $\{\mathbf{X}, \mathbf{Y}\}$, $\mathbf{X} \in V_1$ and $\mathbf{Y} \in V_2$, to the real field for two real vector spaces V_1 and V_2. Define the matrix of such a function and a corresponding bilinear form. What is the generalization of Theorem 6.1 in such a case? If $V_1 = R^n$ and $V_2 = R^m$, is there any statement that relates a general bilinear mapping to an inner product as in (6.4)?

6.2 Quadratic Forms

We shall defer a discussion of the applications of bilinear forms and consider at this time an important special case

If we replace $[y_1, y_2, \ldots, y_n]^\top$ by $[x_1, x_2, \ldots, x_n]^\top$ in the bilinear form

$$B(\mathbf{X}, \mathbf{Y}) = \sum_{i,j=1}^{n} x_i a_{ij} y_j = [x_1, x_2, \ldots, x_n] A [y_1, y_2, \ldots, y_n]^\top,$$

where A is an $n \times n$ real matrix, we obtain a *real quadratic form*,

$$[x_1, x_2, \ldots, x_n] A [x_1, x_2, \ldots, x_n]^\top = \sum_{i,j=1}^{n} x_i a_{ij} x_j.$$

A quadratic form will be denoted by $Q(\mathbf{X})$, where again we may use this notation either for the given form or for a real number obtained by assigning real values to $x_1, x_2, \ldots, x_n$.

When we wish to draw particular attention to the $\{x_i\}$ or to the number of them, we describe $Q(\mathbf{X})$ as a *quadratic form in n variables*, $x_1, x_2, \ldots, x_n$.

A quadratic form may be obtained from any bilinear mapping B on a real vector space V by introducing a basis $\{\mathbf{X}_i\}$ of V, letting the basis $\{\mathbf{Y}_i\}$ be the same as the basis $\{\mathbf{X}_i\}$ in the discussion preceding (6.3), and writing

$$Q(\mathbf{X}) = B(\mathbf{X}, \mathbf{X}) = \sum_{i,j=1}^{n} x_i a_{ij} x_j. \tag{6.5}$$

Moreover, any quadratic form may be obtained as such a reduction of a bilinear mapping; it is only necessary to construct the mapping B having the matrix $A = [a_{ij}]$ relative to a basis $\{\mathbf{X}_i\}$ and then specialize.

In the case $V = R^n$, and where the basis $\{\mathbf{X}_i\}$ chosen to represent a bilinear mapping is the natural basis $\{\mathbf{E}_i\}$, we have

$$Q(\mathbf{X}) = B(\mathbf{X}, \mathbf{X}) = \mathbf{X}A\mathbf{X}^\top = \mathbf{X}(A\mathbf{X}^\top) = (\mathbf{X}, A\mathbf{X}^\top), \tag{6.6}$$

where $\mathbf{X} = [x_1, x_2, \ldots, x_n]$ and $A = [a_{ij}]$.

Example 1. The bilinear form,

$$B(\mathbf{X}, \mathbf{Y}) = [x_1, x_2] \begin{bmatrix} 1 & 5 \\ 2 & 1 \end{bmatrix} \begin{bmatrix} y_1 \\ y_2 \end{bmatrix} = x_1 y_1 + x_2 y_2 + 2x_1 y_2 + 5x_2 y_1,$$

gives rise to the quadratic form

$$Q(\mathbf{X}) = x_1^2 + x_2^2 + 2x_1 x_2 + 5x_2 x_1.$$

We have, of course, the matrix expression

$$Q(\mathbf{X}) = B(\mathbf{X}, \mathbf{X}) = [x_1, x_2]\begin{bmatrix} 1 & 5 \\ 2 & 1 \end{bmatrix}\begin{bmatrix} x_1 \\ x_2 \end{bmatrix} = ([x_1 + 2x_2, 5x_1 + x_2], [x_1, x_2]).$$

Equally well, we could have combined the terms $2x_1x_2$ and $5x_2x_1$ in $Q(\mathbf{X})$ and written

$$Q(\mathbf{X}) = [x_1, x_2]\begin{bmatrix} 1 & 0 \\ 7 & 1 \end{bmatrix}\begin{bmatrix} x_1 \\ x_2 \end{bmatrix} = ([x_1 + 7x_2, x_2], [x_1, x_2]).$$

Or, yet again, we could have "averaged" the terms $2x_1x_2$ and $5x_2x_1$ and written

$$Q(\mathbf{X}) = [x_1, x_2]\begin{bmatrix} 1 & \frac{7}{2} \\ \frac{7}{2} & 1 \end{bmatrix}\begin{bmatrix} x_1 \\ x_2 \end{bmatrix} = ([x_1 + \tfrac{7}{2}x_2, \tfrac{7}{2}x_1 + x_2], [x_1, x_2]).$$

In Example 1 we have an illustration of the general situation; many different bilinear forms give rise to the same quadratic form. However, the last matrix expression is typical. For $i \neq j$, the simple expedient of replacing $x_ia_{ij}x_j + x_ja_{ji}x_i$ by

$$x_i\left(\frac{a_{ij} + a_{ji}}{2}\right)x_j + x_j\left(\frac{a_{ij} + a_{ji}}{2}\right)x_i$$

allows us to assume without any loss of generality that the quadratic form,

$$Q(\mathbf{X}) = \sum_{i,j=1}^{n} x_ia_{ij}x_j, \tag{6.7}$$

has the property that $a_{ij} = a_{ji}$ for $i \neq j$. Henceforth we shall always make this assumption. Then with each quadratic form we associate the symmetric matrix $A = [a_{ij}] = A^{\mathsf{T}}$. We then think of $Q(\mathbf{X})$ as being derived from a specialization of the *symmetric* bilinear form

$$B(\mathbf{X}, \mathbf{Y}) = \sum_{i,j=1}^{n} x_ia_{ij}y_j.$$

Before proceeding with our discussion of quadratic forms, we shall indicate a few places where quadratic forms arise in mathematics.

The student of plane analytic geometry is familiar with the concept of an ellipse or a hyperbola (with center at the origin) as the locus of all points (x_1, x_2) that satisfy an equation of the form

$$a_{11}x_1^2 + 2a_{12}x_1x_2 + a_{22}x_2^2 = 1.$$

The left member of the preceding equation is a quadratic form. There are analogs (the quadric surfaces) in three-dimensional spaces, and we shall now extend the consideration to n-dimensional spaces. The classification of quadratic forms will be considered in the remainder of this chapter.

Another use of quadratic forms is the generalization of the distance formula. In terms of the $\mathbf{E}_i$ bases, we can give a representation of the distance between two points X, Y in the plane or in space by denoting the vectors from the origin to the respective points by $\mathbf{X}$, $\mathbf{Y}$ and defining $d(X, Y) = \|\mathbf{Y} - \mathbf{X}\| = \sqrt{(\mathbf{Y} - \mathbf{X}, \mathbf{Y} - \mathbf{X})}$. One is tempted to use the generalization offered by the bilinear mappings and to define the square of a "distance" as

$$Q(\mathbf{Y} - \mathbf{X}) = [y_1 - x_1, y_2 - x_2, \ldots, y_n - x_n]A[y_1 - x_1, y_2 - x_2, \ldots, y_n - x_n]^{\mathsf{T}}.$$

It is not quite that simple since we must at least guarantee that $Q(\mathbf{Y} - \mathbf{X})$ is positive when $\mathbf{Y} \neq \mathbf{X}$. Thus special restrictions on A are needed in addition to the possibility of selecting A as a symmetric matrix, which we have already mentioned.

Quadratic forms also play a role in the determination of maxima and minima of functions of more than one variable. Such problems are important in many fields of applied mathematics.

We begin our direct discussion with the idea of a *linear change of variables* in a quadratic form. The concept is closely related to the changing of bases and we shall investigate the connection, but it will be more direct to start from the quadratic form because the procedure will be familiar to the reader who has transformed equations of conic sections in analytic geometry.

Example 2. Refer to Example 1 and use the symmetric matrix form:

$$\begin{aligned} x_1^2 + x_2^2 2x_1x_2 + 5x_2x_1 &= x_1^2 + x_2^2 + 7x_1x_2 \\ &= [x_1, x_2]\begin{bmatrix} 1 & \frac{7}{2} \\ \frac{7}{2} & 1 \end{bmatrix}\begin{bmatrix} x_1 \\ x_2 \end{bmatrix}. \end{aligned}$$

Now, let

$$\begin{aligned} x_1 &= y_1, \\ x_2 &= -\tfrac{7}{2}y_1 + y_2, \end{aligned}$$

or, in matrix form,

$$\begin{bmatrix} x_1 \\ x_2 \end{bmatrix} = \begin{bmatrix} 1 & 0 \\ -\frac{7}{2} & 1 \end{bmatrix}\begin{bmatrix} y_1 \\ y_2 \end{bmatrix} \quad \text{or} \quad [x_1, x_2] = [y_1, y_2]\begin{bmatrix} 1 & 0 \\ -\frac{7}{2} & 1 \end{bmatrix}^{\mathsf{T}}.$$

Then

$$\begin{aligned} [x_1, x_2]\begin{bmatrix} 1 & \frac{7}{2} \\ \frac{7}{2} & 1 \end{bmatrix}\begin{bmatrix} x_1 \\ x_2 \end{bmatrix} &= [y_1, y_2]\begin{bmatrix} 1 & -\frac{7}{2} \\ 0 & 1 \end{bmatrix}\begin{bmatrix} 1 & \frac{7}{2} \\ \frac{7}{2} & 1 \end{bmatrix}\begin{bmatrix} 1 & 0 \\ -\frac{7}{2} & 1 \end{bmatrix}\begin{bmatrix} y_1 \\ y_2 \end{bmatrix} \\ &= [y_1, y_2]\begin{bmatrix} -\frac{45}{4} & 0 \\ 0 & 1 \end{bmatrix}\begin{bmatrix} y_1 \\ y_2 \end{bmatrix} \\ &= -\tfrac{45}{4}y_1^2 + y_2^2. \end{aligned}$$

DEFINITION 6.1. Two real quadratic forms,

$$\sum_{i,j=1}^{n} x_i a_{ij} x_j \quad \textit{and} \quad \sum_{i,j=1}^{n} y_i b_{ij} y_j$$

are said to be EQUIVALENT *over the real field if there exists a linear change of variables,*

$$\begin{bmatrix} x_1 \\ x_2 \\ \vdots \\ x_n \end{bmatrix} = P\begin{bmatrix} y_1 \\ y_2 \\ \vdots \\ y_n \end{bmatrix}, \tag{6.8}$$

where $P = [p_{ij}]$ is a real nonsingular matrix that transforms the first quadratic form into the second.

Thus, by Example 2, the forms $x_1^2 + x_2^2 + 7x_1x_2$ and $-\frac{45}{4}y_1^2 + y_2^2$ are equivalent.

It is clear that the net result of a linear change of variables is to change one symmetric matrix, $A = A^{\mathsf{T}}$, to another.

Let us carry out the calculations in the general case.

$$[x_1, x_2, \ldots, x_n]A\begin{bmatrix} x_1 \\ x_2 \\ \vdots \\ x_n \end{bmatrix} = ([y_1, y_2, \ldots, y_n]P^{\mathsf{T}})A\left(P\begin{bmatrix} y_1 \\ y_2 \\ \vdots \\ y_n \end{bmatrix}\right).$$

If we regroup terms, we have

$$[x_1, x_2, \ldots, x_n]A \begin{bmatrix} x_1 \\ x_2 \\ \vdots \\ x_n \end{bmatrix} = [y_1, y_2, \ldots, y_n](P^{\mathsf{T}}AP) \begin{bmatrix} y_1 \\ y_2 \\ \vdots \\ y_n \end{bmatrix}. \qquad (6.9)$$

Thus the effect is to replace A by $P^{\mathsf{T}}AP$. Note that $B = P^{\mathsf{T}}AP$ is symmetric if A is; the proof is left as an exercise.

Conversely, if B, A are symmetric matrices satisfying $B = P^{\mathsf{T}}AP$, then the forms associated with A and B can be seen to be equivalent as follows. If $[y_1, y_2, \ldots, y_n]B[y_1, y_2, \ldots, y_n]^{\mathsf{T}}$ is the form associated with B, define new variables $\{x_i\}$ by $[x_1, x_2, \ldots, x_n]^{\mathsf{T}} = P[y_1, y_2, \ldots, y_n]^{\mathsf{T}}$. Then, multiplying by P^{-1} and transposing,

$$[y_1, y_2, \ldots, y_n]^{\mathsf{T}} = P^{-1}[x_1, x_2, \ldots, x_n]^{\mathsf{T}}. \qquad (6.10)$$

Now,

$$[y_1, y_2, \ldots, y_n]B \begin{bmatrix} y_1 \\ y_2 \\ \vdots \\ y_n \end{bmatrix} = [x_1, x_2, \ldots, x_n](P^{-1})^{\mathsf{T}}BP^{-1} \begin{bmatrix} x_1 \\ x_2 \\ \vdots \\ x_n \end{bmatrix}$$

$$= [x_1, x_2, \ldots, x_n](P^{\mathsf{T}})^{-1}P^{\mathsf{T}}APP^{-1} \begin{bmatrix} x_1 \\ x_2 \\ \vdots \\ x_n \end{bmatrix}$$

$$= [x_1, x_2, \ldots, x_n]A \begin{bmatrix} x_1 \\ x_2 \\ \vdots \\ x_n \end{bmatrix}.$$

And thus the forms associated with A and B are equivalent, reflecting the change of variables (6.10). We sum up the preceding discussion in a theorem.

THEOREM 6.2. *Two real quadratic forms are equivalent if and only if the symmetric matrices associated with these forms are related by an equation $B = P^{\mathsf{T}}AP$, where P is a real nonsingular matrix.*

The above procedure can be expressed in vector form by replacing Q(**X**) with the special bilinear mapping B(**X**, **X**) (B will have special restrictions derived from the symmetric nature of Q). Suppose we regard B as being calculated with respect to a specific basis $\{\mathbf{X}_i\}$ for both arguments and make a change of basis to $\{\mathbf{Y}_i\}$ with matrix P. We saw in Chapter 3 that if

$$\mathbf{X} = x_1\mathbf{X}_1 + x_2\mathbf{X}_2 + \cdots + x_n\mathbf{X}_n,$$

then

$$\mathbf{X} = y_1\mathbf{Y}_1 + y_2\mathbf{Y}_2 + \cdots + y_n\mathbf{Y}_n,$$

where

$$[y_1, y_2, \ldots, y_n]^{\mathsf{T}} = P[x_1, x_2, \ldots, x_n]^{\mathsf{T}}.$$

Thus the change in the matrix from A to $P^{\mathsf{T}}AP$ can be regarded as resulting from a change of basis from $\{\mathbf{X}_i\}$ to $\{\mathbf{Y}_i\}$ with P the matrix of change of basis. The similarity to the idea of the change of basis in its effect on the matrix of a linear transformation should be observed. Here we do not use the inverse of P because we never "go back" to the original; we have only the matrix of change of basis on one side and its transpose (reflecting the transpose of the column vector) on the other side.

The essential problem in most applications is to determine the simplest form to which $Q(\mathbf{X})$ can be reduced when certain transformations of variables are permitted. In the next section we shall discuss the case in which we allow P (the matrix of change of variables) to be *any* real nonsingular matrix. In Chapter 8 we shall discuss the restriction of P to orthogonal matrices (that is, to rotations and reflections).

Exercises

1. What are the quadratic forms represented by the following matrix products?

(a) $[x_1, x_2]\begin{bmatrix} 1 & -3 \\ -3 & 4 \end{bmatrix}\begin{bmatrix} x_1 \\ x_2 \end{bmatrix}$,

(b) $[x_1, x_2, x_3]\begin{bmatrix} 1 & -2 & 3 \\ -2 & 4 & 1 \\ 3 & 1 & 5 \end{bmatrix}\begin{bmatrix} x_1 \\ x_2 \\ x_3 \end{bmatrix}$.

2. Express the following quadratic forms as matrix products:
(a) $2x_1^2 - 8x_1x_2 + 3x_2^2$,
(b) $3x_1^2 - 2x_2^2 + 5x_3^2 + 6x_1x_2 - 4x_2x_3 + 8x_1x_3$.

3. Let the quadratic form $x_1^2 + 4x_1x_2 + 3x_2^2$ be transformed by the change of variables

$$x_1 = 3y_1 + 2y_2,$$
$$x_2 = y_1 - y_2.$$

(a) What is the transformed quadratic form $Q^*(\mathbf{Y})$?
(b) Express the quadratic form of (a) as a matrix product $P^{\mathsf{T}}AP$.

4. Replace the distance formula for E_2 by defining the distance from (x_1, x_2) to (y_1, y_2) to be

$$\{d(X, Y)\}^2 = [y_1 - x_1, y_2 - x_2]\begin{bmatrix} 1 & 2 \\ 2 & 5 \end{bmatrix}\begin{bmatrix} y_1 - x_1 \\ y_2 - x_2 \end{bmatrix}.$$

Show that $d(X, Y) > 0$ unless $X = Y$; $d(X, Y) = d(Y, X)$.

5. For the quadratic form

$$Q([x_1, x_2]) = [x_1, x_2]\begin{bmatrix} a & b \\ b & c \end{bmatrix}\begin{bmatrix} x_1 \\ x_2 \end{bmatrix},$$

with $\begin{bmatrix} a & b \\ b & c \end{bmatrix} \neq 0$, show that there always exists a change of variables that yields a form $Q^*(\mathbf{Y})$ in which the coefficient of y_1y_2 is 0.

6. Show that the quadratic forms

$$Q([x_1, x_2]) = x_1^2 + x_2^2 + 8x_1x_2,$$
$$Q^*([y_1, y_2]) = y_1^2 - 14y_2^2 + 2y_1y_2,$$

are equivalent under the change of variables given by

$$\begin{bmatrix} x_1 \\ x_2 \end{bmatrix} = \begin{bmatrix} 1 & -3 \\ 0 & 1 \end{bmatrix}\begin{bmatrix} y_1 \\ y_2 \end{bmatrix}.$$

7. What is the expression of the quadratic form (relative to the $\{\mathbf{E}_i\}$ basis)

$$Q([x_1, x_2, x_3]) = x_1^2 + x_2^2 - 3x_3^2 + 4x_1x_2 + 2x_2x_3 + 6x_1x_3$$

relative to the basis $\mathbf{X}_1^* = [1, 2, -1]$, $\mathbf{X}_2^* = [1, 0, 2]$, $\mathbf{X}_3^* = [1, -1, 2]$?

8. Show that $P^{\mathsf{T}}AP$ is symmetric if A is symmetric.
9. The set of all real numbers $Q(\mathbf{X})$ as $\mathbf{X}$ runs through all vectors of R^n is called the range of values of the quadratic form $Q(\mathbf{X})$. Prove that the range of values of two equivalent quadratic forms is the same.
10. Let B be a symmetric bilinear mapping of R^n; that is, $B(\mathbf{X}, \mathbf{Y}) = B(\mathbf{Y}, \mathbf{X})$ for all vectors $\mathbf{X}, \mathbf{Y}$ of R^n. If $Q(\mathbf{X}) = B(\mathbf{X}, \mathbf{X})$, show that

$$B(\mathbf{X}, \mathbf{Y}) = \tfrac{1}{2}\{Q(\mathbf{X} + \mathbf{Y}) - Q(\mathbf{X}) - Q(\mathbf{Y})\}.$$

6.3 Equivalence of Quadratic Forms; Congruence of Matrices

The problem of the equivalence of two quadratic forms has been reduced to the study of matrix equations of the form $B = P^{\mathsf{T}}AP$. For the moment, let us study this type of equation in general, without requiring A to be symmetric. To this end we introduce the notion of *congruence of matrices*.

DEFINITION 6.2. If two real matrices A and B have the property that there exists a real nonsingular matrix P such that

$$B = P^{\mathsf{T}}AP, \tag{6.11}$$

then B is said to be CONGRUENT *to A over the real field.*

Congruence is an equivalence relation on the set of all $n \times n$ real matrices. (Why do we have to restrict our attention to square matrices?) To establish this fact, we must check reflexivity, symmetry, and transitivity.

1. $A = I^{\mathsf{T}}AI$, hence A is congruent to A.
2. If $B = P^{\mathsf{T}}AP$, $(P^{\mathsf{T}})^{-1}BP^{-1} = (P^{\mathsf{T}})^{-1}P^{\mathsf{T}}APP^{-1} = A$.

But $(P^{\mathsf{T}})^{-1} = (P^{-1})^{\mathsf{T}}$ and $A = (P^{-1})^{\mathsf{T}}BP^{-1}$. Thus, if B is congruent to A, A is congruent to B.

3. If $B = P^{\mathsf{T}}AP$ and $C = Q^{\mathsf{T}}BQ$, then $C = Q^{\mathsf{T}}P^{\mathsf{T}}APQ = (PQ)^{\mathsf{T}}A(PQ)$ and PQ is nonsingular because both P and Q are. Thus if B is congruent to A and C is congruent to B, then C is congruent to A.

With the establishment of congruence as an equivalence relation, we return to the restriction that A be symmetric. Any matrix congruent to a symmetric matrix is symmetric. This remark was made in the last section in terms of equivalent quadratic forms and the proof was posed as Exercise 8 of that section.

Let $E(A)$ be the set of all matrices congruent to a particular symmetric matrix A in S, the set of all real symmetric matrices. That is, $E(A) = \{P^{\mathsf{T}}AP \mid P \text{ nonsingular}\}$. Any equivalence relation partitions the set on which it is defined into disjoint subsets (see Section 3.10). In the present case these subsets of S have the following properties:

(i) Every symmetric matrix is in some E-subset.
(ii) Two matrices A and B are congruent if and only if $E(A) = E(B)$.
(iii) Either $E(A) = E(B)$ or $E(A) \cap E(B) = \emptyset$ (the empty set).

The relation of congruence for symmetric matrices (in view of the properties listed above) partitions the set S of all $n \times n$ symmetric matrices into non-intersecting subsets. Crudely, we may picture the situation as shown in Figure 6.1.

If we now select one matrix from each distinct subset $E(M)$ to represent

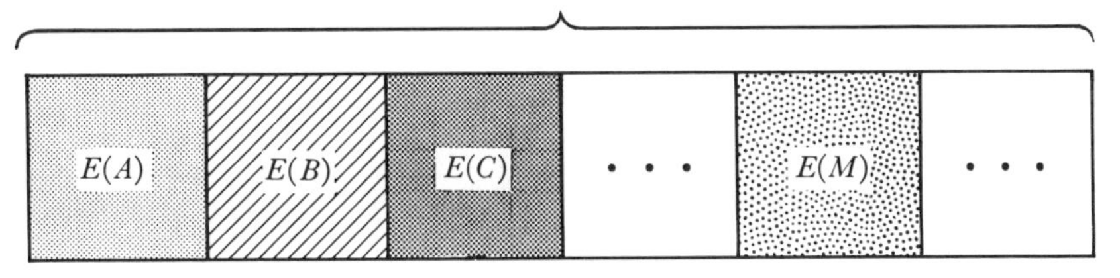

FIGURE 6.1

that subset, every $n \times n$ symmetric matrix will be congruent to one and only one of our selected representatives. In terms of quadratic forms, we associate with each representative matrix the corresponding quadratic form in n variables, and then *every* quadratic form in n variables is equivalent to one and only one of these representative forms by a suitable change of variables.

The two general problems in the equivalence of quadratic forms in n variables can now be stated in terms of the subsets $E(M)$ and the choice of representatives:

Problem 1. Does there exist a simple, convenient choice of a representative matrix for each subset $E(M)$?

Problem 2. Do there exist some features (numbers, rank, order, etc.) of an arbitrary symmetric matrix A that will determine which subset contains A and consequently whether A is congruent to a particular representative?

SOLUTION OF PROBLEM 1. We shall show first that each subset $E(M)$ contains diagonal matrices, and then our choice for a representative matrix of each subset $E(M)$ will be a particular diagonal matrix.

Our demonstration will use induction on the order n of the symmetric matrices involved. For $n = 1$, we have nothing to prove, since any matrix $[a_{11}]$ of a subset $E(M)$ is a diagonal matrix. The inductive assumption is that every subset $E(M_1)$ of $(n - 1) \times (n - 1)$ symmetric matrices contains a diagonal matrix.

Now let $A = [a_{ij}]$ be an $n \times n$ symmetric matrix in a subset $E(M)$ and consider the associated quadratic form

$$Q(\mathbf{X}) = \sum_{i,j=1}^{n} x_i a_{ij} x_j. \tag{6.12}$$

We think of $Q(\mathbf{X})$ as arising from a bilinear mapping B of R^n, where

$$\mathrm{B}(\mathbf{X}, \mathbf{Y}) = \sum_{i,j=1}^{n} x_i a_{ij} y_j = (\mathbf{X}, A\mathbf{Y}^{\mathsf{T}}) \tag{6.13}$$

is the expression for $\mathrm{B}(\mathbf{X}, \mathbf{Y})$ relative to the natural basis $\{\mathbf{E}_1, \mathbf{E}_2, \ldots, \mathbf{E}_n\}$ and

$$\mathbf{X} = x_1\mathbf{E}_1 + \cdots + x_n\mathbf{E}_n, \qquad \mathbf{Y} = y_1\mathbf{E}_1 + \cdots + y_n\mathbf{E}_n.$$

For the bilinear mapping B of (6.13), we may assume that there is a vector $\mathbf{X}_1$ such that $\mathrm{B}(\mathbf{X}_1, \mathbf{X}_1) \neq 0$. Otherwise, from the relation

$$\mathrm{B}(\mathbf{X}, \mathbf{Y}) = \tfrac{1}{2}\{\mathrm{B}(\mathbf{X} + \mathbf{Y}, \mathbf{X} + \mathbf{Y}) - \mathrm{B}(\mathbf{X}, \mathbf{X}) - \mathrm{B}(\mathbf{Y}, \mathbf{Y})\}$$

(Exercise 10, Section 6.2), we would have $B(\mathbf{X}, \mathbf{Y}) = 0$ for all vectors $\mathbf{X}$ and $\mathbf{Y}$ of R^n, and consequently the matrix $[a_{ij}] = [0]$ would already be a diagonal matrix.

We select $\mathbf{X}_1$ as the first vector of a new basis for R^n, with respect to which we shall evaluate $B(\mathbf{X}, \mathbf{X})$. Our next step will be to select the remaining vectors of this new basis.

The set of all vectors $\mathbf{Z}$ of R^n such that $B(\mathbf{Z}, \mathbf{X}_1) = 0$ is a subspace V of R^n. In fact, we see from (6.13) that V consists of all those vectors $\mathbf{Z} = [z_1, z_2, \ldots, z_n]$ for which $(\mathbf{Z}, A\mathbf{X}_1^{\mathsf{T}}) = 0$. Now we selected $\mathbf{X}_1$ such that $A\mathbf{X}_1 \neq \mathbf{0}$, hence V is the space of vectors orthogonal to $A\mathbf{X}_1^{\mathsf{T}}$ and has dimension $n - 1$. (See Theorem 2.13.) We select vectors $\mathbf{X}_2, \mathbf{X}_3, \ldots, \mathbf{X}_n$ as a basis for V, and, together with $\mathbf{X}_1$, we use $\{\mathbf{X}_i\}$ as a basis for R^n. Note that $B(\mathbf{X}_k, \mathbf{X}_1) = 0$ for $k \neq 1$. Then we find the matrix of B in this basis. If

$$\mathbf{X} = [x_1, x_2, \ldots, x_n] = x_1'\mathbf{X}_1 + x_2'\mathbf{X}_2 + \cdots + x_n'\mathbf{X}_n,$$

$$B(\mathbf{X}, \mathbf{X}) = \sum_{i,j=1}^{n} x_i' B(\mathbf{X}_i, \mathbf{X}_j) x_j'.$$

But

$$B(\mathbf{X}_i, \mathbf{X}_1) = B(\mathbf{X}_1, \mathbf{X}_i) = 0 \qquad \text{for } i > 1.$$

Thus, if we write the matrix of B in its new form, the first row and first column will be zero except for the leading element.

$$\begin{bmatrix} B(\mathbf{X}_1, \mathbf{X}_1) & 0 & \cdots & 0 \\ 0 & B(\mathbf{X}_2, \mathbf{X}_2) & \cdots & B(\mathbf{X}_2, \mathbf{X}_n) \\ \vdots & & & \vdots \\ 0 & B(\mathbf{X}_n, \mathbf{X}_2) & \cdots & B(\mathbf{X}_n, \mathbf{X}_n) \end{bmatrix} = P^{\mathsf{T}}[a_{ij}]P, \qquad (6.14)$$

where P is the matrix of the change of basis from $\{\mathbf{X}_i\}$ to $\{\mathbf{E}_i\}$.

Now the $(n - 1) \times (n - 1)$ matrix in the lower right corner of the matrix in (6.14) is a symmetric matrix which we may call A_1. Our induction assumption applies to A_1, and we know there is a nonsingular $(n - 1) \times (n - 1)$ matrix Q_1 such that $Q_1^{\mathsf{T}} A_1 Q_1$ is diagonal.

We make an $n \times n$ nonsingular matrix Q as follows. The first row and column have a 1 in the leading position and zeros elsewhere. The remainder of Q is Q_1 unchanged:

$$Q = \begin{bmatrix} 1 & 0 & 0 & \cdots & 0 \\ 0 & & & & \\ 0 & & & & \\ \vdots & & & Q_1 & \\ 0 & & & & \end{bmatrix}.$$

If $Q_1^{\mathsf{T}} A_1 Q_1 = \text{diagonal } [d_2, d_3, \ldots, d_n]$, a matrix multiplication shows that

$$Q^{\mathsf{T}}(P^{\mathsf{T}}[a_{ij}]P)Q = \text{Diagonal } [B(\mathbf{X}_1, \mathbf{X}_1), d_2, d_3, \ldots, d_n].$$

Thus $(PQ)^{\mathsf{T}}[a_{ij}](PQ)$ is a diagonal matrix belonging to our subset $E(M)$.

Example 1. Let

$$A = \begin{bmatrix} 0 & 4 & 3 \\ 4 & 2 & 1 \\ 3 & 1 & 0 \end{bmatrix}$$

correspond to the quadratic form $2x_2^2 + 8x_1x_2 + 6x_1x_3 + 2x_2x_3$. We pass to the bilinear form

$$B(X, Y) = [x_1, x_2, x_3] \begin{bmatrix} 0 & 4 & 3 \\ 4 & 2 & 1 \\ 3 & 1 & 0 \end{bmatrix} \begin{bmatrix} y_1 \\ y_2 \\ y_3 \end{bmatrix}.$$

Now we look for a vector $\mathbf{X}_1$ such that $B(\mathbf{X}_1, \mathbf{X}_1) \neq 0$. Our first try, $\mathbf{E}_1$, doesn't work; we next try $\mathbf{E}_2 = [0, 1, 0]$ and find that $B(\mathbf{E}_2, \mathbf{E}_2) = 2 \neq 0$. Thus $\mathbf{X}_1 = \mathbf{E}_2$.

The next step is to find a basis for the space orthogonal to $AE_2^{\mathsf{T}} = [4, 2, 1]^{\mathsf{T}}$. Any vectors $\mathbf{Z}_1 = [z_1, z_2, z_3]$ such that $4z_1 + 2z_2 + z_3 = 0$ will do. We select $\mathbf{X}_2 = [1, 0, -4]$ and $\mathbf{X}_3 = [1, -2, 0]$.

$$\begin{aligned} \mathbf{X}_1 &= \mathbf{E}_2, \\ \mathbf{X}_2 &= \mathbf{E}_1 - 4\mathbf{E}_3, \\ \mathbf{X}_3 &= \mathbf{E}_1 - 2\mathbf{E}_2. \end{aligned}$$

So the matrix of change of basis P is

$$P = \begin{bmatrix} 0 & 1 & 1 \\ 1 & 0 & -2 \\ 0 & -4 & 0 \end{bmatrix}.$$

Then

$$P^{\mathsf{T}}AP = \begin{bmatrix} 0 & 1 & 0 \\ 1 & 0 & -4 \\ 1 & -2 & 0 \end{bmatrix} \begin{bmatrix} 0 & 4 & 3 \\ 4 & 2 & 1 \\ 3 & 1 & 0 \end{bmatrix} \begin{bmatrix} 0 & 1 & 1 \\ 1 & 0 & -2 \\ 0 & -4 & 0 \end{bmatrix} = \begin{bmatrix} 2 & 0 & 0 \\ 0 & -24 & -12 \\ 0 & -12 & -8 \end{bmatrix}.$$

The matrix A_1 in this case is $\begin{bmatrix} -24 & -12 \\ -12 & -8 \end{bmatrix}$ and we need a matrix Q_1 that will put it in diagonal form. The matrix A_1 could be interpreted as the matrix of a quadratic form $-24y_1^2 - 8y_2^2 - 24y_1y_2$. Take $[0, 1] = [y_1, y_2]$ as a vector such that

$$[y_1, y_2]A_1 \begin{bmatrix} y_1 \\ y_2 \end{bmatrix} \neq 0$$

and find the space orthogonal to

$$A_1 \begin{bmatrix} 0 \\ 1 \end{bmatrix} = \begin{bmatrix} -12 \\ -8 \end{bmatrix}.$$

We need a vector $[z_1, z_2]$ such that $-12z_1 - 8z_2 = 0$, and we select $z_1 = 1$, $z_2 = -\frac{3}{2}$.

The matrix Q_1 in the proof, then, can be

$$\begin{bmatrix} 0 & 1 \\ 1 & -\frac{3}{2} \end{bmatrix} \quad \text{and} \quad \begin{bmatrix} 0 & 1 \\ 1 & -\frac{3}{2} \end{bmatrix} \begin{bmatrix} -24 & -12 \\ -12 & -8 \end{bmatrix} \begin{bmatrix} 0 & 1 \\ 1 & -\frac{3}{2} \end{bmatrix} = \begin{bmatrix} -8 & 0 \\ 0 & -6 \end{bmatrix}.$$

Finally,

$$\begin{bmatrix} 1 & 0 & 0 \\ 0 & 0 & 1 \\ 0 & 1 & -\frac{3}{2} \end{bmatrix} \begin{bmatrix} 2 & 0 & 0 \\ 0 & -24 & -12 \\ 0 & -12 & -8 \end{bmatrix} \begin{bmatrix} 1 & 0 & 0 \\ 0 & 0 & 1 \\ 0 & 1 & -\frac{3}{2} \end{bmatrix} = \begin{bmatrix} 2 & 0 & 0 \\ 0 & -8 & 0 \\ 0 & 0 & -6 \end{bmatrix},$$

which is a diagonal matrix in the same equivalence class as the first one.

So far, we know that each equivalence class $E(M)$ contains a diagonal matrix

$$D^* = \text{Diagonal } [d_1, d_2, \ldots, d_n].$$

Now we wish to collect the positive elements among the d_i's in the leading positions, the negative elements next, and the zero values last. This may be accomplished by using a sequence of elementary matrices of the second kind. (See Section 4.2.) If P_{ij} is the matrix obtained from the identity by interchanging the ith and jth rows of the identity matrix, then

$$(P_{ij})^{\mathsf{T}} \begin{bmatrix} d_1 & 0 & 0 & \cdots & & 0 \\ 0 & \ddots & & & & \\ 0 & & d_i & \cdots & & \\ & & \vdots & \ddots & & \\ & & \cdots & d_j & & \\ & & & & \ddots & \\ 0 & & & & & d_n \end{bmatrix} P_{ij} = \begin{bmatrix} d_1 & 0 & 0 & \cdots & & 0 \\ 0 & \ddots & & & & \\ 0 & & d_j & \cdots & & \\ & & \vdots & \ddots & & \\ & & \cdots & d_i & & \\ & & & & \ddots & \\ 0 & & & & & d_n \end{bmatrix}.$$

Thus by using a suitable sequence of P_{ij}'s we may arrange the diagonal elements in any order desired.

Next, we show that the elements along the diagonal can actually be chosen to be $+1$, -1, or 0. Assume for definiteness that

$$D^* = \text{diagonal } [d_1, d_2, \ldots, d_n],$$

$$d_1, d_2, \ldots, d_p > 0,$$

$$d_{p+1}, d_{p+2}, \ldots, d_r < 0$$

and

$$d_{r+1}, d_{r+2}, \ldots, d_n = 0.$$

We choose one more matrix,

$$P = P^{\mathsf{T}} = \text{diagonal } [1/\sqrt{d_1}, 1/\sqrt{d_2}, \ldots, 1/\sqrt{d_p}, \\ 1/\sqrt{-d_{p+1}}, \ldots, 1/\sqrt{-d_r}, 1, 1, \ldots, 1].$$

Now

$$P^{\mathsf{T}}D^*P = D = \text{Diagonal } [1, 1, \ldots, 1, -1, -1, \ldots, -1, 0, 0, \ldots, 0] \tag{6.15}$$

with p ones, r minus ones and $n - r$ zeros. Thus every symmetric matrix is congruent to a matrix of the form (6.15). Phrased in terms of quadratic forms, we have the following result:

THEOREM 6.3. Every quadratic form

$$Q(X) = \sum_{i,j=1}^{n} x_i a_{ij} x_j$$

is equivalent over the real field to a form

$$y_1^2 + y_2^2 + \cdots + y_p^2 - y_{p+1}^2 - \cdots - y_r^2$$

by means of a change of variables

$$\begin{bmatrix} y_1 \\ y_2 \\ \vdots \\ y_n \end{bmatrix} = P \begin{bmatrix} x_1 \\ x_2 \\ \vdots \\ x_n \end{bmatrix},$$

where P is a nonsingular matrix.

SOLUTION OF PROBLEM 2 (CANONICAL FORMS AND INVARIANTS). The representative matrix selected from a particular subset is called a *canonical form* for the members of $E(M)$. A set of such matrices which includes precisely one element from each set $E(M)$ is called a *set of canonical forms*. The question still remains whether the set of all matrices of the form D of (6.15) is a set of canonical forms. We know that there is at least one matrix D in each subset $E(M)$ and we shall show later that there is only one.

It is possible to have different sets of canonical forms for the same equivalence relation. For the congruence of symmetric matrices some people might find it more esthetic to put the zeros first, or perhaps in the middle, rather than last, as we have in (6.15). All we can say is that a given set of representatives of the subsets $E(M)$ is a set of canonical forms for a particular equivalence relation. In our case the matrices D of (6.15) are canonical for the *congruence of symmetric matrices*.

A proof that there is precisely one matrix D in each subset $E(M)$ proceeds as follows:

First, we have noted that multiplication of a matrix A by a nonsingular matrix P on either left or right does not change the rank, so that all congruent matrices (members of $E(M)$) have the same rank. Hence, if two matrices D_1 and D_2 of the form of (6.15) were in one subset $E(M)$, both would have the same rank: the total number of positive and negative units.

It only remains to show that the number of plus signs is identical in both cases to see that $D_1 = D_2$. Suppose that

$$D_1 = \text{Diagonal}\,[\underbrace{1, 1, \ldots, 1}_{p},\ \underbrace{-1, -1, \ldots, -1}_{r-p},\ 0, 0, \ldots, 0],$$

$$D_2 = \text{Diagonal}\,[\underbrace{1, 1, \ldots, 1}_{q},\ \underbrace{-1, -1, \ldots, -1}_{r-q},\ 0, 0, \ldots, 0],$$

and that $p \neq q$, say $p > q$. If D_1 and D_2 are in the same equivalence class, there is a matrix P such that $D_1 = P^{\mathsf{T}}D_2P$. For any nonzero vector

$$\mathbf{X} = [x_1, x_2, \ldots, x_p, 0, 0, \ldots, 0]$$

of R^n, $\mathbf{X}D_1\mathbf{X}^{\mathsf{T}}$ will have the value

$$x_1^2 + x_2^2 + \cdots + x_p^2 > 0$$

These vectors (with $\mathbf{0}$) form a p-dimensional subspace V_1. Hence the set of vectors of the form $P\mathbf{X}^{\mathsf{T}}$, with $\mathbf{X}$ in V_1, form another subspace V_2 of dimension p. Then for $\mathbf{X}$ in V_1, $\mathbf{X} \neq \mathbf{0}$,

$$\mathbf{X}P^{\mathsf{T}}D_2P\mathbf{X}^{\mathsf{T}} = \mathbf{X}D_1\mathbf{X}^{\mathsf{T}} > 0.$$

So for every nonzero vector $\mathbf{Z} = P\mathbf{X}^{\mathsf{T}}$ in V_2, $\mathbf{Z}D_2\mathbf{Z}^{\mathsf{T}} > 0$.

Consider the effect on a vector $\mathbf{Y} = [0, 0, \ldots, 0, y_{q+1}, \ldots, y_n]$:

$$\mathbf{Y}D_2\mathbf{Y}^{\mathsf{T}} = -y_{q+1}^2 - y_{q+2}^2 - \cdots - y_r^2 \leq 0.$$

The set of vectors of this form is a subspace V_3 of dimension $n - q$. Since the effect of D_2 on any nonzero vector in V_2 is positive, V_2 and V_3 can have only the zero vector in common.

Now we know that

$$\text{dimension } V_2 + \text{dimension } V_3 = \text{dimension } (V_2 + V_3) + \text{dimension } (V_2 \cap V_3)$$

by Theorem 2.11. Of the various quantities in the equation we know dimension $V_2 = p$, dimension $V_3 = n - q$, dimension $(V_2 + V_3) \le n$, and dimension $(V_2 \cap V_3) = 0$. Thus $p + n - q =$ dimension $(V_2 + V_3) \le n$ or $p \le q$, a contradiction.

The net result is that D is truly canonical. There is one and only one matrix of the type of D in each equivalence class of matrices.

The preceding method of proof suggests an interpretation for the number of positive 1's occurring in a canonical form D of (6.15). First, a definition:

DEFINITION 6.3. A quadratic form

$$Q(\mathbf{X}) = \sum_{i,j=1}^{n} x_i a_{ij} x_j$$

is said to be POSITIVE DEFINITE *on a subspace V of R^n if $Q(\mathbf{X}) > 0$ for all nonzero vectors $\mathbf{X}$ of V. Similarly $Q(\mathbf{X})$ is said to be* NEGATIVE DEFINITE *on a subspace V of R^n if $Q(\mathbf{X}) < 0$ for all nonzero vectors $\mathbf{X}$ of V.*

If $Q_1(\mathbf{X})$ is the quadratic form whose associated matrix is D_1 of the preceding proof, then Q_1 is certainly positive definite on V_1. Moreover, if $D_1 = P^{\mathsf{T}}BP$ and V_2 consists of vectors $P\mathbf{X}^{\mathsf{T}}$ for $\mathbf{X} \in V_1$, while B is the symmetric matrix associated with the quadratic form $Q_2(X)$, then $Q_2(\mathbf{X})$ is positive definite on V_2 since

$$Q_2(P\mathbf{X}^{\mathsf{T}}) = (P\mathbf{X}^{\mathsf{T}}, BP\mathbf{X}^{\mathsf{T}}) = (\mathbf{X}, P^{\mathsf{T}}BP\mathbf{X}^{\mathsf{T}}) = (\mathbf{X}, D_1\mathbf{X}) > 0.$$

Thus any quadratic form $Q(\mathbf{X})$ with a matrix congruent to D_1 is positive definite on a subspace of dimension p. On the other hand, a simple reversal of this argument shows that no subspace of larger dimension has this property.

THEOREM 6.4. Let t be the largest dimension of any subspace V on which the quadratic form $Q(\mathbf{X})$ is positive definite. If $Q(\mathbf{X})$ is equivalent to the canonical form

$$y_1^2 + y_2^2 + \cdots + y_p^2 - y_{p+1}^2 - \cdots - y_r^2,$$

then $t = p$.

For historical reasons the number $(2p - r) = p + (p - r)$ is called the *signature* of a quadratic form or its associated symmetric matrix. The signature, rank, and order of a symmetric matrix A determine which subset $E(M)$ contains A. We say that these numbers constitute a *complete set of invariants* for symmetric matrices under congruence. Two symmetric matrices will be congruent if and only if they have the same rank, signature, and order. We now have the answer to Problem 2 and we formalize our discussion in two theorems, with which we shall conclude this section.

THEOREM 6.5. Every quadratic form $Q(\mathbf{X}) = \sum_{i,j=1}^{n} x_i a_{ij} x_j$ is equivalent over R to a UNIQUE *form*

$$y_1^2 + y_2^2 + \cdots + y_p^2 - y_{p+1}^2 - \cdots - y_r^2,$$

where r is the rank of the symmetric matrix $A = [a_{ij}]$ and p is the largest dimension of any subspace V on which $Q(\mathbf{X})$ is positive definite.

THEOREM 6.6. Two $n \times n$ symmetric matrices A and B are congruent if and only if they have the same rank and signature.

Exercises

1. Show that the matrices

$$A = \begin{bmatrix} 1 & 2 & 3 \\ 2 & -2 & 1 \\ 3 & 1 & 0 \end{bmatrix} \quad \text{and} \quad B = \begin{bmatrix} 12 & 6 & 10 \\ 6 & 1 & 6 \\ 10 & 6 & 7 \end{bmatrix}$$

are congruent to each other.

2. Reduce the quadratic form

$$Q(\mathbf{X}) = x_2^2 + 3x_3^2 - 6x_1x_2 + 4x_2x_3 + 8x_1x_3$$

to canonical (diagonal) form.

3. Show that the quadratic form

$$Q^*(\mathbf{Y}) = 7y_2^2 + 11y_3^2 - 6y_1y_2 + 8y_1y_3 - 10y_2y_3$$

is equivalent to the quadratic form of Exercise 2.

4. How many subsets $E(M)$ are there for the set of all 3×3 symmetric matrices under the equivalence relation of congruence?
5. Find a matrix P such that

$$P^T \begin{bmatrix} -1 & 0 & 0 \\ 0 & 0 & 0 \\ 0 & 0 & 1 \end{bmatrix} P = \begin{bmatrix} 1 & 0 & 0 \\ 0 & -1 & 0 \\ 0 & 0 & 0 \end{bmatrix}.$$

6. Prove that the number of nonequivalent real quadratic forms in n variables is

$$\frac{(n+1)(n+2)}{2}.$$

7. Provide a proof for Theorem 6.6.
8. Give a proof that the number of (-1)'s in the canonical form (6.15) of a quadratic form $Q(\mathbf{X})$ is equal to the largest dimension of any vector subspace of R^n on which $Q(\mathbf{X})$ is negative definite.
9. Prove that for any $\mathbf{X} \in R^n$, $Q(\mathbf{X}) \geq 0$ if the rank of $Q(\mathbf{X})$ is equal to its signature.
10. Prove that a quadratic form $Q(\mathbf{X})$ is positive definite for all of R^n if and only if its canonical (diagonal) matrix is Diagonal $[1, 1, \ldots, 1]$.
11. Show that the quadratic forms

$$Q_1(\mathbf{X}) = [x_1, x_2, x_3] \begin{bmatrix} 6 & 1 & 1 \\ 1 & 10 & 3 \\ 1 & 3 & 1 \end{bmatrix} \begin{bmatrix} x_1 \\ x_2 \\ x_3 \end{bmatrix},$$

$$Q_2(\mathbf{X}) = [x_1, x_2, x_3] \begin{bmatrix} 1 & 2 & -1 \\ 2 & 5 & 0 \\ -1 & 0 & 6 \end{bmatrix} \begin{bmatrix} x_1 \\ x_2 \\ x_3 \end{bmatrix},$$

are positive definite for all of R^n.

12. Show that a quadratic form $Q(\mathbf{X})$ associated with $A = [a_{ij}]$ is positive definite on the subspace of all vectors of the form $[x_1, x_2, \ldots, x_k, 0, 0, \ldots, 0]$ if and only if the quadratic form $\sum_{i,j=1}^{k} x_i a_{ij} x_j$ is positive definite on R^k.

6.4 A Geometric Interpretation of Equivalence of Quadratic Forms

The equivalence of a quadratic form

$$Q(\mathbf{X}) = \sum_{i,j=1}^{n} x_i a_{ij} x_j$$

to a diagonal form

$$y_1^2 + \cdots + y_p^2 - y_{p+1}^2 - \cdots - y_r^2$$

has a simple geometrical interpretation. An illustration of the ideas in the plane will be of value.

We assume that we have a Cartesian coordinate system in a plane and use the association of points $X(x_1, x_2)$ with vectors $[x_1, x_2]$. The coordinates of $X(x_1, x_2)$ are the components of $[x_1, x_2]$ relative to the natural basis.

Now let us consider those points in the plane for which

$$Q(\mathbf{X}) = [x_1, x_2] \begin{bmatrix} a_{11} & a_{12} \\ a_{21} & a_{22} \end{bmatrix} \begin{bmatrix} x_1 \\ x_2 \end{bmatrix} = 1. \tag{6.16}$$

We have already discussed the fact that the locus of all points satisfying (6.16) will be a conic C. We plot the graph of C in the plane.

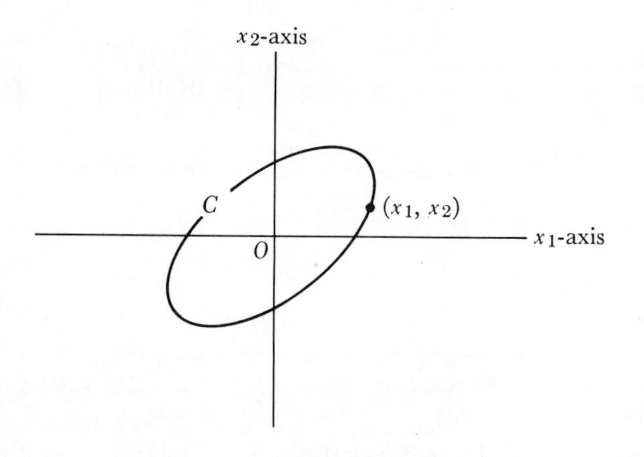

FIGURE 6.2

If $P = [p_{ij}]$ is the nonsingular matrix such that $P^{\mathsf{T}}AP =$ Diagonal $[d_1, d_2]$ (where $d_1, d_2 = \pm 1, 0$), we let the points (p_{11}, p_{21}) and (p_{12}, p_{22}) be the unit points of a new coordinate system with the origin unchanged. The new coordinates of a point whose old coordinates were (x_1, x_2) are obtained from the relation

$$\begin{bmatrix} x_1 \\ x_2 \end{bmatrix} = \begin{bmatrix} p_{11} & p_{12} \\ p_{12} & p_{22} \end{bmatrix} \begin{bmatrix} y_1 \\ y_2 \end{bmatrix}$$

by inverting the matrix P or solving the system of equations.

Graphically, we have the situation of Figure 6.3. Now, the old coordinates of a point on C are (x_1, x_2) and the new coordinates are (y, y_2). The equation of the conic (6.16) in terms of the new coordinates is

$$[y_1, y_2] \begin{bmatrix} p_{11} & p_{21} \\ p_{12} & p_{22} \end{bmatrix} \begin{bmatrix} a_{11} & a_{12} \\ a_{21} & a_{22} \end{bmatrix} \begin{bmatrix} p_{11} & p_{12} \\ p_{21} & p_{22} \end{bmatrix} \begin{bmatrix} y_1 \\ y_2 \end{bmatrix} = 1$$

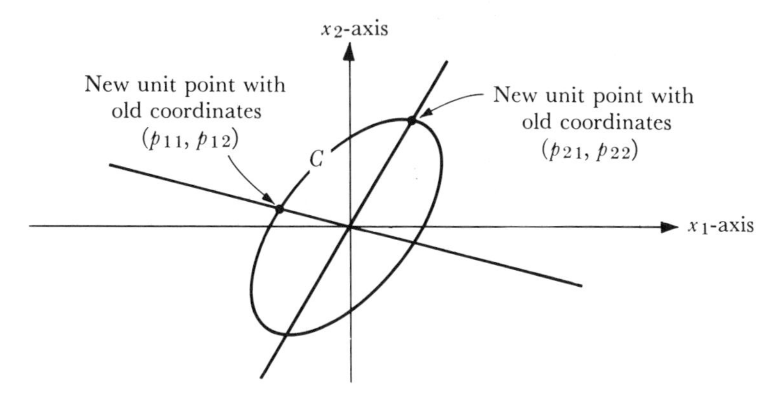

FIGURE 6.3

or

$$[y_1, y_2]\begin{bmatrix} d_1 & 0 \\ 0 & d_2 \end{bmatrix}\begin{bmatrix} y_1 \\ y_2 \end{bmatrix} = 1.$$

In general the new system will not be Cartesian.

The possible matrices diagonal $[d_1, d_2]$ and the resulting equations are

(a) $\begin{bmatrix} 1 & 0 \\ 0 & 1 \end{bmatrix}$, $y_1^2 + y_2^2 = 1$.

(b) $\begin{bmatrix} 1 & 0 \\ 0 & -1 \end{bmatrix}$, $y_1^2 - y_2^2 = 1$.

(c) $\begin{bmatrix} 1 & 0 \\ 0 & 0 \end{bmatrix}$, $y_1^2 = 1$.

(d) $\begin{bmatrix} -1 & 0 \\ 0 & 0 \end{bmatrix}$, $-y_1^2 = 1$.

(e) $\begin{bmatrix} 0 & 0 \\ 0 & 0 \end{bmatrix}$, $0 = 1$.

Case (e) may be ignored since it will occur only if the original matrix A was 0. (Why?) Case (a) is the equation of a circle if we have a Cartesian system but can represent an ellipse in a general system. Case (b) is a hyperbola with the lines $y_1 = \pm y_2$ (in the new system) as asymptotes. Case (c) is a pair of parallel lines (parallel to the new y_2-axis). Case (d) has no locus.

Certain "degenerate" conic sections and one nondegenerate section are not included in this classification. The degenerate cases are those for which the equation $Q(X) = 0$ applies; that is, when there is no "constant" term. In the cases (a)–(e) above, the right-hand member may be replaced by a 0 and the graphs are seen to be (a) point (0, 0); (b) intersecting lines; (c) one line; (d) one line; (e) all points in the plane.

The parabola is not included because we cannot bring its equation into the form $Q(\mathbf{X}) = 1$ or 0. If we begin with $y = x^2$, no translation $x' = x - h$, $y' = y - k$ will get rid of the term in y.

Example 1. A conic has the form

$$ax_1^2 + 2bx_1x_2 + cx_2^2 = 1,$$

with $a \neq 0$. What are the conditions on the coefficients that the conic is a circle or ellipse?

We follow our basic pattern for reduction. The matrix

$$A = \begin{bmatrix} a & b \\ b & c \end{bmatrix}$$

satisfies $[1, 0]A[1, 0]^{\mathsf{T}} = a \neq 0$ so we may take one new unit point also at $(1, 0)$ in the old system. Next we want a vector $[z_1, z_2]$ orthogonal to

$$A\mathbf{E}_1^{\mathsf{T}} = [a, b]^{\mathsf{T}}$$

or

$$az_1 + bz_2 = 0, \qquad z_1 = -(b/a)z_2.$$

Select $z_2 = a$, $z_1 = -b$. Then $\mathbf{Z} = [-b, a]^{\mathsf{T}}$ and $(\mathbf{Z}, \mathbf{Z}) = b^2 + a^2 \neq 0$. Our first new matrix is then

$$\begin{bmatrix} 1 & 0 \\ -b & a \end{bmatrix} \begin{bmatrix} a & b \\ b & c \end{bmatrix} \begin{bmatrix} 1 & -b \\ 0 & a \end{bmatrix} = \begin{bmatrix} a & 0 \\ 0 & -ab^2 + a^2c \end{bmatrix}.$$

If this matrix is to reduce in the further steps to $\begin{bmatrix} 1 & 0 \\ 0 & 1 \end{bmatrix}$, both diagonal terms must be positive. Hence $a > 0$, $ac > b^2$ are the requirements which must be met.

We will conclude this section with a brief look at the nondegenerate cases for three-dimensional space. The possible matrices without a zero on the diagonal and the resulting equations are:

(a) Diagonal $[1, 1, 1]$: $y_1^2 + y_2^2 + y_3^2 = 1$.
(b) Diagonal $[1, 1, -1]$: $y_1^2 + y_2^2 - y_3^2 = 1$.
(c) Diagonal $[1, -1, -1]$: $y_1^2 - y_2^2 - y_3^2 = 1$.

There are, thus, three basically different "central quadrics" in three-space.

A quadric of type (a) is called an ellipsoid (spheres and footballs are examples). A quadric of type (b) is called an elliptic hyperboloid of one sheet. A quadric of type (c) is an elliptic hyperboloid of two sheets. The latter two surfaces are sketched in Figures 6.4 and 6.5, respectively.

The results of this section may be generalized to higher-dimensional spaces but, of course, the direct geometrical figures could not be drawn.

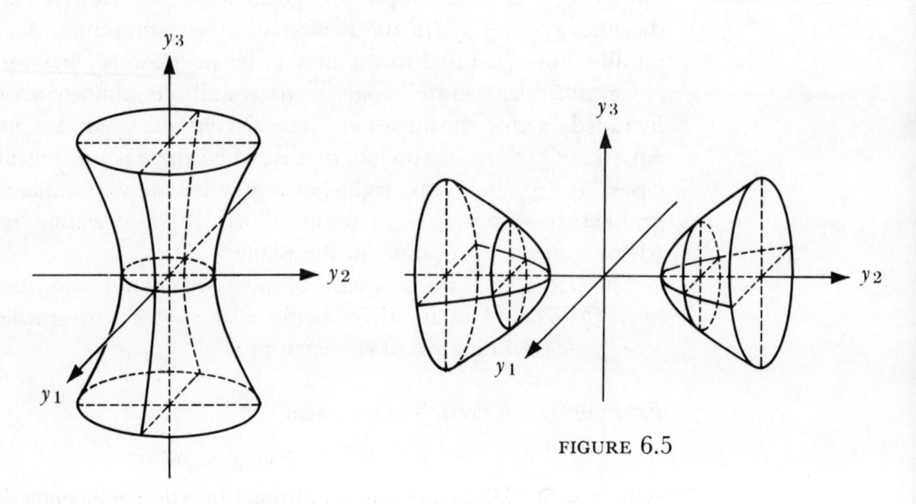

FIGURE 6.4

FIGURE 6.5

As remarked above, we shall return to the subject in Chapter 8 with a procedure that will enable us to distinguish, for example, between an ellipse and a circle.

Exercise

What types of curve or quadric surface (within the limits of this section) are represented by the following equations?
(a) $x_1^2 - 2x_1x_2 + 3x_2^2 = 1$,
(b) $x_1^2 + x_2^2 + x_3^2 - 4x_1x_2 + 2x_1x_3 = 1$,
(c) $2x_1x_2 + 2x_1x_3 + 2x_2x_3 = 1$.

6.5 Geometric Applications of Bilinear and Quadratic Forms

We shall now discuss briefly a point that we mentioned before: possible alternatives for an inner product in R^n.

Let us consider the bilinear form

$$\mathrm{B}(\mathbf{X}, \mathbf{Y}) = \sum_{i,j=1}^{n} x_i a_{ij} y_j = (\mathbf{X}, A\mathbf{Y}^{\mathsf{T}}), \tag{6.17}$$

where

$$\mathbf{X} = [x_1, x_2, \ldots, x_n],$$
$$\mathbf{Y} = [y_1, y_2, \ldots, y_n],$$
$$A = [a_{ij}].$$

We consider using $\mathrm{B}(\mathbf{X}, \mathbf{Y})$ as a new "inner product." To justify this we must be able to guarantee that $(\mathbf{X}, A\mathbf{Y}^{\mathsf{T}})$ has the basic properties of an inner product that were listed in Section 2.9.

First, we want $\mathrm{B}(\mathbf{X}, \mathbf{Y}) = \mathrm{B}(\mathbf{Y}, \mathbf{X})$ for all vectors of R^n. By choosing $X = \mathbf{E}_i$, $\mathbf{Y} = \mathbf{E}_j$, we get

$$\mathrm{B}(\mathbf{X}, \mathbf{Y}) = a_{ij} = \mathrm{B}(\mathbf{Y}, \mathbf{X}) = a_{ji}.$$

Thus the matrix A must be symmetric. This is our first restriction.

Then, if every nonzero vector is to have a positive "length," $\mathrm{B}(\mathbf{X}, \mathbf{X})$ must be positive if $\mathbf{X} \neq \mathbf{0}$ and thus the quadratic form $\mathrm{Q}(\mathbf{X}) = \mathrm{B}(\mathbf{X}, \mathbf{X})$ must be positive definite on all of R^n.

We may extend the idea of a positive definite form to matrices by saying that a real symmetric matrix A is *positive definite* if $\mathrm{Q}(\mathbf{X}) = (\mathbf{X}, A\mathbf{X}^{\mathsf{T}})$ is a positive definite quadratic form on all of R^n.

We then define a new inner product in the following manner:

DEFINITION 6.4. Let A be an $n \times n$ positive definite matrix and define a bilinear form

$$\mathrm{B}(\mathbf{X}, \mathbf{Y}) = \sum_{i,j=1}^{n} x_i a_{ij} y_j = (\mathbf{X}, A\mathbf{Y}^{\mathsf{T}})$$

*for all vectors X, Y of R^n. We call (X, AY^{T}) the A-*INNER PRODUCT *for R^n.*

All the properties desired for a general inner product are satisfied by the A-inner product on R^n. By A-orthogonality we would mean that the vectors $\mathbf{X}$ and $\mathbf{Y}$ are A-orthogonal if $(\mathbf{X}, A\mathbf{Y}^{\mathsf{T}}) = 0$. Then we could seek an A-orthogonal basis for R^n (even an A-orthonormal basis, as we have a new length, $(\mathbf{X}, A\mathbf{X}^{\mathsf{T}})^{1/2}$, as well). The existence of such a basis could be demonstrated in a straightforward manner as in Example 1 following, or we could provide the equivalent of the Gram-Schmidt process for A-orthogonality. The theorems on orthogonal subspaces also carry directly over to our new setting.

We shall give a proof of the Schwarz inequality in terms of the A-inner product. This important inequality (see Exercise 7, Section 2.9) in its original form may be written

$$(\mathbf{X}, \mathbf{Y})^2 \le (\mathbf{X}, \mathbf{X})(\mathbf{Y}, \mathbf{Y}).$$

In the form that we shall prove, it reads

$$(\mathbf{X}, A\mathbf{Y}^{\mathsf{T}})^2 \le (\mathbf{X}, A\mathbf{X}^{\mathsf{T}})(\mathbf{Y}, A\mathbf{Y}^{\mathsf{T}}) \tag{6.18}$$

for all vectors X, Y of R^n and any $n \times n$ positive definite matrix A.

To begin the proof, we note that for any real x,

$$(x\mathbf{X} + \mathbf{Y})A(x\mathbf{X} + \mathbf{Y})^{\mathsf{T}} \ge 0,$$

because A is positive definite. Using the linearity properties and collecting terms, this last expression becomes

$$x^2(\mathbf{X}A\mathbf{X}^{\mathsf{T}}) + 2x(\mathbf{X}A\mathbf{Y}^{\mathsf{T}}) + (\mathbf{Y}A\mathbf{Y}^{\mathsf{T}}) \ge 0.$$

For convenience of notation, set

$$(\mathbf{X}A\mathbf{X}^{\mathsf{T}}) = a, \qquad (\mathbf{X}A\mathbf{Y}^{\mathsf{T}}) = b, \quad \text{and} \quad (\mathbf{Y}A\mathbf{Y}^{\mathsf{T}}) = c,$$

$ax^2 + 2bx + c \ge 0$ for all real x. This means that if we draw the parabola $y = ax^2 + 2bx + c$ it must never go below the x-axis. This will be true if both $a > 0$ and $ax^2 + 2bx + c = 0$ has at most one real root. We have automatically that $a = \mathbf{X}A\mathbf{X}^{\mathsf{T}} > 0$ for $\mathbf{X} \ne \mathbf{0}$, and the second condition holds if the discriminant $4b^2 - 4ac$ is zero or negative. Thus $b^2 - ac \le 0$ or $b^2 \le ac$. Replacing the lowercase letters by their vector definitions completes the proof.

Example 1. Let us determine an A-orthogonal basis of R^3 for A the positive definite matrix

$$\begin{bmatrix} 1 & 2 & -1 \\ 2 & 5 & 0 \\ -1 & 0 & 6 \end{bmatrix}.$$

We choose as a first basis vector $\mathbf{X}_1 = [1, 0, 0]$. If $\mathbf{X}_2$ and $\mathbf{X}_3$ are to be A-orthogonal to $\mathbf{X}_1$ we must have

$$(\mathbf{X}_2, A[1, 0, 0]^{\mathsf{T}}) = (\mathbf{X}_3, A[1, 0, 0]^{\mathsf{T}}) = 0;$$

so the possibilities for $\mathbf{X}_2$ and $\mathbf{X}_3$ are solutions of

$$[x_1, x_2, x_3]\begin{bmatrix} 1 \\ 2 \\ -1 \end{bmatrix} = 0,$$

$$x_1 + 2x_2 - x_3 = 0.$$

We may choose $\mathbf{X}_2 = [2, -1, 0]$. Then $\mathbf{X}_3 = [x_1, x_2, x_3]$ must satisfy two equations:

$$x_1 + 2x_2 - x_3 = 0,$$

and

$$[x_1, x_2, x_3]A\begin{bmatrix} 2 \\ -1 \\ 0 \end{bmatrix} = 0$$

or

$$-x_2 - 2x_3 = 0.$$

A solution to this pair of equations is $\mathbf{X}_3 = [5, -2, 1]$.

The concept of A-inner product has many useful applications, both in physical and in mathematical settings. It is used, for example, to reduce quadratic forms to diagonal form in the theory of small vibrations, and to define distance in a generalized version of Euclidean geometry.

Lastly, we mention that the concepts discussed in this section could be referred to a change of basis rather than to a direct generalization of the inner product. It is a problem in the exercises to prove that A is positive definite if and only if it is of the form $A = P^{\mathsf{T}}P$, where P is nonsingular. Then

$$\begin{aligned}(\mathbf{X}, A\mathbf{Y}^{\mathsf{T}}) &= (\mathbf{X}, P^{\mathsf{T}}P\mathbf{Y}^{\mathsf{T}}) \\ &= \mathbf{X}P^{\mathsf{T}}P\mathbf{Y}^{\mathsf{T}} \\ &= (P\mathbf{X}^{\mathsf{T}})^{\mathsf{T}}P\mathbf{Y}^{\mathsf{T}} \\ &= (P\mathbf{X}^{\mathsf{T}}, P\mathbf{Y}^{\mathsf{T}}).\end{aligned}$$

The net result of this is that the "generalized" inner product is the old inner product of the vectors transformed by P, that is, after a change of basis.

Exercises

1. Determine an A-orthogonal basis for R^3, where A is the matrix of Example 1, by using the generalized Gram-Schmidt process and the initial basis $\{\mathbf{E}_i\}$.
2. Prove that a real symmetric matrix A is positive definite if and only if $A = P^{\mathsf{T}}P$, where P is a real nonsingular matrix.
3. For the positive definite matrix

$$B = \begin{bmatrix} 1 & -1 & 2 \\ -1 & 2 & -2 \\ 2 & -2 & 5 \end{bmatrix},$$

   (a) find P such that $B = P^{\mathsf{T}}P$,
   (b) find a B-orthogonal basis for R^3 by a transformation of the standard basis using part (a).
4. Find the A-orthogonal subspace to $L\{[1, 2, 0, 0], [1, -1, 0, 0]\}$ in R^4 where

$$A = \begin{bmatrix} 1 & -1 & 1 & 1 \\ -1 & 5 & -1 & -1 \\ 1 & -1 & 2 & 0 \\ 1 & -1 & 0 & 3 \end{bmatrix}.$$

5. If a real symmetric matrix is positive definite, then its determinant is positive (prove). Give an example that shows the converse to be false.

*6. Prove that a real symmetric matrix A is positive definite if and only if *all* the determinants

$$\Delta_k = \det\left(\begin{bmatrix} a_{11} & a_{12} & \cdots & a_{1k} \\ a_{21} & a_{22} & \cdots & a_{2k} \\ \vdots & & & \vdots \\ a_{k1} & & \cdots & a_{kk} \end{bmatrix}\right)$$

   are positive for $k = 1, 2, \ldots, n$.

*7. Show that there always exists a real number c such that $cI + A$ is positive definite for any real symmetric matrix A.

Complex Numbers and Polynomial Rings

In Chapters 8 and 9 we shall study the behavior of matrices under similarity ($B = PAP^{-1}$). To this end, it will be necessary to introduce certain polynomials associated with a matrix or a linear transformation. The resulting theory depends crucially on the roots and the factorization of the resulting polynomials. Therefore we will need to use some of the theory of factorization of polynomials. Furthermore, as real polynomials may have complex roots, it is also essential to use complex numbers.

The purpose of this chapter, then, is to introduce the necessary material on complex numbers and polynomials. As such, this chapter is an aside from the development of linear algebra. Many readers will already be familiar with this material and may wish to skim or omit this chapter.

7.1 The Complex Number Field *C*

We have assumed in some of the problems throughout the text that the student is familiar with complex numbers $a + bi$, where a and b are real numbers and $i^2 = -1$. In a somewhat vague sense, the complex numbers provide a field containing the real number field and solutions of the equation $x^2 + 1 = 0$. An extension of the real numbers is necessary if a solution of the equation $x^2 + 1 = 0$ is desired; the properties of order for the real numbers imply that there are no elements of R satisfying this equation. In order to make the relationship between complex numbers and real numbers more precise, we shall define the complex number field C in a more formal manner.

Take as elements of the complex number field C ordered pairs of real numbers $[a, b]$. Thus the elements of C have the same notation as the vectors of R^2, and we shall retain for the elements of C the definitions of equality and addition that they have as elements of R^2. Specifically,

DEFINITION 7.1 (EQUALITY). $[a, b] = [c, d]$ *if and only if* $a = c$, $b = d$.

DEFINITION 7.2 (ADDITION). $[a, b] + [c, d] = [a + c, b + d]$.

Now, in order to obtain a number system satisfying the postulates of a field (Section 1.3), we provide a multiplication of elements of C by means of the following definition:

DEFINITION 7.3 (MULTIPLICATION). $[a, b] \times [c, d] = [ac - bd, ad + bc]$.

There is nothing to verify for the postulates of addition because the definitions of equality and addition are those of R^2 and we know them to be satisfied.

We may compute

$$[0, 0] + [a, b] = [a, b] + [0, 0] = [a, b],$$
$$[1, 0] \times [a, b] = [a, b] \times [1, 0] = [a, b],$$

and consequently $[0, 0]$ and $[1, 0]$ play the role in C that 0 and 1 play for the real number field R. We say that $[0, 0]$ is the zero element and $[1, 0]$ is the unity, or identity, element of C.

For associativity, let $[a, b]$, $[c, d]$, and $[e, f]$ be three arbitrary elements of C and compute

$$\begin{aligned}
([a, b] \times [c, d]) \times [e, f] \\
&= [ac - bd, ad + bc] \times [e, f] \\
&= [(ac - bd)e - (ad + bc)f, (ac - bd)f + (ad + bc)e] \\
&= [ace - bde - adf - bcf, acf - bdf + ade + bce]; \\
[a, b] \times ([c, d] \times [e, f]) \\
&= [a, b] \times [ce - df, cf + de] \\
&= [a(ce - df) - b(cf + de), a(cf + de) + b(ce - df)] \\
&= [ace - adf - bcf - bde, acf + ade + bce - bdf].
\end{aligned}$$

We observe that the final forms of these associations are equal so that associativity is valid for the multiplication of elements of C. It should be noted that the distributive, associative, and commutative laws for real numbers have been used extensively in making the reductions above.

We shall show that every nonzero element $[a, b]$ has an inverse.

Given $[a, b] \neq [0, 0]$, we seek an element $[x, y]$ such that

$$[a, b] \times [x, y] = [1, 0];$$

or, after applying the definition of multiplication, such that

$$[ax - by, ay + bx] = [1, 0].$$

The last equality leads to the system of linear equations

$$ax - by = 1,$$
$$bx + ay = 0.$$

Since $[a, b] \neq [0, 0]$, $a^2 + b^2 \neq 0$, and these equations have the unique solution

$$x = \frac{a}{a^2 + b^2}, \qquad y = \frac{-b}{a^2 + b^2}.$$

A straightforward computation yields

$$\begin{aligned}
[a, b] \times \left[\frac{a}{a^2 + b^2}, \frac{-b}{a^2 + b^2}\right] \\
&= \left[\frac{a^2}{a^2 + b^2} + \frac{b^2}{a^2 + b^2}, \frac{-ab}{a^2 + b^2} + \frac{ab}{a^2 + b^2}\right] = [1, 0],
\end{aligned}$$

and we have shown the existence of $[a, b]^{-1}$.

Example 1. We shall illustrate the commutative law of multiplication and the distributive laws. These postulates comprise the unverified portions of the proof of the theorem to follow. Their verification is left to the student.

Let $[3, 2]$, $[1, 4]$, $[-1, 1]$ be elements of C. We calculate

$$\begin{aligned}[3, 2][1, 4] &= [3 - 8, 12 + 2] = [-5, 14] = [1, 4][3, 2];\\ ([3, 2] + [1, 4])[-1, 1] &= [4, 6][-1, 1] = [-10, -2],\\ ([3, 2] + [1, 4])[-1, 1] &= [3, 2][-1, 1] + [1, 4][-1, 1]\\ &= [-5, 1] + [-5, -3] = [-10, -2].\end{aligned}$$

Our foregoing discussion leads to the following theorem:

THEOREM 7.1. *The set C of all ordered pairs of real numbers $[a, b]$ together with the definitions of addition (Definition 7.2) and multiplication (Definition 7.3) forms a field which we shall call the complex number field C.*

The elements of C of the form $[a, 0]$ have the following rules of operation:

$$\begin{aligned}[a, 0] + [b, 0] &= [a + b, 0],\\ [a, 0][b, 0] &= [ab, 0].\end{aligned}$$

Ignoring the second component, 0, we see that the elements of C of the form $[a, 0]$ add and multiply like real numbers. More accurately, if we establish the one-to-one mapping T, defined by $[a, 0] \xrightarrow{T} a$, between the complex numbers of the form $[a, 0]$ and the real numbers, we see that

$$\text{if } \begin{cases}[a, 0] \xrightarrow{T} a,\\ [b, 0] \xrightarrow{T} b,\end{cases} \quad \text{then } \begin{cases}[a, 0] + [b, 0] \xrightarrow{T} a + b,\\ [a, 0][b, 0] \xrightarrow{T} ab.\end{cases}$$

This preservation of algebraic operations under the mapping T is reminiscent of the situation in the case of linear transformations and matrices, and again we speak of the two systems as being isomorphic.

In general, two fields, F (with operations $+$ and $\cdot$) and F^* (with operations $\oplus$ and $\otimes$), are *isomorphic* if there exists a one-to-one mapping T of F onto F^* such that

$$\begin{aligned}T(a + b) &= T(a) \oplus T(b),\\ T(ab) &= T(a) \otimes T(b).\end{aligned}$$

It is in this sense that we say (somewhat loosely) that the complex number field C contains the real numbers; actually C contains a subset that is isomorphic to the real number field R.

We see easily that

$$\begin{aligned}[a, b] &= [a, 0] + [b, 0][0, 1],\\ [0, 1] \times [0, 1] &= [-1, 0],\end{aligned}$$

so that, by making the identification of $[a, 0]$ with the real number a, we can write every number of C in the familiar form

$$[a, b] = a + bi,$$

where $i = [0, 1]$ and $i^2 + [1, 0] = [0, 0]$, or i is a solution of the equation $x^2 + 1 = 0$.

When a complex number is written in the form $a + bi$, we refer to a as the real part and to b as the imaginary part of the complex number $a + bi$.

We have observed that complex numbers $[a, b]$ have the same definitions of equality and addition as the vectors of R^2, and so it should not be surprising that the vectors in the plane provide a convenient geometric interpretation for complex numbers. We establish a Cartesian coordinate system for the plane and refer to the x_1-axis as the real axis and the x_2-axis as the imaginary axis. We may now associate the complex number $z = a + bi$ with the point (a, b). It should be clear that this establishes a one-to-one mapping between points in the plane and complex numbers. (Figure 7.1.)

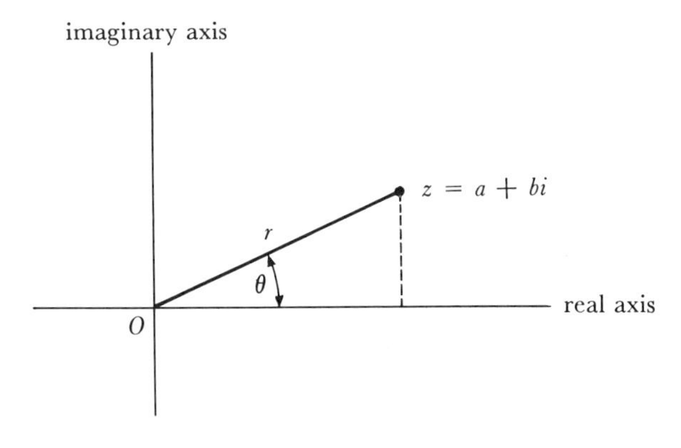

FIGURE 7.1

The length of the vector $[a, b]$, or, equivalently, the length of the line segment from the origin to the point (a, b), is called the *absolute value*, or *modulus*, of the complex number $z = a + bi$. We denote the absolute value of the complex number $z = a + bi$ by

$$|z| = |a + bi| = (a^2 + b^2)^{1/2} \tag{7.1}$$

and will often refer to the line segment from O to the point (a, b), as well as to the absolute value of $z = a + bi$, by r.

If $z = a + bi$, the complex number $\bar{z} = a - bi$ is called the *conjugate* of z. Note that $z\bar{z} = |z|^2$.

The angle θ from the positive real axis to the line segment r, measured in a counterclockwise direction, is called the *amplitude* of the complex number $z = a + bi$. We see from Figure 7.1 that

$$\theta = \tan^{-1} b/a$$

and that any complex number $z = a + bi$ may be written in the *polar form*

$$z = |z|(\cos\theta + i\sin\theta) = r(\cos\theta + i\sin\theta). \tag{7.2}$$

Example 2. The complex number $z = 1 + \sqrt{3}i$ may be written in the polar form

$$1 + \sqrt{3}i = 2(\cos 60^\circ + i\sin 60^\circ).$$

We have arranged the association of complex numbers with points in the plane so that we can think of the complex number $a + bi$ as corresponding to the vector $[a, b]$. Since the addition of complex numbers corresponds to the addition of vectors, we have already established a geometrical interpretation for complex addition in Section 2.3. If z_1 and z_2 are complex numbers, this geometrical interpretation of addition in terms of the three sides of a triangle readily establishes the relation

$$|z_1 + z_2| \leq |z_1| + |z_2|.$$

The interesting geometrical interpretation for multiplication is best obtained from the polar form of complex numbers. Thus, if

$$z_1 = |z_1|(\cos\theta + i\sin\theta),$$
$$z_2 = |z_2|(\cos\beta + i\sin\beta),$$

then

$$\begin{aligned} z_1 z_2 &= |z_1|\,|z_2|(\cos\theta + i\sin\theta)(\cos\beta + i\sin\beta) \\ &= |z_1|\,|z_2|[\cos\theta\cos\beta - \sin\theta\sin\beta + i(\cos\theta\sin\beta + \sin\theta\cos\beta)] \\ &= |z_1|\,|z_2|[\cos(\theta + \beta) + i\sin(\theta + \beta)]. \end{aligned} \tag{7.3}$$

Hence the amplitude of the product of two complex numbers is the sum of their amplitudes and the absolute value is the product of their absolute values.

Example 3. Let $z_1 = 1 + \sqrt{3}i$, $z_2 = 1 + i$; then

$$z_1 = 2(\cos 60^\circ + i\sin 60^\circ),$$
$$z_2 = \sqrt{2}(\cos 45^\circ + i\sin 45^\circ),$$

and

$$z_1 z_2 = 2\sqrt{2}(\cos 105^\circ + i\sin 105^\circ).$$

If we take $z_1 = z_2 = z$ in formula (7.3), we obtain

$$z^2 = |z|^2(\cos 2\theta + i\sin 2\theta),$$

and a simple induction argument gives the more general formula

$$z^n = |z|^n(\cos n\theta + i\sin n\theta), \qquad n = 1, 2, \ldots. \tag{7.4}$$

We can use formula (7.4) quite effectively to obtain the nth roots of any complex number. Let $z_0 = r_0(\cos\phi + i\sin\phi)$ and assume that we wish to find those complex numbers z such that

$$z^n = r_0(\cos\phi + i\sin\phi). \tag{7.5}$$

We substitute from (7.4) to obtain the relation

$$|z|^n(\cos n\theta + i\sin n\theta) = r_0(\cos\phi + i\sin\phi),$$

where $r_0 \geq 0$ and, consequently, $|z|$, being positive, must be a real positive nth root of r_0. As is easily seen, the amplitudes of equal complex numbers must be equal and hence

$$|z|^n = r_0, \quad \text{or} \quad |z| = r_0^{1/n}.$$

We must also satisfy the relations

$$\cos n\theta = \cos\phi,$$
$$\sin n\theta = \sin\phi.$$

There is no unique solution for θ since

$$\cos n\theta = \cos n\left(\theta + \frac{2k\pi}{n}\right)$$

for any integer k. However, we see that only the following values of θ,

$$\theta = \frac{\phi}{n} + \frac{2k\pi}{n},$$

for $k = 0, 1, \ldots, n - 1$, yield distinct values for z. (Why?) Hence there are precisely n solutions of Equation (7.5), and these nth roots of $z_0 = r_0(\cos\theta + i\sin\theta)$ are

$$z = r_0^{1/n}\left[\cos\left(\frac{\phi}{n} + \frac{2k\pi}{n}\right) + i\sin\left(\frac{\phi}{n} + \frac{2k\pi}{n}\right)\right]$$

for $k = 0, 1, 2, \ldots, n - 1$.

Example 4. Let us solve $z^3 = 1$. We write

$$1 = 1(\cos 0° + i \sin 0°),$$

and then the cube roots of 1 are

$$\begin{aligned} z_1 &= (\cos 0° + i \sin 0°), \\ z_2 &= (\cos 120° + i \sin 120°), \\ z_3 &= (\cos 240° + i \sin 240°). \end{aligned}$$

Exercises

1. Perform the indicated operation on the complex numbers.
   (a) $[3, 4] + [1, -2]$, (b) $[1, 6][2, -1]$,
   (c) $(3 + 4i) + (1 - 2i)$, (d) $(1 + 6i)(2 - i)$.
2. Verify the distributive laws for the field of complex numbers.
3. Convert the following complex numbers to polar form:
   (a) $1 - i$, (b) $-1 + i$,
   (c) $-3i$, (d) $\sqrt{3} + i$,
   (e) $3 + 4i$, (f) $2 - i$.
4. Convert the following complex numbers in polar form to the form $a + bi$:
   (a) $4(\cos 30° + i \sin 30°)$, (b) $2(\cos 90° + i \sin 90°)$,
   (c) $1(\cos 60° + i \sin 60°)$, (d) $\sqrt{3}(\cos 45° + i \sin 45°)$.
5. Determine a geometrical construction for the product of two complex numbers.
6. Determine a geometrical construction for the quotient of two complex numbers.
7. Give a complete proof for the formula

$$z^n = |z|^n(\cos n\theta + i \sin n\theta), \qquad n = 1, 2, \ldots.$$

   (This is commonly known as Demoivre's formula.)
8. Determine the inverse of a complex number $z = r(\cos \theta + i \sin \theta)$ in polar form.
9. What is the formula for z_1/z_2 in polar form?
10. Determine the solutions of the following equations:
    (a) $x^5 = 1$, (b) $x^2 = -1 - i$,
    (c) $x^4 = 625$, (d) $x^3 = -27$,
    (e) $x^2 = 1 + \sqrt{3}i$, (f) $x^3 = -i$.
11. Determine an expression for z^{-1} in terms of $|z|$ and the conjugate $\bar{z}$.
12. Show that $z + \bar{z}$ is always real and that $z - \bar{z}$ is a complex number with real part zero.
13. Prove that the complex nth roots of 1 form a group of n elements for any positive integer n, where the group operation is multiplication.
14. If $z = \cos 2\pi/n + i \sin 2\pi/n$, show that $z^k = 1$ if and only if n divides k.
15. Among the sixth roots of 1, find those complex numbers that are also cube roots of 1; square roots of 1.
16. Those nth roots of 1 which are not at the same time mth roots of 1 for $m < n$ are called primitive nth roots of 1. How many primitive sixth roots of 1 are there?
17. Prove that every nth root of 1 may be expressed as a power of any primitive nth root of 1.

7.2 Polynomial Rings

We have frequently assumed a working knowledge of polynomial algebra in our illustrations and examples. We wish now to give a careful development of this algebra in order to apply it directly to the theory of canonical forms of matrices. In particular, we will want polynomials with coefficients from fields F which may not be always the real field R. There are cases when we will wish to restrict attention to the rational field Q or to extend to the complex field C.

When we attempt to give a definition of a "polynomial with coefficients in F" we find a surprising amount of difficulty if we wish to avoid circularity and confusion between polynomials and functions defined by polynomial equations. Standard simple definitions lead to questions such as "What is x?" Answer, "x is an indeterminate or monomial." "What is that?"

There are two standard ways to avoid confusion. One is a "recursive definition," where specific entities are defined as polynomials and polynomials in general are defined as the result of specific operations on these entities. The other, which we shall adopt, uses infinite sequences over F. Technically an infinite sequence is a mapping from the set of nonnegative integers to a given set, in our case F. It is standard practice to write $a_0, a_1, \ldots,$ in place of $a(0)$, $a(1), \ldots,$ to indicate the values assigned to $0, 1, \ldots,$ and to give a "function table" in the form $[a_0, a_1, a_2, \ldots, a_n, \ldots]$. There will be no ambiguity if we call the table or list $[a_0, a_1, \ldots]$ a sequence, since it defines and is defined by the sequence function.

DEFINITION 7.4. A POLYNOMIAL OVER F *is a sequence with values in* F *in which all but a finite number of the values are* 0. *Two polynomials are equal if and only if the respective functions are equal, i.e.,*

(i) $[a_0, a_1, a_2, \ldots] = [b_0, b_1, b_2, \ldots]$ *if and only if* $a_i = b_i \; i = 0, 1, \ldots.$ *Three operations, addition, scalar multiplication, and product (multiplication), are defined for polynomials. Addition is simply the addition of functions:*

(ii) $[a_0, a_1, a_2, \ldots] + [b_0, b_1, b_2, \ldots] = [a_0 + b_0, a_1 + b_1, a_2 + b_2, \ldots].$ *Scalar multiplication is similarly defined:*

(iii) $a[a_0, a_1, a_2, \ldots] = [aa_0, aa_1, aa_2, \ldots]$, $a \in F$. *The product has a more complicated definition:*

(iv) $[a_0, a_1, a_2, \ldots][b_0, b_1, b_2, \ldots] = [c_0, c_1, c_2, \ldots]$ *where*

$$c_i = a_0b_i + a_1b_{i-1} + a_2b_{i-2} + \cdots + a_{i-1}b_1 + a_ib_0.$$

In order to verify that the definition does not contradict itself, we must be sure that the sum, scalar multiple, and product of polynomials are polynomials. It is clear that the sum cannot have more nonzero elements than the sum of the number of nonzero elements in each addend. Similarly, it is clear that the scalar multiple either consists entirely of zero values or has exactly the same number of nonzero values as the original polynomial.

The case of the product needs a little more attention. If there are only a finite number of nonzero values, there must be a *last* nonzero value, say a_n for the first polynomial and b_m for the second; $a_r = 0$, $r > n$ and $b_s = 0$ for $s > m$. If we consider c_k for $k > m + n$,

$$c_k = (a_kb_0 + a_{k-1}b_1 + \cdots + a_{k-m}b_m) + (a_{k-m-1}b_{m+1} + \cdots + a_1b_{n-1} + a_0b_k)$$

we see that every term in the first group is 0 because

$$a_k = a_{k-1} = \cdots = a_{k-m} = 0$$

and every term in the second group is 0 because $b_{m+1} = \cdots = b_{k-1} = b_k = 0$. Thus $c_k = 0$ and $c_{m+n} = a_nb_m$ is the *last* nonzero term in the product.

The set S of polynomials over F is

(a) A vector space over F.
(b) A ring (commutative with multiplicative identity).
(c) An algebra over F.

The verification of the various postulates is straightforward but somewhat lengthy. The details, as usual in such cases, are left to the exercises. We shall simply point out some basic features of the algebraic structures. In this discussion it will be convenient to use the notation $[a_0, a_1, \ldots, a_n, 0, 0, \ldots]$ to indicate a polynomial whose last nonzero value is a_n.

As a basis we naturally select the $\{\mathbf{E}_i\}$ system:

$$\mathbf{E}_1 = [1, 0, 0, \ldots], \qquad \mathbf{E}_2 = [0, 1, 0, 0, \ldots], \ldots.$$

It is clear that each $\mathbf{E}_i$ having only *one* nonzero element *is* a polynomial and that every finite subset of the $\{\mathbf{E}_i\}$ is linearly independent. Further, by addition and scalar multiplication any polynomial is a linear combination of a finite subset of the $\{\mathbf{E}_i\}$. In this sense, we say that the $\{\mathbf{E}_i\}$ do, in fact, form a basis of the vector space. However, it should be clear that this space is *not* a finite-dimensional space. (If we had a finite basis, no larger set could be linearly independent. If there were a basis of n elements, the set $\{\mathbf{E}_1, \mathbf{E}_2, \ldots, \mathbf{E}_{n+1}\}$ would furnish a contradiction).

It is more convenient to start counting with 0 in the case of polynomials, and we rename the basis by defining $\mathbf{X}_i = \mathbf{E}_{i+1}$, $i = 0, 1, \ldots$. Then

$$[a_0, a_1, \ldots, a_n, 0, 0, \ldots] = a_0\mathbf{X}_0 + a_1\mathbf{X}_1 + \cdots + a_n\mathbf{X}_n.$$

The multiplicative identity is easily seen to be $\mathbf{X}_0$. Indeed, viewed as a ring, S obviously contains an isomorphic copy of F under the mapping $a\mathbf{X}_0 \to a$. This phenomenon we have seen with every algebra we have studied; if there is a multiplicative unit I, we always have the results $(aI)(bI) = (ab)I$ and $aI + bI = (a + b)I$. These establish a morphism from the algebra to the field F, and in all the cases we have looked at, the morphism has been one-to-one.

The student who practices using the formal definitions will find that computing a product is somewhat of a bookkeeping chore without the familiar "powers of x" to guide him. In fact one of the two uses of the "powers of x" is as such a guide and we shall soon resort to them.

Example 1. We compute the product

$$\begin{aligned}
&[1, 2, 3, 0, 0, \ldots][2, -1, 1, 0, 0, \ldots] \\
&\quad = [1\cdot 2, 1(-1) + 2\cdot 2, 1\cdot 1 + 2(-1) + 3(2), 1\cdot 0 + 2\cdot 1 + 3(-1) \\
&\qquad\qquad + 0\cdot 2, 1\cdot 0 + 2\cdot 0 + 3\cdot 1 + 0(-1) + 0\cdot 2, 0, 0, \ldots] \\
&\quad = [2, 3, 5, -1, 3, 0, 0, \ldots].
\end{aligned}$$

In order to regain the standard notation, we first note that $(\mathbf{X}_1)^n = \mathbf{X}_n$. This fact is easily demonstrated by mathematical induction. It is obvious for $n = 1$. Assume the statement valid for $n = k - 1$; then

$$\mathbf{X}_1^k = \mathbf{X}_1(\mathbf{X}_1^{k-1}) = [0, 1, 0, 0, \ldots][0, 0, \ldots, \underset{\substack{\uparrow \\ k-1 \text{ place}}}{1}, 0, 0, \ldots].$$

The only nonzero term in any element of the product can occur when a summand of the type a_1b_{k-1} appears. This is, by the definition of the product, in the kth place and the value there is 1.

Then we can write

$$[a_0, a_1, a_2, \ldots, a_n, 0, 0, \ldots] = a_0\mathbf{X}_0 + a_1\mathbf{X}_1 + a_2\mathbf{X}_1^2 + \cdots + a_n\mathbf{X}_1^n.$$

If we make the identification of a_0 with $a_0\mathbf{X}_0$, the sequence may be rewritten

$$a_0 + a_1\mathbf{X}_1 + a_2\mathbf{X}_1^2 + \cdots + a_n\mathbf{X}_1^n.$$

Example 2. Let us repeat the product of Example 1 in the new notation.

$$\begin{aligned}(1 + 2\mathbf{X}_1 + 3\mathbf{X}_1^2)(2 - \mathbf{X}_1 + \mathbf{X}_1^2) = 2 + 4\mathbf{X}_1 &+ 6\mathbf{X}_1^2 \\ - \mathbf{X}_1 &- 2\mathbf{X}_1^2 - 3\mathbf{X}_1^3 \\ &\quad\;\; \mathbf{X}_1^2 + 2\mathbf{X}_1^3 + 3\mathbf{X}_1^4 \\ \hline 2 + 3\mathbf{X}_1 &+ 5\mathbf{X}_1^2 - \mathbf{X}_1^3 + 3\mathbf{X}_1^4\end{aligned}$$

When the elements of S are written in the form $a_0 + a_1\mathbf{X}_1 + \cdots + a_n\mathbf{X}_1^n$, the student will readily note that the definitions (7.4) comprise the familiar rules of equality, addition, and multiplication of polynomials with the element $\mathbf{X}_1$ of S playing the role of x in $a_0 + a_1x + a_2x^2 + \cdots + a_nx^n$.

We will now identify the element $\mathbf{X}_1$ of S with x and denote S, as an algebra, by $F[x]$. We call $F[x]$ *a polynomial ring* (or algebra) *over the field F*. The elements of $F[x]$ now appear in the more familiar form as *polynomials*

$$a_0 + a_1x + \cdots + a_nx^n,$$

with the *coefficients* $a_i \in F$. The symbol x is often called an *indeterminate*. Frequently an abbreviation such as $p(x)$ will be used for an element of $F[x]$.

Example 3. The polynomial

$$p(x) = 1 + \tfrac{1}{2}x + 3x^2$$

is an element of $Q[x]$ but

$$q(x) = \sqrt{2} - x + (3 + \sqrt{2})x^2$$

is not. On the other hand, both $p(x)$ and $q(x)$ are in $R[x]$.

Exercises

1. The set S of this section, as a vector space, does not have a finite basis. A subset X of S is said to be a basis of S if any finite number of elements from X are linearly independent and every element of S can be written as a linear combination of a finite number of elements from X. Show that $X = \{\mathbf{X}_0, \mathbf{X}_1, \mathbf{X}_2, \ldots\}$ is a basis for S.
2. Show that

$$[1, 2, -1, 1, 0, 0, \ldots][1, 0, 3, 0, 0, \ldots] = [1, 0, 3, 0, 0, \ldots][1, 2, -1, 1, 0, 0, \ldots].$$

3. Prove, in general, that the product of elements of S (as defined by Definition 7.4 (iv)) is commutative.
4. Show that $(\mathbf{AB})\mathbf{C} = \mathbf{A}(\mathbf{BC})$ for the elements

$$\begin{aligned}\mathbf{A} &= [1, 0, -1, 0, 0, \ldots],\\ \mathbf{B} &= [0, 1, 2, 0, 0, \ldots],\\ \mathbf{C} &= [1, -1, 2, 0, 0, \ldots]\end{aligned}$$

of S.

5. Prove, in general, that the product of elements of S is associative. *Hint:* If

$$\mathbf{A} = [a_0, a_1, a_2, \ldots],$$
$$\mathbf{B} = [b_0, b_1, b_2, \ldots],$$

and

$$\mathbf{C} = [c_0, c_1, c_2, \ldots],$$

then show that the mth component of $(\mathbf{AB})\mathbf{C}$ and $\mathbf{A}(\mathbf{BC})$ is

$$\left(\sum_{i+j+k=m} a_i b_j c_k\right).$$

6. Verify the distributive laws for S as a ring.
7. How would you show that the relation $p(x)q(x) = 0$ for elements $p(x)$ and $q(x)$ of $F[x]$ implies either $p(x) = 0$ or $q(x) = 0$? Note that the proof for a field in Section 1.3 is not valid. (A proof of this exercise is suggested at the beginning of the next section.)

7.3 Division Algorithm for Polynomials

We are primarily interested in developing a theory of factorization of polynomials over F (where F is normally the reals or the rationals) comparable to the factoring of an integer into prime factors. We proceed to develop the necessary tools.

The *degree* of the polynomial

$$p(x) = a_0 + a_1x + \cdots + a_mx^m$$

is defined to be m if $m > 0$. If $m = 0$ and $a_0 \neq 0$, the degree is defined as 0. The zero polynomial, $p(x) = 0$, has no degree. We see from Definition 7.4 that if $p(x)$ and $q(x) = b_0 + \cdots + b_nx^n$ have degrees, then so does $p(x) \cdot q(x)$, and the degree of $p(x) \cdot q(x)$ is the sum of the degrees of $p(x)$ and $q(x)$; the coefficient of x^{m+n} in $p(x) \cdot q(x)$ is $a_mb_n \neq 0$. The student should apply this result to show that the product of two nonzero polynomials is nonzero.

The familiar process of dividing one polynomial by another one is formalized in the following theorem:

THEOREM 7.2 (DIVISION ALGORITHM). Let $f(x)$ and $g(x) \neq 0$ be two polynomials of $F[x]$. We can find two new polynomials of $F[x]$, $q(x)$ (quotient) and $r(x)$ (remainder), such that

$$f(x) = q(x)g(x) + r(x),$$

where $r(x)$ is either zero or the degree of $r(x)$ is less than the degree of $g(x)$. Moreover, $q(x)$ and $r(x)$ are uniquely determined by $f(x)$ and $g(x)$.

PROOF. If the degree of $f(x)$ is less than the degree of $g(x)$ or if $f(x) = 0$, take $q(x) = 0$, $r(x) = f(x)$. If $f(x)$ and $g(x)$ are both of degree zero: $f(x) = a_0$, $g(x) = b_0 \neq 0$; then $q(x) = a_0/b_0$ and $r(x) = 0$.

Now we may proceed by induction. Specifically, if

$$f(x) = a_0 + a_1x + \cdots + a_mx^m, \qquad g(x) = b_0 + b_1x + \cdots + b_nx^n,$$

and $m \geq n$, we assume the existence of a unique quotient and remainder for the division of all polynomials $f_1(x)$ of degree less than m by any polynomial $g(x)$. Form the polynomial:

$$f_1(x) = f(x) - a_mb_n^{-1}x^{m-n}g(x). \tag{7.6}$$

The coefficient of x^m in $f_1(x)$ is $a_m - (a_m b_n^{-1}) b_n = 0$; no coefficient of x^k for $k > m$ appears in $f_1(x)$; hence $f_1(x)$ has degree less than m. By our induction hypothesis, we may find $q_1(x)$ and $r(x)$ in $F[x]$ such that

$$f_1(x) = q_1(x) g(x) + r(x),$$

where $r(x)$ is zero or of degree less than that of $g(x)$. Now, substituting for $f_1(x)$ in (7.6),

$$q_1(x) g(x) + r(x) = f(x) - a_m b_n^{-1} x^{m-n} g(x),$$

or

$$f(x) = (a_m b_n^{-1} x^{m-n} + q_1(x)) g(x) + r(x),$$

and we have shown the existence of at least one polynomial

$$q(x) = (a_m b_n^{-1} x^{m-n} + q_1(x))$$

and a polynomial $r(x)$ satisfying the division algorithm.

Now we need to show the uniqueness of $q(x)$ and $r(x)$. Suppose that we have two results:

$$f(x) = q(x) g(x) + r(x),$$
$$f(x) = q^*(x) g(x) + r^*(x).$$

Subtracting,

$$(q^*(x) - q(x)) g(x) = r(x) - r^*(x). \tag{7.7}$$

If $q^*(x) \neq q(x)$, the degree of the polynomial on the left-hand side of (7.7) is at least as great as n since the degree of $q^*(x) - q(x)$ will be at least zero. Since the degree of the right-hand side cannot be as large as n, the result is impossible. Then $q^*(x) - q(x) = 0$; hence $r(x) - r^*(x) = 0$. Therefore the two results are identical; the division algorithm gives a unique result.

Example 1. Let

$$f(x) = 3 - 2x + 4x^2 - x^3 + 2x^4,$$
$$g(x) = 1 - x + x^2.$$

Then it is easy to see that

$$(3 - 2x + 4x^2 - x^3 + 2x^4) = (3 + x + 2x^2)(1 - x + x^2),$$

and the remainder $r(x)$ is zero.

If $f(x)$ and $g(x) \neq 0$ are two polynomials such that upon division of $f(x)$ by $g(x)$ the remainder $r(x) = 0$, we have the relation

$$f(x) = q(x) g(x). \tag{7.8}$$

In this case we say that $f(x)$ is a *multiple* of $g(x)$, or $g(x)$ divides $f(x)$, or $g(x)$ is a *divisor* or *factor* of $f(x)$ in $F[x]$.

DEFINITION 7.5. Let $f_1(x)$ and $f_2(x)$ be two polynomials of $F[x]$ not both zero. A polynomial of $F[x]$ that divides $f_1(x)$ and $f_2(x)$ is called a common divisor of $f_1(x)$ and $f_2(x)$. A polynomial $d(x)$ of $F[x]$ is called a GREATEST COMMON DIVISOR (GCD) *of $f_1(x)$ and $f_2(x)$ if*

(i) *$d(x)$ is a common divisor of $f_1(x)$ and $f_2(x)$;*
(ii) *every common divisor of $f_1(x)$ and $f_2(x)$ divides $d(x)$.*

It is not clear that a GCD exists for every two polynomials of $F[x]$. We shall demonstrate this fact and leave to the student the generalization of a GCD for any finite number of polynomials.

Let $f_1(x)$ and $f_2(x)$ be two polynomials not both zero and consider the set S^* of all polynomials of the form $p_1(x)f_1(x) + p_2(x)f_2(x)$, where $p_1(x)$ and $p_2(x)$ are arbitrary polynomials of $F[x]$. Certainly the set S^* contains some nonzero polynomials; pick one of least possible degree:

$$d(x) = p_1^*(x)f_1(x) + p_2^*(x)f_2(x). \tag{7.9}$$

We can show that $d(x)$ is a GCD of $f_1(x)$ and $f_2(x)$.

First, $d(x)$ must divide $f_1(x)$, for if not,

$$f_1(x) = q_1(x)d(x) + r_1(x),$$

where $r_1(x)$ is not zero but is of degree less than that of $d(x)$. But

$$\begin{aligned} r_1(x) &= -q_1(x)[p_1^*(x)f_1(x) + p_2^*(x)f_2(x)] + f_1(x) \\ &= [1 - q_1(x)p_1^*(x)]f_1(x) + [-q_1(x)p_2^*(x)]f_2(x), \end{aligned}$$

and thus $r_1(x)$ is in S^*, contradicting the minimality of the degree of $d(x)$.

Similarly it can be shown that $d(x)$ divides $f_2(x)$. We have then satisfied condition (i) of the definition of a GCD.

Next suppose $d_1(x)$ is any common divisor of $f_1(x)$ and $f_2(x)$; in fact, let

$$f_1(x) = d_1(x)f_1^*(x) \quad \text{and} \quad f_2(x) = d_1(x)f_2^*(x).$$

Then

$$\begin{aligned} d(x) &= p_1^*(x)d_1(x)f_1^*(x) + p_2^*(x)d_1(x)f_2^*(x) \\ &= d_1(x)[p_1^*(x)f_1^*(x) + p_2^*(x)f_2^*(x)]. \end{aligned}$$

That is, $d(x)$ is a multiple of $d_1(x)$. Thus both conditions for a GCD are fulfilled by $d(x)$.

Of course the GCD of two polynomials is not unique. If $d(x)$ is one GCD, $cd(x)$ is another, where c is an arbitrary element of F. This is the only latitude allowed since, if $d_1(x)$ and $d_2(x)$ are both GCD's of $f_1(x)$ and $f_2(x)$, condition (ii) implies that each divides the other:

$$d_1(x) = m(x)d_2(x); \qquad d_2(x) = n(x)d_1(x),$$

or

$$d_1(x) = m(x)n(x)d_1(x), \qquad [1 - m(x)n(x)]d_1(x) = 0.$$

Since the product of two nonzero polynomials is nonzero, we conclude that $m(x)n(x) - 1 = 0$ because $d_1(x) \neq 0$ and the assumption that $m(x)n(x) - 1 \neq 0$ would lead to a contradiction. Thus the sum of the degrees of $m(x)$ and $n(x)$ is 0 so the degree of each must be 0; that is, $m(x)$ and $n(x)$ are both elements of F.

Two polynomials which are multiples of one another and, by the argument just given, have a quotient which is an element of F are called *associates*. If

$$p(x) = a_0 + a_1x + a_2x^2 + \cdots + a_mx^m \neq 0,$$

there is precisely one associate of $p(x)$ that has 1 as the coefficient of x^m, namely $a_m^{-1}p(x)$. Such a polynomial is called *monic;* there is a unique *monic* GCD of every pair of polynomials that are not both zero. To summarize, we state the following theorem:

THEOREM 7.3. If $f_1(x)$ and $f_2(x)$ are any two polynomials of $F[x]$ which are not both zero, they have a greatest common divisor. Any two greatest common divisors of $f_1(x)$

and $f_2(x)$ are multiples of each other; their ratio is an element of F. Any greatest common divisor $d(x)$ may be written in the form

$$d(x) = p_1^*(x) f_1(x) + p_2^*(x) f_2(x),$$

where $p_1^*(x)$ and $p_2^*(x)$ are polynomials of $F[x]$.

The proof given for Theorem 7.3 is a *nonconstructive existence* proof. The existence of $d(x)$ was demonstrated, but no practicable or even possible method was given to find $d(x)$. We cannot really look over the infinite collection of members of S^* and select one of the minimum degree. In special cases it may be possible to select a reasonable-looking member of S^* and then, by other reasoning, *prove* that no smaller degree can arise than that of the selected polynomial, but no general prescription exists.

There is available an alternative proof of the existence of a GCD that is *constructive* in that it provides a method of computing the GCD in a finite number of steps. We shall state the result and leave the formal proof for the exercises.

THEOREM 7.4 (EUCLID'S ALGORITHM). Let $f_1(x)$ and $f_2(x)$ be two polynomials of $F[x]$ with degree $f_1(x) \geq$ degree $f_2(x) > 0$. Let

$$\begin{aligned}
f_1(x) &= q_1(x) f_2(x) + r_2(x), & 0 &< \text{degree } r_2(x) < \text{degree } f_2(x),\\
f_2(x) &= q_2(x) r_2(x) + r_3(x), & 0 &< \text{degree } r_3(x) < \text{degree } r_2(x),\\
r_2(x) &= q_3(x) r_3(x) + r_4(x), & 0 &< \text{degree } r_4(x) < \text{degree } r_3(x),\\
&\vdots & &\vdots\\
r_{k-2}(x) &= q_{k-1}(x) r_{k-1}(x) + r_k(x), & 0 &\leq \text{degree } r_k(x) < \text{degree } r_{k-1}(x),\\
r_{k-1}(x) &= q_k(x) r_k(x),\\
r_{k+1}(x) &= 0.
\end{aligned}$$

Then $r_k(x)$ is a GCD of $f_1(x)$ and $f_2(x)$.

Example 2. We will find a GCD of

$$\begin{aligned}
f_1(x) &= -2 - 3x + x^2 + 3x^3 + x^4,\\
f_2(x) &= -8 - 4x + 2x^2 + x^3.
\end{aligned}$$

Omitting the details, we state for the student the values of $q_i(x)$ and $r_i(x)$ obtained by applying Theorem 7.4.

$$\begin{aligned}
q_1(x) &= (1 + x), & r_2(x) &= 6 + 9x + 3x^2;\\
q_2(x) &= (-\tfrac{1}{3} + \tfrac{1}{3}x), & r_3(x) &= (-6 - 3x);\\
q_3(x) &= (-1 - x), & r_4(x) &= 0.
\end{aligned}$$

Thus, $(-6 - 3x)$ or the unique monic polynomial $2 + x$ is a GCD of $f_1(x)$ and $f_2(x)$.

By rewriting

$$f_2(x) = q_2(x) r_2(x) + r_3(x)$$

as

$$r_3(x) = f_2(x) - q_2(x) r_2(x)$$

and then substituting

$$f_1(x) - q_1(x) f_2(x) \quad \text{for} \quad r_2(x)$$

we have

$$\begin{aligned}
r_3(x) &= f_2(x) - q_2(x)[f_1(x) - q_1(x) f_2(x)]\\
&= -q_2(x) f_1(x) + (1 + q_2(x) q_1(x)) f_2(x).
\end{aligned}$$

Thus we have expressed the GCD of $f_1(x)$ and $f_2(x)$ as stated in Theorem 7.3. A similar reversal of the division steps with proper substitution is possible to obtain the GCD of any two polynomials $f_1(x)$ and $f_2(x)$ as an expression

$$p_1^*(x)f_1(x) + p_2^*(x)f_2(x) = r_k(x) = d(x).$$

Exercises

1. Show that the degree of the sum of two nonzero polynomials is equal to or less than the larger of the degrees of the individual summands when the sum is nonzero.
2. Find the quotient and remainder when the division algorithm is applied to the following pairs of polynomials:
   (a) $1 + (\sqrt{2} + \sqrt{3})x + x^2$ divided by $x + \sqrt{3}$,
   (b) $1 - x^n$ divided by $-1 + x$,
   (c) $1 + x + 2x^2 + 4x^3 - x^4$ divided by $1 - 2x + x^2 + x^3$,
   (d) $3 - 5x - 5x^2 + 5x^3 + 3x^4$ divided by $-2 + x + x^2$.
3. Find the GCD of the following pairs of polynomials:
   (a) $1 - x^2$ and $2 + (2 + \sqrt{2})x + \sqrt{2}x^2$,
   (b) $1 - 4x + 2x^2 - x^3$ and $1 - x^2 + x^4$,
   (c) $2 + 2x + 3x^2 + x^3 + x^4$ and $-2 - x^2 + 2x^3 + x^5$,
   (d) $45 - 12x + 2x^2 - 4x^3 + x^4$ and $-12 + 4x - 12x^2 + 4x^3$.
4. For each of the parts of Exercise 3, express the GCD in the form

$$d(x) = p_1(x)f_1(x) + p_2(x)f_2(x).$$

5. In the notation of Theorem 7.4, prove that a GCD of $f_1(x)$ and $f_2(x)$ is a GCD of $f_2(x)$ and $r_2(x)$. Now show that a GCD of $f_2(x)$ and $r_2(x)$ is a GCD of $r_2(x)$ and $r_3(x)$. Finally, show (by iterating this procedure) that the process terminates and $r_k(x)$ is a GCD of $f_1(x)$ and $f_2(x)$.
6. Define a GCD of a finite set of polynomials $\{f_1(x), f_2(x), \ldots, f_n(x)\}$, not all zero. Prove that this GCD exists. *Hint:* From the set S^* of all polynomials $p_1(x)f_1(x) + \cdots + p_n(x)f_n(x)$ choose one of smallest degree for $d(x)$.

7.4 Factorization of Polynomials

A polynomial $p(x) \in F[x]$ is said to be *reducible* over F if there exist polynomials $p_1(x)$ and $p_2(x)$ of degree > 0 in $F[x]$ such that $p(x) = p_1(x) \cdot p_2(x)$. Otherwise, $p(x)$ is said to be *irreducible* over F.

The field F plays a dominant role in the reducibility or irreducibility of a polynomial. For example, let $p(x) = 2 - x^2$ be a polynomial viewed first as an element of $R[x]$, then as an element of $Q[x]$. We have

$$2 - x^2 = (\sqrt{2} - x)(\sqrt{2} + x),$$

but neither $(\sqrt{2} - x)$ nor $(\sqrt{2} + x)$ is a polynomial of $Q[x]$. Now if we were able to show that this is the only way to express $2 - x^2$ as the product of polynomials of degree 1 in $R[x]$, then we could conclude that $2 - x^2$ is *irreducible* over the rational field Q. These details will be supplied later (Theorem 7.6), but for the present, note that $2 - x^2$ as a polynomial of $R[x]$ is reducible.

Two polynomials $f_1(x)$ and $f_2(x)$ are said to be *relatively prime* if any GCD of $f_1(x)$ and $f_2(x)$ is an element of F.

Theorem 7.3 asserts that, for relatively prime polynomials $f_1(x)$ and $f_2(x)$, it is possible to find polynomials $p_1(x)$ and $p_2(x)$ of $F[x]$ such that

$$1 = p_1(x)f_1(x) + p_2(x)f_2(x). \tag{7.10}$$

We shall make use of this property in the proof of the following theorem:

THEOREM 7.5. If $p(x)$ is an irreducible polynomial over F and $p(x)$ divides $r(x) \cdot s(x)$, where $r(x)$ and $s(x)$ are elements of $F[x]$, then $p(x)$ divides either $r(x)$ or $s(x)$.

PROOF. Let us assume that $p(x)$ does not divide $r(x)$. Then $p(x)$ must be relatively prime to $r(x)$ because, if the GCD of $p(x)$ and $r(x)$ were $d(x)$, not an element of F, $p(x) = q(x)d(x)$ and $p(x)$ would be reducible.

Thus, we may apply (7.10) to obtain

$$1 = p_1(x)r(x) + p_2(x)p(x).$$

Now we multiply both sides by $s(x)$ to obtain

$$s(x) = p_1(x)r(x)s(x) + p_2(x)s(x)p(x).$$

Our hypothesis is that for some $q(x)$,

$$r(x) \cdot s(x) = q(x) \cdot p(x);$$

hence

$$s(x) = p_1(x)q(x)p(x) + p_2(x)s(x)p(x) = [p_1(x) \cdot q(x) + p_2(x) \cdot s(x)]p(x),$$

and so $p(x)$ divides $s(x)$.

THEOREM 7.6. Let $p(x)$ be a polynomial of degree >0 in $F[x]$. Then $p(x)$ may be expressed as a product

$$p(x) = ap_1(x)p_2(x)\cdots p_k(x),$$

where $p_i(x)$ are monic irreducible polynomials of $F[x]$ and a is an element of F. Except for the order, these factors are unique.

PROOF. We prove our theorem by induction on the degree of $p(x)$. If $p(x)$ is of degree 1, then

$$p(x) = ax + b = a(x + a^{-1}b).$$

The uniqueness of this expression is easily shown.

Now assume that $p(x)$ is of degree m. Our induction hypothesis is that every polynomial of degree $<m$ satisfies the theorem. If $p(x)$ is irreducible, we are through after factoring out the coefficient of the largest power of x as a. Otherwise $p(x)$ is reducible and is the product of two polynomials of lower degree; that is,

$$p(x) = q(x) \cdot q^*(x).$$

By induction

$$q(x) = a_1p_1(x)p_2(x)\cdots p_h(x),$$
$$q^*(x) = a_2p_{h+1}(x)\cdots p_k(x),$$

where a_1 and a_2 are contained in F and the $p_i(x)$ are monic irreducible polynomials. Thus,

$$p(x) = a_1a_2p_1(x)p_2(x)\cdots p_k(x),$$

and we have at least one factorization satisfying the conditions of our theorem.

The uniqueness of the factors remains to be shown. Let us assume that we have two factorizations of $p(x)$ into monic irreducible factors,

$$p(x) = ap_1(x)p_2(x) \cdots p_k(x),$$
$$p(x) = bq_1(x)q_2(x) \cdots q_r(x).$$

First, $a = b$ since each must be the coefficient of the highest power of x occurring in $p(x)$. We then have

$$p_1(x)p_2(x) \cdots p_k(x) = q_1(x)q_2(x) \cdots q_r(x). \tag{7.11}$$

From (7.11), we see that $p_1(x)$ divides $q_1(x)q_2(x) \cdots q_r(x)$, and from Theorem 7.5 we may argue that $p_1(x)$ must divide one of the $q_i(x)$. Actually, since both are monic they must be identical or $q_i(x)$ would be reducible. For convenience (renumbering if necessary) let $p_1(x) = q_1(x)$ so that

$$p_1(x)p_2(x) \cdots p_k(x) = p_1(x)q_2(x) \cdots q_r(x)$$

or

$$p_1(x)[p_2(x)p_3(x) \cdots p_k(x) - q_2(x)q_3(x) \cdots q_r(x)] = 0.$$

In the last expression $p_1(x) \neq 0$, and we may conclude that

$$p_2(x) \cdots p_k(x) = q_2(x) \cdots q_r(x).$$

We iterate the argument and, if $k < r$, we ultimately arrive at the situation

$$1 = q_{k+1}(x) \cdots q_r(x).$$

But then the factors $q_{k+1}(x), \ldots, q_r(x)$ must all be 1, and our proof is complete.

Exercise

Let $p(x)$ and $q(x)$ be polynomials of $F[x]$, where F is a proper subfield of C. Show that if $p(x)$ and $q(x)$ are relatively prime in $F[x]$, then they are relatively prime in $C[x]$.

7.5 Factorization of Polynomials in $C[x]$ and $R[x]$

In the previous sections we have been viewing $F[x]$ as a strictly algebraic object (that is, as a precisely defined set together with some algebraic structure). It is also possible, and indeed fruitful, to view elements of $F[x]$ as functions from F to F and to investigate the properties of these functions. We shall now adopt the latter approach in order to gain information about the factorization of polynomials in $C[x]$ and $R[x]$. In this section, as in the rest of this chapter, we shall confine our attention primarily to the fields R and C.

If

$$p(x) = a_0 + a_1x + \cdots + a_mx^m$$

is a particular polynomial, we define a mapping or function on the underlying field by

$$p(x): c \rightarrow a_0 + a_1c + a_2c^2 + \cdots + a_mc^m.$$

Thus the real polynomial $p(x) = 2 + 3x - x^2$ maps π to $2 + 3\pi - \pi^2$ and 1 to 4. Because of the obvious similarity, it is usual to write $p(c)$ for the value of this function at c. That is, we write

$$p(c) = a_0 + a_1c + \cdots + a_mc^m.$$

We shall also change the order of presenting a polynomial and write

$$p(x) = a_m x^m + \cdots + a_1 x + a_0$$

in the sequel.

For a fixed polynomial $p(x)$, considerable interest is attached to finding those elements c such that $p(c) = 0$. The standard terminology is to say that, when $p(c) = 0$, c is a *zero of* $p(x)$, *or a root of the equation* $p(x) = 0$.

Example 1. Let

$$p(x) = x^3 - 3x^2 + 4x - 2.$$

We find

$$\begin{aligned} p(1) &= 1^3 - 3 \cdot 1^2 + 4 \cdot 1 - 2 = 0, \\ p(1+i) &= (1+i)^3 - 3(1+i)^2 + 4(1+i) - 2, \\ &= 1 + 3i - 3 - i - 6i + 4 + 4i - 2 = 0, \\ p(1-i) &= (1-i)^3 - 3(1-i)^2 + 4(1-i) - 2 = 0. \end{aligned}$$

Thus 1, $1+i$, $1-i$ are zeros of the polynomial $p(x)$ or roots of the equation $x^3 - 3x^2 + 4x - 2 = 0$.

If the reader were unaware of irrational real numbers, it would seem logical to say that the equation $x^2 - 2 = 0$ has no roots. Likewise, if the real numbers were the extent of the reader's knowledge of fields, the polynomial $p(x) = x^2 + 3$ would appear to have no zeros. In each case, the zeros of the polynomials $p(x) = x^2 - 2$, $p(x) = x^2 + 3$, are in a larger field. A natural question is, "Are there polynomials of $C[x]$ that have no zeros in the complex number field C?" For example, if

$$p(x) = (\sqrt{3} + i)x^3 - (2 + i)x - [(7 - 2\sqrt{3}) + (2 - 9\sqrt{3})i], \tag{7.12}$$

does $p(x)$ have a zero in C? If not, can a larger field be constructed that contains C and in which $p(x)$ will have a zero? The latter question need not be considered; we do not have to go on constructing fields indefinitely. The polynomial of (7.12) does have the zero $(\sqrt{3} - i)$. It illustrates the following theorem:

THEOREM 7.7. *Let $p(x)$ be an arbitrary polynomial of degree ≥ 1 of $C[x]$. Then there exists an element c of C such that $p(c) = 0$.*

This theorem is often given the title "The Fundamental Theorem of Algebra." Although many proofs of this theorem are available, they involve concepts beyond the scope of this text. Therefore we shall assume its validity without proof. (The interested reader will find a proof of elementary nature in *The American Mathematical Monthly*, Volume 64 (1957), pages 582–585.)

If c is an arbitrary complex number, $p(x)$ a polynomial of $C[x]$, the division algorithm yields

$$p(x) = q(x)(x - c) + r,$$

where the remainder r is in C. We may determine r by setting $x = c$. Thus, $p(c) = q(c)(c - c) + r = r$. We substitute $r = p(c)$ in the equation above to obtain

$$p(x) = q(x)(x - c) + p(c). \tag{7.13}$$

The relation (7.13) is often called the remainder theorem. It yields the following information:

A polynomial $p(x)$ is divisible by $(x - c)$ if and only if c is a zero of $p(x)$.

We may use Theorem 7.7 and the observation above to determine the nature of irreducible polynomials of $C[x]$. First, the polynomials of degree 1 are certainly irreducible. Now, if $p(x)$ is a polynomial of degree >1, it has a zero in C from Theorem 7.7. Hence $p(x)$ is divisible by $(x - c)$ and $p(x)$ is not irreducible. Therefore the only irreducible polynomials of $C[x]$ are the linear polynomials $p(x) = ax + b$.

The factorization of a polynomial as a product of irreducible polynomials (Theorem 7.6) gives the following theorem for polynomials of $C[x]$:

THEOREM 7.8. *Let*

$$p(x) = a_m x^m + a_{m-1}x^{m-1} + \cdots + a_1 x + a_0$$

be a polynomial of degree m of $C[x]$. Then $p(x)$ has the unique factorization (except for order of factors)

$$p(x) = a_m(x - c_1)(x - c_2)\cdots(x - c_m),$$

where $c_1, c_2, \ldots, c_m$ are zeros of $p(x)$.

COROLLARY. *A polynomial of degree m has at most m zeros.*

PROOF. The corollary is verified by observing that, if $c \neq c_1, c_2, \ldots, c_m$, $p(c) = a_m(c - c_1)(c - c_2)\cdots(c - c_m)$ is the product of nonzero elements and $p(c) \neq 0$.

An alternative proof of Theorem 7.8 can be given directly by the use of Theorem 7.7, the remark following (7.13), and induction. Thus, let $p(x)$ be an arbitrary polynomial. Since $p(x) = 0$ for some c, we know that $p(x)$ is divisible by $(x - c)$. Hence $p(x) = q(x)(x - c)$. Now use induction on $q(x)$.

Example 2. If we again let

$$p(x) = x^3 - 3x^2 + 4x - 2$$

as in Example 1, we have already determined the zeros of $p(x)$ so that

$$x^3 - 3x^2 + 4x - 2 = (x - 1)[x - (1 + i)][x - (1 - i)].$$

A straightforward multiplication will verify this relation.

Let us now determine the factorization of a polynomial of $R[x]$ into its irreducible factors The student may recall that if a complex number $a + bi$ is a zero of a polynomial with real coefficients, then the conjugate complex number $a - bi$ is also a zero of $p(x)$. We will demonstrate the validity of this statement in terms of concepts that we have developed. We note that the mapping $a + bi \xrightarrow{T} a - bi$ is a one-to-one mapping of the complex field C onto itself. Under this mapping, a real number maps upon itself. Now, if

$$a + bi \xrightarrow{T} a - bi, \qquad c + di \xrightarrow{T} c - di,$$

then

$$\begin{aligned}(a + bi) + (c + di) &= (a + c) + (b + d)i \xrightarrow{T} (a + c) - (b + d)i \\ &= (a - bi) + (c - di), \\ (a + bi)(c + di) &= (ac - bd) + (ad + bc)i \xrightarrow{T} (ac - bd) - (ad + bc)i \\ &= (a - bi)(c - di).\end{aligned}$$

Hence, we have a mapping of C onto itself that preserves sums and products. Any algebraic theorem involving sums and products will be true if, throughout, a complex number is replaced by its conjugate. Thus, the algebraic statement that $p(a + bi) = 0$ implies that $p(a - bi) = 0$, if all coefficients of $p(x)$ are real so that they map upon themselves. Briefly, the mapping

$$a + bi \xrightarrow{T} a - bi$$

is an isomorphism of the complex field C with itself under which the real numbers are mapped upon themselves identically.

Let us consider a polynomial $p(x)$ of $R[x]$ as an element of $C[x]$ and obtain from Theorem 7.8 the factorization

$$p(x) = a_m(x - c_1)(x - c_2) \cdots (x - c_m)$$

in $C[x]$. Unfortunately, if c_i is a complex number and not a real number, the linear factor $(x - c_i)$ is not in $R[x]$. However, we know that the conjugate of c_i is also a root. For convenience, let us assume that $c_1 = a + bi$; $c_2 = a - bi$, where, of course, a and $b \neq 0$ are in R. We consider the product of the linear factors

$$[x - (a + bi)][x - (a - bi)] = x^2 - 2ax + a^2 + b^2.$$

Certainly $x^2 - 2ax + a^2 + b^2$ is in $R[x]$ and, since its zeros are $a + bi$ and $a - bi$, irreducible over R. (Otherwise it would have a linear factor in $R[x]$ and consequently a real zero.) By the division algorithm, we may write

$$p(x) = q(x)(x^2 - 2ax + a^2 + b^2) + (dx + f), \tag{7.14}$$

where $q(x) \in R[x]$ and $d, f \in R$. Replacing x by $a + bi$ and $a - bi$ in (7.14), we obtain

$$\begin{aligned} d(a + bi) + f &= 0, \\ d(a - bi) + f &= 0. \end{aligned}$$

By subtracting the second of these equations from the first we get $2dbi = 0$ and, since $b \neq 0$, $d = 0$. Then $f = 0$ and (7.14) becomes

$$p(x) = q(x)(x^2 - 2ax + a^2 + b^2),$$

with $q(x) \in R[x]$. We complete the proof of the following theorem by mathematical induction.

THEOREM 7.9. *Let*

$$p(x) = a_m x^m + a_{m-1}x^{m-1} + \cdots + a_1 x + a_0$$

be a polynomial of $R[x]$ of degree m. Then, over R, $p(x)$ may be factored uniquely (except for order of factors) into irreducible factors:

$$p(x) = a_m(x^2 + r_1 x + s_1) \cdots (x^2 + r_k x + s_k)(x - c_{2k+1}) \cdots (x - c_m),$$

where $x^2 + r_i x + s_i \in R[x]$ and $c_{2k+1}, \ldots, c_m$ are real.

This theorem states that the only irreducible polynomials of $R[x]$ are either linear or quadratic.

Example 3. For the polynomial

$$p(x) = x^3 - 3x^2 + 4x - 2$$

of Example 1, the irreducible factorization over R would be

$$x^3 - 3x^2 + 4x - 2 = (x - 1)(x^2 - 2x + 2).$$

In the factorization of a polynomial given in Theorem 7.8,

$$p(x) = a_m(x - c_1)(x - c_2)\cdots(x - c_m),$$

the c_i may not be distinct. Let $c_1, c_2, \ldots, c_k$ be the distinct zeros. Then,

$$p(x) = a_m(x - c_1)^{p_1}(x - c_2)^{p_2}\cdots(x - c_k)^{p_k},$$

where p_i is the number of times that the zero c_i is repeated. The p_i are integers ≥ 1, and

$$p_1 + p_2 + \cdots + p_k = m.$$

A zero c_i with $p_i > 1$ is called a *multiple zero* (or multiple root) of $p(x)$, and p_i is the *multiplicity*. A zero with multiplicity 1 is called a *simple zero*. We see that if a zero is counted according to its multiplicity, a polynomial of degree m has exactly m zeros in the complex field C.

Example 4. Let

$$p(x) = (x - 2)^3(x - 1)^2(x + i)(x - i).$$

Then 2 is a zero of multiplicity 3; 1 is a zero of multiplicity 2; i and $-i$ are simple zeros. Counting according to multiplicities, $p(x)$ has 7 zeros of which 4 are distinct.

Exercises

1. Give an alternative proof of Theorem 7.8 following the sketch of the text. Furnish complete details.
2. If $2 - 3i$, $2 + 3i$, 1, 5, $1 - i$, and $1 + i$ are the zeros of a polynomial $p(x)$ of degree 6 of $C[x]$, what are the irreducible factors of $p(x)$ in $C[x]$ and in $R[x]$?
3. Prove that a polynomial $p(x)$ of $R[x]$ is divisible by the square of a polynomial $g(x)$ of $R[x]$ if and only if $p(x)$ has multiple zeros. The multiple zeros need not be real.
4. Prove that, if $a_0 \neq 0$ in

$$p(x) = a_m x^m + a_{m-1}x^{m-1} + \cdots + a_1 x + a_0,$$

then

$$q(x) = a_0 x^m + a_1 x^{m-1} + \cdots + a_{m-1}x + a_m$$

is a polynomial whose zeros are the reciprocals of those of $p(x)$; that is, if $p(c) = 0$, then $q(1/c) = 0$.
5. Prove that, if $p(x)$ is as in Exercise 4, the product of the zeros of $p(x)$ is $(-1)^m a_0/a_m$ and the sum of the zeros is $-a_1/a_m$.

7.6 The Practical Determination of Roots of Algebraic Equations

The previous section provides us with no practical way of determining the roots of an arbitrary algebraic equation

$$p(x) = a_m x^m + a_{m-1}x^{m-1} + \cdots + a_1 x + a_0 = 0.$$

We may reduce the problem to that of a polynomial with simple zeros by means of the following theorem:

THEOREM 7.10. *Let $p(x)$ have a zero c of multiplicity $r > 1$. Then the derivative $p'(x)$ has c as a zero of multiplicity $r - 1$. A simple zero of $p(x)$ is not a zero of $p'(x)$.*

PROOF. Let $p(x) = q(x)(x - c)^r$, where $q(c) \neq 0$. We know that $(x - c)$ does not divide $q(x)$ or c would be a zero of multiplicity $> r$. Now take the derivative of $p(x)$, thus

$$\begin{aligned} p'(x) &= rq(x)(x - c)^{r-1} + q'(x)(x - c)^r \\ &= [rq(x) + q'(x)(x - c)](x - c)^{r-1}. \end{aligned}$$

Since

$$rq(c) + q'(c)(c - c) = rq(c) \neq 0,$$

we see that c is a zero of multiplicity $r - 1$ of $p'(x)$ when $r > 1$ and c is not a zero of $p'(x)$ when c is a simple zero of $p(x)$.

COROLLARY. *Let $d(x)$ be a* GCD *of $p(x)$ and $p'(x)$. Then $p(x)/d(x)$ has only simple zeros and these zeros are the distinct zeros of $p(x)$.*

PROOF. Let the factored form of $p(x)$ in $C[x]$ be

$$p(x) = a_m(x - c_1)^{p_1}(x - c_2)^{p_2} \cdots (x - c_k)^{p_k}(x - c_{k+1}) \cdots (x - c_t),$$

where $p_i > 1$ and $c_1, c_2, \ldots, c_k$ are multiple zeros of $p(x)$. A zero c_i (for $i = 1, 2, \ldots, k$) is a zero of multiplicity $p_i - 1$ of $p'(x)$, and the zero c_j (for $j = k + 1, \ldots, t$) is not a zero of $p'(x)$. Thus,

$$p'(x) = q(x)(x - c_1)^{p_1 - 1}(x - c_2)^{p_2 - 1} \cdots (x - c_k)^{p_k - 1},$$

where $q(c_i) \neq 0$ for $i = 1, 2, \ldots, t$. It is easy to see that a GCD of $p(x)$ and $p'(x)$ is

$$d(x) = (x - c_1)^{p_1 - 1}(x - c_2)^{p_2 - 1} \cdots (x - c_k)^{p_k - 1}.$$

Therefore,

$$p(x)/d(x) = a_m(x - c_1)(x - c_2) \cdots (x - c_t).$$

Example 1. Let

$$p(x) = (x - 1)^3(x^2 + 1) = x^5 - 3x^4 + 4x^3 - 4x^2 + 3x - 1,$$

so that 1 is a zero of multiplicity 3 and i, $-i$ are simple zeros of $p(x)$. Now,

$$p'(x) = 5x^4 - 12x^3 + 12x^2 - 8x + 3$$

and $p'(i) = -4 + 4i$, $p'(-i) = -4 - 4i$, so that the simple zeros of $p(x)$ are not zeros of $p'(x)$.

Next we note that $p'(1) = 0$ and that $p'(x)$ is divisible by $(x - 1)$. We compute

$$p'(x) = (5x^3 - 7x^2 + 5x - 3)(x - 1).$$

For $q(x) = 5x^3 - 7x^2 + 5x - 3$, we have $q(1) = 0$ or

$$q(x) = (5x^2 - 2x + 3)(x - 1),$$

and $5 \cdot 1^2 - 2 \cdot 1 + 3 = 6 \neq 0$. Thus,

$$p'(x) = (5x^2 - 2x + 3)(x - 1)^2,$$

and 1 is a zero of multiplicity 2 for $p'(x)$. Moreover, the GCD of $p(x)$ and $p'(x)$ is $(x - 1)^2$ so that

$$p(x)/d(x) = (x - 1)(x^2 + 1) = x^3 - x^2 + x - 1$$

has only simple zeros.

Actually, the removal of multiple zeros from a polynomial may be done without prior knowledge of its zeros. We have merely to find the GCD of $p(x)$ and $p'(x)$ and divide this into $p(x)$ to obtain the required quotient. The process of finding the GCD by Euclid's algorithm involves no knowledge of the zeros.

Example 2. Let us assume that we are given the polynomial of Example 1 in its unfactored form. Then

$$\begin{aligned} p(x) &= x^5 - 3x^4 + 4x^3 - 4x^2 + 3x - 1, \\ p'(x) &= 5x^4 - 12x^3 + 12x^2 - 8x + 3, \end{aligned}$$

and we have as the first step in Euclid's algorithm

$$\begin{aligned} &(x^5 - 3x^4 + 4x^3 - 4x^2 + 3x - 1) \\ &\quad = (\tfrac{1}{5}x - \tfrac{3}{25})(5x^4 - 12x^3 + 12x^2 - 8x + 3) + \tfrac{4}{25}(x^3 - 6x^2 + 9x - 4). \end{aligned}$$

Certainly the constant $\frac{4}{25}$ is not going to change the GCD, and it may be ignored in the next division,

$$\begin{aligned} &(5x^4 - 12x^3 + 12x^2 - 8x + 3) \\ &\quad = (5x + 18)(x^3 - 6x^2 + 9x - 4) + 75(x^2 - 2x + 1). \end{aligned}$$

Again the constant 75 may be ignored, so that

$$(x^3 - 6x^2 + 9x - 4) = (x - 4)(x^2 - 2x + 1).$$

The last nonzero remainder is $(x^2 - 2x + 1)$ and this is the GCD of $p(x)$ and $p'(x)$. Now,

$$p(x)/d(x) = x^3 - x^2 + x - 1,$$

and this agrees with the result of Example 1, but this time we used no prior knowledge of the zeros of $p(x)$.

We have reduced the problem of finding the roots of $p(x) = 0$ to that of finding the roots of an equation having simple roots, but our problem is far from solved.

The student is probably familiar with the formula

$$r = \frac{-b \pm \sqrt{b^2 - 4ac}}{2a},$$

which provides the answer to the problem of solving the equation

$$ax^2 + bx + c = 0,$$

where a, b, and c are real. The extension of the result to complex coefficients is in the exercises. Now, we might hope that similar formulas exist for equations of all degrees.

The roots of the equations

$$\begin{aligned} ax^3 + bx^2 + cx + d &= 0, \\ ax^4 + bx^3 + cx^2 + dx + e &= 0, \end{aligned}$$

may be given by formulas involving radicals and the coefficients. Unfortunately, however, it can be shown that beyond the fourth degree such formulas are impossible. A proof of this fact is an important result of the theory of fields. There have been attempts to provide elementary proofs for this result, but they are quite long and require extensive preparation.

The more elegant proofs are much more satisfying. They are, however, beyond the scope of this book and we therefore content ourselves with the bare statement of the facts.

Assuming that there is no algebraic formula involving the coefficients that gives the roots of equations of degree larger than 4, how do we find the roots?

Quite frankly, except for special polynomials, there is no other way than to approximate the root as closely as possible. Normally, we would obtain upper and lower bounds for the real roots and then apply various methods to determine intervals on the real axis containing these roots. Then Newton's method, Horner's method, or other methods may be used to approximate the root. With high-speed computers many refinements of these methods are available. These are discussed in texts in numerical analysis.

For our purposes, it will be desirable to establish for the student a method of determining whether a polynomial has integral or rational zeros. Exercises in later chapters will require a determination of zeros of special polynomials, and the following theorem will prove valuable:

THEOREM 7.11. *Let*

$$p(x) = a_m x^m + a_{m-1}x^{m-1} + \cdots + a_1 x + a_0$$

be a polynomial whose coefficients are integers. A rational zero of $p(x)$ *must have the form* s/t, *where* s *is an integer that divides* a_0 *and* t *is an integer that divides* a_m.

COROLLARY. *Rational zeros of a monic polynomial* $p(x) = x^m + \cdots + a_0$ *with integral coefficients must be integers which divide* a_0.

Proof of Theorem 7.11. Let the zero $r = s/t$ of $p(x)$ be reduced to lowest terms. Thus, s and t have no common divisors except ± 1. Then,

$$0 = t^m p(s/t) = a_m s^m + a_{m-1}s^{m-1}t + \cdots + a_1 s t^{m-1} + a_0 t^m.$$

Now

$$-a_m s^m = (a_{m-1}s^{m-1} + \cdots + a_1 s t^{m-2} + a_0 t^{m-1})t,$$

and t divides $-a_m s^m$.

We now use a theorem for integers analogous to Theorem 7.5 and, since s^m and t have no common divisors except ± 1, t divides a_m.

In a similar manner it can be shown that s divides a_0.

The corollary is the special case $a_m = 1$.

Example 3. Let

$$p(x) = 6x^3 - 2x^2 + 3x + 4.$$

The possible rational zeros s/t must have $s = \pm 1, \pm 2, \pm 4$ and $t = \pm 1, \pm 2, \pm 3, \pm 6$. The distinct possible values are

$$s/t = \pm 1, \pm\tfrac{1}{2}, \pm\tfrac{1}{3}, \pm\tfrac{1}{6}, \pm 2, \pm\tfrac{2}{3}, \pm 4, \pm\tfrac{4}{3}.$$

For all these sixteen values $p(s/t) \neq 0$; hence $p(x)$ has no rational zeros.

Exercises

1. Determine a polynomial having as simple zeros the distinct zeros of

$$p(x) = 4x^4 + 8x^3 + 9x^2 + 5x + 1.$$

2. Solve the equation $z^2 = a + bi$ by setting $z = x + iy$ and equating coefficients to obtain

$$x^2 - y^2 = a,$$
$$2xy = b.$$

3. Solve

$$(2 + i)x^2 + 3x + (-5 + 7i) = 0$$

by the quadratic formula and a *correct* application of Exercise 2.

4. Find all rational roots of the following equations. Where possible, solve completely.
   (a) $x^3 - 2x^2 + 3x - 6 = 0$,
   (b) $2x^3 - 9x^2 + 12x - 5 = 0$,
   (c) $2x^3 + 3x^2 + 9x + 4 = 0$,
   (d) $x^4 + 4x^2 - 8x + 12 = 0$,
   (e) $x^4 + 2x^2 + 1 = 0$.

5. If $p(x) = a_m x^m + a_{m-1}x^{m-1} + \cdots + a_0$, show that

$$q(x) = a_m x^m - a_{m-1}x^{m-1} + a_{m-2}x^{m-2} + \cdots + (-1)^m a_0$$

has zeros that are the negatives of the zeros of $p(x)$.

6. Show that the equation

$$p(x) = a_m x^m + a_{m-1}x^{m-1} + \cdots + a_0 = 0,$$

with integral coefficients has no integral roots if $p(0)$ and $p(1)$ are both odd integers.

7. Show that the equation $x^m - 1 = 0$ has no multiple roots.

Characteristic Values and Vectors of Linear Transformations

We now return to the consideration of linear transformations and their matrices. In the present chapter we study the concepts of characteristic values and vectors and use these ideas to achieve a simplification of matrices under similarity and under an orthonormal change of basis. In this chapter, as in the next one, we shall consider only transformations from a space V to the same space; correspondingly, the matrices to be considered will be square.

8.1 Characteristic Values and Vectors

The length of a vector $\mathbf{X}$ of R^n has been defined as $(\mathbf{X}, \mathbf{X})^{1/2}$; the direction of $\mathbf{X}$ may be specified by the cosines of the angles between $\mathbf{X}$ and the basis vectors $\mathbf{E}_1, \mathbf{E}_2, \ldots, \mathbf{E}_n$. (These cosines are called direction cosines in analytic geometry.) If T is a linear transformation, T$\mathbf{X}$ normally differs from $\mathbf{X}$ both in length and direction. For some vectors, however, T may act in such a way that the direction remains fixed: T$\mathbf{X} = \lambda\mathbf{X}$ for some scalar λ. (If $\lambda < 0$ the direction is actually reversed and if $\lambda = 0$ any sense of direction is annihilated, but we include these cases since they fit our algebraic purposes, as will soon be evident.)

Such vectors are easily seen to be important. Suppose we can accumulate enough of them to form a basis: $R^n = L\{\mathbf{X}_1, \mathbf{X}_2, \ldots, \mathbf{X}_n\}$, T$\mathbf{X}_i = \lambda_i\mathbf{X}_i$. Then, if $\mathbf{Y}$ is any vector of R^n,

$$\begin{aligned} \mathbf{Y} &= a_1\mathbf{X}_1 + a_2\mathbf{X}_2 + \cdots + a_n\mathbf{X}_n, \\ \mathrm{T}\mathbf{Y} &= a_1 T\mathbf{X}_1 + a_2 T\mathbf{X}_2 + \cdots + a_n T\mathbf{X}_n \\ &= a_1\lambda_1\mathbf{X}_1 + a_2\lambda_2\mathbf{X}_2 + \cdots + a_n\lambda_n\mathbf{X}_n. \end{aligned}$$

The matrix of T with respect to the $\{\mathbf{X}_i\}$ basis, then, is simply Diagonal $[\lambda_1, \lambda_2, \ldots, \lambda_n]$. Clearly one of our basic questions will be to find out under what circumstances such a basis exists and how we can find one in this case.

DEFINITION 8.1. Let T *be a linear transformation on a real vector space* V. *A real number* λ *is a* CHARACTERISTIC VALUE *of the linear transformation if*

$$\mathbf{TX} = \lambda\mathbf{X} \tag{8.1}$$

for some nonzero vector $\mathbf{X} \in V$. *A nonzero vector satisfying* (8.1) *is called a* CHARACTERISTIC VECTOR *of* T (*belonging to the characteristic value* λ).

The names characteristic vector and characteristic value are standard in American mathematical terminology. Other adjectives occasionally replace "characteristic." In British usage we frequently find "latent" while "proper" is used in both British and American literature. A peculiar half-translation is very common, giving the terms *eigenvector* and *eigenvalue* (from the German words for characteristic vector and characteristic value, Eigenvektor and Eigenwert). These latter terms have the advantage of being shorter than "characteristic" and are extensively used colloquially.

Example 1. Let T be the linear transformation that multiplies every vector of R^n by 2. Every nonzero vector of R^n is a characteristic vector and 2 is the only characteristic value.

Example 2. In R^3 define T by

$$T[x_1, x_2, x_3] = [x_1, 2x_2, 2x_3].$$

Any nonzero vector of the form $[x_1, 0, 0]$ is left unchanged by T so such vectors are characteristic vectors belonging to the characteristic value 1. Any nonzero vector of the form $[0, x_2, x_3]$ is doubled by T and thus is a characteristic vector belonging to the characteristic value 2. $\{\mathbf{E}_1, \mathbf{E}_2, \mathbf{E}_3\}$ is a basis of characteristic vectors.

Example 3. In R^2 define T by

$$\mathrm{T}[x_1, x_2] = [-x_2, x_1].$$

T is orthogonal, i.e., the length of the transformed vector is the same as the length of the original vector. However *all* nonzero vectors have their directions changed by T. T is, in fact, a rotation through $\pi/2$. In the notation of Section 3.1, $\mathrm{T} = \mathrm{T}_{\pi/2}$. There are *no* characteristic vectors of T.

Example 4. In R^3 define T by

$$\mathrm{T}[x_1, x_2, x_3] = [-x_2 - 3x_3, 2x_1 + 3x_2 + 3x_3, -2x_1 + x_2 + x_3].$$

We note

$$\begin{aligned} \mathrm{T}[a, -a, -a] &= 4[a, -a, -a], \\ \mathrm{T}[a, a, -a] &= 2[a, a, -a], \\ \mathrm{T}[a, -a, a] &= -2[a, -a, a]. \end{aligned}$$

Thus all nonzero vectors $[a, -a, -a]$, $[a, a, -a]$, $[a, -a, a]$ are characteristic vectors with associated characteristic values 4, 2, -2. The basis

$$\{[1, -1, -1], [1, 1, -1], [1, -1, 1]\}$$

consists of characteristic vectors.

In each of these examples, we see that the addition of $\mathbf{0}$ to the set of characteristic vectors belonging to a particular characteristic value yields a subspace. We shall prove a somewhat more general theorem.

THEOREM 8.1. Let V be a real vector space and T *a linear transformation on V. The set M_λ of all vectors* **X** *such that* $\mathrm{T}\mathbf{X} = \lambda\mathbf{X}$, *for a real number* λ, *forms a subspace of V. Moreover* $M_\lambda \cap M_\mu = \{\mathbf{0}\}$ *if* $\lambda \neq \mu$.

PROOF. Since $\mathrm{T}\mathbf{0} = \mathbf{0} = \lambda\mathbf{0}$ for all $\lambda \in R$, $\mathbf{0} \in M_\lambda$. If λ is not a characteristic value there are no nonzero vectors in M_λ, so that $M_\lambda = \{\mathbf{0}\}$.

If λ is a characteristic value and

$$\mathrm{T}\mathbf{X} = \lambda\mathbf{X}, \qquad \mathrm{T}\mathbf{Y} = \lambda\mathbf{Y};$$

$$\mathrm{T}(a\mathbf{X} + b\mathbf{Y}) = a\mathrm{T}\mathbf{X} + b\mathrm{T}\mathbf{Y} = a\lambda\mathbf{X} + b\lambda\mathbf{Y} = \lambda(a\mathbf{X} + b\mathbf{Y}).$$

Thus, $a\mathbf{X} + b\mathbf{Y}$ is in M_λ and M_λ is a subspace.

Finally, if $\mathbf{X} \in M_\lambda$, $\mathbf{X} \in M_\mu$,

$$\mathrm{T}\mathbf{X} = \lambda\mathbf{X} = \mu\mathbf{X};$$
$$(\lambda - \mu)\mathbf{X} = \mathbf{0}.$$

Thus either $\lambda = \mu$ or $\mathbf{X} = \mathbf{0}$.

The deliberate exclusion of **0** as a characteristic vector often causes extra verbiage in statements and proofs. The exclusion nevertheless seems to be the best of a bad bargain. If **0** were admitted as a characteristic vector more trouble would arise than is caused by excluding it. For example, if **0** were allowed, all numbers would be characteristic values, since, if $\lambda \in R$, $T\mathbf{0} = \lambda\mathbf{0}$, as we have already remarked.

The real number 0 was *not* excluded as a characteristic value. The kernel of T is the union of $\{\mathbf{0}\}$ and the set of vectors that are characteristic vectors belonging to 0.

Example 3 illustrates that a linear transformation may have no characteristic values as defined. This feature is closely related to the fact that a real polynomial equation may have no real roots.

In Examples 1 and 2, the answers are reasonably evident from the specification of T. In Example 3 and, more particularly, Example 4, it is not at all clear how the results are obtained. Let us examine the problem more closely. We begin with Example 3 and assume we do *not* immediately recognize T as $\mathrm{T}_{\pi/2}$ but seek a characteristic vector from first principles. We want a real number λ such that $\mathrm{T}\mathbf{X} = \lambda\mathbf{X}$, or

$$\mathrm{T}[x_1, x_2] = [\lambda x_1, \lambda_2] = [x_2, -x_1].$$

Thus

$$[\lambda x_1, \lambda x_2] = [x_2, -x_1], \quad \text{or} \quad \lambda x_1 = x_2,\ \lambda x_2 = -x_1.$$

This is a system of two homogeneous equations and will have a solution different from $[x_1, x_2] = [0, 0]$ if the determinant of the coefficients is 0. The determinant is $\lambda^2 + 1$. Thus T has no real characteristic value.

Let us look at Example 4 in the same way.

$$\mathrm{T}[x_1, x_2, x_3] = [\lambda x_1, \lambda x_2, \lambda x_3],$$

or

$$[-x_2 - 3x_3, 2x_1 + 3x_2 + 3x_3, -2x_1 + x_2 + x_3] = [\lambda x_1, \lambda x_2, \lambda x_3],$$

$$[-\lambda x_1 - x_2 - 3x_3, 2x_1 + (3 - \lambda)x_2 + 3x_3, -2x_1 + x_2 + (1 - \lambda)x_3] = [0, 0, 0],$$

$$\begin{aligned} -\lambda x_1 - x_2 - 3x_3 &= 0, \\ 2x_1 + (3 - \lambda)x_2 + 3x_3 &= 0, \\ -2x_1 + x_2 + (1 - \lambda)x_3 &= 0. \end{aligned}$$

This system of three homogeneous equations will have solutions different from zero if the following determinant is zero:

$$\begin{vmatrix} -\lambda & -1 & -3 \\ 2 & 3-\lambda & 3 \\ -2 & 1 & 1-\lambda \end{vmatrix}.$$

Evaluating the determinant:

$$-\lambda^3 + 4\lambda^2 + 4\lambda - 16 = 0,$$
$$-(\lambda - 4)(\lambda - 2)(\lambda + 2) = 0.$$

We find characteristic vectors if and only if λ has one of the characteristic values 4, 2, or -2. For example, for $\lambda = 4$, the equations become

$$\begin{aligned} -4x_1 - x_2 - 3x_3 &= 0, \\ 2x_1 - x_2 + 3x_3 &= 0, \\ -2x_1 + x_2 - 3x_3 &= 0. \end{aligned}$$

The first and second equations give the values $x_1 = -x_2 = -x_3$ so that $[a, -a, -a]$ is a characteristic vector belonging to 4. Similar results follow for other characteristic values.

Exercises

1. For the linear transformations T defined by the following equations, find the characteristic values and vectors of T.
   (a) $T[x_1, x_2] = [x_1, x_2]$,
   (b) $T[x_1, x_2] = [x_1, 2x_1 - 3x_2]$,
   (c) $T[x_1, x_2, x_3] = [x_2 - x_1, x_3 - x_2, x_1 - x_3]$,
   (d) $T[x_1, x_2, x_3] = [x_1, -2x_1 - x_2, x_1 + 3x_2 + 2x_3]$.
2. Let T be the transformation on R^2 defined by letting $T\mathbf{X}$ be the orthogonal projection of $\mathbf{X}$ on the line $x = y$ (see Exercise 8, Section 2.9). What are the characteristic values and vectors of T?
3. T_θ is the rotation of R^2 by an angle θ. For which values of θ will T_θ have characteristic values?
4. (a) What are the subspaces M_λ for the transformation T in Exercise 1(d)?
   (b) Is it possible to find a basis $\{\mathbf{X}_1, \mathbf{X}_2, \mathbf{X}_3\}$ for R^3, with respect to which the matrix of T is diagonal?
5. If λ is a characteristic value of T, show that λ^2 is a characteristic value of T^2.
6. Let T be the 45° shear on R^2 defined in Section 3.1:

$$T[x_1, x_2] = [x_1 + x_2, x_2].$$

   What are the characteristic values of T?
7. If D is the differentiation operator on the space, P^n, of polynomials of degree at most $n - 1$, what are the characteristic values and vectors of D?

8.2 Characteristic Values of Matrices

In this section we shall give definitions of characteristic vectors and characteristic values of an arbitrary square matrix when no particular transformation is preassigned. The resulting theory will also yield information about linear transformations.

Given an arbitrary square matrix A, one is tempted simply to consider the linear transformation T defined by $\mathbf{TX} = A\mathbf{X}$ and then define the characteristic values and vectors of A to be those of T. This method is equivalent to the definition we present, but we seek a purely algebraic formulation. Let us consider an example. If A is the matrix

$$\begin{bmatrix} 0 & -1 & -3 \\ 2 & 3 & 3 \\ -2 & 1 & 1 \end{bmatrix},$$

then, as we saw in Example 4 of the previous section, the characteristic values of the associated linear transformation T are just the roots of the equation

$$\det(A - \lambda I) = \begin{vmatrix} -\lambda & -1 & -3 \\ 2 & 3-\lambda & 3 \\ -2 & 1 & 1-\lambda \end{vmatrix} = -(\lambda - 4)(\lambda - 2)(\lambda + 2) = 0.$$

It should be clear that the method of this example is completely general. That is, if A is a square matrix, T the linear transformation associated with A with respect to the standard basis, then the characteristic values of T are the roots of the polynomial $p(\lambda) = \det(A - \lambda I)$.

There are minor technical difficulties in this procedure since we have defined determinants only for matrices with elements in a field F. The determinant, then, was also an element of F.

One way around this difficulty is to extend our considerations to the field of "rational functions," the quotients of polynomials of $F[x]$. (This field is constructed from $F[x]$ in the same manner as the rational numbers are constructed from the integers.) In this new field $F(\lambda)$, the determinants we consider will have values in $F[\lambda]$ as all "denominators" in our determinants will be 1. A simpler way around the difficulty is to observe that the definition of the determinant function makes perfectly good sense for a matrix over any commutative ring with identity.

A more troublesome difficulty is that the roots of $\det(A - \lambda I) = 0$ may not lie in the original field. As an example, take A to be the matrix of Example 3 of the previous section:

$$A = \begin{bmatrix} 0 & 1 \\ -1 & 0 \end{bmatrix}, \quad A - \lambda I = \begin{bmatrix} -\lambda & 1 \\ -1 & -\lambda \end{bmatrix}.$$

Then $\det(A - \lambda I) = \lambda^2 + 1 = 0$ has no roots in the real field. We overcome this difficulty in the sequel by assuming that A has values in a subfield F of C, the complex numbers, and then we allow the complex roots of $\det(A - \lambda I) = 0$ to be characteristic values. Without further ado we give the definition.

DEFINITION 8.2. *If A is an $n \times n$ matrix with elements in a field $F \subseteq C$, the polynomial $p(\lambda) = \det(A - \lambda I)$ is called the* CHARACTERISTIC POLYNOMIAL *of A. The roots of $p(\lambda) = 0$ are called the* CHARACTERISTIC VALUES *of A. For any such value λ, the vectors $\mathbf{X}$ in C^n such that $(A - \lambda I)\mathbf{X} = 0$ are called* CHARACTERISTIC VECTORS *of A.*

Example 1. If $A = \begin{bmatrix} 0 & 1 \\ -1 & 0 \end{bmatrix}$, the characteristic polynomial of A is $\lambda^2 + 1$. The characteristic values of A are i and $-i$. Characteristic vectors are: for i, $[\alpha, i\alpha]$; for $-i$, $[\alpha, -i\alpha]$, where α is any nonzero complex scalar.

Example 2. Take A to be the matrix

$$\begin{bmatrix} 1 & 2 & 1 \\ 2 & 0 & -2 \\ -1 & 2 & 3 \end{bmatrix}.$$

Then $\det(A - \lambda I) = -\lambda(\lambda - 2)^2$, the characteristic polynomial of A. The characteristic values are 0 and 2. The characteristic vectors of A corresponding to 0 are the nonzero vectors satisfying

$$A\mathbf{X} = \mathbf{0} \quad \text{or} \quad \begin{aligned} x_1 + 2x_2 + x_3 &= 0, \\ 2x_1 \qquad\quad - 2x_3 &= 0, \\ -x_1 + 2x_2 + 3x_3 &= 0. \end{aligned}$$

Solving the linear system, we obtain $X = [a, -a, a]$. Similarly, the vectors corresponding to 2 may be found to be vectors of the form $[a, 0, a]$.

We conclude this section with an investigation of the relationship of characteristic polynomials, values, and vectors of similar matrices, that is, of matrices corresponding to the same linear transformation.

THEOREM 8.2. If $B = P^{-1}AP$ is an $n \times n$ matrix and P is any $n \times n$ nonsingular matrix, then

(i) *A and B have the same characteristic polynomial.*
(ii) *A and B have the same characteristic values.*
(iii) *If X is a characteristic vector of A, $P^{-1}X$ is a characteristic vector of B corresponding to the same characteristic value.*

PROOF. For (i) and (ii),

$$\begin{aligned} \det(B - \lambda I) &= \det(P^{-1}AP - \lambda I) \\ &= \det(P^{-1}AP - \lambda P^{-1}IP) \\ &= \det(P^{-1}(A - \lambda I)P) \\ &= \det(P^{-1}) \det(A - \lambda I) \det(P) \\ &= \det(A - \lambda I). \end{aligned}$$

The last line results from the fact that $\det(P^{-1}) \det(P) = \det(P^{-1}P) = \det(I) = 1$. Therefore the characteristic polynomials of A and B are the same, and consequently they have the same zeros.

For (iii) we have $A\mathbf{X} = \lambda\mathbf{X}$; then

$$\begin{aligned} BP^{-1}\mathbf{X} = (P^{-1}AP)P^{-1}\mathbf{X} = P^{-1}A(PP^{-1})\mathbf{X} &= P^{-1}A\mathbf{X} \\ &= P^{-1}(\lambda\mathbf{X}) \\ &= \lambda P^{-1}\mathbf{X}. \end{aligned}$$

This completes the proof.

The result of Theorem 8.2 allows us to extend the idea of the characteristic polynomial to linear transformations. We see that all matrices representing a given linear transformation T have the same characteristic polynomial. We say, then, that this polynomial is the characteristic polynomial of T.

Example 3. If D is differentiation on the space P^3 of real quadratic polynomials, we choose the basis $\{x^2, 2x, 2\}$; the matrix of D is

$$A = \begin{bmatrix} 0 & 0 & 0 \\ 1 & 0 & 0 \\ 0 & 1 & 0 \end{bmatrix}.$$

The characteristic polynomial of D is then

$$\det(A - \lambda I) = \begin{vmatrix} -\lambda & 0 & 0 \\ 1 & -\lambda & 0 \\ 0 & 1 & -\lambda \end{vmatrix} = -\lambda^3.$$

Exercises

1. Find the characteristic polynomial, values, and vectors of

$$\begin{bmatrix} 0 & 0 & 0 \\ 2 & 0 & 0 \\ 0 & 1 & 0 \end{bmatrix}.$$

Use Theorem 8.2 to relate this to the matrix of Example 3.

2. Find the characteristic polynomial, values, and vectors of the following matrices:

(a) $\begin{bmatrix} 1 & 2 \\ 3 & 2 \end{bmatrix}$, (b) $\begin{bmatrix} 2 & -1 & 1 \\ 1 & 0 & 3 \\ 0 & 0 & 2 \end{bmatrix}$,

(c) $\begin{bmatrix} 2 & -2 \\ 3 & -2 \end{bmatrix}$. (This will involve complex numbers.)

3. Prove that the characteristic values of any triangular matrix are the diagonal elements.
4. Prove that a matrix and its transpose have the same characteristic values.
5. If λ is a characteristic value of the matrix A and $\mathbf{X}$ a corresponding characteristic vector, show that $A^2\mathbf{X} = \lambda^2\mathbf{X}$. What does this prove about the characteristic values of the matrix A^2? Without further proof, is it correct to conclude that all the characteristic values of A^2 are the squares of the characteristic values of A?
6. Generalize Exercise 5 and show that a characteristic value of the matrix

$$a_0 I + a_1 A + \cdots + a_m A^m$$

is

$$a_0 + a_1\lambda + a_2\lambda^2 + \cdots + a_m\lambda^m,$$

where λ is a characteristic value of A.

7. Prove that all real characteristic values of an orthogonal matrix are ± 1.
8. Prove that if $A^m = 0$, the only characteristic value of A is 0. Give examples of such *nilpotent* matrices.
9. Prove that two characteristic vectors belonging to distinct characteristic values λ_1 and λ_2 of a linear transformation T of R^n are linearly independent.
10. If A is a nonsingular matrix, prove that AB and BA have the same characteristic values.
11. Give an example to show that similar matrices do not have the same characteristic vectors.

8.3 Similarity and Diagonal Matrices

We have just seen that any matrix similar to a matrix A has the same characteristic polynomial and values as A. The converse is *not* true. Two matrices may have the same characteristic polynomial and not be similar. For example,

$$A = \begin{bmatrix} 1 & 1 \\ 0 & 1 \end{bmatrix}$$

has the same characteristic polynomial as

$$I = \begin{bmatrix} 1 & 0 \\ 0 & 1 \end{bmatrix}, (1 - \lambda)^2.$$

But $P^{-1}IP = I$ for any P, so that A is not similar to I.

In the present section we wish to investigate circumstances under which matrices are similar to diagonal matrices. In doing this, we must remind the reader that the answer may depend on the field that he is willing to admit. Referring back to Example 1 of the last section, a matrix $\begin{bmatrix} 0 & 1 \\ -1 & 0 \end{bmatrix}$ was considered which is *not* similar to any *real* diagonal matrix but which *is* similar to $\begin{bmatrix} 2i & 0 \\ 0 & -2i \end{bmatrix}$ if we operate in

$$C\colon \begin{bmatrix} 1 & -i \\ -i & 1 \end{bmatrix} \begin{bmatrix} 0 & 1 \\ -1 & 0 \end{bmatrix} \begin{bmatrix} 1 & i \\ i & 1 \end{bmatrix} = \begin{bmatrix} 2i & 0 \\ 0 & -2i \end{bmatrix}.$$

The reader who wishes to use only real matrices, values, and vectors will have to place these restrictions automatically on all the statements considered.

The cue for our answer is found at the beginning of the first section, where it was remarked that, if V had a basis consisting of characteristic vectors, the transformation T had a representation by a diagonal matrix with respect to that basis.

Now suppose we start with an $n \times n$ matrix A. If F^n has a basis of characteristic vectors of A, $\{\mathbf{X}_1, \mathbf{X}_2, \ldots, \mathbf{X}_n\}$, $A\mathbf{X}_i^{\mathsf{T}} = \lambda_i \mathbf{X}_i^{\mathsf{T}}$ (where the λ_i need not be distinct), then we may regard A as the matrix of a transformation T with respect to the $\{\mathbf{E}_i\}$ basis and find the matrix of T with respect to the $\{\mathbf{X}_i\}$ basis. From the basic results of Chapter 3, we know that this new matrix will be $B = P^{-1}AP$, where P is the matrix of the change of basis from $\{\mathbf{X}_i\}$ to $\{\mathbf{E}_i\}$. But B is a diagonal matrix by our previous result.

On the other hand, suppose A is similar to some diagonal matrix,

$$C = Q^{-1}AQ = \text{Diagonal } [\lambda_1, \lambda_2, \ldots, \lambda_n].$$

Then

$$C\mathbf{E}_i^{\mathsf{T}} = \lambda_i \mathbf{E}_i^{\mathsf{T}}, \qquad i = 1, 2, \ldots, n.$$

This means that the $\{\mathbf{E}_i\}$ basis is a basis of characteristic vectors of C. Thus the set of vectors $\{Q\mathbf{E}_i^{\mathsf{T}}\}$ is a set of characteristic vectors of A by Theorem 8.2 and $A = QCQ^{-1}$. This set is a basis of F^n since Q is nonsingular.

It can happen that an examination of the characteristic *values* of a matrix will not reveal whether or not a basis of characteristic vectors can be found. If an $n \times n$ matrix A has n *distinct* characteristic values, however, we can show that there will automatically be a basis of characteristic vectors. Assume that $\{\lambda_i\}$ are the n characteristic values, and $\{\mathbf{X}_i\}$ is a set of nonzero vectors with $A\mathbf{X}_i^{\mathsf{T}} = \lambda_i \mathbf{X}_i^{\mathsf{T}}$. We shall show that $\{\mathbf{X}_i\}$ are linearly independent, and thus form a basis of characteristic vectors. Assume that $\{\mathbf{X}_i\}$ is linearly dependent, in fact, that $\mathbf{X}_k$ is the first vector dependent on previous $\mathbf{X}_i$'s. Then we have

$$\mathbf{X}_k = c_1\mathbf{X}_1 + c_2\mathbf{X}_2 + \cdots + c_{k-1}\mathbf{X}_{k-1}, \tag{8.2}$$

where $\mathbf{X}_1, \mathbf{X}_2, \ldots, \mathbf{X}_{k-1}$ are linearly independent. Applying A to both sides of (8.2) yields

$$A\mathbf{X}_k^{\mathsf{T}} = c_1 A\mathbf{X}_1^{\mathsf{T}} + \cdots + c_{k-1}A\mathbf{X}_{k-1}^{\mathsf{T}}$$

or

$$\lambda_k\mathbf{X}_k = c_1\lambda_1\mathbf{X}_1 + \cdots + c_{k-1}\lambda_{k-1}\mathbf{X}_{k-1}; \tag{8.3}$$

now multiply Equation (8.2) by λ_k and subtract from (8.3). The result is

$$\mathbf{0} = c_1(\lambda_1 - \lambda_k)\mathbf{X}_1 + \cdots + c_{k-1}(\lambda_{k-1} - \lambda_k)\mathbf{X}_{k-1}.$$

As $\mathbf{X}_1, \mathbf{X}_2, \ldots, \mathbf{X}_{k-1}$ are linearly independent and $\lambda_k \neq \lambda_i$, $i = 1, 2, \ldots, k - 1$, we have

$$c_1 = c_2 = \cdots = c_{k-1} = 0,$$

a contradiction. We state our results formally.

THEOREM 8.3. A matrix A over F is similar to a diagonal matrix if and only if the characteristic vectors of A lie in and generate F^n. The characteristic values of A are the diagonal elements of the resulting diagonal matrix.

COROLLARY. An $n \times n$ matrix with n distinct characteristic values in F is similar to a diagonal matrix.

Example 1. The matrix

$$A = \begin{bmatrix} 1 & 2 & 1 \\ 2 & 0 & -2 \\ -1 & 2 & 3 \end{bmatrix}$$

of Example 2, Section 8.2, was seen to have characteristic vectors either of the form $[a, -a, a]$ or $[a, 0, a]$. As it is impossible to construct a basis for R^3 from such vectors (try writing $[1, 0, 0]$ as a linear combination of such vectors), this matrix is not similar to a diagonal matrix over the reals. Note, also, that even if we consider A as a matrix over the complex numbers, it is not possible to find a basis of characteristic vectors.

The actual procedure of finding a diagonal matrix similar to a given matrix A is indicated by the argument leading to the theorem. First we find the characteristic values by finding the zeros of the characteristic polynomial. Then we attempt to find a basis of F^n consisting of characteristic vectors. We then find the matrix of the change of basis from the new basis to $\{\mathbf{E}_i\}$ and we have P such that $P^{-1}AP$ is diagonal.

Example 2. Let

$$A = \begin{bmatrix} 1 & 1 & -1 \\ 0 & 0 & 1 \\ 0 & -2 & -3 \end{bmatrix}.$$

The characteristic polynomial of A is

$$\det \begin{bmatrix} 1 - \lambda & 1 & -1 \\ 0 & -\lambda & 1 \\ 0 & -2 & -3 - \lambda \end{bmatrix} = -(\lambda - 1)(\lambda + 1)(\lambda + 2),$$

so that there are three characteristic values, 1, -1, -2. For the value 1, we solve $A\mathbf{X}^{\mathsf{T}} = \mathbf{X}^{\mathsf{T}}$ or

$$\begin{aligned} x_1 + x_2 - x_3 &= x_1, \\ x_3 &= x_2, \\ -2x_2 - 3x_3 &= x_3, \end{aligned}$$

which lead to $x_2 = x_3 = 0$. A typical characteristic vector is $[1, 0, 0] = \mathbf{X}_1$.

For -1, $A\mathbf{X}^{\mathsf{T}} = -\mathbf{X}^{\mathsf{T}}$

$$\begin{aligned} x_1 + x_2 - x_3 &= -x_1, \\ x_3 &= -x_2, \\ -2x_2 - 3x_3 &= -x_3. \end{aligned}$$

These equations lead to $x_3 = -x_2 = x_1$ and a characteristic vector is $[1, -1, 1] = \mathbf{X}_2$. Then, for -2,

$$\begin{aligned} x_1 + x_2 - x_3 &= -2x_1, \\ x_3 &= -2x_2, \\ -2x_2 - 3x_3 &= -2x_3, \end{aligned}$$

which give $x_3 = -2x_2, x_1 = -x_2$. A characteristic vector is $[1, -1, 2] = \mathbf{X}_3$.

The vectors $\mathbf{X}_1, \mathbf{X}_2, \mathbf{X}_3$ are independent and form a basis.

$$\begin{aligned} \mathbf{X}_1 &= \mathbf{E}_1, \\ \mathbf{X}_2 &= \mathbf{E}_1 - \mathbf{E}_2 + \mathbf{E}_3, \\ \mathbf{X}_3 &= \mathbf{E}_1 - \mathbf{E}_2 + 2\mathbf{E}_3, \end{aligned}$$

are the equations of change of basis from the $\{\mathbf{X}_i\}$ to $\{\mathbf{E}_i\}$. The matrix consists simply of the matrix whose column vectors are the $\mathbf{X}_i$.

$$P = \begin{bmatrix} 1 & 1 & 1 \\ 0 & -1 & -1 \\ 0 & 1 & 2 \end{bmatrix}.$$

We solve for P^{-1}:

$$P^{-1} = \begin{bmatrix} 1 & 1 & 0 \\ 0 & -2 & -1 \\ 0 & 1 & 1 \end{bmatrix},$$

and compute

$$P^{-1}AP = \text{Diagonal } [1, -1, 2].$$

The reader may object that the process given above, although simple enough in theory, would be impractical in cases where the zeros of the characteristic polynomial were not so readily found. Indeed, the very computation of the characteristic polynomial would become difficult for matrices larger than 4×4. These objections are well taken. Numerical methods exist to approximate characteristic values and characteristic vectors but there is no really simple or quick method. Due to the large number of applications to differential equations and other problems of applied mathematics, the problem of finding characteristic values and vectors has become "big business" and vast sums of money in terms of high-speed computer time are expended on their computation.

Note also that we made a more or less arbitrary choice of characteristic vectors in each case of Example 2 and used the values in a particular order. The student should try other choices of vectors and of order of values. Naturally, a change in the order of the values (corresponding to an interchange in columns of P and rows of P^{-1}) will produce a change in the order of the diagonal elements in the resulting matrix.

If we wish to establish a pattern for "canonical" matrices so that we may have one for each possible equivalence class under similarity, we must choose some definite order for the characteristic values. One method of doing this for real matrices with real characteristic values is illustrated in Exercise 5.

We give one more example to illustrate how the process of diagonalization may be carried out in the complex field.

Example 3. Let

$$A = \begin{bmatrix} 1 & 2 \\ -1 & -1 \end{bmatrix}.$$

The characteristic polynomial is $\lambda^2 + 1$. The characteristic values in C are $i, -i$. For i, we solve $A\mathbf{X}^{\mathsf{T}} = i\mathbf{X}^{\mathsf{T}}$

$$\begin{aligned} x_1 + 2x_2 &= ix_1, \\ -x_1 - x_2 &= ix_2. \end{aligned}$$

Both these equations give

$$x_1 = (-1 - i)x_2 \quad \text{or} \quad x_2 = -\tfrac{1}{2}(1 - i)x_1.$$

We select $\mathbf{X}_1 = [1 + i, -1]$. For $-i$, we have $A\mathbf{X}^{\mathsf{T}} = -i\mathbf{X}^{\mathsf{T}}$,

$$\begin{aligned} x_1 + 2x_2 &= -ix_1, \\ -x_1 - x_2 &= -ix_2. \end{aligned}$$

These give $x_1 = (-1 + i)x_2$ and we select $\mathbf{X}_2 = [1 - i, -1]$. Then

$$P = \begin{bmatrix} 1 + i & 1 - i \\ -1 & -1 \end{bmatrix}, \quad P^{-1} = \frac{-1}{2i}\begin{bmatrix} -1 & -1 + i \\ +1 & 1 + i \end{bmatrix}$$

$$= \frac{i}{2}\begin{bmatrix} -1 & -1 + i \\ 1 & 1 + i \end{bmatrix},$$

$$\frac{i}{2}\begin{bmatrix} -1 & -1 + i \\ 1 & 1 + i \end{bmatrix}\begin{bmatrix} 1 & 2 \\ -1 & -1 \end{bmatrix}\begin{bmatrix} 1 + i & 1 - i \\ -1 & -1 \end{bmatrix}$$

$$= \frac{i}{2}\begin{bmatrix} -i & -1 - i \\ -i & 1 - i \end{bmatrix}\begin{bmatrix} 1 + i & 1 - i \\ -1 & -1 \end{bmatrix}$$

$$= \frac{i}{2}\begin{bmatrix} 2 & 0 \\ 0 & -2 \end{bmatrix} = \begin{bmatrix} i & 0 \\ 0 & -i \end{bmatrix}.$$

Exercises

1. Find the diagonal matrices similar to

$$\text{(a)} \begin{bmatrix} 0 & 1 \\ 0 & 1 \end{bmatrix}, \quad \text{(b)} \begin{bmatrix} 1 & -5 & 9 \\ 2 & 0 & -1 \\ 1 & 2 & -4 \end{bmatrix}, \quad \text{(c)} \begin{bmatrix} -1 & 4 & -2 \\ 0 & 3 & -2 \\ 0 & 4 & -3 \end{bmatrix}.$$

2. Show that $\begin{bmatrix} 0 & 5 & -3 \\ 1 & 0 & 1 \\ 2 & -4 & 4 \end{bmatrix}$ is not similar to a diagonal matrix.

3. Using matrices with complex elements if necessary, diagonalize

$$\begin{bmatrix} 1 & -1 \\ 1 & 2 \end{bmatrix}.$$

4. If the characteristic vectors of a matrix A generate R^n, show that a basis for R^n consisting of characteristic vectors of A must contain a vector associated with every characteristic value of A.
5. Finish the proof that, for real matrices with real characteristic values of the type considered in this section, the matrix Diagonal $[\lambda_1, \lambda_2, \ldots, \lambda_n]$, such that $\lambda_i \geq \lambda_j$ for $i \geq j$, is canonical for similarity transformations. That is, there are not two such diagonal matrices in the same equivalence class.
6. Show that the only matrices which have $\mathbf{E}_1, \mathbf{E}_2, \ldots, \mathbf{E}_n$ as characteristic vectors are the diagonal matrices.

7. If a matrix A is similar to a diagonal matrix, show that the polynomial matrix
$$f(A) = a_m A^m + a_{m-1}A^{m-1} + \cdots + a_1 A + a_0 I$$
has as characteristic values
$$a_m c^m + a_{m-1}c^{m-1} + \cdots + a_1 c + a_0 c,$$
where c ranges over the characteristic values of A. (See also Exercise 6, Section 8.2.)
8. What conclusions can you draw from Exercise 7 if the polynomial
$$f(\lambda) = a_n\lambda^n + a_{n-1}\lambda^{n-1} + \cdots + a_1\lambda + a_0$$
used to form $f(A)$ is the characteristic polynomial of A?
9. If A is a real matrix with only real characteristic values, is it possible that for no matrix P over the reals, PAP^{-1} is diagonal, yet such a P can be found with complex entries?

8.4 Orthogonal Reduction of Symmetric Matrices

In the preceding section we considered the circumstances under which a matrix is *similar* to a diagonal matrix; in Chapter 6 we found that every symmetric matrix is *congruent* to a diagonal matrix, in fact to one whose diagonal elements are ± 1 or 0. The concepts of similarity ($B = P^{-1}AP$) and congruence ($B = P^{\mathsf{T}}AP$) overlap in the case that $P^{\mathsf{T}} = P^{-1}$; that is, if P is an orthogonal matrix. We shall now establish the result that any real symmetric matrix is simultaneously similar and congruent to a diagonal matrix.

We begin by proving the following theorem about the characteristic values of symmetric matrices.

THEOREM 8.4. If A is a real symmetric matrix, the characteristic values of A are real.

PROOF. Let λ be a (possibly complex) characteristic value of A, with a nonzero characteristic vector $\mathbf{Z} = [z_1, z_2, \ldots, z_n]$ in C^n. We shall use $\overline{\mathbf{Z}}$ to denote the vector $\overline{\mathbf{Z}} = [\bar{z}_1, \bar{z}_2, \ldots, \bar{z}_n]$. We consider the product $\overline{\mathbf{Z}}A\mathbf{Z}^{\mathsf{T}}$. Assume $A = [a_{ij}]$.

$$\overline{\mathbf{Z}}A\mathbf{Z}^{\mathsf{T}} = \sum_{i=1}^{n} \bar{z}_i \sum_{j=1}^{n} a_{ij}z_j = \sum_{j=1}^{n} z_j \sum_{i=1}^{n} a_{ij}\bar{z}_i = \mathbf{Z}A^{\mathsf{T}}\overline{\mathbf{Z}}^{\mathsf{T}}. \tag{8.4}$$

Because $A\mathbf{Z}^{\mathsf{T}} = \lambda\mathbf{Z}^{\mathsf{T}}$, we have $\overline{\mathbf{Z}}A\mathbf{Z}^{\mathsf{T}} = \lambda\overline{\mathbf{Z}}\mathbf{Z}^{\mathsf{T}}$. But $A^{\mathsf{T}} = A$ and A is real, so
$$A^{\mathsf{T}}\overline{\mathbf{Z}}^{\mathsf{T}} = A\overline{\mathbf{Z}}^{\mathsf{T}} = (\overline{A\mathbf{Z}^{\mathsf{T}}}) = (\overline{\lambda\mathbf{Z}^{\mathsf{T}}}) = \bar{\lambda}\overline{\mathbf{Z}}^{\mathsf{T}}.$$
Thus (8.4) becomes
$$\lambda\overline{\mathbf{Z}}\mathbf{Z}^{\mathsf{T}} = \mathbf{Z}\bar{\lambda}\overline{\mathbf{Z}}^{\mathsf{T}} = \bar{\lambda}\mathbf{Z}\overline{\mathbf{Z}}^{\mathsf{T}}.$$
As $\overline{\mathbf{Z}}\mathbf{Z}^{\mathsf{T}} = \mathbf{Z}\overline{\mathbf{Z}}^{\mathsf{T}} \neq 0$, we have $\lambda = \bar{\lambda}$, or λ is real.

The next step is to show that two characteristic vectors of A belonging to different characteristic values are orthogonal.

THEOREM 8.5. If A is a real symmetric matrix and $\mathbf{X}$, $\mathbf{Y}$ are characteristic vectors of A corresponding to distinct values λ_1, λ_2, then $\mathbf{X}$ and $\mathbf{Y}$ are orthogonal.

PROOF. We compute $\mathbf{X}A\mathbf{Y}^{\mathsf{T}}$ in two ways. $\mathbf{X}(A\mathbf{Y}^{\mathsf{T}}) = \mathbf{X}(\lambda_2\mathbf{Y}^{\mathsf{T}}) = \lambda_2\mathbf{X}\mathbf{Y}^{\mathsf{T}} = \lambda_2(\mathbf{X}, \mathbf{Y})$:

$$\mathbf{X}A\mathbf{Y}^{\mathsf{T}} = \mathbf{X}A^{\mathsf{T}}\mathbf{Y}^{\mathsf{T}} = (A\mathbf{X}^{\mathsf{T}})^{\mathsf{T}}\mathbf{Y}^{\mathsf{T}} = (\lambda_1\mathbf{X}^{\mathsf{T}})^{\mathsf{T}}\mathbf{Y}^{\mathsf{T}} = \lambda_1\mathbf{X}\mathbf{Y}^{\mathsf{T}} = \lambda_1(\mathbf{X}, \mathbf{Y}).$$

Thus $(\lambda_1 - \lambda_2)(\mathbf{X}, \mathbf{Y}) = 0$ and it follows that $(\mathbf{X}, \mathbf{Y}) = 0$ since $\lambda_1 - \lambda_2 \neq 0$.

It might seem that we are essentially done. All we have to do is to make up orthonormal bases for each space M_λ, put them together as a basis for R^n and we have the columns for an orthogonal matrix P such that $P^{-1}AP = P^{\mathsf{T}}AP$ is diagonal. In practice, this is just what we do, but in theory there is a gap. How can we be sure that the sum of the dimensions of the spaces M_λ is n? We have already seen matrices like $\begin{bmatrix} 1 & 1 \\ 0 & 1 \end{bmatrix}$ where the characteristic vectors do not span the space. Perhaps there are symmetric matrices like this? There are not and we can prove our theorem.

THEOREM 8.6. If A is a real symmetric matrix, then there is an orthogonal matrix P such that $P^{-1}AP$ is a diagonal matrix.

PROOF. As in Theorem 6.11, we will use mathematical induction, which will avoid having to add the dimensions of the M_λ. The induction argument begins with $n = 1$; $A = [a_{11}]$ is already diagonal.

Now we assume the theorem proved for $(n - 1) \times (n - 1)$ matrices and prove it for $n \times n$ symmetric matrices. As usual, we associate with A the linear transformation T defined by $\mathrm{T}\mathbf{X} = A\mathbf{X}^{\mathsf{T}}$, so that A is the matrix of T with respect to the $\{\mathbf{E}_i\}$ basis. Now let λ_1 be a characteristic value of A and thus of T. Choose a unit vector $\mathbf{X}_1$ belonging to λ_1, $\mathrm{T}\mathbf{X}_1 = A\mathbf{X}_1^{\mathsf{T}} = \lambda_1\mathbf{X}_1^{\mathsf{T}}$.

Next, let V be the orthogonal complement of $L\{\mathbf{X}_1\}$ in R^n; dimension $V = n - 1$. Find an orthonormal basis of V, $\{\mathbf{X}_2, \mathbf{X}_3, \ldots, \mathbf{X}_n\}$. We claim that any vector of V is transformed by T into another vector of V. To see this, we prove that the transformed vector is orthogonal to $\mathbf{X}_1$. For any vector $\mathbf{X}$ of V,

$$(\mathbf{X}_1, \mathrm{T}\mathbf{X}) = \mathbf{X}_1A\mathbf{X}^{\mathsf{T}} = \mathbf{X}_1A^{\mathsf{T}}\mathbf{X}^{\mathsf{T}} = (A\mathbf{X}_1^{\mathsf{T}})^{\mathsf{T}}\mathbf{X}^{\mathsf{T}} = (\lambda_1\mathbf{X}_1^{\mathsf{T}})^{\mathsf{T}}\mathbf{X}^{\mathsf{T}} = \lambda_1(\mathbf{X}_1, \mathbf{X}) = 0.$$

In particular, the basis vectors $\mathbf{X}_2, \mathbf{X}_3, \ldots, \mathbf{X}_n$ are transformed by T into vectors of V, that is, into linear combinations of $\mathbf{X}_2, \mathbf{X}_3, \ldots, \mathbf{X}_n$. Then the matrix of T with respect to the basis $\{\mathbf{X}_1, \mathbf{X}_2, \ldots, \mathbf{X}_n\}$ of R^n has a matrix of the form

$$B = \begin{bmatrix} \lambda_1 & 0 & \cdots & 0 \\ 0 & & & \\ \vdots & & A^* & \\ 0 & & & \end{bmatrix}.$$

Now, B is the result of a change of orthonormal bases from $\{\mathbf{E}_i\}$ to $\{\mathbf{X}_i\}$ so $B = R^{-1}AR$, where R is orthogonal. Furthermore A^* is symmetric because

$$B^{\mathsf{T}} = R^{\mathsf{T}}A^{\mathsf{T}}(R^{-1})^{\mathsf{T}} = R^{-1}AR = B$$

since $R^{-1} = R^{\mathsf{T}}$.

We know by the induction hypothesis that there is an $(n - 1) \times (n - 1)$ orthogonal matrix Q^* such that $(Q^*)^{-1}A^*Q^*$ is diagonal. Define an $n \times n$ orthogonal matrix

$$Q = \begin{bmatrix} 1 & 0 & \cdots & 0 \\ 0 & & & \\ \vdots & & [Q^*] & \\ 0 & & & \end{bmatrix}$$

and compute $Q^{-1}BQ$. If

$$\begin{aligned}(Q^*)^{-1}A^*Q^* &= \text{Diagonal } [\lambda_2, \ldots, \lambda_n],\\ Q^{-1}BQ &= \text{Diagonal } [\lambda_1, \lambda_2, \ldots, \lambda_n].\end{aligned}$$

Then $Q^{-1}R^{-1}ARQ$ is diagonal, and we may choose $P = RQ$. P is orthogonal since it is the product of orthogonal matrices.

Example 1. We mentioned that, in practice, now that we know things will work out, we simply compute orthonormal bases of the M_λ. Let us demonstrate this computation on

$$A = \begin{bmatrix} 1 & -4 & 2 \\ -4 & 1 & -2 \\ 2 & -2 & -2 \end{bmatrix}.$$

Our first job is to find the characteristic values from the characteristic polynomial:

$$\det \begin{bmatrix} 1-\lambda & -4 & 2 \\ -4 & 1-\lambda & -2 \\ 2 & -2 & -2-\lambda \end{bmatrix} = -\lambda^3 + 27\lambda + 54 = -(\lambda+3)^2(\lambda-6).$$

There are two values, -3, 6.

For -3 we solve

$$\begin{bmatrix} 4 & -4 & 2 \\ -4 & 4 & -2 \\ 2 & -2 & 1 \end{bmatrix} \begin{bmatrix} x_1 \\ x_2 \\ x_3 \end{bmatrix} = 0$$

or $2x_1 - 2x_2 + x_3 = 0$.

There are, of course, infinitely many ways to choose an orthogonal basis of M_{-3}. The choice of $[2, 1, -2]$, $[1, 2, 2]$ is made with the idea of avoiding radicals in the computation, since these vectors have length 3.

For $\lambda = 6$,

$$\begin{bmatrix} -5 & -4 & 2 \\ -4 & -5 & -2 \\ 2 & -2 & -8 \end{bmatrix} \begin{bmatrix} x_1 \\ x_2 \\ x_3 \end{bmatrix} = 0;$$

$$\begin{aligned} -5x_1 - 4x_2 + 2x_3 &= 0,\\ -4x_1 - 5x_2 - 2x_3 &= 0,\\ 2x_1 - 2x_2 - 8x_3 &= 0. \end{aligned}$$

This system may be solved by standard methods and the results are $x_1 = -x_2 = 2x_3$. Again we choose a vector of length 3 by taking $x_3 = 1$: $M_6 = L\{[2, -2, 1]\}$. The orthonormal system is, then,

$$[\tfrac{2}{3}, \tfrac{1}{3}, -\tfrac{2}{3}], [\tfrac{1}{3}, \tfrac{2}{3}, \tfrac{2}{3}], [\tfrac{2}{3}, -\tfrac{2}{3}, \tfrac{1}{3}]$$

and

$$P^{\mathsf{T}}AP = P^{-1}AP = \begin{bmatrix} \frac{2}{3} & \frac{1}{3} & -\frac{2}{3} \\ \frac{1}{3} & \frac{2}{3} & \frac{2}{3} \\ \frac{2}{3} & -\frac{2}{3} & \frac{1}{3} \end{bmatrix} \begin{bmatrix} 1 & -4 & 2 \\ -4 & 1 & -2 \\ 2 & -2 & -2 \end{bmatrix} \begin{bmatrix} \frac{2}{3} & \frac{1}{3} & \frac{2}{3} \\ \frac{1}{3} & \frac{2}{3} & -\frac{2}{3} \\ -\frac{2}{3} & \frac{2}{3} & \frac{1}{3} \end{bmatrix}$$

$$= \text{Diagonal } [-3, -3, 6].$$

The reader may find it instructive to carry out the same reduction with other bases for M_{-3}. See, for example, Exercise 1.

Exercises

1. In Example 1, use as a basis for M_{-3} the orthogonal vectors [1, 1, 0] and [1, −1, −4]. Now finish the process by constructing a matrix P such that

$$P^{-1}AP = P^{\mathsf{T}}AP = \text{Diagonal}\,[-3, -3, 6].$$

2. (a) Find a diagonal matrix D orthogonally similar to the matrix

$$A = \begin{bmatrix} 1 & \frac{1}{3} & 0 \\ \frac{1}{3} & 1 & \frac{1}{4} \\ 0 & \frac{1}{4} & 1 \end{bmatrix}.$$

   (b) Verify Theorems 8.4 and 8.5 for the matrix A.
   (c) Find a matrix P such that $P^{-1}AP = D$.
3. Discuss the question of canonical forms for real symmetric matrices under the equivalence relation of orthogonal similarity; that is, $B = P^{-1}AP$, where $P^{-1} = P^{\mathsf{T}}$.
4. Suppose that the characteristic polynomial of a symmetric matrix A in its factored form is

$$(\lambda - \lambda_1)^{m_1}(\lambda - \lambda_2)^{m_2}\cdots(\lambda - \lambda_k)^{m_k};$$

$$m_1 + m_2 + \cdots + m_k = n.$$

Show that the subspace M_{λ_i} of Theorem 8.1 associated with the characteristic value λ_i has dimension m_i. *Hint:* Let

$$P^{-1}AP = \text{Diagonal}\,[\underbrace{\lambda_1, \lambda_1, \ldots, \lambda_1}_{m_1 \text{ times}}, \underbrace{\lambda_2, \lambda_2, \ldots, \lambda_2}_{m_2 \text{ times}}, \ldots].$$

Now consider the subspace generated by $P\mathbf{E}_i^{\mathsf{T}}$ for $i = 1, 2, \ldots, m_1$. Why are we sure λ_1 will appear exactly m_1 times in the diagonal matrix?

8.5 Quadratic Forms and Quadratic Surfaces

We have considered the geometric interpretation of a change of variables in a real quadratic form in Section 6.4. Although we are limiting our discussion to two and three dimensions, a generalized geometry could easily be constructed. However, the advantages of visualization would be lost. We desire now to restrict attention to orthogonal change of variables. That is, we will allow only orthogonal matrices P to change the form

$$Q(\mathbf{X}) = \sum_{i,j=1}^{n} x_i a_{ij} x_j \tag{8.5}$$

to

$$Q^*(\mathbf{Y}) = \sum_{i,j=1}^{n} y_i a_{ij}^* y_j \tag{8.6}$$

by

$$[x_1, x_2, \ldots, x_n]^{\mathsf{T}} = P[y_1, y_2, \ldots, y_n]^{\mathsf{T}}. \tag{8.7}$$

Effectively, we could limit our attention to rotations since, if det $P = -1$, a new matrix can be formed from P by multiplying a column by -1, which is still orthogonal, has a similar effect to the first matrix, and has determinant 1. The difference is hardly worth the bother.

Let us look at the situation in two dimensions. In texts on elementary analytic geometry it is shown that if we have a conic with an equation of the type

$$ax^2 + 2bxy + cy^2 = 1,$$

we can obtain an equation

$$a^*(x^*)^2 + c^*(y^*)^2 = 1$$

by a rotation through an angle θ where

$$\theta = \tfrac{1}{2} \arctan \frac{2b}{a - c}.$$

This result can also be obtained by matrix methods but direct application of the procedures of the preceding section will replace the trigonometrical computations by simpler algebraic equivalents.

Texts in analytic geometry rarely carry out the similar process in three dimensions because the formulation of the trigonometry is too complicated. In matrix terms we have an essentially simpler formulation, but it masks a practical difficulty in that the solution of a third-degree polynomial equation is assumed. If we have

$$[x_1, x_2, x_3]A \begin{bmatrix} x_1 \\ x_2 \\ x_3 \end{bmatrix} = 1$$

and find an orthogonal matrix P such that $P^{\mathsf{T}}AP = \text{Diagonal } [\lambda_1, \lambda_2, \lambda_3]$, then the substitution

$$P \begin{bmatrix} y_1 \\ y_2 \\ y_3 \end{bmatrix} = \begin{bmatrix} x_1 \\ x_2 \\ x_3 \end{bmatrix}$$

will lead to the new form

$$[y_1, y_2, y_3]P^{\mathsf{T}}AP \begin{bmatrix} y_1 \\ y_2 \\ y_3 \end{bmatrix} = 1,$$

or $\lambda_1 y_1^2 + \lambda_2 y_2^2 + \lambda_3 y_3^2 = 1$.

Example 1. Consider the equation defined by

$$x^2 - 4xy - 2y^2 = 1.$$

The analytic geometry text would have us rotate through an angle $\frac{1}{2} \arctan -\frac{4}{3}$. If we write the equation

$$[x, y] \begin{bmatrix} 1 & -2 \\ -2 & -2 \end{bmatrix} \begin{bmatrix} x \\ y \end{bmatrix} = 1,$$

we see that the characteristic polynomial is

$$\det \begin{bmatrix} 1 - \lambda & -2 \\ -2 & -2 - \lambda \end{bmatrix} = -6 + \lambda + \lambda^2 = (\lambda - 2)(\lambda + 3).$$

A basis for M_{-3} is given by $\begin{bmatrix} 4 & -2 \\ -2 & 1 \end{bmatrix} \begin{bmatrix} x_1 \\ x_2 \end{bmatrix} = 0$, or $-2x_1 + x_2 = 0$, $x_2 = 2x_1$; we choose $[1, 2]$, which, when normalized, becomes $[1/\sqrt{5}, 2/\sqrt{5}]$. A basis for M_2, similarly, is $[-2/\sqrt{5}, +1/\sqrt{5}]$, and

$$P = \frac{1}{\sqrt{5}} \begin{bmatrix} 1 & -2 \\ 2 & 1 \end{bmatrix}.$$

Then

$$[x^*, y^*] \frac{1}{\sqrt{5}} \begin{bmatrix} 1 & 2 \\ -2 & 1 \end{bmatrix} \begin{bmatrix} 1 & -2 \\ -2 & -2 \end{bmatrix} \frac{1}{\sqrt{5}} \begin{bmatrix} 1 & -2 \\ 2 & 1 \end{bmatrix} \begin{bmatrix} x^* \\ y^* \end{bmatrix} = 1$$

or

$$[x^*, y^*]\left(\frac{1}{5}\right)\begin{bmatrix}-15 & 0\\ 0 & 10\end{bmatrix}\begin{bmatrix}x^*\\ y^*\end{bmatrix} = 1,$$

$$-3(x^*)^2 + 2(y^*)^2 = 1.$$

We knew the answer above as soon as we had solved $\lambda^2 + \lambda - 6 = 0$. Why did we bother to find P? It wasn't to verify our ability to multiply matrices. Let us look at the geometry and write explicitly the equations given by $\begin{bmatrix}x\\ y\end{bmatrix} = P\begin{bmatrix}x^*\\ y^*\end{bmatrix}$:

$$x = \frac{1}{\sqrt{5}}(x^* - 2y^*),$$

$$y = \frac{1}{\sqrt{5}}(2x^* + y^*).$$

If

$$(x^*, y^*) = (1, 0), \qquad (x, y) = \left(\frac{1}{\sqrt{5}}, \frac{2}{\sqrt{5}}\right).$$

If

$$(x^*, y^*) = (0, 1), \qquad (x, y) = \left(-\frac{2}{\sqrt{5}}, \frac{1}{\sqrt{5}}\right).$$

These points are marked P and Q in Figure 8.1. They are the unit points on the new (x^*, y^*)-axis. Without finding P we would not have known the orientation of these axes to the old ones.

We can now easily sketch the hyperbola represented by

$$-3(x^*)^2 + 2(y^*)^2 = 1$$

on the new axes. It cuts the y^*-axis at $(0, \pm\sqrt{2}/2)$ in the new coordinates and has asymptotes given by

$$y^* = \pm\frac{\sqrt{3}}{\sqrt{2}}x^* = \pm\frac{\sqrt{6}}{2}x^*.$$

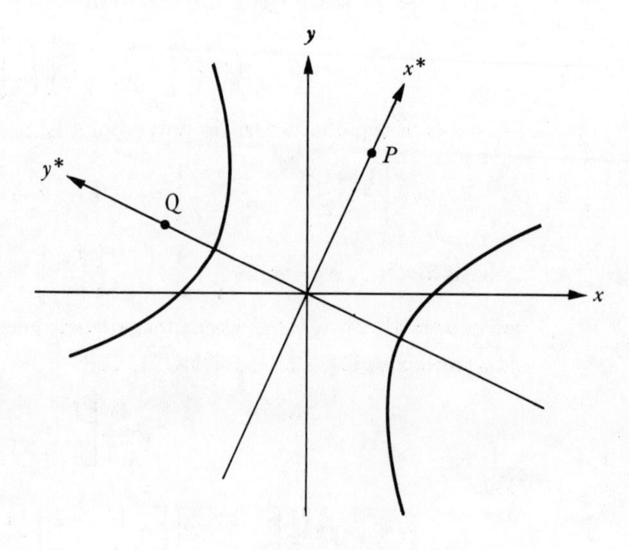

FIGURE 8.1

The reader is invited to use the trigonometric method to compare the work, keeping in mind that the actual matrix multiplication performed was wasted effort.

Example 2. Consider the quadratic form

$$Q(\mathbf{X}) = [x_1, x_2, x_3]\begin{bmatrix} -1 & -4 & 2 \\ -4 & 1 & -2 \\ 2 & -2 & -2 \end{bmatrix}\begin{bmatrix} x_1 \\ x_2 \\ x_3 \end{bmatrix} = \mathbf{X}A\mathbf{X}^{\mathsf{T}}.$$

The matrix A is the matrix considered in Example 1, Section 8.4, and we have seen that for the matrix

$$P = \begin{bmatrix} \frac{2}{3} & \frac{1}{3} & \frac{2}{3} \\ \frac{1}{3} & \frac{2}{3} & -\frac{2}{3} \\ -\frac{2}{3} & \frac{2}{3} & \frac{1}{3} \end{bmatrix}$$

$P^{\mathsf{T}}AP = \text{Diagonal }[-3, -3, 6]$.

Therefore if we make the change of variables

$$\begin{bmatrix} x_1 \\ x_2 \\ x_3 \end{bmatrix} = \begin{bmatrix} \frac{2}{3} & \frac{1}{3} & \frac{2}{3} \\ \frac{1}{3} & \frac{2}{3} & -\frac{2}{3} \\ -\frac{2}{3} & \frac{2}{3} & \frac{1}{3} \end{bmatrix}\begin{bmatrix} y_1 \\ y_2 \\ y_3 \end{bmatrix},$$

the quadratic form $Q(\mathbf{X})$ is replaced by

$$Q(P\mathbf{Y}) = Q^*(\mathbf{Y}) = -3y_1^2 - 3y_2^2 + 6y_3^2.$$

Designate the new unit points

$$(y_1, y_2, y_3) = (1, 0, 0), (0, 1, 0), (0, 0, 1)$$

by $P_1^{(1)}, P_1^{(2)}, P_1^{(3)}$, respectively. From the matrix equation of the change of variables, we can read off the coordinates in the old system (x_1, x_2, x_3). For each case $P_1^{(1)}, P_1^{(2)}, P_1^{(3)}$ they are, respectively,

$$(\tfrac{2}{3}, \tfrac{1}{3}, -\tfrac{2}{3}), (\tfrac{1}{3}, \tfrac{2}{3}, \tfrac{2}{3}) \text{ and } (\tfrac{2}{3}, -\tfrac{2}{3}, \tfrac{1}{3}).$$

If we now consider the equation $Q(\mathbf{X}) = 1$ in the old coordinates as transformed to

$$Q^*(\mathbf{Y}) = -3y_1^2 - 3y_2^2 + 6y_3^2 = 1$$

in the new system, we see that the surface cuts the y_3-axis in the points $(0, 0, \pm 1/\sqrt{6})$, while it does not cut the y_1- or the y_2-axis. See Figure 8.2.

We will give now a general discussion using the last example as an illustration. We shall use geometrical language although the geometrical entities can be visualized only in two or three dimensions. Any reader who wishes to do so may assume that n is 2 or 3.

We begin with (8.5) and find an orthogonal matrix P such that, by the change of variables (8.7), all terms in (8.6) of the form $y_i a_{ij}^* y_j$, $i \neq j$, are 0. The new unit points have coordinates in the original system which are obtained from the respective columns of P:

$$P_{(1)}^{j} = (p_{1j}, p_{2j}, \ldots, p_{nj}).$$

The transformed quadratic form $Q^*(\mathbf{Y})$ has the form

$$Q^*(\mathbf{Y}) = \lambda_1 y_1^2 + \lambda_2 y_2^2 + \cdots + \lambda_n y_n^2, \tag{8.8}$$

where the λ_i (not necessarily distinct) are the characteristic values of the matrix $A = [a_{ij}]$ defined by (8.5). If we consider the equation $Q(\mathbf{X}) = 1$ as being

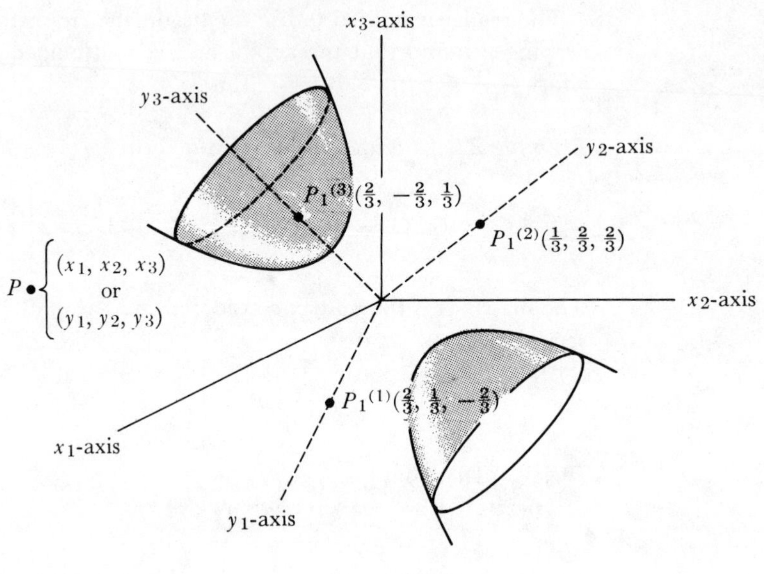

FIGURE 8.2

transformed to $Q^*(\mathbf{Y}) = 1$, the surface will cut the y_i-axis in points whose ith coordinate is $\pm 1/\sqrt{\lambda_i}$ when $\lambda_i > 0$. (In Example 2, $\lambda_3 = 6$.)

The new axes (the y_i-axes) are called the *principal axes* of the surface. When two or more of the λ_i are equal in (8.8), any system of orthogonal axes defined by an orthogonal basis of M_{λ_i} will serve as principal axes. (In Example 2, $\lambda_1 = \lambda_2 = -3$; we have already pointed out the arbitrariness of our selection of the first two columns of P in this case.) The principal axes are defined by characteristic vectors of A belonging to λ_i. We may think of such a vector as being defined by the vector from the origin to the point $P_1^{(i)}$.

The line segment from the origin to the point on the y_i-axis with ith coordinate $1/\sqrt{\lambda_i}$, $\lambda_i > 0$ is called a *semiaxis*. This point satisfies the equation $Q^*(\mathbf{Y}) = 1$ or, on transformation to the old system, $Q(\mathbf{X}) = 1$.

We shall now turn to some results whose detailed proofs require the use of the calculus; we shall give a motivation that does not depend on the calculus and state the results, leaving the proofs to the exercises where they will not be difficult for those readers who are familiar with the calculus of several variables.

Suppose $\mathbf{X}_0 = [x_1^0, x_2^0, \ldots, x_n^0]$ is a vector such that $Q(\mathbf{X}_0) = 1$; we say that $\mathbf{X}_0 = (x_1^0, x_2^0, \ldots, x_n^0)$ is a *point* on the surface $Q(\mathbf{X}) = 1$. Let $\mathbf{X} = [x_1, x_2, \ldots, x_n]$ similarly define another point (not necessarily on the surface); what is the equation of the line joining $\mathbf{X}$ and $\mathbf{X}_0$? This question was answered (at least for $n = 2$ and 3) in Chapter 2. If $\mathbf{Y} = [y_1, y_2, \ldots, y_n]$ is another point on the line, then for some t, $\mathbf{Y} = \mathbf{X}_0 + t(\mathbf{X} - \mathbf{X}_0)$. Where does this line intersect the surface $Q(\mathbf{X}) = 1$? In any point $\mathbf{Y}$ such that $Q(\mathbf{Y}) = 1$ or

$$(\mathbf{X}_0 + t(\mathbf{X} - \mathbf{X}_0))A(\mathbf{X}_0 + t(\mathbf{X} - \mathbf{X}_0))^{\mathsf{T}} = 1,$$

or

$$\mathbf{X}_0 A \mathbf{X}_0^{\mathsf{T}} + t\mathbf{X}_0 A(\mathbf{X} - \mathbf{X}_0)^{\mathsf{T}} + t(\mathbf{X} - \mathbf{X}_0)A\mathbf{X}_0^{\mathsf{T}} + t^2(\mathbf{X} - \mathbf{X}_0)A(\mathbf{X} - \mathbf{X}_0)^{\mathsf{T}} = 1.$$

We recall that $\mathbf{X}_0 A \mathbf{X}_0^{\mathsf{T}} = 1$ by definition of $\mathbf{X}_0$ and that

$$\mathbf{X}_0 A(\mathbf{X} - \mathbf{X}_0)^{\mathsf{T}} = (\mathbf{X} - \mathbf{X}_0)A\mathbf{X}_0^{\mathsf{T}}$$

by reason of the symmetry of A. Then

$$2t\mathbf{X}_0A(\mathbf{X} - \mathbf{X}_0)^{\mathsf{T}} + t^2(\mathbf{X} - \mathbf{X}_0)A(\mathbf{X} - \mathbf{X}_0)^{\mathsf{T}} = 0.$$

The condition that the line be tangent to the surface may be described by requiring that it intersect the surface only once. Normally the equation above gives *two* values of t which would represent intersections, 0 and

$$\frac{-2\mathbf{X}_0A(\mathbf{X} - \mathbf{X}_0)^{\mathsf{T}}}{(\mathbf{X} - \mathbf{X}_0)A(\mathbf{X} - \mathbf{X}_0)^{\mathsf{T}}}.$$

We assume that the denominator can be made nonzero by a proper choice of $\mathbf{X}$ and we see that we will have only one intersection if and only if both values are 0, that is, exactly when the numerator is 0.

The condition $\mathbf{X}_0A(\mathbf{X} - \mathbf{X}_0)^{\mathsf{T}} = 0$ reduces to

$$\mathbf{X}_0A\mathbf{X}^{\mathsf{T}} = 1. \tag{8.9}$$

When $n = 2$, it gives the tangent line to the curve at $\mathbf{X}_0$; when $n \geq 3$, it gives the tangent plane to the surface at $\mathbf{X}_0$; for $n > 3$ we say that $\mathbf{X}_0A\mathbf{X}^{\mathsf{T}} = 1$ is the equation of the tangent *hyperplane* to the "surface" at $\mathbf{X}_0$.

In Example 2, the point whose new coordinates are $(0, 0, 1/\sqrt{6})$ was on the surface. The old coordinates of that point are given by

$$P\left[0, 0, \frac{1}{\sqrt{6}}\right]^{\mathsf{T}} = \frac{1}{\sqrt{6}}\left[\frac{2}{3}, -\frac{2}{3}, \frac{1}{3}\right]^{\mathsf{T}}.$$

Thus, in the original system, the tangent plane to $Q(\mathbf{X}) = 1$ at this point is given by

$$[\tfrac{2}{3}, -\tfrac{2}{3}, \tfrac{1}{3}]\begin{bmatrix} -1 & -4 & 2 \\ -4 & 1 & -2 \\ 2 & -2 & -2 \end{bmatrix}\begin{bmatrix} x_1 \\ x_2 \\ x_3 \end{bmatrix} = 1,$$

or

$$\tfrac{8}{3}x_1 - \tfrac{12}{3}x_2 + \tfrac{6}{3}x_3 = 1,$$

or

$$8x_1 - 12x_2 + 6x_3 = 3.$$

Suppose, as just above, we choose $\mathbf{X}_0$ as defining some semiaxis, so that $\mathbf{X}_0$ is a characteristic vector of A and $\mathbf{X}_0A = \lambda_i\mathbf{X}_0$. Then the condition that $\mathbf{X}_0A(\mathbf{X} - \mathbf{X}_0)^{\mathsf{T}} = 0$ becomes

$$\lambda_i\mathbf{X}_0(\mathbf{X} - \mathbf{X}_0)^{\mathsf{T}} = 0$$

or

$$(\mathbf{X}_0, \mathbf{X} - \mathbf{X}_0) = 0.$$

This means that the vector $\mathbf{X} - \mathbf{X}_0$ in the direction of the tangent line we defined from $\mathbf{X}$ to $\mathbf{X}_0$ is perpendicular to the semiaxis. Thus the whole tangent plane is perpendicular to the semiaxis since all the lines in it through $\mathbf{X}_0$ are perpendicular.

The distance from the origin to this tangent plane at the end of the semiaxis is clearly $1/\sqrt{\lambda_i}$ and, in the case of the example, $1/\sqrt{6}$ is the shortest distance from the origin to the surface (Figure 8.2).

If all characteristic values are positive, it may be shown analytically that the shortest distance to the quadratic surface from the origin is along the principal axis associated with the largest characteristic value, and that the longest distance is along the principal axis associated with the smallest characteristic value. (See Exercise 5.)

Exercises

1. Use the method of this section to find a rotation which will bring $x_1^2 + 8x_1x_2 + 7x_2^2 = 3$ into a form containing no x_1x_2 term. Check your result by the trigonometric formula of plane geometry.
2. Find the principal axes and transform to reduced form:

$$2x_1^2 + 2x_1x_2 + x_2^2 + 2x_3^2 = 1.$$

3. Prove that for positive characteristic values one end of a semiaxis lies on a generalized quadratic surface.
4. Prove (using calculus) that the equation of the tangent hyperplane to the surface $Q(\mathbf{X}) = \mathbf{X}A\mathbf{X}^{\mathsf{T}} = 1$, at the point $P(p_1, p_2, \ldots, p_n)$ on the surface, is $\mathbf{P}A\mathbf{X}^{\mathsf{T}} = 1$.
5. Prove analytically that the minimum distance from the origin to the generalized quadratic surface is $1/\sqrt{\lambda_i}$, where λ_i is the maximum characteristic value >0.

8.6 Unitary and Hermitian Matrices

In the first five sections of this chapter we were primarily interested in transformations on R^n (on real matrices, if you wish). We shall now consider the generalizations of these results to transformations on C^n, or equivalently, to complex matrices.

We begin by considering the inner product in C^n. The reader will recall from Section 2.9 the definition

$$([x_1, x_2, \ldots, x_n], [y_1, y_2, \ldots, y_n]) = x_1\bar{y}_1 + x_2\bar{y}_2 + \cdots + x_n\bar{y}_n,$$

where the bar denotes complex conjugation. The complex conjugation in this definition seems strange at first. For instance, we lose commutativity: $(X, Y) = \overline{(Y, X)}$. The reason for introducing the conjugation is that we have $(X, X) > 0$ for all nonzero X (that is, (X, X) is *real* and positive). This allows us to use "order" properties, which were used in many of our previous theorems.

With this definition we can reformulate almost all the algebraic structure involving inner products. We can prove equivalents of the Schwarz inequality, the Gram-Schmidt process, etc. Moreover, the fact that "orthogonality" is available (two vectors are perpendicular if their inner product is 0) allows us to generalize many geometrical theorems. It is this last fact that makes the study of inner product spaces so rich and interesting.

Without further ado, let us consider the analogs of symmetric matrices and orthogonal linear transformations.

DEFINITION 8.3. If $A = [a_{ij}]$ is a complex $m \times n$ matrix, we define the CONJUGATE TRANSPOSE, *$B = [b_{ij}]$ of A, by $b_{ij} = \bar{a}_{ji}$. We write $B = A^*$.*

DEFINITION 8.4. A transformation T on C^n is said to be UNITARY *if $(T\mathbf{X}, T\mathbf{Y}) = (\mathbf{X}, \mathbf{Y})$ for all $\mathbf{X}$, $\mathbf{Y}$ in C^n.*

What can be said about the matrices that represent unitary transformations? If A is the matrix of such a transformation, T, with respect to the standard basis we have

$$(\mathbf{X}, \mathbf{Y}) = (\mathrm{T}\mathbf{X}, \mathrm{T}\mathbf{Y}) = (A\mathbf{X}^{\mathsf{T}}, A\mathbf{Y}^{\mathsf{T}}) = (A\mathbf{X}^{\mathsf{T}})^{\mathsf{T}}(A\mathbf{Y}^{\mathsf{T}})^{*\mathsf{T}} = \mathbf{X}A^{\mathsf{T}}A^{*\mathsf{T}}\mathbf{Y}^*$$

for all $\mathbf{X}$ in C^n. It follows that $A^*A = I$ (see Exercise 4), or $A^{-1} = A^*$. We use this property to define a unitary matrix; that is, we shall say that A is *unitary* if its inverse and its conjugate transpose are equal.

It is easy to see that unitary transformations are represented by unitary matrices with respect to any orthonormal basis, and that the rows and columns of unitary matrices are orthonormal sets of vectors in C^n.

It should be clear by now that the complex generalization of a real symmetric matrix is not a complex symmetric matrix but rather a matrix such that $A = A^*$. Matrices with this property are called *Hermitian*. Theorems concerning symmetric real matrices generally carry over directly to statements about Hermitian matrices. We begin by noting that $(A\mathbf{X}^{\mathsf{T}}, \mathbf{Y}^{\mathsf{T}}) = (\mathbf{X}^{\mathsf{T}}, A^*\mathbf{Y}^{\mathsf{T}})$ for any A and any vectors $\mathbf{X}, \mathbf{Y}$ in C^n. The proof of this fact consists in simply expanding both sides of the equation; but, in spite of its innocent appearance, this equation is an important technical device. We use it in the following theorem.

THEOREM 8.7. If A is Hermitian, then the characteristic values of A are real, and there exists a unitary matrix U such that $UAU^{-1} = UAU^*$ is a real diagonal matrix.

PROOF. If λ is a characteristic value of A, with characteristic vector, X, we have

$$(\lambda\mathbf{X}, \mathbf{X}) = (A\mathbf{X}^{\mathsf{T}}, \mathbf{X}^{\mathsf{T}}) = (\mathbf{X}^{\mathsf{T}}, A^*\mathbf{X}^{\mathsf{T}}) = (\mathbf{X}^{\mathsf{T}}, A\mathbf{X}^{\mathsf{T}}) = (\mathbf{X}, \lambda\mathbf{X}).$$

But
$$(\lambda\mathbf{X}, \mathbf{X}) = \lambda(\mathbf{X}, \mathbf{X})$$
and
$$(\mathbf{X}, \lambda\mathbf{X}) = \bar{\lambda}(\mathbf{X}, \mathbf{X}).$$

As $(\mathbf{X}, \mathbf{X}) \neq 0$ this means $\lambda = \bar{\lambda}$ or λ is real. (The astute reader will notice that this is exactly the proof we gave in the case of a real, symmetric matrix; it looks simpler because our notation is better.) The remainder of the proof is exactly as in the real, symmetric case; pick an orthonormal basis of characteristic vectors and let U be the matrix of change of basis.

In the preceding sketch, we have omitted proofs not because they are difficult but simply because they would be almost word-for-word repetitions of existing proofs with "conjugate transpose" replacing "transpose" and with a little care for the order of inner products. The student is urged to take a theorem such as the Gram-Schmidt process, Theorem 2.13, or one of the theorems of Section 8.4 and carry out the proofs for the complex case.

For complete details, the interested reader should consult other books such as *Finite Dimensional Vector Spaces*, by P. R. Halmos (New York: Van Nostrand Reinhold, 1958).

Exercises

1. State the Schwarz inequality adapted to vectors in C^n.
2. State the Gram-Schmidt process theorem for the complex case and find an orthonormal basis for the subspace of C^4 spanned by $\{[1, 0, i, -i], [0, i, 1, i], [1, 1, 1, 0]\}$.
3. Given $A = \begin{bmatrix} 1 & i \\ -i & 1 \end{bmatrix}$, find a unitary matrix P such that PAP^* is a real diagonal matrix.
4. If B is a complex $n \times n$ matrix that satisfies $(\mathbf{X}, \mathbf{Y}) = \mathbf{X}B\mathbf{Y}^*$ for all $\mathbf{X}, \mathbf{Y}$ in C^n, show that B is the identity matrix. *Hint:* Try specific vectors for $\mathbf{X}$, $\mathbf{Y}$, such as the standard basis vectors.

Canonical Forms

Let T be a linear transformation on V with a characteristic value λ. If we regard T as a linear transformation on the subspace of characteristic vectors M_λ, the restriction of T to M_λ has a particularly simple matrix. For any basis whatever, the matrix of T restricted to M_λ is just λI. As we saw in the previous chapter, if the subspaces M_λ span V, then we can "paste" these matrices together to obtain a diagonal matrix representing T. We wish to find a "nice" matrix representation for transformations in general. The plan is to find a generalization of the subspaces M_λ and to make precise the statement about "pasting" smaller matrices together.

9.1 Invariant Subspaces

In this section we study subspaces M associated with a linear transformation which generalize the characteristic subspaces of Chapter 8. As we wish to consider the transformation obtained by restricting the given transformation T to the subspace M, the subspaces must have the property that $\mathrm{T}(M) \subseteq M$. This property is given a name.

DEFINITION 9.1. *If* T *is a linear transformation on* V *and* M *is a subspace of* V *with the property that* $\mathrm{T}(M) \subseteq M$, *then* M *is said to be an* INVARIANT SUBSPACE *for* T.

Example 1. Let A be the matrix

$$\begin{bmatrix} 3 & -2 & -2 \\ -1 & 2 & 1 \\ 3 & -3 & -2 \end{bmatrix}$$

and define a linear transformation T on $\mathbf{R}^3$ by $\mathrm{T}\mathbf{X} = A\mathbf{X}^{\mathrm{T}}$.

Consider $\mathbf{X} = [1, 0, 0]$.

$$\mathrm{T}\mathbf{X} = [3, -1, 3]$$

and

$$T^2\mathbf{X} = T[3, -1, 3] = [5, -2, 6] = -[1, 0, 0] + 2[3, -1, 3].$$

It is now easy to see that $T^k\mathbf{X}$ is a linear combination of $[1, 0, 0]$ and $[3, -1, 3]$ for any $k = 0, 1, 2, \ldots$. For example,

$$T^3\mathbf{X} = [7, -3, 9] = -2[1, 0, 0] + 3[3, -1, 3].$$

It is a simple induction to conclude that $T^k\mathbf{X} = -(k-1)\mathbf{X} + kT\mathbf{X}$. If we let M be the subspace $L\{\mathbf{X}, T\mathbf{X}\}$, then M is an invariant subspace for T.

It is interesting to note that M is *not* a characteristic subspace. This is probably most easily seen by observing that $T[1, 0, 0] = [3, -1, 3]$ is not a multiple of $[1, 0, 0]$; thus $[1, 0, 0]$ is not a characteristic vector of T for any λ.

The value of invariant subspaces in finding simple matrix representations of a linear transformation is illustrated in the following example.

Example 2. Let T be the linear transformation whose matrix relative to the standard basis is

$$\begin{bmatrix} 3 & 1 & 1 \\ 1 & 3 & -1 \\ 0 & 0 & 4 \end{bmatrix}.$$

We begin with $\mathbf{X} = [1, 0, 0]$ and calculate $T\mathbf{X} = [3, 1, 0]$, $T^2[\mathbf{X}] = [10, 6, 0]$. Note that $T^2[\mathbf{X}] = -8\mathbf{X} + 6T\mathbf{X}$, and thus the subspace $M_1 = L\{\mathbf{X}, T\mathbf{X}\}$ is invariant under T (why?). If we let T_1 be the restriction of T to M_1 and calculate the matrix of T_1 relative to the basis $\mathbf{X}, T\mathbf{X}$, we have

$$\begin{aligned} T_1\mathbf{X} &= T\mathbf{X} &&= 0 \cdot \mathbf{X} + 1 \cdot T_1\mathbf{X}, \\ T_1(T\mathbf{X}) &= T^2\mathbf{X} &&= -8 \cdot \mathbf{X} + 6 \cdot T_1\mathbf{X}. \end{aligned}$$

The matrix of T_1 is then

$$\begin{bmatrix} 0 & -8 \\ 1 & 6 \end{bmatrix}.$$

We now note the fact that $T[1, 0, 1] = [4, 0, 4]$ and thus the subspace $M_2 = L\{[1, 0, 1]\}$ is also invariant under T. The matrix of T_2, the restriction of T to M_2, is just $[4]$ relative to the basis $\{[1, 0, 1]\}$.

Now, what is the matrix of T relative to the basis $[1, 0, 0], [3, 1, 0], [1, 0, 1]$? Repeating the calculations above we obtain

$$\begin{bmatrix} 0 & -8 & 0 \\ 1 & 6 & 0 \\ 0 & 0 & 4 \end{bmatrix}.$$

The procedure in Example 2 will always work (providing the invariant subspaces can be found). That is, if T is a linear transformation on $V = M_1 \oplus M_2$, the matrix of T restricted to M_1 is A, and the matrix of T restricted to M_2 is B, then by "stringing" together the bases for M_1 and M_2 one will obtain a matrix for T of the form

$$\begin{bmatrix} A & \bigcirc \\ \bigcirc & B \end{bmatrix}.$$

The large zeros in the above matrix again represent blocks of zeros. This will be our fundamental technique for finding simple matrix representations of a given transformation. We state the technique as a theorem.

THEOREM 9.1. If T *is a linear transformation on* $V = M_1 \oplus M_2 \oplus \cdots \oplus M_k$ *and each* M_i *is an invariant subspace for* T, *then there is a choice of basis of* V *with respect to which the matrix of* T *is given by*

$$\begin{bmatrix} A_1 & \bigcirc & \cdots & \bigcirc \\ \bigcirc & A_2 & \cdots & \bigcirc \\ \vdots & \vdots & & \vdots \\ \bigcirc & \bigcirc & \cdots & A_k \end{bmatrix}.$$

Here the large zeros stand for blocks of zeros and A_j *is any matrix of the restriction of* T *to* M_j.

PROOF. Exactly as in the case of two subspaces, assume that A_j is the matrix of T restricted to M_j relative to the basis $\{\mathbf{X}_1^j, \mathbf{X}_2^j, \ldots, \mathbf{X}_{n_j}^j\}$ and then calculate the matrix of T relative to the basis obtained by "stringing" these bases together; namely, relative to the basis

$$\{\mathbf{X}_1^1, \mathbf{X}_2^1, \ldots, \mathbf{X}_{n_1}^1, \mathbf{X}_1^2, \mathbf{X}_2^2, \ldots, \mathbf{X}_{n_k}^k\}.$$

Matrices such as the one in Theorem 9.1 are called *block diagonal* matrices and will appear throughout this chapter. In the sequel we will often omit the large zeros.

Theorem 9.1 allows us to find a simple matrix representing a linear transformation assuming that we have suitable invariant subspaces available. We now turn to the problem of finding these subspaces.

Let us begin by picking an arbitrary vector $\mathbf{X} \in V$, and try to find an invariant subspace for T containing $\mathbf{X}$. The subspace must contain $\mathrm{T}\mathbf{X}$, and then $\mathrm{T}^2\mathbf{X}$, and so on. Consider the set of vectors $\{\mathbf{X}, \mathrm{T}\mathbf{X}, \mathrm{T}^2\mathbf{X}, \ldots, \mathrm{T}^n\mathbf{X}\}$, where n is the dimension of V. Since our set contains $n + 1$ vectors, some vector must be a linear combination of previous vectors. Let us say that $\mathrm{T}^k\mathbf{X}$ is the first such vector. We have a relationship of the form

$$\mathrm{T}^k\mathbf{X} + a_{k-1}\mathrm{T}^{k-1}\mathbf{X} + a_{k-2}\mathrm{T}^{k-2}\mathbf{X} + \cdots + a_0\mathbf{X} = 0. \tag{9.1}$$

We claim that $M = L\{\mathbf{X}, \mathrm{T}\mathbf{X}, \ldots, \mathrm{T}^{k-1}\mathbf{X}\}$ is invariant for T. This is easily seen, for if $\mathbf{Y}$ is any vector in M, then for some scalars $b_0, b_1, \ldots, b_{k-1}$ we have $\mathbf{Y} = b_0\mathbf{X} + b_1\mathrm{T}\mathbf{X} + \cdots + b_{k-1}\mathrm{T}^{k-1}\mathbf{X}$ and

$$\begin{aligned} \mathrm{T}\mathbf{Y} &= \mathrm{T}(b_0\mathbf{X} + \cdots + b_{k-1}\mathrm{T}^{k-1}\mathbf{X}) = b_0\mathrm{T}\mathbf{X} + \cdots + b_{k-2}\mathrm{T}^{k-1}\mathbf{X} + b_{k-1}\mathrm{T}^k\mathbf{X} \\ &= b_0\mathrm{T}\mathbf{X} + \cdots + b_{k-2}\mathrm{T}^{k-1}\mathbf{X} \\ &\quad + b_{k-1}(-a_0\mathbf{X} - a_1\mathrm{T}\mathbf{X} - \cdots - a_{k-1}\mathrm{T}^{k-1}\mathbf{X}). \end{aligned}$$

The last expression is clearly in M. If we choose $\{\mathbf{X}, \mathrm{T}\mathbf{X}, \ldots, \mathrm{T}^{k-1}\mathbf{X}\}$ as a basis of M, what is the matrix of T? We have

$$\begin{aligned} \mathrm{T}\mathbf{X} &= 0\cdot\mathbf{X} + 1\cdot\mathrm{T}\mathbf{X} + 0\cdot\mathrm{T}^2\mathbf{X} + \cdots + 0\cdot\mathrm{T}^{k-1}\mathbf{X}, \\ \mathrm{T}(\mathrm{T}\mathbf{X}) &= 0\cdot\mathbf{X} + 0\cdot\mathrm{T}\mathbf{X} + 1\cdot\mathrm{T}^2\mathbf{X} + 0\cdot\mathrm{T}^3\mathbf{X} + \cdots + 0\cdot\mathrm{T}^{k-1}\mathbf{X}, \\ &\vdots \\ \mathrm{T}(\mathrm{T}^{k-2}\mathbf{X}) &= 0\cdot\mathbf{X} + \cdots + 0\cdot\mathrm{T}^{k-2}\mathbf{X} + 1\cdot\mathrm{T}^{k-1}\mathbf{X}, \\ \mathrm{T}(\mathrm{T}^{k-1}\mathbf{X}) &= -a_0\mathbf{X} - a_1\mathrm{T}\mathbf{X} - \cdots - a_{k-1}\mathrm{T}^{k-1}\mathbf{X}. \end{aligned}$$

Thus the matrix of T is

$$\begin{bmatrix} 0 & 0 & 0 & \cdots & & 0 & -a_0 \\ 1 & 0 & 0 & \cdots & & 0 & -a_1 \\ 0 & 1 & 0 & \cdots & & 0 & -a_2 \\ \vdots & & & & & & \vdots \\ 0 & 0 & 0 & \cdots & 0 & 1 & -a_{k-1} \end{bmatrix}.$$

As the previous discussion is fundamental to our future work, we formalize it with two definitions.

DEFINITION 9.2. If M is a subspace of V which is invariant for T *and of the form* $M = L\{\mathbf{X}, \mathrm{T}\mathbf{X}, \ldots, \mathrm{T}^{k-1}\mathbf{X}\}$ *for some* $\mathbf{X}$, *we say that M is a* CYCLIC SUBSPACE *with respect to* T. $\mathbf{X}$ *is said to* GENERATE M.

For brevity we shall often denote a cyclic subspace by $L\{\mathrm{T}^i\mathbf{X}\}$ or $L\{A^i\mathbf{X}^\mathsf{T}\}$ if A is a matrix. It is usually not necessary to specify the dimension k.

DEFINITION 9.3. Given a polynomial $p(x) = a_0 + a_1x + a_2x^2 + \cdots + a_{k-1}x^{k-1}$, *the matrix*

$$\begin{bmatrix} 0 & 0 & 0 & \cdots & 0 & -a_0 \\ 1 & 0 & 0 & \cdots & 0 & -a_1 \\ 0 & 1 & 0 & \cdots & 0 & -a_2 \\ 0 & 0 & 1 & \cdots & 0 & -a_3 \\ \vdots & & & & & \vdots \\ 0 & 0 & 0 & \cdots & 1 & -a_{k-1} \end{bmatrix}$$

is called the COMPANION MATRIX *of* $p(x)$, *and this matrix will be denoted by* $C(p(x))$.

Example 3. The companion matrix of $x^4 + 2x^3 - 3x^2 + x - 1$ is

$$\begin{bmatrix} 0 & 0 & 0 & 1 \\ 1 & 0 & 0 & -1 \\ 0 & 1 & 0 & 3 \\ 0 & 0 & 1 & -2 \end{bmatrix},$$

that of $x + 2$ is $[-2]$, and that of $(x - 2)^2 = x^2 - 4x + 4$ is $\begin{bmatrix} 0 & -4 \\ 1 & 4 \end{bmatrix}$. To illustrate the connection between the companion matrix and our work on cyclic subspaces, let us consider the transformation T whose matrix relative to the $\{E_i\}$ basis is

$$\begin{bmatrix} 0 & -4 & -4 \\ \frac{1}{2} & 3 & 1 \\ \frac{1}{2} & 1 & 3 \end{bmatrix}.$$

Note that

$$\mathrm{T}[1, 0, 0] = [0, \tfrac{1}{2}, \tfrac{1}{2}]$$

and

$$\mathrm{T}[0, \tfrac{1}{2}, \tfrac{1}{2}] = [-4, 2, 2] = -4[1, 0, 0] + 4[0, \tfrac{1}{2}, \tfrac{1}{2}],$$

and thus the cyclic subspace generated by $[1, 0, 0]$ is $L\{[1, 0, 0], [0, \frac{1}{2}, \frac{1}{2}]\}$. Further, the matrix of T restricted to $L\{\mathrm{T}^i[1, 0, 0]\}$ with respect to the basis $\{[1, 0, 0], [0, \frac{1}{2}, \frac{1}{2}]\}$ is

$$\begin{bmatrix} 0 & -4 \\ 1 & 4 \end{bmatrix} = C(x^2 - 4x + 4).$$

The connection between the polynomial $x^2 - 4x + 4$ and T is just that

$$\mathrm{T}^2[1, 0, 0] = 4\mathrm{T}[1, 0, 0] - 4[1, 0, 0]$$

or

$$\mathrm{T}^2[1, 0, 0] - 4\mathrm{T}[1, 0, 0] + 4[1, 0, 0] = 0;$$

or $[\mathrm{T}^2 - 4\mathrm{T} + 4\mathrm{I}][1, 0, 0] = 0$.

In the preceding example, we were led to considering a "polynomial in a transformation." In the next section we pause to consider this concept carefully, and to study polynomials that arise naturally from linear transformations.

Exercises

1. Let T be the linear transformation whose matrix relative to the standard basis is
$$A = \begin{bmatrix} 0 & -2 & -2 \\ 2 & 3 & 0 \\ -1 & 0 & 3 \end{bmatrix}.$$
   (a) What is the dimension of the cyclic subspace
$$V_1 = L\{\mathrm{T}^i[1, 0, 0]\} = L\{A^i[1, 0, 0]^{\mathrm{T}}\}?$$
   (b) What is the dimension of the cyclic subspace
$$V_2 = L\{\mathrm{T}^i[1, -1, 0]\} = L\{A^i[1, -1, 0]^{\mathrm{T}}\}?$$
   (c) What is the dimension of $V_1 \cap V_2$?
2. Let D be the differentiation operator on P^n, the polynomials of degree less than n.
   (a) Describe the cyclic subspace for D generated by x^3.
   (b) Describe the cyclic subspace for D generated by $2x^3 + x^2$.
   (c) If $p(x)$ is a polynomial in P^n, describe the cyclic subspace for D generated by $p(x)$.
   (d) Note that
$$x^{n-1}, (n-1)x^{n-2}, (n-1)(n-2)x^{n-3}, \ldots, (n-1)!$$
   are a basis for P^n. What is the matrix of D in this basis? For what polynomial is this matrix the companion matrix?
3. Let T be rotation of the plane (R^2) by 90° in the counterclockwise direction. Does T have any invariant subspaces besides $\{0\}$ and R^2? What is the matrix of T with respect to the basis $\{[1, 0], \mathrm{T}[1, 0]\}$? For what polynomial is the last matrix the companion matrix?
4. Show that if T is a nonsingular linear transformation, then any invariant subspace for T is also invariant for T^{-1}.
5. Show that for any linear transformation T with characteristic value λ, the subspace M_λ is invariant.

9.2 The Minimal Polynomial

In this section we consider certain polynomials associated with a linear transformation. The reader may not see the importance of these polynomials until the next section, where they will provide the key to our problem of finding a simple matrix for a given transformation.

We saw previously that any element c in a field F gives rise to a mapping from $F[x]$ to F: namely $p(x) \to p(c)$. This idea can be extended to give mappings from $F[x]$ to the algebra of linear transformations on F^n or to the algebra of $n \times n$ matrices over F. The procedure is as follows: if we have a polynomial $a_0 + a_1x + a_2x^2 + \cdots + a_mx^m$, and a linear transformation T on F^n, the mapping
$$a_0 + a_1x + a_2x^2 + \cdots + a_mx^m \to a_0\mathrm{I} + a_1\mathrm{T} + a_2\mathrm{T}^2 + \cdots + a_m\mathrm{T}^m$$
defines a morphism from the algebra $F[x]$ into the algebra Hom (F^n, F^n).

The same result applies to matrices. For example, if $A = \begin{bmatrix} 1 & -1 \\ 2 & 0 \end{bmatrix}$, then

$$1 - x + 2x^2 \to \begin{bmatrix} 1 & 0 \\ 0 & 1 \end{bmatrix} - \begin{bmatrix} 1 & -1 \\ 2 & 0 \end{bmatrix} + 2\begin{bmatrix} 1 & -1 \\ 2 & 0 \end{bmatrix}^2$$
$$= \begin{bmatrix} 1 & 0 \\ 0 & 1 \end{bmatrix} - \begin{bmatrix} 1 & -1 \\ 2 & 0 \end{bmatrix} + \begin{bmatrix} -1 & -1 \\ 2 & -2 \end{bmatrix}$$
$$= \begin{bmatrix} -1 & 0 \\ 0 & -1 \end{bmatrix}$$

and

$$2 - x + 2x^2 \to \begin{bmatrix} 0 & 0 \\ 0 & 0 \end{bmatrix}.$$

The verifications that these mappings are truly morphisms will be left to the exercises. (Any expected difficulty with commutativity disappears since we are dealing with powers of a single transformation or matrix and $T^mT^n = T^nT^m = T^{m+n}$.) We state the definition using the common notation for polynomials.

DEFINITION 9.4. Let $p(x) = a_0 + a_1x + \cdots + a_mx^m$ be an element of $F[x]$, and let T be a linear transformation of a vector space V over F. Furthermore, let $A = [a_{ij}]$ be an $n \times n$ matrix over F.

We define $p(T)$ to be the linear transformation

$$a_0I + a_1T + \cdots + a_mT^m \text{ on } V$$

and we define $p(A)$ to be the matrix

$$a_0I + a_1A + \cdots + a_mA^m.$$

Our first application of polynomials in transformations will be to show that each vector **X** in V has an associated unique *minimal polynomial* with respect to a fixed transformation on V. This minimal polynomial is the monic polynomial of least degree that satisfies $m(T)\mathbf{X} = 0$.

Our discussion about cyclic subspaces showed that there is at least one monic polynomial $m(x) \in F[x]$ such that $m(T)\mathbf{X} = \mathbf{0}$, $m(x) = x^k + a_{k-1}x^{k-1} + \cdots + a_0$. (See Equation (9.1).) If there were a monic polynomial of lower degree with the desired property, say of degree $r < k$, then we would have $T^r\mathbf{X}$ dependent on previous vectors, contradicting the choice of $T^k\mathbf{X}$ in the discussion preceding (9.1). If there were *two* monic polynomials $m_1(x)$ and $m_2(x)$ with the property $m_1(T)\mathbf{X} = m_2(T)\mathbf{X} = \mathbf{0}$, then $(m_1(T) - m_2(T))\mathbf{X} = \mathbf{0}$ and $m_1(x) - m_2(x)$ is a polynomial of lower degree. A scalar multiple of $m_1(x) - m_2(x)$ would then be monic and still annihilate **X**.

DEFINITION 9.5. The monic polynomial $m(x)$ of least degree such that $m(T)\mathbf{X} = \mathbf{0}$ is called the RELATIVE MINIMAL POLYNOMIAL *of* **X** *for* T.

Example 1. If T is the linear transformation of Example 3 in the preceding section and $\mathbf{X} = [1, 0, 0]$, then $x^2 - 4x + 4$ is the relative minimal polynomial of **X** because $T^2\mathbf{X} - 4T\mathbf{X} + 4I = \mathbf{0}$ and no polynomial in T of degree one can annihilate **X** (why?). What is the relative minimal polynomial of $\mathbf{Y} = [-2, 1, 0]$?

$$\begin{bmatrix} 0 & -4 & -4 \\ \frac{1}{2} & 3 & 1 \\ \frac{1}{2} & 1 & 3 \end{bmatrix} \begin{bmatrix} -2 \\ 1 \\ 0 \end{bmatrix} = \begin{bmatrix} -4 \\ 2 \\ 0 \end{bmatrix}.$$

Thus $$\mathrm{T}[-2, 1, 0] = [-4, 2, 0] = 2[-2, 1, 0],$$

or $$\mathrm{T}[-2, 1, 0] - 2[-2, 1, 0] = \mathbf{0},$$
$$[\mathrm{T} - 2\mathrm{I}][-2, 1, 0] = \mathbf{0}.$$

If $p(x) = x - 2$, we have then that $p(\mathrm{T})\mathbf{Y} = \mathbf{0}$. As no monic zero-degree polynomial has this property, $x - 2$ is the desired relative minimal polynomial.

Let us return to the general case and suppose that $p(x)$ is some other polynomial that annihilates $\mathbf{X}$, that is, such that $p(\mathrm{T})\mathbf{X} = \mathbf{0}$. We claim that $m(x)$ divides $p(x)$ in $F[x]$. In fact, applying the division algorithm,

$$p(x) = q(x)m(x) + r(x),$$

where $r(x)$ is either zero or of degree less than $m(x)$. But

$$\mathbf{0} = p(\mathrm{T})\mathbf{X} = [q(\mathrm{T})m(\mathrm{T}) + r(\mathrm{T})]\mathbf{X} = q(\mathrm{T})m(\mathrm{T})\mathbf{X} + r(\mathrm{T})\mathbf{X} = r(\mathrm{T})\mathbf{X},$$

so that $r(\mathrm{T})$ annihilates $\mathbf{X}$. If $r(x)$ were not zero, multiplying by the inverse of its leading coefficient would yield a monic polynomial of degree less than $m(x)$, which annihilated $\mathbf{X}$. Hence $r(x) = 0$.

THEOREM 9.2. *Let* T *be a linear transformation on V and* $\mathbf{X}$ *a vector in V. Then*

(i) $M = L\{\mathrm{T}^i\mathbf{X}\}$ *is an invariant subspace for* T.
(ii) *There exists a unique monic polynomial $m(x)$ of least degree such that* $m(\mathrm{T})\mathbf{X} = \mathbf{0}$.
(iii) *The dimension of M is equal to the degree of $m(x)$.*
(iv) *The polynomial $m(x)$ divides every polynomial $p(x)$ that satisfies* $p(\mathrm{T})\mathbf{X} = \mathbf{0}$.

Example 2. The relative minimal polynomial of $\mathbf{X} = [1, 0, 0]$ with respect to the transformation T that has the matrix (relative to $\{E_i\}$)

$$A = \begin{bmatrix} 3 & -2 & -2 \\ -1 & 2 & 1 \\ 3 & -3 & -2 \end{bmatrix} \quad \text{is} \quad x^2 - 2x + 1.$$

This may be seen by following the procedure outlined in the text.

$$A\mathbf{X}^{\mathsf{T}} = [3, -1, 3]^{\mathsf{T}}, \qquad A^2\mathbf{X}^{\mathsf{T}} = [5, -2, 6]^{\mathsf{T}} = -[1, 0, 0]^{\mathsf{T}} + 2[3, -1, 3]^{\mathsf{T}}.$$

Thus $\mathbf{X}$, $\mathrm{T}\mathbf{X}$ are linearly independent and $\mathrm{T}^2\mathbf{X} = -\mathbf{X} + 2\mathrm{T}\mathbf{X}$.

The preceding discussion gives us many polynomials associated with a transformation T. There is another important polynomial depending only on T; the monic polynomial $m(x)$ of least degree such that $m(\mathrm{T}) = \mathbf{0}$.

THEOREM 9.3. *Associated with each linear transformation* T *on V is a polynomial $m(x)$ with the following properties.*

(i) *$m(x)$ is the unique monic polynomial of minimal degree that satisfies* $m(\mathrm{T}) = \mathbf{0}$.
(ii) *$m(x)$ divides every polynomial $p(x)$ such that* $p(\mathrm{T}) = \mathbf{0}$.

PROOF. The uniqueness of $m(x)$ and part (ii) can be proved by mimicking the proofs of the similar statements in Theorem 9.2, once we have established that there is at least one polynomial that annihilates T. Recall that if V has dimension n, then Hom (V, V) has dimension n^2; thus the set $\{\mathrm{I}, \mathrm{T}, \mathrm{T}^2, \ldots, \mathrm{T}^{n^2}\}$ must be linearly dependent. There is, then, a relationship

$$a_0\mathrm{I} + a_1\mathrm{T} + \cdots + a_{n^2}\mathrm{T}^{n^2} = \mathbf{0}$$

and the polynomial

$$p(x) = a_0 + a_1 x + \cdots + a_{n^2} x^{n^2}$$

annihilates T. Another proof of the existence of at least one such polynomial is suggested in Exercise 7.

DEFINITION 9.6. *The monic polynomial of least degree $m(x)$ that satisfies $m(\mathrm{T}) = 0$ is called the minimal polynomial of* T. *A similar definition applies to an $n \times n$ matrix A.*

Note that if A represents T, then $p(\mathrm{T}) = 0$ if and only if $p(A) = 0$. Thus the minimal polynomial of T is the same as the minimal polynomial of any matrix that represents T.

Note that if $\mathbf{X}$ is any vector in V with relative minimal polynomial $m_1(x)$ for T and $m(x)$ is the minimal polynomial of T, then $m_1(x)$ divides $m(x)$. This fact is often helpful in practice.

Example 3. Let us return to the transformation T of Example 1. We seek the minimal polynomial $m(x)$ of T. We know that $(x-2)^2$ must divide $m(x)$ by the remark preceding this example. We consider $(\mathrm{T}-2)^2$. Its matrix relative to the $\{E_i\}$ basis is

$$\left(\begin{bmatrix} 0 & -4 & -4 \\ \frac{1}{2} & 3 & 1 \\ \frac{1}{2} & 1 & 3 \end{bmatrix} - \begin{bmatrix} 2 & 0 & 0 \\ 0 & 2 & 0 \\ 0 & 0 & 2 \end{bmatrix}\right)^2 = \begin{bmatrix} -2 & -4 & -4 \\ \frac{1}{2} & 1 & 1 \\ \frac{1}{2} & 1 & 1 \end{bmatrix}^2 = \begin{bmatrix} 0 & 0 & 0 \\ 0 & 0 & 0 \\ 0 & 0 & 0 \end{bmatrix}.$$

Thus $(\mathrm{T}-2)^2 = 0$, and the minimal polynomial is $(x-2)^2$ as $(x-2)^2$ does not divide any lower degree polynomial.

Our program for finding a canonical form for a transformation T on V will consist of finding cyclic subspaces whose direct sum is V. In the previous chapter this process was facilitated by the fact that, if $\lambda_1 \neq \lambda_2$, then $M_{\lambda_1} \cap M_{\lambda_2} = \mathbf{0}$. Thus if the characteristic spaces spanned V, their sum was direct. It is unfortunately *not* true in general that two different cyclic subspaces have $\{0\}$ as intersection. In Example 1 of Section 9.1, the cyclic subspace generated by $[1, 0, 0]$ has a basis $\{[1, 0, 0], [3, -1, 3]\}$. That generated by $[0, 1, 0]$ has a basis $\{[0, 1, 0], [-2, 2, -3]\}$. Since these subspaces are of dimension two in R^3, they must have a one-dimensional intersection. This problem will cause us grave difficulties; nonetheless, in the following we shall see that it is always possible to find a set of vectors $\mathbf{X}_1, \ldots, \mathbf{X}_s$ such that

$$V = L\{\mathrm{T}^i\mathbf{X}_1\} \oplus L\{\mathrm{T}^i\mathbf{X}_2\} \oplus \cdots \oplus L\{\mathrm{T}^i\mathbf{X}_s\}.$$

Exercises

1. Let T be the transformation on R^4 whose matrix relative to the $\{\mathbf{E}_i\}$ basis is

$$\begin{bmatrix} 3 & 1 & 1 & 0 \\ -1 & 1 & 0 & -1 \\ -1 & -1 & 0 & 1 \\ -2 & -1 & -1 & 1 \end{bmatrix}.$$

   (a) Find the relative minimal polynomial of $\mathbf{X}_1 = [1, -1, -1, 0]$ and $\mathbf{X}_2 = [1, 0, -1, -1]$.
   (b) Find the minimal polynomial of T.

2. Let T be a linear transformation on R^n and $m_1(x), m_2(x), \ldots, m_n(x)$ the relative minimal polynomials of the standard basis vectors $\mathbf{E}_1, \mathbf{E}_2, \ldots, \mathbf{E}_n$. If $m(x)$ is the least common multiple of $m_1(x), m_2(x), \ldots, m_n(x)$ show that $m(x)$ is the minimal polynomial of T.
3. Let a linear transformation T on R^4 be defined by $\mathrm{T}\mathbf{X} = A\mathbf{X}^{\mathsf{T}}$, where

$$A = \begin{bmatrix} -2 & 0 & 0 & -1 \\ 4 & 1 & 0 & 0 \\ 1 & 0 & 1 & -1 \\ 1 & 0 & 0 & 0 \end{bmatrix}.$$

   (a) What are the relative minimal polynomials of $\mathbf{E}_1, \mathbf{E}_2, \mathbf{E}_3, \mathbf{E}_4$?
   (b) What is the minimal polynomial of T?
4. Use Exercise 2 to show that

$$A = \begin{bmatrix} 3 & 1 & 1 & 0 \\ -1 & 1 & 0 & -1 \\ -1 & -1 & 0 & 1 \\ -2 & -1 & -1 & 1 \end{bmatrix}$$

   has minimal polynomial $(x - 1)^2(x - 2)$.
5. Find the minimal polynomial of the matrix A in Exercise 1, Section 9.1.
6. Show that if a linear transformation T on R^n has n distinct characteristic values, the minimal polynomial of T has degree n. (What is the minimal polynomial?)
7. Use Exercise 2 to show that for any linear transformation T there is a polynomial $p(x)$ such that $p(\mathrm{T}) = 0$.
8. If $m(x)$ is an arbitrary polynomial and $B = P^{-1}AP$, show that $P^{-1}m(A)P = m(B)$. Use this to show directly that the minimal polynomials of similar matrices are equal.
9. Prove that if λ is a characteristic value of T, then $(x - \lambda)$ divides the minimal polynomial of T.
10. Write out the proof of Theorem 9.3.

9.3 The Rational Canonical Form

In this section we shall finish the program started in Section 9.1: to find a simple matrix representation for any linear transformation. Some of the proofs are technical and involved, particularly those of Lemma 1 and Theorem 9.5. As we feel that it is more important to understand the statement of these results than to be able to master the details of their proofs, we urge the reader to skip these two proofs on first reading. Having seen the power of the results, the reader will perhaps be motivated to work through their proofs. We begin by considering the special case of a linear transformation whose minimal polynomial is a power of an irreducible polynomial.

LEMMA 1. Let T *be a linear transformation on V with minimal polynomial $p(x)^l$, where $p(x)$ is monic irreducible, and let $\mathbf{X} \in V$ be such that $p(\mathrm{T})^{l-1}\mathbf{X} \neq \mathbf{0}$. Then there is at least one subspace W of V, invariant for* T, *with $V = L\{\mathrm{T}^i\mathbf{X}\} \oplus W$.*

PROOF. There is certainly at least one subspace W that is invariant under T and satisfies $W \cap L\{\mathrm{T}^i\mathbf{X}\} = \{0\}$, namely the subspace $\{0\}$. Let W be a subspace with these two properties having largest dimension. We claim that such a W satisfies $V = L\{T^i\mathbf{X}\} \oplus W$. The idea of the proof is to show that if there were a vector $\mathbf{Y} \in V - L\{T^i\mathbf{X}\} \oplus W$, then W could be enlarged while preserving invariances and independence, contradicting the maximality of W. To this end, let $\mathbf{Y} \in V - (\{L\{T^i\mathbf{X}\} + W\})$. If $(L\{T^i x\} + W) \cap L\{T^i\mathbf{Y}\} = \{0\}$ we are done, since we have enlarged W. Unfortunately this may not be the case. We shall show, however, that a suitable modification of $\mathbf{Y}$ will work.

Start by letting $r(x)$ be the monic polynomial of least degree with the property that

$$r(T)\mathbf{Y} \in L\{T^i\mathbf{X}\} + W.$$

Set

$$r(T)\mathbf{Y} = g(T)\mathbf{X} + \mathbf{Z},$$

where $\mathbf{Z} \in W$. Note that if $q(x)$ is any polynomial such that

$$q(T)\mathbf{Y} \in L\{T^i\mathbf{X}\} + W,$$

then $r(x)$ divides $q(x)$; for if

$$q(x) = r(x)h(x) + s(x),$$

then

$$q(T)\mathbf{Y} = r(T)h(T)\mathbf{Y} + s(T)\mathbf{Y}.$$

But this implies

$$s(T)\mathbf{Y} \in L\{T^i\mathbf{X}\} + W,$$

and since the degree of $s(x)$ is less than that of $r(x)$, $s(x)$ must be zero. Thus $r(x)$ must be a power of $p(x)$, since

$$p(T)^l\mathbf{Y} = 0 \in L\{T^i\mathbf{X}\} + W.$$

Let us say that $r(x) = p(x)^k$. We now claim that $r(x)$ actually divides $g(x)$. Apply $p(T)^{l-k}$ to the vector $r(T)\mathbf{Y}$:

$$0 = p(T)^{l-k}p(T)^k\mathbf{Y} = p(T)^{l-k}g(T)\mathbf{X} + p(T)^{l-k}\mathbf{Z}$$

so

$$p(T)^{l-k}g(T)\mathbf{X} = -p(T)^{l-k}\mathbf{Z}.$$

Since W is invariant, the right-hand side of the last equation is in W; the left-hand side is clearly in $L\{T^i\mathbf{X}\}$. As the intersection of these two subspaces is $\mathbf{0}$ alone we have

$$p(T)^{l-k}g(T)\mathbf{X} = \mathbf{0}.$$

Of course, $p(x)^l$ is the relative minimal polynomial of $\mathbf{X}$, so we now have that $p(x)^l$ divides $p(x)^{l-k}g(x)$. This means that $g(x)$ is divisible by $p(x)^k = r(x)$. Write $g(x) = r(x)d(x)$.

We now define $\mathbf{Y}^* = \mathbf{Y} - d(T)\mathbf{X}$. Note that any polynomial that maps $\mathbf{Y}^*$ into $L\{T^i\mathbf{X}\} \oplus W$ also maps $\mathbf{Y}$ into $L\{T^i\mathbf{X}\} \oplus W$ and hence is divisible by $r(x)$. We claim that

$$L\{T^i\mathbf{X}\} \cap (W + L\{T^i\mathbf{Y}^*\}) = \{0\}.$$

Let $\mathbf{Z}_1$ be any vector in this intersection, say

$$\mathbf{Z}_1 = f_1(T)\mathbf{X} = \mathbf{Z}_2 + f_2(T)\mathbf{Y}^*$$

for some polynomials f_1, f_2 and some $\mathbf{Z}_2 \in W$. $f_2(x)$ is divisible by $r(x)$, say $f_2(x) = f_3(x)r(x)$.

$$\begin{aligned} f_2(T)\mathbf{Y}^* &= f_3(T)r(T)\mathbf{Y}^* = f_3(T)[r(T)\mathbf{Y} - r(T)d(T)\mathbf{X}] \\ &= f_3(T)[r(T)d(T)\mathbf{X} + \mathbf{Z} - r(T)d(T)\mathbf{X}] = f_3(T)\mathbf{Z}. \end{aligned}$$

But $\mathbf{Z}$ is in W, so $f_3(\mathrm{T})\mathbf{Z}$ is too. Then $f_1(\mathrm{T})\mathbf{X} = \mathbf{Z}_2 + f_3(\mathrm{T})\mathbf{Z}$ is in W. Since $L\{\mathrm{T}^i\mathbf{X}\} \cap W = \{0\}$, this means $\mathbf{Z}_1$ must be zero and the lemma is finally established.

THEOREM 9.4. Let T *be a linear transformation on* V *with minimal polynomial* $p(x)^l$, *where* $p(x)$ *is monic irreducible. There exist integers* $l = l_1 \geq l_2 \geq \cdots \geq l_k$ *and vectors* $\mathbf{X}_1, \ldots, \mathbf{X}_k$ *such that*

$$V = L\{\mathrm{T}^i\mathbf{X}_1\} \oplus \cdots \oplus L\{\mathrm{T}^i\mathbf{X}_k\}.$$

Further, the relative minimal polynomial of $\mathbf{X}_i$ *is* $p(x)^{l_i}$.

PROOF. Pick $\mathbf{X}_1$ such that $p(\mathrm{T})^{l-1}\mathbf{X}_1 \neq \mathbf{0}$. By Lemma 1 we can find a subspace W_1 that is invariant for T, such that $V = L\{\mathrm{T}^i\mathbf{X}\} \oplus W_1$. Now consider the restriction of T to W_1. The minimal polynomial of T restricted to W_1 is a power of $p(x)$ because $p(\mathrm{T})^l W_1 = \{0\}$. Let us call this minimal polynomial $p(x)^{l_2}$. If we choose $\mathbf{X}_2 \in W_1$ such that $p(\mathrm{T})^{l_2-1}\mathbf{X}_2 \neq 0$, then by Lemma 1 we can find W_2, invariant under T, with

$$W_1 = L\{\mathrm{T}^i\mathbf{X}_2\} \oplus W_2.$$

Thus we have

$$V = L\{\mathrm{T}^i\mathbf{X}_1\} \oplus L\{\mathrm{T}^i\mathbf{X}_2\} \oplus W_2.$$

We now continue the process with W_2. After a finite number of steps (by induction if you wish) this process will terminate because each $L\{\mathrm{T}^i\mathbf{X}_j\}$ is of dimension at least one. Note that $l_1 + l_2 + \cdots + l_k =$ dimension V.

COROLLARY. If T *is as in Theorem* 9.4, *then there is a basis of* V *with respect to which the matrix of* T *is given by*

$$\begin{bmatrix} C(p(x)^{l_1}) & & & \\ & C(p(x)^{l_2}) & & \\ & & \ddots & \\ & & & C(p(x)^{l_k}) \end{bmatrix}$$

where the l_i*'s are also as in Theorem* 9.4.

PROOF OF COROLLARY. We write

$$V = L\{\mathrm{T}^i\mathbf{X}_1\} \oplus \cdots \oplus L\{\mathrm{T}^i\mathbf{X}_k\}$$

by Theorem 9.4. If we now choose the basis $\{\mathbf{X}_j, \mathrm{T}\mathbf{X}_j, \ldots, \mathrm{T}^{r_j}\mathbf{X}_j\}$ for $L\{\mathrm{T}^i\mathbf{X}_j\}$ (r_j here is one less than the dimension of $L\{\mathrm{T}^i\mathbf{X}_j\}$), then the matrix of T restricted to $L\{\mathrm{T}^i\mathbf{X}_j\}$ will be $C(p(x)^{l_j})$. Now the corollary follows by Theorem 9.1.

Example 1. If T is the linear transformation of R^3 whose matrix relative to the standard basis is

$$\begin{bmatrix} 3 & -2 & -2 \\ -1 & 2 & 1 \\ 3 & -3 & -2 \end{bmatrix},$$

then T has minimal polynomial $(x - 1)^2$. What is the matrix of T guaranteed by the corollary above? We note that

$$(\mathrm{T} - \mathrm{I})[1, 0, 0] = [2, -1, 3] \neq 0;$$

thus

$$L\{[1, 0, 0], \mathrm{T}[1, 0, 0]\} = L\{[1, 0, 0], [3, -1, 3]\}$$

is a maximal cyclic subspace of R^3 for T (see Exercise 3 of this section). Further, $T[1, 0, 1] = [1, 0, 1]$, so $L\{[1, 0, 1]\}$ is invariant under T. As

$$L\{[1, 0, 1]\} \cap L\{[1, 0, 0], [3, -1, 3]\} = \{0\},$$

we have

$$R^3 = L\{[1, 0, 0], [2, -1, 3]\} \oplus L\{[1, 0, 1]\}$$

and the matrix of T relative to the basis $\{[1, 0, 0], [3, -1, 3], [1, 0, 1]\}$ is

$$\begin{bmatrix} 0 & -1 & 0 \\ 1 & 2 & 0 \\ 0 & 0 & 1 \end{bmatrix} = \begin{bmatrix} C((x-1)^2) & \\ & C(x-1) \end{bmatrix}.$$

The next theorem serves to reduce the general case to the special case of Theorem 9.4.

THEOREM 9.5. *Let* T *be a linear transformation on* V *with minimal polynomial*

$$m(x) = p_1(x)^{l_1} p_2(x)^{l_2} \cdots p_n(x)^{l_n},$$

where each $p_i(x)$ *is monic irreducible. Define* $V_i = \{\mathbf{X} \in V \mid p_i(T)^{l_i}\mathbf{X} = \mathbf{0}\}$ *for each* $i = 1, 2, \ldots, n$. *Then the following hold:*

(i) *Each* V_i *is invariant for* T.

(ii) $V = V_1 \oplus V_2 \oplus \cdots \oplus V_n$.

(iii) *The minimal polynomial of the restriction of* T *to* V_i *is* $p_i(x)^{l_i}$.

DEFINITION 9.7. *The* V_i *of Theorem* 9.5 *are called the* PRINCIPAL COMPONENTS *of* T.

Example 2. Let A be the matrix of Exercise 4, Section 9.2, and T the linear transformation it defines in the standard basis.

T was seen to have minimal polynomial, $m(x) = (x - 1)^2(x - 2)$; thus T has two principal components:

$$V_1 = \{\mathbf{X} \in R^4 \mid (T - I)^2\mathbf{X} = \mathbf{0}\} \quad \text{and} \quad V_2 = \{\mathbf{X} \in R^4 \mid (T - 2I)\mathbf{X} = \mathbf{0}\}.$$

We solve for V_1, V_2 explicitly. If $\mathbf{X} = [x_1, x_2, x_3, x_4]$ is in V_1 we must have

$$\left(\begin{bmatrix} 3 & 1 & 1 & 0 \\ -1 & 1 & 0 & -1 \\ -1 & -1 & 0 & 1 \\ -2 & -1 & -1 & 1 \end{bmatrix} - \begin{bmatrix} 1 & 0 & 0 & 0 \\ 0 & 1 & 0 & 0 \\ 0 & 0 & 1 & 0 \\ 0 & 0 & 0 & 1 \end{bmatrix}\right)^2 \begin{bmatrix} x_1 \\ x_2 \\ x_3 \\ x_4 \end{bmatrix} = \mathbf{0}$$

or

$$\begin{bmatrix} 2 & 1 & 1 & 0 \\ 0 & 0 & 0 & 0 \\ -2 & -1 & -1 & 0 \\ -2 & -1 & -1 & 0 \end{bmatrix} \begin{bmatrix} x_1 \\ x_2 \\ x_3 \\ x_4 \end{bmatrix} = \mathbf{0},$$

$$\begin{aligned} 2x_1 + x_2 + x_3 &= 0, \\ 0 &= 0, \\ -2x_1 - x_2 - x_3 &= 0, \\ -2x_1 - x_2 - x_3 &= 0. \end{aligned}$$

It is clear that x_2, x_3, x_4 may be arbitrarily chosen and then $x_1 = -\frac{1}{2}(x_2 + x_3)$. Thus V_1 is the set of all vectors of the form $[-\frac{1}{2}(x_2 + x_3), x_2, x_3, x_4]$ and is clearly three-dimensional. Solving for V_2,

$$\left(\begin{bmatrix} 3 & 1 & 1 & 0 \\ -1 & 1 & 0 & -1 \\ -1 & -1 & 0 & 1 \\ -2 & -1 & -1 & 1 \end{bmatrix} - \begin{bmatrix} 2 & 0 & 0 & 0 \\ 0 & 2 & 0 & 0 \\ 0 & 0 & 2 & 0 \\ 0 & 0 & 0 & 2 \end{bmatrix}\right) \begin{bmatrix} x_1 \\ x_2 \\ x_3 \\ x_4 \end{bmatrix} = \mathbf{0},$$

which is equivalent to the system

$$\begin{aligned} x_1 + x_2 + x_3 \qquad &= 0, \\ -x_1 - x_2 \qquad - x_4 &= 0, \\ -x_1 - x_2 - 2x_3 + x_4 &= 0, \\ -2x_1 - x_2 - x_3 - x_4 &= 0. \end{aligned}$$

Adding multiples of the first equation to the others yields

$$\begin{aligned} x_1 + x_2 + x_3 \qquad &= 0, \\ x_3 - x_4 &= 0, \\ - x_3 + x_4 &= 0, \\ x_2 + x_3 - x_4 &= 0. \end{aligned}$$

Thus $x_3 = x_4$ (second equation), $x_2 = 0$ (fourth equation), and $x_1 = -x_3 = -x_4$ (first equation); and V_2 is the set of all vectors of the form $[-x_4, 0, x_4, x_4]$. The reader should convince himself that $V_1 \oplus V_2 = R^4$ as guaranteed by the theorem.

PROOF OF THEOREM 9.5. To verify (i), let $\mathbf{X}$ be any vector in V_i. We know $p_i(\mathrm{T})^{l_i}\mathbf{X} = \mathbf{0}$; thus

$$p_i(\mathrm{T})^{l_i}(\mathrm{T}\mathbf{X}) = \mathrm{T}(p_i(\mathrm{T})^{l_i}\mathbf{X}) = \mathrm{T}(\mathbf{0}) = \mathbf{0}$$

and $\mathrm{T}\mathbf{X}$ is in V_i.

To establish (ii) we introduce the polynomials $q_i(x) = m(x)/p_i(x)^{l_i}$. We claim that the $q_i(x)$ are relatively prime. Any nonconstant polynomial $h(x)$ that divides

$$q_1(x) = p_2(x)^{l_2}p_3(x)^{l_3}\cdots p_n(x)^{l_n}$$

must be divisible by one of $p_2(x), p_3(x), \ldots, p_n(x)$; say $p_k(x)$. But then $h(x)$ does not divide $q_k(x)$. Thus there exist polynomials $h_1(x), h_2(x), \ldots, h_n(x)$ such that

$$h_1(x)q_1(x) + h_2(x)q_2(x) + \cdots + h_n(x)q_n(x) = 1.$$

We also note that for any $\mathbf{X} \in V$, $q_i(\mathrm{T})\mathbf{X} \in V_i$ for

$$p_i(\mathrm{T})^{l_i}q_i(\mathrm{T})\mathbf{X} = m(\mathrm{T})\mathbf{X} = \mathbf{0}.$$

We now show that $V = V_1 + V_2 + \cdots + V_n$. Let $\mathbf{X}$ be any vector in V, and write

$$\begin{aligned} \mathbf{X} = 1\mathbf{X} &= [h_1(\mathrm{T})q_1(\mathrm{T}) + \cdots + h_n(\mathrm{T})q_n(\mathrm{T})]\mathbf{X} \\ &= h_1(\mathrm{T})q_1(\mathrm{T})\mathbf{X} + \cdots + h_n(\mathrm{T})q_n(\mathrm{T})\mathbf{X}. \end{aligned}$$

As $q_i(\mathrm{T})\mathbf{X} \in V_i$ and each V_i is invariant under T, this proves that $V = V_1 + \cdots + V_n$. To see that the sum is direct we must show that

$$V_k \cap (V_1 + V_2 + \cdots + V_{k-1} + V_{k+1} + \cdots + V_n) = \{\mathbf{0}\}.$$

If $\mathbf{X}$ is in this intersection then $p_k(\mathrm{T})^{l_k}\mathbf{X} = \mathbf{0}$ because $\mathbf{X} \in V_k$ and $q_k(\mathrm{T})\mathbf{X} = \mathbf{0}$ since $\mathbf{X}$ is in

$$V_1 + V_2 + \cdots + V_{k-1} + V_{k+1} + \cdots + V_n.$$

Thus the relative minimal polynomial of $\mathbf{X}$ divides both $p_k(x)^{l_k}$ and $q_k(x)$. As these polynomials have no nonconstant irreducible factors in common, this means that the relative minimal polynomial of $\mathbf{X}$ is 1, i.e., $1\mathbf{X} = \mathbf{X} = \mathbf{0}$.

By the very definition of V_i, the restriction of T to V_i satisfies $p_i(x)^{l_i}$; hence has minimal polynomial $p_i(x)^k$ for some $k \leq l_i$. But if $p_i(\mathrm{T})^k V_i = \{\mathbf{0}\}$ for some $k < l_i$, then $p_i(\mathrm{T})^k q_i(\mathrm{T})$ would annihilate all of V. (Why?) This contradicts the fact that $m(x)$ is the minimal polynomial of T.

COROLLARY. *If* T *is a linear transformation on* V *with minimal polynomial* $p_1(x)^{l_1} p_2(x)^{l_2} \cdots p_n(x)^{l_n}$, *then there is a basis of* V *with respect to which the matrix of* T *is given by*

$$\begin{bmatrix} D_1 & & & \\ & D_2 & & \\ & & \ddots & \\ & & & D_n \end{bmatrix} \tag{9.2}$$

where each D_i *is of the form*

$$D_i = \begin{bmatrix} C(p_i(x)^{l_{i1}}) & & & \\ & C(p_i(x)^{l_{i2}}) & & \\ & & \ddots & \\ & & & C(p_i(x)^{l_{ik_i}}) \end{bmatrix}.$$

Here $l_i = l_{i1} \geq l_{i2} \geq \cdots \geq l_{ik_i}$.

PROOF. By Theorem 9.5, $V = V_1 \oplus V_2 \oplus \cdots \oplus V_n$ with each V_i invariant under T, and the minimal polynomial of T restricted to V_i is $p_i(x)^{l_i}$. Applying the corollary of Theorem 9.4 to the restriction of T to V_i, we obtain D_i as promised. Now another application of Theorem 9.1 completes the proof.

Example 3. Let T be the linear transformation of Example 2. What is the matrix of T guaranteed by the corollary? We note that $\mathbf{X}_1 = [0, 1, -1, 1]$ is in V_1 and $(\mathrm{T} - \mathrm{I})\mathbf{X}_1 = [0, -1, 1, 0] \neq 0$ so that the relative minimal polynomial of $\mathbf{X}_1$ must be $(x - 1)^2$. (Why?) Thus $L\{\mathbf{X}_1, \mathrm{T}\mathbf{X}_1\}$ is a maximal cyclic subspace of V_1 (if there were such a subspace of dimension three, the generating vector would have a relative minimal polynomial of degree three, contradicting the fact that $(\mathrm{T} - \mathrm{I})^2$ annihilates V_1). We must now find W such that $V_1 = L\{\mathbf{X}_1, \mathrm{T}\mathbf{X}_1\} \oplus W$ with W invariant for T. A generator $\mathbf{X}_2$ for such a W must satisfy $(\mathrm{T} - \mathrm{I})\mathbf{X}_2 = \mathbf{0}$. Using this fact and the definition of V_1, a little searching gives $\mathbf{X}_2 = [1, -1, -1, -1]$. The reader should verify that

$$V_1 = L\{[0, 1, -1, 1], [0, -1, 1, 0]\} \oplus L\{[1, -1, -1, -1]\}$$

and that the matrix of T restricted to V_1 relative to the basis $\{\mathbf{X}_1, \mathrm{T}\mathbf{X}_1, \mathbf{X}_2\}$ is

$$\begin{bmatrix} 0 & -1 & 0 \\ 1 & 2 & 0 \\ 0 & 0 & 1 \end{bmatrix} = \begin{bmatrix} C((x-1)^2) & \\ & C(x-1) \end{bmatrix} = D_1.$$

Recalling the definition of V_2 from Example 2 we pick $\mathbf{X}_3 = [-1, 0, 1, 1]$. Then $\mathrm{T}\mathbf{X}_3 = 2\mathbf{X}_3$, so

$$V = V_1 \oplus V_2 = L\{\mathbf{X}_1, \mathrm{T}\mathbf{X}_1\} \oplus L\{\mathbf{X}_2\} \oplus L\{\mathbf{X}_3\}$$

and the matrix of T relative to the basis $\{\mathbf{X}_1, \mathrm{T}\mathbf{X}_1, \mathbf{X}_2, \mathbf{X}_3\}$ is

$$\begin{bmatrix} D_1 & \\ & D_2 \end{bmatrix} = \begin{bmatrix} C((x-1)^2) & & \\ & C((x-1)) & \\ & & C((x-2)) \end{bmatrix} = \begin{bmatrix} 0 & -1 & 0 & 0 \\ 1 & 2 & 0 & 0 \\ 0 & 0 & 1 & 0 \\ 0 & 0 & 0 & 2 \end{bmatrix}.$$

DEFINITION 9.8. The matrix (9.2) *of* T *given in the corollary to Theorem* 9.5 *is called the* RATIONAL CANONICAL FORM *of* T, *and the polynomials*

$$p_1(x)^{l_{11}}, p_1(x)^{l_{12}}, \ldots, p_1(x)^{l_{1k_1}}, p_2(x)^{l_{21}} \cdots p_n(x)^{l_{nk_n}}$$

are called the ELEMENTARY DIVISORS *of* T.

Definition 9.8 implicitly states two things that we have yet to prove. First that T determines only one matrix of the form of the corollary to Theorem 9.3 (up to interchanging the blocks), and second, that the polynomials of the definition are invariants in some sense. It is time to establish these facts.

THEOREM 9.6. Two linear transformations T, S *on V are similar if and only if they have the same rational canonical form.*

PROOF. If two transformations have the same matrix (with respect to different bases) they are easily seen to be similar; thus we need only show that similar transformations have the same rational canonical form. As similar matrices have the same minimal polynomial, the spaces V_i of Theorem 9.5 for S and T will have the same dimension. Thus we need only show that the corresponding D_i are the same. We can assume, then, that we are dealing with two similar linear transformations with minimal polynomial $p(x)^l$ for some monic irreducible $p(x)$. Thus we assume that

$$\begin{aligned} V &= W_1 \oplus W_2 \oplus \cdots \oplus W_s \\ &= U_1 \oplus U_2 \oplus \cdots \oplus U_t, \end{aligned}$$

and the matrix of T restricted to W_i is $C(p(x)^{m_i})$ while that of S restricted to U_i is $C(p(x)^{n_i}$ (of course $m_1 = n_1 = l$ and $m_1 \geq m_2 \geq \cdots \geq m_s$, $n_1 \geq n_2 \geq \cdots \geq n_t$). If we show that $s = t$ and $m_i = n_i$ for $i = 1, 2, \ldots, s$, then we will be done, as all of the companion matrices in the forms of S and T will be the same. Assume that k is the first integer such that $m_k \neq n_k$ and that degree $p(x) = d$. Certainly

$$d(m_1 + m_2 + \cdots + m_s) = d(n_1 + n_2 + \cdots + n_t) = \text{dimension of } V$$

and there is no harm in assuming $m_k > n_k$. As S and T are similar, so are $p(\mathrm{T})^{n_k}$ and $p(\mathrm{S})^{n_k}$ (prove!). Thus $p(\mathrm{T})^{n_k}V$ and $p(\mathrm{S})^{n_k}V$ have the same dimension. But

$$\begin{aligned} \dim p(\mathrm{T})^{n_k}V &= \dim p(\mathrm{T})^{n_k}W_1 + \dim p(\mathrm{T})^{n_k}W_2 + \cdots + \dim p(\mathrm{T})^{n_k}W_s \\ &\geq \dim p(\mathrm{T})^{n_k}W_1 + \cdots + \dim p(\mathrm{T})^{n_k}W_k \end{aligned}$$

and

$$\begin{aligned} \dim p(\mathrm{S})^{n_k}V &= \dim p(\mathrm{S})^{n_k}U_1 + \dim p(\mathrm{S})^{n_k}U_2 + \cdots + \dim p(\mathrm{S})^{n_k}U_t \\ &= \dim p(\mathrm{S})^{n_k}U_1 + \cdots + \dim p(\mathrm{S})^{n_k}U_{k-1}. \end{aligned}$$

The last equation is the result of the fact that $p(\mathrm{S})^{n_k}$ annihilates U_i for $i \geq k$. As $n_k < m_k$, $\dim p(\mathrm{T})^{n_k}W_k > 0$ and we also have that $\dim p(\mathrm{T})^{n_k}W_i = \dim p(\mathrm{S})^{n_k}U_i$ for $i < k$. Thus $\dim p(\mathrm{T})^{n_k}V > \dim p(\mathrm{S})^{n_k}V$, a contradiction.

As an immediate consequence of Theorem 9.6 we have:

THEOREM 9.7. Two linear transformations on V are similar if and only if they have the same elementary divisors.

Note that if a matrix A corresponds to linear transformations T and S with respect to bases $\{\mathbf{X}_i\}$ and $\{\mathbf{Y}_i\}$, respectively, then T and S are similar (define a transformation U by $UX_i = Y_i$; then $T = U^{-1}SU$). Thus given a matrix we can speak of its rational canonical form and its elementary divisors.

DEFINITION 9.9. The ELEMENTARY DIVISORS *of a matrix A are the elementary divisors of any linear transformation to which A corresponds. Similarly, the* RATIONAL CANONICAL FORM *of A is the rational form of any transformation corresponding to A.*

Example 4. The elementary divisors of the transformation in Example 3 are $(x - 1)^2$, $(x - 1)$, and $(x - 2)$.

Example 5. Let D be the differentiation operator on P^4, the polynomials in x with real coefficients whose degree is at most 3. Find the rational form and the elementary divisors of D. We must find the minimal polynomial of D. Noting that $D^4 = 0$ (taking the derivative four times maps all of these polynomials to zero), we have that the minimal polynomial is x^n for some $n \leq 4$. As $D^3(x^3) = 6 \neq 0$, the minimal polynomial is x^4. This means that V_1 is four-dimensional and hence all of P^4! As we know $D^3(x^3) \neq 0$, we pick $\mathbf{X}_1 = x^3$ and we have

$$P^4 = L\{\mathbf{X}_1, D\mathbf{X}_1, D^2\mathbf{X}_1, D^3\mathbf{X}_1\} = L\{x^3, 3x^2, 6x, 6\}.$$

The form of D is

$$\begin{bmatrix} 0 & 0 & 0 & 0 \\ 1 & 0 & 0 & 0 \\ 0 & 1 & 0 & 0 \\ 0 & 0 & 1 & 0 \end{bmatrix} = C(x^4).$$

D then has only one elementary divisor x^4.

Exercises

1. Find the rational canonical form of the matrix

$$A = \begin{bmatrix} 1 & 0 & 2 \\ -3 & 1 & 4 \\ -1 & 2 & 2 \end{bmatrix}.$$

2. Find the rational canonical form of the matrix

$$A = \begin{bmatrix} -2 & 4 & 1 & 1 \\ 0 & 1 & 0 & 0 \\ 0 & 0 & 1 & 0 \\ -1 & 0 & 1 & 0 \end{bmatrix}.$$

3. If the minimal polynomial of T is of degree n, show that the maximal cyclic subspace of T has dimension n.
4. Give an example of a matrix which has the elementary divisors

$$(x - 1)^2, (x - 1), (x - 1), (x + 1), (x + 1), (x + 1).$$

5. Determine if the following matrices are similar and, if so, find a matrix P such that $A = PBP^{-1}$:

$$A = \begin{bmatrix} 2 & 1 & 5 \\ -1 & 3 & 1 \\ 1 & -2 & 0 \end{bmatrix}, \quad B = \begin{bmatrix} 3 & -1 & 1 \\ -2 & 5 & 8 \\ 1 & -2 & -3 \end{bmatrix}.$$

Hint: Reduce both A and B to rational form.

6. Suppose that R^n is itself a cyclic subspace for a matrix A. What is the rational form of A?
7. Under what conditions on a matrix A is the rational form a diagonal matrix?
8. Prove Theorem 9.7.

*9. Prove that a matrix A is always similar to A^T.

9.4 The Jordan Canonical Form

The rational canonical form is very general, and in many special cases we can find a simpler form. Consider the matrix $A = \begin{bmatrix} 1 & 0 \\ 1 & 1 \end{bmatrix}$, for example. Its minimal polynomial is $(x - 1)^2 = x^2 - 2x + 1$ and thus its rational form is $\begin{bmatrix} 0 & -1 \\ 1 & 2 \end{bmatrix}$. Note that the rational form is not simpler than A; in fact, the characteristic values are more apparent from A than from the rational form. We seek a canonical form that would leave A unchanged. The key to our work lies in an observation to be made about Example 5 of the previous section. The differentiation operator of this example has minimal polynomial x^4 and rational form

$$\begin{bmatrix} 0 & 0 & 0 & 0 \\ 1 & 0 & 0 & 0 \\ 0 & 1 & 0 & 0 \\ 0 & 0 & 1 & 0 \end{bmatrix}.$$

Note that in this case the rational form is particularly simple and the characteristic value of D (0 alone) is immediately apparent. We consider transformations similar to D and then use them to find a canonical form for a larger class of matrices (including A above).

DEFINITION 9.10. *A linear transformation* T *that satisfies* $T^k = 0$ *for some* k *is said to be* NILPOTENT. *The smallest integer* n *such that* $T^n = 0$ *is said to be the* INDEX OF NILPOTENCE *of* T. *Nilpotency and index of nilpotence are defined similarly for a matrix* A.

Nilpotent transformations (or matrices) have particularly simple rational canonical forms. For reference, we restate the corollary to Theorem 9.5 for this special case.

THEOREM 9.8. *If* T *is a nilpotent linear transformation on* V *of index* k, *then there is a choice of basis of* V *that gives the matrix of* T *as*

$$\begin{bmatrix} N_{k_1} & & & \\ & N_{k_2} & & \\ & & \ddots & \\ & & & N_{k_m} \end{bmatrix}. \tag{9.3}$$

Here each N_{k_i} *is a* $k_i \times k_i$ *matrix of the form*

$$N_{k_i} = \begin{bmatrix} 0 & 0 & \cdots & & 0 \\ 1 & 0 & \cdots & & 0 \\ 0 & 1 & \cdots & & 0 \\ \vdots & & & & \vdots \\ 0 & 0 & \cdots & 0 \quad 1 & 0 \end{bmatrix}.$$

Further, $k = k_1 \geq k_2 \geq \cdots \geq k_m$ *and* $k_1 + k_2 + \cdots + k_m = \dim V$.

Now, let us consider a linear transformation T on R^2 whose matrix relative to the standard basis is $A = \begin{bmatrix} 1 & 0 \\ 1 & 1 \end{bmatrix}$. How can we relate Theorem 9.8 to T? We know that the minimum polynomial of T is $(x - 1)^2$, so $(T - I)^2 = 0$. But this is just the statement that $(T - I)$ is nilpotent! If we apply Theorem 9.8 to $T - I$, we get a basis $\{\mathbf{X}_1, \mathbf{X}_2\}$ of R^2 for which the matrix of $T - I$ is $\begin{bmatrix} 0 & 0 \\ 1 & 0 \end{bmatrix}$. Since the matrix of I is $\begin{bmatrix} 1 & 0 \\ 0 & 1 \end{bmatrix}$ in this basis (in any basis for that matter) and $T = (T - I) + I$, the matrix of T with respect to $\{\mathbf{X}_1, \mathbf{X}_2\}$ is just

$$\begin{bmatrix} 0 & 0 \\ 1 & 0 \end{bmatrix} + \begin{bmatrix} 1 & 0 \\ 0 & 1 \end{bmatrix} = \begin{bmatrix} 1 & 0 \\ 1 & 1 \end{bmatrix}.$$

Further, this method will work for any linear transformation with minimum polynomial of the form $(x - a)^k$. Before giving the details of this case, we pause for a definition.

DEFINITION 9.11. If a is a scalar and n an integer, the JORDAN BLOCK *of size n corresponding to a is the n × n matrix*

$$J_n = \begin{bmatrix} a & 0 & 0 & \cdots & & 0 \\ 1 & a & 0 & \cdots & & 0 \\ 0 & 1 & a & \cdots & & 0 \\ \vdots & & & & & \vdots \\ & & & & a & 0 \\ 0 & 0 & 0 & \cdots & 1 & a \end{bmatrix}.$$

THEOREM 9.9. If T *is a linear transformation on V with minimum polynomial $(x - a)^k$, then there is a choice of basis of V with respect to which the matrix of* T *is of the form*

$$\begin{bmatrix} J_{k_1} & & & \\ & J_{k_2} & & \\ & & \ddots & \\ & & & J_{k_m} \end{bmatrix}, \tag{9.4}$$

where $J_{k_i}(a)$ is the $k_i \times k_i$ Jordan block corresponding to a,

$$k = k_1 \geq k_2 \geq \cdots \geq k_m$$

and

$$k_1 + k_2 + \cdots + k_m = \dim V.$$

PROOF. We have that $(T - aI)$ is nilpotent of index k. Applying Theorem 9.8 to $(T - aI)$ we get a basis $\{\mathbf{X}_1, \mathbf{X}_2, \ldots, \mathbf{X}_n\}$ for V with respect to which the matrix of $(T - aI)$ is of the form (9.3). The matrix of aI in this basis is just

$$A = \begin{bmatrix} a & 0 & 0 & \cdots & 0 \\ 0 & a & 0 & \cdots & 0 \\ 0 & 0 & a & \cdots & 0 \\ \vdots & & & & \vdots \\ 0 & 0 & 0 & \cdots & a \end{bmatrix}.$$

Thus the matrix of T with respect to the basis $\{\mathbf{X}_1, \mathbf{X}_2, \ldots, \mathbf{X}_n\}$ is just the sum of A and a matrix of the form (9.3). A moment's reflection reveals that this gives a matrix of the desired form.

Example 1. If T is the linear transformation of Example 1, Section 9.3, what is the matrix of T guaranteed by Theorem 9.9? As the minimal polynomial is $(x - 1)^2$, the first Jordan block is 2×2, and the final matrix is 3×3, the only possibility is

$$\begin{bmatrix} 1 & 0 & 0 \\ 1 & 1 & 0 \\ 0 & 0 & 1 \end{bmatrix} = \begin{bmatrix} J_2 & \\ & J_1 \end{bmatrix}.$$

If we want the basis which gives this matrix, a little more work is involved. The technique is to find the basis which puts T − I (not T!) into rational form.

$$\begin{bmatrix} 3 & -2 & -2 \\ -1 & 2 & 1 \\ 3 & -3 & -2 \end{bmatrix} - \begin{bmatrix} 1 & 0 & 0 \\ 0 & 1 & 0 \\ 0 & 0 & 1 \end{bmatrix} = \begin{bmatrix} 2 & -2 & -2 \\ -1 & 1 & 1 \\ 3 & -3 & -3 \end{bmatrix}.$$

Thus $(\mathrm{T} - \mathrm{I})[1, 0, 0] = [2, -1, 3] \neq \mathbf{0}$ and we may start our basis with $[1, 0, 0], [2, -1, 3]$.

$$L\{[1, 0, 0], [2, -1, 3]\} = L\{(\mathrm{T} - \mathrm{I})^i[1, 0, 0]\}$$

is a cyclic subspace for T − I of maximal dimension. For our third basis vector we must pick a vector $\mathbf{X}$ such that $(\mathrm{T} - \mathrm{I})\mathbf{X} = \mathbf{0}$ and such that $\mathbf{X} \notin L\{[1, 0, 0], [2, -1, 3]\}$. The calculations done in Example 1, Section 9.3, show that $[1, 0, 1]$ is such a vector. Thus $\{[1, 0, 0], [2, -1, 3], [1, 0, 1]\}$ is the desired basis.

THEOREM 9.10. *If* T *is a linear transformation on* V *with minimal polynomial*

$$m(x) = (x - a_1)^{k_1}(x - a_2)^{k_2} \cdots (x - a_m)^{k_m},$$

then for some choice of basis, T *is represented by the matrix*

$$\begin{bmatrix} K_1 & & & \\ & K_2 & & \\ & & \ddots & \\ & & & K_m \end{bmatrix}, \tag{9.5}$$

where K_i *is a* $k_i \times k_i$ *matrix of the form* (9.4) *with its Jordan blocks corresponding to* a_i.

PROOF. If V_i is the principal component of V corresponding to $(x - a_i)^{k_i}$, then the minimum polynomial of T restricted to V_i is just $(x - a_i)^{k_i}$. Applying Theorem 9.9 and Theorem 9.1 yields the desired result.

DEFINITION 9.12. *The matrix* (9.5) *of* T *is called the* JORDAN CANONICAL FORM *of* T.

Example 2. If T is the linear transformation whose matrix is given in Example 2, Section 9.3, then T has minimum polynomial $(x - 1)^2(x - 2)$. The principal component of $(x - 1)^2$ was seen to be of dimension three, that of $(x - 2)$ of dimension one. Thus the only possibility for the Jordan form is

$$\begin{bmatrix} 1 & 0 & 0 & 0 \\ 1 & 1 & 0 & 0 \\ 0 & 0 & 1 & 0 \\ 0 & 0 & 0 & 2 \end{bmatrix}.$$

Example 3. Let T be a linear transformation on R^5 with invariant factors $(x - 1)^2$, $(x - 1)$, $(x - 2)^2$.

What is the Jordan form of T? It must be

$$\begin{bmatrix} 1 & 0 & 0 & 0 & 0 \\ 1 & 1 & 0 & 0 & 0 \\ 0 & 0 & 1 & 0 & 0 \\ 0 & 0 & 0 & 2 & 0 \\ 0 & 0 & 0 & 1 & 2 \end{bmatrix}.$$

Why? Because to an invariant factor $(x - a)^k$ corresponds a subspace invariant for T on which the matrix of T is J_k.

THEOREM 9.11. *If* T, S *have minimal polynomials which are products of linear factors, then* T *and* S *are similar if and only if they have the same Jordan canonical form.*

PROOF. Certainly if T and S have the same form they are similar. If T and S are similar, they have the same invariant factors (Theorem 9.7) and then, by the remark in Example 3, they have the same Jordan form.

Note that if A is a matrix, then Theorem 9.11 assures us that we may speak of *the* Jordan canonical form of A; namely, it is the Jordan form of any transformation corresponding to A.

If we are considering a real matrix (or a transformation on R^n), the Jordan form may not exist. However, when considering complex matrices (transformations on C^n) the minimal polynomial will always be a product of linear factors and thus the Jordan form is always available.

Example 4. Consider the matrix $A = \begin{bmatrix} 0 & 1 \\ -1 & 0 \end{bmatrix}$. If we are considering matrices over the real numbers (transformations on R^2), then the minimum polynomial is $x^2 + 1$; and A has no Jordan canonical form. If, however, our underlying field is C, then A has minimal polynomial $(x - i)(x + i)$ and Jordan form $\begin{bmatrix} i & 0 \\ 0 & -i \end{bmatrix}$.

The canonical forms that we have developed allow us to prove an important classical result that is known as the Cayley-Hamilton theorem. We start by relating the elementary divisors of a matrix to its characteristic polynomial.

THEOREM 9.12. *If A is an $n \times n$ matrix, the characteristic polynomial of A* det $(A - xI)$, *is either the product of the elementary divisors of A or the negative of this product.*

PROOF. If J_n is the $n \times n$ Jordan block corresponding to a, what is det $(J_n - xI)$? Since $J_n - xI$ is triangular, clearly

$$\det (J_n - xI) = (a - x)^n = (-1)^n(x - a)^n.$$

Now, if A has a Jordan form J, we will have $\det (A - xI) = \det (J - xI)$ and $\det (J - xI)$ will have a block J_k for each elementary divisor $(x - a)^k$. Thus $\det (J - xI)$ and the product of the elementary divisors will differ at most by a factor of -1 (the determinant of $J - xI$ will be the product of the determinants of the Jordan blocks).

What if A is a real matrix (more precisely, if we are considering R as our underlying field) that has no Jordan form? One method of proof is to show that

$$\det [C(p(y)) - xI] = \pm p(x).$$

Another method is to pass to the complex numbers. Then A will have a Jordan form, and while the elementary divisors are different, their product is the same (why?), and the proof above will work.

COROLLARY 1. *The minimal polynomial of an $n \times n$ matrix (of a linear transformation) divides the characteristic polynomial.*

COROLLARY 2. *(Cayley-Hamilton) If $p(x) = \det (A - xI)$, where A is a square matrix, then $p(A) = 0$.*

The Cayley-Hamilton theorem, appearing at the end of a long development, may seem almost trivial. Nonetheless, it is difficult to prove without canonical forms even if it is simple with them. Another important theorem follows from our development.

THEOREM 9.13. *The minimal polynomial and the characteristic polynomial of a square matrix A have the same elementary divisors.*

PROOF. By Corollary 1, every factor of the minimal polynomial divides the characteristic polynomial. If $p(x)$ is an elementary divisor of the characteristic polynomial, then by Theorem 9.12 it must divide one of the elementary divisors of A and of any transformation corresponding to A. This means that if T is a linear transformation corresponding to A, there is a vector $\mathbf{X}$ with relative minimal polynomial $p(x)^k$ for some $k \geq 1$ ($\mathbf{X}$ is a generator of the cyclic subspace corresponding to the elementary divisor in question). But then $p(x)^k$, and hence $p(x)$, divides the minimal polynomial of T and thus that of A.

Example 5. If a matrix A has characteristic polynomial $(x - 1)(x - 2) \times (x - 3)^2$, what are the possible minimal polynomials of A? By Theorem 9.13 the minimal polynomial has $(x - 1)$, $(x - 2)$, and $(x - 3)$ as factors. As it must divide the characteristic polynomial the only possibilities are $(x - 1)(x - 2)(x - 3)$ and $(x - 1)(x - 2)(x - 3)^2$.

The reader will recall that when we first defined the minimal polynomial of an $n \times n$ matrix A (a transformation T on F^n) we proved that it was of degree at most n^2. Using the Cayley-Hamilton theorem we now know that the degree of the minimal polynomial of A (of T) is at most n.

Exercises

1. Consider the linear transformation T on R^2 whose matrix relative to the standard basis is $\begin{bmatrix} 4 & 4 \\ -1 & 0 \end{bmatrix}$.
   (a) Find the characteristic polynomial and the minimal polynomial of T.
   (b) What is the Jordan canonical form for T?
   (c) Find a basis of R^2 with respect to which T is represented by the matrix in part (b).

2. Find the Jordan canonical form of the matrix

$$A = \begin{bmatrix} 3 & 1 & 1 & 0 \\ -1 & 1 & 0 & -1 \\ -1 & -1 & 0 & 1 \\ -2 & -1 & -1 & 1 \end{bmatrix}.$$

   Hint: The characteristic values of A are 1 and 2.

3. If the characteristic polynomial of a linear transformation R^4 is $x^4 - 4$, what are the possibilities for the minimal polynomial?
4. (a) If A is a 4×4 matrix that is nilpotent of index 3, how many possibilities are there for the Jordan form of A?
   (b) What is the number of similarity classes of 4×4 nilpotent matrices?
5. Is it possible to find a 3×3 matrix which has minimal polynomial $x^2 + 1$ over the reals?
6. Find the most general matrix which commutes with the matrix J_n of Definition 9.11.
7. Prove that the answer to Exercise 6 may be written as a polynomial in J_n.

*8. Generalize Exercise 7 as follows. If A is a matrix having a single elementary divisor, any matrix commuting with A is a polynomial in A.

10 Applications

10.1 Basic Solutions and Pivoting

In this section we are interested in systems of linear equations with more variables than equations. As we saw in Section 4.4, such systems usually have many solutions. The structure of these solutions was given in Chapter 4; we are interested here primarily in the computational aspects, that is, we will want to go from one solution to another, make certain variables zero, etc. This work is critical in problems that involve finding solutions to systems of equations that have another property as well (e.g., finding a solution that maximizes a particular function).

As usual, we shall consider the system $A\mathbf{X}^{\mathsf{T}} = \mathbf{B}$, and will denote the column vectors of A by $\mathbf{A}^1, \mathbf{A}^2, \ldots, \mathbf{A}^n$. Thus the system may also be thought of as

$$x_1\mathbf{A}^1 + x_2\mathbf{A}^2 + \cdots + x_n\mathbf{A}^n = \mathbf{B}, \tag{10.1}$$

where $\mathbf{X} = [x_1, x_2, \ldots, x_n]$. If we are looking for simple solutions to (10.1) it seems natural to make as many of the x_i's zero as possible. Such a solution is called a *basic solution.* To be precise, a solution $\mathbf{X} = [x_1, x_2, \ldots, x_n]$ with $x_{i_1} = x_{i_2} = \cdots = x_{i_k} = 0$ is basic if there is no solution having more zero entries than $\mathbf{X}$ *and* having its $i_1, i_2, \ldots, i_k$th entries zero. While this definition makes it clear why basic solutions are of interest, it is hard to check in practice. The following proposition gives an easy criterion to check.

PROPOSITION 1. *A solution $\mathbf{X} = [x_1, x_2, \ldots, x_n]$ with nonzero entries $x_{j_1}, x_{j_2}, \ldots, x_{j_k}$ is basic if and only if the vectors $\mathbf{A}^{j_1}, \mathbf{A}^{j_2}, \ldots, \mathbf{A}^{j_k}$ are linearly independent.*

PROOF. If the vectors $A^{j_1}, A^{j_2}, \ldots, A^{j_k}$ are linearly independent, then the representation of $\mathbf{B}$ as

$$x_{j_1}\mathbf{A}^{j_1} + x_{j_2}\mathbf{A}^{j_2} + \cdots + x_{j_k}\mathbf{A}^{j_k} = \mathbf{B}$$

is unique, and thus *no* other linear combination of $\mathbf{A}^{j_1}, \mathbf{A}^{j_k}$ will yield $\mathbf{B}$. Certainly, then, we cannot make one of $x_{j_1}, \ldots, x_{j_k}$ equal to zero.

Conversely, suppose $\mathbf{X}$ is a basic solution, and the vectors $\mathbf{A}^{j_1}, \mathbf{A}^{j_2}, \ldots, \mathbf{A}^{j_k}$ are linearly dependent, say,

$$\mathbf{A}^{j_1} = \alpha_2 \mathbf{A}^{j_2} + \cdots + \alpha_k \mathbf{A}^{j_k}.$$

Then we have

$$\begin{aligned} x_{j_1}\mathbf{A}^{j_1} + x_{j_2}\mathbf{A}^{j_2} + \cdots + x_{j_k}\mathbf{A}^{j_k} &= \mathbf{B}, \\ x_{j_1}(\alpha_2\mathbf{A}^{j_2} + \cdots + \alpha_k\mathbf{A}^{j_k}) + x_{j_2}\mathbf{A}^{j_2} + \cdots + x_{j_k}\mathbf{A}^{j_k} &= \mathbf{B}, \\ (x_{j_1}\alpha_2 + x_{j_2})\mathbf{A}^{j_2} + (x_{j_1}\alpha_3 + x_{j_3})\mathbf{A}^{j_3} + \cdots + (x_{j_1}\alpha_k + x_{j_k})\mathbf{A}^{j_k} &= \mathbf{B}, \end{aligned}$$

contradicting the fact that $\mathbf{X}$ is basic.

Example 1. Consider the system

$$\begin{aligned} x_1 \qquad + x_3 &= 1, \\ x_1 + x_2 \qquad &= 0; \end{aligned}$$

we rewrite the system in another form:

$$x_1 \begin{bmatrix} 1 \\ 1 \end{bmatrix} + x_2 \begin{bmatrix} 0 \\ 1 \end{bmatrix} + x_3 \begin{bmatrix} 1 \\ 0 \end{bmatrix} = \begin{bmatrix} 1 \\ 0 \end{bmatrix}.$$

One solution is $x_1 = 2, x_2 = -2, x_3 = -1$. This solution is not basic, as no set of three vectors in R^2 can be linearly independent. If we make $x_3 = 0$, we get $x_1 = 1, x_2 = -1$, giving a basic solution, since $[1, 1]^{\mathsf{T}}, [0, 1]^{\mathsf{T}}$ are linearly independent. Note that this is the *only* solution with $x_3 = 0$. If we set $x_1 = 0$ we get $x_2 = 0, x_3 = 1$, another basic solution. Observe that the number of nonzero variables is different in our two basic solutions.

The problem we shall now consider is how to go from one basic solution to another. The way to view the problem is as follows. We are given a vector $\mathbf{B}$ as a linear combination of vectors $A^{j_1}, A^{j_2}, \ldots, A^{j_k}$, and we wish to express it in terms of some other set of vectors (that is, in terms of other columns of A). To this end we introduce a table of coefficients.

DEFINITION 10.1. Let $\mathbf{A}^1, \mathbf{A}^2, \ldots, \mathbf{A}^m$ *be a linearly independent set of vectors, and* $\mathbf{B}^1, \mathbf{B}^2, \ldots, \mathbf{B}^n$ *be any set of vectors in the span of* $\{\mathbf{A}^i\}$. *We say that the matrix* $T = [t_{ij}]$ *is the* TABLEAU *of the* $\mathbf{B}^i$ *with respect to the* $\mathbf{A}^i$ *if*

$$\mathbf{B}^j = \sum_{i=1}^{m} t_{ij}\mathbf{A}^i.$$

For convenience we display the tableau as follows:

	$\mathbf{B}^1$	$\mathbf{B}^2$		$\mathbf{B}^n$
$\mathbf{A}^1$	t_{11}	t_{12}	$\cdots$	t_{1n}
$\mathbf{A}^2$	t_{21}	t_{22}	$\cdots$	t_{2n}
	$\vdots$			
$\mathbf{A}^m$	t_{m1}	t_{m2}	$\cdots$	t_{mn}

The meaning of the definition, then, is that the column under $\mathbf{B}^i$ gives the coefficients of $\mathbf{B}^i$ with respect to the basis $\mathbf{A}^1, \mathbf{A}^2, \ldots, \mathbf{A}^m$.

Example 2. The simplest tableau to construct is when the $\mathbf{A}^i$'s are the standard basis elements. In the future we shall denote by $\mathbf{E}^i$ the column vector with all zeros except for a 1 in the ith position (i.e., $\mathbf{E}^i = \mathbf{E}_i^{\mathsf{T}}$). Suppose

$$\mathbf{B}^1 = \begin{bmatrix} 1 \\ -1 \\ 2 \end{bmatrix}, \quad \mathbf{B}^2 = \begin{bmatrix} 1 \\ 0 \\ -1 \end{bmatrix}, \quad \mathbf{B}^3 = \begin{bmatrix} 1 \\ 6 \\ 2 \end{bmatrix}, \quad \mathbf{B}^4 = \begin{bmatrix} -2 \\ 1 \\ 0 \end{bmatrix}.$$

The tableau in this case is just

	$\mathbf{B}^1$	$\mathbf{B}^2$	$\mathbf{B}^3$	$\mathbf{B}^4$
$\mathbf{E}^1$	1	1	1	-2
$\mathbf{E}^2$	-1	0	6	1
$\mathbf{E}^3$	2	-1	2	0

Before leaving this example, let us ask another question. What is the tableau of $\mathbf{B}^1$, $\mathbf{B}^2$, $\mathbf{B}^3$, $\mathbf{B}^4$ with respect to the vectors $\{\mathbf{B}^3, \mathbf{E}^2, \mathbf{E}^3\}$? Certainly $\mathbf{B}^3 = 1 \cdot \mathbf{B}^3 + 0 \cdot \mathbf{E}^2 + 0 \cdot \mathbf{E}^3$, and thus the third column of our tableau will be $\begin{bmatrix} 1 \\ 0 \\ 0 \end{bmatrix}$. To find the first column we must solve the system

$$x_1\mathbf{B}^3 + x_2\mathbf{E}^2 + x_3\mathbf{E}^3 = \mathbf{B}^1,$$

$$\begin{aligned} x_1 \qquad\qquad &= 1, \\ 6x_1 + x_2 \qquad &= -1, \\ 2x_1 \qquad + x_3 &= 2. \end{aligned}$$

Thus $x_1 = 1$, $x_2 = -7$, $x_3 = 0$. Solving two more systems of this form yields the tableau

	$\mathbf{B}^1$	$\mathbf{B}^2$	$\mathbf{B}^3$	$\mathbf{B}^4$
$\mathbf{B}^3$	1	1	1	-2
$\mathbf{E}^2$	-7	-6	0	13
$\mathbf{E}^3$	0	-3	0	4

The reader who followed the calculations in Example 2 certainly noticed that it took a tremendous amount of calculation to go from the first tableau to the second. A careful perusal of the two tableaus reveals an easy procedure: Use the first row and row reduction beginning with the original tableau to "zero out" the last two entries of the third column; the result is the new tableau. This procedure always works.

PROPOSITION 2. *If T is the tableau of $\mathbf{B}^1, \mathbf{B}^2, \ldots, \mathbf{B}^n$ with respect to $\mathbf{A}^1, \mathbf{A}^2, \ldots, \mathbf{A}^m$ and S is the tableau of the $\{\mathbf{B}^i\}$ with respect to $\mathbf{A}^1, \mathbf{A}^2, \ldots, \mathbf{A}^{i-1}, \mathbf{B}^j, \mathbf{A}^{i+1}, \ldots, \mathbf{A}^m$, then S may be obtained from T as follows:*

(1) *multiply the ith row of T by $1/t_{ij}$.*

(2) *use elementary row operations to make all entries of the jth column zero save for the ith one.*

This proposition may look a little formidable, but it is quite easy to remember. Simply use row operations to make the jth column correct; the other columns will then be correct automatically. The proof is simply a matter of keeping the subscripts and superscripts straight, and we omit it.

Example 3. We use Proposition 2 to find the inverse of the matrix

$$A = \begin{bmatrix} 1 & 0 & 2 \\ -1 & 1 & -1 \\ 3 & 0 & 5 \end{bmatrix}.$$

If $\mathbf{X} = \begin{bmatrix} x_1 \\ x_2 \\ x_3 \end{bmatrix}$ is the first column of A^{-1}, then

$$x_1 \begin{bmatrix} 1 \\ -1 \\ 3 \end{bmatrix} + x_2 \begin{bmatrix} 0 \\ 1 \\ 0 \end{bmatrix} + x_3 \begin{bmatrix} 2 \\ -1 \\ 5 \end{bmatrix} = \begin{bmatrix} 1 \\ 0 \\ 0 \end{bmatrix}.$$

Similarly, to find the second and third columns of A^{-1}, we must express $\mathbf{E}^2$ and $\mathbf{E}^3$ as linear combinations of the columns of A. To this end we introduce the tableau

	$\mathbf{A}^1$	$\mathbf{A}^2$	$\mathbf{A}^3$	$\mathbf{E}^1$	$\mathbf{E}^2$	$\mathbf{E}^3$
$\mathbf{E}^1$	(1)	0	2	1	0	0
$\mathbf{E}^2$	−1	1	−1	0	1	0
$\mathbf{E}^3$	3	0	5	0	0	1

We now use Proposition 2 to replace $\mathbf{E}^1$ by $\mathbf{A}^1$; for convenience we have circled the element used to reduce the first column to zero.

	$\mathbf{A}^1$	$\mathbf{A}^2$	$\mathbf{A}^3$	$\mathbf{E}^1$	$\mathbf{E}^2$	$\mathbf{E}^3$
$\mathbf{A}^1$	1	0	2	1	0	0
$\mathbf{E}^2$	0	1	(1)	1	1	0
$\mathbf{E}^3$	0	0	−1	−3	0	1

Let us now replace $\mathbf{E}^2$ by $\mathbf{A}^3$

	$\mathbf{A}^1$	$\mathbf{A}^2$	$\mathbf{A}^3$	$\mathbf{E}^1$	$\mathbf{E}^2$	$\mathbf{E}^3$
$\mathbf{A}^1$	1	−2	0	−1	−2	0
$\mathbf{A}^3$	0	1	1	1	1	0
$\mathbf{E}^3$	0	(1)	0	−2	1	1

	$\mathbf{A}^1$	$\mathbf{A}^2$	$\mathbf{A}^3$	$\mathbf{E}^1$	$\mathbf{E}^2$	$\mathbf{E}^3$
$\mathbf{A}^1$	1	0	0	−5	0	2
$\mathbf{A}^3$	0	0	1	3	0	−1
$\mathbf{A}^2$	0	1	0	−2	1	1

We now know that

$$\mathbf{E}^1 = \begin{bmatrix}1\\0\\0\end{bmatrix} = -5\mathbf{A}^1 - 2\mathbf{A}^2 + 3\mathbf{A}^3,$$

$$\mathbf{E}^2 = \begin{bmatrix}0\\1\\0\end{bmatrix} = 0 \cdot \mathbf{A}^1 + 1 \cdot \mathbf{A}^2 + 0 \cdot \mathbf{A}^3,$$

$$\mathbf{E}^3 = \begin{bmatrix}0\\0\\1\end{bmatrix} = 2\mathbf{A}^1 + 1\mathbf{A}^2 - 1\mathbf{A}^3,$$

or,

$$A^{-1} = \begin{bmatrix}-5 & 0 & 2\\-2 & 1 & 1\\3 & 0 & -1\end{bmatrix}.$$

We conclude this section by introducing some terminology. The process outlined in Proposition 2 is called *pivoting* and the element circled above is often called the *pivot element.*

Exercises

1. Consider the system

$$\begin{aligned}-2x_1 - x_2 + x_3 + x_4 &= 2,\\ -4x_1 + x_2 - x_3 + 2x_4 &= 1,\\ 2x_1 - x_2 + x_3 + x_4 &= 0.\end{aligned}$$

Which of the following are basic solutions?

(a) $x_1 = 0, x_2 = 2, x_3 = 3, x_4 = 1$.

(b) $x_1 = 0, x_2 = 0, x_3 = -1, x_4 = 1$.

(c) $x_1 = -\frac{1}{2}, x_2 = -2, x_3 = -1, x_4 = 0$.

2. Use Proposition 2 to express the vector $[1, -2, 3]$ in terms of the basis $\{[1, 0, 1], [1, -1, 1], [0, 1, 1]\}$. *Hint:* Start with the tableau

	$\mathbf{A}^1$	$\mathbf{A}^2$	$\mathbf{A}^3$	$\mathbf{X}$
$\mathbf{E}^1$	1	1	0	1
$\mathbf{E}^2$	0	−1	1	−2
$\mathbf{E}^3$	1	1	1	3

3. Use the techniques of this section to find the inverses of the following matrices.

(a) $\begin{bmatrix} 1 & 2 \\ -1 & 1 \end{bmatrix}$. (b) $\begin{bmatrix} 1 & 0 & -1 \\ 1 & 2 & 0 \\ 2 & -1 & 3 \end{bmatrix}$.

4. The system

$$\begin{aligned} x_1 + x_2 + x_3 \qquad &= 0, \\ x_2 - x_3 + x_4 &= 4, \\ -x_1 + x_2 \qquad + x_4 &= 3, \end{aligned}$$

has one solution $x_1 = 0, x_2 = 1, x_3 = -1, x_4 = 2$. Use Proposition 2 and the following tableau to find a solution with $x_3 = 0$.

	$\mathbf{A}^1$	$\mathbf{A}^2$	$\mathbf{A}^3$	$\mathbf{A}^4$	$\mathbf{B}$
$\mathbf{A}^2$	2	1	0	0	1
$\mathbf{A}^3$	−1	0	1	0	−1
$\mathbf{A}^4$	−3	0	0	1	2

5. Show that if $A\mathbf{X}^{\mathsf{T}} = \mathbf{B}$ has a solution, then it has a basic solution.

6. Note that if T is the tableau of $\mathbf{X}_1, \mathbf{X}_2, \ldots, \mathbf{X}_n$ with respect to $\mathbf{Y}_1, \mathbf{Y}_2, \ldots, \mathbf{Y}_m$, and $t_{ij} = 0$ for a fixed i and j, then it is impossible to replace $\mathbf{Y}_i$ by $\mathbf{X}_j$ using Proposition 2. Prove that in this case $\mathbf{Y}_1, \mathbf{Y}_2, \ldots, \mathbf{Y}_{i-1}, \mathbf{X}_j, \mathbf{Y}_{i+1}, \ldots, \mathbf{Y}_m$ are linearly dependent.

10.2 Linear Programs

In economics and in many other areas, one is often faced with the problem of maximizing or minimizing some quantity subject to certain restrictions or constraints. If both the constraints and the quantity to be minimized (or maximized) are linear functions of the variables involved, such a problem is called a *linear program*. The purpose of this section is to give several examples of such problems and show how they can be formulated mathematically. We shall make no attempt to solve the problems until the next section.

The reader may object that the problems are unrealistically simple. We hasten to point out that we have simplified the problems only in that the number of variables has been reduced and the numbers chosen are simple so as to clarify the exposition. In practice, a large number of variables and "messy" numbers present no difficulties because the actual calculations are done by machine. The basic techniques and concepts involved in practical situations are just as in our examples.

Example 1. A pharmaceutical firm wishes to manufacture pills containing both Vitamin C and iron by mixing three ingredients, R_1, R_2, and R_3. The ingredients contain different amounts of Vitamin C and iron and have different costs. It is required that each pill contain 100 units of Vitamin C and 150 units of iron. The problem is to determine the amounts of the three ingredients so as to minimize the cost (to the manufacturer).

For definiteness, we have assumed the quantities involved are as in the following table.

Ingredient:	R_1	R_2	R_3
Vitamin C per gram	1000 units	0 units	500 units
Iron per gram	0 units	750 units	250 units
Cost per gram	4¢	3¢	2¢

To formulate the problem mathematically, we first assume that the manufacturer decides to use x_1 grams of R_1, x_2 grams of R_2, and x_3 grams of R_3. The constraints then become the following equations:

$$\begin{aligned} 1000x_1 \qquad\quad + 500x_3 &= 100, \\ 750x_2 + 250x_3 &= 150. \end{aligned}$$

The first equation reflects the fact that each pill must contain 100 units of Vitamin C; the second, the constraint that each pill contain 150 units of iron. The function we are trying to minimize is $C(x_1, x_2, x_3) = 4x_1 + 3x_2 + 2x_3$, since this is the cost of each pill. Actually, there is another constraint implicit in the problem: none of the x_i's can be negative.

The following definitions simply serve to introduce terminology related to the previous example.

DEFINITION 10.2. *A vector* $\mathbf{X} = [x_1, x_2, \ldots, x_n]$ *is said to be* NONNEGATIVE, *written* $\mathbf{X} \geq 0$, *if each of its coordinates is a nonnegative number. We will write* $\mathbf{X} \geq \mathbf{Y}$ *if* $\mathbf{X} - \mathbf{Y}$ *is nonnegative.*

DEFINITION 10.3. *A problem of the form: Find a nonnegative vector* $\mathbf{X} = [x_1, x_2, \ldots, x_n]$ *that will minimize* $f_1(x_1, x_2, \ldots, x_n) = c_1x_1 + c_2x_2 + \cdots + c_nx_n$ *subject to*

$$A\mathbf{X}^{\mathsf{T}} = \mathbf{B}, \tag{10.2}$$

where A *is an* $m \times n$ *matrix with real entries and* $\mathbf{B}$ *is a column vector with* m *real entries, is called a* CANONICAL MINIMUM PROGRAM. *The function* f *is often called the* OBJECTIVE FUNCTION. *A nonnegative vector satisfying* (10.2) *is called a* FEASIBLE SOLUTION, *and a feasible solution that minimizes the objective function is called an* OPTIMAL SOLUTION.

A *canonical maximum program* is defined similarly except that it is desired to maximize the objective function. The value of the objective function at an optimal solution will be called the *value* of the program.

Example 2. The Diet Problem. When putting together a balanced diet, a nutritionist has available a number of different foods, each containing various amounts of nutrients. Usually there are constraints on the minimum amount of each nutrient. The problem, then, is to determine a diet that satisfies the constraints (that is, has at least the minimum amount of each nutrient) and at the same time minimizes the cost. Let us construct a hypothetical example that will serve to illustrate the principle involved, even though it may not be particularly realistic. As before, we give the quantities involved in tabular form.

Nutrient	Meat	Potatoes	Beans	Cheese	Minimum amount required
Carbohydrates	20	40	10	10	100
Protein	40	05	40	40	100
Vitamins	10	01	02	15	10
Cost	2.50	0.10	0.20	1.00	

To obtain a mathematical formulation, we assume that x_1 is the amount of meat to be used, x_2 the amount of potatoes, x_3 the amount of beans, and x_4 the amount of cheese. The cost of the diet is then given by

$$2.50x_1 + 0.10x_2 + 0.20x_3 + 1.00x_4. \tag{10.3}$$

The constraints take the form of inequalities

$$\begin{aligned} 20x_1 + 40x_2 + 10x_3 + 10x_4 &\geq 100, \\ 40x_1 + 5x_2 + 40x_3 + 40x_4 &\geq 100, \\ 10x_1 + x_2 + 2x_3 + 15x_4 &\geq 10. \end{aligned} \tag{10.4}$$

For example, the first inequality above reflects the fact that the diet contains at least 100 units of carbohydrates. In mathematical terms, then, the problem reads: Find the nonnegative vector $X = [x_1, x_2, x_3, x_4]$ which satisfies the inequalities (10.4) and at the same time minimizes the linear expression (10.3).

The problem in Example 2 is just one of many whose mathematical formulation conforms to the following definition.

DEFINITION 10.4. *The* STANDARD MINIMUM PROGRAM *is to find that nonnegative vector* $\mathbf{X} = [x_1, x_2, \ldots, x_n]$ *which minimizes*

$$c_1x_1 + c_2x_2 + \cdots + c_nx_n$$

subject to the constraints

$$A\mathbf{X}^{\mathsf{T}} \geq \mathbf{B},$$

where A *is an* $m \times n$ *matrix of constraints and* $\mathbf{B}$ *is a column vector of* m *numbers.*

Of course, there may not be any nonnegative vectors that satisfy the constraints (such a problem is called infeasible). If a nonnegative vector satisfies the constraints we call it a *feasible solution* as before; similarly, a feasible solution that minimizes the objective function is called an *optimal solution.*

For completeness, we give another definition at this time.

DEFINITION 10.5. *The* STANDARD MAXIMUM PROGRAM *is to find a nonnegative vector* $\mathbf{Y} = [y_1, y_2, \ldots, y_n]$ *that maximizes*

$$b_1y_1 + b_2y_2 + \cdots + b_my_m$$

subject to the constraints

$$\mathbf{Y}A \leq \mathbf{C},$$

where A *is an* $m \times n$ *matrix of constants and* $\mathbf{C}$ *is an* n*-vector of constants.*

Example 3. We give an abstract example of a standard maximum program. Find a nonnegative vector $\mathbf{Y} = [y_1, y_2, y_3]$ that maximizes

$$2y_1 + 3y_2 + 6y_3$$

subject to the restrictions

$$\begin{aligned} y_1 + y_2 + 3y_3 &\leq 6, \\ 2y_1 + y_2 \quad &\leq 3, \\ y_1 + 2y_2 + y_3 &\leq 4. \end{aligned}$$

Here the matrix A is

$$A = \begin{bmatrix} 1 & 2 & 1 \\ 1 & 1 & 2 \\ 3 & 0 & 1 \end{bmatrix}.$$

If we set $\mathbf{C} = [6, 3, 4]$, then the constraints may be written $\mathbf{Y}A \leq \mathbf{C}$ as in Definition 10.5.

In the next section we turn to the problem of *solving* these linear programming programs.

Exercises

In each exercise, formulate the given problem as a linear program, and determine if the problem is a canonical or a standard program. Do not attempt to solve the programs.

1. An oil company has two refineries that it wishes to use to fill an order for 30 million barrels of high-octane gas and 50 million barrels of low-octane gas. The first refinery produces 2 million barrels of high octane per day and 3 million barrels of low octane per day, and costs \$2000 a day to operate. The second refinery produces 3 and 6 million barrels per day of high and low octane, respectively, and costs \$3000 a day to operate. How many days should each plant be operated to produce the desired amount of gasoline most economically?
2. A shipper of fruit has a truck with a capacity of 800 boxes of fruit and a maximum load of 1600 pounds of cargo. Oranges weigh 25 pounds a box and return 25¢ a box profit, tangerines weigh 30 pounds a box and return 30¢ a box, and apples weigh 15 pounds a box, returning 20¢ a box in profit. How should the shipper load his truck?
3. An oil company wishes to make an oil with viscosity 23 and surface tension 106 by mixing three grades of oil, G_1, G_2, and G_3. G_1 has viscosity 30, surface tension 100, and costs 20¢ a quart. G_2 has viscosity 15, surface tension 80, and costs 15¢ a quart. G_3 has viscosity 10, surface tension 150, and costs 10¢ a quart. Assuming that the viscosity and surface tension of the mixture are the averages of those of the ingredients, in what proportions should the ingredients be mixed so as to minimize the cost?

10.3 The Simplex Method I

We now turn to the solution of linear programs by the simplex method. This celebrated procedure was invented by G. B. Dantzig in the 1940s and has since become one of the most powerful tools in economics. In this section we consider the method applied to canonical programs, leaving the extension to other programs for the next section. We shall be mainly concerned with the actual computational procedure, the objective being to develop proficiency in solving linear programs. Thus, while we give heuristic explanations for the method, we shall not dwell on the underlying theory.

We turn, then, to the canonical minimum program: To find the nonnegative vector $\mathbf{X} = [x_1, x_2, \ldots, x_n]$ that minimizes $c_1x_1 + c_2x_2 + \cdots + c_nx_n$ subject to

$$\begin{aligned} a_{11}x_1 + a_{12}x_2 + \cdots + a_{1n}x_n &= b_1, \\ a_{21}x_1 + a_{22}x_2 + \cdots + a_{2n}x_n &= b_2, \\ &\vdots \\ a_{m1}x_1 + a_{m2}x_2 + \cdots + a_{mn}x_n &= b_m. \end{aligned} \tag{10.5}$$

We shall assume in most of this section that we are given a feasible basic solution as a starting point. We also will make the theoretical assumption that there exists a basic optimal solution. Our efforts will be directed at finding an optimal basic solution from this starting point.

One way of solving the problem, given these assumptions, would be to look at all basic solutions to the constraint equation and then, from this finite set, pick the nonnegative one that minimized the objective function.

Example 1. Consider the program of Example 1 of the previous section.

$$\begin{aligned} 1000x_1 \qquad\quad + 500x_3 &= 100, \\ 750x_2 + 250x_3 &= 150. \\ \text{Minimize } 4x_1 + 3x_2 + 2x_3. \end{aligned}$$

The basic solutions to the constraint equations are: $\mathbf{X}_1 = [\frac{1}{10}, \frac{1}{5}, 0]$, $\mathbf{X}_2 = [-\frac{1}{5}, 0, \frac{3}{5}]$, $\mathbf{X}_3 = [0, \frac{2}{15}, \frac{1}{5}]$. $\mathbf{X}_2$ is out because it has a negative coordinate; the values of the objective function at $\mathbf{X}_1$ and $\mathbf{X}_3$ are 1 and $\frac{4}{5}$, respectively. Thus, assuming that there is *some* basic optimal solution, an optimal solution is given by: $x_1 = 0$, $x_2 = \frac{2}{15}$, and $x_3 = \frac{1}{5}$.

The difficulty with the procedure illustrated in Example 1 is that, for programs of any size, the number of basic solutions is very large. For example, if the constraints determine five equations in ten unknowns, there could conceivably be $10!/5!(10 - 5)! = 252$ basic solutions. For larger problems, the number of basic solutions is so large as to be prohibitive even with the use of high-speed computers.

The underlying idea of the simplex method is to proceed from a given basic solution to the optimal basic solution in an orderly fashion. Essentially, it gives us a procedure for going from a given feasible solution to a better feasible solution. Thus, rather than checking all basic solutions exhaustively, we proceed from one solution to another, always improving the value of the objective function. After relatively few steps we arrive at an optimal solution. The key to the method is the technique for deciding how to improve a given feasible solution.

Let us be more specific. Assume we have a basic feasible solution to (10.5) with (for simplicity) the last $n - m$ coordinates of $\mathbf{X}$ equal to zero. This means that the first m columns $\mathbf{A}^1, \mathbf{A}^2, \ldots, \mathbf{A}^m$ of $A = [a_{ij}]$ are linearly independent and we can construct the following tableau.

	$\mathbf{A}^1$	$\mathbf{A}^2$	$\cdots$	$\mathbf{A}^m$	$\mathbf{A}^{m+1}$	$\cdots$	$\mathbf{A}^n$	$\mathbf{B}$
$\mathbf{A}^1$	1	0	$\cdots$	0	$e_{1,m+1}$		e_{1n}	f_1
$\mathbf{A}^2$	0	1	$\cdots$	0	$e_{2,m+1}$		e_{2n}	f_2
$\vdots$	$\vdots$	$\vdots$		$\vdots$			$\vdots$	$\vdots$
$\mathbf{A}^m$	0	0	$\cdots$	1	$e_{m,m+1}$		e_{mn}	f_m

Recall from Section 10.1 that the meaning of this tableau is simply that each column gives the coefficients of the vector at the top of the column in terms of the basis vectors on the left. We are assuming that our initial basic solution is $\mathbf{X}_0 = [f_1, f_2, \ldots, f_m, 0, \ldots, 0]$. The idea of the simplex method is to pass to a new basic feasible solution by replacing *one* of the vectors in the basis on the left by one of the vectors $\mathbf{A}^{m+1}, \ldots, \mathbf{A}^n$ not presently in the basis. In Section 10.2 we saw how to accomplish this operation. But which vector should we bring into the basis? If $\mathbf{A}^j$ is a vector not presently in the basis we know that if one "unit" of $\mathbf{A}^j$ is introduced into the solution, its contribution to the objective function will be c_j. Meanwhile, the tableau gives

$$\mathbf{A}^j = e_{1j}\mathbf{A}^1 + e_{2j}\mathbf{A}^2 + \cdots + e_{mj}\mathbf{A}^m;$$

thus the contribution to the objective function of one "unit" of

$$e_{1j}\mathbf{A}^1 + \cdots + e_{mj}\mathbf{A}^m \quad \text{is} \quad c_1e_{1j} + c_2e_{2j} + \cdots + c_me_{mj}.$$

Thus, intuitively, it would seem that if

$$c_j < c_1e_{1j} + c_2e_{2j} + \cdots + c_me_{mj},$$

then the objective function would be reduced by bringing the vector $\mathbf{A}^j$ into the basis. (This process has also been described as follows: think of $e_{1j}\mathbf{A}^1 + \cdots + e_{mj}\mathbf{A}^m$ as "synthetic" $\mathbf{A}^j$. If the cost of the real thing is less than the cost of the synthetic item, we should bring $\mathbf{A}^j$ into the basis.) If we define

$$\mathbf{Z} = [z_1, z_2, \ldots, z_n]$$

by

$$z_j = c_1e_{1j} + c_2e_{2j} + \cdots + c_me_{mj},$$

the numbers we need to calculate are $z_j - c_j$ for $j = m + 1, m + 2, \ldots, n$. For reasons that will become clear shortly, we add the entire vector $\mathbf{D} = \mathbf{Z} - \mathbf{C}$ as the last row of our tableau.

	$\mathbf{A}^1$	$\mathbf{A}^2$	$\cdots$	$\mathbf{A}^m$	$\mathbf{A}^{m+1}$	$\cdots$	$\mathbf{A}^n$	$\mathbf{B}$
$\mathbf{A}^1$	1	0		0	$e_{1,m+1}$	$\cdots$	e_{1n}	f_1
$\mathbf{A}^2$	0	1	$\cdots$	0	$e_{2,m+1}$	$\cdots$	e_{2n}	f_2
	$\vdots$	$\vdots$		$\vdots$				
$\mathbf{A}^m$	0	0		1	$e_{m,m+1}$		e_{mn}	f_n
$\mathbf{D}$	0	0	$\cdots$	0	d_{m+1}		d_n	

We now decide which vector to bring into the basis simply by examining the numbers d_j and picking a j with d_j positive. Having picked a vector to bring into the basis we face a further obstacle. Which $\mathbf{A}^i$ should we replace? Of course, if e_{ij} is zero we cannot replace $\mathbf{A}^i$ by $\mathbf{A}^j$, but what about the others? Actually, we have no choice. The numbers in the column under $\mathbf{B}$ must remain nonnegative (remember, these are the coordinates of our solution vector), so we cannot choose an i with e_{ij} negative. But, as we shall presently see, the requirement $\mathbf{X} \geq \mathbf{0}$ forces us to choose a particular i.

Assuming i and j are picked, let us see what happens to f_k when we replace $\mathbf{A}^i$ by $\mathbf{A}^j$ in the basis. We multiply the ith row by $1/e_{ij}$, and then subtract this new row, multiplied by e_{kj}, from the kth row. If we denote the new entry in the kth row last column by f_k' we have

$$f_k' = f_k - (e_{kj}/e_{ij})f_i.$$

The requirement that f_k' be nonnegative gives

$$(e_{kj}/e_{ij})f_i \leq f_k$$

or

$$f_i/e_{ij} \leq f_k/e_{kj}.$$

But this must be true for all k! This means that we must examine the ratios f_k/e_{kj} for each $k = 1, 2, \ldots, m$ and select the smallest. This is the row into which we must bring our new vector.

Without further ado, let us apply the method to an example.

Example 2. Let us solve the problem of Example 1 using the simplex method. The vector $\mathbf{X} = [\frac{1}{10}, \frac{1}{5}, 0]$ is an obvious feasible solution, and we use it as a starting point. Recalling that

$$\mathbf{A}^1 = \begin{bmatrix} 1000 \\ 0 \end{bmatrix}, \quad \mathbf{A}^2 = \begin{bmatrix} 0 \\ 750 \end{bmatrix}, \quad \mathbf{A}^3 = \begin{bmatrix} 500 \\ 250 \end{bmatrix}, \quad \mathbf{B} = \begin{bmatrix} 100 \\ 150 \end{bmatrix},$$

we have

$$\mathbf{A}^3 = \tfrac{1}{2}\mathbf{A}^1 + \tfrac{1}{3}\mathbf{A}^2, \mathbf{B} = \tfrac{1}{10}\mathbf{A}^1 + \tfrac{1}{5}\mathbf{A}^2.$$

Our initial tableau is then

	$\mathbf{A}^1$	$\mathbf{A}^2$	$\mathbf{A}^3$	$\mathbf{B}$
$\mathbf{A}^1$	1	0	$\frac{1}{2}$	$\frac{1}{10}$
$\mathbf{A}^2$	0	1	$\frac{1}{3}$	$\frac{1}{5}$
$\mathbf{D}$	0	0	d_3	

We calculate $d_3 = (4 \cdot \frac{1}{2} + 3 \cdot \frac{1}{3}) - 2 = 1 > 0$, which means that $\mathbf{A}^3$ should be brought into the basis. Calculating the ratios f_i/e_{i3}: $\frac{1}{10}/\frac{1}{2} = \frac{1}{5}$, $\frac{1}{5}/\frac{1}{3} = \frac{3}{5}$. This means we must replace $\mathbf{A}^1$. Pivoting on the $\frac{1}{2}$ we obtain

	$\mathbf{A}^1$	$\mathbf{A}^2$	$\mathbf{A}^3$	$\mathbf{B}$
$\mathbf{A}^3$	2	0	1	$\frac{2}{10}$
$\mathbf{A}^2$	$-\frac{2}{3}$	1	0	$\frac{2}{15}$
$\mathbf{D}$	d_1'	0	0	

$d_1' = (2 \cdot 2 + (-\frac{2}{3})3) - 4 = -2 < 0$. And thus we have found the desired solution: $\mathbf{X} = [0, \frac{2}{15}, \frac{2}{10}]$. Note also that the last row of the last tableau can be obtained from the first tableau simply by treating it in the same fashion as the other rows; that is, by applying the row-reduction technique. This turns out to always be the case and the fact is very useful computationally.

Example 3. Find a nonnegative vector $\mathbf{X} = [x_1, x_2, x_3, x_4, x_5]$ that minimizes

$$2x_1 - x_2 + 3x_3 + 4x_4 + 2x_5$$

subject to

$$\begin{aligned} x_1 + x_2 - 2x_3 - x_4 + 2x_5 &= 2, \\ 3x_1 + x_2 - x_3 + x_4 + x_5 &= 4. \end{aligned}$$

To find the initial solution it is usually possible to "guess" a solution (in this case, for example, set $x_3 = x_4 = x_5 = 0$ and solve for x_1 and x_2). A method with somewhat more general applicability is the following. Set up for a tableau of the columns of A and $\mathbf{B}$ in terms of the unit basis vectors $\mathbf{E}^1$, $\mathbf{E}^2$:

	$\mathbf{A}^1$	$\mathbf{A}^2$	$\mathbf{A}^3$	$\mathbf{A}^4$	$\mathbf{A}^5$	$\mathbf{B}$
$\mathbf{E}^1$	1	1	-2	-1	2	2
$\mathbf{E}^2$	3	1	-1	1	1	4

Now use the replacement operation of Section 10.1, being careful that the coefficients in the last column remain nonnegative. For example, if we decide to bring in $\mathbf{A}^4$, we must replace $\mathbf{E}^2$ (why?), yielding

	$\mathbf{A}^1$	$\mathbf{A}^2$	$\mathbf{A}^3$	$\mathbf{A}^4$	$\mathbf{A}^5$	$\mathbf{B}$
$\mathbf{E}^1$	4	2	-3	0	3	6
$\mathbf{A}^4$	3	1	-1	1	1	4

We now replace $\mathbf{E}^1$ by $\mathbf{A}^5$, making our initial tableau the following:

	$\mathbf{A}^1$	$\mathbf{A}^2$	$\mathbf{A}^3$	$\mathbf{A}^4$	$\mathbf{A}^5$	$\mathbf{B}$
$\mathbf{A}^5$	$\frac{4}{3}$	$\frac{2}{3}$	-1	0	1	2
$\mathbf{A}^4$	$\textcircled{\frac{5}{3}}$	$\frac{1}{3}$	0	1	0	2
$\mathbf{D}$	$\frac{22}{3}$	$\frac{11}{3}$	-5	0	0	

We apply the simplex method. Note that in our first step we can bring either $\mathbf{A}^1$ or $\mathbf{A}^2$ into the basis. It is not crucial, but one procedure is to choose the largest entry in the last row. For convenience we have circled the pivot elements.

	$\mathbf{A}^1$	$\mathbf{A}^2$	$\mathbf{A}^3$	$\mathbf{A}^4$	$\mathbf{A}^5$	$\mathbf{B}$
$\mathbf{A}^5$	0	$\textcircled{\frac{2}{5}}$	-1	$-\frac{4}{5}$	1	$\frac{2}{5}$
$\mathbf{A}^1$	1	$\frac{1}{5}$	0	$\frac{3}{5}$	0	$\frac{6}{5}$
$\mathbf{D}$	0	$\frac{11}{5}$	-5	$-\frac{22}{5}$	0	

	$\mathbf{A}^1$	$\mathbf{A}^2$	$\mathbf{A}^3$	$\mathbf{A}^4$	$\mathbf{A}^5$	$\mathbf{B}$
$\mathbf{A}^2$	0	1	$-\frac{5}{2}$	-2	$\frac{5}{2}$	1
$\mathbf{A}^1$	1	0	$\textcircled{\frac{1}{2}}$	1	$-\frac{1}{2}$	1
$\mathbf{D}$	0	0	$\frac{1}{2}$	0	$-\frac{11}{2}$	

	$\mathbf{A}^1$	$\mathbf{A}^2$	$\mathbf{A}^3$	$\mathbf{A}^4$	$\mathbf{A}^5$	$\mathbf{B}$
$\mathbf{A}^2$	5	1	0	3	0	6
$\mathbf{A}^3$	2	0	1	2	-1	2
$\mathbf{D}$	-1	0	0	-1	-5	

The desired solution is [0, 6, 2, 0, 0] and the minimum value of the objective function is 0.

What about solving a canonical *maximum* problem? As we now wish to increase the objective function, the only change in the procedure is to look for negative entries in the last row of the tableau. When all entries are nonnegative, the desired maximum will be reached.

Exercises

1. Use the simplex method to find the minimum value of $3x_1 + 4x_2 + x_3$ subject to

$$\begin{aligned} x_1 \quad + 2x_3 &= 1, \\ x_2 + \ x_3 &= 2, \\ x_1 \geq 0, x_2 \geq 0, x_3 &\geq 0. \end{aligned}$$

2. Solve Exercise 1 by considering all basic solutions.

3. Find the nonnegative $\mathbf{X} = [x_1, x_2, x_3, x_4]$ that minimizes $3x_1 + 4x_2 + 5x_3 + x_4$ subject to

$$\begin{aligned} x_1 + 2x_2 + x_3 + 3x_4 &= 6, \\ 2x_1 + x_2 + 3x_3 + 2x_4 &= 7, \\ 3x_1 + 2x_2 + x_3 + x_4 &= 8, \end{aligned}$$

given the feasible solution $[1, 2, 1, 0]$.
4. Minimize $x_1 + 2x_2 + x_3 + 3x_4$ subject to

$$\begin{aligned} x_1 + x_2 + 3x_3 + x_4 &= 30, \\ 2x_1 + x_3 + 2x_4 &= 24, \\ x_1 + 2x_2 + 3x_4 &= 18, \\ [x_1, x_2, x_3, x_4] &\geq \mathbf{0}. \end{aligned}$$

5. Maximize $2x_1 + 4x_2 + x_3 + x_4$ subject to

$$\begin{aligned} x_1 + 3x_2 + x_4 &= 4, \\ 2x_1 + x_2 &= 3, \\ x_2 + 4x_3 + x_4 &= 3, \\ [x_1, x_2, x_3, x_4] &\geq \mathbf{0}. \end{aligned}$$

6. Let A be an $m \times n$ matrix, I the $m \times m$ identity matrix, $\mathbf{B}$ a column vector of m constants,

$$\mathbf{X} = [x_1, x_2, \ldots, x_n],$$

and

$$\mathbf{X}_1 = [x_1, x_2, \ldots, x_n, y_1, y_2, \ldots, y_m].$$

Show that the linear program:

$$\begin{aligned} &\text{Minimize } y_1 + y_2 + \cdots + y_m \\ &\text{Subject to } [A : I]\mathbf{X}_1^{\mathsf{T}} = \mathbf{B}, \quad \mathbf{X}_1 \geq \mathbf{0} \end{aligned}$$

has an optimal solution with the objective function 0, if and only if the system $A\mathbf{X}^{\mathsf{T}} = \mathbf{B}$ has a nonnegative solution. Use this and the simplex method to find a nonnegative solution to the system

$$\begin{aligned} x_1 - x_2 + 2x_3 + x_4 &= 5, \\ x_1 + 2x_2 - x_3 + 2x_4 &= 3, \\ x_2 + x_3 - x_4 &= 0. \end{aligned}$$

7. Solve the program in Exercise 3, Section 10.2.

10.4 The Simplex Method II

We conclude our discussion of the simplex method by showing how to solve the standard linear programs. We shall see that the standard maximum program can easily be changed into an equivalent canonical program, which can then be solved using the techniques of the previous section. The standard minimum program will be treated using the concept of *duality*, an important tool in the theory as well as in the practice of linear programming.

To solve a standard maximum program we simply add some new variables that change the problem to a canonical program. The procedure is probably best understood through a simple example.

Example 1. Consider the standard maximum program of maximizing $y_1 + y_2 + 3y_3 + 2y_4$ subject to the constraints

$$\begin{aligned} 2y_1 + y_2 + y_3 &\le 10, \\ y_1 + 2y_2 + y_4 &\le 20, \\ y_2 + y_3 + 2y_4 &\le 40, \end{aligned}$$

and

$$[y_1, y_2, y_3, y_4] \ge \mathbf{0}.$$

We change the problem to a canonical program by adding three new variables z_1, z_2, z_3 (called *slack variables*).

$$\begin{aligned} 2y_1 + y_2 + y_3 + z_1 &= 10, \\ y_1 + 2y_2 + y_4 + z_2 &= 20, \\ y_2 + y_3 + 2y_4 + z_3 &= 40, \end{aligned}$$

$$[y_1, y_2, y_3, y_4, z_1, z_2, z_3] \ge \mathbf{0}.$$

We retain the same objective function, or, if you wish, we now use $y_1 + y_2 + 3y_3 + 2y_4 + 0 \cdot z_1 + 0 \cdot z_2 + 0 \cdot z_3$. Certainly any solution to the equations above will give us a solution to the system of inequalities since the z_i's are nonnegative. Similarly any solution to the original constraints will give us a solution to the equations with the proper choice of z_1, z_2, z_3. In other words, the systems are equivalent: solving one solves the other. Note also that one feasible solution to the system of equations is obvious; namely, $z_1 = 10$, $z_2 = 20$, and $z_3 = 40$. We write down the initial tableau.

	$\mathbf{A}^1$	$\mathbf{A}^2$	$\mathbf{A}^3$	$\mathbf{A}^4$	$\mathbf{E}^1$	$\mathbf{E}^2$	$\mathbf{E}^3$	$\mathbf{C}$
$\mathbf{E}^1$	2	1	(1)	0	1	0	0	10
$\mathbf{E}^2$	1	2	0	1	0	1	0	20
$\mathbf{E}^3$	0	1	1	2	0	0	1	40
$\mathbf{D}$	-1	-1	-3	-2	0	0	0	

As always, we have circled the pivot element. Because we are maximizing, we look for negative entries in the last row.

	$\mathbf{A}^1$	$\mathbf{A}^2$	$\mathbf{A}^3$	$\mathbf{A}^4$	$\mathbf{E}^1$	$\mathbf{E}^2$	$\mathbf{E}^3$	$\mathbf{C}$
$\mathbf{A}^3$	2	1	1	0	1	0	0	10
$\mathbf{E}^2$	1	2	0	1	0	1	0	20
$\mathbf{E}^3$	-2	0	0	(2)	-1	0	1	30
$\mathbf{D}$	5	2	0	-2	3	0	0	

	$\mathbf{A}^1$	$\mathbf{A}^2$	$\mathbf{A}^3$	$\mathbf{A}^4$	$\mathbf{E}^1$	$\mathbf{E}^2$	$\mathbf{E}^3$	$\mathbf{C}$
$\mathbf{A}^3$	2	1	1	0	1	0	0	10
$\mathbf{E}^2$	2	2	0	0	$\frac{1}{2}$	1	$-\frac{1}{2}$	5
$\mathbf{A}^4$	-1	0	0	1	$-\frac{1}{2}$	0	$\frac{1}{2}$	15
$\mathbf{D}$	3	2	0	0	2	0	1	

We are now finished; the answer to the original program is $y_1 = y_2 = 0$, $y_3 = 10$, and $y_4 = 15$. The value of the program is $3 \cdot 10 + 2 \cdot 15 = 60$. The reader should convince himself that if there were a solution to the original inequalities with a larger value, then there would be a solution to the equalities with the same (higher) value.

The reader no doubt wondered why the standard maximum and minimum problem were stated in different forms (why not just reverse inequalities and change "maximum" to "minimum"?). The following discussion should answer this question. We assume that $A = [a_{ij}]$ is a given $m \times n$ matrix of constants, and $\mathbf{B} \in R^m$, $\mathbf{C} \in R^n$ are fixed. As always, $\mathbf{X} = [x_1, x_2, \ldots, x_n]$, $\mathbf{Y} = [y_1, y_2, \ldots, y_m]$ are our "variables."

DEFINITION 10.6. *The* DUAL *of the standard maximum program:*

$$\begin{aligned} &\textit{Maximize } (\mathbf{Y}, \mathbf{B}) = b_1 y_1 + b_2 y_2 + \cdots + b_m y_m \\ &\textit{Subject to } \mathbf{Y}A \leq \mathbf{C}, \qquad \mathbf{Y} \geq \mathbf{0} \end{aligned} \tag{10.6}$$

is the following standard minimum program:

$$\begin{aligned} &\textit{Minimize } (\mathbf{X}, \mathbf{C}) = c_1 x_1 + c_2 x_2 + \cdots + c_n x_n \\ &\textit{Subject to } A\mathbf{X}^{\mathsf{T}} \geq \mathbf{B}, \qquad \mathbf{X} \geq \mathbf{0}; \end{aligned} \tag{10.7}$$

we also say that (10.6) *is the* DUAL *of* (10.7).

The implication of the previous definition is that the two programs are somehow related. We proceed to investigate this relation.

Example 2. Consider the maximum program of Example 1. What is its dual? We have

$$A = \begin{bmatrix} 2 & 1 & 0 \\ 1 & 2 & 1 \\ 1 & 0 & 1 \\ 0 & 1 & 2 \end{bmatrix}$$

from the inequalities given in that example. $\mathbf{X}$ must, therefore, be a 3-vector, and also $B = [1, 1, 3, 2]$. Writing out $A\mathbf{X}^{\mathsf{T}} \geq \mathbf{B}$,

$$\begin{aligned} 2x_1 + x_2 \phantom{{}+ x_3} &\geq 1, \\ x_1 + 2x_2 + x_3 &\geq 1, \\ x_1 \phantom{{}+ 2x_2} + x_3 &\geq 3, \\ x_2 + 2x_3 &\geq 2. \end{aligned}$$

The objective function $(\mathbf{X}, \mathbf{C})$ is $10x_1 + 20x_2 + 40x_3$. Recall, from Example 1, the entries in the last row of the last tableau obtained. The reader may have wondered why we carried the values under the $\mathbf{E}^i$'s along. We claim that the last three entries solve the dual! That is, that $x_1 = 2$, $x_2 = 0$, $x_3 = 1$ solves the minimum program above. The proof will come shortly; for now, let us be satisfied by noting that $[2, 0, 1]$ is a feasible solution, and that the value of the minimum problem $10 \cdot 2 + 20 \cdot 0 + 40 \cdot 1 = 60$ is the same as the value of the dual, maximum problem.

PROPOSITION 3. *If* A, $\mathbf{B}$, $\mathbf{C}$ *are as in Definition* 10.6 *and* $\mathbf{X}_0$, $\mathbf{Y}_0$ *are two non-negative vectors that satisfy*

$$A\mathbf{X}_0^{\mathsf{T}} \geq \mathbf{B}, \qquad \mathbf{Y}_0 A \leq \mathbf{C}$$

and $(\mathbf{X}_0, \mathbf{C}) = (\mathbf{Y}_0, \mathbf{B})$, *then* $\mathbf{X}_0$ *is an optimal solution of the minimum problem* (10.7) *and* $\mathbf{Y}_0$ *is an optimal solution to the maximum problem* (10.6).

PROOF. The content of the proposition is that if one can find feasible solutions of a program and its dual that yield the same values, then one has solved *both* programs. The proof is really quite easy. Let $\mathbf{Y}_1$ be any feasible solution to (10.6); then $\mathbf{Y}_1\mathbf{A} \leq \mathbf{C}$. Multiply both sides of the equation by $\mathbf{X}_0^{\mathsf{T}}$:

$$\mathbf{Y}_1 A\mathbf{X}^{\mathsf{T}} \leq \mathbf{C}\mathbf{X}_0^{\mathsf{T}} = (\mathbf{C}, \mathbf{X}_0) = (\mathbf{Y}_0, \mathbf{B}).$$

But, since $\mathbf{Y}_1$ is nonnegative and $A\mathbf{X}^{\mathsf{T}} \geq \mathbf{B}^{\mathsf{T}}$, we have

$$(\mathbf{Y}_1, \mathbf{B}) \leq (\mathbf{Y}_1, (A\mathbf{X}^{\mathsf{T}})^{\mathsf{T}}) = \mathbf{Y}_1 A\mathbf{X}^{\mathsf{T}} \leq (\mathbf{Y}_0, \mathbf{B})$$

or $(\mathbf{Y}_1, \mathbf{B}) \leq (\mathbf{Y}_0, \mathbf{B})$. This means that $\mathbf{Y}_0$ is optimal! The proof that $\mathbf{X}_0$ is optimal is similar, and we leave it as an exercise.

And, suddenly, we have a technique for finding the solution to a standard minimum program. Write down the dual and solve it as in Example 1; the final tableau gives the solution of both programs.

Example 3. Find the minimum of $3x_1 + 2x_2 + 5x_3$ subject to the constraints

$$\begin{aligned} x_1 + 3x_2 + x_3 &\geq 4, \\ x_1 + x_2 + x_3 &\geq 6, \\ x_1 \quad + 2x_3 &\geq 2, \qquad [x_1, x_2, x_3] \geq \mathbf{0}. \end{aligned}$$

We write out the dual program.
Maximize $4y_1 + 6y_2 + 2y_3$ subject to

$$\begin{aligned} y_1 + y_2 + y_3 &\leq 3, \\ 3y_1 + y_2 \quad &\leq 2, \\ y_1 + y_2 + 2y_3 &\leq 5, \qquad [y_1, y_2, y_3] \geq \mathbf{0}. \end{aligned}$$

Add the slack variables

$$\begin{aligned} y_1 + y_2 + y_3 + z_1 \qquad &= 3, \\ 3y_1 + y_2 \qquad + z_2 \quad &= 2, \\ y_1 + y_2 + 2y_3 \qquad + z_3 &= 5. \end{aligned}$$

The simplex method:

	$\mathbf{A}^1$	$\mathbf{A}^2$	$\mathbf{A}^3$	$\mathbf{E}^1$	$\mathbf{E}^2$	$\mathbf{E}^3$	$\mathbf{C}$
$\mathbf{E}^1$	1	1	1	1	0	0	3
$\mathbf{E}^2$	3	(1)	0	0	1	0	2
$\mathbf{E}^3$	1	1	2	0	0	1	5
$\mathbf{D}$	−4	−6	−2	0	0	0	

	$\mathbf{A}^1$	$\mathbf{A}^2$	$\mathbf{A}^3$	$\mathbf{E}^1$	$\mathbf{E}^2$	$\mathbf{E}^3$	$\mathbf{C}$
$\mathbf{E}^1$	−2	0	(1)	1	−1	0	1
$\mathbf{A}^2$	3	1	0	0	1	0	2
$\mathbf{E}^2$	−2	0	2	0	−1	1	3
$\mathbf{D}$	14	0	−2	0	6	0	

	$\mathbf{A}^1$	$\mathbf{A}^2$	$\mathbf{A}^3$	$\mathbf{E}^1$	$\mathbf{E}^2$	$\mathbf{E}^3$	$\mathbf{C}$
$\mathbf{A}^3$	−2	0	1	1	−1	0	1
$\mathbf{A}^2$	3	1	0	0	1	0	2
$\mathbf{E}^3$	2	0	0	−2	1	1	1
$\mathbf{D}$	10	0	0	2	4	0	

The result indicates that the maximum program has optimal solution $y_1 = 0$, $y_2 = 2$, $y_3 = 1$, and the minimum program has solution $x_1 = 2$, $x_2 = 4$, $x_3 = 0$. A convenient way to check the answer is to compute both values; we see that the value in both cases is 14. Proposition 1 then assures us that we have indeed found the optimal solutions.

Throughout our discussion of linear programs we have assumed that the problems under consideration did, in fact, have an answer. It is quite easy to construct programs that are either infeasible or have no optimal solution. For example, consider the two programs

I. Minimize $x_1 + x_2$
Subject to
$$-x_1 + x_2 \geq 1,$$
$$x_1 - x_2 \geq 2.$$

II. Maximize $x_1 + x_2$
Subject to
$$x_1 - x_2 \leq 2,$$
$$-x_1 + x_2 \leq 1.$$

Program I has no feasible solutions, for the first inequality may be written $x_1 \leq x_2 - 1$, while the second may be written as $x_1 \geq x_2 + 2$. No matter what you choose for x_2, no value of x_1 will satisfy both of these inequalities. In the second program, pick $x_1 = x_2 = N$ and the value of $x_1 + x_2$ is $2N$. Thus the objective function can be made arbitrarily large. One of the most important theorems guaranteeing existence of a solution to linear programs is the following.

THEOREM 10.1. If A, $\mathbf{B}$, $\mathbf{C}$ are such that both of the programs in Definition 10.6 have a feasible solution, then both programs have an optimal solution, and the values of the two programs are equal.

The above theorem is often called the fundamental theorem and has a long and interesting history. It was first proved by the great mathematician J. von Neumann using sophisticated techniques. Several different proofs have been given since, leading up to the present proofs, which are elementary, if somewhat involved. It is the concept of duality that has simplified the proof to such an extent. We refer the interested reader to the excellent and complete treatment in *The Theory of Linear Economic Models*, by David Gale (McGraw-Hill, New York, 1960).

Exercises

1. Maximize $2x_1 + x_2$ subject to

$$2x_1 + 3x_2 \leq 4,$$
$$3x_1 + x_2 \leq 3.$$

2. Maximize $x_1 + 2x_2 - x_3$ subject to

$$2x_1 + x_2 + x_3 \leq 6,$$
$$x_1 + x_2 - x_3 \leq 3,$$
$$x_1 \geq 0, x_2 \geq 0, x_3 \geq 0$$

3. Minimize $4x_1 + 5x_2 + 2x_3$ subject to

$$x_1 + x_2 + x_3 \geq 6,$$
$$3x_1 + x_3 \geq 1,$$
$$x_1 + x_2 \geq 2,$$
$$x_1 + 2x_2 \geq 1,$$
$$x_1 \geq 0, x_2 \geq 0, x_3 \geq 0.$$

4. Solve the program of Exercise 2, Section 10.2.
5. Prove that the vector $\mathbf{X}_0$ of Proposition 1 is an optimal solution to its minimum program.
6. If $\mathbf{Y}_1$, $\mathbf{X}_1$ are any feasible solutions to the standard maximum program, (10.6), and the standard minimum program, (10.7), respectively, show that $(\mathbf{Y}_1, \mathbf{B}) \leq (\mathbf{X}_1, \mathbf{C})$. That is, the value corresponding to a feasible solution of a maximum program is less than or equal to the value of any feasible solution of the dual. *Hint:* Use the technique in the proof of Proposition 1.

10.5 Linear Least-Square Curve Fitting

In this section we consider the problem of fitting a polynomial to a given set of data points. This problem typically arises when one tries to interpret data from a scientific experiment. Let us illustrate the idea with a simple example. In a physics laboratory, a student studies the behavior of a spring by hanging several known weights from the spring and noting the distance that the spring stretches in each case. The weights are 1, 2, 3, 4, and 5 pounds, and the spring stretches 2.15, 4.41, 6.60, 8.76, and 10.9 inches, respectively. We graph the amount of elongation of the spring versus the applied force in Figure 10.1.

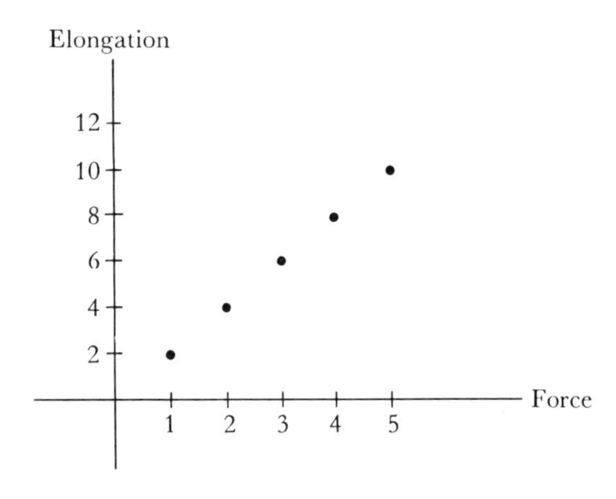

FIGURE 10.1

In the figure, the points appear to lie on a straight line. Unfortunately, calculation shows that the first three points are not collinear. But, of course, the numbers involved are not exact. The individual weights may be slightly off, the measurement of elongation is subject to error, etc. Thus, it is reasonable to conclude that a straight line describes the physical situation even though our points do not lie exactly on a line. (The reader who has studied physics will recall that this principle is called Hooke's law.) Finally, we come to our problem: Since it is impossible to draw a straight line through our five points, which straight line should we pick as best representing the given data? A straight line is just the graph of a function of the form $f(x) = ax + b$, where a and b are fixed constants; so the problem can also be viewed as determining the values of a and b such that the graph of f best "fits" the data. Of course, before we can solve this problem we must decide what we mean by "best"; that is, we must give a quantitative expression for the distance from our data to a given line.

In many experiments, the data are not linear, and then we must look to more complicated functions to approximate the data. The functions we consider in this section are the polynomials, and without further ado we state the problem we shall solve.

Assume we are given m data points $(x_1, y_1), (x_2, y_2), \ldots, (x_m, y_m)$ and we desire to approximate this data by a polynomial $a_0 + a_1 x + a_2 x^2 + \cdots + a_n x^n$ (n is *fixed* in each problem). The *least-squares polynomial* is that polynomial $p(x)$ of degree n which minimizes the square root of the sum of the squares of the errors:

$$\left[\sum_{i=1}^{m} (y_i - p(x_i))^2\right]^{1/2}. \tag{10.8}$$

Geometrically, the problem may be viewed as follows: let the "distance" from a function $f(x)$ to the set of data be defined as

$$\left[\sum_{i=1}^{m} (y_i - f(x_i))^2\right]^{1/2}.$$

We then seek the polynomial of degree n that is "closest" to our set of data. We begin the solution of the problem with a lemma.

LEMMA. *Let V be a subspace of R^n, and $\mathbf{X}_0$ a point of R^n not in V. A necessary and sufficient condition that $\mathbf{Y}_0 \in V$ be the closest point in V to $\mathbf{X}_0$ is that the vector $\mathbf{X}_0 - \mathbf{Y}_0$ is perpendicular to every vector in V.*

PROOF. As usual, we denote the inner product of two vectors by $(\mathbf{X}, \mathbf{Y})$, and we denote the distance between two vectors by $d(\mathbf{X}, \mathbf{Y})$. The formula $d(\mathbf{X}, \mathbf{Y})^2 = (\mathbf{X} - \mathbf{Y}, \mathbf{X} - \mathbf{Y})$ should also be recalled. Assume first that $\mathbf{X}_0 - \mathbf{Y}_0$ is perpendicular to every vector in V, and let $\mathbf{Y}$ be an arbitrary vector in V.

$$\begin{aligned}
&(\mathbf{X}_0 - \mathbf{Y}, \mathbf{X}_0 - \mathbf{Y}) \\
&\quad = (\mathbf{X}_0 - \mathbf{Y}_0 + \mathbf{Y}_0 - \mathbf{Y}, \mathbf{X}_0 - \mathbf{Y}_0 + \mathbf{Y}_0 - \mathbf{Y}) \\
&\quad = (\mathbf{X}_0 - \mathbf{Y}_0, \mathbf{X}_0 - \mathbf{Y}_0 + \mathbf{Y}_0 - \mathbf{Y}) + (\mathbf{Y}_0 - \mathbf{Y}, \mathbf{X}_0 - \mathbf{Y}_0 + \mathbf{Y}_0 - \mathbf{Y}) \\
&\quad = (\mathbf{X}_0 - \mathbf{Y}_0, \mathbf{X}_0 - \mathbf{Y}_0) + 2(\mathbf{X}_0 - \mathbf{Y}_0, \mathbf{Y}_0 - \mathbf{Y}) + (\mathbf{Y}_0 - \mathbf{Y}, \mathbf{Y}_0 - \mathbf{Y}).
\end{aligned}$$

But $\mathbf{Y}_0 - \mathbf{Y}$ is in V, and thus the last equation becomes

$$d(\mathbf{X}_0, \mathbf{Y})^2 = d(\mathbf{X}_0, \mathbf{Y}_0)^2 + d(\mathbf{Y}_0, \mathbf{Y})^2$$

or

$$d(\mathbf{X}_0, \mathbf{Y}) \geq d(\mathbf{X}_0, \mathbf{Y}_0)$$

and thus $\mathbf{Y}_0$ is at least as close to $\mathbf{X}_0$ as $\mathbf{Y}$ is. Conversely assume that $\mathbf{Y}_0$ is the closest point to $\mathbf{X}_0$, and that $\mathbf{Y}_1$ is a vector in V such that $(\mathbf{X}_0 - \mathbf{Y}_0, \mathbf{Y}_1) = \alpha \neq 0$. We can assume that $\mathbf{Y}_1$ has length 1 (why?). Define $\mathbf{Y}_2$ by $\mathbf{Y}_2 = \mathbf{Y}_0 + \alpha \mathbf{Y}_1$. It is clear that $\mathbf{Y}_2$ is in V, and we claim that it is closer than $\mathbf{Y}_0$ to $\mathbf{X}_0$.

$$\begin{aligned}
d(\mathbf{X}_0, \mathbf{Y}_2)^2 &= (\mathbf{X}_0 - \mathbf{Y}_2, \mathbf{X}_0 - \mathbf{Y}_2) \\
&= (\mathbf{X}_0 - \mathbf{Y}_0 - \alpha \mathbf{Y}_1, \mathbf{X}_0 - \mathbf{Y}_0 - \alpha \mathbf{Y}_1) \\
&= (\mathbf{X}_0 - \mathbf{Y}_0, \mathbf{X}_0 - \mathbf{Y}_0) - 2\alpha(\mathbf{X}_0 - \mathbf{Y}_0, \mathbf{Y}_1) + \alpha^2(\mathbf{Y}_1, \mathbf{Y}_1) \\
&= d(\mathbf{X}_0, \mathbf{Y}_0)^2 - 2\alpha^2 + \alpha^2 \\
&= d(\mathbf{X}_0, \mathbf{Y}_0)^2 - \alpha^2.
\end{aligned}$$

COROLLARY. A necessary and sufficient condition that $\mathbf{Y}_0$ *be the closest point in* V *to* $\mathbf{X}_0$ *is that*

$$\begin{aligned}(\mathbf{X}_0, \mathbf{Z}_1) &= (\mathbf{Y}_0, \mathbf{Z}_1)\\ (\mathbf{X}_0, \mathbf{Z}_2) &= (\mathbf{Y}_0, \mathbf{Z}_2)\\ &\vdots\\ (\mathbf{X}_0, \mathbf{Z}_k) &= (\mathbf{Y}_0, \mathbf{Z}_k)\end{aligned} \tag{10.9}$$

where $\mathbf{Z}_1, \mathbf{Z}_2, \ldots, \mathbf{Z}_k$ *is a set of vectors that span* V.

We leave the proof of the corollary as an exercise. The equations (10.9) are known as the *normal equations* and are the key to solving our approximation problem.

Example 1. Find the distance from (3, 1) to the straight line $y = 2x$. We consider the straight line as a subspace of R^2 with basis $\{[1, 2]\}$. In this case we have only one normal equation $([3, 1], [1, 2]) = 5 = (\mathbf{Y}_0, [1, 2])$. As $\mathbf{Y}_0$ is in V, it is of the form $[y_1, 2y_1]$, so the normal equation becomes $5y_1 = 5$ or $\mathbf{Y}_0 = [1, 2]$, and the required distance is $\sqrt{(3 - 1)^2 + (1 - 2)^2} = \sqrt{5}$.

Returning to our general approximation problem, we seek to write it in matrix form. Assume for a moment that there is a polynomial that fits the data exactly. We would have the following system:

$$\begin{aligned}a_0 + a_1x_1 + a_2x_1^2 + \cdots + a_nx_1^n &= y_1,\\ a_0 + a_1x_2 + a_2x_2^2 + \cdots + a_nx_2^n &= y_2,\\ \vdots \qquad\qquad &\quad \vdots\\ a_0 + a_1x_m + a_2x_m^2 + \cdots + a_nx_m^n &= y_m.\end{aligned}$$

Since we are trying to determine the numbers $a_0, a_1, \ldots, a_n$ we define an $m \times n$ matrix A and two column vectors $\mathbf{U}, \mathbf{Y}_0$ by

$$A = \begin{bmatrix} 1 & x_1 & x_1^2 & \cdots & x_1^n \\ 1 & x_2 & x_2^2 & \cdots & x_2^n \\ \vdots & & & & \vdots \\ 1 & x_m & x_m^2 & \cdots & x_m^n \end{bmatrix}, \qquad \mathbf{U} = \begin{bmatrix} a_0 \\ a_1 \\ a_2 \\ \vdots \\ a_n \end{bmatrix}, \qquad \mathbf{Y}_0 = \begin{bmatrix} y_1 \\ y_2 \\ \vdots \\ y_m \end{bmatrix}.$$

The equation we are trying to solve may now be written

$$A\mathbf{U} = \mathbf{Y}_0. \tag{10.10}$$

Of course, the case of most interest is when $m > n$ and (10.10) has no solution. What do we seek in this case? We are trying to find the vector $\mathbf{U}_0$ that minimizes the expression (10.8). But, in our new notation, the quantity we are trying to minimize is just the distance from $A\mathbf{U}$ to $\mathbf{Y}_0$! As the set of all vectors of the form $A\mathbf{U}$ is a subspace of R^n (the span of the columns of A), we can apply the corollary of this section. If we denote the columns of A by $\mathbf{A}^1, \mathbf{A}^2, \ldots, \mathbf{A}^{n+1}$, the normal equations become

$$\begin{aligned}(A\mathbf{U}, \mathbf{A}^1) &= (\mathbf{Y}_0, \mathbf{A}^1)\\ (A\mathbf{U}, \mathbf{A}^2) &= (\mathbf{Y}_0, \mathbf{A}^2)\\ &\vdots\\ (A\mathbf{U}, \mathbf{A}^{n+1}) &= (\mathbf{Y}_0, \mathbf{A}^{n+1}).\end{aligned}$$

If the reader writes out the above equations, he will see that they can be compactly written as a single matrix equation, namely

$$A^{\mathsf{T}}A\mathbf{U} = A^{\mathsf{T}}\mathbf{Y}_0.$$

But this is simply a system of linear equations, which we may solve by Gaussian elimination or any other convenient method.

Example 2. Consider the problem of finding the straight line that best fits the data plotted in Figure 10.1. The matrix A is given by

$$A = \begin{bmatrix} 1 & 1 \\ 1 & 2 \\ 1 & 3 \\ 1 & 4 \\ 1 & 5 \end{bmatrix}.$$

So
$$A^{\mathrm{T}}A\mathbf{U} = \begin{bmatrix} 5 & 15 \\ 15 & 55 \end{bmatrix} \mathbf{U} = A^{\mathrm{T}} \begin{bmatrix} 2.15 \\ 4.41 \\ 6.60 \\ 8.76 \\ 10.9 \end{bmatrix} = \begin{bmatrix} 32.82 \\ 120.31 \end{bmatrix}.$$

Solving this system by elimination yields $a_0 = 0.009$, $a_1 = 2.185$, and the straight line desired is the graph of $y = 0.009 + 2.185x$.

Example 3. Find the quadratic that best fits the data

$$\{(1, 1), (2, 3), (0, 1), (3, 7)\}.$$

The matrix A is

$$A = \begin{bmatrix} 1 & 1 & 1 \\ 1 & 2 & 4 \\ 1 & 0 & 0 \\ 1 & 3 & 9 \end{bmatrix}.$$

The normal equations:

$$A^{\mathrm{T}}A\mathbf{U} = \begin{bmatrix} 4 & 6 & 14 \\ 6 & 14 & 36 \\ 14 & 36 & 98 \end{bmatrix} \mathbf{U} = A^{\mathrm{T}} \begin{bmatrix} 1 \\ 3 \\ 1 \\ 7 \end{bmatrix} = \begin{bmatrix} 12 \\ 28 \\ 76 \end{bmatrix}.$$

Solving by elimination yields $a_0 = a_2 = 1$, $a_1 = -1$ and the desired quadratic is $y = 1 - x + x^2$. How good is the fit?

Note that $A^{\mathrm{T}}A$ is *always* symmetric and thus one need only calculate the entries in the upper triangle.

Exercises

1. Use the methods of this section to find the straight lines that best fit the following sets of data:
   (a) $\{(1, 2), (4, \frac{1}{2})\}$.
   (b) $\{(1, 2), (2, 4), (3, 5.9)\}$.
   (c) $\{(1, 2), (2, 1), (3, 6), (4, 5)\}$.
2. Use the methods of this section to find the quadratics that best fit the following sets of data:
   (a) $\{(0, 3), (1, 6), (2, 13)\}$.
   (b) $\{(0, 1), (1, 2), (2, 2), (3, \frac{1}{2})\}$.

3. Consider the plane π: $2x + 3y - z = 0$ and the point $\mathbf{X}_0 = [-1, -2, 6]$.
   (a) Find a basis for the plane when it is considered as a subspace of R^3.
   (b) Find the normal equations for your basis and the point $\mathbf{X}_0$.
   (c) Find the point on π closest to $\mathbf{X}_0$.

4. (a) If $A = \begin{bmatrix} 1 & x_1 & x_1^2 \\ 1 & x_2 & x_2^2 \\ 1 & x_3 & x_3^2 \end{bmatrix}$, show that

$$\det(A) = (x_1 - x_2)(x_2 - x_3)(x_3 - x_1).$$

   (b) Use part (a) to show that a quadratic can be passed through *any* three points with different x coordinates.

5. Prove the corollary of this section.

10.6 Difference Equations

Suppose one knows that a sequence of numbers $\{x_n\}$ satisfies the conditions:

$$\begin{aligned} x_n &= ax_{n-1} + bx_{n-2}, \\ x_1 &= c_1, \qquad x_2 = c_2, \end{aligned} \tag{10.11}$$

where a, b, c_1, and c_2 are known constants and it is desired to find a formula for the nth term x_n in terms of n. An equation of the form (10.11) is called a *second-order difference equation.* The "second-order" refers to the fact that each term depends on two previous terms, and the equations $x_1 = c_1$, $x_2 = c_2$ are often called *initial conditions.* Problems of this type occur in many areas of applied mathematics. The most famous example is probably the sequence of Fibonacci numbers first studied by Leonardo Fibonacci while investigating a problem on the population of rabbits. In this instance the numbers are defined by $x_1 = x_2 = 1$ and $x_n = x_{n-1} + x_{n-2}$. The first few terms of the sequence are 1, 1, 2, 3, 5, 8, ... To formulate the problem in matrix terms we add a seemingly superfluous equation:

$$\begin{aligned} x_n &= x_{n-1} + x_{n-2}, \\ x_{n-1} &= x_{n-1}. \end{aligned} \tag{10.12}$$

We now write (10.12) in matrix form

$$\begin{bmatrix} x_n \\ x_{n-1} \end{bmatrix} = \begin{bmatrix} 1 & 1 \\ 1 & 0 \end{bmatrix} \begin{bmatrix} x_{n-1} \\ x_{n-2} \end{bmatrix} = A \begin{bmatrix} x_{n-1} \\ x_{n-2} \end{bmatrix}.$$

Of course, we also have that

$$\begin{bmatrix} x_{n-1} \\ x_{n-2} \end{bmatrix} = A \begin{bmatrix} x_{n-2} \\ x_{n-3} \end{bmatrix}.$$

Repeated application of this principle yields

$$\begin{bmatrix} x_n \\ x_{n-1} \end{bmatrix} = A^{n-2} \begin{bmatrix} x_2 \\ x_1 \end{bmatrix}.$$

Thus if we can find an expression for the nth power of the matrix A, we will have solved the problem. What do we know about the higher powers of a matrix? In Chapter 9 we studied polynomials involving a matrix; for our present purposes we need only recall the Cayley-Hamilton theorem that a matrix satisfies its characteristic polynomial.

Start with the polynomial $p(x) = x^n$, and divide by the characteristic polynomial $c(x)$ of the matrix under consideration:

$$x^n = c(x)q(x) + r(x), \tag{10.13}$$

where the degree of the remainder $r(x)$ is less than the degree of $c(x)$. Substituting A into the equation we obtain

$$A^n = c(A)q(A) + r(A) = 0 \cdot q(A) + r(A) = r(A).$$

Thus we have reduced the problem to finding the polynomial $r(x)$. (Note that the coefficients of $r(x)$ depend on n as well as A.)

Returning to our example, the characteristic polynomial is $C(x) = x^2 - x - 1$, and the equation we are interested in is

$$x^n = (x^2 - x - 1)q(x) + b_1 + b_2 x.$$

The problem is to find b_1 and b_2 in terms of n.

The two roots of $x^2 - x - 1$ are $\lambda_1 = \frac{1}{2}(1 + \sqrt{5})$ and $\lambda_2 = \frac{1}{2}(1 - \sqrt{5})$. Note that if we substitute these two numbers into the previous equation we will obtain two equations in the unknowns b_1, b_2.

$$\lambda_1^n = b_1 + b_2\lambda_1,$$
$$\lambda_2^n = b_1 + b_2\lambda_2;$$

solving for b_1 and b_2 yields

$$b_1 = \frac{\lambda_1\lambda_2^n - \lambda_2\lambda_1^n}{\lambda_1 - \lambda_2}, \qquad b_2 = \frac{\lambda_1^n - \lambda_2^n}{\lambda_1 - \lambda_2}.$$

We now know

$$\begin{bmatrix} 1 & 1 \\ 1 & 0 \end{bmatrix}^n = b_1 \begin{bmatrix} 1 & 0 \\ 0 & 1 \end{bmatrix} + b_2 \begin{bmatrix} 1 & 1 \\ 1 & 0 \end{bmatrix} = \begin{bmatrix} b_1 + b_2 & b_2 \\ b_2 & b_1 \end{bmatrix}.$$

Since we have an expression for A^n, let us use the equation

$$\begin{bmatrix} x_{n+2} \\ x_{n+1} \end{bmatrix} = A^n \begin{bmatrix} x_2 \\ x_1 \end{bmatrix} = \begin{bmatrix} b_1 + b_2 & b_2 \\ b_2 & b_1 \end{bmatrix} \begin{bmatrix} 1 \\ 1 \end{bmatrix}$$

to find the general term of the sequence. We have $x_{n+1} = b_2 + b_1$ or

$$x_{n+1} = \frac{\lambda_1\lambda_2^n - \lambda_2\lambda_1^n + \lambda_1^n - \lambda_2^n}{\lambda_1 - \lambda_2} = \frac{\lambda_1^n(1 - \lambda_2) + \lambda_2^n(\lambda_1 - 1)}{\lambda_1 - \lambda_2}.$$

For our particular values of λ_1, λ_2 we have $1 - \lambda_2 = \lambda_1$ and $\lambda_1 - 1 = -\lambda_2$, and our final answer is

$$x_{n+1} = \frac{1}{\sqrt{5}}\left(\left(\frac{1 + \sqrt{5}}{2}\right)^{n+1} - \left(\frac{1 - \sqrt{5}}{2}\right)^{n+1}\right).$$

The above procedure will work for any matrix A that has two distinct characteristic values λ_1, λ_2. What can be done if A has only one characteristic value? The characteristic equation in this case is $(x - \lambda)^2$ and Equation (10.13) becomes

$$x^n = (x - \lambda)^2 q(x) + b_1 + b_2 x. \tag{10.14}$$

The problem is that we have only one equation in the two unknowns, namely $\lambda^n = b_1 + b_2\lambda$. To obtain another equation, differentiate (10.14).

$$nx^{n-1} = 2(x - \lambda)q(x) + (x - \lambda)^2 q'(x) + b_2;$$

substituting λ into this equation yields $n\lambda^{n-1} = b_2$.

We summarize our results in the following theorem.

THEOREM 10.2. *If A is a 2×2 matrix, the nth power of A is given by*

$$A^n = b_1 I + b_2 A,$$

where b_1, b_2 are the following functions of n and the characteristic values λ_1, λ_2 of A.

(i) *If* $\lambda_1 \neq \lambda_2$: $b_1 = \dfrac{\lambda_1\lambda_2^n - \lambda_2\lambda_1^n}{\lambda_1 - \lambda_2}$, $\quad b_2 = \dfrac{\lambda_1^n - \lambda_2^n}{\lambda_1 - \lambda_2}$.

(ii) *If* $\lambda_1 = \lambda_2$: $b_1 = (1 - n)\lambda_1^n$, $\quad b_2 = n\lambda_1^{n-1}$.

Another problem which can be solved using Theorem 10.2 is a *first-order difference equation*:

$$x_n = ax_{n-1} + b, \qquad x_1 = c.$$

We add a dummy equation:

$$\begin{aligned} x_n &= ax_{n-1} + b \cdot 1, \\ 1 &= 0 \cdot x_{n-1} + 1 \cdot 1, \end{aligned}$$

which we rewrite as

$$\begin{bmatrix} x_n \\ 1 \end{bmatrix} = \begin{bmatrix} a & b \\ 0 & 1 \end{bmatrix} \begin{bmatrix} x_{n-1} \\ 1 \end{bmatrix}.$$

We then have

$$\begin{bmatrix} x_n \\ 1 \end{bmatrix} = A^{n-1} \begin{bmatrix} x_1 \\ 1 \end{bmatrix}, \qquad A = \begin{bmatrix} a & b \\ 0 & 1 \end{bmatrix},$$

and we can apply the theorem, the characteristic values being a and 1.

Example 1. In a typical retirement plan, the employee makes a fixed contribution C at each pay period. The company pays interest at a rate r on the balance at the end of the previous period; this interest along with the contribution C is added to the employee's account. Find a formula for the balance of the account after n periods. We have

$$B_1 = C, \qquad B_2 = (C + rC) + C,$$
$$B_3 = (C + rC + C) + r(C + rC + C) + C, \quad \text{etc.}$$

The balances are related by the formula $B_n = B_{n-1} + rB_{n-1} + C = (1 + r)B_{n-1} + C$. Our matrix A is

$$A = \begin{bmatrix} 1 + r & C \\ 0 & 1 \end{bmatrix}.$$

As usual, it is easiest to write a formula for x_{n+1} using

$$\begin{bmatrix} x_{n+1} \\ 1 \end{bmatrix} = A^n \begin{bmatrix} C \\ 1 \end{bmatrix} = \begin{bmatrix} b_1 + b_2(1 + r) & b_2 C \\ 0 & b_1 + b_2 \end{bmatrix} \begin{bmatrix} C \\ 1 \end{bmatrix}.$$

$$x_{n+1} = [b_1 + b_2(1 + r)]C + b_2 C;$$

substituting

$$b_1 = \frac{(1 + r) - (1 + r)^n}{r} \quad \text{and} \quad b_2 = \frac{(1 + r)^n - 1}{r},$$

$$x_{n+1} = C\left[\frac{(1 + r)^{n+1} - 1}{r}\right].$$

A plan of this type is called an *ordinary annuity*. Difference equations arise in many situations involving compound interest; a further example is contained in Exercise 9.

Exercises

Use the methods of this section to solve the difference equations in Exercises 1 through 6.

1. $x_n = x_{n-1} + x_{n-2}$, $x_1 = 2$, $x_2 = 1$.
2. $x_n = x_{n-1} + x_{n-2}$, $x_1 = 1$, $x_2 = 0$.
3. $x_n = 3x_{n-1} + 3x_{n-2}$, $x_1 = 0$, $x_2 = 1$.
4. $x_n = 3x_{n-1}$, $x_1 = 2$.
5. $x_n = 2x_{n-1} + 3$, $x_1 = 1$.
6. $x_n = rx_{n-1}$, $x_1 = c$.
7. Two sequences of numbers $\{x_n\}$ and $\{y_n\}$ are related by

$$x_n = x_{n-1} + 3y_{n-1},$$
$$y_n = 3x_{n-1} + y_{n-1}.$$

If $x_1 = y_1 = 1$, find a formula for x_n. *Hint:* Rewrite the system as a matrix equation, and use the methods of this section.

8. It is possible that the matrix A arising from a system such as the one in Exercise 7 will have complex characteristic values even though the two sequences are real numbers. For example, solve the system

$$x_n = -y_{n-1}, \qquad y_n = x_{n-1}, \qquad x_1 = y_1 = 1.$$

9. On a typical loan, the lender charges interest at a rate r on the unpaid balance at the end of each month, and the borrower pays an amount p at the end of each month. If the initial balance is B_1 find a formula for the balance after n months. Intuitively, it is clear that, if the payment p is less than the first month's interest rB_1, then the balance will be increasing. Does your formula reflect this?

Answers to Selected Exercises

§1.1, page 3

1. (a) $\{2, -2\}$. (b) $\{1\}$. (c) $\{\pm 1, \pm 2, \pm 3, \pm 4, \pm 6, \pm 8, \pm 12, \pm 24\}$.
3. (a) Positive multiples of 6.
   (b) Positive integers that are either even or multiples of 3.
   (c) Odd positive multiples of 3.
   (d) Same as (b).
4. (a) (3, 2) and (1, 6). (b) 16.

§1.2, page 8

1. Injective mapping of P into P.
4. Yes; when the set is infinite.
5. Yes; no.
6. 6; $n!$.
7. No; no.
8. No.
10. (a) $(F \circ G)(2) = 4$, $(G \circ F)(2) = 2$.

§1.3, page 14

1. (a) c, c, a. (b) a, b, c. (c) Yes. (d) Yes.
2. (a) No. (b) No. (c) No, Yes.
3. (a) Not A3, A4, M4. (b) Not M4. (c) All.
10. All. Yes.
11. (a) 27. (b) 54. (c) a, b. (d) b, c.
12. (a) D, C, B. (b) Yes. (c) Yes; no.

§2.1, page 23

1. (a) $0, 1, \frac{5}{8}, \frac{19}{8}, -\frac{21}{8}, \frac{3}{7}$.
   (b) $-3, 5, 0, 61, -19$.
2. $x' = (x + 3)/8$.

3. (a) $(-2, 2), (-1, 2), (1, 1), (0, 3)$.
   (b) $(2, 1), (3, 3), (3, 0), (5, 3)$.
   (c) $x' = x - y, y' = y$.
8. $[(x_1 - x_2)^2 + 2(x_1 - x_2)(y_1 - y_2) + 2(y_1 - y_2)^2]^{1/2}$.

§2.2, page 26

1. $r_1 = 1 + t, r_2 = 1 - 2t, r_3 = 1 + 2t; [r_1, r_2, r_3], [-r_1, -r_2, -r_3]$.
2. $r_1 = 2 + 3t, r_2 = 3 - 5t, r_3 = -4 + 4t;$
   $[r_1 - 2, r_2 - 3, r_3 + 4], [2 - r_1, 3 - r_2, -4 - r_3]$.
3. (a) $(\frac{3}{2}, 1, 1)$. (b) $(\frac{5}{4}, -\frac{1}{2}, 2)$. (c) $(3, 10, -5)$. (d) $(0, -8, 7)$.
4. $[2, 2, 2]; [-1, -1, -2]; [1, 1, 0]$.

§2.3, page 29

1. (a) $[3, 6, 0]$. (b) $[1, 3, 1]$. (c) $[a + b, 2a + 3b, -a + b]$.
2. $[-1, 1, 0]; [\frac{1}{2}, \frac{1}{2}, 0]$.
3. Yes.
4. $[3, 5, -3]$.

§2.4, page 32

1. (a) $[4, 7, -1, 3]$. (b) $[5, 7, -3, 16]$. (c) $[2a + b, 3a + 2b, -a, 5a - b]$.
2. (a) $[3, i, 1, i]$. (b) $[5, 3i, -5, 7i]$. (c) $[2a + bi, ai, -a + 2bi, b + 2ai]$.
3. 81.
5. (a) $\mathbf{R} = [2, 3, -4] + t[3, -5, 4]$. (b) $\mathbf{R} = (1 - t)[1, 1, 1] + t[2, -1, 3]$.
   (c) $\mathbf{R} = [1 + t, -2 + 6t, 3 - 4t]$.
6. $[-1, 1, 0]; [\frac{1}{2}, \frac{1}{2}, 0]$.
7. $[3, 5, -3]$.

§2.5, page 34

1. The sets in (a) and (b) are vector spaces.
2. (a) Vectors of the form $[a, 0, 0, 0]$ for $a \in R$.
   (b) Vectors of the form $[a, 2a, 0, a + b]$ for $a, b \in R$.
   (c) Vectors of the form $[a + b, a, 0, 0]$ for $a, b \in R$.
3. Yes.
4. The set of all polynomials of degree ≤ 5.
5. All indicated sets are subspaces except (d).
7. Yes; no; Equations of the form $ax_1 + bx_2 + cx_3 = 0$, where a, b, c are real constants.
8. Yes.

§2.6, page 42

1. Yes.
2. Yes, if it is the zero vector.
3. (a) $\mathbf{A}_3 = 5\mathbf{A}_1 - 3\mathbf{A}_2$. (b) $\mathbf{A}_3 = -\mathbf{A}_1 + 6\mathbf{A}_2$. (c) Independent.
4. Yes.
5. (a) $\{[1, -1, 0, 1, 1], [0, 3, 0, -1, -3], [0, 1, -1, -1, -3], [0, 0, 3, 2, 6]\}$.
   (b) $\{[1, -1, 0, 1, 1], [2, 1, 0, 1, -1], [1, 1, 1, 1, 1], [2, -1, -1, 1, -1]\}$.
6. $k = 1$ is the only value that will make the indicated vectors dependent.

§2.7, page 45

1. (a) No. (b) Yes.
4. All values of k except $0, 1, -\frac{4}{3}$.
8. (b) $[a + 2b, -a + b, -b, a] \rightarrow [a, b]$.

§2.8, page 49

1. $S \cap T = L\{[1, 2, -1]\}$, $S + T = R^3$.
2. The dimensions are 2, 3, 1, 4, respectively.
5. $\mathbf{Y} = [5, 1, -2]$, $\mathbf{Z} = [-1, 0, -1]$.
6. $\mathbf{X} \in T$, $\mathbf{X} \in S$, respectively.
8. $S + T = R^4$; $S \cap T$ consists of all vectors of the form $[2a, b, a, b]$.

§2.9, page 56

1. (a) -1. (b) 0.
2. $-1, \frac{1}{3}$.
3. $[1, 2, -1, 0]$, $[\frac{1}{2}, -1, -\frac{3}{2}, 1]$, $[\frac{1}{9}, \frac{1}{9}, \frac{1}{3}, \frac{5}{9}]$.
8. $[0, -\frac{8}{5}, \frac{16}{5}, 0]$.

§2.10, page 59

2. (a) $\mathbf{f}_1, \mathbf{f}_2, \ldots, \mathbf{f}_n$; where $\mathbf{f}_i(a_1\mathbf{E}_1 + a_2\mathbf{E}_2 + \cdots + a_n\mathbf{E}_n) = a_i$.
   (b) $\mathbf{f}_1, \mathbf{f}_2, \ldots, \mathbf{f}_n$; where $\mathbf{f}_i(\mathbf{X}) = (\mathbf{X}, \mathbf{E}_i)$. Note that these are the same functions as in (a).

§3.1, page 64

1. (a) Equal segment on OY.
   (b) Segment on line $y = -x$.
   (c) Segment on OX twice as long as original.
2. (a) and (c); image of (b) is the line $y = -x$.
4. Line shrinks to the point $(1, -1)$.
5. One-to-one but not onto.
6. (b), (c), and (d).
9. $\mathrm{T}[x_1, x_2, x_3] = [x_1, x_2, -x_3]$.

§3.2, page 69

1. $\mathrm{T}[x_1, x_2, x_3] = [2x_1 + x_3, x_1 + x_2 + x_3]$; the null space is spanned by $[1, 1, -2]$; the image is R^2.
2. Image: $L\{[1, 1, -1], [1, -1, 1]\}$; null space: $L\{[1, -2, 1]\}$.
3. Image: nonzero multiples of x; null space: $\{0\}$.
4. Image: $L\{[0, 1, 0, 0], [2, 1, 2, 1]\}$; null space: $L\{1, 2, -4\}$.
5. $\mathrm{T}[1, 0, 0] = [4, 4, 4, 2]$, $\mathrm{T}[0, 1, 0] = [-6, -8, -6, -3]$, $\mathrm{T}[0, 0, 1] = [-2, -3, -2, -1]$.
7. $\mathrm{T}\mathbf{X}_1 = 2\mathbf{X}_1 - \mathbf{X}_2 - \mathbf{X}_3$, $\mathrm{T}\mathbf{X}_2 = -\frac{1}{3}\mathbf{X}_1 + \frac{1}{3}\mathbf{X}_2 + \frac{2}{3}\mathbf{X}_3$, $\mathrm{T}\mathbf{X}_3 = -\frac{1}{3}\mathbf{X}_1 - \frac{2}{3}\mathbf{X}_2 + \frac{2}{3}\mathbf{X}_3$.
8. W and U, respectively.

§3.3, page 74

1. (a) (i) $[1, 1, 2]$; (ii) $[0, 0, 1]$; (iii) $[3, -1, 2]$; (iv) $[-1, 3, 1]$; (v) $[2, 2, 3]$; (vi) $[-3, 1]$.
   (b) $[x_1 - 2x_2, x_2, x_1 - x_2]$.
   (c) $[x_2, x_1 - 2x_2, x_1]$.
   (d) $[x_1, x_1, 2x_1 + x_2]$.
   (e) $[x_1 - x_2, x_1 - x_2, 2x_1 - x_2]$.
2. (a) $\mathrm{T}_1\mathrm{T}_3\mathbf{X}_1 = 2\mathbf{X}_1' - \mathbf{X}_2' + \mathbf{X}_3'$,
   $\mathrm{T}_1\mathrm{T}_3\mathbf{X}_2 = \mathbf{X}_1'$,
   $\mathrm{T}_1\mathrm{T}_3\mathbf{X}_3 = \mathbf{X}_1' + \mathbf{X}_2' + \mathbf{X}_3' + \mathbf{X}_4'$.
   (b) $(\mathrm{T}_1 + \mathrm{T}_2)\mathbf{X}_1 = 2\mathbf{X}_1' - \mathbf{X}_2' + 3\mathbf{X}_3'$,
   $(\mathrm{T}_1 + \mathrm{T}_2)\mathbf{X}_2 = 2\mathbf{X}_1' - \mathbf{X}_2' - \mathbf{X}_3' + \mathbf{X}_4'$,
   $(\mathrm{T}_1 + \mathrm{T}_2)\mathbf{X}_3 = 2\mathbf{X}_2' + \mathbf{X}_3' + \mathbf{X}_4'$.

(c) $$\begin{aligned}
T_1E_1 &= 2E_2' - E_3' + E_4',\\
T_1E_2 &= E_1' + E_3',\\
T_1E_3 &= E_1' - E_2' + 2E_3',\\
T_2E_1 &= -3E_1' + 7E_2' + E_3' + E_4',\\
T_2E_2 &= -2E_1' + 4E_2',\\
T_2E_3 &= 3E_1' - 4E_2' + E_3',\\
T_3E_1 &= 2E_1 - 3E_2,\\
T_3E_2 &= E_1 - E_2,\\
T_3E_3 &= 2E_2 + 2E_3.
\end{aligned}$$

(d) $$\begin{aligned}
T_1T_3E_1 &= -3E_1' + 4E_2' - 5E_3' + 2E_4',\\
T_1T_3E_2 &= -E_1' + 2E_2' - 2E_3' + E_4',\\
T_1T_3E_3 &= 4E_1' - 2E_2' + 6E_3'.
\end{aligned}$$

3. $\theta_1 = -\theta_2, \theta_3 = 0.$
4. $T_{11}X_1 = X_1'; T_{12}X_1 = 0; T_{13}X_1 = X_3'; T_{14}X_1 = 0;$
$T_{11}X_2 = X_1'; T_{12}X_2 = -X_2'; T_{13}X_2 = 0; T_{14}X_2 = 0;$
$T_{11}X_3 = 0; T_{12}X_3 = X_2'; T_{13}X_3 = 0; T_{14}X_3 = X_4'.$
6. No. All but one distributive law.
9. (a) The identity transformation. (b) 0. (c) T_1. (d) T_2.

§3.4, page 78

1. $T_1: \begin{bmatrix} 1 & -1 \\ 0 & 1 \end{bmatrix}, \quad T_2: \begin{bmatrix} 1 & -1 \\ 0 & 1 \\ 1 & 0 \end{bmatrix}, \quad T_3: \begin{bmatrix} 0 & 1 \\ 1 & -1 \\ 1 & 1 \end{bmatrix}.$

2. $T_2: \begin{bmatrix} 1 & 1 & 0 \\ -1 & 0 & 1 \\ 2 & -1 & 1 \\ 0 & 1 & 0 \end{bmatrix}, \quad T_3: \begin{bmatrix} 1 & 0 & 1 \\ 1 & 1 & 0 \\ 0 & 1 & 1 \end{bmatrix}.$

3. $T_1: \begin{bmatrix} 0 & 1 & 1 \\ 2 & 0 & -1 \\ -1 & 1 & 2 \\ 1 & 0 & 0 \end{bmatrix}, \quad T_2: \begin{bmatrix} -3 & -2 & 3 \\ 7 & 4 & -4 \\ 1 & 0 & 1 \\ 1 & 0 & 0 \end{bmatrix}, \quad T_3: \begin{bmatrix} 2 & 1 & 0 \\ -3 & -1 & 2 \\ 0 & 0 & 2 \end{bmatrix}.$

5. $\begin{bmatrix} 0 & 1 & 0 & 0 \\ 0 & 0 & 2 & 0 \\ 0 & 0 & 0 & 3 \\ 0 & 0 & 0 & 0 \end{bmatrix}$ and $\begin{bmatrix} 0 & 1 & 2 & 3 \\ 0 & 0 & 2 & 6 \\ 0 & 0 & 0 & 3 \\ 0 & 0 & 0 & 0 \end{bmatrix}$, respectively.

6. (a) $3X_1' + 3X_2'$. (b) $-X_1' + 5X_2'$.

§3.5, page 82

1. (a) $\begin{bmatrix} 0 & 1 \\ 5 & 1 \end{bmatrix}$. (b) $\begin{bmatrix} 2 & 5 & 4 \\ 2 & 5 & 9 \end{bmatrix}$.

4. (a) No answer. (b), (c) $\begin{bmatrix} 2 & -4 & -3 \\ -1 & 22 & 14 \end{bmatrix}$. (d) $\begin{bmatrix} 2 & 5 \\ 5 & 13 \end{bmatrix}$.

(e) $\begin{bmatrix} 12 & 13 \\ 31 & 34 \end{bmatrix}$. (f) $\begin{bmatrix} -3 & -8 \\ 19 & 49 \end{bmatrix}$. (g) No answer.

(h) $\begin{bmatrix} -1 & -4 \\ 8 & 7 \end{bmatrix}$.

6. (a) $[-1, 1, -2]$. (b) $[-4, 1, 0]$. (c) $\begin{bmatrix} 0 & 4 & -1 \\ 3 & 2 & 1 \\ 2 & 2 & 0 \end{bmatrix}$.

(d) $\begin{bmatrix} 2 & 1 & 0 \\ 2 & 2 & 1 \\ 1 & 3 & 1 \end{bmatrix}$. (e) $[-4, 1, 0]$.

7. No.
8. (a) When $\sin\theta \neq 0$, commuting matrices have the form $\begin{bmatrix} a & b \\ -b & a \end{bmatrix}$.

§3.6, page 89

1. $c_1 = c_3, c_2 = -c_3, c_3$ arbitrary.
2. $[3, 1, -2] - [2, 3, 1] + [-1, 2, 3] = [0, 0, 0]$.
3. (a) $\mathbf{A}_3 = 5\mathbf{A}_1 - 3\mathbf{A}_2$. (b) $\mathbf{A}_3 = -\mathbf{A}_1 + 6\mathbf{A}_2$. (c) Independent.
4. $c_1 = -7, c_2 + 8, c_3 = 5c_2 - 2c_4 - 2, c_2, c_4$ arbitrary.
5. Yes.
6. $c_1 = c_2 = c_3 = 0$. Vectors are independent.
7. $c_1 = 19t, c_2 = 21t, c_3 = 9t, c_4 = -4t, t$ arbitrary.
9. $K = 1$.

§3.7, page 93

1. $\mathrm{T}^{-1}[x_1, x_2] = [\frac{1}{2}(x_1 + x_2), \frac{1}{2}(-x_1 + x_2)]$.
2. $\mathrm{T}^{-1}[x_1, x_2, x_3] = [x_1 - x_2, x_2 - x_3, x_3]$.
3. $\begin{bmatrix} 1 & 1 \\ -1 & 1 \end{bmatrix}, \quad \begin{bmatrix} \frac{1}{2} & -\frac{1}{2} \\ \frac{1}{2} & \frac{1}{2} \end{bmatrix}$.
4. $\mathrm{T}^{-1}[x_1, x_2, x_3] = [x_1 + 2, x_2, x_3 - x_1 - 2]$.
5. (b) T_1 is onto; T_2 is one-to-one.
6. The left-hand matrix is nonsingular.

§3.8, page 99

1. (a) $[2, 7, 1]$. (b) $[18, 36, 6]$. (c) $[-1, 1, 0]$. (d) $[2, 3, 1]$.
2. $\begin{bmatrix} -4 & -4 & -4 \\ 4 & 5 & 7 \\ 0 & 0 & -1 \end{bmatrix}$. (a) $-8\mathbf{X}_1 + 13\mathbf{X}_2 - 2\mathbf{X}_3$.

   (b) $-8\mathbf{X}_1 + 4\mathbf{X}_2 + 2\mathbf{X}_3$. (c) $16\mathbf{X}_1 + 31\mathbf{X}_2 - 6\mathbf{X}_3$.
3. (a) From $\mathbf{X}_i$ to $\mathbf{Y}_i$: $\frac{1}{2}\begin{bmatrix} 1 & 1 & -1 \\ -1 & 1 & 1 \\ 1 & -1 & 1 \end{bmatrix}$; from $\mathbf{Y}_i$ to $\mathbf{X}_i$: $\begin{bmatrix} 1 & 0 & 1 \\ 1 & 1 & 0 \\ 0 & 1 & 1 \end{bmatrix}$.

   (b) $\mathbf{Z} = 2\mathbf{Y}_1 - \mathbf{Y}_3$. (c) $c_1' + c_2' + c_3' = 0$.
4. (a) $\begin{bmatrix} -6 & \frac{3}{2} & \frac{7}{2} \\ 3 & -\frac{1}{2} & -\frac{3}{2} \\ -1 & \frac{1}{2} & \frac{1}{2} \end{bmatrix}$.

   (b) Coefficients are
   $[\frac{15}{2}, -\frac{5}{2}, \frac{3}{2}]$, $[\frac{79}{2}, -\frac{33}{2}, \frac{15}{2}]$
   $[-\frac{25}{2}, \frac{11}{2}, -\frac{5}{2}]$, $[-6a + \frac{3}{2}b + \frac{7}{2}c, 3a - \frac{1}{2}b - \frac{3}{2}c, -a + \frac{1}{2}b + \frac{1}{2}c]$.
5. (a) $\begin{bmatrix} 1 & 1 & 1 & 1 \\ 0 & 1 & 2 & 3 \\ 0 & 0 & 1 & 3 \\ 0 & 0 & 0 & 1 \end{bmatrix}$.

   (b) $3x^3 + 2x^2 - x + 4 = 8 + 12(x - 1) + 11(x - 1)^2 + 3(x - 1)^3$.

§3.9, page 105

1. $P = \begin{bmatrix} 1 & 1 \\ 1 & 2 \end{bmatrix}, \quad Q = \begin{bmatrix} 1 & -1 & 3 \\ 1 & -1 & 0 \\ 1 & 1 & -1 \end{bmatrix}.$

2. $P^{-1} = \begin{bmatrix} 2 & -1 \\ -1 & 1 \end{bmatrix}, \quad Q^{-1} = \frac{1}{6}\begin{bmatrix} 1 & 2 & 3 \\ 1 & -4 & 3 \\ 2 & -2 & 0 \end{bmatrix}.$

3. $\begin{bmatrix} -10 & 4 \\ -1 & 1 \\ 6 & 2 \end{bmatrix}.$

4. $\mathbf{Z} = -13\mathbf{X}_1 + 5\mathbf{X}_2 = -8\mathbf{Y}_1 - 3\mathbf{Y}_2$; $\mathbf{TZ} = [-4, 254, -118]$ in standard form.

5. $\frac{1}{5}\begin{bmatrix} 6 & -13 \\ 1 & -11 \end{bmatrix}.$

6. $\frac{1}{3}\begin{bmatrix} -1 & -4 & -1 \\ 2 & 8 & 2 \\ 5 & -1 & -1 \end{bmatrix}.$

7. $A = \begin{bmatrix} 0 & 1 & 0 \\ 0 & 0 & 2 \\ 0 & 0 & 0 \end{bmatrix}, \quad B = \begin{bmatrix} 0 & 0 & 0 \\ 1 & 0 & 0 \\ 0 & 1 & 0 \end{bmatrix}, \quad P = \begin{bmatrix} 0 & 0 & 2 \\ 0 & 2 & 0 \\ 1 & 0 & 0 \end{bmatrix}.$

8. $\begin{bmatrix} 0 & 0 & \cdots & 0 & 0 \\ 1 & 0 & \cdots & 0 & 0 \\ 0 & 1 & \cdots & 0 & 0 \\ \cdots & \cdots & \cdots & \cdots & \cdots \\ 0 & 0 & \cdots & 1 & 0 \end{bmatrix}.$

§3.10, page 109

3. (a) (iii). (b) (i) and (iii). (c) None. (d) (ii). (e) All. (f) All. (g) (ii).
5. No.
6. Consider $a = 1$.

§4.2, page 117

1. (a) $E = S_{32}(1)$; $AE = B$.
   (b) $E = P_{23}$; $EA = B$.
   (c) $E = D_1(2)$; $AE = B$.

3. (a) $\frac{1}{20}\begin{bmatrix} -1 & -1 & 6 \\ -13 & 7 & -2 \\ 4 & 4 & -4 \end{bmatrix}$; (b) $\frac{1}{33}\begin{bmatrix} 8 & 13 & -1 \\ -7 & 1 & 5 \\ -9 & 6 & -3 \end{bmatrix}.$

6. (a) $\frac{1}{6}\begin{bmatrix} 8 & 2 & -6 & 0 \\ -19 & 2 & 3 & 12 \\ -6 & 0 & 0 & 6 \\ -3 & 0 & 3 & 0 \end{bmatrix}$; (b) $\frac{1}{35}\begin{bmatrix} 25 & -15 & 15 & -5 \\ -7 & 14 & -7 & 7 \\ 9 & -18 & 4 & 1 \\ -6 & 12 & -26 & 11 \end{bmatrix}.$

§4.3, page 123

1. Ranks are: (a) 3; (b) 2; (c) 3; (d) 3.
2. Rank is 3 unless $h = 3, k = 1$; in this case rank is 2.

4. $P = \begin{bmatrix} \frac{1}{a} & 0 \\ -\frac{c}{a} & 1 \end{bmatrix}$, $Q = \begin{bmatrix} 1 & -\frac{b}{a} \\ 0 & 1 \end{bmatrix}$ is one answer pair.

§4.4, page 125

1. See Exercise 1, preceding section.
3. See Exercise 3, preceding section.
4. (a) One pair is $\{x, x^2, x^3, x^4, 1\}$, $\{1, 2x, 3x^2, 4x^3, x^4\}$.
5. 5; $\min(m, n) + 1$.

§4.5, page 131

1. The sets in (b) and (d) are groups.
5. $$\begin{bmatrix} \frac{1}{2} & -\frac{1}{2} & \frac{1}{\sqrt{2}} \\ \frac{5}{6} & \frac{1}{2} & -\frac{1}{3\sqrt{2}} \\ -\frac{1}{3\sqrt{2}} & \frac{1}{\sqrt{2}} & \frac{2}{3} \end{bmatrix}.$$

§5.2, page 136

1. (a) -7. (b) 19. (c) ab.
2. (a) -2. (b) -2. (c) -4.
4. $\Delta(\mathbf{X}_1) = x_1$ where $\mathbf{X}_1 = [x_1]$.

§5.3, page 140

1. (a) $-12, -6, -3$. (b) $-12, 6, -3$.
2. (a) -9. (b) 0. (c) -174.
3. (a) $a_{11}a_{22}\cdots a_{nn}$. (b) $(-1)^{\frac{n(n-1)}{2}} a_{1n}a_{2,n-1}\cdots a_{n1}$.

§5.4, page 144

1. (a) 3 inversions; 3 transpositions. (b) 5 inversions; 3 transpositions.
   (c) 9 inversions; 5 transpositions. (d) 4 inversions; 2 transpositions.
   (e) 24 inversions; 8 transpositions. (f) 25 inversions; 7 transpositions.
   (g) 28 inversions; 4 transpositions. (h) 13 inversions; 5 transpositions.
2. (a) $f_P = f_I$; 4 inversions.
   (b) $f_P = -f_I$; 3 inversions.
   (c) $f_P = -f_I$; 3 inversions.
   (d) $f_P = f_I$; 6 inversions.
4. (a) $-$. (b) $+$. (c) $-$. There would be 720 terms.
5. (a) -2. (b) 0.
9. Rules (i) and (iii) are satisfied.

§5.5, page 149

1. (a) 3. (b) -2. (c) -26. (d) 3.
2. (a) P1. (b) P3. (c) Theorem 5.3. (d) P4. (e) P3.

§5.6, page 153

1. (a) Dependent. (b) Dependent. (c) Dependent for all values of x.
8. (a) $y = \frac{14}{11}$. (b) $z = 0$. (c) No unique solution.
(d) $x = 1, y = z = t = w = 0$.

§6.1, page 158

1. (a) $[x_1, x_2] \begin{bmatrix} 2 & 3 \\ -4 & 1 \end{bmatrix} [y_1, y_2]^{\mathsf{T}}$.

(b) $[x_1, x_2] \begin{bmatrix} 5 & 0 \\ -1 & 2 \end{bmatrix} \begin{bmatrix} y_1 \\ y_2 \end{bmatrix}$.

(c) $[x_1, x_2, x_3] \begin{bmatrix} 1 & 1 & -1 \\ 2 & 0 & -1 \\ 0 & 0 & 0 \end{bmatrix} [y_1, y_2, y_3]^{\mathsf{T}}$.

2. $\begin{bmatrix} 1 & 2 \\ -4 & 3 \end{bmatrix}$.

3. (a) 3; 21.

(b) $\begin{bmatrix} -1 & 1 \\ -5 & 14 \end{bmatrix}$.

4. Condition $b_{ij} = b_{ji}$ is necessary and sufficient.

§6.2, page 163

1. (a) $x_1^2 - 6x_1x_2 + 4x_2^2$. (b) $x_1^2 + 4x_2^2 + 5x_3^2 - 4x_1x_2 + 6x_1x_3 + 2x_2x_3$.

2. (a) $[x_1, x_2] \begin{bmatrix} 2 & -4 \\ -4 & 3 \end{bmatrix} \begin{bmatrix} x_1 \\ x_2 \end{bmatrix}$.

(b) $[x_1, x_2, x_3] \begin{bmatrix} 3 & 3 & 4 \\ 3 & -2 & -2 \\ 4 & -2 & 5 \end{bmatrix} \begin{bmatrix} x_1 \\ x_2 \\ x_3 \end{bmatrix}$.

3. (a) $24y_1^2 + 2y_1y_2 - y_2^2$.

(b) $\begin{bmatrix} 3 & 1 \\ 2 & -1 \end{bmatrix} \begin{bmatrix} 1 & 2 \\ 2 & 3 \end{bmatrix} \begin{bmatrix} 3 & 2 \\ 1 & -1 \end{bmatrix} = \begin{bmatrix} 24 & 1 \\ 1 & -1 \end{bmatrix}$

7. $x_2^{*2} - 6x_3^{*2} + 36x_1^*x_2^* + 30x_1^*x_3^* - 6x_2^*x_3^*$.

§6.3, page 171

1. Both are congruent to $\begin{bmatrix} 1 & 0 & 0 \\ 0 & -1 & 0 \\ 0 & 0 & -1 \end{bmatrix}$.

2. $y_1^2 + y_2^2 - y_3^2$.
4. 10.

§6.4, page 175

1. (a) Ellipse. (b) Elliptic hyperboloid of one sheet.
(c) Elliptic hyperboloid of one sheet.

§6.5, page 177

1. $\{[1, 0, 0], [-2, 1, 0], [5, -2, 1]\}$.

3. (a) $\begin{bmatrix} 1 & -1 & 2 \\ 0 & 1 & 0 \\ 0 & 0 & -1 \end{bmatrix}$. (b) $\{[1, 0, 0], [1, 1, 0], [2, 0, -1]\}$.

4. $L\{[1, 0, -1, 0], [1, 0, 0, -1]\}$.

§7.1, page 183

1. (a) $[4, 2]$. (b) $[8, 11]$. (c) $4 + 2i$. (d) $8 + 11i$.

3. (a) $\sqrt{2}\left(\cos \frac{7\pi}{4} + i \sin \frac{7\pi}{4}\right)$. (b) $\sqrt{2}\left(\cos \frac{3\pi}{4} + i \sin \frac{3\pi}{4}\right)$.

   (c) $3\left(\cos \frac{3\pi}{2} + i \sin \frac{3\pi}{2}\right)$. (d) $2\left(\cos \frac{\pi}{6} + i \sin \frac{\pi}{6}\right)$.

   (e) $5\{\cos(\cos^{-1} \frac{3}{5}) + i \sin(\cos^{-1} \frac{3}{5})\}$.
   (f) $\sqrt{5}\{\cos(\tan^{-1}(-\frac{1}{2})) + i \sin(\tan^{-1}(-\frac{1}{2}))\}$.

4. (a) $2\sqrt{3} + 2i$. (b) $2i$. (c) $\frac{1}{2} + \frac{\sqrt{3}}{2} i$. (d) $\frac{\sqrt{3}}{\sqrt{2}} + \frac{\sqrt{3}}{\sqrt{2}} i$.

8. $r^{-1}\{\cos(2\pi - \theta) + i \sin(2\pi - \theta)\}$, or $\frac{1}{r}(\cos\theta - i \sin\theta)$.

9. $\frac{r_1}{r_2}\{\cos(\theta_1 - \theta_2) - i \sin(\theta_1 - \theta_2)\}$.

10. (a) $\cos \frac{2k\pi}{5} + i \sin \frac{2k\pi}{5}$; $k = 0, 1, \ldots, 4$.

    (b) $2^{1/4}\left(\cos \frac{5\pi}{8} + i \sin \frac{5\pi}{8}\right)$, $2^{1/4}\left(\cos \frac{13\pi}{8} + i \sin \frac{13\pi}{8}\right)$.

    (c) ± 5, $\pm 5i$.

    (d) $-3\left(\cos \frac{2k\pi}{3} + i \sin \frac{2k\pi}{3}\right)$, $k = 0, 1, 2$.

    (e) $\pm\left(\frac{\sqrt{3}}{\sqrt{2}} + \frac{1}{\sqrt{2}} i\right)$.

    (f) $\cos\left(\frac{\pi}{2} + \frac{2k\pi}{3}\right) + i \sin\left(\frac{\pi}{2} + \frac{2k\pi}{3}\right)$, $k = 0, 1, 2$.

11. $z^{-1} = \frac{\bar{z}}{|z|^2}$.

15. $\cos \frac{2\pi}{3} + i \sin \frac{2\pi}{3}$, $\cos \frac{4\pi}{3} + i \sin \frac{4\pi}{3}$, 1 are cube roots of 1; ± 1 are square roots of 1.

16. 2.

§7.3, page 191

2. (a) $q(x) = x + \sqrt{2}$; $r(x) = 1 - \sqrt{6}$.
   (b) $q(x) = -1 - x - x^2 - \cdots - x^{n-1}$; $r(x) = 0$.
   (c) $q(x) = 5 - x$; $r(x) = -4 + 12x - 5x^2$.
   (d) $q(x) = -1 + 2x + 3x^2$; $r(x) = 1$.

3. (a) $x + 1$. (b) 1. (c) $2 + 2x + 3x^2 + 2x^3 + 2x^4$. (d) $x - 3$.

4. (a) $p_1(x) = \dfrac{\sqrt{2}}{\sqrt{2} + 2}$; $p_2(x) = \dfrac{1}{\sqrt{2} + 2}$.

   (b) $p_1(x) = \frac{1}{14}(-3 - 4x + 2x^2 + 5x^3)$; $p_2(x) = \frac{1}{14}(17 - 8x + 5x^2)$.
   (c) $p_1(x) = 1$; $p_2(x) = 0$.
   (d) $p_1(x) = \frac{1}{100}(-7 + x)$; $p_2(x) = \frac{1}{400}(-5 + 8x - x^2)$.

§7.5, page 197

2. In $C[x]$: $(x - 2 + 3i)$, $(x - 2 - 3i)$, $(x - 1)$, $(x - 5)$, $(x - 1 + i)$, $(x - 1 - i)$; in $R[x]$: $(x^2 - 4x + 13)$, $(x^2 - 2x + 2)$, $(x - 1)$, $(x - 5)$.

§7.6, page 200

1. $2x^3 + 3x^2 + 3x + 1$.
3. $x = 1 - i, \frac{1}{5}(-11 + 8i)$.
4. (a) $2, \pm\sqrt{3}$. (b) $1, 2, \frac{5}{2}$.

   (c) $-\frac{1}{2}, \dfrac{-1 \pm i\sqrt{15}}{2}$.

   (d) No rational roots. (e) No rational roots, roots are $\pm i$.

§8.1, page 205

1. (a) Value, 1. Vectors, all nonzero vectors.
   (b) Values, $+1, -3$. Vectors, $[2a, a]$, $[0, a]$, $a \neq 0$.
   (c) Values, 0. Vectors, $[a, a, a]$, $a \neq 0$.
   (d) Values, $\pm 1, 2$. Vectors, $[a, -a, 2a]$, $[0, a, -a]$, $[0, 0, a]$, $a \neq 0$.
2. Values, 0, 1. Vectors $[a, -a]$, $[a, a]$, $a \neq 0$.
3. $0, \pi$.
4. (a) $M_1 = L\{[1, -1, 2]\}$, $M_1 = L\{[0, 1, -1]\}$, $M_2 = L\{[0, 0, 1]\}$.
   (b) Yes, $\mathbf{X}_1 = [1, -1, 2]$, $\mathbf{X}_2 = [0, 1, -1]$, $\mathbf{X}_3 = [0, 0, 1]$ is one of many possible answers.
6. Value, 1.
7. Value, 0. Vectors, any nonzero constant polynomial.

§8.2, page 208

1. $-\lambda^3$; 0; $[0, 0, a]$, $a \neq 0$.
2. (a) $\lambda^2 - 3\lambda - 4$; $-1, 4$; $[3a, -2a]$, $[a, a]$, $a \neq 0$.
   (b) $-\lambda^3 + 4\lambda^2 - 5\lambda + 2$; 1, 2; $[a, -a, 2a]$, $[0, 0, a]$, $a \neq 0$.

   (c) $\lambda^2 + 2$; $\pm\sqrt{2}\,i$; $\left[a, \left(\dfrac{-2 + \sqrt{2}\,i}{3}\right) a\right]$, $\left[a, \left(\dfrac{-2 - \sqrt{2}\,i}{3}\right) a\right]$, $a \neq 0$.

§8.3, page 212

1. (a) Diagonal $[1, 0]$. (b) Diagonal $[1, -1, -3]$. (c) Diagonal $[1, -1, -1]$.
2. Characteristic vectors are $[a, -3a, 2a]$ and $[0, -2a, a]$; these do not generate $V_3(R)$.

3. $$\begin{bmatrix} 1 & \dfrac{1 + \sqrt{3}i}{2} \\ 1 & \dfrac{1 - \sqrt{3}i}{2} \end{bmatrix} \begin{bmatrix} 1 & -1 \\ 1 & 2 \end{bmatrix} \begin{bmatrix} \dfrac{\sqrt{3} + i}{2\sqrt{3}} & \dfrac{\sqrt{3} - i}{2\sqrt{3}} \\ -\dfrac{i}{\sqrt{3}} & \dfrac{i}{\sqrt{3}} \end{bmatrix} = \begin{bmatrix} \dfrac{3 + \sqrt{3}i}{2} & 0 \\ 0 & \dfrac{3 - \sqrt{3}i}{2} \end{bmatrix}.$$

§8.4, page 216

1. $P = \begin{bmatrix} \frac{1}{\sqrt{2}} & \frac{1}{\sqrt{2}} & 0 \\ \frac{1}{3\sqrt{2}} & -\frac{1}{3\sqrt{2}} & -\frac{4}{3\sqrt{2}} \\ \frac{2}{3} & -\frac{2}{3} & \frac{1}{3} \end{bmatrix}.$

2. (a) Diagonal $[1, \frac{17}{12}, \frac{5}{12}]$.
   (b) $\lambda_1 = 1, \lambda_2 = \frac{17}{12}, \lambda_3 = \frac{5}{12}$; corresponding characteristic vectors are $[3, 0, -4]$, $[4, 5, 3]$, $[4, -5, 3]$, which are orthogonal.
   (c) $\begin{bmatrix} \frac{3}{5} & 0 & -\frac{4}{5} \\ \frac{4}{5\sqrt{2}} & \frac{1}{\sqrt{2}} & \frac{3}{5\sqrt{2}} \\ \frac{4}{5\sqrt{2}} & -\frac{1}{\sqrt{2}} & \frac{3}{5\sqrt{2}} \end{bmatrix}.$

§8.5, page 222

1. $[x_1, x_2] = [y_1, y_2] \begin{bmatrix} \frac{1}{\sqrt{5}} & \frac{2}{\sqrt{5}} \\ -\frac{2}{\sqrt{5}} & \frac{1}{\sqrt{5}} \end{bmatrix}.$

2. Principal axes are in directions indicated by $[0, 0, 1]$, $\left[1, \frac{-1+\sqrt{5}}{2}, 0\right]$, $\left[1, \frac{-1-\sqrt{5}}{2}, 0\right]$. Reduced form is $2y_1^2 + \frac{3+\sqrt{5}}{2}y_2^2 + \frac{3-\sqrt{5}}{2}y_3^2 = 1$.

(c) 1.
(c) Polynomials of degree no higher than $p(x)$.

$- 2)$. (b) $(x - 1)^2, (x - 2)$.
$- 1, x - 1, x - 1, x^3 + x^2 - x - 1$;
(b) $x^3 + x^2 - x - 1$.

5. $x^3 - 6x^2 + 11x - 6$.

§9.3, page 239

1. $\begin{bmatrix} 0 & 0 & -16 \\ 1 & 0 & 1 \\ 0 & 1 & 4 \end{bmatrix}$.

2. $\begin{bmatrix} 0 & 0 & 1 & 0 \\ 1 & 0 & 1 & 0 \\ 0 & 1 & -1 & 0 \\ 0 & 0 & 0 & 1 \end{bmatrix}$.

5. Yes.
6. The companion matrix of the minimum polynomial of A.
7. All elementary divisors are linear.

§9.4, page 244

1. (a) $(x-2)^2$. (b) $\begin{bmatrix} 2 & 0 \\ 1 & 2 \end{bmatrix}$. (c) One answer is $\begin{bmatrix} 1 & 2 \\ 0 & -1 \end{bmatrix}$.

2. $\begin{bmatrix} 1 & 0 & 0 & 0 \\ 1 & 1 & 0 & 0 \\ 0 & 1 & 1 & 0 \\ 0 & 0 & 0 & 2 \end{bmatrix}$.

3. $x^4 - 4$.
4. (a) Essentially one; interchanging first and last rows, two.
   (b) 5.
5. Yes.
6. Lower triangular with equal elements along diagonal and subdiagonal.

§10.1, page 249

1. Only (b) is a basic solution.
2. $[1, -2, 3] = -3[1, 0, 1] + 4[1, -1, 1] + 2[0, 1, 1]$.
3. (a) $\begin{bmatrix} \frac{1}{3} & -\frac{2}{3} \\ \frac{1}{3} & \frac{1}{3} \end{bmatrix}$ (b) $\frac{1}{22}\begin{bmatrix} 12 & 2 & 4 \\ -6 & 10 & -2 \\ -10 & 2 & 4 \end{bmatrix}$.

§10.2, page 253

1. Canonical minimum.
2. Standard maximum.
3. Canonical minimum.

§10.3, page 257

1. $x_1 = 0, x_2 = \frac{3}{2}, x_3 = \frac{1}{2}$; value $= \frac{13}{2}$.
3. $x_1 = \frac{9}{4}, x_2 = 0, x_3 = 0, x_4 = \frac{5}{4}$; value $= 8$.
4. $x_1 = \frac{102}{11}, x_2 = \frac{48}{11}, x_3 = \frac{60}{11}, x_4 = 0$; value $= \frac{258}{11}$.
5. $x_1 = 1, x_2 = 1, x_3 = \frac{1}{2}, x_4 = 0$; value $= \frac{13}{2}$.
7. The oils G_1, G_2, G_3 should be used in fractions $\frac{3}{5}, \frac{1}{5}, \frac{1}{5}$, respectively.

§10.4, page 262

1. $x_1 = \frac{5}{7}, x_2 = \frac{6}{7}$; value $= \frac{16}{7}$.
2. $x_1 = 0, x_2 = \frac{9}{2}, x_3 = \frac{3}{2}$; value $= \frac{15}{2}$.
3. $x_1 = 2, x_2 = 0, x_3 = 4$; value $= 16$.
4. The shipper should take all apples; that is, 106 boxes of apples.

§10.5, page 266

1. (a) $y = -\frac{1}{2}x + \frac{5}{2}$. (b) $y = 1.95x + \frac{2}{30}$. (c) $y = \frac{7}{5}x$.
2. (a) $y = 2x^2 + x + 3$. (b) $y = -\frac{5}{8}x^2 + \frac{69}{40}x + \frac{39}{20}$.
3. (a) $\{[3, -2, 0], [1, 0, 2]\}$.
   (b) $3(x + 1) - 2(y + 2) = 0, x + 1 + 2(z - 6) = 0$.
   (c) $[10, \frac{29}{2}, \frac{1}{2}]$.
   Note: Parts (a) and (b) have many possible solutions.

§10.6, page 270

1. $x_{n+1} = \left(\frac{1 + \sqrt{5}}{2}\right)^n + \left(\frac{1 - \sqrt{5}}{2}\right)^n$.

2. $x_{n+1} = \frac{1}{\sqrt{5}}\left(\left(\frac{1 + \sqrt{5}}{2}\right)^{n-1} - \left(\frac{1 - \sqrt{5}}{2}\right)^{n-1}\right)$.

3. $x_{n+1} = \frac{1}{\sqrt{21}}\left(\left(\frac{3 + \sqrt{21}}{2}\right)^n - \left(\frac{3 - \sqrt{21}}{2}\right)^n\right)$.

4. $x_n = 2(3)^{n-1}$.
5. $x_n = 2^{n+1} - 3$.
6. $x_n = cr^{n-1}$.
7. $x_n = 4^{n-1}$.

8. $x_{n+1} = \frac{(-i)^n(i + 1) + i^n(i - 1)}{2i}$; n even, $x_{n+1} = (-1)^{n/2}$, n odd,

   $x_{n+1} = (-1)^{(n+1)/2}$.

9. $B_{n+1} = \frac{1}{r}[(1 + r)^n(B_1 r - P) + P]$, P is the payment.

Index

A B C D E F G H 7 9 8 7 6 5 4